AI-Powered Assessments for Quality and Integrity in Global Higher Education

Oluwatoyin Ayodele Ajani
https://orcid.org/0000-0001-6545-0203
University of KwaZulu-Natal, South Africa

IGI Global
Scientific Publishing
Publishing Tomorrow's Research Today

VP of Publishing Ethics & Research Integrity	Melissa Wagner
Director of Acquisitions	Mikaela Felty
Director of Book Development	Jocelynn Hessler
Production Manager	Mike Brehm
Cover Design	Jose Rosado

Published in the United States of America by
IGI Global Scientific Publishing
701 East Chocolate Avenue
Hershey, PA, 17033, USA
Tel: 717-533-8845 | Fax: 717-533-7115
Website: https://www.igi-global.com E-mail: cust@igi-global.com

Library of Congress Cataloging-in-Publication Data

Names: Ajani, Oluwatoyin Ayodele, 1972- editor
Title: AI-powered assessments for quality and integrity in global higher education / Edited by Oluwatoyin Ayodele Ajani.
Description: Hershey, PA : IGI Global Scientific Publishing, [2027] | Includes bibliographical references and index. | Summary: "This book aims to advance critical, contextually grounded scholarship on the use of artificial intelligence in higher education"-- Provided by publisher.

Identifiers: LCCN 2026004301 (print) | LCCN 2026004302 (ebook) | ISBN 9798337389394 hardcover | ISBN 9798337389400 paperback | ISBN 9798337389417 ebook
Subjects: LCSH: Educational tests and measurements--Technological innovations | Artificial intelligence--Educational applications | Education, Higher--Evaluation | Education and globalization
Classification: LCC LB3060.5 .A55 2026 (print) | LCC LB3060.5 (ebook)
LC record available at https://lccn.loc.gov/2026004301
LC ebook record available at https://lccn.loc.gov/2026004302

British Cataloguing in Publication Data
A Cataloguing in Publication record for this book is available from the British Library.

Table of Contents

Detailed Table of Contents

Artificial intelligence (AI) is rapidly changing how assessment is designed and conducted in higher education. While AI tools can improve feedback, efficiency, and personalization, they also raise serious concerns related to academic integrity, fairness, transparency, privacy, and trust. This chapter critically examines AI-powered assessment as not just a technical process, but a socio-pedagogical and ethical practice. It highlights the limitations of surveillance-based and detection-focused approaches and argues for a shift toward authentic, integrity-driven assessment. Special attention is given to Global South and resource-constrained contexts, where issues of access, bias, and inequality are more pronounced. The chapter proposes guiding principles for responsible AI use that prioritize learning, equity, student agency, and human judgment in higher education assessment.

This chapter critically examines the growing use of AI-mediated assessment in higher education and its implications for academic integrity, judgement, and institutional trust. While technologies such as automated grading, plagiarism detection, and remote proctoring are promoted for efficiency and consistency, their adoption represents a deeper sociotechnical shift that redistributes authority and reshapes accountability in assessment practices. Drawing on assessment theory, academic integrity scholarship, and algorithmic governance studies, the chapter argues that automation often reframes students as risks to be monitored rather than learners to be supported, raising concerns related to fairness and transparency. Rather than rejecting, the chapter advances a trust-centred framework emphasizing judgement, concluding that assessment quality cannot be secured through technological control.

The rapid growth of Generative Artificial Intelligence in higher education has made assessment more complex. Its importance lies in protecting genuine learning and academic integrity in AI rich environments. The main objective of this chapter is to explain how assessment and feedback practices can be redesigned to measure real understanding instead of automated output. The chapter shows that authentic tasks, staged submissions, reflection, and oral interaction improve validity and fairness. Key findings suggest that formative feedback, clear AI guidelines, and process based evaluation strengthen integrity. The chapter concludes that thoughtful redesign helps institutions maintain standards while adapting to technological change.

Generative artificial intelligence (GenAI) has destabilised conventional assessment arrangements in higher education by lowering the cost of producing plausible academic texts and solutions. In this context, institutional responses have frequently concentrated on detection and surveillance, or on narrow policy prohibitions, approaches that risk eroding trust, amplifying inequities, and misrecognising assessment as a socio-pedagogical practice shaped by institutional cultures, disciplinary norms, and unequal access to resources. This chapter advances a theoretically informed redesign agenda that re-centres authentic assessment and assessment-for-learning (AfL) as complementary foundations for quality and integrity in AI-rich environments. Rather than treating GenAI as an external threat to be "controlled," the chapter conceptualises GenAI as a socio-technical mediator within learners' activity systems and academic literacies, requiring assessment designs that make learning processes visible, uphold fairness and accountability, and preserve students' epistemic agency.

The rapid integration of AI into higher education assessment is reshaping academic integrity, quality assurance, and trust. While AI offers efficiency, scalability, and personalized feedback, it also raises ethical and equity concerns such as bias, surveillance, and inequity. This chapter argues that academic integrity cannot be ensured through technology alone, but must be treated as a socio-pedagogical practice shaped by institutional culture and global contexts. It proposes a Socio-Pedagogical Integrity Framework (SPIF) comprising pedagogical design, ethical AI use, assessment literacy, and contextual equitability. The framework promotes a shift from surveillance-based compliance to trust-based, learning-focused assessment practices.

Artificial intelligence (AI) is increasingly shaping assessment practices in higher education through tools such as automated grading systems, AI-generated feedback, learning analytics, and technologies designed to detect academic dishonesty. While these innovations promise greater efficiency, scalability, and consistency in evaluating student performance, they also introduce significant challenges related to fairness, transparency, academic integrity, and institutional governance. This chapter argues that the central challenge of AI-mediated assessment is not purely technological but lies in the governance of trust within assessment systems. Furthermore, it examines how AI reshapes power relations among

such as intelligent tutoring systems, automated grading platforms, and predictive learning analytics offer opportunities for personalized learning, improved efficiency, and enhanced academic outcomes. However, the increasing reliance on these technologies also raises important contractual, regulatory, and liability concerns, particularly within the evolving legal framework of the Indian education sector. This study examines the contractual governance and liability allocation associated with AI educational technologies by analyzing stakeholder perceptions of contractual clarity, regulatory compliance, ethical safeguards, and institutional support mechanisms. Using an empirical mixed-methods research design, data were collected from 300 stakeholders including AI developers, educational administrators, teachers, and students across four South Indian states.

The findings show that although AI holds considerable promise for enhancing assessment efficiency and feedback quality, its actual impact is heavily conditioned by infrastructural deficits, ethical issues, and uneven institutional capacity across the Global South. This review offers evidence-informed insights into how AI is shaping higher education assessment and underscores the importance of contextually responsive strategies that confront structural inequities. It also guides policy and institutional decision-making by foregrounding fair and sustainable approaches to integrating AI into assessment. Additionally, the study outlines key avenues for future research on AI-mediated assessment in under-resourced higher education systems.

A combination of pressure points that question traditional approaches to evaluation is experienced in the Global South and low-density rural higher education contexts. The chapter explores the AI-enabled assessment for the Global South, rural and resource-constrained higher education. It draws together cross-sectional evidence about approaches to architecture, governance, pedagogy and equity in order to explore how AI can support assessment whilst respecting local goals and limitations. The Principal Analysis spots four design levers, namely: lightweight and offline-capable assessment tools; governance and data sovereignty-based data collection; modular architectures through capacity building and evidence across domains. But there will be growing dangers in relation to data privacy, algorithmic bias, inequalities in language and culture, as well as dependency on suppliers. The chapter ends with policy, university governance and sustainable scaling implications focused on learner rights and educational justice that is locally stewarded.

This chapter examines the implications of generative artificial intelligence for assessment practices, academic integrity and quality assurance in South African higher education institutions. As AI-powered tools such as ChatGPT, SciSpace, Gemini, and Copilot become embedded in teaching, learning and assessment, they offer opportunities to enhance efficiency, feedback and assessment design while raising ethical concerns about misconduct, authorship, transparency and assessment validity. Drawing on the Theory of Planned Behaviour and the Utilitarian Theory of Ethics, the chapter adopts a conceptual and critical approach to analyse how the literature portrays academics' and students' perceptions, adoption and justification of the ethical or unethical use of generative artificial intelligence in assessment contexts. Particular attention is given to challenges surrounding originality, intellectual property, and authenticity, which, in turn, have implications for assessment outcomes.

The rapid adoption of generative artificial intelligence in higher education has transformed assessment faster than academic development has adapted. This conceptual chapter examines preparedness for artificial intelligence driven assessment in South African universities, where policies have expanded since 2023 but staff development remains uneven. Drawing on Technological Pedagogical Content Knowledge, the Artificial Intelligence Assessment Scale, Diffusion of Innovations Theory, and the Technology Acceptance Model, supported by emerging South African evidence, it argues that preparedness extends beyond technical competence. It proposes a four dimensional model comprising technological and pedagogical fluency, assessment design capability, academic integrity, and institutional readiness, with implications for policy, academic development, and future research. It emphasises assessment redesign, ethical practice, and institutional investment to strengthen quality and implementation now.

Assessment plays a pivotal contentious role in language education, in African contexts, where colonial-era epistemologies and monolingual standards have shaped prevailing practices. Assessment frameworks for African languages often mirror those designed for dominant global languages, neglecting learners' sociolinguistic realities. Concurrently, the rise of generative artificial intelligence tools has catalysed discussions about academic integrity and assessment validity, in English-medium higher education. This chapter addresses a significant gap in the discourse on African languages and generative AI by examining how authentic assessment and assessment for learning can be redefined in these contexts. The chapter suggests that GenAI can serve as a transformative catalyst that challenges conventional

This will create the learning environment for each connected with this platform and real time learning uniquely with proper feedback system. The experts will guide the students on each level and encourage them for the higher education with proper academic progression. This type of platform beneficial for students for proper engagement and advance level of learning method, predictive analysis and progress report on each level. This platform is easy to handle for educators and focus on unlimited time interaction with students. This will be fostering critical thinking and stimulating creativity while encouraging self-paced learning. This allows for less administrative hassle, gains insights for the tutors to check the student progress, and offers online meetings.

Preface

INTRODUCTION

The rapid emergence of artificial intelligence (AI) is reshaping the landscape of higher education, with assessment representing one of the areas in which the implications of this transformation are most immediate and far-reaching. AI-powered technologies are increasingly being used to support automated and adaptive assessment, feedback generation, learning analytics, plagiarism detection, remote proctoring, curriculum development, and personalized learning. These developments offer considerable possibilities for improving the efficiency, responsiveness, scalability, and accessibility of assessment practices. At the same time, they have introduced fundamental questions concerning what constitutes valid evidence of learning, how academic integrity should be understood in AI-rich environments, who should be accountable for assessment decisions, and how trust between students, academics, institutions, and technological systems can be sustained. This edited volume, *AI-Powered Assessments for Quality and Integrity in Global Higher Education*, responds to these questions by bringing together diverse scholarly perspectives on the opportunities, challenges, ethical tensions, and governance implications associated with AI-mediated assessment.

The central premise of this volume is that AI-powered assessment cannot be understood solely as a technological innovation. Rather, it is a complex socio-pedagogical, ethical, institutional, and cultural development that affects the purposes and practices of higher education. Assessment is not simply a mechanism for assigning grades; it communicates institutional values, shapes learning behaviours, establishes relationships of authority, and provides evidence upon which important educational decisions are made. The introduction of AI therefore has implications extending beyond efficiency and automation. Questions of algorithmic bias, transparency, privacy, surveillance, data ownership, accessibility, authorship, cultural and linguistic representation, and professional judgment become inseparable from questions of assessment quality and integrity. Across the chapters, contributors consequently examine AI not merely as a tool to be adopted or resisted, but as a force requiring thoughtful reconsideration of assessment design, academic practice, institutional governance, and the educational relationship between human actors and intelligent technologies.

An important feature of this collection is its global orientation. Much of the emerging discourse on AI in education has been shaped by institutions and technological ecosystems in relatively well-resourced contexts, while the realities of the Global South, rural institutions, multilingual educational environments, and resource-constrained universities can differ substantially. The chapters in this volume deliberately broaden the conversation by drawing on experiences and scholarship from Africa, Asia, the Middle East, Australia, Canada, and other contexts. Particular attention is given to South African and wider African higher education, Indian higher education, multilingual and language-learning contexts, and resource-constrained environments. This geographical diversity enables the volume to consider how infrastructure, institutional capacity, language, culture, educational histories, regulation, and socioeconomic inequalities influence the implementation and consequences of AI-powered assessment. In doing so, the volume emphasizes that responsible AI adoption cannot rely on universal solutions detached from local educational realities.

The book also moves beyond a narrow understanding of academic integrity as the prevention and detection of student misconduct. Several contributors argue for a broader conception in which integrity is embedded within assessment design, institutional culture, professional judgment, transparency, fairness, and shared responsibility. Authentic assessment, assessment for learning, formative feedback, process-oriented evaluation, human oversight, privacy by design, and responsible innovation consequently emerge as important themes throughout the collection. The contributors collectively invite readers to reconsider whether technological surveillance alone can preserve trust and quality, and instead explore how assessment systems can be redesigned so that integrity becomes an outcome of sound pedagogy and equitable institutional practice. The volume is therefore intended not simply as a discussion of current technologies, but as a contribution to the wider rethinking of quality assurance, academic integrity, and educational practice in an increasingly AI-mediated higher education landscape.

OVERVIEW OF THE CHAPTERS

The volume opens with a focused examination of AI-powered assessment and integrity in Cantonese as a second language education, providing an important linguistic and culturally situated entry point into the broader discussion. The chapter by Siu-lun Lee considers how AI-driven diagnostics, adaptive testing, and automated feedback may respond to learner diversity and proficiency benchmarking in Cantonese education in Hong Kong. At the same time, it draws attention to algorithmic bias, cultural insensitivity, and the possible erosion of authentic communicative interaction. By emphasizing authenticity, fairness, transparency, and trust, the chapter establishes an important principle for the volume: AI-supported assessment must remain responsive to the linguistic, cultural, and communicative contexts in which learning occurs.

Chapter 1, "AI-Enabled Assessment: Transforming Higher Education Pedagogy," by Welile Msimango and Siyacela Nzuza, examines AI-enabled assessment through the lens of Assessment for Learning (AfL). The chapter synthesizes research on personalized feedback, adaptive learning, learner engagement, and data-informed instructional decision-making. It also addresses algorithmic bias, academic integrity, transparency, and data privacy, positioning AI as a potential contributor to learner-centred pedagogical transformation when embedded within appropriate ethical and pedagogical frameworks.

Chapter 2, "Artificial Intelligence–Supported Assessment: Advancing Equity, Integrity, and Curriculum Innovation," by Ratan Sarkar, extends the discussion by conceptualizing AI-mediated assessment as a socio-pedagogical practice. Particular attention is given to equity, inclusion, curriculum governance, and the risks of surveillance, opacity, automation bias, and diminished professional judgment. The chapter's layered ecosystem model emphasizes the need for transparent and human-centred implementation, especially in resource-constrained and Global South contexts.

Chapter 3, "Reframing Quality and Integrity in AI-Powered Assessment: A Global and Ethical Perspective on Higher Education," by Sohom Saha and Mahendra Kumar Singh, further develops the ethical dimension of AI assessment. The authors question approaches that rely excessively on surveillance and detection and advocate assessment practices centred on authenticity, student agency, equity, and human judgment. The chapter is particularly attentive to the circumstances of Global South institutions, where inequalities in access and resources can shape the consequences of AI adoption.

Chapter 4, "AI-Mediated Assessment in Global Higher Education: Trust and Integrity Quality Assurance Challenges," by Neha Guliani and Nidhi Shukla, examines the redistribution of authority and accountability that accompanies automated grading, plagiarism detection, and remote proctoring. The chapter considers how automation can alter the relationship between students and institutions and emphasizes trust-centred approaches to judgment and quality assurance rather than technological control alone.

Chapter 5, "Redesigning Authentic Assessment and Feedback Practices in the Generative AI Era," by Sushil Bhardwaj, Sweta Rana, Indu Sharma, and Rohit Markan, turns specifically to the implications of generative AI for assessment design. The authors highlight authentic tasks, staged submissions, reflection, oral interaction, formative feedback, and clear institutional AI guidelines as mechanisms through which assessment can continue to provide meaningful evidence of student learning. The chapter underscores the importance of assessing processes of learning rather than merely evaluating final products.

Chapter 6, "Authentic Assessment and Assessment-for-Learning in the Generative AI Era," by Tendai Charles and Siham Abukhalaf, similarly challenges assessment approaches dominated by detection and surveillance. The chapter conceptualizes generative AI as a socio-technical mediator and argues for assessment designs that make learning processes visible while preserving student agency, fairness, and accountability. Its emphasis on authentic assessment and AfL contributes to the volume's broader movement from prohibition toward pedagogical redesign.

Chapter 7, "Reframing Academic Integrity in the Age of AI using a Socio-Pedagogical Framework for Quality and Trust in Higher Education Assessment," by Viji J, M. Sasikala, and M. Hemalatha, proposes a Socio-Pedagogical Integrity Framework. The framework brings together pedagogical design, ethical AI use, assessment literacy, and contextual equitability. In doing so, the chapter emphasizes that integrity is produced through relationships among technology, pedagogy, institutional culture, and educational context rather than guaranteed through technological mechanisms alone.

Chapter 8, "Assessing Trust, Quality, Integrity, and Power in AI-Mediated Higher Education Assessment," by Salam Al-E'mari, Yousef Sanjalawe, and Fadi Fataftah, places trust and power at the centre of the analysis. The authors explore how automated assessment, analytics, and integrity technologies reshape relationships among students, educators, institutions, and technological systems. The chapter is particularly significant in drawing attention to the power relations and governance structures that accompany the increasing use of AI in assessment.

Chapter 9, "Beyond Efficiency: Reimagining Assessment as an Ethical AI Practice in Higher Education," by Siyacela Nzuza, approaches AI-mediated assessment through the Responsible Innovation framework. The chapter considers governance, human oversight, stakeholder participation, transparency, and ongoing evaluation as necessary components of responsible implementation. It reinforces the argument that responsible AI adoption requires institutional processes capable of identifying and responding to emerging consequences.

Chapter 10, "From Cheating Prevention to Integrity Innovation in AI-Based Assessment: From Surveillance to Systemic Integrity," by Naveen Nandal, Deepak Chahal, Rajesh Dhaka, Raman Joshi, and Suraj Yadav, develops the concept of *integrity innovation*. Rather than treating academic integrity primarily as an individual compliance problem, the chapter positions it as a systemic outcome of assessment design, governance, and institutional culture. Its focus on shared responsibility and assessment redesign adds another dimension to the volume's sustained critique of surveillance-centred approaches.

Chapter 11, "Contractual and Liability Issues in AI Educational Technologies," by Azash S. MD., Mamatha G.M., and Yusuf Hayath Md, broadens the discussion into legal and contractual territory. Focusing particularly on the Indian educational context, the chapter examines contractual governance, regulatory compliance, ethical safeguards, and liability allocation surrounding AI educational technologies. Its empirical mixed-methods approach, involving 300 stakeholders across four South Indian states, provides a stakeholder-oriented perspective on the institutional and legal responsibilities associated with AI adoption.

Chapter 12, "A Systematic Review of AI-Powered Assessment in the Global South: Opportunities and Challenges in Resource-Constrained Higher Education Contexts," by Nontobeko Khumalo and Ntandokamenzi Dlamini, explicitly foregrounds the structural conditions under which AI-powered assessment is implemented. The chapter examines infrastructural limitations, institutional capacity, ethical concerns, and uneven access to AI technologies. It argues for contextually responsive approaches that address structural inequities while informing sustainable policy and institutional decision-making.

Chapter 13, "AI and Assessment in Global South, Rural, and Resource-Constrained Higher Education Contexts," by Michael Oyenuga, complements this systematic review by focusing on practical design and governance considerations. The chapter identifies lightweight and offline-capable systems, data sovereignty, modular architectures, capacity building, and evidence-based implementation as important design considerations. It also addresses risks involving privacy, algorithmic bias, language and cultural inequalities, and technological dependency.

Chapter 14, "Generative Artificial Intelligence in South African Higher Education: Ethical Challenges, Misuse and Implications for Assessment Outcomes and Academic Integrity," by Patrick Nyathi and Nokuthula Nkosi, brings the discussion specifically into South African higher education. Drawing on the Theory of Planned Behaviour and Utilitarian Theory of Ethics, the chapter considers perceptions and uses of generative AI in assessment, with particular attention to authorship, originality, intellectual property, authenticity, and assessment validity. It provides an important contextual contribution to understanding the ethical dimensions of GenAI adoption within South African institutions.

Chapter 15, "Preparing Higher Education Academics for Artificial Intelligence-Driven Assessment in South African Higher Education," by Oluwatoyin Ajani, shifts attention from technology and student behaviour to academic preparedness. The chapter proposes a four-dimensional model encompassing technological and pedagogical fluency, assessment design capability, academic integrity, and institutional readiness. Its emphasis on professional development and institutional investment highlights the importance of preparing academics to make informed pedagogical and ethical decisions in AI-mediated assessment environments.

Chapter 16, "Authentic Assessment and Assessment for Learning in African Languages in the Era of Generative AI: Pedagogical Possibilities, Ethical Tensions, and Epistemic Justice," by Nthabiseng Khoalenyane and Tinashe Matiyenga, introduces questions of language, coloniality, and epistemic justice. The chapter challenges the uncritical application of assessment models developed around dominant languages and considers how generative AI may create both risks and opportunities for African-language education. Its focus on decoloniality and linguistic realities adds an important dimension to the volume's wider concern with contextual equity.

Chapter 17, "Human-AI Collaboration in Pedagogy and Ethical Assessment in GenAI-Integrated Education: Learning Analytics with Privacy by Design," by Sabyasachi Pramanik, develops a framework for human-AI cooperation grounded in psychometrics, algorithmic fairness, data protection, socio-technical systems theory, and critical pedagogy. The chapter presents risk and harm considerations, privacy-by-design controls, discipline-sensitive assessment redesign, and staged governance mechanisms. It positions AI as an augmentative but contestable partner that must remain accountable to students, educators, institutions, and wider communities.

Chapter 18, "Redefining Postgraduate Student-Supervisor Relationships and the Role of Supervisors in the Age of Artificial Intelligence," by Luthando Molefe and Nokubongwa Ntuli, extends the volume beyond conventional assessment settings into postgraduate research and supervision. Drawing on Foucault's conception of power-knowledge relations, the chapter examines how AI tools are changing student-supervisor relationships and potentially shifting traditional mentoring arrangements toward hybrid forms of supervision. It highlights questions concerning independence, critical thinking, accuracy, ethical use, and the evolving responsibilities of supervisors.

Finally, Chapter 19, "The Future of Learning: AI-Driven Educational Platforms for Inclusive and Adaptive Education," by Govind Sharma, Payal Shekhawat, Kunal Shekhawat, and Swarnim Shrivastav, considers the possibilities offered by integrated AI-based educational platforms. The chapter focuses on adaptive learning, self-assessment, personalized feedback, predictive analytics, student engagement, academic progression, and educator support. As the concluding contribution to the chapter sequence, it provides a forward-looking perspective on how AI platforms may contribute to more individualized and accessible learning environments while reinforcing the need for thoughtful educational design.

Taken together, these chapters move across multiple levels of analysis—from individual assessment tasks and classroom practices to institutional governance, legal accountability, professional development, language and culture, and broader questions of educational justice. They also bring together conceptual, theoretical, systematic-review, empirical, and practice-oriented approaches. This diversity is deliberate. AI-powered assessment is not a single problem with a single solution; rather, it is an evolving field in which technological possibilities intersect with disciplinary expectations, institutional cultures, educational inequalities, legal frameworks, and changing conceptions of knowledge and learning.

CONCLUSION

The chapters in this volume collectively demonstrate that the future of AI-powered assessment in higher education cannot be reduced to a question of whether institutions should adopt or prohibit artificial intelligence. The more consequential question concerns *how assessment should be designed, governed, and experienced when AI becomes an increasingly ordinary component of educational environments.* Across the contributions, AI is shown to have the capacity to improve feedback, personalization, scalability, accessibility, learning analytics, and formative assessment. Yet these possibilities coexist with substantial concerns surrounding algorithmic bias, privacy, surveillance, transparency, authorship, cultural representation, inequitable access, professional judgment, and accountability. Quality and integrity therefore depend not on technological sophistication alone, but on the educational and institutional conditions within which technology is deployed.

A recurring message across the collection is the need to move from surveillance-oriented approaches toward assessment systems that foreground authenticity, learning, trust, and shared responsibility. Detection technologies may have a role within institutional integrity strategies, but the chapters demonstrate why they cannot constitute the entirety of an integrity framework. Assessment design itself can create stronger opportunities for authentic demonstrations of learning through staged work, reflection, dialogue, oral interaction, process evidence, formative feedback, and discipline-sensitive tasks. Such approaches do not eliminate the challenges posed by generative AI, but they reposition assessment around its fundamental educational purpose: generating credible and meaningful evidence of what learners know, understand, can do, and are able to develop.

The volume also makes clear that there is no context-free model of responsible AI assessment. The implications of AI differ according to language, culture, infrastructure, institutional capacity, regulatory environments, disciplinary practices, and histories of educational inequality. Contributions addressing the Global South, African languages, South African higher education, Cantonese education, rural institutions, and resource-constrained environments demonstrate the importance of locally responsive implementation. Equity cannot be treated as an afterthought once AI systems have been introduced. Questions concerning data sovereignty, accessibility, language representation, technological dependency, staff preparedness, and institutional capacity must be incorporated into assessment planning from the outset. Responsible AI therefore requires not only technical safeguards but also institutional willingness to recognize and address structural inequalities.

Ultimately, this volume positions trust as a central organizing principle for the future of AI-powered assessment. Trust does not mean the uncritical acceptance of AI systems; rather, it requires transparency about how systems operate, meaningful human oversight, mechanisms for contesting automated decisions, appropriate protection of personal data, clear expectations concerning AI use, and accountability among technology providers, institutions, educators, and students. It also requires investment in assessment literacy and professional development so that academics can make informed decisions about when, where, and how AI should be incorporated into assessment. The future described across these chapters is therefore neither one of unrestricted automation nor one of technological rejection. It is a future in which AI is deliberately situated within pedagogical, ethical, legal, and institutional frameworks that preserve human judgment and educational purpose.

As editors, we hope that this volume contributes to a more nuanced and constructive conversation about AI and higher education assessment. The contributors collectively invite researchers, academics, educational leaders, policymakers, technology developers, and students to view the current transformation not simply as a challenge to existing assessment systems, but as an opportunity to reconsider what quality, integrity, fairness, and learning should mean in the contemporary university. AI may alter the tools through which assessment is conducted, but the responsibility for defining its educational purposes remains fundamentally human. The enduring task is therefore to build assessment ecosystems in which technological innovation supports—not displaces—the principles of fairness, authenticity, inclusion, accountability, academic integrity, and meaningful learning.

Chapter 1
AI-Enabled Assessment:
Transforming Higher Education Pedagogy

Welile Ntombifuthi Msimango
http://orcid.org/0000-0001-6051-4351
University of Zululand, South Africa

Siyacela Thandazani Nzuza
http://orcid.org/0000-0002-3521-7627
University of Zululand, South Africa

ABSTRACT

Artificial Intelligence (AI) is increasingly transforming assessment in higher education by enhancing Assessment for Learning (AfL) through personalized feedback, adaptive learning, and data-informed teaching. This chapter presents a systematic literature review examining how AI-driven assessment is reshaping teaching, learning, and assessment practices. Guided by the AfL framework, the review synthesizes current research on AI applications and their role in pedagogical transformation. Findings indicate that AI enables timely feedback, improves learner engagement, supports personalized learning experiences, and promotes authentic, process-oriented assessment. The review also highlights the increasing integration of AI into curriculum design and instructional decision-making. However, ethical concerns remain, including algorithmic bias, academic integrity, transparency, and data privacy. The chapter concludes that AI can strengthen formative assessment when implemented within sound pedagogical and ethical frameworks, supporting learner-centered transformation in higher education.

INTRODUCTION

Artificial Intelligence (AI) is increasingly being adopted in higher education to support and transform assessment practices, particularly within the paradigm of Assessment for Learning. This shift reflects a broader movement toward leveraging digital technologies to enhance teaching, learning, and assessment in more responsive and data-informed ways. Kasneci et al. (2023) and Yan et al. (2024) argue that the emergence of generative AI (GAI) has the potential to fundamentally reshape educational practices by enabling more dynamic, interactive, and personalized learning experiences. In the context of assessment, AI tools are increasingly used to provide real-time feedback, support adaptive learning pathways, and facilitate continuous monitoring of student progress key principles underpinning Assessment for Learning.

DOI: 10.4018/979-8-3373-8939-4.ch001

The integration of AI into assessment practices signals a shift from traditional, summative approaches toward more formative, learner-centered models. AI-driven systems can analyze large volumes of student data, generate immediate feedback, and identify learning gaps, thereby supporting both lecturers and students in making informed decisions about teaching and learning. This aligns with contemporary pedagogical approaches that emphasize feedback, reflection, and active learner engagement. However, while global trends indicate rapid adoption, the implementation of AI in higher education is uneven across contexts. The South African context reflects many of these global developments, although the pace and nature of adoption differ across institutions.

In the South African context, Patel and Ragolane (2024) highlight that the adoption of AI in education remains relatively limited, with institutions still navigating infrastructural, pedagogical, and policy-related challenges. This limited uptake highlights a critical need for deeper understanding of how AI can be effectively integrated to maximize its educational benefits. Despite these challenges, emerging research points to significant opportunities. For instance, AI technologies have the potential to enhance access to education, improve the quality of feedback, and support innovative teaching practices. Patel and Ragolane (2024) further note that AI integration can contribute to improved efficiency in assessment processes and enable more personalized learning experiences. Moreover, Funda and Piderit (2024) emphasize that AI-powered online platforms offer flexible learning opportunities, particularly for students who may not have access to traditional face-to-face classroom environments. This is especially relevant in contexts characterized by resource constraints and geographical disparities, where technology can play a transformative role in expanding access and supporting inclusive education. AI-driven tools can bridge gaps in teaching and learning by providing scalable solutions that cater to diverse learner needs. Despite these promising developments, the integration of AI into Assessment for Learning raises important questions about its impact on pedagogy. There is a need to critically examine how AI is reshaping teaching practices, assessment design, and the roles of both lecturers and students. Furthermore, concerns related to ethics, data privacy, algorithmic bias, and the potential over-reliance on automated systems highlight the importance of adopting a balanced and critical perspective. This chapter therefore explores the pedagogical changes enabled by AI-driven Assessment for Learning in higher education. It seeks to provide a systematic and critical synthesis of existing literature to better understand how AI is influencing assessment practices and to identify both opportunities and challenges associated with its integration.

This chapter is structured into several key sections. It begins with the background of the study, which provides the contextual foundations and rationale for the systematic review. This is followed by the problem statement, outlining the research gap and the central issue addressed in the review. The chapter then presents a review of relevant literature to situate the study within existing scholarship, followed by a discussion of the theoretical framework underpinning the study. The research questions guiding this systematic review are subsequently outlined. The data analysis section describes how the reviewed studies were systematically analyzed and synthesized, leading into the discussion of findings, where the results are interpreted in relation to the research questions and existing literature. Finally, the chapter concludes with a discussion of the study's limitations, recommendations, and directions for future research. Each of these sections is presented and discussed below.

BACKGROUND OF THE STUDY

Artificial Intelligence (AI) is defined by Alhalalmeh and Al-Tarawneh (2025) as computer systems capable of performing tasks that typically require human intelligence, including learning, problem-solving, and decision-making. Building on this, Singh (2023) highlights that AI has been widely adopted across multiple sectors such as healthcare, finance, transportation, and entertainment, demonstrating its versatility and transformative potential. This widespread application has accelerated the development of AI technologies, leading to their increasing integration into the education sector. Patel and Ragolane (2024) explain that the rapid advancement of AI in recent years has begun to significantly influence higher education institutions, particularly in teaching, learning, and assessment. This progression highlights the growing importance of examining how AI is reshaping pedagogical practices, especially within the context of assessment for learning.

Patel and Ragolane (2024) explain that over the past decades, the emergence and rapid adoption of AI have introduced both challenges and opportunities for higher education globally. Ncube et al. (2026) argue that, in the early stages of AI integration, it was largely perceived as a threat to the quality and integrity of assessment practices, particularly because of concerns related to academic honesty and the authenticity of student work. This initial resistance reflects a broader tension between technological advancement and traditional assessment approaches. However, as understanding of AI has evolved, so too have perspectives on its role in education. Increasingly, AI is being recognized as both a catalyst for change and a potential enabler of innovation in teaching, learning, and assessment. This shift in perception highlights the need to move beyond a deficit view of AI toward exploring how it can be meaningfully integrated to enhance pedagogical practices, particularly within the framework of Assessment for Learning.

Ogwueleka (2025) raises concerns regarding plagiarism, the automation of student work, and the potential erosion of critical thinking, all of which have contributed to a defensive stance among many higher education institutions. However, these perceptions are gradually evolving, as the potential of AI to enhance teaching and learning becomes increasingly evident and warrants further exploration. Contemporary discourse increasingly positions AI as a disruptive force and as a catalyst for pedagogical transformation. Scholars such as Gamage et al. (2023) argue that while AI raises significant concerns regarding academic integrity, it simultaneously offers opportunities to rethink and redesign assessment practices. Similarly, Overono and Ditta (2025) caution that an excessive focus on detecting and penalizing AI use may lead institutions into an unproductive cycle, thereby missing the opportunity to reimagine the purpose and value of assessment in higher education. This shift in perspective encourages educators to move beyond control-driven approaches toward more constructive and pedagogically meaningful integration of AI.

Rahiman and Kodikal (2024) suggest that institutional adoption of AI is largely influenced by stakeholders' understanding of its functionality, perceived usefulness, and the extent to which associated risks are considered manageable. In this regard, Singh (2023) describes AI as a disruptive yet transformative force that is reshaping pedagogical approaches, student learning experiences, and institutional operations. This transformation compels higher education institutions to adapt and develop innovative models that leverage AI to improve teaching, learning, and assessment practices. Within this evolving landscape, there is growing recognition of the potential of AI to support Assessment for Learning by enabling timely feedback, personalized learning pathways, and data-informed decision-making. Despite these advancements, there remains a lack of systematic and consolidated understanding of how AI-driven assessment practices are influencing pedagogy in higher education. This chapter seeks to address this gap by examining the pedagogical changes enabled by AI-driven Assessment for Learning in higher education. Specifically, it aims to critically explore how AI is integrated into assessment practices and how such integration contributes to meaningful transformations in teaching and learning.

PROBLEM STATEMENT

AI technologies hold significant promise for enhancing formative assessment practices, including those grounded in Assessment for Learning. However, there is currently no consolidated framework that clearly explains how these tools collectively contribute to pedagogical transformation in higher education. Existing studies tend to focus on isolated aspects of AI in education, such as academic integrity, technological adoption, or student performance outcomes (e.g., Nakajima, 2025; Abah et al., 2025), rather than providing a comprehensive synthesis of its broader pedagogical implications. This fragmented focus limits a holistic understanding of AI's role in reshaping teaching and assessment practices. The central problem addressed in this chapter is that, although AI offers significant educational benefits, its rapid integration into higher education creates tension between pedagogical innovation and assessment integrity. Khasawneh and Khasawneh (2023) further argue that current assessment frameworks are often not adequately equipped to address issues such as systemic bias and the potential marginalisation of students' work in AI-mediated environments. This situation highlights a critical gap between technological innovation and the readiness of existing assessment systems to respond effectively and ethically. Therefore, there is a pressing need to systematically examine how AI-driven assessment for learning is reshaping pedagogical practices in higher education, with particular attention to both its transformative potential and its associated risks. This chapter responds to this need by synthesizing existing literature to develop a clearer understanding of pedagogical change enabled by AI in assessment contexts.

THE INTERSECTION OF ARTIFICIAL INTELLIGENCE AND ASSESSMENT FOR LEARNING (AFL)

Memarian and Doleck (2024) and Saputra et al. (2024) note that the relationship between Artificial Intelligence (AI) and Assessment for Learning is increasingly recognized as both complementary and transformative. While AfL is grounded in formative assessment principles that emphasize continuous feedback, learner engagement, and adaptive teaching, AI introduces technological capabilities that extend these practices in more scalable and responsive ways. Almutairi et al. (2025) argue that AI strengthens AfL by enabling the rapid collection and analysis of learner data, allowing lecturers to gain deeper insights into students' understanding and progress in real time. This directly supports a core principle of AfL using evidence of learning to inform teaching by making feedback more immediate, personalized, and actionable. Sari et al. (2024) further maintain that automated feedback systems, adaptive learning platforms, and predictive analytics facilitate continuous monitoring of student performance, thereby enabling timely and targeted pedagogical interventions. Yang and Xin (2022) assert that the integration of AI does not replace the pedagogical foundations of AfL but rather amplifies them. Perla and Vinci (2023) emphasize that, although AI enhances efficiency and scalability, the role of the lecturer remains central in interpreting data, guiding learning, and ensuring that assessment practices are contextually relevant and ethically sound. Deneen (2025) adds that AI integration intersects with academic cultures, authority structures, and expectations of formative assessment, highlighting its broader institutional implications. Alfaleh (2026) contends that these developments underscore the pedagogical imperative to embed AI within established learning frameworks rather than treating it as an isolated evaluative tool. Therefore, the intersect of AI and AfL reflects a shift toward a more responsive, data-informed, and learner-centered approach to assessment in higher education, where technology enhances but does not replace pedagogical intent.

METHODOLOGY

A systematic literature review was employed to identify, analyze, and synthesize relevant secondary sources. The review findings were organized into themes to ensure logical presentation and readability. Furthermore, the Preferred Reporting Item for Systematic Review and Meta Analysis is employed to ensure transparency, accurate reporting and quality results. In terms of the search strategy, keywords such as artificial intelligence (AI), assessment, higher education, and pedagogical change were used to discover the relevant data. In addition to that, Boolean operators were applied to narrow down the results. The search primarily focused on studies published between 2015 and 2026 across databases to ensure that the perspectives incorporated into this research are fresh and relevant.

Regarding the eligibility criteria, the priority was placed on scholarly papers that had been peer reviewed and that were written in English to determine inclusion and exclusion. Also, pertaining to the selection process, titles and abstracts were screened initially to determine whether full-text review was required. Furthermore, a quality assessment process was conducted to ensure the careful selection of studies. All papers were systematically evaluated based on methodological quality and validity. Thereafter, only high and medium quality papers were considered for inclusion. Additionally, in extracting and synthesizing data, the key findings were isolated from the selected papers, then the thematic analysis and coding were conducted by identifying overarching themes for reporting. Also, as this chapter was co-authored, an independent collaborative review process was conducted, with application of uniform criteria across papers and throughout the process to minimize bias.

The application of PRISMA provided a structured and transparent methodological approach, ensuring transparency, completeness of this systematic review and meta-analyses chapter.

THEORETICAL FRAMEWORK

The chapter is grounded in the Assessment for Learning (AfL) framework proposed by Black and Wiliam (1998). This framework provides the ideal conceptual framework for 'AI-Enabled Assessment: Transforming Higher Education Pedagogy' because it shifts the focus from static and retrospective assessment to dynamic and iterative growth, reflecting the current capabilities of artificial intelligence. In the context of transforming higher education pedagogy, AfL goes beyond the constraint of human feedback, where teachers often struggle to provide timely and personalized critiques to large groups of students, by taking advantage of AI to offer instant and diagnostic insights. This alignment enables AI to function as a facilitator, carrying out the regular feedback loops and self-regulatory habits vital for effective learning. By framing AI through AfL lens, this chapter argues that technology does not merely automate marking, but necessarily humanizes the learning process by ensuring every student receives the precise and actionable support needed to bridge their specific knowledge gaps.

RESEARCH QUESTIONS

- How is Artificial Intelligence currently being used to support Assessment for Learning practices in higher education?
- In what ways does AI-driven Assessment for Learning contribute to pedagogical change in teaching, learning, and assessment practices in higher education?

DISCUSSION

This study explored how pedagogical change is enabled by AI-driven Assessment for Learning in higher education. The interpretation of findings is guided by the two research questions: 1) how Artificial Intelligence is currently being used to support Assessment for Learning practices in higher education, and 2) the ways in which AI-driven Assessment for Learning contributes to pedagogical change in teaching, learning, and assessment practices in higher education. The analysis revealed four themes. The first is the role of AI-driven tools in facilitating pedagogical change in teaching and learning. The second highlights AI-driven innovations in Assessment for Learning, particularly in relation to enhanced feedback, personalization, and learner engagement. The third examines the reshaping of authentic assessment in higher education, with attention to how AI is transforming assessment design and implementation. The fourth considers the ethical imperatives and risks associated with AI-driven assessment, including concerns of academic integrity, bias, and data privacy.

The Role of AI-Driven Tools in Facilitating Pedagogical Change in Teaching and Learning

Higher education institutions are increasingly encouraged to adopt a hybrid pedagogical framework that integrates Assessment for Learning with Responsible AI ethics to ensure human-centered educational innovation (Luckin, 2018; UNESCO, 2021). Within this framework, AI is positioned not as a replacement for educators, but as an assistive tool that enhances teaching, learning, and assessment practices. Deepshikha (2026) emphasizes that while AI improves efficiency, scalability, and consistency, its greatest value lies in supporting human-AI collaborative models under continuous pedagogical oversight. One significant pedagogical shift involves redesigning assessment around authentic, process-oriented tasks that emphasize metacognition, reflection, and real-world problem-solving. Dawson (2021) argues that such approaches reduce reliance on rote memorization and help mitigate risks associated with automation and academic dishonesty. Selwyn (2019) and Bearman and Luckin (2020) further assert that AI-augmented pedagogy should be understood as a means of supporting teaching rather than replacing it, provided that continuous monitoring and appropriate ethical safeguards are maintained. From an Assessment for Learning perspective, this finding reinforces the principle that assessment should function as an integral component of learning rather than a mechanism for evaluating learning after instruction has occurred. The role assigned to AI within the reviewed studies is therefore consistent with the AfL position advanced by Black and Wiliam (1998), where evidence generated through assessment is continuously used to support learning progression. Instead of replacing lectures, AI expands their capacity to monitor learner development and respond to learning needs in a more timely manner.

Across the literature, there is strong consensus that effective AI integration requires human oversight, institutional governance, and AI literacy development. Deepshikha (2026) highlights the importance of balancing technological automation with pedagogical judgment, while Naraliev (2025) and Sheikh (2024) advocate for structured hybrid human-AI frameworks supported by ethical institutional policies. Similarly, Wu (2026) proposes blended pedagogical models to ensure inclusive curriculum transformation across diverse learning contexts. Institutional readiness is also identified as a critical factor. Nwafor and Ezeugo (2025) and Saaida (2023) stress the need for investment in digital infrastructure and ethical governance frameworks, while Bhatia et al. (2024) and Suchithra and Arya (2025) emphasize continuous staff development and capacity building to support effective AI integration in teaching and learning environments. Rahiman and Kodikal (2024) further argue that curricula must be deliberately redesigned to align with the demands of a technologically advanced educational landscape. The need for curriculum redesign also aligns with AfL's emphasis on using assessment evidence to shape teaching practices. The findings suggest that AI integration is not simply a technological intervention but a catalyst for pedagogical adjustment, where teaching strategies, learning activities, and assessment processes become increasingly interconnected. This reflects Black and Wiliam's (1998) argument that effective assessment should directly inform instructional decisions and curriculum implementation.

AI integration requires curriculum and assessment redesign that promotes higher-order thinking and critical engagement. Gamage et al. (2023) and Perera and Lankathilake (2023) recommend a shift toward authentic, scenario-based assessments supported by clear institutional guidelines for ethical AI use. Similarly, Chukwu et al. (2026) emphasize subject-specific AI integration strategies that promote critical thinking rather than passive knowledge reproduction, while Sajja et al. (2026) advocate for flexible, course-specific AI usage policies rather than blanket restrictions. From a pedagogical perspective, AI is also seen as a tool for enhancing learner engagement and reducing cognitive overload. Nguyen et al. (2022) argue that AI can reduce administrative burdens on lecturers, enabling them to focus on meaningful student interaction and personalized support. Moulavinafchi et al. (2026) further suggest that blended approaches combining traditional instruction with AI tools can improve learning retention while reducing student fatigue. Finally, several scholars highlight the importance of continuous improvement and ethical alignment. Luo et al. (2025) propose iterative development cycles to ensure fairness, transparency, and effectiveness of AI tools across disciplines. Slimi and Villarejo-Carballido (2024) further recommend cross-disciplinary curriculum integration, collaborative policy development, and structured ethical training to support sustainable AI adoption in higher education. Viewed through the Assessment for Learning lens, these developments indicate a movement toward learning environments in which assessment data continuously informs teaching and supports learner development. The findings therefore suggest that AI strengthens the formative function of assessment by enabling lecturers to make more informed pedagogical decisions while maintaining responsibility for learner support and progression.

AI-Driven Innovations in Assessment for Learning

Several studies (Bhatia et al., 2024; Owan et al., 2023; Saaida, 2023) indicate that AI systems are widely used to support the rapid completion of assessment tasks and reduce administrative workload, thereby improving productivity and saving time. Sheikh (2024) further explains that AI functions as a tool that streamlines both the design and implementation of assessment activities, enabling lecturers to manage tasks more efficiently while supporting students in completing them at a faster pace. Nwafor and Ezeugo (2025), Sheikh (2024), and Luo et al. (2025) emphasize that, beyond efficiency, AI is increasingly utilized to provide timely, actionable, and personalized feedback, which is central to Assessment for Learning practices. Automated grading systems and intelligent feedback mechanisms allow students to receive immediate diagnostic insights into their performance, replacing delayed feedback with real-time guidance (Rahiman & Kodikal, 2024). This shift demonstrates how AI is currently being used for assessment automation and for enhancing formative feedback processes that support continuous learning. This finding strongly supports one of the central assumptions of Assessment for Learning. Black and Wiliam (1998) argue that feedback is most effective when it helps learners identify gaps in their understanding and provides guidance for improvement. The immediate and personalized feedback generated through AI systems reflects this principle by enabling students to act on assessment information while learning is still taking place rather than after learning has concluded.

Saaida (2023) indicates that AI applications in assessment are used to generate adaptive learning pathways that respond to individual learner performance data, thereby supporting differentiated instruction. This reflects a shift toward more personalized and responsive assessment practices. Moulavinafchi et al. (2026) further report that AI tools are increasingly integrated into learning environments to support grammar correction, task completion, and personalized learning support, often reducing learner stress and improving engagement. In relation to the second research question on how AI-driven Assessment for Learning contributes to pedagogical change in teaching, learning, and assessment practices, the findings indicate that AI is reshaping traditional assessment by transforming it into a dynamic, data-informed process. Assessment is no longer a static evaluation activity but is increasingly becoming an ongoing diagnostic process that informs teaching in real time. This represents a clear shift from assessment from assessment of learning to assessment for learning. According to the AfL framework, assessment should generate evidence that can be used by both lecturers and students to improve future learning. The reviewed studies demonstrate that AI facilitates this process by producing continuous performance data that can be used to modify instructional approaches and learning strategies as needs emerge. This shift enables lecturers to adjust instruction based on immediate student performance data, thereby strengthening the connection between assessment and teaching practice. Deepshikha (2025) and Singh (2023) argue that AI-driven assessment enhances student engagement and motivation through immediate and personalized feedback. Peddi and Manoharan (2026) and Gamage et al. (2023) further suggest that AI serves as a transformative tool in higher education by reducing repetitive administrative tasks while enabling more meaningful instructional interactions between lecturers and students. These findings extend the Assessment for Learning framework by demonstrating how technological systems can strengthen formative assessment practices at scale. While Black and Wiliam (1998) developed AfL within traditional classroom contexts, the evidence reviewed in this study suggests that AI can enhance the frequency, responsiveness, and individualisation of formative assessment without compromising its pedagogical purpose.

Reshaping of Authentic Assessment in Higher Education

The rapid integration of artificial intelligence into higher education is prompting a significant shift in how student learning is defined and assessed. Increasingly, there is a move away from traditional assessment approaches that prioritize rote memorization, toward more authentic forms of assessment that reflect real-world and AI-enabled professional environments. In a context where AI systems can instantly retrieve information, generate content, and analyze large datasets, the value of testing recall-based knowledge has diminished. As a result, conventional closed-book examinations are becoming less effective and more vulnerable to issues of academic integrity. Supporting this view, Bhatia et al. (2024) note that AI has the capacity to enhance online learning by personalizing student experiences, improving engagement, and streamlining assessment processes. In response to these changes, there is a growing need to redesign curricula in ways that promote "AI-resilient" authentic assessments. Such assessments should prioritize higher-order cognitive skills, including critical thinking, ethical judgment, creativity, and the ability to evaluate and manage AI-generated outputs. These competencies are increasingly essential in contemporary workplaces. Rather than focusing solely on final answers, assessment practices are beginning to emphasize the learning process itself. This includes requiring students to document their reasoning, reflect on their decision-making, justify their use of AI tools, and present their thinking in both written and oral forms. These practices are closely aligned with Assessment for Learning principles because they encourage students to become active participants in evaluating and regulating their own learning. Black and Wiliam (1998) emphasize the importance of learner self-assessment and reflection, both of which are evident in assessment designs requiring students to explain and justify their thinking processes.

The evolving approach ensures that students are not positioned as passive users of AI technologies, but rather as active, critical thinkers capable of engaging with AI as a collaborative tool. From AfL perspective, this shift is significant because it places learner agency at the centre of assessment. Instead of focusing exclusively on assessment outcomes, attention is directed toward how students learn, reflect, and improve throughout the learning process. Such an approach reflects one of the core objectives of Assessment for Learning, namely the development of self-regulated and reflective learners. Authentic assessment in this sense mirrors real professional contexts, where graduates may be expected to use generative AI to support tasks such as report writing, while also critically evaluating outputs for accuracy, bias, and cultural sensitivity. Such tasks foreground durable human capabilities, including metacognition, complex problem-solving, and socio-ethical awareness, ensuring that learning remains relevant in an increasingly automated world. By integrating AI into assessment design rather than excluding it, higher education institutions can foster more meaningful digital literacy and better prepare students to operate confidently and ethically in AI-driven environments. However, Deepshikha (2026) and Zhao (2024) caution that while AI tools such as machine learning and natural language processing perform effectively in structured disciplines like STEM, they are often less responsive to the contextual and interpretive demands of the humanities. In contrast, Chukwu et al. (2026) argue that although usage patterns may differ across disciplines, AI tools have the potential to support learning development across all fields, helping students improve at comparable rates regardless of their area of study. The findings therefore suggest that authentic assessment supported by AI remains fundamentally consistent with the goals of Assessment for Learning, particularly where assessment tasks encourage reflection, ongoing improvement, and meaningful engagement with knowledge rather than simple content reproduction.

The Ethical Imperatives and Risks Associated with AI-Driven Assessment

While AI-driven assessment offers significant pedagogical potential, its adoption in higher education is accompanied by important ethical imperatives and systemic risks that require careful and sustained institutional attention. A key concern relates to transparency and data governance. Chukwu et al. (2026)

emphasize the need for clarity in how AI systems make decisions and how student data is collected, stored, and protected. Without such transparency, trust in AI-mediated assessment processes may be compromized. A further major challenge is algorithmic bias. Many AI systems are trained on historical datasets that may reflect existing social inequalities, leading to the unintended reproduction of bias in assessment outcomes. As a result, certain student groups may be marginalized or unfairly disadvantaged (Ajani et al., 2024; Jobin et al., 2019). This risk is particularly concerning in diverse higher education contexts, where fairness and inclusion are central to assessment integrity. In addition, Gamage et al. (2023) highlight risks related to the difficulty of detecting AI-generated work, potential misuse of generative tools, and the possibility that qualifications may lose credibility if academic dishonesty becomes widespread. Deepshikha (2025, 2026), Sheikh (2024), and Awadallah Alkouk and Khlaif (2024) similarly point to persistent challenges, including the "black-box" nature of AI systems, concerns about data privacy, and limited interpretability of AI decision-making processes. Luo et al. (2025) further caution that over-reliance on AI may reduce students' critical thinking capacity and lead to the uncritical adoption of embedded biases. These concerns are particularly important when viewed through the Assessment for Learning framework. AfL assumes that assessment should support learner growth, autonomy, and meaningful engagement with knowledge. If AI systems encourage passive acceptance of automated outputs, the formative purpose of assessment may be weakened, limiting opportunities for reflection, self-regulation, and critical thinking.

Institutional challenges also remain significant. Nwafor and Ezeugo (2025) note that although lecturers may find AI tools useful, barriers such as inadequate infrastructure, high costs, and ongoing privacy concerns continue to hinder effective implementation (Rizvi, 2023). Accordingly, Rahiman and Kodikal (2024) argue that successful integration requires technological readiness and strong ethical governance, institutional support, and investment in infrastructure. If these challenges remain unaddressed, AI-driven assessment may reinforce existing inequities by disadvantaging students based on language, culture, or socio-economic background. Naraliev (2025) warns that AI systems may incorrectly flag non-native English speakers as dishonest, while Primi et al. (2026) highlight ongoing concerns around cross-cultural fairness, interpretability, and the recognition of novel or unconventional student thinking. Similarly, Es-sarghini and Boumahdi (2026) observe that while AI systems may align with human judgment in structured tasks, they demonstrate limitations in evaluating qualitative or nuanced academic work. Sajja et al. (2026) further note that students often experience ethical uncertainty, particularly around whether AI use constitutes acceptable learning support or academic misconduct. Scholars emphasize the importance of embedding Responsible AI Ethics into curriculum design and institutional policy frameworks, ensuring transparency, fairness, and accountability in AI use (UNESCO, 2021). Saaida (2023) and Xu (2026) similarly stress that effective implementation must prioritize data privacy and ethical safeguards, while Peddi and Manoharan (2026) argue that AI's benefits must be carefully balanced against risks such as bias and security vulnerabilities. Wu (2026) reinforces the need for clear ethical principles and robust institutional data governance structures. From a theoretical standpoint, these findings indicate that the successful integration of AI within Assessment for Learning depends not only on technological effectiveness but also on the extent to which AI-supported assessment promotes fairness, learner participation, and educational improvement. Where transparency, equity, and trust are compromised, the fundamental aims of Assessment for Learning become difficult to achieve.

Collectively, these findings demonstrate strong alignment between AI-driven assessment practices and the principles of Assessment for Learning. Across all themes, AI was found to support the continuous collection of learning evidence, the provision of timely feedback, the personalization of learning experiences, and the use of assessment information to guide teaching decisions. These functions correspond directly with the central propositions of Black and Wiliam (1998), who argue that assessment should actively support learning improvement. At the same time, the findings extend the AfL framework by illustrating how digital technologies can increase the scale, speed, and responsiveness of formative assessment processes. However, the review also highlights that the educational value of AI remains dependent on human judgment, ethical implementation, and learner engagement. Consequently, AI should be understood not as a replacement for Assessment for Learning, but as a mechanism through which its principles can be implemented more effectively within contemporary higher education contexts.

LIMITATIONS OF THE STUDY

Although this systematic review provides valuable insights into AI-enabled Assessment for Learning in higher education, several limitations should be acknowledged. Firstly, the study is limited by its reliance on secondary data sources, meaning that findings are dependent on the quality, scope, and methodological rigor of existing literature. As a result, the conclusions drawn may reflect biases present in published studies, particularly those favoring positive outcomes of AI integration. Secondly, the review may be constrained by database selection and search strategy limitations, which could have resulted in the exclusion of relevant studies not indexed in the selected databases or published in non-English contexts. This may limit the comprehensiveness and global representation of findings. Finally, the rapid evolution of Artificial Intelligence means that the literature included in this review may quickly become outdated, particularly in relation to generative AI tools and emerging assessment technologies within Educational Technology.

RECOMMENDATIONS

Based on the findings, several recommendations are proposed for higher education institutions and policymakers.

- Institutions should adopt a hybrid pedagogical model integrating Assessment for Learning with responsible AI governance frameworks to ensure ethical and pedagogically sound implementation.
- Clear institutional policies should be developed to guide the ethical use of AI in assessment, with specific attention to academic integrity, transparency, and data privacy.
- Continuous professional development programs should be implemented to equip lecturers with AI literacy, enabling them to design authentic, AI-integrated assessment tasks.
- Assessment practices should be redesigned to emphasize higher-order thinking skills, including critical thinking, reflection, and problem-solving, rather than rote memorization.
- Institutions should invest in digital infrastructure and support systems to ensure equitable access to AI tools across diverse student populations.

FUTURE RESEARCH DIRECTIONS

This study identifies several important directions for future research. Empirical studies are needed to examine the actual classroom implementation of AI-driven Assessment for Learning, particularly its impact on student learning outcomes and lecturer practices. Comparative studies across disciplines (e.g., STEM vs humanities) could provide deeper insights into discipline-specific pedagogical transformations enabled by AI. Further research should explore student and lecturer perceptions of AI-assisted assessment, particularly regarding trust, fairness, and academic integrity. There is also a need for research in resource-constrained contexts, particularly in African higher education systems, to understand how AI can be equitably and effectively implemented. Finally, future studies should develop and test ethical AI assessment frameworks that ensure transparency, inclusivity, and pedagogical alignment.

CONCLUSION

This synthesis indicates that AI is driving a shift toward a hybrid human AI model in higher education, where technology enhances efficiency, feedback, and assessment design, while human pedagogical judgment remains central. Within this context, Assessment for Learning plays a crucial role in ensuring that assessment continues to prioritize learning, reflection, and metacognitive development through authentic, process-oriented tasks. However, the study also identifies ongoing ethical concerns, including bias, data privacy, transparency, and academic integrity, which require careful institutional attention. The chapter concludes that meaningful pedagogical transformation depends on balancing AI-driven innovation with human judgment and ethical responsibility to support fair, effective, and learner-centered assessment practices in higher education.

REFERENCES

Abah, J. A., Terungwa, U. D., & Chinaka, T. W. (2025). Conceptualizing the Influence of Artificial Intelligence on Students' Academic Integrity. *Journal of Mathematics Instruction. Social Research & Opinion*, *4*(2), 257–290.

Ajani, O. A., Gamede, B., & Matiyenga, T. C. (2024). Leveraging artificial intelligence to enhance teaching and learning in higher education: Promoting quality education and critical engagement. *Journal of Pedagogical Sociology and Psychology*, *7*(1), 54–69. DOI: 10.33902/JPSP.202528400

Alfaleh, M. (2026). Sustainable AI-Driven Assessment in Higher Education: A Systematic Review of Fairness, Transparency, Pedagogical Innovation, and Governance. *Sustainability (Basel)*, *18*(2), 785. DOI: 10.3390/su18020785

Alhalalmeh, A. H., & Al-Tarawneh, A. (2025). Artificial intelligence and the law: the complexities of technology and legalities. In A. Hannoon., & A Mahmood (Eds.). *Intelligence-Driven Circular Economy: Regeneration Towards Sustainability & Social Responsibility*, Volume 2 (pp. 641-649). Cham: Springer Nature Switzerland. DOI: 10.1007/978-3-031-74220-0_50

Almutairi, M., Alamry, A., Rahman, G., & Mudhsh, B. A. (2025). The role of AI-powered learning analytics in enhancing EFL curriculum design and learning outcomes in higher education. *International Journal of Innovative Research and Scientific Studies*, *8*(7), 477–487. DOI: 10.53894/ijirss.v8i7.10480

Awadallah Alkouk, W., & Khlaif, Z. N. (2024). AI-resistant assessments in higher education: Practical insights from faculty training workshops. [). Frontiers Media SA.]. *Frontiers in Education*, *9*, 1499495. DOI: 10.3389/feduc.2024.1499495

Bhatia, A., Bhatia, P., & Sood, D. (2024). Leveraging AI to transform online higher education: Focusing on personalized learning, assessment, and student engagement. *International Journal of Management and Humanities (IJMH) Volume-11 Issue-1.*

Black, P., & Wiliam, D. (1998). Assessment and classroom learning. *Assessment in Education: Principles, Policy & Practice*, *5*(1), 7–74. DOI: 10.1080/0969595980050102

Chukwu, C. O., Chukwu, J. C., & Odey, F. A. (2026). AI-Powered Learning Tools on Measurement of Student Engagement Across Academic Disciplines: Implications of Age and Gender. *Educational Point*, *3*(1), e144. DOI: 10.71176/edup/17782

Deepshikha, D. (2025). A comprehensive review of AI-powered grading and tailored feedback in universities. *Discover Artificial Intelligence*, *5*(1), 251. DOI: 10.1007/s44163-025-00517-0

Deepshikha, D. (2026). A systematic review on the future of educational assessment: AI-driven grading and personalised feedback in higher education. In *Artificial Intelligence in Education* (Vol. 2, No. 2, pp. 75-115). Emerald Publishing Limited.

Deneen, C. (2025). Artificial intelligence and educational assessment: Opportunities and threats. *Learning Letters*, *4*, 38–38. DOI: 10.59453/ll.v4.38

Es-sarghini, A., & Boumahdi, A. (2026). Introducing sentinel assessment: An AI-powered approach for evaluating writing competence in French as a Foreign Language. *Language Education & Assessment*, *9*, 103686–103686. DOI: 10.29140/lea.v9.103686

Funda, V., & Piderit, R. (2024, March). A review of the application of artificial intelligence in South African Higher Education. In *2024 Conference on Information Communications Technology and Society (ICTAS)* (pp. 44-50). IEEE. DOI: 10.1109/ICTAS59620.2024.10507113

Gamage, K. A., Dehideniya, S. C., Xu, Z., & Tang, X. (2023). ChatGPT and higher education assessments: More opportunities than concerns? *Journal of Applied Learning & Teaching*, *6*(2), 358–369.

Kasneci, E., Seßler, K., Küchemann, S., Bannert, M., Dementieva, D., Fischer, F., Gasser, U., Groh, G., Günnemann, S., Hüllermeier, E., Krusche, S., Kutyniok, G., Michaeli, T., Nerdel, C., Pfeffer, J., Poquet, O., Sailer, M., Schmidt, A., Seidel, T., & Kasneci, G. (2023). ChatGPT for good? On opportunities and challenges of large language models for education. *Learning and Individual Differences*, *103*, 102274. DOI: 10.1016/j.lindif.2023.102274

Khasawneh, M. A. S., & Khasawneh, Y. J. A. (2023). *Achieving assessment equity and fairness: Identifying and eliminating bias in assessment tools and practices.*

Luo, J., Zheng, C., Yin, J., & Teo, H. H. (2025). Design and assessment of AI-based learning tools in higher education: A systematic review. *International Journal of Educational Technology in Higher Education*, *22*(1), 42. DOI: 10.1186/s41239-025-00540-2

Memarian, B., & Doleck, T. (2024). A review of assessment for learning with artificial intelligence. *Computers in Human Behavior: Artificial Humans*, *2*(1), 100040. DOI: 10.1016/j.chbah.2023.100040

Moulavinafchi, A., Alhaideri, S. A. A., & Alfawwaz, S. N. M. (2026). The impact of an AI-powered Flipped classroom on grammar competence and language anxiety in EFL learners. *International Journal of Instruction*, *19*(1), 105–130. DOI: 10.29333/iji.2026.1916a

Nakajima, G. T. (2025). *Impact of AI Tools On Students' Learning and Academic Integrity: A Case Study at Africa University.*

Naraliev, A. (2025). The Impact Of Ai-Powered Tools On Language Learning And Assessment In Higher Education. In *International Conference on Global Trends and Innovations in Multidisciplinary Research* (Vol. 1, No. 4, pp. 146-149).

Ncube, P. D., Dzvapatsva, G. P., Matobobo, C., & Ranga, M. M. (2026). Redefining student assessment in AI-infused learning environments: A systematic review of challenges and strategies for academic integrity. *AI and Ethics*, *6*(1), 68. DOI: 10.1007/s43681-025-00871-w

Nguyen, T. H., Tran, D. N., Vo, D. L., Mai, V. H., & Dao, X. Q. (2022). AI-powered university: Design and deployment of robot assistant for smart universities. *Journal of Advances in Information Technology*, *13*(1). Advance online publication. DOI: 10.12720/jait.13.1.78-84

Nwafor, O. F., & Ezeugo, C. R. (2025). Roles of AI-Powered Assessments in Enhancing the Professional Development of Academic Staff in Public Universities in Rivers State. *International Journal of Educational Management, Rivers State University.*, *1*(2), 170-180.

Ogwueleka, F. N. (2025). Plagiarism detection in the age of artificial intelligence: current technologies and future directions. *AI & Ethics, Academic Integrity & the Future of Quality Assurance in Higher Education*, 10.

Overono, A. L., & Ditta, A. S. (2025). The rise of artificial intelligence: A clarion call for higher education to redefine learning and reimagine assessment. *College Teaching*, *73*(2), 123–126. DOI: 10.1080/87567555.2023.2233653

Owan, V. J., Abang, K. B., Idika, D. O., Etta, E. O., & Bassey, B. A. (2023). Exploring the potential of artificial intelligence tools in educational measurement and assessment. *Eurasia Journal of Mathematics, Science and Technology Education*, *19*(8), em2307. DOI: 10.29333/ejmste/13428

Patel, S., & Ragolane, M. (2024). The implementation of artificial intelligence in South African higher education institutions: Opportunities and challenges. *Technium Education & Humanities*, *9*, 51–65. DOI: 10.47577/teh.v9i.11452

Peddi, S., & Manoharan, G. (2026). Ethical Guidelines for the thoughtful Implementation of AI in Higher Education. *EthAIca: Journal of Ethics. AI and Critical Analysis*, (5), 409.

Perera, P., & Lankathilake, M. (2023). AI in higher education: A literature review of ChatGPT and guidelines for responsible implementation.

Perla, L., & Vinci, V. (2023). Enhancing authentic assessment in higher education: Leveraging digital transformation and artificial intelligence. *AIxEDU, 1.*

Primi, R., Beaty, R. E., Benedek, M., Dumas, D., Organisciak, P., Patterson, J. D., Calico, T., & Piacentini, M. (2026). AI-Powered Scoring for Creative Thinking: Methods and Challenges in PISA Assessment. *The Journal of Creative Behavior*, *60*(1), e70082. DOI: 10.1002/jocb.70082

Rahiman, H. U., & Kodikal, R. (2024). Revolutionizing education: Artificial intelligence empowered learning in higher education. *Cogent Education*, *11*(1), 2293431. DOI: 10.1080/2331186X.2023.2293431

Saaida, M. B. (2023). AI-Driven transformations in higher education: Opportunities and challenges. *International journal of educational research and studies, 5*(1), 29-36.

Sajja, R., Sermet, Y., Fodale, B., & Demir, I. (2026). Evaluating AI-powered learning assistants in engineering higher education with implications for student engagement, ethics, and policy. *Scientific Reports*, *16*(1), 7565. DOI: 10.1038/s41598-026-39237-5

Saputra, I., Kurniawan, A., Yanita, M., Putri, E. Y., & Mahniza, M. (2024). The evolution of educational assessment: How artificial intelligence is shaping the trends and future of learning evaluation. *Indonesian Journal of Computer Science*, *13*(6). Advance online publication. DOI: 10.33022/ijcs.v13i6.4465

Sari, H. E., Tumanggor, B., & Efron, D. (2024). Improving educational outcomes through adaptive learning systems using AI. *International Transactions on Artificial Intelligence*, *3*(1), 21–31. DOI: 10.33050/italic.v3i1.647

Selwyn, N. (2019). *Should robots replace teachers?: AI and the future of education.* John Wiley & Sons.

Sheikh, F. (2024). AI-powered assessment and feedback: Enhancing student engagement and performance. *AI Edify Journal*, *1*(4), 30–37.

Singh, R. J. (2023). Transforming higher education: The power of artificial intelligence. *International Journal of Multidisciplinary Research in Arts. Science and Technology*, *1*(3), 13–18.

Slimi, Z., & Villarejo-Carballido, B. (2024). Unveiling the potential: Experts' perspectives on artificial intelligence integration in higher education. *European Journal of Educational Research*, *13*(4), 1477–1492. DOI: 10.12973/eu-jer.13.4.1477

Suchithra, V. G., & Arya, C. S. (2025). The study on ethics and biases in AI-powered education. *European Journal of Contemporary Education and E-Learning*, *3*(2), 37–43. DOI: 10.59324/ejceel.2025.3(2).04

UNESCO. (2021). *Recommendation on the ethics of artificial intelligence*. https://bsu.buap.mx/b2m

Wu, Z. (2026). Evaluating the impact of AI tools on academic performance and student satisfaction. *Journal of Computer Assisted Learning*, *42*(2), e70225. DOI: 10.1002/jcal.70225

Xu, H. (2026). AI-powered technologies in physical education: Impact on physical and psycho-emotional well-being of students. *The Journal of General Psychology*, *153*(1), 130–151. DOI: 10.1080/00221309.2025.2541585

Yan, L., Sha, L., Zhao, L., Li, Y., Martinez-Maldonado, R., Chen, G., Li, X., Jin, Y., & Gašević, D. (2024). Practical and ethical challenges of large language models in education: A systematic scoping review. *British Journal of Educational Technology*, *55*(1), 90–112. DOI: 10.1111/bjet.13370

Yang, L. P., & Xin, T. (2022). Changing educational assessments in the post-COVID-19 era: From assessment of learning (AoL) to assessment as learning (AaL). *Educational Measurement: Issues and Practice*, *41*(1), 54–60. DOI: 10.1111/emip.12492

Zhao, C. (2024). AI-assisted assessment in higher education: A systematic review. *Journal of Educational Technology and Innovation*, *6*(4). Advance online publication. DOI: 10.61414/jeti.v6i4.209

Chapter 2
Artificial Intelligence–Supported Assessment: Advancing Equity, Integrity, and Curriculum Innovation

Ratan Sarkar
http://orcid.org/0009-0008-5480-0165
Tezpur University, India

ABSTRACT

This chapter critically examines AI-supported assessment as a transformative yet ethically complex development in higher education. It frames AI-mediated assessment as a socio-pedagogical practice shaped by equity, integrity, and curriculum governance. While tools such as automated grading, learning analytics, and generative feedback can enhance formative assessment, constructive alignment, and inclusion, they also pose risks of bias, surveillance, opacity, automation bias, and weakened professional judgment—especially in resource-constrained and Global South contexts. Drawing on inclusive education, assessment-for-learning, and human-centered AI frameworks, the chapter proposes a layered ecosystem model for responsible implementation. It argues that AI can strengthen quality and trust only when embedded in transparent, ethically governed, and pedagogically grounded systems that uphold human dignity and educational justice.

INTRODUCTION

Assessment occupies a central position in higher education, shaping not only what students learn but also how knowledge, competence, and academic success are defined. In recent years, artificial intelligence (AI) has emerged as a powerful force influencing assessment design, grading, feedback, and academic integrity monitoring (Miller, 2024). From automated scoring systems and learning analytics to generative AI–supported feedback mechanisms, assessment practices are undergoing significant transformation (Williamson, Eynon, & Potter, 2020).

While proponents emphasize efficiency and scalability, assessment cannot be understood merely as a technical process. Contemporary scholarship increasingly recognizes assessment as a pedagogical, ethical, and cultural practice embedded within institutional values, power relations, and social contexts

DOI: 10.4018/979-8-3373-8939-4.ch002

(Boud & Falchikov, 2007). The integration of AI therefore raises fundamental questions regarding fairness, trust, transparency, and educational purpose.

Equity remains a persistent challenge in higher education assessment systems. Traditional assessment models often privilege particular linguistic, cultural, and cognitive norms, marginalizing learners from diverse socio-economic and educational backgrounds (Klinger, DeLuca, & Miller, 2015). AI-supported assessment holds potential to address some of these inequities through adaptive feedback, flexible assessment formats, and personalized learning pathways. However, without careful governance, AI may also reproduce or intensify structural inequalities through biased data and opaque algorithms (Benjamin, 2019).

Academic integrity represents another critical concern. The rise of generative AI tools has destabilized conventional understandings of authorship, originality, and misconduct (Eaton, 2023). Institutions now face the challenge of maintaining trust while avoiding surveillance-driven assessment cultures that undermine learner autonomy.

Simultaneously, curriculum structures are being reshaped by AI-informed assessment strategies. Assessment increasingly functions not merely as measurement but as a driver of curriculum innovation, emphasizing formative feedback, competency-based learning, and alignment between learning outcomes and real-world application (Biggs & Tang, 2011).

This chapter situates AI-supported assessment within these intersecting concerns, arguing that meaningful innovation must prioritize equity, integrity, and curriculum coherence rather than automation alone.

Rationale

The rationale for this chapter emerges from the growing gap between technological adoption and pedagogical preparedness in higher education. Although AI tools are rapidly being introduced into assessment systems, institutional frameworks for ethical governance and inclusive practice often lag behind (OECD, 2021).

Research on assessment for learning emphasizes that assessment should enhance learning rather than merely certify achievement (Black & Wiliam, 2009). AI-supported assessment has the capacity to strengthen formative practices through timely feedback, diagnostic insights, and personalized learning support. However, when deployed uncritically, such systems risk narrowing learning to measurable outputs and reinforcing performative cultures (Swiecki et al., 2022).

Equity-oriented assessment requires sensitivity to learner diversity, contextual constraints, and systemic inequalities. In Global South contexts, challenges such as uneven digital access, limited infrastructure, and policy constraints complicate AI integration (UNESCO, 2021). Thus, AI adoption cannot rely on universal models developed in well-resourced systems.

Integrity concerns further necessitate scholarly attention. Automated plagiarism detection and proctoring technologies have raised ethical debates regarding surveillance, student rights, and algorithmic transparency (Selwyn, 2019). Integrity must be understood not solely as compliance but as a relational practice grounded in trust, assessment design, and institutional culture.

Curriculum innovation offers a productive pathway forward. AI-informed assessment strategies can support authentic assessment, reflective learning, and interdisciplinary competence development when aligned with curriculum goals (Boud et al., 2018). This chapter therefore argues for a pedagogically anchored approach that integrates assessment, curriculum, and ethical governance.

Objectives

The objectives of this chapter are to:

1. Critically examine artificial intelligence–supported assessment as a pedagogical and ethical practice.
2. Analyze the potential of AI to promote equity and inclusion in higher education assessment.
3. Explore challenges related to academic integrity, transparency, and trust in AI-mediated assessment.
4. Examine how AI-informed assessment strategies contribute to curriculum innovation and alignment.
5. Propose a conceptual framework for responsible, equitable, and integrity-driven AI-supported assessment.

ARTIFICIAL INTELLIGENCE–SUPPORTED ASSESSMENT AS A PEDAGOGICAL AND ETHICAL PRACTICE

Artificial intelligence–supported assessment cannot be understood as a mere technological enhancement to conventional evaluation systems. Rather, it constitutes a structural reconfiguration of how knowledge is validated, how academic authority is exercised, and how institutional trust is sustained (Mütterlein et al., 2024). As higher education institutions increasingly adopt AI-driven grading systems, predictive analytics, automated feedback mechanisms, and surveillance technologies, assessment is shifting from a human-centered interpretive practice to a data-mediated governance mechanism. This transformation demands critical examination (Verwoerd, 2025).

Assessment has always been more than a technical procedure. It shapes academic identities, structures motivation, and defines what counts as legitimate knowledge. The introduction of AI therefore intervenes not only in grading efficiency but in the epistemological foundations of higher education itself (Ardito, 2023). When algorithms evaluate essays, flag "at-risk" students, or monitor examination behavior, they participate in shaping normative expectations of performance, compliance, and success.

Thus, AI-supported assessment must be interrogated as a pedagogical and ethical practice situated within power relations and institutional governance structures.

Pedagogical Reconfiguration: Augmentation or Reduction?

AI systems are frequently promoted for their capacity to enhance formative assessment. Automated feedback tools can provide immediate responses, adaptive scaffolding, and personalized learning pathways (Dockens & Shelton, 2025). In large classes, such systems may democratize access to feedback that human instructors cannot feasibly provide at scale. Learning analytics dashboards may allow early identification of struggling students, enabling targeted support (Agrawal et al., 2024).

However, this promise coexists with pedagogical risks. Automated essay scoring systems often rely on linguistic features and structural markers that may privilege dominant academic writing norms (Bai et al., 2022). Higher-order thinking, creativity, and contextual nuance are difficult to quantify. When assessment systems prioritize what is computationally measurable, curriculum design may gradually conform to algorithmic logic.

Automation bias further complicates matters. Educators may defer excessively to AI outputs, especially when institutional pressure prioritizes efficiency (Bhavana. et al., 2024). This can erode professional judgment and interpretive nuance. Assessment risks becoming procedural rather than dialogic.

AI therefore operates within a tension between pedagogical augmentation and pedagogical reduction. Its ethical legitimacy depends on whether it enhances reflective learning or narrows intellectual engagement.

Equity, Bias, and Algorithmic Power

Equity concerns are central to critical examination. Traditional assessment systems have historically privileged certain linguistic, cultural, and cognitive norms. AI systems, trained on existing data, may replicate and institutionalize such inequalities (Sulthana et al., 2025).

Algorithmic bias emerges when training datasets reflect dominant social patterns. Automated scoring tools may penalize non-native English speakers. Predictive analytics systems may disproportionately categorize marginalized students as academically vulnerable (Praveenkumar et al., 2025). Facial-recognition-based proctoring systems have demonstrated racial inaccuracies.

In this context, claims of algorithmic neutrality are ethically untenable. AI does not eliminate bias; it can obscure and amplify it under the guise of objectivity.

In Global South contexts, infrastructural disparities further complicate equity. Students without stable internet access or high-performance devices may face disadvantages in AI-mediated assessments. Digital literacy divides may intensify stratification.

Equity in AI-supported assessment must therefore be understood at three interconnected levels:

a) Algorithmic fairness
b) Infrastructural access
c) Cultural representation

Without attention to these dimensions, AI may deepen educational inequality.

Academic Integrity: From Surveillance to Relational Ethics

The rise of generative AI has unsettled established academic integrity frameworks. Detection-based approaches—plagiarism checkers and AI-authorship detection tools—are increasingly inadequate. Institutions have responded by expanding surveillance technologies, including remote proctoring systems that monitor gaze patterns, background environments, and behavioral signals (Song, 2024).

Such surveillance introduces ethical concerns regarding privacy, consent, and presumption of suspicion. Surveillance-driven integrity models may undermine trust and disproportionately impact marginalized students who lack private examination spaces.

Integrity must instead be reframed as a relational and pedagogical practice. Assessment design plays a critical role. Authentic tasks, oral examinations, iterative drafts, and reflective components can reduce reliance on detection technologies while strengthening learning engagement (Shishavan, 2024).

Thus, ethical AI-supported assessment shifts focus from technological policing to pedagogical redesign.

Curriculum Coherence and Epistemic Consequences

AI-supported assessment influences curriculum architecture (Luckin, 2017). When institutions adopt AI systems capable of evaluating discrete competencies, curricula may gradually shift toward measurable skill fragments rather than holistic intellectual development.

This creates epistemic risks:

- Over-standardization
- Reduction of qualitative judgment
- Marginalization of interpretive disciplines

However, AI can also support curriculum innovation when aligned with constructive alignment principles. Continuous formative feedback cycles, competency-based progression, and data-informed curriculum revision may strengthen coherence (Chu & Ashraf, 2025).

The ethical imperative is to ensure that curriculum intentionality precedes technological adoption. AI should support pedagogical goals rather than define them.

Below is a structured analytical table synthesizing pedagogical benefits, ethical risks, and critical considerations.

Table 1. Analytical Summary Table

Dimension	*Potential Pedagogical Gains*	*Ethical & Structural Risks*	*Critical Safeguards*
Automated Feedback	Timely, scalable formative feedback	Over-standardization; superficial evaluation	Human moderation; qualitative oversight
Learning Analytics	Early identification of learning gaps	Predictive labeling; data profiling	Transparent algorithms; student consent
Automated Grading	Consistency; workload reduction	Reduction of complex cognition	Faculty override authority
Proctoring Technologies	Exam integrity monitoring	Surveillance; privacy violations	Limited use; rights-based protocols
Generative AI Tools	Draft support; reflective iteration	Authorship ambiguity; dependency	Integrity-by-design assessment

This table illustrates that AI-supported assessment cannot be judged in binary terms. Each technological intervention carries both pedagogical affordances and ethical vulnerabilities.

Figure 1. Conceptual Graphical Model for Inclusion

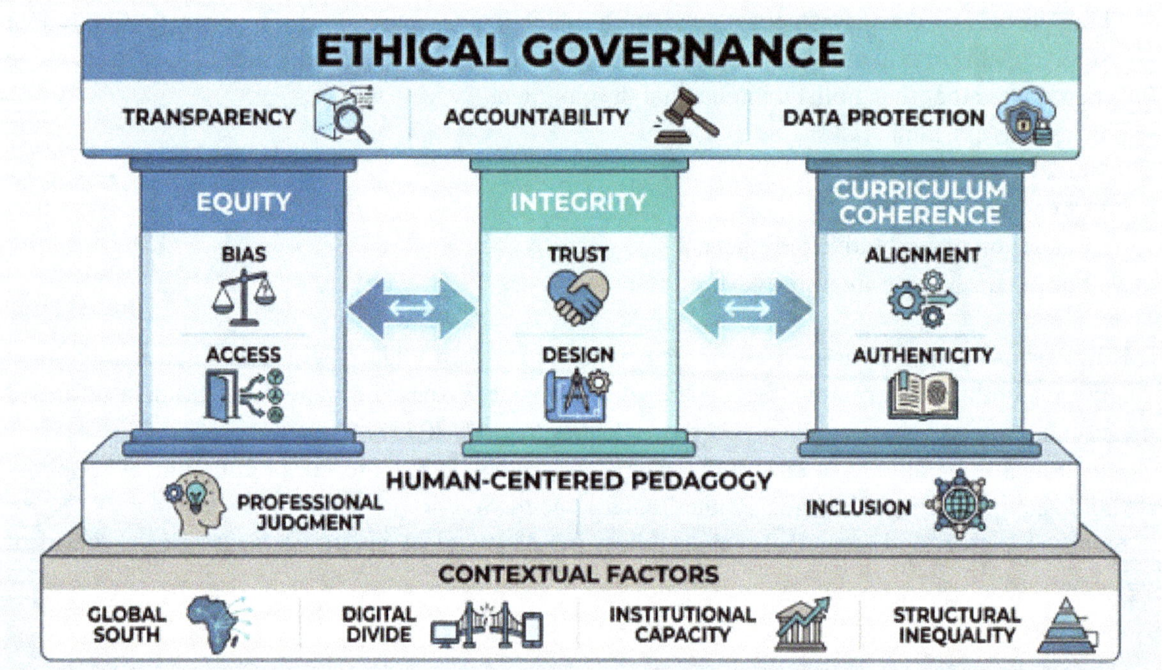

This conceptual model frames inclusion as an interconnected system grounded in ethical governance—defined by transparency, accountability, and data protection—which establishes the foundation for trust and responsible practice. At its base lies human-centered pedagogy, emphasizing professional judgment and inclusive action in lived educational contexts. At the core, equity (addressing bias and access), integrity (ensuring trust and responsible design), and curriculum coherence (maintaining alignment and authenticity) function as interdependent pillars, each reinforcing and stabilizing the others. Ethical governance sustains this balance, while broader contextual realities- including the Global South, the digital divide, institutional capacity, and structural inequality- shape the feasibility and depth of implementation. As an ecosystem model, it underscores the necessity of equilibrium: when surveillance intensifies, integrity weakens; when bias persists, equity erodes; and when curriculum alignment is neglected, innovation risks becoming superficial rather than transformative.

Professional Judgment and Institutional Responsibility

AI-supported assessment intersects with academic labor and professional autonomy. When algorithmic systems mediate grading, educators risk becoming supervisors of technological processes rather than interpretive evaluators (Gnanaprakasam & Lourdusamy, 2024). Institutional management may prioritize efficiency metrics over pedagogical depth.

A critical position insists that AI remain subordinate to professional expertise. Faculty must retain interpretive authority and capacity to contest algorithmic outputs.

Institutional responsibility includes:

- Continuous bias auditing
- Faculty AI literacy training
- Student transparency rights
- Participatory governance structures

AI cannot self-regulate; governance must be human-directed.

Critical Synthesis

A critical reading of AI-supported assessment reveals a paradox at its core: it is simultaneously technologically transformative, pedagogically disruptive, ethically complex, and politically embedded (Perkins et al., 2024). While its technical capacity promises efficiency, scalability, and data-driven precision, these affordances do not exist in a neutral vacuum. AI reconfigures assessment logics—shifting authority from professional judgment toward algorithmic mediation and embedding evaluative power within opaque computational systems. In doing so, it unsettles established pedagogical relationships, reframes what counts as evidence of learning, and redistributes control over evaluative processes (Al-Amin et al., 2024).

Its legitimacy, therefore, cannot be measured by sophistication, predictive accuracy, or automation capacity alone. Rather, it depends on alignment with foundational educational values. Efficiency cannot supersede equity without reproducing structural disadvantage. Surveillance cannot substitute for trust without weakening the relational fabric of learning environments (Peddi & Manoharan, 2025). Automation cannot replace professional judgment without narrowing the interpretive, contextual, and ethical dimensions of assessment. When optimization becomes the dominant logic, the risk is not merely technical error but epistemic reductionism—where complex human learning is compressed into quantifiable proxies (Zhang, 2025).

AI-supported assessment must consequently be conceptualized as a negotiated pedagogical practice rather than a technical solution. This requires reflexivity about embedded biases, ethical commitment to fairness and transparency, and contextual sensitivity to institutional capacity and socio-economic disparities (Agrawal et al., 2025). Its integration demands governance structures capable of scrutinizing not only outputs but underlying assumptions, data infrastructures, and power dynamics.

Artificial intelligence does not merely assist assessment; it reshapes the conditions under which learning is evaluated, authority is exercised, and accountability is enforced (Agrawal et al., 2025). Uncritically deployed, it risks intensifying structural inequality, normalizing surveillance cultures, and eroding institutional trust through opacity and datafication. However, when embedded within inclusive, ethically governed, and pedagogically grounded ecosystems, it may enhance formative feedback, strengthen curriculum coherence, and broaden equitable participation.

The central challenge is therefore not technological capacity but moral intentionality. The question is not whether AI can assess, but whether it should—and under what ethical, pedagogical, and political conditions its use advances rather than constrains educational justice.

POTENTIAL OF AI TO PROMOTE EQUITY AND INCLUSION IN HIGHER EDUCATION ASSESSMENT

Artificial intelligence (AI) is increasingly positioned as a transformative force in higher education assessment, often framed as a mechanism for enhancing fairness, personalization, and efficiency (Murgatroyd, 2024). Yet its potential to promote equity and inclusion is neither automatic nor politically neutral. Rather, AI-supported assessment exists within complex pedagogical, ethical, and socio-structural ecosystems (Kayyali, 2025). A critical analysis must therefore move beyond techno-optimism to interrogate how AI reshapes assessment practices, redistributes authority, and interacts with existing inequalities.

At its most promising, AI can enhance access, responsiveness, and personalization. Adaptive assessment systems can tailor tasks to students' performance levels, providing scaffolded pathways that reduce cognitive overload and support differentiated learning needs (Ahamed, 2025). Automated feedback tools can deliver rapid formative responses, narrowing feedback gaps that disproportionately affect students in large classes or under-resourced institutions. AI-driven analytics can identify patterns of disengagement or performance disparity, enabling early interventions that support students from historically marginalized groups (Main, 2025). In multilingual contexts, AI can facilitate translation, speech recognition, and multimodal interaction, thereby expanding participation for students whose linguistic or physical abilities may otherwise constrain assessment performance.

Such affordances suggest that AI can help operationalize inclusive assessment principles—flexibility, accessibility, and timely feedback—at scale. In theory, AI can also mitigate certain forms of human bias (Agrawal et al., 2024). Traditional assessment is susceptible to implicit bias, fatigue, and subjective inconsistency. Algorithmic scoring of structured responses may reduce some variability, and large-scale data analysis can illuminate systemic inequities across demographic groups. When used diagnostically, AI can surface patterns that institutions might otherwise overlook, prompting policy reform and targeted support initiatives (Vangibhuratha, 2025).

However, these benefits must be critically contextualized. AI systems are trained on historical datasets that reflect entrenched social inequities. As such, algorithmic systems risk encoding and amplifying bias under the appearance of objectivity (Entschew, 2024). If training data underrepresent certain linguistic styles, cultural expressions, or epistemic traditions, automated scoring may systematically disadvantage students who deviate from dominant norms. What is framed as "neutral" evaluation can, in practice, privilege particular forms of knowledge production aligned with Western, standardized, or technocratic epistemologies (Vangibhuratha, 2025).

Moreover, AI-supported assessment may reconfigure power relations within higher education. The introduction of automated grading and predictive analytics shifts authority from professional academic judgment toward algorithmic mediation. While faculty expertise is inherently interpretive and context-sensitive, algorithmic systems operate through pattern recognition and probabilistic inference (Miller, 2024). This shift risks narrowing assessment criteria to what is computationally measurable, thereby marginalizing complex, dialogic, and culturally situated forms of learning. When efficiency becomes the primary metric of success, assessment may drift toward standardization at the expense of authenticity.

Concerns about surveillance and datafication further complicate AI's equity claims. Automated proctoring technologies, behavioral tracking systems, and predictive analytics can generate environments of heightened monitoring. Such surveillance disproportionately affects students with limited access to private spaces, stable internet connectivity, or high-quality hardware—conditions frequently associated with socioeconomic inequality and the Global South (Diene, 2024). Students from marginalized communities may experience increased anxiety or misidentification due to facial recognition inaccuracies or algorithmic flagging systems. In these cases, AI does not merely fail to promote equity; it actively intensifies structural disadvantage (Praveenkumar et al., 2025).

The digital divide represents another critical dimension. Access to AI-enhanced assessment presupposes reliable technological infrastructure, institutional capacity, and digital literacy. Institutions in resource-constrained contexts may lack the technical expertise required to audit algorithms or manage data governance responsibly (Agrawal et al., 2025). Without adequate oversight, external vendors may exercise disproportionate control over assessment systems, embedding commercial interests within academic evaluation. Equity cannot be realized where institutions lack the structural capacity to ensure transparency, accountability, and contextual adaptation (Agrawal et al., 2025).

Therefore, the equity potential of AI is contingent upon ethical governance and participatory design (Kumar & Sanjaya, 2025). Transparent algorithmic processes, routine bias audits, and inclusive stakeholder engagement are necessary safeguards. Students and faculty must have avenues to question, challenge, and understand automated decisions. Professional judgment should remain central, with AI functioning as augmentation rather than substitution (Agrawal et al., 2025). Inclusive assessment requires interpretive nuance—an understanding of cultural context, disciplinary norms, and individual student trajectories—that no algorithm can fully replicate.

Critically, AI-supported assessment should be conceptualized not as a technological solution but as a negotiated pedagogical practice (Perkins, Furze, et al., 2024). Its integration must be guided by normative commitments to justice, fairness, and trust. This entails continuous reflexivity regarding whose knowledge is validated, whose performance is privileged, and whose vulnerabilities are amplified. Institutions must resist equating innovation with progress; technological advancement does not inherently produce social inclusion (Agrawal et al., 2024).

Ultimately, AI has the potential to enhance equity and inclusion in higher education assessment by expanding accessibility, personalizing feedback, and illuminating systemic disparities. Yet these possibilities remain fragile. When implemented uncritically, AI may entrench surveillance cultures, reinforce epistemic hierarchies, and reproduce structural inequality under the guise of neutrality (Kayyali, 2025). The decisive issue is not whether AI can technically improve assessment processes, but whether its deployment aligns with educational values centered on dignity, fairness, and human development.

Equity in AI-supported assessment is therefore less a function of algorithmic sophistication than of moral intentionality and institutional responsibility. Only when embedded within ethically governed, contextually responsive, and pedagogically grounded ecosystems can AI move from being a disruptive technology to a genuinely inclusive educational instrument (Praveenkumar et al., 2025).

Table 2. Analytical Framework: AI and Equity in Higher Education Assessment

Dimension	*Equity & Inclusion Potential*	*Risks / Limitations*	*Conditions for Ethical Implementation*	*Implications for Higher Education*
Accessibility & Universal Design	Adaptive testing; multimodal responses (text, audio, speech); assistive technologies; multilingual feedback	Digital divide; unequal device access; unstable connectivity; algorithmic misrecognition (e.g., speech or facial recognition bias)	Investment in infrastructure; inclusive design standards; offline alternatives; accessibility audits	Can broaden participation if structural access gaps are addressed
Personalization & Differentiation	Tailored feedback; scaffolded assessments; individualized pacing; early identification of at-risk students	Risk of labeling; deficit framing; predictive bias reinforcing stereotypes	Transparent predictive models; human oversight; contextual interpretation of analytics	Supports retention and engagement when framed as support rather than surveillance
Bias Mitigation in Grading	Reduced human fatigue bias; consistency in scoring structured tasks; detection of systemic performance gaps	Embedded data bias; privileging dominant linguistic/cultural norms; opacity of scoring algorithms	Regular bias audits; diverse training datasets; explainable AI systems; participatory review	Can enhance fairness only if algorithmic neutrality is critically examined
Feedback Efficiency & Scale	Rapid formative feedback; scalable support in large classes; continuous assessment analytics	Over-standardization; shallow feedback; replacement of dialogic engagement	AI as augmentation, not substitution; integration with human mentoring	Enhances formative assessment when relational pedagogy remains central
Curriculum Alignment & Coherence	Data-informed curriculum refinement; learning analytics aligned to outcomes	Teaching-to-the-algorithm; narrowing of measurable competencies; neglect of creativity and criticality	Balanced assessment models; preservation of authentic, higher-order tasks	Risk of epistemic reductionism if measurement dominates meaning
Surveillance & Academic Integrity	Detection of plagiarism; automated proctoring; integrity monitoring	Privacy invasion; racial/gender misidentification; heightened anxiety; normalization of surveillance culture	Data protection frameworks; minimal data collection; consent and transparency; alternative assessment design	Institutional trust may erode if surveillance supersedes relational accountability
Governance & Data Ethics	Improved transparency through structured analytics; traceable assessment processes	Vendor dependency; opaque proprietary algorithms; commercialization of academic data	Institutional AI policies; open standards; independent auditing; regulatory compliance	Legitimacy depends on ethical governance rather than technological sophistication
Professional Judgment	Augmented decision-making through analytics; evidence-informed evaluation	Deprofessionalization; erosion of academic autonomy; algorithmic authority displacement	Faculty training; shared governance; AI as decision-support tool	Sustains integrity only when human interpretive authority remains primary
Structural Inequality & Global Context	Potential to expand reach in under-resourced regions through scalable digital tools	Reinforcement of Global North epistemologies; infrastructural disparities; contextual misalignment	Local adaptation; capacity-building; culturally responsive datasets	Equity claims must be context-sensitive rather than universally assumed
Student Agency & Participation	Opportunities for self-assessment analytics; feedback dashboards; learner autonomy	Data determinism; reduced agency if students cannot challenge algorithmic decisions	Transparent appeals processes; student co-design; algorithmic literacy initiatives	Inclusion requires empowering students as stakeholders, not data subjects

The table 2 demonstrates that AI-supported assessment contains dual potentialities: it can enhance accessibility, consistency, and early intervention, yet it can simultaneously intensify surveillance, embed bias, and reconfigure power asymmetries. The determining factor is not algorithmic capability but governance architecture, pedagogical integration, and contextual responsiveness. From a systems perspective, AI intersects with four overarching domains:

1. **Technological Infrastructure** – access, reliability, and design inclusivity
2. **Pedagogical Integrity** – alignment with authentic learning and professional judgment
3. **Ethical Governance** – transparency, accountability, data protection
4. **Socio-Structural Context** – digital divides, institutional capacity, global inequities

Critically, equity is not produced by automation alone. It emerges through intentional design, reflexive practice, and regulatory oversight. Without these safeguards, AI risks transforming assessment into a data-driven surveillance apparatus that privileges efficiency over justice. Thus, the analysis affirms that AI can support inclusive assessment only when embedded within ethically governed, human-centered, and contextually adaptive educational ecosystems.

CHALLENGES RELATED TO ACADEMIC INTEGRITY, TRANSPARENCY, AND TRUST IN AI-MEDIATED ASSESSMENT

The incorporation of artificial intelligence into higher education assessment does not simply introduce new tools; it reconfigures the moral, epistemic, and relational foundations upon which academic integrity, transparency, and trust are built (Peddi & Manoharan, 2025). While AI-mediated systems are frequently presented as neutral mechanisms for enhancing fairness and efficiency, a critical perspective reveals that they redistribute power, redefine authorship, and recalibrate the balance between surveillance and pedagogical care (Bearman et al., 2022).

Academic Integrity: From Ethical Culture to Algorithmic Policing

AI-driven plagiarism detection, authorship verification, and automated proctoring systems are often justified as safeguards of academic integrity. However, these technologies tend to conceptualize integrity as a problem of technical detection rather than ethical formation (Fisk, 2024). Instead of cultivating scholarly responsibility and critical engagement, institutions may shift toward surveillance infrastructures that monitor, flag, and discipline. Integrity becomes procedural compliance rather than a relational and developmental value (Drinan & Gallant, 2008).

Automated proctoring technologies, for instance, rely on behavioral analytics—eye movement tracking, facial recognition, environmental scanning—that embed suspicion into assessment environments. Such systems disproportionately burden students who lack stable technological infrastructure or private spaces, reinforcing socioeconomic disparities (Oravec, 2022). Moreover, algorithmic misidentification and false positives can criminalize ordinary behaviors, particularly among neurodiverse students or those whose cultural norms diverge from standardized behavioral expectations. The presumption of dishonesty embedded in surveillance technologies risks eroding the very trust that integrity frameworks seek to uphold (Barrett, 2021).

Generative AI further destabilizes conventional notions of authorship. As AI-assisted writing becomes ubiquitous, binary distinctions between "original" and "inauthentic" work become increasingly untenable. Institutions face a critical dilemma: whether to prohibit AI tools and risk irrelevance, or to integrate them and reconceptualize intellectual contribution (Bozkurt, n.d.). Overly punitive responses may entrench inequities, as students with greater technological literacy gain advantage, while rigid enforcement frameworks may fail to account for legitimate assistive uses. Academic integrity, therefore, requires reframing—not as control over tools, but as clarity regarding intellectual accountability and cognitive engagement (Hutson, 2024).

Transparency: The Problem of Algorithmic Opacity

Transparency is foundational to procedural justice in assessment. Students must understand how judgments are made and retain the ability to contest them. Yet AI systems often operate through opaque computational models, particularly when proprietary algorithms are deployed through commercial vendors (Fakokunde, 2025). These "black box" systems obscure decision-making processes, rendering grades or risk classifications difficult to interpret or challenge.

Opacity undermines accountability. If neither educators nor administrators fully understand how an algorithm weighs variables or identifies anomalies, institutional oversight becomes superficial (McConvey et al., 2023). The authority of the algorithm may supersede professional judgment, not because it is infallible, but because it appears technically sophisticated. These dynamic risks epistemic displacement, where computational outputs are privileged over contextual expertise (Mishara, 2024).

Furthermore, explainability is not merely a technical issue but a pedagogical one. If AI-generated feedback lacks interpretive depth or contextual nuance, students may perceive it as mechanistic and impersonal. Transparency must therefore extend beyond disclosing system architecture (Thai et al., 2024); it must ensure that assessment rationales are meaningful, intelligible, and open to dialogue. Without this, AI-mediated assessment may reinforce hierarchical asymmetries between system designers and educational participants.

Trust: Fragility in Datafied Educational Ecosystems

Trust is relational, historically constructed, and institutionally sustained. AI-mediated assessment introduces tensions that can both bolster and undermine this trust. On one hand, consistent grading and structured analytics may enhance perceptions of procedural fairness (Jackson & Panteli, 2022). On the other, pervasive data collection and behavioral monitoring can cultivate climates of suspicion.

The normalization of surveillance risks transforming educational environments into compliance regimes. When students perceive those algorithms, rather than educators, determine their academic trajectory, assessment becomes depersonalized (Mishara, 2024). Faculty autonomy may also be constrained if algorithmic recommendations are treated as authoritative. In such contexts, trust is displaced by technological determinism (Radjabov & Ravshanov, 2024).

Moreover, trust is acutely vulnerable to error. Algorithmic misclassification, data breaches, or biased outputs can rapidly erode institutional credibility. Unlike human error, algorithmic error often carries the aura of objectivity, making contestation more difficult and remediation slower (Lahusen et al., 2024). Restoring trust requires transparent acknowledgment of limitations, participatory governance structures, and accessible appeals processes.

Intersections and Normative Implications

Academic integrity, transparency, and trust are interdependent. Surveillance-heavy approaches to integrity weaken trust. Opaque algorithms compromise transparency, which in turn destabilizes legitimacy (Ross & Macleod, 2018). The critical issue is not whether AI can enhance monitoring capacity, but whether such enhancement aligns with educational values grounded in dignity, fairness, and intellectual growth.

To navigate these tensions, institutions must resist equating technological capability with ethical progress. AI-mediated assessment should be embedded within frameworks that prioritize human oversight, contextual sensitivity, and regulatory accountability (A. B. Kumar & Sanjaya, 2025). Faculty judgment must remain central, and students must be recognized as active stakeholders rather than passive data subjects.

Ultimately, the challenge is moral rather than technical. AI does not inherently erode integrity, transparency, or trust—but its uncritical deployment can. If implemented reflexively, with clear governance and participatory oversight, AI may support credible and trustworthy assessment ecosystems (Verwoerd, 2025). If deployed as a mechanism of efficiency and control, however, it risks institutionalizing surveillance, obscuring accountability, and weakening the relational foundations upon which higher education depends.

AI-INFORMED ASSESSMENT AS A CATALYST FOR CURRICULUM INNOVATION AND CONSTRUCTIVE ALIGNMENT

AI-informed assessment strategies are increasingly positioned as catalysts for curriculum innovation and improved alignment in higher education. By leveraging learning analytics, adaptive systems, and automated feedback mechanisms, AI has the capacity to reshape how curricula are designed, delivered, and evaluated (Torrisi-Steele, 2025). However, its contribution is not inherently progressive; it depends on how assessment data are interpreted, governed, and pedagogically integrated.

At a structural level, AI can enhance constructive alignment by linking learning outcomes, instructional activities, and assessment tasks through continuous data feedback loops. Learning analytics systems can identify patterns in student performance across modules, revealing misalignments between intended outcomes and assessed competencies (Chu & Ashraf, 2025). For example, if students consistently underperform in higher-order analytical tasks, this may signal gaps in instructional scaffolding or curriculum sequencing. AI-driven dashboards enable curriculum designers to detect such trends at scale, facilitating evidence-informed revision rather than reactive adjustment. In this sense, AI supports coherence by making curriculum performance visible and measurable (Kirange & Chaudhari, 2025).

AI also contributes to curriculum innovation through adaptive and formative assessment models. Traditional curricula often rely on summative evaluations at fixed intervals. AI-enabled systems, by contrast, allow for continuous formative feedback, personalized learning pathways, and dynamic assessment design (Dockens & Shelton, 2025). Adaptive testing platforms can adjust task difficulty based on student responses, promoting differentiated learning experiences. This adaptability encourages curricular flexibility, shifting from static content delivery toward responsive and iterative learning environments.

Moreover, AI-informed assessment can promote interdisciplinary innovation. Data analytics can reveal connections between competencies across courses, highlighting transferable skills such as critical thinking, communication, or quantitative reasoning. Such insights may prompt curriculum integration across departments, supporting competency-based frameworks rather than siloed disciplinary structures (Agrawal et al., 2025). In competency-based education models, AI can map student progress against defined skill matrices, enhancing curricular transparency and progression pathways.

However, the relationship between AI and curriculum alignment must be examined critically. AI systems privilege what is measurable, and this can narrow curricular priorities. When assessment analytics focus primarily on quantifiable outcomes, curricula may drift toward standardized, easily assessable competencies at the expense of creativity, ethical reasoning, and contextual knowledge (Pusporini & Nurdiyanto, 2024). This phenomenon risks producing epistemic reductionism—where complex intellectual development is compressed into data points. Curriculum innovation, in such contexts, may become data-driven optimization rather than pedagogical transformation.

There is also a risk of teaching to the algorithm. If faculty adapt instruction primarily to improve analytics metrics or automated scoring performance, curricular depth may be compromised. Overreliance on algorithmic indicators can marginalize professional judgment and diminish the interpretive dimensions of curriculum design (Olmos & Corrin, 2011). Innovation then becomes reactive to system outputs rather than grounded in scholarly inquiry or disciplinary evolution.

Transparency and governance are therefore central. For AI-informed assessment to meaningfully support curriculum alignment, institutions must ensure that analytics are interpretable, contextualized, and subject to human oversight (Zhang, 2025). Faculty engagement in reviewing AI-generated insights is essential to prevent technocratic determinism. Curriculum alignment should remain anchored in disciplinary standards, societal relevance, and inclusive educational values—not solely in algorithmic performance metrics (Yani & Rosita, 2025).

Furthermore, AI's contribution to alignment must consider equity implications. If predictive analytics identify "at-risk" students without contextual sensitivity, curricular adjustments may unintentionally reinforce deficit narratives (Praveenkumar et al., 2025). Conversely, when used reflexively, AI can illuminate systemic disparities within curriculum pathways, prompting inclusive redesign and targeted support mechanisms.

Ultimately, AI-informed assessment strategies can strengthen curriculum innovation and alignment by enabling continuous feedback, adaptive learning, and evidence-informed revision (Agrawal et al., 2025). Yet their transformative potential depends on maintaining pedagogical integrity and safeguarding against reductive measurement logics. AI should function as an analytical lens rather than a prescriptive authority—supporting reflective curriculum development while preserving the complexity, creativity, and ethical grounding that define higher education (Sarita & Rajeev, 2025).

A CONCEPTUAL FRAMEWORK FOR RESPONSIBLE, EQUITABLE, AND INTEGRITY-DRIVEN AI-SUPPORTED ASSESSMENT

The integration of artificial intelligence into assessment systems represents not merely a technological enhancement but a structural transformation in how authority, accountability, and epistemic legitimacy are constructed in higher education. AI-supported assessment reshapes who evaluates learning, how evidence is interpreted, and under what conditions fairness and credibility are secured. Therefore, proposing a responsible framework requires moving beyond technical optimization toward an ethically grounded, pedagogically anchored, and contextually responsive model.

This section proposes a *Layered Ecosystem Framework* for responsible, equitable, and integrity-driven AI-supported assessment. The framework conceptualizes AI as a mediating intelligence embedded within human-centered pedagogy, stabilized by governance and equity safeguards, and continuously refined through reflexive alignment processes. Responsibility, equity, and integrity are positioned as structural design principles—not supplementary considerations.

Conceptual Foundation

At its core, assessment is relational and interpretive. It involves professional judgment, disciplinary standards, and dialogic engagement between educators and learners. AI systems—adaptive platforms, predictive analytics, automated feedback engines—introduce scalability and analytical precision, yet they also introduce risks: algorithmic opacity, bias amplification, surveillance normalization, and epistemic reductionism (Wang et al.,2024). Accordingly, AI is positioned within this framework not as an autonomous evaluator, but as a *decision-support mechanism* operating within a carefully regulated ecosystem. Responsible AI-supported assessment requires dynamic balance across six interdependent domains:

1) Pedagogical Integrity
2) AI Operational Systems
3) Ethical Governance
4) Equity Safeguards
5) Integrity Architecture
6) Contextual Responsiveness

These domains function interactively rather than hierarchically.

Table 3. Ecosystem Framework for Responsible AI-Supported Assessment

Domain	*Core Function*	*Contribution to Equity & Integrity*	*Risks if Unchecked*	*Safeguarding Mechanisms*
Human-Centered Pedagogy	Anchors assessment in professional judgment and disciplinary values	Preserves interpretive nuance; protects authentic assessment	Deprofessionalization; over-automation	Faculty oversight; dialogic feedback; authentic assessment design
AI Operational Systems	Provides analytics, adaptive pathways, automated feedback	Enhances formative responsiveness and scalability	Algorithmic determinism; epistemic reductionism	Human validation; contextual interpretation; transparency
Ethical Governance	Ensures accountability and procedural fairness	Protects due process; sustains trust	Opaque algorithms; vendor dependency	Bias audits; explainability standards; data protection policies
Equity Safeguards	Embeds inclusion structurally in design	Expands access; mitigates systemic bias	Digital exclusion; stratification	Universal Design for Learning; participatory design; infrastructure investment

continued on following page

Table 3. Continued

Domain	*Core Function*	*Contribution to Equity & Integrity*	*Risks if Unchecked*	*Safeguarding Mechanisms*
Integrity Architecture	Reframes academic honesty frameworks	Builds trust beyond surveillance	Over-monitoring; punitive compliance culture	AI literacy; transparent AI-use policies; authentic assessment strategies
Contextual Environment	Shapes implementation feasibility	Aligns system with local realities	Technological imposition; Global North bias	Local adaptation; regulatory alignment; institutional capacity-building

Table 3 demonstrates that each domain both contributes to and constrains the system. Responsibility emerges from maintaining equilibrium across these interacting elements.

Figure 2. Layered Ecosystem Model of AI in Education

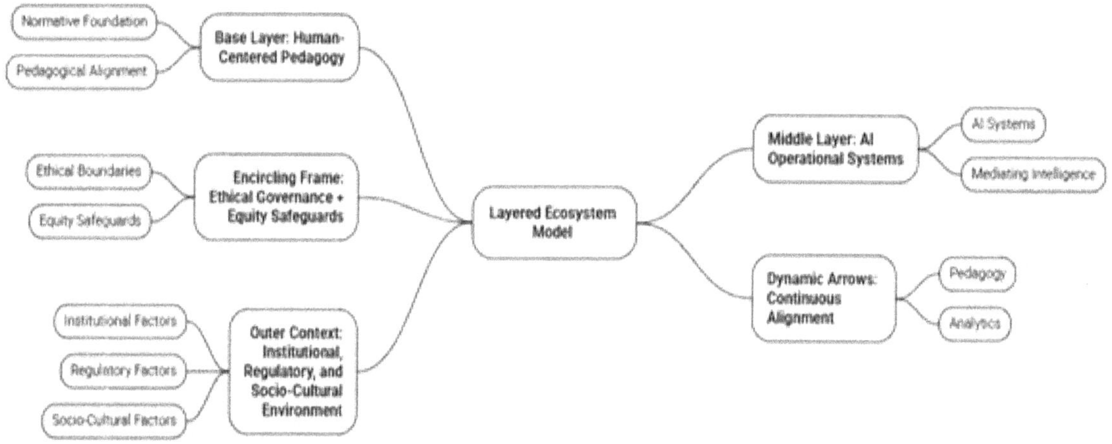

Figure 2 conceptualizes AI-supported assessment as a layered ecosystem, emphasizing balance rather than technological dominance.

At the base layer lies *human-centered pedagogy*, which forms the normative foundation. Assessment remains grounded in educational values, professional judgment, inclusive principles, and constructive alignment. This positioning ensures that pedagogical purpose precedes technological adoption.

The middle layer consists of *AI operational systems*—including automated grading, learning analytics, adaptive feedback tools, and integrity monitoring mechanisms. AI is deliberately placed in the middle to symbolize mediation and augmentation rather than authority. It supports assessment processes but does not replace human decision-making.

Encircling these layers is a protective frame of ethical governance and equity safeguards. This stabilizing structure includes transparency, bias auditing, data protection, accessibility standards, and accountability mechanisms. Governance ensures that AI remains ethically bounded and aligned with educational goals.

Dynamic arrows between pedagogy and AI represent continuous alignment, indicating that analytics inform teaching practice while pedagogical priorities shape technological configuration.

Finally, the entire ecosystem operates within a broader institutional, regulatory, and socio-cultural environment, acknowledging that policy frameworks, digital infrastructure, and contextual inequalities influence implementation—particularly in Global South contexts.

By positioning AI within, rather than above, pedagogy and governance, the framework affirms that artificial intelligence should augment human-centered assessment systems, not dominate them.

Conceptual Logic

Figure 3 illustrates the dynamic and iterative functioning of AI-supported assessment within the broader pedagogical ecosystem. Rather than depicting a linear pipeline in which data flows unidirectionally toward decision-making, the model presents a reflexive alignment loop that sustains curriculum coherence and ethical accountability.

Figure 3. Reflexive Alignment Feedback Loop

The loop (figure 3) unfolds as follows: *Learning Outcomes Teaching Practices AI-Mediated Assessment Analytics Interpretation Curriculum & Policy Revision (return to) Learning Outcomes* This structure emphasizes that assessment is embedded within a continuous cycle of reflection and recalibration.

Figure 2 conceptualizes AI-supported assessment as a dynamic and iterative process embedded within a reflexive pedagogical cycle. Rather than presenting assessment as a linear sequence driven by technological outputs, the model illustrates a continuous alignment loop that safeguards educational purpose and human interpretive authority.

The cycle begins with learning outcomes, which articulate the intended knowledge, skills, values, and competencies that a curriculum seeks to cultivate. These outcomes are normatively determined through disciplinary standards, institutional missions, and broader educational commitments. They represent the ethical and intellectual aspirations of the learning process. Importantly, within this framework, learning outcomes are pedagogically grounded and institutionally deliberated; they are not generated by algorithmic systems.

Learning outcomes are operationalized through teaching practices. Instructional design, classroom engagement, learning activities, and formative interactions translate abstract objectives into concrete pedagogical experiences. This stage ensures coherence between intention and implementation, reinforcing the principle of constructive alignment. Teaching practices mediate between institutional goals and student learning, providing the context within which assessment acquires meaning.

Following instructional engagement, AI-mediated assessment enters the cycle. At this stage, AI tools—such as automated grading systems, adaptive testing platforms, or analytics dashboards—process student performance data. These systems generate insights regarding patterns of achievement, areas of difficulty, and potential inequities. AI functions here as mediating intelligence: it aggregates and interprets data at scale, offering analytical visibility that may otherwise be difficult to achieve.

However, the model emphasizes that AI outputs are not self-validating conclusions. They are probabilistic representations shaped by historical data, design assumptions, and algorithmic parameters. Consequently, the next stage—analytics interpretation—is crucial. Faculty members, administrators, and academic leaders interpret AI-generated insights through professional judgment and contextual knowledge. Human actors assess whether patterns indicate curricular misalignment, pedagogical gaps, inequitable outcomes, or systemic barriers.

This interpretive stage ensures that analytics serve as reflective input rather than prescriptive authority. Without human mediation, analytics risk becoming deterministic, potentially narrowing curriculum or reinforcing biases embedded in data.

Insights derived from reflective interpretation inform curriculum and policy revision. Patterns of persistent misunderstanding may prompt redesign of learning activities. Disparities in achievement may lead to the adoption of more inclusive assessment formats. Institutional policies governing AI use, transparency, or academic integrity may be refined in response to evidence. Importantly, revision is deliberative and ethical; it is guided by educational values rather than automated optimization.

The loop ultimately returns to learning outcomes, completing the cycle. Outcomes may be recalibrated to better reflect evolving competencies, disciplinary developments, or equity commitments. This recursive movement sustains alignment across curriculum, pedagogy, and assessment.

Theoretical Significance

The reflexive alignment feedback loop embodies three critical principles. First, it preserves human interpretive authority at every stage. AI contributes insight but does not determine curricular direction. Second, it reinforces continuous alignment, ensuring that analytics inform reflective practice rather than dictating reform. Third, it situates AI-supported assessment within a living educational system, where innovation emerges through dialogue, deliberation, and ethical judgment. By conceptualizing AI within a reflexive loop rather than as a top-down driver of reform, the model resists technological determinism. It affirms that curriculum innovation remains a human endeavor guided by pedagogical purpose and ethical responsibility. In this framework, AI becomes transformative not because it predicts performance more efficiently, but because it supports sustained, reflective recalibration of educational practice grounded in equity, integrity, and coherence.

Narrative Integration of the Framework

The proposed framework conceptualizes AI-supported assessment as a layered ecosystem grounded in pedagogical integrity, mediated by artificial intelligence, stabilized through governance, and shaped by contextual realities. Its structure resists technocentric hierarchies and instead emphasizes ethical balance and educational intentionality.

Pedagogical Integrity as Foundation

Assessment is not merely a technical procedure; it is a moral act of recognition. It shapes learner identity, allocates opportunity, and sustains institutional credibility (Falchikov & Boud, 2007). Decisions about grading, feedback, and progression influence students' academic trajectories and self-perception. For this reason, pedagogy occupies the foundational layer of the framework.

Positioning human-centered pedagogy at the base ensures that artificial intelligence remains subordinate to educational purpose. Without this normative anchor, assessment risks becoming an exercise in data optimization—privileging efficiency, scalability, and measurable outputs over meaning, dialogue, and intellectual growth (LaFrance, 2025). The framework therefore insists that assessment design, constructive alignment, and professional judgment must precede technological integration. AI must serve learning; learning must not be redesigned to serve AI.

AI as Mediating Intelligence

Within this pedagogical foundation, AI functions as mediating intelligence. It enhances scale, responsiveness, and pattern detection. Learning analytics can illuminate curricular misalignment, identify performance disparities, and generate timely formative feedback (Mishra, 2025). Automated systems can support large cohorts in ways previously unattainable.

Yet AI outputs are probabilistic and historically conditioned. Algorithms interpret patterns based on training data that may embed structural inequalities. Their conclusions are statistical approximations rather than pedagogical truths (Selwyn, 2024). Responsible deployment therefore requires human validation, contextual interpretation, and the preservation of professional discretion.

In this model, AI informs—it does not determine. It augments interpretive practice rather than replacing it. The placement of AI in the middle layer symbolizes this mediation: positioned neither as foundational nor supreme, but as a tool operating within pedagogical and ethical boundaries.

Governance as Legitimizing Structure

Encircling pedagogy and AI operations is the stabilizing structure of ethical governance. Governance legitimizes technological integration by ensuring transparency, explainability, and accountability. Without mechanisms for bias auditing, consent, and oversight, algorithmic systems risk becoming opaque authorities that undermine trust (Al-Omari et al., 2025).

Governance protects procedural fairness. It establishes standards for data protection, clarifies student rights, and enables contestation of algorithmic decisions. In its absence, technological authority may exceed ethical oversight, allowing efficiency-driven logics to overshadow institutional responsibility (Peddi & Manoharan, 2025).

Thus, governance is not peripheral but constitutive. It provides the boundary within which AI operates legitimately. Ethical oversight ensures that innovation remains accountable to educational values rather than market pressures or managerial imperatives.

Equity as Structural Design Principle

Equity must be embedded at the inception of system design rather than treated as a corrective measure after implementation. Inclusive datasets, multimodal assessment pathways, and principles drawn from Universal Design for Learning help prevent algorithmic stratification (Roscoe, 2023). Equity requires recognition of linguistic diversity, cultural variation, and differential access to digital infrastructure.

Beyond algorithmic fairness, equity demands structural awareness. In resource-constrained contexts, unstable internet access, limited device availability, and uneven digital literacy may distort AI-mediated assessment (Praveenkumar et al., 2025). Without attention to these realities, technological reform risks amplifying inequality.

Equity is therefore not an auxiliary goal but a structural design principle. It shapes dataset construction, interface design, feedback mechanisms, and implementation timelines. Responsible AI-supported assessment cannot claim legitimacy without equity safeguards embedded throughout the ecosystem.

Integrity Beyond Surveillance

The proliferation of generative AI has intensified institutional anxieties about academic misconduct. However, integrity cannot be reduced to automated detection systems. Surveillance-heavy models—particularly remote proctoring and opaque AI-detection software—risk eroding relational trust and creating adversarial assessment cultures (Perkins et al., 2023).

Integrity must be understood as developmental rather than punitive. Authentic assessment design, reflective components, iterative drafting processes, and AI literacy initiatives foster shared responsibility (Hook et al., 2024). Students become participants in ethical learning cultures rather than subjects of suspicion.

When integrity is rooted in assessment design and dialogue rather than surveillance, AI becomes a support mechanism rather than a policing instrument. Trust strengthens institutional credibility more effectively than technological monitoring.

Contextual Responsiveness

AI-supported assessment does not operate in a vacuum. Its implementation is shaped by institutional capacity, regulatory frameworks, socio-cultural norms, and global knowledge asymmetries (Al-Amin et al., 2024). What is viable in highly resourced institutions may be unsustainable elsewhere.

Responsible AI cannot be universally imposed; it must be locally negotiated. Contextual responsiveness requires adaptation to policy regimes, infrastructural realities, and cultural expectations regarding privacy, authority, and educational values (Agrawal et al., 2025).

In Global South contexts, particular attention must be paid to digital divides and data governance vulnerabilities. Responsible adoption demands gradual integration, capacity-building, and participatory decision-making.

Critical Synthesis

The framework emphasizes systemic balance. Its layered structure highlights interdependence:

- If governance weakens, transparency collapses.
- If equity safeguards fail, bias intensifies.
- If pedagogy is displaced, automation supersedes professional judgment.
- If surveillance dominates, trust erodes.
- If context is ignored, innovation becomes inequitable.

Responsible AI-supported assessment is therefore a negotiated equilibrium among technological innovation, ethical oversight, and human judgment. Its legitimacy derives not from computational sophistication but from alignment with educational justice, dignity, and relational trust.

Artificial intelligence becomes transformative only when embedded within a morally intentional, pedagogically grounded, and equity-centered ecosystem (Murugesan & Kumar, 2023). The central question is not whether AI can assess more efficiently, but whether its integration strengthens the ethical and relational foundations of higher education.

DISCUSSION

The analysis undertaken in this chapter demonstrates that artificial intelligence–supported assessment must be understood not as a neutral technological innovation but as a structural transformation in the governance of knowledge, authority, and accountability within higher education. AI systems intervene directly in the evaluative core of academic life, shaping how learning is measured, how competence is recognized, and how institutional trust is sustained (Dignum, 2021). As such, the implications of AI integration extend far beyond efficiency gains or feedback automation; they reach into the ethical and epistemological foundations of assessment itself.

A critical reading of the findings reveals a persistent tension between technological instrumentalism and pedagogical intentionality. On one level, AI-supported systems offer compelling advantages. Automated feedback tools can enhance formative assessment practices at scale, learning analytics can illuminate patterns of disengagement, and adaptive systems can personalize learning pathways in ways that were previously impractical (Han et al., 2023). In resource-constrained environments, particularly within Global South contexts, such scalability may appear transformative. Yet these promises must be interpreted cautiously. The capacity to process data efficiently does not inherently align with the normative aims of education. When optimization, prediction, and performance metrics become dominant logics, assessment risks being reframed as a data-governance mechanism rather than a dialogic pedagogical practice.

The equity dimension of AI-supported assessment illustrates this paradox most vividly. The chapter highlights the potential of AI to enhance accessibility, flexibility, and early intervention, particularly for diverse learners. However, these benefits are contingent upon careful governance. Algorithms trained on historically biased datasets risk institutionalizing structural inequalities under the guise of objectivity. Predictive analytics may reproduce deficit narratives by labeling certain students as "at risk" without adequate contextual interpretation (Diene, 2024). Automated scoring systems may privilege dominant linguistic norms while marginalizing alternative forms of expression. Infrastructural disparities further complicate implementation, as digital divides and uneven institutional capacity shape who benefits from AI-mediated systems and who is disadvantaged. Thus, equity emerges not from automation alone but from deliberate, context-sensitive design (Praveenkumar et al., 2025).

Concerns surrounding academic integrity further underscore the ethical complexity of AI integration. The proliferation of generative AI tools has destabilized traditional understandings of authorship and originality, prompting institutions to expand detection technologies and surveillance infrastructures. While such systems may deter certain forms of misconduct, they also risk cultivating suspicion-driven cultures that erode relational trust (Rimban, 2025). The normalization of behavioral monitoring and opaque authorship-detection algorithms reframes integrity as a problem of technological policing rather than ethical formation. The analysis suggests that a more sustainable response lies in redesigning assessment practices—emphasizing authenticity, iterative development, and reflective engagement—rather than escalating surveillance. Integrity, in this sense, becomes a relational and pedagogical commitment rather than a compliance-based regime (Rimban, 2025).

Transparency and trust emerge as interdependent conditions for legitimacy. Algorithmic opacity undermines procedural fairness when students and educators cannot meaningfully understand or challenge automated decisions. Proprietary systems further complicate accountability, limiting institutional oversight. When algorithmic outputs are treated as authoritative without sufficient interpretive scrutiny, professional judgment risks displacement (Farooqi, 2025). Trust is particularly fragile in such contexts; errors, biases, or data breaches can quickly erode institutional credibility. The discussion therefore affirms that transparency must extend beyond technical disclosure to include explainability, participatory governance, and accessible avenues for contestation.

The chapter also situates AI-supported assessment within broader debates on curriculum innovation and alignment. AI-informed analytics can enhance constructive alignment by revealing discrepancies between intended learning outcomes and observed performance patterns. Continuous feedback loops may support evidence-informed curriculum revision and interdisciplinary integration. However, there is a parallel risk that curricular priorities become subordinated to what is computationally measurable (Alone & Mishra, 2025). When analytics privilege quantifiable competencies, complex intellectual capacities—ethical reasoning, creativity, critical dissent—may be marginalized. This epistemic narrowing reflects a deeper tension between data-driven optimization and holistic educational development. Curriculum innovation must therefore remain grounded in disciplinary values and societal relevance rather than algorithmic efficiency (Sarita & Rajeev, 2025).

Across these dimensions, a consistent theme emerges: AI-supported assessment is not inherently emancipatory or oppressive; its impact depends on the moral architecture within which it operates. The layered ecosystem framework proposed in the chapter offers a conceptual means of maintaining equilibrium among pedagogical integrity, governance, equity safeguards, and contextual responsiveness. Yet such balance is not static (Lim et al., 2023). It requires continuous reflexivity, institutional vigilance, and participatory engagement. If governance weakens, transparency collapses. If equity safeguards erode, bias intensifies. If pedagogy is displaced, automation supersedes professional judgment. If surveillance dominates, trust deteriorates (Sarita & Rajeev, 2025).

Ultimately, the discussion affirms that the legitimacy of AI-supported assessment derives not from predictive accuracy or technological sophistication but from alignment with educational justice. Artificial intelligence reshapes the conditions under which learning is evaluated and authority is exercised (Main, 2025). The central challenge for higher education is therefore not whether AI can assess more efficiently, but whether its integration strengthens the ethical, relational, and inclusive foundations upon which educational practice depends (Ilieva et al., 2025). In this respect, AI becomes transformative only when embedded within human-centered, transparently governed, and equity-oriented assessment ecosystems that prioritize dignity and intellectual growth over algorithmic control.

POLICY IMPLICATIONS

The findings of this chapter suggest that the integration of AI-supported assessment in higher education cannot be governed through ad hoc institutional experimentation or purely technical regulation. Because AI reshapes authority, accountability, and epistemic legitimacy within assessment systems, policy responses must be systemic, ethically grounded, and contextually responsive. Policy frameworks must move beyond adoption guidelines toward comprehensive governance architectures that embed equity, transparency, integrity, and pedagogical integrity as foundational principles.

First, policy must clearly establish that AI-supported assessment remains subordinate to human professional judgment. Regulatory frameworks should affirm faculty authority over final evaluative decisions and prohibit fully autonomous grading systems without human oversight. Institutional policies must mandate that AI tools function as decision-support systems rather than decision-makers. This safeguards against automation bias and prevents the displacement of interpretive expertise.

Second, transparency and explainability should be codified as non-negotiable policy requirements. Institutions adopting AI assessment technologies must require algorithmic documentation, explainable decision pathways, and accessible appeals mechanisms for students. Procurement policies should include contractual clauses ensuring transparency from vendors, including the right to audit algorithms for bias and fairness. Without such requirements, higher education institutions risk becoming dependent on opaque commercial systems that undermine accountability.

Third, equity must be embedded at the policy design stage rather than treated as an afterthought. Policies should mandate bias audits, inclusive dataset standards, and regular equity impact assessments prior to and following AI implementation. In Global South and resource-constrained contexts, AI policy must also address infrastructural realities. Investment in digital infrastructure, faculty training, and student digital literacy should accompany technological adoption. Without parallel capacity-building initiatives, AI integration may exacerbate structural inequalities rather than mitigate them.

Fourth, academic integrity policies require substantive revision. Detection-driven approaches alone are insufficient in an era of generative AI. Policies should shift toward integrity-by-design frameworks that promote authentic assessment, iterative drafting, reflective components, and AI literacy education. Surveillance-heavy proctoring policies should be critically reassessed, particularly where privacy risks outweigh demonstrated benefits. Integrity must be reframed as an educational commitment supported by transparent AI-use guidelines rather than enforced solely through algorithmic monitoring.

Fifth, data governance policies must be strengthened. AI-supported assessment generates extensive student data, including behavioral patterns and predictive analytics. Clear policies regarding data minimization, storage limitations, informed consent, and third-party access are essential. Students should retain rights to access, correct, and challenge data-driven decisions that affect their academic progression. In contexts where data protection regulations are weak or unevenly enforced, institutional self-regulation becomes particularly critical.

Sixth, participatory governance should be institutionalized. AI policy development must involve faculty, students, technologists, and ethics committees. Shared governance structures enhance legitimacy and ensure that AI integration aligns with educational values rather than managerial imperatives. Policy should encourage ongoing review processes rather than one-time adoption approvals, recognizing that AI systems evolve and require continuous oversight.

Seventh, national and international policy bodies should develop context-sensitive frameworks rather than universal mandates. Educational systems vary significantly in infrastructural capacity, regulatory maturity, and socio-cultural norms. Policy transfer from highly resourced systems to under-resourced contexts without adaptation risks reproducing Global North biases. International cooperation should focus on knowledge exchange, capacity building, and ethical benchmarking rather than prescriptive standardization.

Finally, policy must articulate a clear normative stance: AI-supported assessment is legitimate only when it advances educational justice, protects human dignity, and sustains trust. Efficiency gains cannot justify erosion of transparency. Predictive analytics cannot supersede equity commitments. Surveillance cannot replace pedagogical engagement. Policies should explicitly state that technological innovation is a means to strengthen educational values—not redefine them.

In sum, the policy implications of this chapter underscore that AI-supported assessment requires robust, multi-layered governance frameworks. Effective policy must integrate professional autonomy, transparency mandates, equity safeguards, data protection, integrity redesign, and participatory oversight. Without such comprehensive regulation, AI risks entrenching inequality and undermining institutional credibility. With thoughtful and ethically grounded policy, however, AI can be aligned with inclusive, integrity-driven, and curriculum-coherent educational futures.

CONCLUSION

Artificial intelligence–supported assessment is reshaping higher education by transforming how learning is evaluated, feedback is delivered, and academic integrity is maintained. As this chapter has argued, AI must be understood not merely as a technological tool but as a socio-pedagogical intervention that influences equity, authority, and curriculum design. While AI offers significant benefits—such as scalable formative feedback, adaptive learning pathways, and data-informed curriculum alignment—these advantages are not inherently equitable or ethically neutral.

Without strong governance and human oversight, AI systems risk reinforcing structural inequalities, embedding algorithmic bias, and normalizing surveillance practices that undermine trust. Automated decision-making can marginalize professional judgment, and opaque algorithms may weaken transparency and accountability. In resource-constrained contexts, digital divides further complicate equitable implementation.

Therefore, the value of AI-supported assessment depends on moral intentionality rather than technical sophistication. AI must remain grounded in human-centered pedagogy, supported by transparent governance, equity safeguards, and integrity-by-design assessment practices. When embedded within inclusive and ethically regulated ecosystems, AI can strengthen feedback, curriculum coherence, and institutional trust. Ultimately, the future of AI in assessment will be defined not by automation alone, but by the educational values institutions choose to uphold.

ACKNOWLEDGEMENTS

The author expresses sincere gratitude to colleagues and peers for their intellectual engagement and encouragement during the development of this chapter.

REFERENCES

Agrawal, A., Banerjee, A. R. S., Jhariya, M. K., Garg, N., Hashmi, I., Brar, V., Gupta, D., & Mishra, D. K. (2025). AI-powered student assessment in higher education. In *Research Gate* (pp. 177–202). DOI: 10.4018/979-8-3373-2130-1.ch006

Agrawal, A., Bhadhouriya, S., Pandey, A. K., Bhadoriya, S., Shrivastava, D., Dubey, G., Dubey, M., Sengar, H., Shakywar, K., & Shrivastava, V. (2024). Transforming student assessment in higher education. In *Advances in Educational Technologies and Instructional Design Book Series* (pp. 363–386). DOI: 10.4018/979-8-3693-6170-2.ch013

Ahamed, F. I. (2025). The transformative role of artificial intelligence in modern education. *World Journal of Advanced Research and Reviews*, *26*(1), 3239–3247. DOI: 10.30574/wjarr.2025.26.1.1453

Al-Amin, M., Saqui, F. Z., & Khan, M. R. (2024). Enhancing assessment systems in higher education. In *Advances in Educational Technologies and Instructional Design Book Series* (pp. 28–56). DOI: 10.4018/979-8-3693-2145-4.ch002

Al-Omari, O., Alyousef, A., Fati, S., Shannaq, F., & Omari, A. (2025). Governance and ethical frameworks for AI integration in higher education: Enhancing personalized learning and legal compliance. *Journal of Ecohumanism*, *4*(2). Advance online publication. DOI: 10.62754/joe.v4i2.5781

Alone, V. N., & Mishra, K. C. (2025). Role of learning analytics and AI in measuring learning outcomes and student performance. In *Research Gate* (pp. 62–90). DOI: 10.71443/9789349552685-03

Ardito, C. G. (2023). *Contra generative AI detection in higher education assessments*. arXiv. /arxiv.2312.05241DOI: 10.48550

Bai, J. Y. H., Zawacki-Richter, O., Bozkurt, A., Lee, K., Fanguy, M., Sari, B. C., & Marin, V. I. (2022). Automated essay scoring (AES) systems: Opportunities and challenges for open and distance education. In *Tenth Pan-Commonwealth Forum on Open Learning*. DOI: 10.56059/pcf10.8339

Barrett, L. (2021). *Rejecting test surveillance in higher education.* SSRN Electronic Journal. DOI: 10.2139/ssrn.3871423

Bearman, M., Ryan, J., & Ajjawi, R. (2022). Discourses of artificial intelligence in higher education: A critical literature review. *Higher Education*, *86*(2), 369–385. DOI: 10.1007/s10734-022-00937-2

Bhavana, S., Jayashree, K., & Rao, T. V. N. (2024). Navigating AI biases in education. In *Advances in Educational Marketing* (pp. 135–160). Administration, and Leadership Book Series., DOI: 10.4018/979-8-3693-5443-8.ch005

Biggs, J., & Tang, C. (2011). *Teaching for quality learning at university* (4th ed.). Open University Press.

Black, P., & Wiliam, D. (2009). Developing the theory of formative assessment. *Educational Assessment, Evaluation and Accountability*, *21*(1), 5–31.

Boud, D., & Falchikov, N. (2007). *Rethinking assessment in higher education*. Routledge.

Boud, D., Ajjawi, R., Dawson, P., & Tai, J. (2018). *Developing evaluative judgement in higher education*. Routledge.

Bozkurt, A. (n.d.). *GenAI et al.: Cocreation, authorship, ownership, academic ethics and integrity in a time of generative AI*. Open Praxis., DOI: 10.55982/openpraxis.16.1.654

Chu, T. S., & Ashraf, M. (2025). Artificial intelligence in curriculum design: A data-driven approach to higher education innovation. *Knowledge (Beverly Hills, Calif.)*, *5*(3), 14. DOI: 10.3390/knowledge5030014

Diene, A. (2024). AI and equity in higher education. In *Advances in Computational Intelligence and Robotics Book Series* (pp. 1–12). DOI: 10.4018/979-8-3693-1565-1.ch001

Dignum, V. (2021). The role and challenges of education for responsible AI. *London Review of Education*, *19*(1). Advance online publication. DOI: 10.14324/lre.19.1.01

Dockens, A. L., & Shelton, K. (2025). AI for formative and summative assessment. In *Advances in Computational Intelligence and Robotics Book Series* (pp. 353–386). DOI: 10.4018/979-8-3373-5102-5.ch013

Drinan, P. M., & Gallant, T. B. (2008). Plagiarism and academic integrity systems. *Journal of Library Administration*, *47*(3–4), 125–140. DOI: 10.1080/01930820802186472

Eaton, S. E. (2023). *Plagiarism in higher education: Tackling tough topics in academic integrity*. Springer.

Entschew, E. M. (2024). Discriminatory data yields discriminatory systems: When AI biases harm human beings. In *Edward Elgar Publishing eBooks* (pp. 37–65). DOI: 10.4337/9781803928241.00009

Fakokunde, A. (2025). Ethics, privacy, and transparency in AI-assisted teaching: Evaluating NoteGrade.ai against global standards. *Preprints.org*. DOI: 10.20944/preprints202509.1148.v1

Falchikov, N., & Boud, D. (2007). The role of assessment in preparing for lifelong learning: Problems and challenges. In *Research Gate* (pp. 97–110). DOI: 10.4324/9780203942185-14

Farooqi, S. A. (2025). Ethical framework for AI in education. In *Advances in Computational Intelligence and Robotics Book Series* (pp. 153–188). DOI: 10.4018/979-8-3373-5550-4.ch007

Fisk, G. D. (2024). AI or human? Finding and responding to artificial intelligence in student work. *Teaching of Psychology*, *52*(3), 314–318. DOI: 10.1177/00986283241251855

Gnanaprakasam, J., & Lourdusamy, R. (2024). The role of AI in automating grading: Enhancing feedback and efficiency. In *Artificial intelligence*. DOI: 10.5772/intechopen.1005025

Han, B., Nawaz, S., Buchanan, G., & McKay, D. (2023). Ethical and pedagogical impacts of AI in education. In *Lecture Notes in Computer Science* (pp. 667–673). DOI: 10.1007/978-3-031-36272-9_54

Hook, J., Junor, A., Sell, C., & Sapsed, C. (2024). Navigating integrity and innovation. In *ASCILITE Publications* (pp. 165–172). DOI: 10.14742/apubs.2024.1234

Hutson, J. (2024). Rethinking plagiarism in the era of generative AI. *Journal of International Communication, 3*(2). Advance online publication. DOI: 10.54963/jic.v3i2.220

Ilieva, G., Yankova, T., Ruseva, M., & Kabaivanov, S. (2025). A framework for generative AI-driven assessment in higher education. *Preprints.org*. DOI: 10.20944/preprints202505.0800.v1

Jackson, S., & Panteli, N. (2022). Trust or mistrust in algorithmic grading? An embedded agency perspective. *International Journal of Information Management, 69*, 102555. DOI: 10.1016/j.ijinfomgt.2022.102555

Kayyali, M. (2025). AI in higher education. In *IGI Global* (pp. 57–82). DOI: 10.4018/979-8-3373-2685-6.ch003

Kirange, D. Y., & Chaudhari, Y. N. (2025). A review of data-driven decision-making approaches in curriculum design. *International Journal of Innovative Research in Engineering, 26–29*. Advance online publication. DOI: 10.59256/ijire.20250604004

Klinger, D. A., DeLuca, C., & Miller, T. (2015). The evolving culture of assessment. *Assessment in Education: Principles, Policy & Practice, 22*(4), 395–411.

Kumar, A. B., & Sanjaya, K. (2025). AI and social justice. In *Advances in Social Networking and Online Communities Book Series* (pp. 163–190). DOI: 10.4018/979-8-3693-9904-0.ch008

Kumar, R. (2024). Beyond reproach: Navigating usage, detection, and future pathways of AI in education. *Brock Education Journal, 33*(3). Advance online publication. DOI: 10.26522/brocked.v33i3.1173

LaFrance, J. (2025). The power and perils of AI-driven assessment in higher education. In *Advances in Computational Intelligence and Robotics Book Series* (pp. 267–296). DOI: 10.4018/979-8-3693-7873-1.ch010

Lahusen, C., Maggetti, M., & Slavkovik, M. (2024). Trust, trustworthiness and AI governance. *Scientific Reports, 14*(1), 20752. DOI: 10.1038/s41598-024-71761-0 PMID: 39237635

Lim, T., Gottipati, S., & Cheong, M. L. F. (2023). Ethical considerations for artificial intelligence in educational assessments. In *Advances in Educational Technologies and Instructional Design Book Series* (pp. 32–79). DOI: 10.4018/979-8-3693-0205-7.ch003

Longworth, J. (2021). Benjamin Ruha (2019) *Race after technology: Abolitionist tools for the new Jim Code*. Medford: Polity Press. 172 pages. eISBN: 9781509526437. *Science & Technology Studies, 34*(2), 92–94. DOI: 10.23987/sts.102639

Luckin, R. (2017). Towards artificial intelligence-based assessment systems. *Nature Human Behaviour, 1*(3). Advance online publication. DOI: 10.1038/s41562-016-0028

Main, P. (2025). AI and student assessment. *International Journal of Science and Research Archive, 16*(2), 305–313. DOI: 10.30574/ijsra.2025.16.2.2225

McConvey, K., Guha, S., & Kuzminykh, A. (2023). A human-centered review of algorithms in decision-making in higher education. In *Proceedings of the ACM Conference* (pp. 1–15). DOI: 10.1145/3544548.3580658

. Miller, W. (2024). Adapting to AI: Reimagining the role of assessment professionals. *Intersection: A Journal at the Intersection of Assessment and Learning, 5*(4). DOI: 10.61669/001c.121439

Mishara, P. (2024). The ethical implications of AI in education: Privacy, bias, and accountability. *Journal of Informatics Education and Research, 4*(2). Advance online publication. DOI: 10.52783/jier.v4i2.1827

Mishra, S. (2025). Artificial intelligence as a mediator between educator and learner: The new paradigm shift. *International Journal of Research and Innovation in Applied Science, 10*(7), 91–95. DOI: 10.51584/ijrias.2025.100700008

Murgatroyd, S. (2024). Artificial intelligence and future of higher education. [REPED]. *Revista Paraguaya de Educación a Distancia, 5*(1), 4–11. DOI: 10.56152/reped2024-vol5num1-art1

Murugesan, S., & Cherukuri, A. K. (2023). The rise of generative artificial intelligence and its impact on education: The promises and perils. *Computer, 56*(5), 116–121. DOI: 10.1109/MC.2023.3253292

. Mütterlein, J., Ranner, T., & Müller, M. (2024). Artificial intelligence at universities: Impact on grades, student experience, and teaching. DOI: 10.56843/jm001tr002

Olmos, M., & Corrin, L. (2011). Academic analytics in a medical curriculum. In *ASCILITE Publications* (pp. 930–941). DOI: 10.14742/apubs.2011.1731

Oravec, J. A. (2022). AI, biometric analysis, and emerging cheating detection systems: The engineering of academic integrity? *Education Policy Analysis Archives, 30*. Advance online publication. DOI: 10.14507/epaa.30.5765

Organisation for Economic Co-operation and Development. (2021). *AI in education: Challenges and opportunities*. OECD Publishing.

. *Pandemic politics, pedagogies and practices: Digital technologies and distance education during the coronavirus emergency.* (n.d.). Taylor & Francis.

Peddi, S., & Manoharan, G. (2025). Ethical guidelines for the thoughtful implementation of AI in higher education. *EthAIca, 5*, 409. DOI: 10.56294/ai2026409

Perkins, M., Furze, L., Roe, J., & MacVaugh, J. (2023). The AI assessment scale (AIAS): A framework for ethical integration of generative AI in educational assessment. *arXiv*. /arXiv.2312.07086DOI: 10.48550

Perkins, M., Furze, L., Roe, J., & MacVaugh, J. (2024). The artificial intelligence assessment scale (AIAS): A framework for ethical integration of generative AI in educational assessment. *Journal of University Teaching & Learning Practice, 21*(6). Advance online publication. DOI: 10.53761/q3azde36

Perkins, M., Roe, J., & Furze, L. (2024). The AI assessment scale revisited: A framework for educational assessment. *arXiv*. /arXiv.2412.09029DOI: 10.48550

Praveenkumar, S., Anute, N., Vaissnave, V., Ragupathi, T., Fardale, S., Selvakumar, P., & Manjunath, T. C. (2025). Risks of AI bias and inequities in learning. In *Advances in Computational Intelligence and Robotics Book Series* (pp. 257–284). DOI: 10.4018/979-8-3373-2302-2.ch009

Pusporini, W., & Nurdiyanto, H. (2024). Utilization of artificial intelligence in outcome-based curriculum evaluation and development. *Journal of Research in Social Science and Humanities*, *4*(2), 132–134. DOI: 10.47679/jrssh.v4i1.109

Radjabov, S., & Ravshanov, F. (2024). Implementation of AI-based algorithm and its complications and security constraints in higher education systems. In *IEEE Xplore Conference Proceedings* (pp. 1597–1602). DOI: 10.1109/icacite60783.2024.10616878

Rimban, E. (2025). Ethics in the time of artificial intelligence: Rethinking integrity in the classroom. *Preprints.org*. DOI: 10.20944/preprints202505.0913.v1

. Roscoe, R. D. (2023). Building inclusive and equitable artificial intelligence for education. *XRDS: Crossroads, the ACM Magazine for Students, 29*(3), 22–25. DOI: 10.1145/3589637

Ross, J., & Macleod, H. (2018). Surveillance, (dis)trust and teaching with plagiarism detection technology. In *Proceedings of the International Conference on Networked Learning, 11*, 235–242. DOI: 10.54337/nlc.v11.8760

. Sarita, & Rajeev. (2025). AI-powered learning analytics: Exploring opportunities and risks for student development. *Research Review: International Journal of Multidisciplinary, 10*(8), 66–68. DOI: 10.31305/rrijm.2025.v10.n8.009

Selwyn, N. (2019). Should robots replace teachers? *British Journal of Educational Technology*, *50*(3), 1033–1046.

Selwyn, N. (2024). On the limits of artificial intelligence (AI) in education. *Nordisk Tidsskrift for Pedagogikk og Kritikk*, *10*(1). Advance online publication. DOI: 10.23865/ntpk.v10.6062

Shishavan, H. B. (2024). AI in higher education. In *ASCILITE Publications* (pp. 118–126). DOI: 10.14742/apubs.2024.1205

Song, N. (2024). Higher education crisis: Academic misconduct with generative AI. *Journal of Contingencies and Crisis Management*, *32*(1). Advance online publication. DOI: 10.1111/1468-5973.12532

Sulthana, K. F., Rajeshwari, B. S., Ashok, M., & Joel, M. R. (2025). Ensuring fairness in AI-driven university assessments. In *Advances in Computational Intelligence and Robotics Book Series* (pp. 77–108). DOI: 10.4018/979-8-3373-6018-8.ch004

Swiecki, Z., Khosravi, H., Chen, G., Martinez-Maldonado, R., Lodge, J. M., Milligan, S., Selwyn, N., & Gašević, D. (2022). Assessment in the age of artificial intelligence. *Computers and Education: Artificial Intelligence*, *3*, 100075. DOI: 10.1016/j.caeai.2022.100075

Thai, H., Nguyen, M., Nguyen, H. T. T., Vo, D. T. H., Thanh, B. N., Nguyen, K., Ha, S., & Le, T. V. A. (2024). Educational technology and responsible automated essay scoring in the generative AI era. In *Practice, Progress, and Proficiency in Sustainability* (pp. 325–356). DOI: 10.4018/979-8-3693-2827-9.ch011

Torrisi-Steele, G. (2025). AI and curriculum. In *Advances in Computational Intelligence and Robotics Book Series* (pp. 147–170). DOI: 10.4018/979-8-3373-2397-8.ch006

United Nations Educational, Scientific and Cultural Organization. (2021). *AI and education: Guidance for policymakers*. UNESCO.

Vangibhuratha, S. K. (2025). The impact of generative AI on educational assessment. *International Journal of Innovative Research in Engineering & Multidisciplinary Physical Sciences*, *13*(4). Advance online publication. DOI: 10.37082/ijirmps.v13.i4.232678

Verwoerd, J. C. (2025). Balancing innovation and ethics: A framework for responsible AI integration in educational assessment. *Preprints.org*. DOI: 10.20944/preprints202508.1696.v1

Wang, S., Wang, F., Zhu, Z., Wang, J., Tran, T., & Du, Z. (2024). Artificial intelligence in education: A systematic literature review. *Expert Systems with Applications*, *252*, 124167. DOI: 10.1016/j.eswa.2024.124167

Yani, A., & Rosita, R. (2025). Integrating AI in outcome-based education. In *Advances in Computational Intelligence and Robotics Book Series* (pp. 133–162). DOI: 10.4018/979-8-3373-1062-6.ch005

Zhang, X. (2025). Fairness and effectiveness in AI-driven educational assessments: Challenges and mitigation strategies. *Journal of Innovation and Development*, *11*(1), 7–10. DOI: 10.54097/adcxze34

Declarations

- Ethical compliance: Follows academic and ethical standards.
- Consent to participate/publication: Not applicable.
- Conflict of interest: None declared.
- Funding: No external funding.
- Data availability: Not applicable.
- Use of AI Tools: *Grammarly* and *Paperpal* (Premium) were used only for language refinement and readability improvement.

Chapter 3
Reframing Quality and Integrity in AI-Powered Assessment:
A Global and Ethical Perspective on Higher Education

Sohom Saha
http://orcid.org/0009-0006-9438-1554
Lakshmibai National Institute of Physical Education, India

Mahendra Kumar Singh
http://orcid.org/0000-0001-9989-9420
Lakshmibai National Institute of Physical Education, India

ABSTRACT

Artificial intelligence (AI) is rapidly changing how assessment is designed and conducted in higher education. While AI tools can improve feedback, efficiency, and personalization, they also raise serious concerns related to academic integrity, fairness, transparency, privacy, and trust. This chapter critically examines AI-powered assessment as not just a technical process, but a socio-pedagogical and ethical practice. It highlights the limitations of surveillance-based and detection-focused approaches and argues for a shift toward authentic, integrity-driven assessment. Special attention is given to Global South and resource-constrained contexts, where issues of access, bias, and inequality are more pronounced. The chapter proposes guiding principles for responsible AI use that prioritize learning, equity, student agency, and human judgment in higher education assessment.

1. INTRODUCTION AND BACKGROUND

Higher education assessment has never been merely a technical process of grading, but it is a pedagogical, ethical, and institutional process which determines how learning should be valued, measured and legitimate (Boud & Soler, 2016). Over the past several years, the principles of artificial intelligence (AI), especially generative AI, automated feedback systems, and algorithmic detectors of misconduct, have begun to shape the assessment design and evaluation and quality assurance processes in assessment systems around the world in a fundamentally different way (Bearman et al., 2022; Gasevic et al., 2023).

DOI: 10.4018/979-8-3373-8939-4.ch003

Even though the developments are likely to bring efficiency, scalability, and personalization, they also exacerbate the old issues regarding academic integrity, fairness, transparency, surveillance, and trust (Dawson, 2021; Eaton, 2023).

The development of large language models like ChatGPT and other generative AI applications has now given rise to what some researchers call an assessment crisis in higher education (Sullivan et al., 2023). Such technologies are capable of creating advanced written answers, finding complex solutions, and writing code, which are essentially disruptive to the conventional notion of authorship, originality, and independent work done by students (Perkins et al., 2023). At the same time, the AI-driven proctoring systems and plagiarism detecting tools have spread, which raises questions about the process of surveillance, privacy, and loss of trust between the students and the institutions (Swauger, 2020; Nguyen et al., 2022). Quality and integrity in assessment should be rediscovered in a critical manner as AI-driven tools are integrated into the assessment processes.

AI-mediated assessment is neither a neutral nor purely technical intervention; rather, it is shaped by institutional cultures, regulatory frameworks, disciplinary conventions, and broader social and economic inequalities (Williamson & Eynon, 2020). Such dynamics are especially acute in the Global South and situations of resource limitation, where infrastructural constraints, policy-related marginalizations, and disproportional access to technology can enhance the threat of exclusion, discrimination, and inequity (Miao & Holmes, 2021; Zawacki-Richter et al., 2019). Although there is accumulating research on the topic of AI in higher education, much of the current literature is focused on well-resourced institutions and Global North scenarios (Chan & Hu, 2023).

As a result, there is a dire need of an approach to context-sensitive, globally representative scholarship, questioning the ways AI-enabled evaluation meets the quality assurance and academic integrity in various educational systems. In addition, numerous researchers focus on technical competence and have a weak theoretical foundation of governance, ethics, and pedagogical consistency (Holmes & Porayska-Pomsta, 2022). The chapter addresses these gaps by redefining AI-powered assessment as a socio-pedagogical and ethical practice, but not as an entirely technological solution. It anticipates quality and integrity as the principles of responsible AI application and locates evaluation in global higher education environments which are characterized by diversity, inequality, and institutional strengths and weaknesses.

The distinctive contribution of this chapter lies in its integration of dimensions that are often discussed separately in the literature on AI-powered assessment. Rather than treating assessment quality, academic integrity, ethical governance, student agency, and Global South perspectives as independent concerns, the chapter brings these dimensions together within a socio-pedagogical framework for responsible AI-powered assessment in higher education. This integrated perspective shifts the discussion from a narrow emphasis on detecting misconduct or adopting AI technologies toward a broader consideration of how assessment can remain valid, equitable, transparent, trustworthy, and educationally meaningful in AI-rich environments. The chapter therefore contributes a holistic framework that connects technological possibilities with pedagogical purposes, institutional responsibilities, student rights, and contextual realities.

2. PURPOSE AND OBJECTIVES OF THE CHAPTER

This chapter is primarily aimed at critical analysis of the opportunities that AI-driven assessment practices have to improve the quality of education and academic integrity in higher education and meet the ethical, cultural, and contextual challenges of the world environments. Instead of focusing on AI as the panacea, the chapter reiterates the importance of responsible and context-specific integration consistent with pedagogical objectives and institutional values (Miao et al., 2024).

Three considerations provide the rationale for this chapter. First, quality assurance systems need to be updated to address AI-mediated assessment without compromising academic standards and learner confidence (Newton & Boud, 2023). Second, academic integrity needs to be reconsidered in the context of generative AI, moving beyond surveillance-oriented approaches toward pedagogically meaningful and authentic assessment practices (Bretag, 2023; Stoesz & Eaton, 2023). Third, higher education institutions, particularly those in the Global South, require governance models and policy frameworks that recognize local realities, resource constraints, and social inequalities (Selwyn et al., 2020).

Specific objectives include:

- Examining AI-powered assessment as a socio-pedagogical and ethical practice in higher education
- Analyzing how AI-mediated assessment influences quality assurance and academic integrity
- Exploring issues of fairness, transparency, bias, and trust in AI-driven assessment systems
- Critically assessing the implications of AI-powered misconduct detection and surveillance practices
- Highlighting Global South and resource-constrained perspectives on AI in assessment
- Proposing principles and frameworks for responsible, integrity-driven AI-powered assessment

By integrating theoretical perspectives, policy analysis, and global considerations, this chapter provides a holistic framework for understanding and guiding AI-powered assessment practices in higher education.

3. AI-POWERED ASSESSMENT AND THE RECONCEPTUALIZATION OF QUALITY

Quality assessment in higher education has always been linked with validity, reliability, consistency and adherence to the learning outcomes (Bloxham and Boyd, 2007). These are the set quality indicators that focus on the degree to which appraisals gauge what they purport to gauge, generate consistent outcomes, and facilitate significant learning (Carless, 2015). The use of AI-based tools opens up the new aspects of quality, as it provides adaptive feedback, learning analytics, and scaled assessment design (Boud et al., 2018; Pardo et al., 2019).

Nonetheless, AI-mediated assessment also disrupts traditional quality indicators as it creates the illusion of veiled information, algorithmic decision-making, and dependence on proprietary systems whose functioning is not accessible to educators and students (Bayne, 2015; Selwyn, 2019). The lack of transparency and comprehension of the mechanisms of evaluation that characterizes many AI systems leads to basic questions about how quality is guaranteed when the mechanisms of the evaluation are not fully apparent (Burrell, 2016).

3.1 Expanding Quality Frameworks

The AI-powered assessment needs to be quality assured, which means it should be even more than technically accurate, pedagogical, and ethically responsible, and, above all, contextually relevant (Gasevic et al., 2023). This broadened definition of quality has a number of critical dimensions. First, pedagogical validity entails that AI tools can actually justify the learning goals as opposed to automating the already existing processes (Dawson et al., 2019). In the case of automated essay scoring systems, they should be tested not only according to their capability to grade and assess essays in the same way as a human being but also whether they can offer the students feedback, which would promote student learning (Shermis, 2014). Second, explainability and transparency are all-important quality measures in AI-mediated assessment (Holstein & Doroudi, 2021).

The students and educators should have the chance to know how AI systems come to conclusions, what the criteria are used, and how the decision may be challenged or reconsidered (Felten et al., 2019). The General Data Protection Regulation (GDPR) of the European Union has laid significant precedents of the concept of the right to explanation in automated decision-making, but it is still inconsistent when applied in the educational setting (Kaminski, 2019). Third, fairness and bias mitigation are some of the key quality requirements (Baker & Hawn, 2022). The AI systems operating on historical data can reinforce the current forms of inequality or disadvantage some groups of students due to linguistics or cultural allusions, writing styles that do not correspond to the general patterns (O'Neil, 2016). Quality assurance procedures should consequently involve continual monitoring of AI tools to perform efficiently on various groups of students and in a variety of contexts (Kizilcec & Lee, 2022).

3.2 Global Perspectives on Quality

Quality should be compared to equity, access, and cultural appropriateness in the global context, as well (Joshi et al., 2021). It is possible that AI-based assessment systems designed with English-language and Western educational settings in mind will not work well or even suit the case of multilingual and multicultural settings (Shultz & Guaglianone, 2015). Tasks that are centred on individualistic learning cultures are not always compatible with the collaborative or community othering pedagogical traditions found in most of the Global South (Twum-Danso Imoh and Gupta, 2021).

Moreover, the aspect of the quality of AI-based assessment cannot be divorced with the concerns that emerge regarding the possibility of infrastructural and digital access (Czerniewicz et al., 2020). Even the best AI tools can increase, instead of decrease, educational inequalities in environments where students lack access to the internet or cannot use their devices or lack any type of technical support (Schleicher, 2020). The quality assurance structures should thus be context sensitive and sensitive to the material circumstances that the assessment takes place.

4. ACADEMIC INTEGRITY, GENERATIVE AI, AND THE SHIFT FROM SURVEILLANCE TO AUTHENTICITY

Academic integrity is one of the most disputable topics of AI-driven assessment. Generative AI has challenged the conventional ideas of authorship, originality, and misconduct, and AI-driven detection software provokes the issues of false positives, bias and student rights (Perkins et al., 2023; Sullivan et al., 2023). The swift development of AI systems, such as ChatGPT, GPT-4, and academic specific AI systems, has completely undermined the definition of academic misconduct (Lancaster, 2023).

4.1 The Limitations of Detection-Based Approaches

Generative AI has received many institutional reactions based on technologies that detect content created by AI (Weber-Wulff et al., 2023). The study has however shown serious short coming in the accuracy and reliability of these tools. Research has demonstrated that AI detection detectors generate high-rates of false positives, especially with students who are not native speakers of English, students with disabilities relying on assistive technologies, or students who do not conform to general academic writing norms (Liang et al., 2023; Wang et al., 2023).

In addition, detection-based methods also pose a danger of establishing adversarial relationships between universities and students, which is detrimental to meaningful learning communities (Eaton & Turner, 2020). It has been argued that such surveillance-oriented practices as AI-enhanced proctoring systems that track the eye movements, facial expressions of students, and physical settings can be seen as invasive, discriminatory, and dehumanizing toward students (Swauger, 2020; Coghlan et al., 2021).

4.2 Reframing Integrity Through Authentic Assessment

The chapter suggests a change in the models based on punitive approaches and detection-oriented models to integrity-based assessment model that puts emphasis on authenticity, process evidence, reflection, and learning (Stoesz & Eaton, 2023; Bretag, 2023). The tasks that are considered to be authentic are the ones that reflect the reality, demand the use of knowledge in new situations, and make plagiarism or AI-generation directly counterproductive or strategically challenging (Villarroel et al., 2018; Ashford-Rowe et al., 2014). Such methods of integrity are the portfolio-based assessment, which captures learning processes over time, oral exams, which demand real-time demonstration of comprehension, and project-based assessments, which are based on regional contexts and would be hard to meaningfully tackle with generic AI systems (Dawson & Sutherland-Smith, 2018).

With the aid of evidence of a genuine engagement, process-oriented assessment models that demand students to send draft, reflections and record of their research and development activity can support learning (Boud, 2000). Academic integrity is not only posed as compliance to rules but as a collective moral obligation through the clear and equitable evaluation procedures (Fishman, 2016). Such view is connected to the educational philosophy that interprets integrity as part of the learning experience rather than the external limitation that must be imposed on students with the help of surveillance (Macfarlane et al., 2014).

5. ALGORITHMIC BIAS, FAIRNESS, AND THE IMPERATIVE OF TRANSPARENCY

The design of AI systems is influenced by the data, assumptions, and power structures (Noble, 2018; Benjamin, 2019). Algorithms bias in an assessment situation can lead to the disadvantage of students with a certain linguistic, cultural, or social-economic background. Lack of transparency and explainability is thus a critical factor to address when it comes to fairness and accountability (Holstein & Doroudi, 2021).

5.1 Sources and Manifestations of Bias

Assessment bias may be algorithmic and have various sources. Training data bias is the situation when the datasets to create AI systems underrepresent or misrepresent the distinct groups (Barocas & Selbst, 2016). As an illustration, automated essay scoring systems that are trained on writing samples of native English speakers are likely to systematically undergraduate, even when the essay shows advanced thinking and relevant knowledge in the discipline, multilingual students (Ballier et al., 2019).

The concept of design bias has to do with the assumptions and priorities of the developers of a system, who can focus on efficiency or standardization rather than pedagogical subtlety or cultural sensitivity (Green, 2021). Deployment bias is a phenomenon where tools created to be used in a particular environment are used in a new environment without due validation or adaptation (Prinsloo & Slade, 2017). These types of algorithmic bias can further reinforce existing inequalities in Global South contexts, where students might be already disadvantaged by systemic inequities (such as language policy or resource access), colonial histories in education, and so on (Keet et al., 2017).

5.2 Transparency as a Precondition for Fairness

Transparency works on various levels in AI-powered assessment. Technical transparency means how the algorithms and training data of AI systems, as well as their decision-making processes, are inspectable (Felten et al., 2019). Operational transparency means that there is a transparency of communication regarding the usage of AI tools in assessment, what they are informing, and how human reviewing opportunities can be offered (Slade and Prinsloo, 2013). Pedagogical transparency means that students know what is assessed and how the AI generated feedback is to be viewed and what is the role played by AI in the assessment (Carless & Boud, 2018).

In the presence of this multilayered transparency, students will be unable to challenge unjust judgments, teachers will be unable to make sure that the pedagogical objectives are being met, and institutions will be unable to fulfill their responsibilities (Whitelock et al., 2015). AI-assessment requires checks and balances to be fair and improve with time (Kizilcec & Lee, 2022). Institutions should apply the mechanism of identifying and managing disparate impacts on the various groups of students, such as disaggregated examination of AI tool performance in students with varied backgrounds (Baker & Hawn, 2022). This necessitates institutional cooperation in preferences towards a data governance that is more equitable and readiness to abolish or remodel AI tools that yield unfair results.

5.3 Student Agency, Voice, and Participation in AI-Mediated Assessment

The incorporation of AI in the evaluation procedures is a paradigm shift in changing the relationship between study participants, educators, and evaluation systems. Although institutions, efficiency, and technical potential are also discussed widely in relation to AI in education, little has been said about how students experience it and exercise agency and participation in AI-mediated assessment settings (Cukurova et al., 2019). Algorithms are not the focus of AI-powered assessment but a stakeholder, and students should have their views, interests, and rights that should inform the design, implementation, and governance of AI-powered assessment (Bayne et al., 2020).

The Erosion of Student Agency in Algorithmic Systems

The traditional assessment, although limited, usually maintains the room of student agency, ability to make choices, judgment, and affect evaluation procedures (Tannock, 2017). Students have the option to clarify on assignment expectations, bargain deadlines in unique situations, justify situational aspects that influence their work, and appeal against grades that they think are unjustified. Such possibilities of conversation, clarification, and request are inherent to the assessment as an educational, not necessarily bureaucratic activity (Carless and Winstone, 2023).

The assessment process led by AI poses a threat to these spaces of student agency in a number of ways. Automated grading systems can offer grades without a chance to explain the context and reflect the mitigating circumstances (Williamson et al., 2020). Plagiarism detectors are algorithms that alert students of work that is considered problematic according to obscure criteria, which puts them in the defensive posture of proving their innocence instead of assuming that they acted ethically (Eaton & Turner, 2020). Facial recognition, eye-tracking, and behavioral analysis systems in the proctoring systems expose students to surveillance regimes that grant no substantive agency and privacy (Selwyn et al., 2021).

A study of student experiences with AI-based proctoring in the COVID-19 pandemic found that students were experiencing significant anxiety, expressed mistrust and concern about their dignity and privacy (Marzouk et al., 2021). Students claimed to have found such systems dehumanizing and infantilizing, and they have been exposed to test-taking settings more characterized by stress than the environments that allow students to exhibit learning (Nguyen et al., 2020). These experiences are a basic disregard of the relational trust that ought to inform the assessment of education (Knight, 2022).

Student Perspectives on Generative AI and Assessment Integrity

The recent studies of student attitude to generative AI demonstrate that this phenomenon is complex and nuanced and may not be described as a simplistic narrative about student motivation and integrity (Crawford et al., 2023). Whereas, some students believe that AI tools are a means to take shortcuts or cheat, a good number of students consider them as valid learning resources, similar to a calculator, spell-checker, or a search engine (Perkins, 2023). Students mention that they use AI to brainstorm, get over writer's block, learn to write better, learn to understand hard points, and learn through the example of AI (Baskara & Mukarto, 2023).

Such diverse applications demonstrate the existence of a critical divide between institutional policy that typically considers any AI usage as malpractice and student behavior that incorporates AI into lawful learning processes (Sullivan et al., 2023). In case of instability, restraint, or irrelevance of institutional guidance to disciplinary norms, students will experience ambiguity regarding the use of AI (Chan & Lee, 2023). It is especially problematic with international students, multilingual students, and students with disabilities, as they might be required to use AI tools to break the language barrier or look through learning resources (Fuchs, 2023).

In addition to that, students have useful information regarding the effect of assessment design on academic integrity. A study suggests that students tend to be more misbehaved when they feel that an assessment is not fair, related to learning objectives, or memorization instead of comprehension (Newton, 2018). According to the student feedback, preferences are always to be given to the authentic and relevant assessment tasks that relate to the real-world application and enable to demonstrate actual learning

(Villarroel et al., 2020). Institutions ought to base their redesign of assessment on these student views in reaction to AI instead of being locked out of the discussion on policy (Amigud & Lancaster, 2019).

Participatory Design and Co-Creation of AI Assessment Policies

To ensure the meaningful student engagement in AI governance, it is necessary to shift the presence of tokens instead of meaningful consultation to the co-creation of policies and practices (Matthews et al., 2019). Students as partners in participatory design methods will help reveal concerns, find unexpected effects, and make sure that AI implementation will meet student needs and experiences (Dollinger et al., 2019). There are a number of institutions starting to experiment with student partnership forms of AI policy development. Such programs engage students in collaborative efforts with faculty and administrations to create guidelines, AI tests, and learning materials on the responsible use of AI (Dawson, 2023).

Student partners can provide an indispensable insight into the ways the policies will work in practice, the support students require, and the ways of communicating expectations properly (Bovill et al., 2016). Co-creation strategies as well construct student AI literacy and critical awareness of algorithmic systems (Long & Magerko, 2020). When students are engaged in the assessment of AI assessment tools, evaluation of their constraints, and the determination of possible biases, they gain more advanced perceptions about the AI capabilities, as well as the values of education (Akgun & Greenhow, 2022). It is important because this critical AI literacy prepares students to work in algorithmically-mediated environments in both their academic and professional lives (Pangrazio & Sefton-Green, 2021). While student agency requires meaningful participation in assessment and AI-related decision-making, agency also depends on clearly defined rights that protect students when AI systems influence assessment processes. The following section therefore considers the specific rights students should retain in AI-mediated assessment environments.

Student Rights in AI-Mediated Assessment

The most basic way to retain educational relationships based on respect and trust is to make the student rights in relation to AI-powered assessment clear (Prinsloo & Slade, 2016). These rights are supposed to entail a number of dimensions. To begin with, students are entitled to the transparency regarding the time and the methods of applying AI systems in their assessment (Tsai et al., 2020). This involves transparent data on the nature of data collected, the process of forming algorithmic judgments, and the input of human assessors in the ultimate decision (Slade & Prinsloo, 2013). Second, AI-generated verdicts should be subjected to meaningful rights of contestation and appeal by the student (Regan & Jesse, 2019). This needs to have available tools to be reviewed by humans, especially those that involve high stakes tests, and sensible timeframes to solve the problems (Whitelock et al., 2015). The onus of proof cannot be primarily placed on the students to prove any error in the algorithm and instead the schools have the responsibility of making sure that their assessment systems are working in a fair and accurate manner (Holmes et al., 2022).

Third, learners have rights to data related to the educational data gathered by systems of AI (Ifenthaler & Schumacher, 2016). Although the formulation of particular legal frameworks may differ, institutional data governance must be based on the principles of data minimization, a purpose limitation, and control by individuals (Pardo & Siemens, 2014). Students must know what is done with their assessment information, how long is it kept, who is allowed to access it, and is it utilized in other objectives than instant evaluation (Tsai et al., 2021).

Fourth, the students have a right to the assessment environment that considers their dignity and psychological wellbeing (Stowell & Bennett, 2010). Proctoring systems which rely on surveillance of bodies, environments, and behaviors of students cause severe apprehension of dignity, privacy, and the circumstances under which they can show learning (Swauger, 2020). These institutions should critically decide any perceived advantages of such systems against the harmful effects they have had on the well-being of students and their discriminatory consequences on students with disabilities, students of color, and students who live in challenging living conditions (Coghlan et al., 2021).

Culturally Responsive Approaches to Student Engagement

The idea of student agency and participation should be interpreted in terms of cultures, which define educational relations, the principles of communication, and power structures (Gay, 2018). Direct student confrontations to institutional policies are not often or even encouraged in certain educational cultures, but does not reflect satisfaction or indifference (Heng, 2018). Institutions then have to use diversified channels of student feedback, surveys, focus groups, student representatives, anonymous feedback and proactively view silence not as agreement but as a possible reflection of some impediment to participation (Gravett & Ajjawi, 2022).

The international students and non-Western educational background students can be subjected to AI-driven assessment through prismatic perspectives of various cultural values in terms of technology, privacy, and educational authority (Zhang & Perez-Paredes, 2021). The views of these students are especially appreciated considering that most AI assessment technology is coded with Western academic norms and assumptions (Buckingham Shum et al., 2019). Cultural humility and the understanding that the mainstream method of evaluation and AI adoption might not be universal or the best will be needed to create inclusive environments that allow a wide range of student voices to be heard (Madge et al., 2019).

Building Student Assessment Literacy for AI Contexts

To justify agency in students, it is necessary to invest in assessment literacy, knowledge of assessment purposes, processes, and quality standards in students (Carless & Chan, 2023). The assessment literacy needs to be broadened in AI-rich settings and encompass the critical knowledge of the algorithmic systems, their strengths and weaknesses, and the approaches to learning successful with the assistance of AI tools (Popenici & Kerr, 2017). The idea of assessment literacy is meant to assist students with becoming more metacognitive about their learning activities and the way the AI tools may assist or hinder in the process of authentic learning (Winstone & Carless, 2020).

It involves assisting students in differentiating between the application of AI to solve short-term challenges and its application in the forms that do not allow the acquisition of critical abilities (Lodge et al., 2018). Instead of merely banning the use of AI, teachers can instruct students on how to make considerate choices concerning the timing and application of various tools in achieving their objectives in the learning process (Bearman et al., 2022). The student assessment literacy is among the areas where peer learning methods can be efficient (Dawson et al., 2019). As students take part in calibration tasks, analyzing sample works and discussing quality criteria, they gain more robust evaluative judgment enabling them to self-assess and be able to judge AI-generated pieces of content (Tai et al., 2018). Those abilities become more and more critical as students are exposed to AI-generated information in every sphere of their academic and professional life. The preceding discussion demonstrates that responsible AI-powered assessment requires attention not only to technological capability and institutional policy but also to the experiences, rights, and agency of learners. These considerations become particularly important when assessment systems are implemented across contexts with substantial differences in infrastructure, language, institutional capacity, and access to technology. The following section therefore examines the Global South and resource-constrained contexts as a central dimension of responsible AI-powered assessment.

6. GLOBAL SOUTH AND RESOURCE-CONSTRAINED PERSPECTIVES

Higher education systems differ substantially in terms of infrastructure, policy maturity, digital capacity, and institutional resources (Altbach et al., 2019). In Global South and rural settings, the implementation of AI is often accompanied by challenges related to connectivity, staff capacity, digital literacy, and regulatory transparency (Miao & Holmes, 2021). These realities reinforce the need for context-sensitive approaches to AI-powered assessment rather than universal technological solutions that may not reflect local educational conditions.

6.1 Infrastructural and Resource Constraints

Digital divide is one of the key obstacles to fair AI-based assessment (Czerniewicz et al., 2020). The resource-strained setting can result in students in such a scenario who have no trustworthy internet access, lack devices to use, or a place to study online without distractions (Mhlanga, 2021). These inequalities became especially obvious during the COVID-19 pandemic when institutions quickly switched to online evaluation, and the results were catastrophic in the case of students who lacked sufficient technological access (Adedoyin & Soykan, 2020).

Intelligent evaluation tools commonly presuppose the high-bandwidth connection, the use of the latest computing equipment, and continuous connectivity, which cannot be considered in numerous cases (Schleicher, 2020). Furthermore, proprietary AI evaluation systems can be expensive, which restricts the accessibility of less-resource-rich institutions to advanced tools, forming a two-tier system where well-endowed universities can access advanced tools and the rest cannot (Selwyn et al., 2020).

6.2 Cultural and Linguistic Considerations

Assessment systems that are based on AI and trained mostly in English and adapted to the Western culture and pedagogy might malfunction in a culturally and linguistically diverse environment (Shultz & Guaglianone, 2015). Different cultures use different writing conventions, rhetorical devices, and knowledge organization, but a lot of AI products embed specific Western standards of academic writing standards as universal (Lillis & Curry, 2010). Such cultural bias may disadvantage students whose academic communication reflects different, but equally valid, epistemological traditions, rhetorical conventions, and communicative practices (Keet et al., 2017).

Multilingual approach offers certain challenges and opportunities to AI-powered assessment (Ballier et al., 2019). Whereas some AI tools can now serve a variety of languages, they perform worse than all other languages, and even then, better results are typically achieved in well-resourced languages and worse in languages with fewer training data (Joshi et al., 2020). The use of code-switching and translanguaging that is typically seen in most multilingual education environments can be interpreted by AI systems as a mistake or anomaly (Garcia & Wei, 2014).

6.3 Amplifying Underrepresented Perspectives

The active centering of voices and experience in underrepresented contexts is the requirement of responsible AI integration instead of considering Global South perspectives peripheral or exceptional (Arday & Mirza, 2018). This includes funding locally-based researches on AI in evaluation, making sure that the governance systems take into account the various stakeholder views, and preventing the unquestioning importation of technologies and practices across the prevailing settings (Chan & Hu, 2023).

Resource-constrained institutions have typically been resourceful and robust in modifying technologies to localization and creating low-tech options as well as focusing on pedagogical connections rather than technological ones (Czerniewicz & Brown, 2013). These methods provide useful insights to every field of education regarding the need to sustain human-oriented practices of assessments in technological-based settings.

7. GOVERNANCE, POLICY, AND INSTITUTIONAL RESPONSIBILITY

The core of the alignment between AI powered assessment and quality and integrity objectives is effective governance (Holmes & Porayska-Pomsta, 2022). The institutions are required to come up with clear policies that will concern data privacy, accountability, academic standards, and ethical use of AI (Miao & Cukurova, 2024). Staff and student capacity building is also necessary to nurture the use of assessment literacy in AI-rich environments (Boud et al., 2018).

7.1 Policy Frameworks and Institutional Guidelines

The institutional policies of AI-powered assessment should also have an overall range of dimensions. First, the policies should introduce clear boundaries on how AI should be used, the authorized tools and the forbidden practices, and because strict regulations can be easily outdated as technologies develop, the policies should take into account that strict regulations may be irrelevant in the near future (Lancaster & Cotarlan, 2021). Other institutions have implemented principles-based strategies, in which the focus is put on learning outcomes, academic integrity, and not trying to list permitted and prohibited technologies (University of Hong Kong, 2023).

Second, the student privacy needs to be safeguarded by the policies of data governance and allow the proper use of learning analytics (Slade & Prinsloo, 2013). This encompasses spelling out what data is eligible to be gathered, the use of the data, access to the data, and rights of students to their educational data (Ifenthaler & Schumacher, 2016). The conflict between a personalized approach to learning that needs in-depth information about students and privacy protection is an old problem that needs to be carefully maneuvered (Pardo & Siemens, 2014).

Third, the accountability systems should be set up based on the policies, which will clarify the roles and responsibilities in making decisions related to AI (Felten et al., 2019). Having AI systems involved in high stakes assessment judgments there should be clear guidelines of how it is under human supervision, appeal mechanisms, and corrective measures (Whitelock et al., 2015).

7.2 Professional Development and Assessment Literacy

Efficient implementation of AI in evaluation demands a lot of investment in the professional development of the teachers (Dawson et al., 2019). Faculty should be assisted in learning to value and use AI tools, create assessment activities that can be used to benefit AI without jeopardizing integrity, and interpret AI-generated analytics and feedback (Bearman et al., 2022). This extends past technical training to include pedagogical reimagination of assessment in AI-rich environments (Gasevic et al., 2023).

There is also a need to improve assessment literacy in students to operate AI-driven evaluation systems (Carless & Boud, 2018). This involves the ability to process automated feedback and the ability to recognize when and how AI applications can rightfully assist in their learning, and their entitlement to algorithmic decision-making (Price & Kirkwood, 2014). Learning and teaching digital literacy, as well as critical AI literacy, should become part of the curriculum to equip students with learning and working in an algorithmically-mediated world (Pangrazio & Selwyn, 2019).

7.3 Participatory Governance and Stakeholder Engagement

Leadership in AI-driven evaluation can be enhanced with the participatory strategies involving various stakeholders, students, faculty, administrators, educational technologists, and community members (Williamson & Eynon, 2020). The student participation plays a very significant role in that matter, in that the most affected by the assessment policies should have a voice in their formulation (Bovill, 2020).

Participatory governance has the potential to bring up issues, point out unintended outcomes, and make sure that technological choices go in line with the values and educational purposes of an institution (Slade & Prinsloo, 2013). It also creates common ownership and knowledge, which facilitates greater execution and continued improvement of AI-associated policies and practices.

8. TOWARD AN INTEGRITY-DRIVEN FRAMEWORK FOR AI-POWERED ASSESSMENT

Based on the above analysis, this section gives a proposal of a framework of integrity-based AI-driven assessment in higher education. This framework combines major principles, which should be used to integrate responsible AI in the context of retaining the focus on educational quality, fairness, and student learning. The proposed framework integrates the major dimensions identified throughout the chapter into a single socio-pedagogical model for responsible AI-powered assessment. Rather than positioning academic integrity as a separate mechanism for detecting misconduct, the framework places integrity within a broader assessment ecosystem that connects pedagogical quality, ethical transparency, fairness and inclusion, student rights and agency, contextual governance, and human professional judgment. The framework therefore emphasizes that responsible AI adoption should be evaluated not only by technological capability but also by its contribution to meaningful learning, equitable participation, institutional accountability, and trust.

Figure 1. Integrity-Driven Socio-Pedagogical Framework for Responsible AI-Powered Assessment in Higher Education

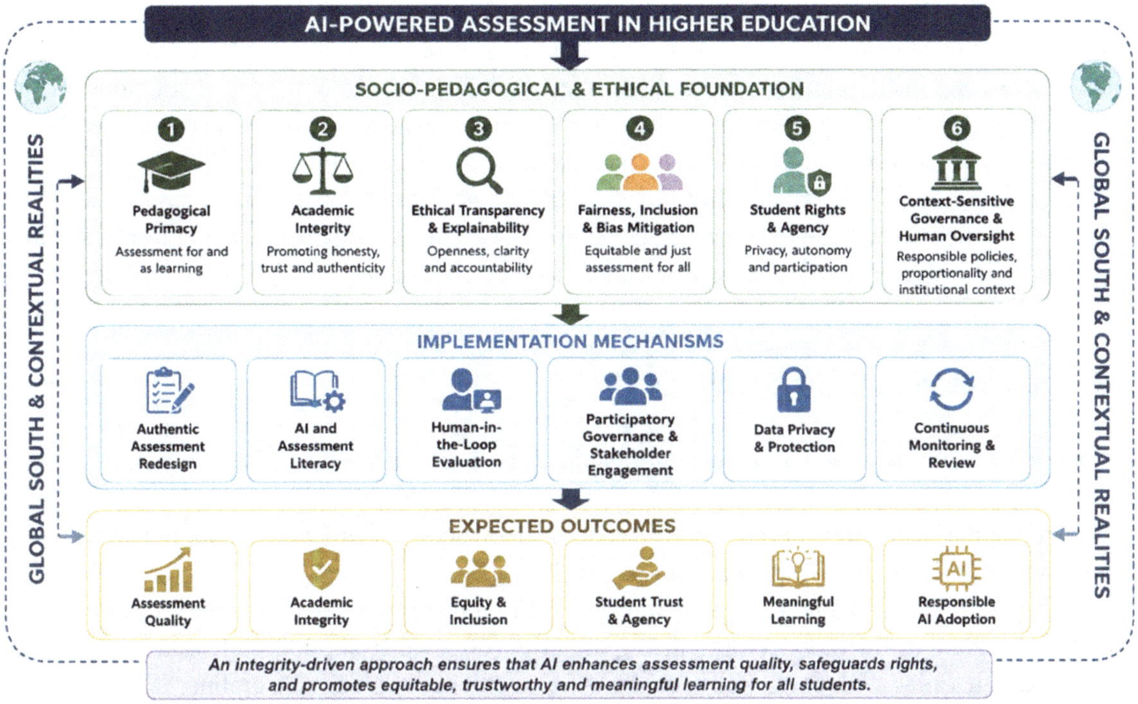

8.1 Core Principles

Pedagogical Primacy and Assessment for Learning. AI-powered assessment tools are to be recommended and deployed with the primary consideration of their ability to promote meaningful learning and not administrative efficiency or cost-cutting (Dawson et al., 2019). The design of assessment must start with well-articulated learning outcomes and instructional plans, in which technology is seen as a means, not an end, of achieving them (Boud & Soler, 2016).

Ethical Transparency and Explainability. The organizations must make sure that AI evaluation systems are transparent, and the manner in which they work, what judgments they inform, and based on what is well-documented (Felten et al., 2019). Automated decisions should be explained to students in terms that they understand, with the chances of clarifying and appealing their verdicts that they perceive as unfair (Holstein & Doroudi, 2021).

Fairness, Inclusion, and Bias Mitigation. The use of AI in assessment has to be regularly reviewed on the differences in its effects on various groups of students, and AIs should be corrected with active steps to minimize bias (Kizilcec & Lee, 2022). This involves disaggregated data analysis and active design processes and readiness to change or eliminate the tools that generate inequitable results (Baker & Hawn, 2022).

Respect for Student Rights and Data Privacy. Educational information of students must be safeguarded with effective governance models that define the rules and regulations in relation to the collection, usage, storage, and sharing of information (Slade & Prinsloo, 2013). Students must be given a meaningful control over their data, and this should be in the form of rights to access and to correct and to delete where applicable (Ifenthaler & Schumacher, 2016).

Context-Sensitive Implementation and Governance. The use of AI should be based on recognition of the fact that educational settings are quite different in terms of the available infrastructural capacity, cultural norms, and institutional priorities (Selwyn et al., 2020). Instead of universal solutions, institutions are advised to customize the AI tools to local conditions and design governance frameworks that are based on their local context and values (Czerniewicz & Brown, 2013).

Human Agency and Professional Judgment. Artificial intelligence must complement, not substitute the human judgment in evaluation (Bearman et al., 2022). Qualified human reviewers must be involved in final decisions regarding high stakes assessment as they are able to exercise contextual sensitivity, detect exceptional cases and provide resourcefulness with educational values (Whitelock et al., 2015).

8.2 Implementation Considerations

Developing such a structure needs institutional investment at several tiers. The leadership will need to develop clear vision of how AI can be used to support the educational mission, invest to develop professions, and infrastructure and create governance frameworks that will allow continuous assessment and improvement (Holmes & Porayska-Pomsta, 2022).

Faculty require time, encouragement, and incentives to transform assessment practices in ways that will put AI to good use without compromising integrity (Gasevic et al., 2023). This will involve experimentation, learning with peers, and exchange of best practices between disciplines and institutions (Dawson et al., 2019).

Students should be involved as active participants in the development of AI-powered assessment, and their experiences and concerns should inform the design, implementation, and continuous improvement of assessment practices (Bovill, 2020). Regular feedback mechanisms, including surveys, focus groups, and student representation in governance bodies, can help ensure that AI implementation remains effective, fair, and responsive to student learning needs.

9. CONCLUSION

Artificial intelligence-based assessment presents significant opportunities as well as complex ethical and pedagogical challenges for higher education. AI can enhance feedback, personalization, learning analytics, and quality assurance, but its educational value depends on how it is designed, governed, implemented, and aligned with educational purposes. This chapter has argued that quality and academic integrity should remain central to assessment innovation and that responsible AI integration requires pedagogical coherence, ethical transparency, inclusive governance, and meaningful human oversight. The increasing use of generative AI requires institutions to reconsider assessment practices rather than respond solely through prohibition or surveillance. Decisions about whether, when, and how AI should be incorporated into assessment should be guided by learning outcomes, assessment purposes, student rights, institutional responsibilities, and the potential effects on equity and inclusion. Such an approach is particularly important across diverse higher education contexts, where differences in infrastructure, language, institutional capacity, and access to technology can shape the consequences of AI adoption.

The experiences of resource-constrained institutions, multilingual learners, and culturally diverse student populations demonstrate the limitations of technology-centred approaches and reinforce the continuing importance of human judgment and educational relationships. Higher education institutions can therefore benefit from AI without compromising academic integrity, equity, or educational purpose by treating AI-powered assessment as a socio-pedagogical and ethical practice rather than as a purely technical process. The integrity-driven framework proposed in this chapter brings together pedagogical primacy, academic integrity, ethical transparency, fairness and inclusion, student rights and agency, context-sensitive governance, and human professional judgment. Its central proposition is that AI should serve assessment and learning rather than determine their purposes. Future implementation should therefore involve continuous evaluation, stakeholder participation, contextual adaptation, and evidence-based revision so that technological possibilities remain subordinate to the broader educational mission of promoting meaningful, equitable, trustworthy, and academically rigorous learning.

REFERENCES

Adedoyin, O. B., & Soykan, E. (2020). Covid-19 pandemic and online learning: The challenges and opportunities. *Interactive Learning Environments*, •••, 1–13. DOI: 10.1080/10494820.2020.1813180

Akgun, S., & Greenhow, C. (2022). Artificial intelligence in education: Addressing ethical challenges in K-12 settings. *AI and Ethics*, *2*(3), 431–440. DOI: 10.1007/s43681-021-00096-7 PMID: 34790956

Altbach, P. G., Reisberg, L., & Rumbley, L. E. (2019). *Trends in global higher education: Tracking an academic revolution*. Brill., DOI: 10.1163/9789004406155

Amigud, A., & Lancaster, T. (2019). 246 reasons to cheat: An analysis of students' reasons for seeking to outsource academic work. *Computers & Education*, *134*, 98–107. DOI: 10.1016/j.compedu.2019.01.017

Arday, J., & Mirza, H. S. (Eds.). (2018). *Dismantling race in higher education: Racism, whiteness and decolonising the academy*. Palgrave Macmillan., DOI: 10.1007/978-3-319-60261-5

Ashford-Rowe, K., Herrington, J., & Brown, C. (2014). Establishing the critical elements that determine authentic assessment. *Assessment & Evaluation in Higher Education*, *39*(2), 205–222. DOI: 10.1080/02602938.2013.819566

Baker, R. S., & Hawn, A. (2022). Algorithmic bias in education. *International Journal of Artificial Intelligence in Education*, *32*(4), 1052–1092. DOI: 10.1007/s40593-021-00285-9

Ballier, N., Pachet, F., Safar, É., & Sagot, B. (2019). Automated language assessment. *Language Assessment Quarterly*, *16*(4-5), 335–354. DOI: 10.1080/15434303.2019.1674316

Barocas, S., & Selbst, A. D. (2016). Big data's disparate impact. *California Law Review*, *104*, 671–732. DOI: 10.15779/Z38BG31

Baskara, F. R., & Mukarto, M. (2023). Exploring the implications of ChatGPT for language learning in higher education. *Indonesian Journal of Applied Linguistics*, *13*(1), 105–117. DOI: 10.17509/ijal.v13i1.53393

Bayne, S. (2015). What's the matter with 'technology-enhanced learning'? *Learning, Media and Technology*, *40*(1), 5–20. DOI: 10.1080/17439884.2014.915851

Bayne, S. (2015). Teacherbot: Interventions in automated teaching. *Teaching in Higher Education*, *20*(4), 455–467. DOI: 10.1080/13562517.2015.1020783

Bayne, S., Evans, P., Ewins, R., Knox, J., Lamb, J., Macleod, H., & Sinclair, C. (2020). The manifold implications of manifold implications of manifold implications of manifold implications of algorithmic proctoring in higher education. *Teaching in Higher Education*, *25*(6), 675–691. DOI: 10.1080/13562517.2020.1760137

Bearman, M., Dawson, P., Ajjawi, R., Tai, J., & Boud, D. (Eds.). (2022). *Re-imagining university assessment in a digital world*. Springer., DOI: 10.1007/978-3-030-41956-1

Bearman, M., Tai, J., Kent, F., Edouard, V., Nestel, D., & Molloy, E. (2022). What should we do about feedback? A participatory approach to feedback research. *Medical Education, 56*(4), 384–392. DOI: 10.1111/medu.14702

Benjamin, R. (2019). *Race after technology: Abolitionist tools for the new Jim Code*. Polity Press., DOI: 10.1093/sf/soz162

Bloxham, S., & Boyd, P. (2007). *Developing effective assessment in higher education: A practical guide*. Open University Press.

Boud, D. (2000). Sustainable assessment: Rethinking assessment for the learning society. *Studies in Continuing Education, 22*(2), 151–167. DOI: 10.1080/713695728

Boud, D., Ajjawi, R., Dawson, P., & Tai, J. (Eds.). (2018). *Developing evaluative judgement in higher education: Assessment for knowing and producing quality work*. Routledge., DOI: 10.4324/9781315109251

Boud, D., & Soler, R. (2016). Sustainable assessment revisited. *Assessment & Evaluation in Higher Education, 41*(3), 400–413. DOI: 10.1080/02602938.2015.1018133

Bovill, C. (2020). Co-creation in learning and teaching: The case for a whole-class approach in higher education. *Higher Education, 79*(6), 1023–1037. DOI: 10.1007/s10734-019-00453-w

Bovill, C., Cook-Sather, A., Felten, P., Millard, L., & Moore-Cherry, N. (2016). Addressing potential challenges in co-creating learning and teaching: Overcoming resistance, navigating institutional norms and ensuring inclusivity in student–staff partnerships. *Higher Education, 71*(2), 195–208. DOI: 10.1007/s10734-015-9896-4

Bretag, T. (2023). Academic integrity in the age of artificial intelligence. *International Journal for Educational Integrity, 19*(1), 1–3. DOI: 10.1007/s40979-015-0004-4

Buckingham Shum, S., Ferguson, R., & Martinez-Maldonado, R. (2019). Human-centred learning analytics. *Journal of Learning Analytics, 6*(2), 1–9. DOI: 10.18608/jla.2019.62.1

Burrell, J. (2016). How the machine 'thinks': Understanding opacity in machine learning algorithms. *Big Data & Society, 3*(1), 1–12. DOI: 10.1177/2053951715622512

Carless, D. (2015). *Excellence in university assessment: Learning from award-winning practice*. Routledge., DOI: 10.4324/9781315740621

Carless, D., & Boud, D. (2018). The development of student feedback literacy: Enabling uptake of feedback. *Assessment & Evaluation in Higher Education, 43*(8), 1315–1325. DOI: 10.1080/02602938.2018.1463354

Carless, D., & Chan, K. K. H. (2023). Student perspectives on assessment feedback: Elaborating the conceptual framework of feedback literacy. *Studies in Higher Education, 48*(1), 133–144. DOI: 10.1080/03075079.2022.2119655

Carless, D., & Winstone, N. (2023). Teacher feedback literacy and its interplay with student feedback literacy. *Teaching in Higher Education, 28*(1), 150–163. DOI: 10.1080/13562517.2020.1782372

Chan, C. K. Y., & Hu, W. (2023). Students' voices on generative AI: Perceptions, benefits, and challenges in higher education. *International Journal of Educational Technology in Higher Education, 20*(1), 43. DOI: 10.1186/s41239-023-00411-8

Chan, C. K. Y., & Lee, K. K. W. (2023). The AI generation gap: Are Gen Z students more interested in adopting generative AI such as ChatGPT in teaching and learning than their Gen X and millennial generation teachers? *Smart Learning Environments, 10*(1), 60. DOI: 10.1186/s40561-023-00269-3

Coghlan, S., Miller, T., & Paterson, J. (2021). Good proctor or "big brother"? Ethics of online exam supervision technologies. *Philosophy & Technology, 34*(4), 1581–1606. DOI: 10.1007/s13347-021-00476-1 PMID: 34485025

Crawford, J., Cowling, M., & Allen, K. A. (2023). Leadership is needed for ethical ChatGPT: Character, assessment, and learning using artificial intelligence (AI). *Journal of University Teaching & Learning Practice, 20*(3), 02. DOI: 10.53761/1.20.3.02

Cukurova, M., Luckin, R., & Kent, C. (2019). Impact of an artificial intelligence research frame on the perceived credibility of educational research evidence. *International Journal of Artificial Intelligence in Education, 29*(4), 205–235. DOI: 10.1007/s40593-019-00182-x

Czerniewicz, L., Agherdien, N., Badenhorst, J., Belluigi, D., Chambers, T., Chili, M., de Villiers, M., Felix, A., Gachago, D., Gokhale, C., Ivala, E., Kramm, N., Madiba, M., Mistri, G., Mgqwashu, E., Pallitt, N., Prinsloo, P., Solomon, K., Strydom, S., & Wissing, G. (2020). A wake-up call: Equity, inequality and Covid-19 emergency remote teaching and learning. *Postdigital Science and Education, 2*(3), 946–967. DOI: 10.1007/s42438-020-00187-4 PMID: 40477091

Czerniewicz, L., & Brown, C. (2013). The habitus of digital "strangers" in higher education. *British Journal of Educational Technology, 44*(1), 44–53. DOI: 10.1111/j.1467-8535.2012.01281.x

Dawson, P. (2021). *Defending assessment security in a digital world: Preventing e-cheating and supporting academic integrity in higher education*. Routledge., DOI: 10.4324/9781003002970

Dawson, P. (2023). *ChatGPT and other AI chatbots: A threat or opportunity for academic integrity?* Centre for Academic Integrity., DOI: 10.5204/intechethics.v10i1.356

Dawson, P., Ajjawi, R., Bearman, M., Boud, D., Tai, J., & Vickers, J. (2019). Strategies for university assessment designers to enhance student learning. In *Strategies for university assessment designers to enhance student learning* (pp. 1–12). Routledge., DOI: 10.4324/9781315109251

Dawson, P., Bearman, M., Boud, D. J., Hall, M., Molloy, E. K., Bennett, S., & Joughin, G. (2019). Assessment might be failing. Can we fix it? *Teaching in Higher Education, 24*(3), 339–357. DOI: 10.1080/13562517.2018.1449742

Dawson, P., & Sutherland-Smith, W. (2018). Can markers detect contract cheating? Results from a pilot study. *Assessment & Evaluation in Higher Education, 43*(2), 286–293. DOI: 10.1080/02602938.2017.1336746

Dollinger, M., Lodge, J. M., & Coates, H. (2019). Co-creation in higher education: Towards a conceptual model. *Journal of Industry-University Collaboration, 3*(1), 3–18. DOI: 10.1108/JIUC-01-2019-0003

Eaton, S. E. (2023). Artificial intelligence and academic integrity: Striking a balance. *International Journal for Educational Integrity*, *19*(1), 1–8. DOI: 10.1007/s40979-023-00144-1

Eaton, S. E., & Turner, K. L. (2020). Exploring academic integrity and mental health during COVID-19: Rapid review. *Journal of Contemporary Education Theory & Research*, *4*(1), 35–41.

Felten, E., Raj, M., & Seamans, R. (2019). The variable impact of artificial intelligence on labor: The role of complementary skills and technologies. *Proceedings - Academy of Management*, *2019*(1), 11925. DOI: 10.5465/AMBPP.2019.11925abstract

Fishman, T. (Ed.). (2016). *The fundamental values of academic integrity* (3rd ed.). International Center for Academic Integrity.

Fuchs, K. (2023). Exploring the opportunities and challenges of NLP models in higher education: Is ChatGPT a blessing or a curse? *Frontiers in Education*, *8*, 1166682. DOI: 10.3389/feduc.2023.1166682

García, O., & Wei, L. (2014). *Translanguaging: Language, bilingualism and education*. Palgrave Macmillan., DOI: 10.1057/9781137385765

Gay, G. (2018). *Culturally responsive teaching: Theory, research, and practice* (3rd ed.). Teachers College Press.

Gravett, K., & Ajjawi, R. (2022). Belonging as situated practice. *Studies in Higher Education*, *47*(7), 1386–1396. DOI: 10.1080/03075079.2021.1894118

Green, B. (2021). Data science as political action: Grounding data science in a politics of justice. MIT Press. DOI: 10.23919/JSC.2021.0029

Heng, T. T. (2018). Different is not deficient: Contradicting stereotypes of Chinese international students in US higher education. *Studies in Higher Education*, *43*(1), 22–36. DOI: 10.1080/03075079.2016.1152466

Holmes, W., Persson, J., Chounta, I. A., Wasson, B., & Dimitrova, V. (2022). *Artificial intelligence and education: A critical view through the lens of human rights, democracy and the rule of law*. Council of Europe Publishing., DOI: 10.1007/978-3-031-32883-1_1

Holmes, W., & Porayska-Pomsta, K. (2022). *The ethics of artificial intelligence in education: Practices, challenges, and debates*. Routledge., DOI: 10.4324/9780429329067

Holstein, K., & Doroudi, S. (2021). Equity and artificial intelligence in education: Will "AIEd" amplify or alleviate inequities in education? *arXiv preprint arXiv:2104.12920*. /arXiv.2104.12920DOI: 10.48550

Ifenthaler, D., & Schumacher, C. (2016). Student perceptions of privacy principles for learning analytics. *Educational Technology Research and Development*, *64*(5), 923–938. DOI: 10.1007/s11423-016-9477-y

Joshi, P., Santy, S., Budhiraja, A., Bali, K., & Choudhury, M. (2020). The state and fate of linguistic diversity and inclusion in the NLP world. *Proceedings of the 58th Annual Meeting of the Association for Computational Linguistics*, 6282-6293. DOI: 10.18653/v1/2020.acl-main.560

Joshi, R. D., Dhakal, C. K., & Pradhan, D. C. (2021). Addressing educational inequalities in the Global South through open and distance learning. *Asian Association of Open Universities Journal*, *16*(2), 201–215. DOI: 10.1108/AAOUJ-02-2021-0029

Kaminski, M. E. (2019). The right to explanation, explained. *Berkeley Technology Law Journal, 34*(1), 189–218. DOI: 10.15779/Z38TD9N83K

Keet, C. M., Alberts, R., Gerber, A., & Chimamiwa, G. (2017). Enhancing web portals with ontology-based data access: The case study of South Africa's accessibility portal for people with disabilities. *OTM Confederated International Conferences*. Springer. DOI: 10.1007/978-3-319-69459-7_36

Kizilcec, R. F., & Lee, H. (2022). Algorithmic fairness in education. In *The ethics of artificial intelligence in education* (pp. 174–202). Routledge., DOI: 10.4324/9780429329067-10

Knight, S. (2022). Building, understanding and using trust in learning analytics: Introducing the BUILD-LAT project. *Journal of Learning Analytics*, *9*(3), 1–6. DOI: 10.18608/jla.2016.33.1

Lancaster, T. (2023). AI tools that can write code: Challenges for academic integrity in computing education. *ACM Inroads*, *14*(2), 30–35. DOI: 10.1145/3597095

Lancaster, T., & Cotarlan, C. (2021). Contract cheating by STEM students through a file sharing website: A COVID-19 pandemic perspective. *International Journal for Educational Integrity*, *17*(1), 1–16. DOI: 10.1007/s40979-021-00070-0

Liang, W., Yuksekgonul, M., Mao, Y., Wu, E., & Zou, J. (2023). GPT detectors are biased against non-native English writers. *Patterns (New York, N.Y.)*, *4*(7), 100779. DOI: 10.1016/j.patter.2023.100779 PMID: 37521038

Lillis, T., & Curry, M. J. (2010). *Academic writing in a global context: The politics and practices of publishing in English.* Routledge., DOI: 10.4324/9780203852217

Lodge, J. M., Kennedy, G., Lockyer, L., Arguel, A., & Pachman, M. (2018). Understanding difficulties and resulting confusion in learning: An integrative review. *Frontiers in Education*, *3*, 49. DOI: 10.3389/feduc.2018.00049

Long, D., & Magerko, B. (2020). What is AI literacy? Competencies and design considerations. *Proceedings of the 2020 CHI Conference on Human Factors in Computing Systems*, 1-16. DOI: 10.1145/3313831.3376727

Macfarlane, B., Zhang, J., & Pun, A. (2014). Academic integrity: A review of the literature. *Studies in Higher Education*, *39*(2), 339–358. DOI: 10.1080/03075079.2012.709495

Madge, C., Breines, M. R., Dalu, M. T. B., Gunter, A., Mittelmeier, J., Prinsloo, P., & Raghuram, P. (2019). WhatsApp use among African international distance education (IDE) students: Transferring, translating and transforming educational experiences. *Learning, Media and Technology*, *44*(3), 267–282. DOI: 10.1080/17439884.2019.1628048

Marzouk, Z., Rakovic, M., Liaqat, A., Vytasek, J., Samadi, D., Stewart-Alonso, J., & Nespenak, M. (2021). What might equity-oriented proctoring systems look like? Critiquing online exam proctoring in the age of COVID. *Canadian Journal of Learning and Technology*, *47*(4), 1–32. DOI: 10.21432/cjlt27854

Matthews, K. E., Dwyer, A., Hine, L., & Turner, J. (2019). Conceptions of students as partners. *Higher Education*, *76*(6), 957–971. DOI: 10.1007/s10734-018-0257-y

Mhlanga, D. (2021). Artificial intelligence in the industry 4.0, and its impact on poverty, innovation, infrastructure development, and the sustainable development goals: Lessons from emerging economies? *Sustainability (Basel), 13*(11), 5788. DOI: 10.3390/su13115788

Miao, F., & Cukurova, M. (2024). *AI competency framework for teachers*. UNESCO. UNESCO official publication

Miao, F., & Holmes, W. (2021). *AI and education: Guidance for policy-makers*. UNESCO Publishing., DOI: 10.54675/PCSP7350

Miao, F., Shiohira, K., & Lao, N. (2024). *AI competency framework for students*. UNESCO. UNESCO official publication

Newton, P. M. (2018). How common is commercial contract cheating in higher education and is it increasing? A systematic review. *Frontiers in Education, 3*, 67. DOI: 10.3389/feduc.2018.00067

Newton, P. M., & Boud, D. (2023). The post-pandemic university and the post-pandemic student: The role of evidence in shaping policy and practice. *Higher Education Research & Development, 42*(1), 3–17. DOI: 10.1080/07294360.2022.2130160

Nguyen, A., Ngo, H. N., Hong, Y., Dang, B., & Nguyen, B. P. T. (2022). Ethical principles for artificial intelligence in education. *Education and Information Technologies, 28*(4), 4221–4241. DOI: 10.1007/s10639-022-11316-w PMID: 36254344

Nguyen, J. G., Keuseman, K. J., & Humston, J. J. (2020). Minimize online cheating for online assessments during COVID-19 pandemic. *Journal of Chemical Education, 97*(9), 3429–3435. DOI: 10.1021/acs.jchemed.0c00790

Noble, S. U. (2018). *Algorithms of oppression: How search engines reinforce racism*. NYU Press., DOI: 10.18574/nyu/9781479833641.001.0001

O'Neil, C. (2016). *Weapons of math destruction: How big data increases inequality and threatens democracy*. Crown.

Pangrazio, L., & Sefton-Green, J. (2021). Digital rights, digital citizenship and digital literacy: What's the difference? *Journal of New Approaches in Educational Research, 10*(1), 15–27. DOI: 10.7821/naer.2021.1.616

Pangrazio, L., & Selwyn, N. (2019). 'Personal data literacies': A critical literacies approach to enhancing understandings of personal digital data. *New Media & Society, 21*(2), 419–437. DOI: 10.1177/1461444818799523

Pardo, A., Jovanovic, J., Dawson, S., Gašević, D., & Mirriahi, N. (2019). Using learning analytics to scale the provision of personalised feedback. *British Journal of Educational Technology, 50*(1), 128–138. DOI: 10.1111/bjet.12592

Pardo, A., & Siemens, G. (2014). Ethical and privacy principles for learning analytics. *British Journal of Educational Technology, 45*(3), 438–450. DOI: 10.1111/bjet.12152

Perkins, M. (2023). Academic integrity considerations of AI Large Language Models in the post-pandemic era: ChatGPT and beyond. *Journal of University Teaching & Learning Practice, 20*(2), 07. DOI: 10.53761/1.20.02.07

Perkins, M., Roe, J., Postma, D., McGaughran, J., & Hickerson, D. (2023). Detection of GPT-4 generated text in higher education: Combining academic judgement and software to identify generative AI tool misuse. *Journal of Academic Ethics*, •••, 1–17. DOI: 10.1007/s10805-023-09505-5

Popenici, S. A., & Kerr, S. (2017). Exploring the impact of artificial intelligence on teaching and learning in higher education. *Research and Practice in Technology Enhanced Learning*, *12*(1), 1–13. DOI: 10.1186/s41039-017-0062-8 PMID: 30595727

Price, M., & Kirkwood, A. (2014). Using technology for assessment for learning in higher education: Student expectations and experiences. *Technology, Pedagogy and Education*, *23*(3), 327–342. DOI: 10.1080/1475939X.2014.894623

Prinsloo, P., & Slade, S. (2016). Student vulnerability, agency, and learning analytics: An exploration. *Journal of Learning Analytics*, *3*(1), 159–182. DOI: 10.18608/jla.2016.31.10

Prinsloo, P., & Slade, S. (2017). Big data, higher education and learning analytics: Beyond justice and ethics. In *Big data and learning analytics in higher education* (pp. 109–124). Springer., DOI: 10.1007/978-3-319-06520-5_8

Regan, P. M., & Jesse, J. (2019). Ethical challenges of edtech, big data and personalized learning: Twenty-first century student sorting and tracking. *Ethics and Information Technology*, *21*(3), 167–179. DOI: 10.1007/s10676-018-9492-2

Schleicher, A. (2020). The impact of COVID-19 on education: Insights from education at a glance 2020. *OECD Journal: Economic Studies*, *2020*(1), 1–31.

Selwyn, N. (2019). What's the problem with learning analytics? *Journal of Learning Analytics*, *6*(3), 11–19. DOI: 10.18608/jla.2019.63.3

Selwyn, N., Hillman, T., Bergviken Rensfeldt, A., & Perrotta, C. (2020). Digital technologies and the automation of education. In *The Routledge international handbook of sociology of education* (pp. 405–414). Routledge., DOI: 10.4324/9781315678825-37

Selwyn, N., O'Neill, C., Smith, G., Andrejevic, M., & Gu, X. (2021). A necessary evil? The rise of online exam proctoring in Australian universities. *Media International Australia, Incorporating Culture & Policy*, *179*(1), 149–164. DOI: 10.1177/1329878X211005862

Shermis, M. D. (2014). State-of-the-art automated essay scoring: Competition, results, and future directions from a United States demonstration. *Assessing Writing*, *20*, 53–76. DOI: 10.1016/j.asw.2013.04.001

Shultz, L., & Guaglianone, L. (2015). Creating spaces for a global dimension in education: Policies and practices in Alberta. *Canadian and International Education. Education Canadienne et Internationale*, *44*(1), 1–14. DOI: 10.5206/cie-eci.v44i1.9252

Slade, S., & Prinsloo, P. (2013). Learning analytics: Ethical issues and dilemmas. *The American Behavioral Scientist*, *57*(10), 1510–1529. DOI: 10.1177/0002764213479366

Stoesz, B. M., & Eaton, S. E. (2023). Academic integrity policies of publicly funded universities in western Canada. *Educational Policy, 08959048231164209*. Advance online publication. DOI: 10.1177/08959048231164209

Stowell, J. R., & Bennett, D. (2010). Effects of online testing on student exam performance and test anxiety. *Journal of Educational Computing Research*, *42*(2), 161–171. DOI: 10.2190/EC.42.2.b

Sullivan, M., Kelly, A., & McLaughlan, P. (2023). ChatGPT in higher education: Considerations for academic integrity and student learning. *Journal of Applied Learning & Teaching*, *6*(1), 1–10. DOI: 10.37074/jalt.2023.6.1.17

Swauger, S. (2020). *Our bodies encoded: Algorithmic test proctoring in higher education*. Hybrid Pedagogy., DOI: 10.21428/3f68b4f3.1fb6fa0e

Tai, J., Ajjawi, R., Boud, D., Dawson, P., & Panadero, E. (2018). Developing evaluative judgement: Enabling students to make decisions about the quality of work. *Higher Education*, *76*(3), 467–481. DOI: 10.1007/s10734-017-0220-3

Tannock, S. (2017). No grades in higher education now! Revisiting the place of graded assessment in the reimagination of the public university. *Studies in Higher Education*, *42*(8), 1345–1357. DOI: 10.1080/03075079.2015.1092131

Tsai, Y. S., Rates, D., Moreno-Marcos, P. M., Muñoz-Merino, P. J., Jivet, I., Scheffel, M., Drachsler, H., Delgado Kloos, C., & Gašević, D. (2020). Learning analytics in European higher education: Trends and barriers. *Computers & Education*, *155*, 103933. DOI: 10.1016/j.compedu.2020.103933

Tsai, Y. S., Whitelock-Wainwright, A., & Gašević, D. (2021). The privacy paradox and its implications for learning analytics. *LAK21: 11th International Learning Analytics and Knowledge Conference*, 71-81. DOI: 10.1145/3448139.3448155

Twum-Danso Imoh, A., & Gupta, N. (Eds.). (2021). *Children's lives in an era of children's rights: The progress of the convention on the rights of the child in Africa*. Routledge., DOI: 10.4324/9781003111719

UNESCO. (2021). *AI and education: Guidance for policy-makers*. UNESCO Publishing.

University of Hong Kong. (2023). *Interim guidance to staff and students on the use of generative AI*. https://tl.hku.hk/generative-ai/

Villarroel, V., Bloxham, S., Bruna, D., Bruna, C., & Herrera-Seda, C. (2018). Authentic assessment: Creating a blueprint for course design. *Assessment & Evaluation in Higher Education*, *43*(5), 840–854. DOI: 10.1080/02602938.2017.1412396

Villarroel, V., Boud, D., Bloxham, S., Bruna, D., & Bruna, C. (2020). Using principles of authentic assessment to redesign written examinations and tests. *Innovations in Education and Teaching International*, *57*(1), 38–49. DOI: 10.1080/14703297.2018.1564882

Wang, Y., Pan, Y., Yan, M., Su, Z., & Luan, T. H. (2023). A survey on ChatGPT: AI-generated contents, challenges, and solutions. *arXiv preprint arXiv:2305.18339*. /arXiv.2305.18339DOI: 10.48550

Weber-Wulff, D., Anohina-Naumeca, A., Bjelobaba, S., Foltýnek, T., Guerrero-Dib, J., Popoola, O., . . . Waddington, L. (2023). Testing of detection tools for AI-generated text. *arXiv preprint arXiv:2306.15666.* /arXiv.2306.15666DOI: 10.48550

Whitelock, D., Gilbert, L., & Gale, V. (2015). *Technology enhanced assessment and feedback.* British Educational Research Association. DOI: 10.13140/RG.2.1.4548.8966

Williamson, B., Bayne, S., & Shay, S. (2020). The datafication of teaching in Higher Education: Critical issues and perspectives. *Teaching in Higher Education, 25*(4), 351–365. DOI: 10.1080/13562517.2020.1748811

Williamson, B., & Eynon, R. (2020). Historical threads, missing links, and future directions in AI in education. *Learning, Media and Technology, 45*(3), 223–235. DOI: 10.1080/17439884.2020.1798995

Winstone, N. E., & Carless, D. (2020). *Designing effective feedback processes in higher education: A learning-focused approach.* Routledge., DOI: 10.4324/9781351115940

Zawacki-Richter, O., Marín, V. I., Bond, M., & Gouverneur, F. (2019). Systematic review of research on artificial intelligence applications in higher education: Where are the educators? *International Journal of Educational Technology in Higher Education, 16*(1), 1–27. DOI: 10.1186/s41239-019-0171-0

Zhang, Z., & Perez-Paredes, P. (2021). Chinese postgraduate EFL learners' self-directed use of mobile English learning resources. *Computer Assisted Language Learning, 34*(8), 1128–1153. DOI: 10.1080/09588221.2019.1662455

Chapter 4

AI-Mediated Assessment in Global Higher Education Trust and Integrity Quality Assurance Challenges:

Integrity and Accountability in AI Systems

Neha Guliani
http://orcid.org/0009-0009-1032-3341
Jagannath University, India

Nidhi Shukla
JIMS, Delhi, India

ABSTRACT

This chapter critically examines the growing use of AI-mediated assessment in higher education and its implications for academic integrity, judgement, and institutional trust. While technologies such as automated grading, plagiarism detection, and remote proctoring are promoted for efficiency and consistency, their adoption represents a deeper sociotechnical shift that redistributes authority and reshapes accountability in assessment practices. Drawing on assessment theory, academic integrity scholarship, and algorithmic governance studies, the chapter argues that automation often reframes students as risks to be monitored rather than learners to be supported, raising concerns related to fairness and transparency. Rather than rejecting, the chapter advances a trust-centred framework emphasizing judgement, concluding that assessment quality cannot be secured through technological control.

INTRODUCTION

Assessment occupies a central position in higher education, not only as a mechanism for grading or certification, but as a practice through which academic authority, institutional credibility, and educational values are enacted. Decisions about assessment shape how learning is defined, how progression is legitimized, and how trust between students, educators, and institutions is sustained. Yet in recent

DOI: 10.4018/979-8-3373-8939-4.ch004

years, assessment has become an increasingly anxious domain of institutional governance, marked by heightened concern over integrity, consistency, and accountability.

This anxiety has coincided with the rapid expansion of AI-mediated assessment systems. Technologies such as automated grading, algorithmic plagiarism detection, predictive analytics, and remote proctoring are now routinely embedded within assessment infrastructures. These systems are often justified on the grounds of efficiency, scalability, and objectivity. However, their significance extends beyond technical functionality. By intervening directly in evaluative processes, AI systems reshape how judgement is exercised and, crucially, where trust is placed. Assessment is no longer governed solely through professional interpretation, but increasingly through algorithmic indicators that claim neutrality while redefining authority.

The acceleration of these technologies cannot be separated from broader structural pressures. The COVID-19 pandemic functioned as a critical catalyst, prompting institutions to adopt remote and automated assessment tools under emergency conditions. In the absence of face-to-face oversight, algorithmic proctoring and detection systems were positioned as substitutes for established trust-based practices. While these measures aimed to preserve academic standards at scale, their rapid deployment often occurred with limited ethical reflection or institutional deliberation. Subsequent disputes ranging from erroneous misconduct allegations to concerns about bias and exclusion revealed that automation did not simply solve integrity problems, but frequently intensified mistrust within academic communities. These developments cannot be adequately explained as technical failures or implementation gaps. Rather, they reflect a deeper transformation in how risk and accountability are governed in contemporary higher education. As universities operate within increasingly audit-driven environments, assessment has become a site where compliance, visibility, and defensibility are prioritized. Drawing on scholarship in audit culture and institutional governance, it becomes evident that technologized controls offer attractive solutions: they are scalable, standardized, and easily documented. Within this logic, AI-based assessment tools function less as pedagogical supports and more as instruments of oversight. Students, in turn, are subtly reframed not as participants in a learning relationship, but as potential risks requiring surveillance and verification.

At the same time, framing AI-mediated assessment purely as an imposed technological threat would be misleading. Many educators and institutions adopt these systems with legitimate intentions, including managing workload pressures, ensuring consistency across large cohorts, and responding to genuine concerns about misconduct. The issue, therefore, is not the existence of AI in assessment, but the assumption that technological control can replace relational trust. As Perrotta and Williamson (2018) observe, educational technologies are never neutral; they carry implicit governance assumptions that redistribute responsibility and reshape professional roles. When these assumptions remain unexamined, technologies introduced to protect academic values may instead weaken them.

This chapter develops its central argument from this tension. It contends that AI-mediated assessment poses fundamental challenges to trust, professional judgement, and quality assurance in higher education challenges that cannot be resolved through increasingly sophisticated systems of detection and enforcement. Efforts to secure integrity or fairness through automation alone overlook the interpretive, contextual, and normative dimensions of assessment. A responsible approach to AI adoption requires not the displacement of academic judgement, but its explicit reassertion within governance frameworks that emphasize transparency, accountability, and institutional responsibility. The contribution of this chapter is conceptual rather than technical. Instead of evaluating specific tools or forecasting future innovations, it examines AI-mediated assessment as a sociotechnical shift with far-reaching implications for educational values and governance. By integrating insights from assessment theory, academic integrity scholarship, algorithmic governance, and quality assurance studies, the chapter advances a trust-centred framework for understanding AI in assessment. Within this framework, trust is not treated as a weakness to be engineered away, but as an essential condition that must be actively sustained through ethical design, participatory decision-making, and sensitivity to institutional and global contexts particularly in systems marked by uneven resources and regulatory capacity.

The chapter proceeds by first revisiting assessment as a historically trust-based and professionally governed practice, identifying both its strengths and inherent limitations prior to widespread automation. AI-mediated systems redistribute authority within assessment practices. In doing so, they also reshape accountability and professional judgement. The discussion subsequently shifts from tools to institutions, examining governance responsibilities, regulatory fragmentation, and quality assurance pressures across diverse higher education contexts.

ASSESSMENT, PROFESSIONAL JUDGEMENT, AND TRUST IN THE PRE-AI ERA

Prior to the widespread introduction of artificial intelligence, assessment in higher education functioned primarily as a human-governed academic practice rooted in professional trust. Although institutional regulations and external accountability mechanisms shaped assessment processes, the legitimacy of evaluative decisions rested largely on confidence in academic expertise rather than technological verification. Grades and credentials derived their authority from disciplinary judgement, ethical responsibility, and institutional reputation. Examining this pre-AI configuration is critical for understanding what contemporary AI-mediated assessment disrupts not only in terms of efficiency or scale, but in relation to authority, discretion, and trust.

Assessment was traditionally understood as an interpretive and situated activity. Evaluating student work required more than applying explicit criteria; it involved contextual judgement, disciplinary sensitivity, and engagement with partially tacit standards of quality (Sadler, 1989). Academic judgement entailed interpreting meaning, intent, and originality within the norms of a field, rather than mechanicaly measuring performance. As Boud and Falchikov (2007) emphasize, assessment practices are inseparable from broader educational values and conceptions of learning. Within this model, professional judgement was foundational. Academics were expected to exercise discretion when applying criteria, to recognize intellectual risk-taking, and to distinguish between conceptual misunderstanding, weak academic practice, and misconduct. This discretion operated within communities of practice, supported by moderation, peer review, and shared disciplinary norms. Rather than undermining reliability, such practices enabled judgement to remain accountable, contestable, and context-sensitive. Trust between students and educators played a central role in sustaining assessment legitimacy. Students generally accepted assessment outcomes because they perceived academics as acting in good faith and possessing relevant expertise. Feedback practices reinforced this relational trust by framing assessment as a developmental dialogue rather than a purely classificatory mechanism (Nicol & Macfarlane-Dick, 2006). Disagreement was possible, but decisions were intelligible and open to explanation. Academic integrity frameworks prior to AI reflected similar trust-oriented assumptions. Integrity breaches were understood as violations of shared scholarly norms rather than primarily as technical infractions detectable through automated means. Educators relied on familiarity with students' writing styles, engagement patterns, and learning trajectories when identifying concerns. Institutional responses typically combined investigation with educational intent, emphasizing proportionality and value reinforcement rather than procedural enforcement (Macfarlane, Zhang, & Pun, 2014).

Quality assurance systems reinforced this model by privileging peer review, disciplinary expertise, and professional accountability. Importantly, trust was sustained not because assessment was error-free, but because its uncertainties were transparent and contestable. Stakeholders recognized that academic judgement involves interpretation and that reasonable disagreement is inherent to scholarly evaluation.

Table 1. Key Features of Pre-AI Assessment in Higher Education

Aspect	Pre-AI (Human-Governed) Assessment
Basis of Judgement	Professional and disciplinary judgement grounded in academic expertise
Nature of Assessment	Interpretive, contextual, and situated evaluation of student work
Role of Trust	Trust between educators and students sustained assessment legitimacy
Quality Assurance	Peer review, moderation, and professional accountability rather than automation

Globally, pre-AI assessment practices were high contextual. Disciplinary traditions, pedagogical norms, and integrity expectations varied across regions and institutions, shaped by local educational cultures. While this diversity complicated standardization, it enabled assessment to remain responsive to purpose and context. International recognition of qualifications relied largely on mutual confidence in professional standards rather than uniform procedural controls (Marginson, 201). Revisiting this landscape highlights two key insights. First, trust and professional judgement were not deficiencies awaiting technological correction; they were constitutive elements of assessment legitimacy. Second, pressures related to scale, globalization, and accountability were already testing trust-based systems, creating conditions under which automation appeared attractive. Understanding this baseline clarifies what is at stake as AI reshapes assessment authority.

AI-Mediated Assessment and Sociotechnical Reconfiguration

AI-mediated assessment is frequently introduced as a pragmatic response to challenges of scale, efficiency, and consistency. Framed as assistive technologies that support educators and enhance objectivity, these systems are often presented as neutral tools. However, their significance lies not in isolated functionalities but in how they reconfigure assessment as a sociotechnical system integrating algorithms, institutional governance, and human actors into new arrangements of authority and responsibility.

At an operational level, AI-mediated assessment includes automated grading, learning analytics, plagiarism detection, authorship analysis, and remote proctoring. These tools process student data to generate scores, flags, predictions, and classifications. What distinguishes them from earlier educational technologies is their growing influence over decision-making rather than mere information management.

AI systems increasingly participate in evaluative judgement by identifying anomalies, ranking performance, and signalling risk. In doing so, they introduce new epistemic assumptions about what constitutes evidence of learning or misconduct. As Williamson (2017) argues, data driven technologies embed calculative logics that reshape how educational phenomena are interpreted and governed. Complex student work is translated into quantifiable indicators optimized for scale and standardization. This translation alters the nature of academic judgement. Whereas pre-AI assessment relied on interpretive engagement with student work, AI-mediated systems operate through statistical inference and pattern recognition. Even when human assessors retain formal authority, algorithmic outputs frequently acquire epistemic weight, subtly redefining what is trusted: not contextual judgement, but system-generated indicators (Kitchin, 2017).

Authority is consequently redistributed. Decision-making shifts away from individual educators toward centralized institutional systems and external vendors. Criteria, thresholds, and risk parameters are encoded into software, often beyond the direct influence of teaching staff. While this aligns with broader governance trends emphasizing standardization and auditability, it narrows the scope for professional discretion. Responsibility is similarly fragmented. Traditional assessment assigned clear roles to educators, institutions, and external bodies. In AI-mediated systems, accountability is dispersed across designers, vendors, administrators, and users. When algorithmic decisions are contested, responsibillity for errors or bias is often unclear, complicating quality assurance processes (Harvey & Williams, 2010).

While automation may enhance procedural consistency, it risks undermining validity. Quality assurance frameworks that prioritize measurable output can conflate reliability with educational quality. As Bearman et al. (2022) note, performance metrics may obscure whether assessment remains pedagogically aligned.

Academic Integrity Under Automation From Pedagogy to Surveillance

Earlier approaches to academic integrity have long been understood as a core educational principle embedded within teaching, assessment design, and disciplinary socialization. In pre-automation contexts, integrity was cultivated through clear expectations, formative feedback, and shared scholarly norms. Although breaches were treated seriously, institutional responses emphasized judgement, proportionality, and educative intent rather than procedural enforcement alone. The increasing automation of assessment has significantly altered this orientation, transforming how integrity is defined, detected, and governed within higher education.This transformation is closely tied to the broader expansion of AI-mediated assessment systems. Plagiarism detection software, authorship verification tools, and algorithmic proctoring technologies are now routinely embedded within assessment infrastructures, often as default institutional requirements rather than optional supports. These systems are typically justified by reference to efficiency, consistency, and objectivity, particularly in large-scale or remote assessment environments. However, their widespread adoption reflects not only technical capability, but a deeper shift in how academic integrity is conceptualized from a pedagogical value to an institutional risk to be managed. Under conditions of automation, integrity increasingly becomes framed as a matter of reputational protection, regulatory compliance, and quality assurance defensibility. Rather than being addressed primarily through assessment design or student engagement, integrity is positioned as a threat that must be monitored and controlled. AI-based tools generate auditable evidence of institutional vigilance, aligning with broader audit cultures in higher education where visible compliance often takes precedence over educational substance. In this context, integrity is redefined less as ethical learning and more as procedural correctness.

A defining feature of automated integrity systems is their probabilistic nature. Similarity scores, authorship likelihoods, and behavioural flags do not establish intent or wrongdoing; they identify patterns that deviate from expected norms. Such indicators struggle to differentiate between deliberate misconduct, weak academic practice, legitimate reuse of disciplinary language, or culturally inflected citation norms. AI-detection systems designed to identify machine-generated text are particularly contested, with growing evidence of high error rates and uneven performance across disciplines and languages (Liang et al., 2023). When probabilistic outputs are treated as authoritative evidence, students may face allegations of misconduct without clear explanation or reliable grounds for contestation. Opacity further intensifies these risks. Many integrity technologies are proprietary, limiting access to information about training data, thresholds, and decision logic. As a result, educators and students often lack meaningful insight into how allegations are generated or how errors can be challenged. This undermines procedural fairness and due process, both of which are central to legitimate academic governance. When responsibility for decisions is obscured split between institutional policy, system outputs, and vendor assurances students are left navigating processes that appear opaque and intimidating rather than educative. Automation also reshapes the professional role of educators in integrity processes. Although institutional policies frequently emphasize that AI systems function in an advisory capacity, practical conditions complicate this ideal.

Importantly, the critique here is not a rejection of enforcement. Detection mechanisms and sanctions have always formed part of academic governance. The issue is balance. Pre-AI integrity frameworks combined enforcement with education, discretion with judgement. Automation disrupts this balance by privileging what can be measured and monitored over what can be taught and cultivated. As O'Neill (2002) cautions, excessive monitoring can paradoxically erode trust by signalling that individuals are not considered worthy of it. Reframing academic integrity in AI-mediated assessment therefore requires resisting its reduction to technical compliance. Integrity is fundamentally relational, developmental, and context-sensitive. It depends on assessment designs that encourage authentic engagement, on feedback practices that support learning, and on institutional cultures that model ethical scholarship. AI tools, where used, must remain subordinate to these educational purposes rather than redefining them. Enforcement alone cannot generate integrity; at best, it can deter certain behaviours while risking new forms of mistrust and disengagement.

Fairness, Bias, and Inclusion in AI-Mediated Assessment

Assertions that AI-mediated assessment enhances fairness and objectivity are among the most persuasive rationales for its institutional adoption. By reducing reliance on individual judgemnt, algorithmic systems are often portrayed as neutral arbiters capable of eliminating inconsistency and bias. However, scholarship across education, data science, and critical algorithm studies increasingly challenges this narrative. Rather than operating outside social context, AI-mediated assessment systems frequently reproduce and at times intensify existing inequalities embedded within data, institutional structures, and global educational hierarchies. Fairness and inclusion therefore cannot be understood as intrinsic properties of technology; they emerge from sociotechnical arrangements that determine whose knowledge, language, and learning conditions are treated as legitimate.

A central source of bias lies in the data on which assessment algorithms are trained. Historical datasets encode patterns of achievement and evaluation shaped by structural inequalities related to language proficiency, socio-economic background, race, gender, and institutional prestige. When such data are used to calibrate models and thresholds, AI systems risk normalizing these inequalities as benchmarks of "acceptable" performance (O'Neil, 2016). In assessment contexts, this can result in systematic advantages for students whose academic practices align with dominant norms, while marginalizing alternative forms of expression and reasoning. Linguistic bias represents one of the most persistent and well-documented challenges. Automated marking and plagiarism detection tools are typically optimized for standardized academic English, privileging grammatical regularity and familiar rhetorical structures. Students who employ non-standard grammar, culturally inflected phrasing, or alternative argumentative styles may be disproportionately penalized. Research on automated essay scoring demonstrates that formulaic writing often receives higher scores than more complex or creative responses, particularly when such systems are trained on narrow datasets (Perelman, 2014). For multilingual students, this creates an assessment environment in which language conformity is conflated with academic ability.

Cultural bias further complicates claims of algorithmic fairness. Academic conventions surrounding citation, collaboration, originality, and authorship vary considerably across educational traditions. AI-mediated integrity systems often operationalize narrow, Western-centric conceptions of scholarly practice, treating deviation from these norms as potential misconduct. Student educated in different academic cultures may therefore be flagged disproportionately, even in the absence of deceptive intent (Macfarlane, Zhang, & Pun, 2014). Automation, in this sense, hardens culturally contingent norms into rigid evaluative rules, reducing the scope for contextual interpretation. Opacity compounds these concerns. Proprietary algorithms limit visibility into how models weight linguistic features, behavioural indicators, or similarity thresholds. Students who experience adverse outcomes may struggle to identify the basis of decisions or to substantiate claims of unfair treatment. Institutions, likewise, may lack the capacity to audit systems or evaluate bias meaningfully. When fairness becomes difficult to contest, procedural justice and institutional trust are undermined.

Global inequalities in higher education further intensify these challenges. AI-mediated assessment technologies are predominantly developed and validated in high-income countries, often within elite institutional contexts. Their deployment across diverse educational systems assumes a level of infrastructural stability, linguistic homogeneity, and regulatory oversight that does not exist universally. In resource-constrained environments, unreliable connectivity, limited technical support, and outdated hardware can disrupt assessment processes, with responsibility often shifted onto individual students rather than institutional systems.

Standardization is frequently presented as a prerequisite for fairness, ensuring that all students are assessed against the same criteria. However, when standards are abstracted from context and enforced algorithmically, they risk erasing legitimate variation in disciplinary practices, institutional missions, and learning pathways. Context-blind uniformity equates fairness with sameness, neglecting equity and responsiveness to difference. In global higher education systems characterized by deep asymmetries, such assumptions exacerbate exclusion rather than mitigate it.

Table 2. highlights key sources of bias and their implications for fairness and inclusion in AI-mediated assessment.

Dimension	How Bias Occurs in AI-Mediated Assessment	Impact on Fairness & Inclusion
Training Data Bias	Algorithms trained on historical data reflecting social and educational inequalities	Normalizes unequal standards and disadvantages marginalized students
Linguistic Bias	Preference for standardized academic English and formulaic writing styles	Penalizes multilingual and non-native English speakers
Cultural Bias	Western-centric norms of citation, originality, and authorship embedded in systems	Flags culturally different academic practices as misconduct
Algorithmic Opacity	Limited access to system logic, thresholds, and decision rules	Students cannot contest decisions; procedural justice weakened
Standardization	Uniform criteria applied without contextual sensitivity	Treats fairness as sameness, ignoring equity and diversity

continued on following page

Table 2. Continued

Dimension	How Bias Occurs in AI-Mediated Assessment	Impact on Fairness & Inclusion
Global Inequality	Systems designed in elite, high-income contexts	Disadvantages students in resource-constrained institutions
Institutional Capacity	Limited ability to audit or evaluate bias in proprietary tools	Shifts responsibility onto students rather than institutions
Student Experience	Assessment outcomes appear arbitrary or unexplained	Reduces trust, inclusion, and sense of academic belonging

Addressing fairness and inclusion in AI-mediated assessment therefore requires more than technical optimization. It demands participatory design processes that involve diverse stakeholders, including students from marginalized groups, and institutional willingness to question whether particular assessment functions should be automated at all. Fairness must be understood as relational and contextual, not computational. Without such reorientation, AI-mediated assessment risks reinforcing existing inequities while presenting them as objective outcomes.

This section has argued that AI-mediated assessment systems frequently reproduce linguistic, cultural, and structural biases, with particularly severe consequences in global and resource-constrained contexts. By embeding narrow standards and opaque decision-making into assessment practices, these systems threaten inclusion and trust.

Transparency, Explainability, and Accountability in Algorithmic Assessment

The legitimacy of assessment in higher education has never depended solely on the correctness of outcomes. It rests on the ability of students and educators to understand how decisions are made, to question them when necessary, and to hold decision-makers accountable. Transparency, explainability, and accountability are therefore foundational conditions of trust rather than optional ethical enhancements. AI-mediated assessment places these conditions under considerable strain by introducing forms of decision-making that are opaque, distributed, and resistant to meaningful scrutiny.

Students subjected to AI-mediated assessment are often presented with numerical scores, similarity indices, or categorical judgements without clear explanation of how these outputs relate to learning criteria. Even when institutions regard such outputs as technically valid, their lack of pedagogical intelligibility can render assessment decisions arbitrary from the student perspective (Burrell, 2016). When students cannot connect evaluation outcomes to assessable aspects of their work, assessment loses its formative function and becomes difficult to trust. This erosion of intelligibility undermines procedural justice. In traditional assessment systems, students could seek clarification from identifiable assessors who could explain how the criteria were applied and where improvement was needed. Algorithmic mediation disrupts this interaction by interposing technical processes that do not translate easily into educational reasoning. As a result, assessment becomes less dialogic and more extractive, weakening its role in learning.

The challenge of explainability is not merely technical but epistemic. Assessment involves normative judgements grounded in disciplinary values and educational purposes. Statistical explanations such as feature weighting or probability scores do not address whether a particular indicator is educationally meaningful or aligned with disciplinary standards. Explainability, therefore, cannot be separated from questions about whose values are embedded in systems and how quality is defined. These issues are particularly acute in cases of academic integrity and misconduct. AI-mediated integrity tools generate probabilistic indicators that are frequently treated as evidence rather than as prompts for further judgement. When students are accused of misconduct based on algorithmic outputs, limited access to system logic, error rates, or contextual assumptions raises serious concerns about due process. Students may be required to disprove allegations without access to the reasoning that produced them, effectively reversing traditional burdens of justification.

Educators' roles are similarly constrained. While instiutional narratives often emphasize that AI systems operate in an advisory capacity, practical realities complicate this ideal. Educators may lack training, documentation, or time to critically evaluate system outputs, particularly in high-volume assessment environments. Under such conditions, algorithmic recommendations can acquire de facto authority, diminishing professional agency.

At the institutional level, accountability becomes fragmented. AI-mediated assessment systems are typically procured from external vendors whose algorithms and training data are protected by commercial confidentiality. When errors, bias, or harm occur, responsibility is distributed across institutional policies, vendor contracts, and user practices. This diffusion of accountability undermines quality assurance frameworks historically built around traceable judgement and identifiable responsibility (Kitchin, 2017). Traditional quality assurance mechanisms struggle to adapt to algorithmic assessment. While metrics such as accuracy or reliability are easily reported, they do not capture educational validity, fairness, or trust. There is a risk that quality assurance becomes aligned with system performance rather than with the quality of learning and assessment itself (Bearman et al., 2022).

Human-in-the-loop models are often presented as safeguards, yet they frequently provide only nominal oversight. Human involvement may be limited to approval stages, with little opportunity to challenge or override algorithmic outputs. Moreover, when systems are framed as objective, human judgement can be portrayed as a source of bias rather than a corrective. This inversion subtly shifts accountability away from systems and onto individuals.

Table 3. illustrates key differences between traditional and AI-mediated assessment practices.

Assessment Aspect	Traditional Assessment	AI-Mediated (Algorithmic) Assessment
Decision Basis	Human judgement based on criteria and context	Algorithmic scores, similarity indices, or risk flags
Transparency	Criteria and feedback explained by educators	Limited explanation of how scores or flags are generated
Explainability	Students can seek clarification from assessors	System logic often opaque or technically inaccessible
Role of Educator	Active evaluator and feedback provider	Reduced to verifier or approver of system outputs
Student Understanding	Clear link between work and evaluation	Weak link between learning effort and final judgement
Accountability	Clearly located with individual assessors and institution	Fragmented between institution, software vendors, and systems
Procedural Justice	Decisions contestable through dialogue	Appeals difficult due to lack of system transparency
Impact on Trust	Supports trust through dialogue and explanation	May reduce trust due to opacity and perceived arbitrariness

Meaningful transparency cannot be achieved through disclosure alone. Overly technical documentation may overwhelm rather than empower students and staff. What is required are explanations that are inteligible, educationally relevant, and connected to institutional values. Transparency must include clarity about system limitations, uncertainty, and avenues for appeal. Without these conditions, transparency risks becoming symbolic compliance rather than a foundation for trust.

This section has argued that opacity, limited explainability, and fragmented accountability undermine the legitimacy of AI-mediated assessment. Addressing these challenges requires governance frameworks that prioritize contestability, preserve professional judgement, and ensure that responsibility remains institutionally grounded. The next section turn to governance structures, examining how responsibility for AI-mediated assessment must be located at the level of institutional decision-making rather than individual users.

Governance and Institutional Responsibility in AI-Mediated Assessment

The challenges posed by AI-mediated assessment cannot be adequately addressed at the level of individual technologies, user behaviour, or isolated ethical principles. They are, at their core, questions of institutional governance. As AI systems become embedded within core assessment processes, higher education institutions are not merely adopting new tools; they are reorganizing how authority, responsibility, and accountability are exercised within assessment regimes. Governance decisions often enacted through procurement processes, policy standardisation, and compliance strategies shape not only assessment outcomes but also the values communicated to students and staff.

A defining feature of AI-mediated assessment governance is the centralization of authority. Historically, assessment authority was distributed across disciplines and academic communities, with educators exercising judgement within institutional and professional frameworks. While institutions provided oversight through quality assurance mechanisms, decisions about assessment design and evaluation were largely situated within disciplinary expertise. AI-based assessment systems, by contrast, tend to operate at an institutional or system-wide scale. Decisions regarding adoption, configuration, thresholds, and intervention protocols are frequently made by senior administrators, IT governance bodies, legal units, or compliance committees, rather than by educators directly engaged in teaching and assessment. This shift reflects broader managerial trends in higher education that prioritize standardization, auditability, and risk mitigation.

Procurement practices often intensify these governance dynamics. Assessment technologies are commonly adopted in response to pressures related to cost efficiency, scalability, reputational risk, and regulatory scrutiny. In such contexts, decisions are driven by functional promises such as accuracy, efficiency, or integrity protection rather than by sustained pedagogical or ethical evaluation. Once implemented, systems may become institutionally entrenched through contractual obligations, integration with learning platforms, and policy mandates, limiting opportunities for critical reassessment.

Ethical oversight within universities is frequently fragmented. Research ethics committees typically focus on scholarly inquiry rather than operational technologies deployed in teaching and assessment. As a result, AI-mediated assessment systems may escape rigorous ethical review despite their significant impact on students' academic progression and institutional trust. Responsibility for evaluating ethical implications is often dispersed across multiple units, reducing accountability and coherence.

Regulatory fragmentation across national and regional contexts further complicates institutional responsibility. Higher education institutions operate within diverse legal frameworks governing data protection, automated decision-making, and student rights. While some jurisdictions impose explicit obligations related to transparency, explainability, and human oversight, others provide limited guidance specific to educational AI. In transnational education contexts, institutions may default to the most permissive regulatory environments, prioritizing operational feasibility over rights-based protection (Veale & Borgesius, 2021).

A governance perspective grounded in rights highlights the inadequacy of treating AI-mediated assessment as a neutral administrative innovation. Assessment decisions shape progression, certification, employability, and students' sense of belonging within academic communities. Governance frameworks that focus narrowly on institutional risk management fail to account for students' rights to fairness, explanation, and meaningful appeal.

Participatory governance represents another unresolved challenge. Students are typically positioned as subjects of AI-mediated assessment rather than as participants in governance deliberations. Educators may be consulted only after systems are selected or policies finalized. Yet legitimate governance requires meaningful involvement of students, faculty, and professional staff in defining acceptable uses of AI in assessment. Participation is not merely consultative; it is foundational to trust and institutional legitimacy.

Crucially, institutional responsibility cannot be outsourced to technology vendors or displaced onto individual users. Policies emphasizing "appropriate use" by educators or "academic honesty" by students obscure the structural nature of governance decisions. Institutions choose to adopt, configure, and mandate AI systems and must therefore remain accountable for their consequences. This includes ongoing evaluation, impact assessment, and the willingness to suspend or withdraw systems that undermine fairness, trust, or educational purpose. Governance must be understood as a continuous and reflexive process rather than a one-time compliance exercise.

In summary, AI-mediated assessment foregrounds governance as the central site of responsibility in contemporary higher education. Centralization of authority, vendor dependence, fragmented ethical oversight, and regulatory diversity collectively reshape how assessment is justified and experienced. Addressing these challenges requires institutions to move beyond tool-centric adoption toward participatory, rights-based, and proportionate governance frameworks that preserve professional judgement and sustain trust.

Toward a Trust-Centred Framework for AI-Mediated Assessment

The preceding sections have demonstrated that the most significant challenges associated with AI-mediated assessment are not technical limitations, but crises of trust, legitimacy, and responsibility. Automation has unsettled long-standing assumptions about who exercises judgement, how decisions are justified, and why assessment outcomes are accepted as fair. This section articulates the chapter's central conceptual contribution: a trust-centred framework for AI-mediated assessment. Rather than treating trust as an indirect outcome of efficiency or compliance, this framework positions trust as the foundational condition guiding the integration of AI into assessment practices.

Trust-centred assessment begins from the recognition that assessment is inherently a moral and relational practice. Assessment decisions communicate institutional values by signalling what counts as knowledge, whose voices are credible, and how uncertainty or error is addressed. Historically, trust in assessment has rested on the expectation that judgements are made by qualified professionals acting in good faith, guided by disciplinary norms and pedagogical purpose. While students may contest outcomes, legitimacy has depended on the belief that decisions are reasoned, contextual, and open to justification. AI-mediated assessment disrupts this moral economy by relocating elements of judgement to algorithmic systems whose rationales are often opaque and whose authority is institutionally imposed rather than professionally earned.

A trust-centred framework explicitly rejects the assumption that trust can be engineered through automation. While AI system may enhance consistency or efficiency, trust does not emerge from technical performance alone. Instead, trust-centred assessment rests on a normative commitment to human-governed evaluation. AI is positiond as a supportive infrastructure that augments professional judgement rather than substituting for it.

Professional judgement constitutes the first pillar of a trust-centred framework. Academic judgement involves interpretive reasoning that cannot be fully formalized or reduced to rule-based processes. It draws on tacit disciplinary knowledge, awareness of student context, and pedagogical intent. Within a trust-centred approach, AI systems may assist by identifying patterns, highlighting anomalies, or supporting formative feedback, but responsibility for final decisions remains explicitly human.

Preserving professional judgement requires supportive governance conditions. Educators must be empowered to question, contextualize, and override algorithmic outputs without institutional penalty. Where policies treat system outputs as presumptively authoritative, human involvement becomes symbolic rather than substantive. Trust-centred assessment therefore demand meaningful human agency, supported by appropriate time, training, and recognition within academic workloads. Without such support, human-in-the-loop models risk functioning as accountability shields rather than genuine safeguards.

Academic integrity is re-imagined within this framework as an educational and relational value rather than a compliance mechanism. Earlier sections demonstrated how AI-based detection tools can recast integrity as risk management, positioning students as potential offenders. Trust-centred assessment resists this adversarial framing, emphasizing integrity cultivation through assessment design, feedback, and institutional culture.

Transparency and explainability form the second core pillar of the framework. Trust requires intelligibility. Students and educators must be able to understand how AI influences assessment decisions, how uncertainty is handled, and where human judgement intervenes. Trust-centre transparency prioritizes explanations that are educationally meaningful rather than technically exhaustive. Students should be able to see assessment decisions as reasoned and contestable, and educators should be able to justify outcomes without deferring responsibility to "the system."

Proportionality represents a further principle of trust-centred assessment. Not all assessment decisions warrant the same degree of automation or oversight. Low-stakes formative tasks may appropriately incorporate greater automation, while high-stakes summative decisions require stronger human involvement and justification. Aligning automation with educational purpose provides a principled basis for determining where AI should be limited or excluded.

Shared responsibility across stakeholders is essential to trust-centred assessment. Trust cannot be imposed through policy; it must be co-constructed. Students, educators, administrators, and professional staff all have legitimate interests in how assessment systems operate. Participatoray governance mechanisms that involve these groups in decisions about AI adoption, acceptable use, and ongoing evaluation are therefore central to legitimacy. Student participation, in particular, strengthens procedural justice even when assessment outcome are contested.

Finally, trust-centred assessment rejects context-blind standardization. What constitutes fair and legitimate assessment varies across disciplines, institutions, and regions. AI systems trained in particular linguistic or cultural contexts may misalign when deployed elsewhere, especially in Global South settings shaped by infrastructural constraints and historical inequalities. Trust-centred frameworks therefore require local adaptation, critical evaluation of transferability, and respect for contextual difference.

Trust-centred assessment also reframes quality assurance. While consistency and reliability remain important, quality cannot be reduced to procedural compliance or system metrics. Legitimate assessment quality depends on whether practices are perceived as fair, meaningful, and educationally justified by those subject to them. Trust thus becomes an indicator of quality rather than a reputational concern to be managed.

This section has articulated a trust-centred framework for AI-mediated assessment that foregrounds professional judgement, transparency, proportionality, participation, and contextual sensitivity. By shifting attention from enforcement and automation to responsibility and relational legitimacy, this framework offers a principled alternative to automation-first approaches. The next section situates this framework within global policy, regulatory, and quality assurance contexts.

Global Policy, Regulation, and Quality Assurance in AI-Mediated Assessment

AI-mediated assessment operates within complex and uneven regulatory environments that were largely designed for human-led evaluation practices. As algorithmic systems become embedded in assessment infrastructures, they intersect with national laws, transnational education markets, and quality assurance (QA) regimes in ways that expose significant governance gaps. This section argues that existing policy and regulatory responses remain fragmented, reactive, and frequently misaligned with the ethical and pedagogical realities of assessment automation.

A central challenge lies in the diversity of legal approaches to artificial intelligence across jurisdictions. Different regions conceptualize automated decision-making, data protection, and individual rights in markedly different ways. In some regulatory environments, education is increasingly recognized as a high-impact domain due to its influence on life chances, social mobility, and credential legitimacy. Emerging frameworks in these contexts emphasize proportionality, transparency, and meaningful human oversight. In contrast, many jurisdictions rely on general data protection laws or non-binding ethicl guidelines that offer limited, education-specific direction. This variation creates uncertainty for institutions, particularly those operating transnationally, and undermines the development of coherent governance practices.

Data protection and privacy regulation constitute another critical policy domain shaping AI-mediated assessment. Assessment technologies routinely process large volumes of student data, including written submissions, behavioural logs, interaction metadata, and, in some cases, biometric information through remote proctoring systems. Although data protection framework typically emphasize principles such as informed consent, purpose limitation, and data minimization, their application in educational assessment contexts is deeply contested. Students often have little meaningful choice regarding participation in AI-mediated assessment, as refusal may jeopardize academic progression or certification. This raises fundamental questions about the legitimacy of consent in settings characterized by institutional power asymmetries.

Regulation of automated decision-making further complicates governance. Many legal regimes differentiate between fully automated decisions and those involving human intervention, granting enhanced rights such as explanation or appeal when decisions are fully automated. In practice, however, AI-mediated assessment frequently occupies an ambiguous space. Systems may generate similarity scores, predictive indicators, or risk flags that heavily influence outcomes without being formally designated as final decisions. Institutions may therefore claim compliance with oversight requirements while relying extensively on algorithmic inference. Trust-centred governance challenges such formalistic interpretations, emphasizing that legitimacy depends on substantive human judgement and meaningful contestability rather than nominal human involvement.

The globalization of educational technology markets intensifies these regulatory difficulties. AI assessment tools are predominantly developed and commercialized by multinational vendors whose operations span multiple legal jurisdictions. Training data may be sourced from diverse educational contexts, while system development and hosting occur far from the institutions where assessment decisions take effect. This diffusion of responsibility creates accountability gaps when systems produce biased, erroneous, or harmful outcomes. While regulators and QA agencies typically focus on institutional compliance, institutions themselves often lack transparency into vendor practices, exposing a structural weakness in current governance arrangements.

Quality assurance frameworks face particular pressure in this context. Traditional QA mechanisms prioritize reliability, consistency, and procedural documentation. While these remain important, they are insufficient for evaluating algorithmic systems characterized by opacity, data dependency, and continuous adaptation. In some cases, institutions adopt AI-mediated assessment precisely because it produces auditable metrics aligned with performance-oriented QA regimes, even when such metrics obscure pedagogical validity or ethical concerns. There is a risk that automation-first approaches become normalized under the banner of quality assurance.

QA agencies are therefore under increasing pressure to expand their evaluative criteria. Beyond technical reliability, assessment practices must now be assessed in terms of transpareny, explainability, fairness, and contestability. Concepts of validity and quality must incorporate sociotechnical dimensions, including how algorithmic systems redistribute judgement, shape authority, and influence stakeholder trust. An assessment process may be statistically consistent yet still perceived as illegitimate by students and educators. Trust-centred QA frameworks recognize that confidence in assessment is a core indicator of quality rather than a peripheral reputational issue.

Global inequalities in regulatory and QA capacity further exacerbate these challenges. Institutions in resource-constrained systems particularly across parts of the Global South face strong incentives to adopt automated assessment technologies in response to large enrolments and limited staffing. At the same time, these contexts may lack robust regulatory oversight, independent QA bodies, or effective mechanisms for student redress. Consequently, students in such systems may be disproportionately exposed to the risks of opaque and poorly governed AI-mediated assessment. Trust-centred approaches explicitly foreground these asymmetries, rejecting assumptions that global standardization can deliver equitable outcomes.

Internationalization trends compound governance complexity. Transnational programmes, online degrees, and cross-border micro-credentials increasingly rely on shared digital assessment infrastructures. While AI-mediated assessment is often promoted as a means of ensuring consistency across dispersed cohorts, uniform technological solutions may conflict with local regulatory requirements, cultural expectations, and pedagogical traditions. QA agencies operating on a national or regional levels may struggle to evaluate assessment practices that are partially outsourced to global platforms and governed through contractual arrangements beyond their jurisdiction.

A trust-centred policy orientation therefore calls for a recalibration of global regulatory and QA priorities. Rather than focusing narrowly on innovation acceleration or compliance, governance frameworks should emphasize proportionality, rights protection, and institutional responsibility. This includes clearer guidance on the use of AI in high-stakes assessment, minimum standards for transparency and explainability, and explicit requirements for meaningful human judgement. QA agencies can do a critical role by embedding these principles into accreditation standards and review processes, shaping institutional behaviour without mandating specific technologies.

In summary, AI-mediated assessment places significant strain on existing global policy, regulatory, and quality assurance frameworks. Legal diversity, vendor globalization, policy lag, and uneven governance capacity shape how assessment automation unfolds across contexts. With out deliberate reorientation, these dynamics risk entrenching automation-first practices that undermine trust and educational values. A trust-centred framework offers a coherent normative basis for aligning policy and quality assurance with the moral and relational foundations of assessment.

IMPLICATIONS FOR EDUCATORS, STUDENTS, AND INSTITUTIONS

The ethical, governance, and policy dynamics surrounding AI-mediated assessment are ultimately experienced in the everyday practices of educators, students, and higher education institutions. While system-level debates often emphasize efficiency, integrity, or compliance, assessment legitimacy is lived and negotiated through routine interactions, expectations, and decisions. This section examines how AI-mediated assessment reshapes professional roles, student experience, and institutional culture, arguing that without deliberate recalibration, automation risks eroding the relationships that sustain trust in higher education.

For educators, AI-mediated assessment introduces both practical efficiencies and profound professional challenges. On one level, automated marking, feedback generation, and misconduct detection promise workload relief, particularly in contexts of mass enrolment and constrained resources. These efficiencies can be valuable. However, they also being raise concerns about the erosion of assessment expertise. Academic judgement develops through sustained engagement with student work, disciplinary standards, and reflective practice. When educators rely heavily on automated systems, opportunities to exercise and refine this judgement may diminish over time. Early-career academics may be socialized into assessment cultures that normalize deference to algorithmic outputs rather than critical evaluation.

AI-mediated assessment also demands new competencies from educators, including data literacy, interpretive skills, and ethical awareness. Yet institutional support for developing these capacities is uneven. Professional development initiatives often prioritize technical operation over critical understanding of system limitations, bias, or governance implications. A trust-centred approach requires institutions to invest in meaningful professional development that empowers educators to question outputs, contextualize results, and participate actively in governence decisions. Without such investment, expectations of responsible human oversight remain largely aspirational.

Students encounter AI-mediated assessment as a central expression of institutional authority. Assessment practices shape not only academic outcomes but also students' perceptions of fairness, recognition, and belonging. When AI systems are introduced without clear explanation or accessible avenues for appeal, assessment may appear opaque or arbitrary. Even technically accurate systems can undermine trust if students do not understand how decisions are made or how they can be challenged.

Trust-centred assessment foregrounds student voice as an essential component of legitimacy. Students are not merely recipients of assessment decisions; they are stakeholders with a legitimate interest in how evaluative systems operate. Excluding students from governance discussions about AI adoption exacerbates mistrust, whereas participatory approaches can foster shared responsibility. Procedural justice being informed, heard, and treated with respect Serves a central functionin sustaining trust even when outcomes are disputed.

At the institutional level, AI-mediated assessment carries significant cultural and strategic implications. Universities operate under growing pressure to demonstrate quality, integrity, and accountability to regulators, funders, and the public. AI tools are often framed as solutions to reputational risk, offering visible indicators of control and compliance. While these motivations are understandable, they risk narrowing institutional conceptions of quality to what is auditable rather than what is educationally meaningful. Over time, this can entrench automation-first strategies that prioritize defensibility over trust.

Institutional cultures are shaped not only by formal policies but by what becomes normalized in daily practice. When AI-mediated assessment is adopted without sustained reflection, assumptions about surveillance, standardization, and algorithmic authority can become embedded. Trust-centred institutions, by contrast, cultivate reflexive cultures that treat AI adoption as an ongoing ethical and pedagogical question rather than a one-time technical solution. This involves creating spaces for dialogue, encouraging critique, and remaining willing to revise or withdraw technologies that undermine educational values.

Rebalancing automation and judgement is therefore a central institutional responsibility. This does not require rejecting AI outright, but situating it within clearly articulated ethical and educational boundaries. Institutions must ask not only what AI can do, but what it should do, and under what conditions. Aligning assessment practices with institutional values, investing in human capacity, and supporting participatory governance are essential to this process. Trust-centred assessment provides a framework for making these choices explicit, contestable, and accountable.

In sum, the implications of AI-mediated assessment are deeply human. For educators, they affect professional autonomy, identity, and ethical agency. For students, they shape experiences of fairness, recognition, and belonging. For institutions, they influence culture, legitimacy, and public trust. Without deliberate intervention, automation risks marginalizing professional judgement and weakening trust across all three domains. A trust-centred approach offers a pathway to rebalancing efficiency with responsibility, ensuring that AI serves educational purposes rather than redefining them.

FUTURE RESEARCH DIRECTIONS AND OPEN QUESTIONS

The rapid expansion of artificial intelligence within higher education assessment has outpaced the development of a sufficiently integrated research base to guide ethical, pedagogical, and governance decisions. While existing scholarship has examined specific tools, integrity technologies, and learning analytics, significant gaps remain particularly in relation to trust, professional judgement, and institutional responsibility. Addressing these gaps is essential for the development of sustainable and legitimate AI-mediated assessment practices.

A first priority for future research concerns student experience and perception. Much of the existing literature evaluates AI systems in terms of technical performance, such as accuracy, efficiency, or detection capability. Far less attention has been paid to how students understand, interpret, and respond to algorithmic involvement in assessment. Trust in assessment is not determined solely by system outputs; it is shaped by whether assessment processes are experienced as fair, transparent, and respectful. Empirical research are needed for the examine how students perceive AI-mediated assessment across different disciplines, cultures, and levels of study, and how these perceptions influence engagement, learning behaviour, and institutional trust. A second critical research gap relates to educators' professional experience. While conceptual work has raised concerns about deskilling, workload redistribution, and shifting authority, there is limited empirical evidence on how AI-mediated assessment reshapes academic judgement in practice. Future studies should explore how educators interpret and negotiate algorithmic outputs, when they defer to or resist system recommendations, and how institutional policies shape these responses. Comparative research across disciplines would be particularly valuable, given the diversity of assessment epistemologies and practices. Such work is essential for designing governance frameworks that genuinely support professional judgement rather than merely asserting its importance.

Research on governance participation represents a further underdeveloped area. Much of the literature focuses on institutional policy statements or top-down implementation strategies, leaving underexplored the processes through which educators and students are included or excluded from decision-making about AI adoption. Trust-centred assessment presupposes participatory governance, yet there is limited empirical insight into how such participation operates in practice or how it affects legitimacy and trust. Future research should examine models of shared governance, including their strengths, limitations, and conditions for success across different institutional contexts. Design-based research offers another promising direction. Many studies evaluate AI tools after deployment, rather than investigating how assessment practices might be co-designed to integrate AI in pedagogically meaningful ways. Trust-centred assessment calls for research that brings together educators, students, and designers to explore how AI can support formative feedback, reflective learning, and disciplinary judgement without undermining trust. Design-based approaches allow for iterative experimentation in authentic educational settings, but require sustained institutional commitment and methodological rigor to generate transferable insights.

Finally, there is a need for further conceptual research that bridges assessment theory, ethics, and governance. Existing work often remains siloed, with technical evaluations disconnected from pedagogical theory and ethical analysis. Developing integrative frameworks that conceptualize assessment as a sociotechnical, moral, and institutional practice is essential for advancing both scholarship and practice. Future research should also explore how trust can be conceptualized and assessed beyond surface indicators such as satisfaction surveys or compliance metrics.

In summary, advancing AI-mediated assessment responsibly requires moving beyond tool-focused evaluation toward interdisciplinary research that foregrounds student experience, professional judgement, participatory governance, and long-term institutional effects. Without such inquiry, higher education risks normalizing assessment practices whose consequences remain poorly understood and difficult to reverse. The next section draws these insights together, reaffirming the centrality of trust in the future of assessment.

CONCLUSION

The increasing integration of artificial intelligence into higher education assessment has reshaped how learning is evaluated, integrity is governed, and authority is exercised within academic institutions. What began as a technological response to challenges of scale, efficiency, and misconduct has evolved into a fundamental transformation of assessment regimes. This chapter has argued that the most pressing challenge of this transformation is not technical performance or regulatory compliance, but the preservation and renewal of trust between students and institutions, between educators and assessment systems, and between higher education and society.

Throughout the chapter, a critical shift has been traced: from integrity as an educationally cultivated value to integrity as a problem of detection and enforcement. When AI tools are deployed primarily as instruments of surveillance and control, students are positioned as risks to be managed rather than learners to be supported. While such approaches may offer short-term reassurance, they often generate longer-term consequences, including student alienation, erosion of professional judgement, and weakened institutional legitimacy. A trust-centred approach challenges this trajectory by reframing integrity as a shared responsibility grounded in pedagogy, ethical judgement, and institutional accountability.

A central insight of this analysis is that assessment is never a neutral technical process. It is a moral, relational, and context-sensitive practice shaped by values, power relations, and institutional choices. AI-mediated systems inevitably encode assumptions about knowledge, authorship, and credibility. Treating these systems as objective or inevitable obscures their governance implications and limits opportunities for critical engagement. Reclaiming trust therefore requires making the assumptions embedded in assessment technologies visible, contestable, and subject to ongoing evaluation.

The chapter has also emphasized the irreplaceable role of professional judgement. While AI systems may assist with pattern recognition, efficiency, or feedback generation, they cannot replicate the contextual understanding, ethical reasoning, and disciplinary sensitivity that educators bring to assessment decisions. Preserving professional judgement is not a nostalgic defence of tradition, but a necessary condition for legitimate assessment in complex and diverse learning environments.

Student experience has emerged as a further cornerstone of trust. Assessment practices shape not only academic outcomes but also students' perceptions of fairness, recognition, and institutional care. Opaque or punitive uses of AI-mediated assessment risk undermining student confidence and engagement. Conversely, when students are informed, consulted, and supported, AI can function as a tool for formative learning rather than as a source of suspicion or anxiety. Trust-centred assessment therefore requires institutions to engage students as partners in the of assessment design and integrity cultivation, rather than passive subjects of technological oversight.

Governance ultimately determines whether AI-mediated assessment strengthens or erodes academic integrity. Policy frameworks focused narrowly on compliance or risk mitigation are insufficient for addressing the sociotechnical complexity of assessment automation. Institutions must instead develop governance arrangements that are participatory, reflexive, and responsive to pedagogical context. This includes clear accountability structures, ongoing impact assessment, and ethical oversight that extends beyond vendor assurances or regulatory minimums. Trust is sustained not through claims of control, but through demonstrable responsibility and openness.

Importantly, this chapter has avoided deterministic narratives that frame AI as either an inevitable threat or a universal solution. AI-mediated assessment is neither inherently corrosive nor inherently transformative. Its effects depend on how technologies are designed, governed, and embedded within institutionl cultures. Integrity innovation does not require for the rejecting AI, but it does require resisting uncritical adoption. By aligning AI deployment with educational purpose, inclusivity, and professional autonomy, institutions can harness technological capabilities while safeguarding core academic values.

In conclusion, rethinking academic integrity in global AI-mediated assessment regimes demands more than technical refinement or policy adjustment. It requires a fundamental reorientation of how learning, trust, and accountability are understood in digitally mediated environments. A trust-centred framework offers a principled and pragmatic pathway forward. By moving from cheating prevention to integrity cultivation, higher education can respond constructively to the challenges posed by AI while reaffirming its commitment to education as a moral, relational, and public good in an age of intelligent systems.

REFERENCES

Bearman, M., Dawson, P., Ajjawi, R., Tai, J., & Boud, D. (2022). Reconsidering assessment for learning in the age of artificial intelligence. *Assessment & Evaluation in Higher Education*, *47*(5), 676–691. DOI: 10.1080/02602938.2021.1930462

Boud, D., & Falchikov, N. (2007). *Rethinking assessment in higher education: Learning for the longer term*. Routledge. DOI: 10.4324/9780203964309

Bretag, T. (2016). Defining academic integrity: International perspectives Introduction. *International Journal for Educational Integrity*, *12*(1), 1–5. DOI: 10.1007/s40979-015-0004-4

Eubanks, V. (2018). *Automating inequality: How high-tech tools profile, police, and punish the poor*. St. Martin's Press.

Kotsiantis, S., Zaharakis, I., & Pintelas, P. (2004). Machine learning: A review of classification and combining techniques. *Artificial Intelligence Review*, *26*(3), 159–190. DOI: 10.1007/s10462-007-9052-3

O'Neil, C. (2016). *Weapons of math destruction: How big data increases inequality and threatens democracy*. Crown Publishing Group.

Sandel, M. J. (2020). *The tyranny of merit: What's become of the common good?* Farrar, Straus and Giroux.

Williamson, B., Eynon, R., & Potter, J. (2020). Pandemic politics, pedagogies and practices: Digital technologies and distance education during the coronavirus emergency. *Learning, Media and Technology*, *45*(2), 107–114. DOI: 10.1080/17439884.2020.1761641

Boud, D. (1995). Assessment and learning: Contradictory or complementary? In Knight, P. (Ed.), *Assessment for learning in higher education* (pp. 35–48). Kogan Page.

Boud, D., & Falchikov, N. (2006). Aligning assessment with long-term learning. *Assessment & Evaluation in Higher Education*, *31*(4), 399–413. DOI: 10.1080/02602930600679050

Broadfoot, P. (1996). *Education, assessment and society: A sociological analysis*. Open University Press.

Eraut, M. (2000). Non-formal learning, implicit learning and tacit knowledge in professional work. *The British Journal of Educational Psychology*, *70*(1), 113–136. DOI: 10.1348/000709900158001 PMID: 10765570

Knight, P. T. (2001). *A briefing on key concepts: Formative and summative, criterion and norm-referenced assessment. Assessment Series*. Learning and Teaching Support Network.

Polanyi, M. (1966). *The tacit dimension*. University of Chicago Press.

Sadler, D. R. (1989). Formative assessment and the design of instructional systems. *Instructional Science*, *18*(2), 119–144. DOI: 10.1007/BF00117714

Shay, S. (2008). Beyond social constructivist perspectives on assessment: The centring of academic judgement. *Teaching in Higher Education*, *13*(5), 595–605. DOI: 10.1080/13562510802334970

Trowler, P. (2014). Depicting and researching disciplines: Strong and moderate essentialist approaches. *Studies in Higher Education, 39*(10), 1720–1731. DOI: 10.1080/03075079.2013.801431

. References for Section 3 (APA 7th Edition)

Bearman, M., & Ajjawi, R. (2023). Learning analytics and the limits of automated judgement in higher education. *Assessment & Evaluation in Higher Education, 48*(4), 567–580. DOI: 10.1080/02602938.2022.2067421

Coates, H., & Galán-Muros, V. (2019). *Performance measurement in universities: Learning from experience.* OECD Publishing.

Dawson, P., Bearman, M., Bennett, S., Hall, M., Molloy, E., & Boud, D. (2023). Assessment reform for the age of artificial intelligence. *Assessment & Evaluation in Higher Education, 48*(3), 357–370. DOI: 10.1080/02602938.2022.2130174

Kitchin, R. (2017). Thinking critically about and researching algorithms. *Information Communication and Society, 20*(1), 14–29. DOI: 10.1080/1369118X.2016.1154087

Mittelstadt, B., Allo, P., Taddeo, M., Wachter, S., & Floridi, L. (2016). The ethics of algorithms: Mapping the debate. *Big Data & Society, 3*(2), 1–21. DOI: 10.1177/2053951716679679

Selwyn, N. (2019). *Should robots replace teachers? AI and the future of education.* Polity Press.

Siemens, G., & Baker, R. S. (2012). Learning analytics and educational data mining: Towards communication and collaboration. In *Proceedings of the 2nd International Conference on Learning Analytics and Knowledge* (pp. 252–254). ACM. DOI: 10.1145/2330601.2330661

Williamson, B. (2017). Big data in education: The digital future of learning, policy and practice. *Sage (Atlanta, Ga.).* Advance online publication. DOI: 10.4135/9781529714920

Williamson, B., & Eynon, R. (2020). Historical threads, missing links, and future directions in AI in education. *Learning, Media and Technology, 45*(3), 223–235. DOI: 10.1080/17439884.2020.1798995

. **Zu**References for Section 4 (APA 7th Edition)

Bretag, T., Harper, R., Burton, M., Ellis, C., Newton, P., Rozenberg, P., Saddiqui, S., & van Haeringen, K. (2019). Contract cheating: A survey of Australian university students. *Studies in Higher Education, 44*(11), 1837–1856. DOI: 10.1080/03075079.2018.1462788

Coghlan, S., Miller, T., & Paterson, J. (2021). Good proctor or "Big Brother"? Ethics of online exam proctoring in higher education. *Ethics and Information Technology, 23*(3), 567–580. DOI: 10.1007/s10676-021-09576-1

Dawson, P., Bearman, M., Boud, D., Hall, M., & Molloy, E. (2020). Reframing assessment for a digital world. *Assessment & Evaluation in Higher Education, 45*(4), 519–533. DOI: 10.1080/02602938.2019.1646270

Foucault, M. (1977). *Discipline and punish: The birth of the prison.* Pantheon Books.

Gilliot, J.-M., & Hénaff, P. (2021). Surveillance technologies and academic integrity: A critical analysis of online proctoring systems. *European Journal of Open. Distance and E-Learning, 24*(1), 1–14.

Newton, P. M. (2016). Academic integrity: A quantitative study of confidence and understanding in students. *Studies in Higher Education, 41*(5), 1–17. DOI: 10.1080/03075079.2014.966111

Selwyn, N., & Gašević, D. (2020). The datafication of higher education: Discussing the promises and problems. *British Journal of Educational Technology, 51*(2), 527–540. DOI: 10.1111/bjet.12946

Sweeney, L. (2013). Discrimination in online ad delivery. *Communications of the ACM, 56*(5), 44–54. DOI: 10.1145/2447976.2447990

Whitley, B. E., & Keith-Spiegel, P. (2002). *Academic dishonesty: An educator's guide*. Lawrence Erlbaum Associates.

. boff, S. (2019). *The age of surveillance capitalism*. PublicAffairs.

. References for Section 5 (APA 7th Edition)

Benjamin, R. (2019). *Race after technology: Abolitionist tools for the new Jim code*. Polity Press.

Buolamwini, J., & Gebru, T. (2018). Gender shades: Intersectional accuracy disparities in commercial gender classification. *Proceedings of Machine Learning Research, 81*, 1–15.

Crenshaw, K. (1991). Mapping the margins: Intersectionality, identity politics, and violence against women of color. *Stanford Law Review, 43*(6), 1241–1299. DOI: 10.2307/1229039

Eubanks, V. (2018). *Automating inequality: How high-tech tools profile, police, and punish the poor*. St. Martin's Press.

Kizilcec, R. F., & Lee, H. (2022). Algorithmic fairness in education. *Educational Psychologist, 57*(1), 1–15. DOI: 10.1080/00461520.2021.1971742

Noble, S. U. (2018). *Algorithms of oppression: How search engines reinforce racism*. NYU Press. DOI: 10.18574/nyu/9781479833641.001.0001

Selwyn, N. (2022). *Education and technology: Key issues and debates* (2nd ed.). Bloomsbury Academic. DOI: 10.5040/9781350145573

UNESCO. (2021). *AI and education: Guidance for policymakers*. UNESCO Publishing.

Williamson, B., & Hogan, A. (2020). Commercialisation and privatisation in/of education in the context of Covid-19. *Journal of Education Policy, 35*(4), 487–507. DOI: 10.1080/02680939.2020.1752031

Zhao, Y., Ni, Y., Zhou, R., & Wu, S. (2021). Accessibility and inclusion challenges in AI-based educational systems. *Computers & Education, 168*, 104195. DOI: 10.1016/j.compedu.2021.104195

. References for Section 6 (APA 7th Edition)

Ananny, M., & Crawford, K. (2018). Seeing without knowing: Limitations of the transparency ideal and its application to algorithmic accountability. *New Media & Society, 20*(3), 973–989. DOI: 10.1177/1461444816676645

Burrell, J. (2016). How the machine "thinks": Understanding opacity in machine learning algorithms. *Big Data & Society, 3*(1), 1–12. DOI: 10.1177/2053951715622512

Floridi, L., Cowls, J., Beltrametti, M., Chatila, R., Chazerand, P., Dignum, V., Luetge, C., Madelin, R., Pagallo, U., Rossi, F., Schafer, B., Valcke, P., & Vayena, E. (2018). AI4People An ethical framework for a good AI society: Opportunities, risks, principles, and recommendations. *Minds and Machines*, *28*(4), 689–707. DOI: 10.1007/s11023-018-9482-5 PMID: 30930541

Kitchin, R. (2017). Thinking critically about and researching algorithms. *Information Communication and Society*, *20*(1), 14–29. DOI: 10.1080/1369118X.2016.1154087

Mittelstadt, B., Russell, C., & Wachter, S. (2019). Explaining explanations in AI. *Proceedings of the ACM Conference on Fairness, Accountability, and Transparency*, 279–288. https://doi.org/DOI: 10.1145/3287560.3287574

Pasquale, F. (2015). *The black box society: The secret algorithms that control money and information*. Harvard University Press. DOI: 10.4159/harvard.9780674736061

Selwyn, N., & Gašević, D. (2020). The datafication of higher education: Discussing the promises and problems. *British Journal of Educational Technology*, *51*(2), 527–540. DOI: 10.1111/bjet.12946

Veale, M., & Edwards, L. (2018). Clarity, surprises, and further questions in the GDPR's "right to explanation". *Computer Law & Security Review*, *34*(2), 398–404. DOI: 10.1016/j.clsr.2017.12.002

Wachter, S., Mittelstadt, B., & Floridi, L. (2017). Why a right to explanation of automated decision-making does not exist in the General Data Protection Regulation. *International Data Privacy Law*, *7*(2), 76–99. DOI: 10.1093/idpl/ipx005

Williamson, B. (2017). Big data in education: The digital future of learning, policy and practice. *Sage (Atlanta, Ga.)*. Advance online publication. DOI: 10.4135/9781529714920

Chapter 5
Redesigning Authentic Assessment and Feedback Practices in the Generative AI Era

Sushil Bhardwaj
http://orcid.org/0000-0001-5184-3866
RIMT University, Punjab, India

Sweta Rana
Chandigarh University, Punjab, India

Indu Sharma
http://orcid.org/0009-0001-9402-4702
Chandigarh University, Punjab, India

Rohit Markan
http://orcid.org/0000-0001-9525-422X
CGC University, Punjab, India

ABSTRACT

The rapid growth of Generative Artificial Intelligence in higher education has made assessment more complex. Its importance lies in protecting genuine learning and academic integrity in AI rich environments. The main objective of this chapter is to explain how assessment and feedback practices can be redesigned to measure real understanding instead of automated output. The chapter shows that authentic tasks, staged submissions, reflection, and oral interaction improve validity and fairness. Key findings suggest that formative feedback, clear AI guidelines, and process based evaluation strengthen integrity. The chapter concludes that thoughtful redesign helps institutions maintain standards while adapting to technological change.

DOI: 10.4018/979-8-3373-8939-4.ch005

INTRODUCTION

Higher education is experiencing rapid transformation due to digital technologies. Among these developments, Generative Artificial Intelligence (Ilieva et al., 2025) has emerged as one of the most influential innovations. AI tools can now generate essays, summaries, reports, programming code, research outlines, and reflective responses within seconds. These tools are available to students all over the web or on phones. Due to this, most academic practices which were previously stable have been subjected to scrutiny.

Assessment plays a central role in higher education. It determines the measurement of learning, the administration of grades and maintenance of standards. Effective assessment instruments are honest and they assist actual learning. Value of degrees is damaged in case there is no assurance of what students actually know. Generative AI causes individuals to fear more that the old forms of evaluation might be no longer estimating true learning (Luo et al., 2024). Written assignments, take-home tests and online submissions are used by many colleges to evaluate students. These were made in the time that we believed students did the work by themselves. It is now possible to get answers written by AI that appear to be well written and organized, raising questions about the person who did the work, who it is an original work or not, and the extent to which the student is a participant. However, Generative AI can also be good. It may assist the students to write, edit, translate, organize thoughts and explain difficult concepts. With responsible application, AI will be able to enhance learning in terms of quality and complexity.

Educators do not have to cease AI implementation; they simply have to alter the assessment procedures to ensure that they are just, useful, and aligned to learning objectives. Both authentic assessment and assessment for learning provide a good way forward. Authentic assessment deals with real life tasks, problem solving, reflection, and application of knowledge (Khlaif et al., 2025). As a means of assessment, assessment for learning provides a continuous feedback and encourages the growth and learning of students. Both are escaping mere memorizing to more understanding and development. They should however be re-engineered to be effective in case AI becomes prevalent (Molloy et al., 2020). This chapter examines the way assessment can be transformed to maintain quality, honesty and fairness in the era of Generative AI. The introduction of the chapter gives the larger context of digital change and new issues that high education confronts.

Novel Contribution of the Chapter

While there are many studies addressing the impact of GenAI in higher education, they have tended to focus on academic integrity, AI detection systems, or ethical considerations related to AI in education. A few fewer studies are those that have suggested a learning model of assessment redesign, formative feedback, academic integrity and authentic learning integrated in one. Fewer still studies have proposed a pedagogical framework that combines assessment redesign, formative feedback, academic integrity, and authentic learning in one. This chapter aims to fill this gap by proposing an integrated solution for the redesign of assessment systems appropriate to an AI-rich learning environment. The heart of this chapter is the holistic assessment redesign framework that integrates Authentic Assessment, Assessment for Learning, ongoing feedback mechanisms and ethical AI integration. This chapter challenges the traditional methods that focus on identifying AI-generated materials and instead proposes a design-based approach where the assessment itself becomes resistant to misuse of AI. The proposed framework involves teachers in moving away from evaluation based on products and towards one that addresses the process of the learning, reasoning, reflection, and collaborative growth, as well as the context of which the knowledge is applied. Another great feature is the hands-on approach taken in the chapter. Instead of abstract conceptual factors, the chapter offers frameworks for assessment, suggestions for implementation, redesign strategies and examples for each of the disciplines that can be adapted. Additionally, it emphasizes institutional duties for sustainable action, such as faculty development, policy creation, and AI literacy programs. The chapter builds on the body of recent research, introduces a novel conceptual framework for the discussion of assessment innovation, and provides concrete recommendations for higher education institutions looking to sustain academic integrity while capitalizing on the educational possibilities opened up by Generative AI.

Methodological Approach

This chapter utilizes a systematic narrative literature review (NNLR) methodology to synthesize the latest scholarly literature on the topics of Generative Artificial Intelligence, authentic assessment, formative assessment, academic integrity, and assessment redesign in higher education. The structured search was done in several scientific databases like Scopus, Web of Science, ERIC, IEEE Xplore, SpringerLink and Google Scholar. Search methodology included using combinations of the following keywords: Generative AI, Academic Integrity, Assessment Redesign, Assessment for Learning, Authentic Assessment, Feedback Practices, AI Literacy, and Artificial Intelligence in Higher Education. The timeframe for the publications was deliberately narrowed to the previous five years (2020-2026) in order to capture the most recent developments in Generative AI technologies, which have been evolving at a rapid pace. The literature selection process went through the following stages: identification of relevant publications, screening of publications based on the abstract and title, eligibility, full-text review of papers, and thematic synthesis. Studies which were only technically orientated to AI algorithms without educational relevance and did not include empirical or conceptual contributions to assessment were excluded. After the literature selection process, thematic analysis was used to analyse the identified literature. The key themes that came to the fore in the review were, AI-aided learning practices, Validity of assessment, Authentic assessment, Formative feedback, Academic integrity, Faculty preparedness, and Institutional policy. The integrated assessment redesign framework developed in this chapter was based on these themes.

The Emergence of Generative AI in Higher Education

Generative Artificial Intelligence refers to systems that can create new content based on patterns learned from large datasets. These systems use advanced language models that respond to user prompts and generate structured outputs (Bernabei et al., 2023). In educational contexts, text generation tools have received particular attention because of their ability to produce essays, research summaries, and analytical responses (Dai et al., 2026). The availability of these tools has changed student behavior. Instead of beginning assignments with independent drafting, some students may generate AI output and then edit or modify it. This shifts the learning process. In some cases, AI may reduce cognitive effort if students rely on it without engaging deeply with the material. In other cases, AI may function as a support system that assists brainstorming and revision.

Faculty members have expressed concerns about the reliability of written assignments. When AI can produce high quality responses, it becomes difficult to determine whether a submission reflects the student's understanding (Kickbusch et al., 2025). This uncertainty affects grading practices and academic trust. Some institutions have responded by adopting AI detection software. However, detection technologies are not fully reliable. They may incorrectly identify human written work as AI generated, or fail to detect modified AI content. Beyond technical challenges, the emergence of Generative AI has created ethical questions. Students may be uncertain about acceptable boundaries of AI use. Some may view AI as similar to a grammar checking tool, while others may use it to generate complete assignments. Without clear guidelines, confusion increases. Faculty members may also vary in their expectations, leading to inconsistency across departments.

The rapid integration of AI into educational environments reflects broader digital transformation (Henderson et al., 2025). Universities are preparing students for workplaces that increasingly incorporate automation and intelligent systems. Therefore, banning AI entirely may not align with professional realities. Instead, institutions must teach students how to use AI responsibly, critically, and ethically. This situation requires a shift in thinking. The central issue is no longer whether AI exists. The more important question is how assessment systems can measure genuine learning when AI tools are widely accessible. If assessment focuses only on final written output, it may fail to capture actual understanding. If assessment emphasizes reasoning, reflection, and contextual application, it becomes more resilient. Thus, the emergence of Generative AI creates both disruption and opportunity. It disrupts traditional assumptions about authorship and originality. It also provides an opportunity to rethink assessment in ways that strengthen learning and authenticity.

The Need for Assessment Redesign in the AI Era

Assessment redesign has become necessary because traditional models were developed under different technological conditions. Many conventional formats prioritize memorization, reproduction of information, and standardized responses. Such approaches were already being questioned before the arrival of AI. The presence of Generative AI has intensified these concerns.

Closed-book tests are examinations that test the memorization under time constraint. They cull AI cheating but prevent deeper involvement and creativeness. Take-home assignments enable free research, although they may be stuffed with text generated by AI. Online multiple-choice tests can only test the lowest level of knowledge, and not actual use or invention of new concepts. In AI-rich environments, the most difficult tasks to automate, such as context interpretation, personal reflection, collaboration, considerations of morality, and oral explanation, ought to be assessed. The presence of students describing their choices, justifying ideas, and reflecting on the learning process is more real. Fairness is also facilitated by redesigning assessment (Kickbusch et al., 2025). In case not all students can use AI extensively and some students do, grades may become skewed.

There are clear rules and tasks that minimize confusion. The students are to understand when it is good to use AI help and how to acknowledge it. Openness creates confidence between the teachers and learners. In addition, redesign is synonymous with contemporary educational aspirations. Colleges have become oriented at critical thinking, problem solving, communication, teamwork and flexibility. Real checks are appropriate to those objectives. They measure knowledge, use and judgment (Zhao et al., 2025). The methods of feedback should be modified. The old systems provide feedback following grading. During the process of making the task, assessment offers feedback continuously. This allows the students to get better gradually. Ethical use of tools and autonomous thinking should also be taught with regards to feedback in the AI age. Institutions must also act.

Regulations must provide direction in all places. Teacher training must make teachers understand AI strength and weaknesses. Newer assessment standards should be used in quality checks. Restructuring assessment does not eliminate rigor. It simply makes learning objectives congruent with assessment. It encourages futile thinking and not encoding. Colleges can maintain integrity by emphasizing learning processes without the sense of surveillance of students.

GENERATIVE AI AND ITS IMPACT ON HIGHER EDUCATION ASSESSMENT

Generative AI has brought a significant shift in universities. It influences the manner of learning by students, the way the teachers teach and the way the schools assess learners. Evaluation systems are being subjected to great pressure. They were prepared keeping in mind that written work demonstrates personal thinking of a student. Generative AI disrupts such a notion and requires careful examination (Bearman et al., 2024). This section explains what Generative AI is and its impact on the learning process of students, the issues it poses on the fair grading process, and the reasons why we should stop merely searching to cheat and reform our assessment methods.

Nature of Generative AI

Generative AI systems are designed to create new content by identifying patterns in large collections of data. These systems are trained using extensive text datasets and advanced machine learning models. When users provide prompts or instructions, the AI system generates responses that are grammatically correct, logically structured, and contextually relevant.

In higher education, text based AI tools are especially significant. They can produce a wide range of academic outputs, including: a) Essays and academic reports b) Literature summaries c) Coding solutions d) Research outlines e) Reflective responses and f) Case analysis. These tools are capable of organizing ideas into structured paragraphs, incorporating formal language, and presenting arguments in a coherent manner. In many cases, the generated responses appear academically sound. They often follow conventional formats, include introductions and conclusions, and use discipline specific terminology.

AI tools can be used by students on a variety of reasons. Others resort to them whenever they are stuck in writer block. There are those who rely on AI to correct grammar, make their writing clear or rearrange the text. The translation can also be assisted by AI, and thus the students will be able to speak their ideas easier in academic English. When it comes to technical subjects, AI can code or debug. Generative AI is attractive due to its flexibility. It is available at any time and provides prompt response. It does not require scheduling as well as it does not require response as is the case with normal help systems. This convenience has made it remain in use among more students. These systems, however, have significant issues too. AI does not actually comprehend the content as a human being. It responds using word patterns and not actual knowledge. That way the answers may appear well but without substance. Students who over use AI may not understand the concepts comprehensively. The key characteristic of Generative AI is that it yields results quickly and in a good fashion. This pace of testing disputes testing systems based on written work as evidence of learning.

Transformation of Student Learning Practices

The availability of Generative AI has influenced how students approach academic tasks. The process of normal learning begins with the students as they read, they search information, plan, write rough copy, revise, and edit. Each step takes thought. In so doing, students get to know how to think and comprehend. Work can be transformed due to the application of AI tools. Other students can even begin by making content using AI before writing a draft by themselves. They then revise or modify the output of AI to suit the assignment. This alters the manner in which learning occurs.

If students rely heavily on AI to produce complete responses, cognitive engagement may decrease. Writing is not only a method of communication but also a method of thinking. The students identify ideas, find connections and evaluate evidence when they formulate arguments themselves. In case AI provides the first argument, that reasoning may diminish. Excessive application of AI may cause superficial learning. Students may turn in a nice work without having to get the ideas. This develops a difference between their appearance and the familiarity with the material (Fischer et al., 2024). High grades may not translate to actual learning. At the same time, AI tools can be used constructively. When students use AI to clarify difficult concepts, generate practice questions, or receive explanations in simpler language, their understanding may improve. AI can function as a supplementary tutor. It can provide examples, suggest alternative perspectives, and assist revision (Kizilcec et al., 2024).

Generative AI has a primary impact on learning that relies on its integration into lessons. In the absence of a proper direction, students may turn to AI to complete the task, rather than studying (Weng et al., 2024). Through proper guidance, AI will be used to assist students with exploration and thinking further. New responsibilities are also placed on the teachers. They should demonstrate the responsible use of AI to the students. They should draw boundaries, encourage integrity, and create the activities that require individual input. The interconnection between technology and instruction gets more complex. Concisely, Generative AI has transformed the learning process of students by altering the sequence and level of cognition. Depending on the manner in which schools establish and direct its usage, it can assist or it can create troubles.

Challenges to Assessment Validity

Assessment validity refers to the degree to which an evaluation accurately measures intended learning outcomes. When AI systems can produce high quality written responses, the validity of traditional assessment formats becomes uncertain.

One of the main concerns is that it is difficult to understand who the author of the work is. Educators might not be in a position to judge the extent to which a paper is the original idea of the student. Authorship cannot be easily graded in case of ambiguity. We also cannot easily evaluate such capabilities as analysis and critical thinking unless we are aware of the person who generated ideas. Hidden AI help is another cause of concern. The students can make use of AI silently (Kizilcec et al., 2024). In case school rules are not explained, students might interpret AI use in various ways. Others understand AI as editing, whereas others have been utilizing it to compose the entire assignment. Such inconsistency renders grades unfair. Routine lack of transparency destroys confidence. When teachers believe that work is not original the relationship becomes strained. Excess suspicion will put the students on their toes. Conversely, lack of monitoring will result in cheating.

A great danger is shallow learning. Students can run risks of not developing the skills of generating their own thoughts in case they focus on AI text. The quality of the AI may then be judged by tests rather than the capability of the student. Achievement does not necessarily correspond to grades. Even without the necessary understanding, students that edit AI text properly can achieve high marks. Unless learners are avoiding AI, they may receive poor grades in case their writing is poor. This is unfair. Consumers are doubting the trustworthiness of home papers and unmonitored assignments. They used to be good methods of putting independent research and writing to test but today automation is posing them a threat. Thus, assessment validity has to be reconsidered. Educators need to enquire whether the existing methods actually gauge what they desire.

Moving from Detection to Redesign

Due to the increase in Generative AI, AI detection software became the initial one used in many schools. These tools attempt to predict the probability of a text being created by an AI. The detection systems are however not flawless. They will be able to confuse the work of humans and AI. They may also overlook AI texts that are carefully edited.

Detection alone cannot solve the underlying problem. Even if detection improves technically, students may find new ways to modify AI output. This creates a continuous cycle of adaptation between generation and detection tools. A more sustainable solution is assessment redesign. Rather than attempting to identify AI usage after submission, institutions should design tasks that require demonstration of understanding and reasoning during the learning process. Redesigned assessment may include a) Staged submissions that document progress b) Reflective explanations of decision making c) Oral presentations or viva sessions d) Context specific case analysis e) Collaborative projects with individual accountability

When assessment focuses on reasoning, interaction, and process documentation, it becomes more resilient. AI may still be used as a tool, but it cannot fully replace personal engagement. Replacing the pursuit of cheating with an adjustment of the manner of instruction also provides a more pleasant learning experience. Schools do not merely believe that students are cheating, but instill good morals. Learners are taught to use AI in a responsible manner rather than just being informed about the need not to abuse AI. This approach agrees that generative AI will remain in schools and work places. It is best to make students know how to use it responsibly rather than get rid of it. To the point, the system of college exams has been altered by generative AI. It challenges the ancient notions of authorship. It transforms the process of learning among students and makes individuals concern with the matters of fairness and truth. Still, it also offers the possibilities of new ideas. The schools can make learning real, honest and useful in our age of AI by abandoning the act of checking cheating in favor of intelligent redesigning.

UNDERSTANDING AUTHENTIC ASSESSMENT AND ASSESSMENT FOR LEARNING

The transformation caused by Generative Artificial Intelligence is that we should have a sound tenure of thoughts before we can develop more progressive testing practices. Two instructional strategies that can be used in this case include authentic assessment and assessment of learning (McGeechan et al., 2025). These concepts were developed many years before AI, yet they continue to provide us with effective instruments with which to address the modern issues. They make the emphasis not on memorization but on understanding the facts, application of the knowledge in actual circumstances and constant development (Nedungadi et al., 2024). True evaluation is founded on the notion that learning must be related to the actual life. The tests are effective when they do not only examine what students know, but they examine how they apply the same knowledge in real-life scenarios. In contrast to old tests into which the main task is to memorize the facts, authentic assessment requires the students to read a problem, use theory, make decisions, and justify their choices.

Concept and Principles of Authentic Assessment

Authentic assessment checks students by assigning to them tasks which are similar to real work, or real problems. It does not ask students to apply ideas based on their own descriptions, but rather asks them to use real situations. The activities may consist of reviewing case studies, fieldwork, project creation, solution design, policy brief writing, or research findings (Weng et al., 2024). Relevance is the major concept of authentic assessment. When students can observe how what they are familiar with can be applied in the outside world, then learning becomes more valuable to them. When students are dealing with actual or simulated real problems, they are forced to transform theory into actual action. That makes learning deeper. Authentic assessment requires students to apply what they know not merely repeat what is in the textbook. Students are forced to read, combine ideas in a variety of sources, and adjust their answers to the circumstances. These are tasks that require critical thinking and intelligence. Problem solving is important as students consider various alternatives as well as reflect on the outcomes prior to making a choice. Working together and talking is another essential component of authentic assessment. Most real work needs teams. So authentic tasks are typically characterized by group work in which students share a job. Nevertheless, every student should be accountable as well. Learners become more proficient speakers when they demonstrate outcomes, justify their reasoning behind that reasoning and respond to questions.

Authentic assessment includes reflection as an element. Students are expected to reflect on how they approached the task, what difficulties have they encountered and what they have learnt. Thinking reflection assists the students to get to know themselves and reflect on the learning. It allows one to evaluate the completed work as well as the path of learning. Authentic assessment is a combination of numerous abilities. Cognitive skills such as analysis and assessment are complemented with practical skills such as writing, presenting, teamwork and reasoning about right and wrong. This combination is comparable to real jobs in which a combination of a number of skills are utilized.

The layered nature of authentic assessment is illustrated in Figure 1.

Figure 1. Core Dimensions of Authentic Assessment

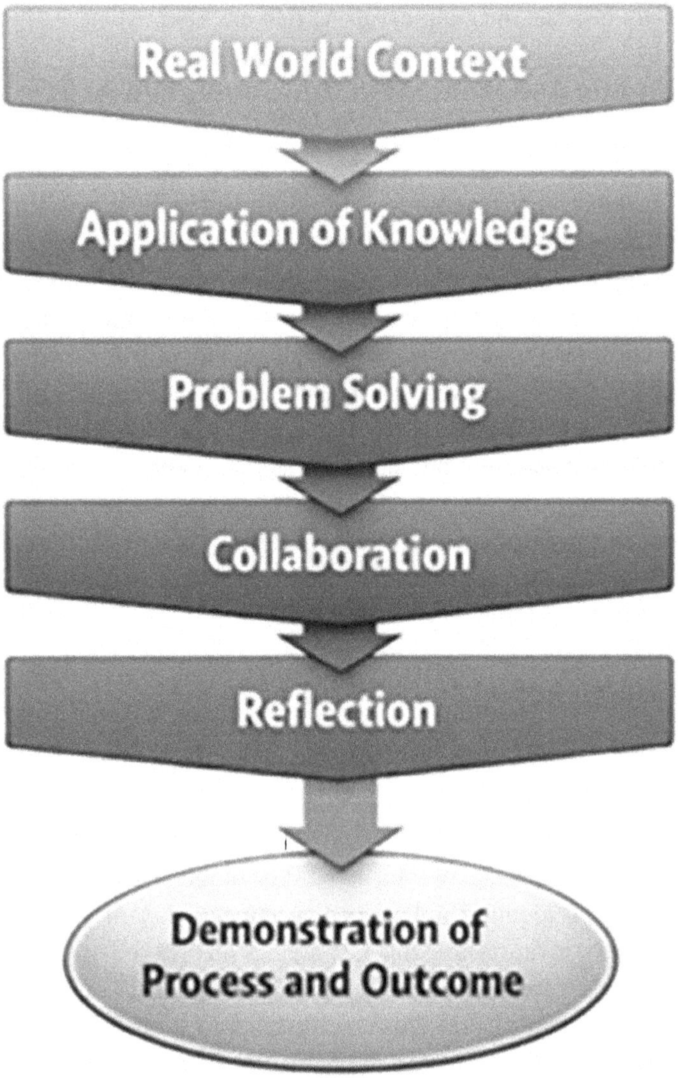

Figure 1 offers authentic assessment as a sequence. The first level points out the fact that meaningful evaluation commences with a real world context. In the absence of contextual basis, tasks are abstract and have no connection to the practical context. The second level entails knowledge application. Students should learn not to memorize but practically apply concepts in new contexts. This phase enhances knowledge transfer. Problem solving is emphasized in the third level. Students process information, find alternatives and make good decisions. The level of thought that is required in this stage is of a higher order. The fourth level brings about cooperation. Authentic tasks are characterized by peer interaction in many cases. Teamwork improves the ability to communicate and mutual responsibility. The fifth level is focused on reflection. Students assess the process of learning. Refraction enhances the comprehension and promotes constant improvement. The last level is an indication of process and result. Authentic assessment does not compare the completed work only. It also takes into account drafts, revisions, explanations, and discussions which expose the way learning took place. The figure indicates that authentic assessment is multidimensional. All the levels are based on each other. The combination of these dimensions forms a strong frame that does not become meaningless in AI rich environments.

Relevance of Authentic Assessment in the Generative AI Era

Authentic assessment is especially significant in the context of the Generative AI era since it makes one less vulnerable to automated content generation. AI systems can easily cope with generic essay prompts. Nonetheless, activities that involve situational adaptation, individualized reflection, and interpersonal elucidation involve human involvement. AI generated responses need to be modified significantly when students need to use the concepts to certain local situations or analyze the existing institutional scenario. In addition, oral presentation and thoughtful aspects render authorship transparent. Students are required to demonstrate their arguments live, and this enhances integrity. The concept of authentic assessment is also in line with the requirements of the modern higher education (Lee et al., 2024). Institutions strive to produce graduates able to think, communicate and adjust to complex settings. Such outcomes can not be quantified using mere rote memorization tests. Nonetheless, valid evaluation must be effectively designed. Task development must be guided by clear learning outcomes. The measures of evaluation must be clear. In the absence of structured rubrics grading can be inconsistent. Training of the faculty is necessary to bring fairness and reliability.

Concept and Principles of Assessment for Learning

Assessment of learning is a form of formative assessment where evaluation is encompassed in the teaching and learning process (Peterson et al.,2025). It does not aim at giving grades but at increasing understanding and facilitating improvement. The style is focused on feedback as a developmental instrument. Clear learning outcomes are conveyed at the start of the instruction in assessment to learning. Students have a sense of what is required and performance measurement. Clear standards decrease misunderstanding and enhance motivation. Feedback strategies are offered at various levels as opposed to the end of submission. Learners are advised on their strengths and areas of improvement. They have the chances to improve and correct their work. This repetitive application enhances the expertise. Learning assessment involves the use of self assessment and peer assessment (Ncube et al., 2026). Students gain responsibility and analytical skills when they review their work or give feedback to their classmates. They are made to be active members of the evaluation process. In the Generative AI scenario, learning assessment assists teachers to see the progress instead of final products alone. The process of learning can be seen through draft submissions, classroom discussions, and interactive feedback sessions. Although AI tools can be utilized, teachers can also track how learners process and learn information.

Integration of Authentic Assessment and Assessment for Learning

Authentic assessment and assessment for learning complement each other. Authentic tasks provide meaningful contexts, while formative feedback ensures continuous development. When combined, they create a comprehensive framework for resilient assessment.

As an example, a project based assignment may be organised into stages. Students can start with a proposal, which describes the goals and the approach. Teachers give feedback to help in refinement. A preliminary report is provided and consulted. Collaborative improvement is promoted through peer feedback. Reflection and presentation is done after final submission. This design allows learning not to be restricted to one submission. The process becomes open. Learners exhibit activity at every level. AI can help in the form of drafting or organizing, however, reasoning and insights have to be presented through engagement and reflections. Ethical awareness is also facilitated through integration. Students adopt responsible habits when expectations of the use of AI are clearly stated and deliberated on during the feedback sessions. They do not conceal AI support but instead get to know how to accept and explain its usage.

An Integrated AI-Resilient Assessment Framework

As Generative AI is becoming more pervasive, assessment models need to maintain the integrity of the academic enterprise, foster meaningful learning, and respect the legitimate educational uses of AI technologies. Assessment practices that address these goals often do so separately. In contrast, authentic assessment is concerned with real-world problem solving, assessment for learning is concerned with ongoing feedback, and institutional integrity policies are primarily focused on ethical behavior. But these dimensions need to work as one in an AI rich environment to be effective. In this regard, the Integrated AI-Resilient Assessment Framework (IARAF) is suggested in this chapter. There are 5 interrelated components in the framework. The first aspect concentrates on the clear learning outcomes, which establish what the students are expected to know, be able to do and act ethically. The second component includes authentic learning activities set in realistic contexts and allows students to try to use theory and not copy information. The third component features staged assessment, which involves making proposals, drafting, peer review, formative feedback, reflective journals and oral defence, allowing teachers to see how things are unfolding in learners' work and not just the end product. The fourth adds the concept of academic integrity with the rules of disclosure, reflection, and rules of institutions about the use of AI. Lastly, institutional support, such as faculty development, AI literacy initiatives, digital infrastructure, and policy frameworks, fosters an environment that enables sustainable implementation. The proposed framework isn't a negative one, but rather a positive one that considers AI as a learning support tool – with an appropriate assessment design, the value of AI in learning is significant. Pedagogy, ethics, and institutional governance are woven together in a single framework that offers a practical roadmap for universities to develop resilient, equitable and future-ready assessment systems.

Reflection as a Bridge Between Learning and Integrity

Reflection serves as a bridge between authentic assessment and assessment for learning. Reflective practices promote reflection among the students. They can describe the way they understood instructions, chosen resources, order of arguments, and feedback reactions. Disclosure of technological assistance can also be part of the reflection in AI supported environments. Students can explain how they used AI technologies to generate ideas or edit and clarify what intellectual contributions they had made independently. This kind of transparency leads to trust and ethical accountability. Long term learning is also facilitated by reflection. Metacognitive awareness is enhanced when the students are able to express their thought processes. Such awareness increases flexibility and problem resolution in different future situations.

LIMITATIONS OF TRADITIONAL ASSESSMENT MODELS IN AI RICH ENVIRONMENTS

Conventional frameworks are structurally weak. These are weaknesses that existed prior to the introduction of Generative Artificial Intelligence, but the influence has been amplified by AI (Page et al., 2024). The assessment systems that have been designed over the previous decades were based on the premise that written work was an indicator of independent intellectual work. This is not an automatic assumption in the AI rich environments. Consequently, a number of weaknesses of conventional assessment models have been more transparent and more prominent.

Focus on Final Output

Most of the tests consider only the finished work. The learners turn in a finished essay, report, assignment or project and are evaluated based on that one piece. The idea development process, decisions to conduct research, drafting, revision, and reflection usually remain unseen. This product oriented approach does not allow the educator to know the way learning took place. This drawback is worse in AI rich environments. Final outputs with the help of generative AI systems can be produced in a short period. It is possible to create a well structured essay in a matter of seconds with an introduction, argument development and conclusion. When evaluation is based on the finished written work, it is hard to rely on the perspective of whether the work is based on real knowledge or mechanical help. Product based appraisal can thus turn out to be inadequate. It gauges what is presented, but not the way it was created. Assessment validity is compromised without the view of the learning process. The grades can be an indication of the quality of created text and not the student understanding. Besides, students can become too efficient and not engaged once they understand that the bottom line is what counts. The educational process is turned into transactional. Students can find the quickest path to a finished paper instead of spending time analyzing and reflecting on it. This changes the aim of learning to intellectual development to completion of tasks. To overcome this shortcoming, evaluation should entail process evidence. The way ideas developed can be identified in draft submissions, progress reports, reflective explanations and oral interactions. These design modifications minimize the reliance on the final product evaluation.

Limited Engagement with Higher Order Thinking

Standard essays and written examinations often emphasize explanation rather than evaluation or creation. Students may be asked to describe theories, summarize concepts, or explain established frameworks. While these tasks test understanding, they may not require advanced analytical reasoning.

Generative AI models are particularly effective at producing descriptive and explanatory responses. They are able to arrange information in a logical manner, to give examples as well as to write in formal academic style. In cases where the job of the assessment tasks involves description, the responses provided by AI can be considered satisfactory. The objectives of higher education include the development of the skills of higher order of thinking i.e. critical thinking, synthesis of ideas, creative problem solving, and ethical thinking (Xia et al., 2024). These dimensions are not necessarily emphasized in traditional formats. During questions, a repetition of the knowledge in the textbook may be promoted instead of the independent interpretation. This is further amplified in AI rich environments. When there is no need in assessment to require originality, reasoning in a situation, or to justify the findings, automated systems can be used to reproduce what is expected. That line between real critical thought and produced description is lost. Hence, evaluation should not be confined to mere elaboration. The work must be the tasks that involve analyzing options, comparing viewpoints, generalizing theories on new situations, and justifying them. Assessment is more resilient when the criteria to evaluate are focused on the depth and the justification of the analysis.

Standardized Questions

AI systems are more capable of responding to repetitive or predictable questions. Most of the traditional tests involve standard prompts that do not vary with a few academic years. These prompts usually take a standard form, i.e., "Discuss the advantages and disadvantages" or "Explain the following concepts." Generic prompts elicit generic responses. Generative AI systems are conditioned with a large amount of data that contains comparable academic frameworks. In instances where the questions are not contextually specific, AI generated answers can be very similar to those that are to be obtained by the student. Standardization helps in maintaining consistency and comparability. Nevertheless, too much standardization minimizes complexity. It might not be as representative of the reality of the world issues. Predictable question patterns make use of AI rich environments more susceptible to automated generation. The second issue is that standardized questions might not take into consideration the local or modern developments. AI systems are also capable of giving generalized explanations, though they do not reflect institution specifics unless asked to do so. When it is needed to evaluate using a local case study, contemporary events or discipline-specific scenarios then it is harder to use generic automation. In order to address this shortage, there must be contextual variation in the design of assessment. These questions must demand that students connect concepts and particular cases, dissect what has recently happened or use their knowledge to situations that are unique to them. Context specific prompts decrease the use of formulaic responses.

Isolation from Real Context

Theoretical questions disconnected from practical application are more vulnerable to automation. When tasks remain abstract, students may treat them as exercises in academic writing rather than opportunities for meaningful learning.

Traditional examinations often separate theory from practice. Students are able to acquire definitions and models, but they might not need to demonstrate how such concepts can be applied to a real life situation. This division cripples the capacity to apply what they are learning elsewhere. In locations where AI is abundant, absence of reality is dangerous. AI is capable of generating explanations that are good since it reads numerous texts. But application of theory in a specific local scenario requires more profound thought. Ineffective assessments are those that associate a study with a real problem. In case the tasks deal with community concerns, business cases, field data or group work among subjects, students will have to be active. This physical foundation enhances the comprehension and makes it difficult to replace AI. The lack of actual context diminishes motivation in students as well. When assessment appears to be unrelated to professional life, there is a loss of interest. Conversely, real tasks make the students feel a sense of ownership and responsibility.

Table 1. Traditional Assessment and AI Resilient Assessment Comparison

Dimension	Traditional Approach	AI Resilient Approach
Evaluation Focus	Final written product	Process and reasoning
Question Type	Generic theoretical	Context specific applied
Feedback Timing	After grading	Continuous and formative
Integrity Strategy	Detection based	Design based prevention
Student Role	Passive responder	Active problem solver

REDESIGNING AUTHENTIC ASSESSMENT IN THE GENERATIVE AI ERA

Redesigning assessment should be scheduled and planned. The emergence of Generative AI should not imply that we should relinquish academic standards. Rather, we must make judgments more viable in order to gauge actual learning, thought, and engagement. Redesign is not a response to fear. It is a cautious instructional method which aligns assessments with the contemporary digital reality (Bearman et l., 2022). Real evaluations provide a solid foundation to this re-design. Nevertheless, actual tests must be established thoroughly. Without clear rules and methods of doing it, the new assessments may fail or be skewed. This section presents simple guidelines on design and basic models that ensure stronger learning in the locations dominated by AI.

Foundational Design Principles

Redesigning authentic assessment begins with core pedagogical principles. These standards ensure that assessment remains connected with learning objectives and maintains academic integrity (Bittle, 2025).

The first principle is alignment between the assessment and learning outcomes. The skills a course desires to develop should be directly tested in the process of assessment. When a course seeks students to think critically, solve a problem or even think about ethics, then the tasks that are assigned in the assessment must require it. Good alignment prevents light, superficial work that may be performed automatically.

The second principle is to look at both the process (and the product) in the end. The process of learning is a developmental process. Assessment that merely examines the outcome in the end will fail to capture the most important actions in cognition. It is all made clear when records of the process, such as drafts, notes, or descriptions of techniques, are added. It also demonstrates the process of thinking and transformation of ideas by students. The third principle is introducing reflection. Reflection is used to enable the student to reflect on her/his own learning (Khlaif et al., 2025). The students can learn more when they describe the way they tackled a task, the challenges they encountered, and the decisions they made. The thinking about the ethics in the AI-utilized environments also allows the students to think. The fourth principle is the staged submissions. Assessment can be divided into distinct steps as opposed to a single end product. All the stages allow teachers to track, provide feedback, and allow the students to revise. The staged tests reduce possibilities of automation in the last moment and maintain a constant learning process. Oral or interactive parts are added in the fifth principle. Brief discussions, viva voices or classroom discussions allow teachers to ensure that they have been understood. Conversing enables students to expound and put questions across board. The sixth principle establishes clear rules of AI use. Students must be aware of when to use AI tools and how. Clarity reduces the chances of confusion and promotes responsible usage. Guidelines must be set between useful application, such as grammatical checking, and actual thinking. The seventh principle is accountable teamwork. Group work depicts actual work environments, yet the role of individual persons should be observed. The presence of a transparent peer-review procedure and assigned roles contributes to its fairness. All these guidelines develop a robust assessment designing structure. They shift attention towards observation to substantial participation.

Project Based Assessment

One of the most appropriate methods to test learning during the Generative AI era is project based assessment. Projects are like real work activities and requires constant effort. Depending on the topic, they may include research, design, analysis, new ideas or problem solving. Projects unlike short essays take weeks or months. Students are forced to make a goal, gather facts, process the received information and present findings. Long time working on them lessens the reliance on a single output. As a rule, a good project is initiated by a proposal. Here students illustrate their subject, objectives, the way it will be done, and what students anticipate. It helps the teachers to review the proposal and confirm that it is original and offer early advice. The second one is literature mapping. Relevant theories, previous researches, or background that is of interest survive among students. Mapping indicates that they have studied scholarly materials and develop a strong conceptual background. Then there is a draft review. Students send early drafts. Teachers provide feedback about the structure, the arguments and the level of clarity of the methods. This is done to enhance the work prior to the end version (Tensen, 2025). The last deliverable is the completion of the project. At this stage, students will provide a completed analysis or solution. Nevertheless, the stage of the judge examines previous stages as well. Reflection notes serve to check students. They describe the way in which they planned the project, what modifications they have made and what they have learned. A presentation through oral presentation makes it real. Students provide their results and respond to questions. This allows teachers to have an idea of how they are well-informed outside of writing. Projects must have consistent participation and accountability. They assist in connecting theory and practice (Page et al., 2024). AI technology can be used to arrange the facts or make writing simpler, yet the entire process requires human evaluation and background.

Case Based Assessment

Case-based assessment requires the student to have a critical examination of particular cases. Those cases may either be based in the local schools, country or globally. They could present business issues, policy discussions, technical malfunctions, ethical dilemmas or social issues. Case tasks require students to apply theory to real life situations. They have to read the facts, locate appropriate ideas, consider various options, and justify their decision. It is important to think independently and make arguments. Case-based assessment is less dangerous in the environment with the prevalence of AI since it demands the information that is appropriate to the case. Generic response may not correspond with the facts. Students are forced to make critical thoughts regarding the information provided. An example is in the field of management where a case concerning a regional company being experiencing leadership conflict should have solutions that are suitable to the situation. In engineering, technical diagnosis is required in a case concerning the failure of a system. A case on curriculum change in education requires a policy review. Written reports and classroom debate can be used in case discussions. Students clarify ways in which they think and respond to what peers say. This renders the learning to become real. Good case materials are required to evaluate a good case. The teachers should maintain the cases simple, pertinent and connected with what the students are to learn. The ability to think logically, apply proofs, and describe should be graded as opposed to the length of the description.

Portfolio Assessment

Portfolio evaluation is a collection of student work over time. It is geared towards development and revision as opposed to a single test. Early drafts, revised work, record of peer feedback, teacher comments and reflective notes can all be included in portfolios (Usher, 2025). The primary benefit of portfolio assessment is that it examines progression across time. Students demonstrate the way of how they cognize things. The educators are able to observe the way the feedback made the students improve. The entire process is presented in portfolios in AI-assisted settings. When students work with AI tools, the modifications to drafts indicate the level of engagement. The reflection notes can document the assistance of AI to organize or edit. Portfolios are good with topics that appreciate innovation, writing, design or research. They assist students to continue learning and be responsible. But portfolios require good direction. Rules shall be used to clarify how the content, order, and reflection should be. Frequent reviews maintain the pace and prevent last-minute work.

Figure 2. Authentic Assessment Redesign Framework

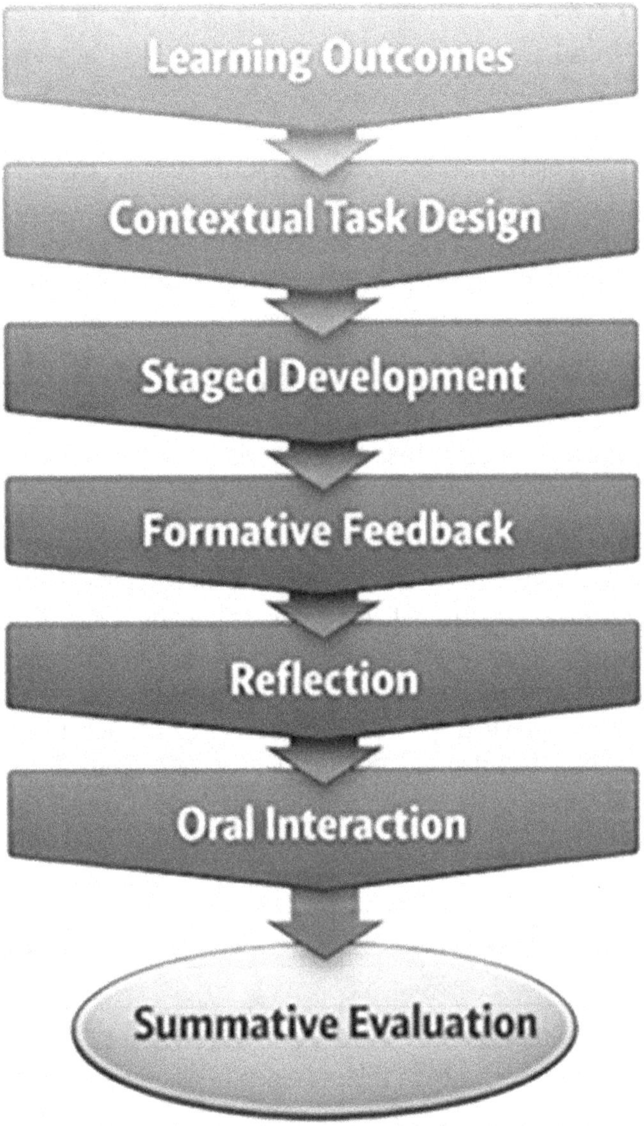

The steps of the new authentic assessment have been depicted in Figure 2. The plan also begins with specific learning objectives. In case the goals are not well stated, the evaluation will be in no direction. The second step is to model tasks which are real life. Theory should be connected to real situations in the tasks. The work becomes more meaningful in context and will not be as easily fooled by automation. The third one will be to construct the assessment phase by phase. The given test is divided into parts, which makes it easier and more interesting. Following that we provide formative feedback. Feedback should also be aimed at assisting the learners to become better but not to judge them. The last stage preceding the judgment is reflection. Reflecting enables the learners to think over morals and comprehend better.

Oral communication will allow learners to describe their work and ensure that they have understood. Last but not the least, the summative evaluation synthesizes all the evidences of the previous steps. This is a step that makes the assessment more valid and authentic.

Oral Defense and Viva

Short interactive sessions confirm understanding. Oral defenses allow them to describe their thought process and the way they respond to abrupt questions. These sessions can be short. A couple of minutes are enough to show the extent of their understanding of the content. Oral sections enhance integrity since students have to recite their thoughts out loud. When there is a discrepancy between what they write and what they say, differences are evident. Communication is also enhanced by the Viva sessions. Students get to know how to justify their arguments and speak in an academic manner. This is in line with expectations of the employers. In order to make it fair, the teachers must have clear question plans and apply the identical grading rules. Being open stops bias.

Reflective Components

Reflection brings work into reality and makes it honest. Students share the way they approached the task, resources they used and strategies they applied. Reflection may refer to the assistance of tech when AI is applied. Students are able to indicate the tools they used and how AI assisted them. They will be in a position to demonstrate what they needed to reflect. They are able to tell what they learned not necessarily through the machine. Transparency builds trust between the students and teachers. Reflection shifts focus from suspicion to responsibility. It encourages ethical integration rather than hidden dependence. Reflective writing will also enable the students to reflect on the way they learn (Urzúa et al., 2025). They explore what they have done good and what they can do better. This keeps them growing.

Table 2. Example Structure of Redesigned Authentic Assessment

Dimension	Traditional Approach	AI Resilient Approach
Stage 1	Proposal	Confirm Originality
Stage 2	Draft Submission	Monitor Development
Stage 3	Feedback Session	Guide Improvement
Stage 4	Final Project	Evaluate Outcome
Stage 5	Reflection	Assess Understanding
Stage 6	Oral Defense	Validate Engagement

A staged assessment redesigning model is presented in Table 2. Stage 1 is when you offer a proposal that makes it clear that your work is original and what direction you are going to. Stage 2 is one in which you hand in a draft in order to track its progress. The third stage is where you get systematic feedback to help you improve. Stage 4 will be the final project assessment. Stage 5 involves reflection in order to determine the extent of understanding. Stage 6, is oral defence to ensure your engagement and line of reasoning. It is a structure that integrates process monitoring and feedbacks and interaction. It minimizes the usage of evaluation of the final product and enhances authenticity.

Illustrative Institutional Case Study

For an illustration of how assessment redesign might occur in an institution, look at the following scenario. A multi-disciplinary university saw a tremendous rise in the amount of students using Generative AI tools to finish written assignments. Students were unclear on what was acceptable for AI to be used for, and faculty members were feeling uncertain about who the author is. The university took a new approach to assessment, instead of only using AI-detection software, they opted for a redesign approach. The traditional assignments were replaced by multi-stage authentic assessments which included the following: project proposals, literature mapping, draft submissions, formative feedback sessions, reflective learning journals, and oral presentations. Students had to report on the use of AI tools at every phase and clarify what were their own ideas and contributions. Professional learning was provided to faculty in the areas of AI literacy, designing authentic assessments, and formative feedback. The institutional policies clearly separated between the use of AI to help student with acceptable activities (such as grammar checking, brainstorm and translating supports) and the use of AI to produce work without critical engagement as an unacceptable practice. Implementing the intervention led to an increase in teachers' confidence when assessing authentic learning and increased student engagement in reflection and reasoning and collaborative learning. The university has not tried to do away with AI in the learning environment, but rather it has been able to integrate AI into the assessment process, while maintaining transparency, continuous feedback and process-based assessment. The following case is illustrative, but does illustrate how assessment redesign can enhance academic integrity and foster responsible AI use in higher education.

REDESIGNING FEEDBACK PRACTICES FOR LEARNING AND INTEGRITY

Good assessment also involves feedback. In most universities, the feedback follows a grade issued. The students submit their work, the teachers mark them, and subsequently provide written comments. It is only a little helpful, and does not give one the chance of learning everything. Feedback should be altered in the new age of Generative AI. The latter should assist students to think more, comprehend how ethics, and not rely heavily on automatic tools. A shift in the manner of providing feedback implies a shift in the role of feedback. It must not just describe the manner in which the grade was determined. Rather it must enable the students to develop as they learn. It is beneficial when feedback is provided continuously, in the form of a dialogue, and makes students to think, in order to remain authentic and full of integrity.

From Summative Comments to Developmental Guidance

Traditional feedback practices are often summative. Comments are provided after final submission, and opportunities for revision may be limited. In such systems, students may focus primarily on marks rather than improvement. Feedback may be read briefly and then ignored.

A large number of AI tools make students seek assistance immediately when they wait to get feedback. Unless they receive timely assistance of teachers, they will spend a lot of time using AI to comprehend assignments or make alterations in drafts. This is capable of restricting actual discussions with teachers. The new feedback techniques should be aimed at supporting the students during their work. The feedback must occur at every stage of a task. Students can also improve gradually when they receive comments during the process of writing a proposal, creating a draft, or revising it. This assists them in the process of understanding. Developmental feedback also reduces anxiety. Students recognize that learning is an ongoing process rather than a one time judgment. In this context, assessment becomes collaborative rather than adversarial.

Characteristics of Effective Feedback in the AI Era

The AI-supported feedback has to possess some major characteristics. It must be fast, clear, useful and be in line with the learning objectives. It is helpful because of quick feedback. When the feedback is immediate after the work of the student or during a project, the student can utilize it immediately. Comments made too late become powerless. Clear feedback matters too. Words that are vague such as make it better, explain more etc do not help. Good feedback demonstrates the student what is good and may be improved and provides particular means of improvement. A friendly voice is an attitude-enhancer. Feedback must include a statement of what the student did in a good manner as well as indicate areas through which the student can improve. The affirming language creates trust. Association between feedback and learning goals makes it significant. The feedback must be in reference to the course objectives and the grading criteria. Once students understand how the comments relate to what they are to learn then those changes that they make become significant. Feedback in the Generative AI age should also speak about responsible usage of technology. In case the use of an AI tool is permitted, teachers can demonstrate to students the application of the tool in a morally sound manner. In case of the risk of cheating, learning goals rather than punishment should be discussed.

Dialog Based Feedback

The feedback change is significant as dialog based feedback is a significant change as compared to the old one-way feedback. It may not just be written notes but an actual back and forth communication between the teacher and the student. This conversation may occur in classroom checks-in, in an online meeting or formal feedback. Students are able to pose questions and clarify. Educators are able to probe into the decision-making process. Feedback is more transparent through dialog based feedback. It reduces the misunderstanding of the comments. Communicating, in the context of AI support, enables teachers to understand how students went about tasks and what assistance they utilized. Accountability is also enhanced through this strategy. The truth can be seen when students demonstrate their reasoning aloud. Conversation fosters respect to each other and lowers suspicions. Dialog based feedback requires time though. It is necessary to ensure that schools offer sufficient resources as well as maintain manageable sizes of classes.

Peer Feedback and Collaborative Learning

Another factor in new feedback methods is peer feedback. When students are able to see the work of other students and examine it with definite criteria they are able to learn how to think and judge. Peer review ensures that students remain engaged in rules of grading. Peer feedback clarifies in AI-rich environments. Students have various perspectives in performing tasks. Instead, they are taught to identify originality, continuity and the extent of thought. Peer feedback must have rules in order to be effective. Students should be aware of what to consider and how to make useful remarks. A lack of structure may result in shallow peer review. Teamwork is also created through peer feedback. It reduces isolation and forms a community of academics. Students feel more accountable when they are aware that their work would be inspected by their fellow students.

AI Assisted Feedback: Opportunities and Boundaries

Generative AI can assist teachers in providing feedback in a fast manner. AI can quickly outline student work, identify what can be improved, and identify issues with the style in which it is written. This can reduce the workload that the teacher is required to undertake in large classes. However, AI feedback is not to be substituted with the teacher judgment. Computer remarks are out of context. They may not pay attention to the regulations of a certain subject or to the requirements of one learner. Be training as an assistant with teacher in charge. Teachers may view the AI recommendations and modify them to comply with the school regulations. Students can also have AI assistance in editing their writings. The students can apply AI to locate grammar errors or get suggestions on what can be changed. This aids in language aptitudes when applied in a prudent manner. Clear guidelines are essential. Students should be aware that AI feedback cannot replace independent thinking. The last piece of work should remain with the student as teachers should emphasize.

The Feedback Loop Model

Redesigned feedback practices can be visualized through a feedback loop model that integrates multiple stages of learning.

Figure 3. Feedback Loop in the Generative AI Era

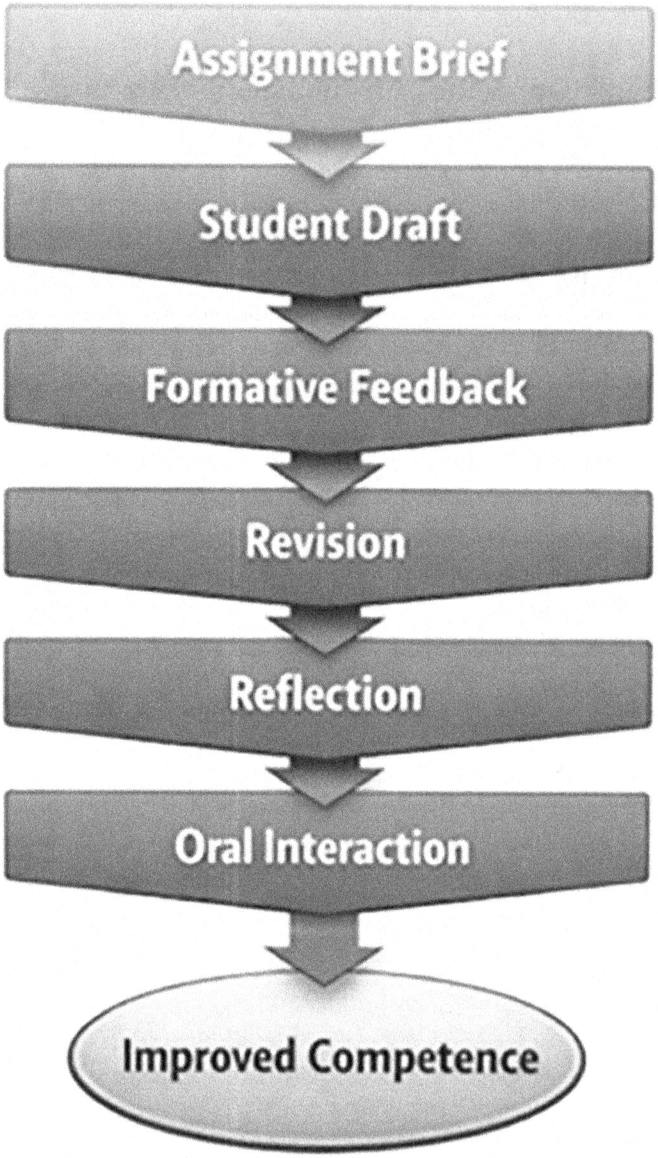

Figure 3 illustrates feedback as a continuous cycle rather than a single event. The process begins with a clear assignment brief that defines expectations and criteria. Students then write a draft. This is the stage where they will be provided with non-formative assessment. The teachers or peers provide feedback and it is geared towards improvement. Students revise their work depending on the feedback. This is an indication of their working and engagement. Having revised, the students consider what and why it changed. This assists them in self-knowledge of learning. There can be a face-to-face conversation to clarify thinking and ensure that all people are on board. This makes things clear. The final product is improved abilities, not only a grade. The cycle emphasizes expansion more than evaluation.

Feedback and Academic Integrity

Feedback is used to maintain academic honesty. Students that are assisted and mentored are less likely to cheat. In case teachers are not clear or too strict on students, it may result in cheating. Clarity of feedback provides students with a clue of what is expected. They get an idea of what a good job is. They are taught that they will improve through efforts, but not cheating. Where AI is extensively used, it is possible to have feedback about how to use technology in an ethical way. Teachers will be able to demonstrate the examples of good and bad usage of tech. Rather than applying just software that would detect cheating, schools would develop a culture of responsibility. When we speak of honesty when we provide feedback, then we make honesty a component of learning rather than simply rules that are implemented.

Institutional Support for Feedback Redesign

Redesigning feedback practices requires institutional commitment. Faculty development programs should train educators in formative assessment techniques and AI literacy (Lye et al., 2024). Digital platforms should support staged submissions and interactive communication.

Workload policies must recognize the time required for meaningful feedback. Without structural support, even well designed feedback models may become impractical (Urzúa et al., 2025). Institutions should also develop consistent guidelines regarding AI usage in feedback. Transparency ensures fairness across departments.

ACADEMIC INTEGRITY AND ETHICAL ASSESSMENT DESIGN

Academic integrity is a foundational principle of higher education. It reflects honesty, responsibility, fairness, and trust in scholarly work. In the Generative AI era, academic integrity requires renewed attention. The availability of AI tools that can generate sophisticated academic content has complicated traditional understandings of authorship and originality. Institutions must therefore rethink integrity not only as a matter of detection and punishment but as a matter of design, education, and culture.

Ethical assessment design presupposes a crucial role in such metamorphosis. When carefully designed assessment systems, these will reduce the chances of academic malpractice and encourage responsible academic behavior. Instead of focusing solely on the detection of transgressions, organizations can avoid them by the encouragement of candor, openness, and the material involvement.

Redefining Academic Integrity in the AI Context

Traditional understandings of academic integrity preempt the prevention of plagiarism, cheating and fabrication. These can still be relevant, but the emergence of generative artificial intelligence creates new complications. Generative AI systems have the ability to generate text that is inherently original and can not be classified as a text of one specific origin, making the plagiarism detection systems in place ineffective. Integrity issues in the case of AI should include the problem of authorship, attribution and transparency. The amount of interaction that can be used by a student should be outlined when using AI assistance. The institutional rules must explain how this kind of help should be recognized and define the line after which AI help is viewed as a replacement of the intellectual effort of the student himself. The redefinition of the parameters of integrity does not imply a decline in the standards in academic practices; more so, it presupposes a clear definition of expectations. Universities should formalize the responsible use of AI in academic work. The policies must clarify the types of AI aid that can be had, including linguistic assistance or ideation aid, and categorize them explicitly as permissible and prohibited, e.g. submission of entirely AI-generated work without substantive student involvement. Foresight eliminates confusion. When learners are made aware of the exact boundaries, they become more oriented to responsible behavior. Ambiguity on the other hand breeds inconsistency and increases the risk of academic malpractice.

Ethical Assessment Design as Preventive Strategy

The design of ethical assessment lays more emphasis on preventive than surveillance methods. In those instances when the assessment activities require evidence of thinking, situational comprehension and reflection, the chances of unethical shortcuts are reduced. Preventive design has a number of elements. Staged submissions will allow the educator to track the process of development over time. Reflective aspects prompt students to reflect on their learning process. Oral presentation or viva voice is used to reinforce knowledge. Generic automation is vulnerable to context-specific tasks. Prevention design also suppresses the use of detection tools. Although detection technologies can help detect irregularities, they must not form the main defence mechanism. Over surveillance may develop mistrust and fear. On the other hand, the prevention-oriented design encourages responsibility. The students are inspired to participate in a genuine way since the assessment framework makes genuine participation conspicuous and treasured.

Transparency and Communication

Transparency is central to maintaining integrity in AI rich environments. Students must clearly understand what constitutes acceptable behavior. Course syllabi should include explicit statements regarding AI use. These statements should describe permitted tools, required disclosures, and potential consequences of misuse.

Communication should occur not only in written policies but also in classroom discussion. Educators can explain the rationale behind guidelines. When students understand why certain restrictions exist, compliance improves.

Transparency also applies to evaluation criteria. Rubrics should specify how reasoning, originality, reflection, and engagement will be assessed. Clear criteria reduce uncertainty and promote fairness.

In addition, institutions should establish consistent policies across departments. Variation in expectations may create confusion. A coordinated framework ensures that integrity standards are applied equitably.

Role of Educators in Upholding Integrity

Educators play a critical role in promoting ethical academic behavior. Their responsibilities extend beyond grading assignments. They model scholarly honesty, clarify expectations, and guide students in responsible technology use.

Educators must become familiar with AI. Being aware of what AI is able to and not allows them to make excellent choices. When they are not aware, they may consider the risks to be too high or too low. Educators ought to be reasonable regarding AI. Being aggressive towards AI can prevent the conversation of AI among students. They can instead make students speculate on what is right as well as what AI could bring them in the future of work. In cases of cheating or any other issues, the teachers must be fair and educate. The formal steps might be required regarding big problems. Advice can be used to correct small mistakes. During the treatment of others, treat them with dignity and respect, which develops trust.

Student Responsibility and Ethical Awareness

It is not the only task of the institution to ensure academic honesty. It is also the duty of students to remain true. Studying should include learning about what is wrong and what is right. During orientation, one may change the lessons that will teach how AI can be used responsibly. Learners are supposed to know how to reference the sources right, mention who assisted them and whether information is reliable. Discussion of rules at work can demonstrate the honesty in school relations to the future jobs. Reflection activities assist the students in thinking of what is right and what is wrong. Students look at their work when explaining the use of AI tools and what ideas they added independently. This makes them feel responsible. The behavior of the classmates is also important. When the class upholds the values of honesty and fairness, the level of cheating reduces. The honor codes, group talks, and glorifying honesty are some methods through which schools can instill good habits.

Limitations of AI Detection Tools

AI detection tools have been widely adopted in response to Generative AI. These tools analyze patterns in writing and estimate probability of AI involvement. While they may provide supportive evidence, they have limitations (Zhao et al.,2025).

Detection tools may falsely identify human written text as AI. They are also able to overlook AI text which has been edited. Depending on them may result in false charges. In addition to this, attention can shift the learning towards punishment. Students will feel monitored rather than assisted. This may destroy the confidence between teachers and students. Detection tools should therefore be used cautiously and as part of a broader integrity framework. Preventive design, transparency, and dialogue remain more sustainable strategies.

Institutional Governance and Policy Development

The administrators of schools should have guidelines that are easily understood to maintain fairness in utilizing AI. The policies must discuss the responsible use of AI, consequences of breaking the rules, and the fact that individuals are provided with a fair opportunity. Tests should be regularly checked on quality. It was possible to have committees that would verify whether assignments abided by fairness rules and learning goals. Teachers need training. They can also be taught in workshops on how to make honest tests and provide fair feedback. Continued training makes the teachers consistent. Technology is an issue that should be considered in schools too. Ethical guidelines and privacy should be followed in safe online systems, plagiarism checkers, and course platforms.

ROLE OF EDUCATORS AND HUMAN JUDGMENT

Technology is becoming extremely strong nowadays. Nevertheless, it is teachers who still play a central role in maintaining college education as good and honest. AI is able to write, categorize information, and even perform like a teacher. However, AI will not be able to substitute the judgment of a human being, his/her comprehension of the situation, moral reasoning, and the sense of responsibility. The existence of AI does not reduce the usefulness of teachers. It simply implies the presence of teachers who consider learning carefully. The teachers should be allowed to interpret the work of the students themselves. Assessment only involves checking whether an answer is correct. We also consider logic, innovativeness, the sense of the work, and suitability. Teachers cogitate and consider the course, the age of grown-up students and the expectations of the subject. All this is not comprehended by AI. It does not seek context but trends. Human judgment is even more important when we apply real- life assessment (Belkina et al., 2025). There should be close interpretation of projects, case studies, written reflections and speaking tasks. Educators have to observe the level of integration of theory and real practice, the level of clarity in the explanation, and the questions answered by the students. Machines cannot do these things completely. Teachers also determine the responsible use of AI by students. Students might be unaware of what AI is capable of doing or not. Teachers should clarify on when students should involve AI technologies and when it is their responsibility. The counsel must be beneficial, not reproving. Students would be likely to behave in an ethical manner when they consider the teachers as their mentors. Strong assessment tasks are another important task of teachers. Thought-provoking work prevents cheating and makes work authentic. The teachers should not just ask the easy questions in the form of quizzes but develop problems that are relevant to the situation. That requires creativity, planning and achievement of the learning objectives. It is essential to learn more about AI. Educators should understand AI operation to detect abuse and develop protective measures. Teamwork, workshops and training can assist them in development. Fairness is also provided by the judgment of teachers. This should be assessed based on the diverse backgrounds and talents of the students. AI is capable of providing an average appearance of works, but it is not capable of considering every situation of a person. The teachers contextualize the performance of students. Communication is also important. In situations where questions on authorship arise in relation to what is written, teachers should discuss it with care. False allegations shatter confidence. The purpose of conversations should not only be to punish but also clarify expectations and learning. Emotional aspect of learning is important. Students are able to become nervous and uncertain. The support and reassurance are provided by teachers. AI is not able to express sympathy or become a mentor. Motivation and confidence are developed through an actual human contact. Teachers demonstrate integrity. They are committed to good scholarship and this influences the behavior of students. Integrity is demonstrated by open communication, proper sources and proper interactions. Concisely, the AI generation reveals that the judgment of teachers remains the central aspect of assessment. Educators create meaningful activities, read complicated responses, mentor morals and maintain impartiality. Artificial intelligence may assist, but it is not capable of substituting professional knowledge. Lasting changes to assessment will require boosting the abilities of teachers.

INSTITUTIONAL POLICIES AND QUALITY ASSURANCE

While educators play a critical role, institutional structures provide the framework within which assessment operates. As the era of Generative AI approaches, school policies and quality check need to evolve to suit the emerging issues. Without the co-ordinated governance, assessment practices may end up being lopsided and useless. Responsible use of AI is anchored on clear school policies. The policies should outline what application of the AI tools are acceptable and what is not in school work. They ought to provide guidelines on how to demonstrate the use of AI, reference it, and repercussions of actions to be taken in case an individual misbehaves. Clear guidelines eliminate confusion and bring a level of fairness to every department. Policies also need balance. Too strict rules may prevent good innovation and cautious usage. Too loose rules may reduce academic standards. The schools need to consider the differences in subjects and still maintain the principles of core honesty. Assessment practices should be under quality checks. Learning goals and honesty rules can be verified through the use of academic committees. Assessment becomes useful with regular reviews since technology evolves. Good quality involves teacher training. Schools ought to provide professional learning in the form of real assessment design, providing helpful feedback, and the understanding of AI. Consistency improves when the teachers are prepared. It is more equal to standardize some steps. As an example, the signs or rules of oral defense meetings have the same templates that schools can use regarding AI disclosure. The difference between flexibility and coordinated cuts cuts upsets. The ethical evaluation should be supported with economic technology. Course management systems must also allow students to work in phases, demonstrate changes with time and assist in providing feedback. Privacy can be ensured using safe digital tools that can store records securely. Schools also help students. It should be oriented on ethical methods of AI use and rules of honesty. It talks things out in the beginning. Complaint and appeal systems should also be fair. Students should have equitable methods of dealing with conflicts. Open reviews keep trust. What makes the institution more powerful is the collaboration amongst departments. Tech support, integrity committees and learning centers should collaborate. It stops split decisions. Leaders must be committed. Leaders of schools need to articulate a clear vision of assessment in the era of AI. Learning and honesty as well as new ideas should be the drive behind the vision and not fear of tech. Policy making can be assisted through working with schools abroad. The global experience and adapting to the local demands can be learned by the schools. Policy plans are enhanced by different cultures.

CRITICAL DISCUSSION AND FUTURE RESEARCH DIRECTIONS

The conclusions drawn from the data throughout this chapter indicate that rather than relying solely on technologies for detecting Generative AI, assessment redesign is a more viable solution. Although there are some tools available for detection, they are still facing criticism for their accuracy in the face of the constantly changing language models and human editing processes. Hence, the validity of the assessment is more and more dependent on the instructional design than the technological surveillance. Authentic Assessment and Assessment for learning offer robust educational support for AI-supported learning. However, this will highly depend on institutional commitment to implement. The faculty should reengineer the evaluation process, give regular formative feedback, create opportunities for reflection, and carry out oral evaluations. This inevitably leads to more workload and a need for constant professional development. Adaptability of institutions to United Nations service is also quite varied from university to university. Factors such as technological infrastructure, faculty AI literacy, students' digital competence, and policy maturity could impact the successful implementation. Moreover, it is important to recognize that there are differences in disciplines, and assessment methods that are effective in engineering, medicine, humanities, or business education might need to be adapted to a particular context. Future studies should involve the empirical validation of integrated assessment framework in different institutional contexts. Longitudinal research on student learning outcomes, academic integrity, development of AI literacy, and faculty adoption would offer useful data to support policy and practice. A comparative examination between disciplines and countries would further enrich knowledge of successful design changes for assessments in the fast-changing world of AI. In the era of Generative AI, sustainable assessment should be considered not only as a technological issue, but also as a pedagogic shift, which needs the concerted action of teachers, institutes, policy makers, and learners.

CONCLUSION

The Generative AI era presents higher education with both challenge and opportunity. Traditional assessment models, which emphasize final written output and memorization, face structural weaknesses in AI rich environments. However, the solution does not lie in excessive surveillance or technological prohibition. Instead, meaningful redesign offers a sustainable pathway forward.

Authentic assessment connects learning to real world contexts and requires application of knowledge, problem solving, collaboration, and reflection. Assessment for learning integrates feedback into the developmental process. Together, these approaches strengthen resilience against automated content generation while promoting deeper engagement.

Redesigning must be planned and methodical. The following are the key points: align the learning objectives, check the way students work and their final, make periodic submissions, promote discussion, and include reflection. Feedback should not be the comments on grading but constant assistance. The academic honesty must be constructed on plain regulations, educating morals and architecture that prevents cheating, not merely on the detecting devices. The most important part of the change is still teachers. AI cannot take the place of their judgments, interpretation of the situation, and mentoring. Checks and policies in school offer some order of consistency. The inclusion is inclusive and context-sensitive by seeing many cultures. AI makes higher education reconsider its central mission. The tests need to measure the knowledge, develop critical thinking, and prepare students to work in responsible roles. Planning rather than responding makes it possible to maintain standards but also to adopt technology in schools. New tech should not struggle with assessment, new technologies should integrate teaching, values and human judgment with the digital. Higher education can transform the AI challenge into the opportunity to discover more relevant, deeper learning with real design, helpful feedback, and school support.

REFERENCES

Bearman, M., Nieminen, J. H., & Ajjawi, R. (2022). Designing assessment in a digital world: An organising framework. *Assessment & Evaluation in Higher Education*, *48*(3), 291–304. DOI: 10.1080/02602938.2022.2069674

Bearman, M., Tai, J., Dawson, P., Boud, D., & Ajjawi, R. (2024). Developing evaluative judgement for a time of generative artificial intelligence. *Assessment & Evaluation in Higher Education*, *49*(6), 893–905. DOI: 10.1080/02602938.2024.2335321

Belkina, M. (2025). Implementing generative AI in higher education teaching and learning: Case studies and integration strategies. *Computers & Education*, *185*, 104781. Advance online publication. DOI: 10.1016/j.compedu.2025.104781

Bernabei, M., Colabianchi, S., Falegnami, A., & Costantino, F. (2023). Students' use of large language models in engineering education: A case study on technology acceptance, perceptions, efficacy, and detection chances. Computers & Education. *Artificial Intelligence*, *5*, 100172. DOI: 10.1016/j.caeai.2023.100172

Bittle, K. (2025). Generative AI and academic integrity in higher education: A systematic literature review. *Information (Basel)*, *16*(4), 296. DOI: 10.3390/info16040296

Dai, K. (2026). Generative AI in higher education: A bibliometric review of the current landscape of research. Computers & Education. *Artificial Intelligence*, *8*, 100311. Advance online publication. DOI: 10.1016/j.caeai.2026.100311

Fischer, I. (2024). Making sense of generative AI for assessments: Student engagement and learning implications. *Teaching in Higher Education*, *29*(4), 456–472. DOI: 10.1080/13562517.2024.15226x

Henderson, M. (2025). Comparing generative AI and teacher feedback: Complementary roles in higher education assessment. *Journal of Learning Analytics*, *12*(1), 144–158. DOI: 10.18608/jla.2025.12212

Ilieva, G., Yankova, T., Ruseva, M., & Kabaivanov, S. (2025). A framework for generative AI-driven assessment in higher education. *Information (Basel)*, *16*(6), 472. DOI: 10.3390/info16060472

Khlaif, Z. N., Alkouk, W. A., Salama, N., & Abu Eideh, B. (2025). Redesigning assessments for AI-enhanced learning: A framework for educators in the generative AI era. *Education Sciences*, *15*(2), 174. DOI: 10.3390/educsci15020174

Kickbusch, S., Ashford-Rowe, K., Kemp, A., Boreland, J., & Huijser, H. (2025). Beyond detection: Redesigning authentic assessment in an AI-mediated world. *Education Sciences*, *15*(11), 1537. DOI: 10.3390/educsci15111537

Kizilcec, R. F., Huber, E., Papanastasiou, E. C., Cram, A., Makridis, C. A., Smolansky, A., Zeivots, S., & Raduescu, C. (2024). Perceived impact of generative AI on assessments: Comparing educator and student perspectives in Australia, Cyprus, and the United States. Computers & Education. *Artificial Intelligence*, *7*, 100269. DOI: 10.1016/j.caeai.2024.100269

Lee, D., Arnold, M., Srivastava, A., Plastow, K., Strelan, P., Ploeckl, F., Lekkas, D., & Palmer, E. (2024). The impact of generative AI on higher education learning and teaching: A study of educators' perspectives. Computers & Education. *Artificial Intelligence*, *6*, 100221. DOI: 10.1016/j.caeai.2024.100221

Luo, J. (2024). A critical review of GenAI policies in higher education assessment: A call to reconsider the "originality" of students' work. *Assessment & Evaluation in Higher Education*, *49*(5), 651–664. DOI: 10.1080/02602938.2024.2309963

Lye, C. Y., & Lim, L. (2024). Generative artificial intelligence in tertiary education: Assessment redesign principles and considerations. Education Sciences, 14(6)*. *Education Sciences*, *569*(6), 569. Advance online publication. DOI: 10.3390/educsci14060569

McGeechan, G. J., & Haste, A. (2026). Authentic assessments as a strategy to address generative AI use in assessment: A case study. *Assessment in Education: Principles, Policy & Practice*. Advance online publication. DOI: 10.14293/FFL26.000027.v1

Molloy, E., Boud, D., & Henderson, M. (2020). Developing a learning-centred framework for feedback literacy. *Assessment & Evaluation in Higher Education*, *45*(4), 527–540. DOI: 10.1080/02602938.2019.1667955

Ncube, P. D. N. (2026). Redefining student assessment in AI-infused learning environments: A scoping review. *AI and Ethics*, *6*(1), 87–103. DOI: 10.1007/s43681-025-00871-w

Nedungadi, P., Tang, K.-Y., & Raman, R. (2024). The transformative power of generative artificial intelligence for achieving the sustainable development goal of quality education. Sustainability, 16(22)*. *Sustainability (Basel)*, *9779*(22), 9779. Advance online publication. DOI: 10.3390/su16229779

Page, E., Meyers, G., & Billings, E. (2024). Theory to practice: An assessment framework for generative AI. Intersection: A Journal at the Intersection of Assessment and Learning, 5(4), 114–126. DOI: 10.61669/001c.124250

Peterson, S. (2025). Generative AI and academic integrity: Developing frameworks for formative assessment and policy. *Frontiers in Education*, *10*, 1610836. DOI: 10.3389/feduc.2025.1610836

Tensen, D. (2025). Using AI to generate formative feedback in doctoral education. *Assessment & Evaluation in Higher Education*. Advance online publication. DOI: 10.1080/02602938.2025.2536558

Urzúa, C. A. C. (2025). Effects of AI-assisted feedback via generative models on student writing and self-monitoring. Education Sciences, 15(10)*, 1396. DOI: 10.3390/educsci15101396

Usher, M. (2025). Generative AI vs. instructor vs. peer assessments: A comparison of grading and feedback. *Assessment & Evaluation in Higher Education*, *50*(6), 912–927. Advance online publication. DOI: 10.1080/02602938.2025.2487495

Weng, X. (2024). A scoping review on current research status and trends in generative AI impact on higher education assessment. Australasian Journal of Educational Technology, 40(5)*, 9540. DOI: 10.14742/ajet.9540

Weng, X., Xia, Q., Gu, M., Rajaram, K., & Chiu, T. K. F. (2024). Assessment and learning outcomes for generative AI in higher education: A scoping review on current research status and trends. Australasian Journal of Educational Technology, 40(6)*. DOI: 10.14742/ajet.9540

Xia, Q., & Weng, X. (2024). A scoping review on how generative artificial intelligence impacts higher education assessment research. *International Journal of Educational Technology in Higher Education*, *21*, 68. Advance online publication. DOI: 10.1186/s41239-024-00468-z

Zhao, J., Chapman, E., & Sabet, P. G. P. (2025). Generative AI and educational assessments: Synthesis of empirical evidence. *Educational Assessment*, *51*, 124–155.

KEY TERMS AND DEFINITIONS

Academic Integrity in the AI Era: Academic integrity in the AI era refers to ethical and transparent engagement with learning and assessment in environments where AI tools are accessible. It emphasizes honesty, responsible technology use, and clear acknowledgment of assistance. Institutions must define acceptable AI practices and disclosure norms. Preventive assessment design supports integrity more effectively than surveillance alone. The approach builds trust and professional responsibility.

Assessment for Learning: Assessment for learning refers to a formative evaluation process that supports continuous student development. It integrates feedback into different stages of learning rather than limiting evaluation to final grading. Students receive guidance, revise their work, and improve gradually. The approach encourages self assessment and peer review. It promotes growth, reflection, and mastery of learning outcomes.

Assessment Validity: Assessment validity refers to the extent to which an evaluation accurately measures the intended learning outcomes. A valid assessment reflects genuine student understanding and competence. In AI rich environments, validity may be threatened when automated systems produce polished outputs. Ensuring validity requires tasks that measure reasoning, application, and reflection. It strengthens fairness and credibility of academic qualifications.

Authentic Assessment: Authentic assessment refers to an evaluation approach that requires students to apply knowledge and skills to real world or realistic contexts. It emphasizes problem solving, critical thinking, and contextual interpretation rather than memorization. Students demonstrate understanding through projects, case analysis, presentations, and reflective tasks. The approach values both process and final outcome. It strengthens relevance, engagement, and practical competence.

Formative Feedback: Formative feedback refers to constructive guidance provided during the learning process to improve performance. It focuses on development rather than judgment. Feedback is specific, timely, and aligned with learning outcomes. Students use it to revise and refine their work. This approach enhances understanding, confidence, and academic integrity.

Generative Artificial Intelligence: Generative Artificial Intelligence refers to advanced computational systems that create new content based on patterns learned from large datasets. These systems generate essays, summaries, reports, code, and analytical responses in structured formats. They operate through probability based language models rather than human understanding. In education, they can assist drafting and revision. However, excessive dependence may reduce independent cognitive engagement.

Chapter 6
Authentic Assessment and Assessment-for-Learning in the Generative AI Era

Tendai Charles
http://orcid.org/0000-0002-0253-5960
The British University in Dubai, UAE

Siham Abukhalaf
http://orcid.org/0009-0000-9894-6264
Deakin University, Australia

ABSTRACT

Generative artificial intelligence (GenAI) has destabilised conventional assessment arrangements in higher education by lowering the cost of producing plausible academic texts and solutions. In this context, institutional responses have frequently concentrated on detection and surveillance, or on narrow policy prohibitions, approaches that risk eroding trust, amplifying inequities, and misrecognising assessment as a socio-pedagogical practice shaped by institutional cultures, disciplinary norms, and unequal access to resources. This chapter advances a theoretically informed redesign agenda that re-centres authentic assessment and assessment-for-learning (AfL) as complementary foundations for quality and integrity in AI-rich environments. Rather than treating GenAI as an external threat to be "controlled," the chapter conceptualises GenAI as a socio-technical mediator within learners' activity systems and academic literacies, requiring assessment designs that make learning processes visible, uphold fairness and accountability, and preserve students' epistemic agency.

INTRODUCTION

Generative artificial intelligence (GenAI), particularly large language models (LLMs) embedded in conversational systems, has rapidly altered the epistemic conditions under which higher education assessment operates. The disruption is not confined to the "risk" that students can outsource production of acceptable prose, code, or worked solutions; it also arises from a broader redistribution of literacy practices and cognitive labour. Students now have low-friction access to tools that can generate plausible

DOI: 10.4018/979-8-3373-8939-4.ch006

outputs, suggest outlines and argument structures, simulate tutoring and feedback, and support rapid iterative revision. Early empirical synthesis on ChatGPT's educational uptake already shows a pattern of simultaneous experimentation and caution, with concerns about reliability, manipulation, and academic misconduct remaining salient (Tlili et al., 2023; Kolade et al., 2024).

Institutional responses have frequently prioritised detection, surveillance, and prohibition. However, evidence indicates that AI-text detection is both technically unstable and socio-educationally risky, including documented bias patterns (e.g., higher false-positive rates for non-native English writers) that threaten equity and due process (Liang et al., 2023). Moreover, conceptual analyses argue that perfect detection faces fundamental challenges and may provoke an "arms race" dynamic, diverting institutional effort away from pedagogical redesign (Májovský et al., 2024; Otterbacher, 2023).

In contrast, recent research argues that in an AI-mediated world, authenticity cannot be policed into existence; it must be redesigned by shifting the assessment focus from surface products to the application of knowledge, judgement, and justification with AI "in the loop" (Kickbusch et al., 2025). This chapter therefore advances a pivot from "integrity by surveillance" to "integrity by design," re-centring authentic assessment and assessment-for-learning (AfL) as complementary foundations for quality and integrity in AI-rich environments.

Building on scholarship on authentic assessment, AfL, feedback literacy, academic integrity (Charles & Hill, 2026), and socio-technical governance, the chapter proposes an evidence-informed conceptual architecture—AI-Resilient Authentic AfL (ARAA)—and derives design principles, assessment patterns, and governance implications suitable for diverse institutional contexts, including resource-constrained and Global South settings (Jin et al., 2025; Tan & Maravilla, 2024).

The argument is not that every assessment must permit unrestricted GenAI use, nor that conventional examinations have become obsolete. Rather, AI-resilient assessment requires deliberate alignment between the intended learning, the permitted role of tools, the evidence students must produce, and the procedures through which judgements are made. A well-designed regime may therefore include AI-restricted tasks, AI-integrated tasks, and hybrid tasks, provided that the rationale for each is educationally defensible and communicated in advance.

This position replaces the binary question of whether AI is allowed with a more precise question: which intellectual work may be delegated, which may be augmented, and which must remain demonstrably attributable to the learner?

The chapter makes three contributions. Conceptually, it integrates authentic assessment and assessment for learning as mutually reinforcing infrastructures for validity and integrity. Practically, it specifies a redesign workflow, an ARAA Canvas, cross-disciplinary assessment patterns, and implementation indicators. Institutionally, it locates assessment redesign within a governance envelope that addresses transparency, privacy, equity, contestability, workload, and capacity. The chapter proceeds from a critical review of the literature to the methodology, model architecture, worked applications, implementation guidance, discussion, and research agenda.

LITERATURE REVIEW

Generative AI, assessment validity, and academic integrity

Empirical work demonstrates that GenAI can generate highly original and high-quality essay-like outputs when prompted, raising challenges for traditional written assignments that rely on product-only evaluation (Kolade et al., 2024). System-level analyses of institutional adoption policies and guidelines further show that higher education providers are attempting to balance integrity, pedagogical opportunity, and equity, while still facing gaps related to privacy, access, and implementation capacity (Jin et al., 2025).

Recent research on academic integrity in the GenAI era highlightss a dual reality: GenAI can lower the cost of misrepresentation while also expanding learning support and feedback opportunities. Consequently, policy strategies focused purely on prohibition risk narrowing legitimate learning benefits and incentivising covert use (Bittle & El-Gayar, 2025).

Detection and surveillance approaches face limitations and risks. Bias evidence suggests AI-text detectors can disproportionately flag non-native English writers (Liang et al., 2023). Conceptual work argues that efforts to achieve perfect detection face fundamental challenges and may rapidly become obsolete as models evolve (Májovský et al., 2024). These findings motivate design-led approaches that incorporate accountable learning processes and human judgement rather than relying on uncertain technical attribution (Otterbacher, 2023).

The central validity problem is therefore not merely authorship attribution. It is that a polished artefact may no longer provide sufficient evidence that the learner has interpreted the task, selected and evaluated evidence, exercised disciplinary judgement, and revised the work responsibly. A prohibition-only response leaves this evidentiary weakness intact because it treats the tool as the principal problem while leaving the product-only design unchanged. By contrast, an assessment-validity response asks what additional evidence is needed for the inference from performance to competence to remain credible (Bittle & El-Gayar, 2025; Kolade et al., 2024).

Detection can occasionally function as a low-weight screening signal, but the literature does not support its use as stand-alone proof. Documented false-positive risks for non-native English writers create a direct equity concern, and model evolution makes stable classification difficult (Liang et al., 2023; Májovský et al., 2024). Otterbacher (2023) therefore argues that technical detection is insufficient without institutional procedures that protect due process. ARAA adopts this position by requiring concerns to be evaluated against multiple forms of evidence, including drafts, revision histories, oral explanation, source verification, and the student's opportunity to respond.

Authentic assessment, assessment for learning, and feedback literacy

Systematic review evidence indicates that authentic assessment can foster employability-related capabilities such as critical thinking, problem-solving, and collaboration, while also identifying implementation challenges including resistance, training needs, and resource constraints (Vlachopoulos & Makri, 2024). In an AI-mediated context, authenticity requires tasks that foreground context, constraints, judgement, and professional reasoning rather than the production of generic texts or solutions (Kickbusch et al., 2025).

AfL positions assessment as a driver of learning through feedback, self-regulation, and iterative improvement. In AI-enhanced contexts, scholars emphasise that formative assessment remains essential, but its practices are reshaped by AI's capacity to generate rapid feedback and to mediate peer- and self-assessment processes (Hopfenbeck et al., 2023). Recent open-access empirical work further suggests that students' self-regulated engagement with GenAI feedback can contribute to feedback literacy development, but that GenAI feedback does not fully replicate human feedback interaction processes, highlighting the need for intentional orchestration of feedback ecologies (Gu et al., 2026).

Systematic review evidence in higher education writing indicates that AI-assisted feedback can support timely guidance and improvements in linguistic aspects of writing; however, scholars caution that such tools should complement human instruction rather than substitute for pedagogical judgement, and that feedback should be oriented toward higher-order thinking rather than mere correction (Urzúa et al., 2025).

Feedback literacy provides the bridge between receiving comments and using them productively. Carless and Boud (2018) define feedback literacy through capacities to appreciate feedback, make evaluative judgements, manage affect, and take action. In GenAI-mediated assessment, these capacities become assessable outcomes because students must distinguish useful from misleading suggestions, compare machine feedback with disciplinary criteria, and explain why particular recommendations were accepted, modified, or rejected. This moves AI-supported feedback away from automated correction and towards the cultivation of evaluative judgement.

Recent evidence strengthens the case for an orchestrated feedback ecology rather than a replacement model. Gu et al. (2026) found that self-regulated engagement with GenAI and human-peer feedback can support feedback-literacy development, while also showing that the interactional qualities of human feedback are not fully reproduced by GenAI. Systematic review evidence on academic writing similarly suggests that AI-assisted feedback can improve timeliness and support linguistic revision, but requires teacher guidance and explicit attention to higher-order reasoning (Urzúa et al., 2025). The implication for assessment design is that feedback sources should have defined roles and that students' use of feedback should itself generate evidence of learning.

Student perspectives, faculty readiness, privacy, and dependency

Student perspectives challenge institutional policies that are framed only around misconduct. In a survey of 399 undergraduate and postgraduate students across disciplines in Hong Kong, participants recognised potential benefits for personalised support, brainstorming, writing, research, and analysis, while also expressing concerns about accuracy, privacy, personal development, career prospects, and social values (Chan & Hu, 2023). These findings do not justify unrestricted use. They show that students already understand GenAI as both support and risk, and that credible policy should incorporate student voice, explain the educational rationale for boundaries, and distinguish responsible assistance from substitution.

Faculty readiness is equally consequential. A mixed-methods study involving qualitative development work and a survey of 538 faculty members in Palestine found that educator AI literacy was associated with AI competencies, perceived usefulness, ease of use, professional development, community support, and prior technological experience (Ayyoub et al., 2025). Assessment redesign is therefore not a one-off technical adjustment. It requires shared exemplars, disciplinary calibration, protected time, professional learning, and support structures that allow staff to interpret policy and redesign tasks without unsustainable workload.

Privacy is a design condition rather than an optional compliance note. Public GenAI systems may retain prompts, process personal or commercially sensitive data, and operate under terms that students and staff do not control. UNESCO's guidance accordingly places human-centred regulation, data privacy, ethical validation, and pedagogical design at the centre of responsible adoption (Miao & Holmes, 2023). In assessment, this means that students should not be required to upload confidential data, unpublished research, protected intellectual property, identifiable learner records, or sensitive case material to public tools. Equivalent non-AI routes and institutionally approved alternatives must remain available.

AI dependency is best understood as a relationship between tool use and the intended cognitive work. The risk is not simply frequent use; it is the displacement of the very reasoning, practice, or judgement that the assessment is meant to develop. The OECD (2026) distinguishes improved task performance from genuine learning and cautions that unguided outsourcing can produce better outputs without corresponding gains in competence. ARAA therefore requires an explicit human-AI division of labour: educators identify which operations may be automated, which should be supported through scaffolding, and which must remain visible as learner performance.

Ethical reviews of large language models in education (Yan et al., 2024) identify related concerns involving bias (Charles & Papadaki, 2025), opacity, inaccurate information, overreliance, data protection, unequal access (Charles & Alshamsi, 2025), and the erosion of human agency. These concerns are interdependent. For example, requiring a premium tool may create access inequity; compensating through a free public tool may introduce privacy risk; and responding through surveillance may undermine trust. The resulting policy problem is socio-technical: institutions must align pedagogy, infrastructure, staff capability, student support, and due process rather than treating each concern in isolation.

Policy, equity, and resource-constrained contexts

Institutional governance is increasingly framed as socio-technical: policies and quality assurance mechanisms must address not only academic integrity rules but also the transparency, privacy, access, and equity conditions under which AI is used. Global policy analyses report uneven institutional readiness and emphasise equity risks when tool access is uneven or when enforcement practices depend on unreliable detection (Jin et al., 2025). Integrity-oriented perspectives argue that GenAI does not have to undermine education if assessment and governance are designed to sustain ethical judgement, accountability, and student agency (Tan & Maravilla, 2024).

Global policy analysis shows uneven institutional readiness and persistent gaps in privacy, access, staff development, and implementation capacity (Jin et al., 2025). These gaps are especially important in resource-constrained settings where students may rely on mobile devices, unstable connectivity, shared accounts, or free-tier systems with limited functionality. ARAA therefore treats equivalence of learning opportunity, rather than identical technological provision, as the relevant equity principle. Institutions can offer low-bandwidth templates, offline process logs, campus access points, non-premium alternatives, and assessment routes that do not penalise students who decline or cannot access a particular tool.

Capacity-sensitive implementation also requires proportionality. Continuous oral defence, detailed prompt capture, or intensive portfolio review may be feasible in small postgraduate classes but unsustainable in large undergraduate modules. The appropriate response is selective rather than total verification: high-stakes decisions receive richer evidence; routine tasks use structured disclosure and sampled checkpoints; and concerns trigger targeted review rather than cohort-wide surveillance. This principle preserves integrity without converting assessment into an administratively unmanageable monitoring system.

Evidence synthesis and unresolved design requirements

Table 1 synthesises the evidence streams most directly informing ARAA. The table is intentionally problem-oriented: it identifies what each stream contributes, where its explanatory or operational reach remains limited, and the design requirement carried forward into the framework.

Table 1. Selected evidence streams, contributions, and design implications

Evidence stream	Core contribution	Requirement carried into ARAA
Detection and attribution	Detector bias and technical instability make stand-alone attribution unsafe (Liang et al., 2023; Májovský et al., 2024; Otterbacher, 2023).	Evidence concerns must be resolved through multiple sources, due process, and student response.
Authentic assessment	Contextualised, consequential tasks can develop higher-order and employability capabilities (Vlachopoulos & Makri, 2024).	Authenticity must include not only task realism but also process visibility and epistemic judgement.
Assessment for learning	Formative assessment supports self-regulation, feedback use, and iterative improvement (Hopfenbeck et al., 2023).	AI feedback requires role definition, critical evaluation, and evidence of action on feedback.
Feedback literacy	Students need capacities to interpret, judge, manage, and act on feedback (Carless & Boud, 2018; Gu et al., 2026).	Feedback uptake and evaluative judgement should be taught and assessed.
Student perspectives	Students value support but identify accuracy, privacy, ethical, and developmental risks (Chan & Hu, 2023).	Policy and task design should incorporate student voice and explain the rationale for boundaries.
Faculty readiness	AI literacy depends on competence, perceived usefulness, professional development, and community support (Ayyoub et al., 2025).	Implementation requires staff development, exemplars, calibration, and workload planning.
Institutional governance	Policies increasingly address integrity, pedagogy, equity, privacy, and training, but readiness is uneven (Chan, 2023; Jin et al., 2025).	Assessment design must be embedded within transparent, contestable, and capacity-sensitive governance.
Hybrid assessment	AI-permitted and AI-restricted components can be combined to protect foundational and higher-order learning (Elshall & Badir, 2025).	The human-AI division of labour should be explicit and aligned with intended outcomes.

Adjacent frameworks and the distinctiveness of ARAA

Several recent frameworks provide important foundations for responsible GenAI use. The Artificial Intelligence Assessment Scale (AIAS) offers five levels from no AI to full AI, giving educators and students a transparent language for specifying permitted use (Perkins et al., 2024). Its pilot implementation at British University Vietnam demonstrates the practical value of a flexible permission scale and stakeholder consultation (Furze et al., 2024). The AIAS primarily answers how much AI use is permitted; ARAA asks what evidence is required for valid judgement at any selected level.

Chan's (2023) AI Ecological Education Policy Framework addresses institutional policy through pedagogical, governance, and operational dimensions and was developed from data collected from 457 students and 180 teachers and staff. It is broader than assessment design and makes stakeholder roles explicit. ARAA complements this policy architecture by specifying the assessment-level mechanisms through which learning becomes visible: contextualised tasks, staged evidence, feedback uptake, justification, and dialogic accountability.

The FACT framework balances fundamental, applied, conceptual, and critical-thinking assessment in environmental data science, combining AI-assisted and non-AI components (Elshall & Badir, 2025). Ilieva et al. (2025) provide a broader framework for GenAI-driven assessment, while Foung et al. (2024) describe opportunities for GenAI-empowered assessment practices. Kickbusch et al. (2025) make the decisive conceptual move from detection to redesigned authenticity. ARAA extends these contributions by integrating three dimensions of authenticity with an assessment-for-learning cycle and a governance envelope.

The literature therefore supports a clear gap statement (*see* Table 2). Existing work offers permission scales, policy architectures, disciplinary exemplars, and arguments for authentic redesign, but these contributions are not yet consistently integrated into a single assessment lifecycle. ARAA addresses that gap by linking what students are asked to do, how their learning trajectory becomes visible, how they justify knowledge claims, how feedback is used, and how institutional rules protect fairness and trust.

Table 2. Comparison of ARAA with adjacent policy and assessment frameworks

Framework	Primary question	Distinctive contribution	ARAA relationship or extension
AI Assessment Scale (Perkins et al., 2024)	Specifies five levels of permitted GenAI use.	Clarity and transparency about permission.	Adds evidence design, feedback processes, epistemic checks, and governance at each level.
AI Ecological Education Policy Framework (Chan, 2023)	Organises institutional policy into pedagogical, governance, and operational dimensions.	Stakeholder roles and whole-institution policy.	Translates policy into assessment mechanisms and auditable evidence requirements.
FACT assessment (Elshall & Badir, 2025)	Balances AI-assisted and non-AI assessment across four learning domains.	Concrete hybrid course design.	Generalises beyond one disciplinary pattern and adds process authenticity and governance.
GenAI-driven assessment framework (Ilieva et al., 2025)	Frames opportunities and requirements for AI-supported assessment.	System-level attention to AI-driven assessment.	Centres the validity of student evidence and the distinction among task, process, and epistemic authenticity.
Beyond Detection (Kickbusch et al., 2025)	Reorients authenticity towards critique, verification, and applied judgement.	Strong integrity-by-design rationale.	Adds an AfL cycle, operational canvas, implementation indicators, and capacity-sensitive governance.
ARAA	Integrates authenticity, AfL, feedback literacy, and socio-technical governance.	Links task design, evidentiary chain, judgement, and institutional conditions.	Requires empirical validation across disciplines, cultures, and resource conditions.

METHODOLOGY

Design-oriented conceptual synthesis

This chapter employs a design-oriented conceptual synthesis methodology aimed at producing a practically useful assessment redesign framework rather than a purely descriptive narrative. In line with methodological guidance on constructing conceptual frameworks and writing conceptual articles, the chapter was developed as a structured theory-synthesis and model-building exercise in which key constructs and relationships were iteratively specified, stress-tested against plausible assessment scenarios, and refined (Jaakkola, 2020; Luft et al., 2022; van der Waldt, 2020). The evidence base prioritised peer-reviewed, open-access publications with DOIs in venues indexed by Scopus, spanning Generative AI adoption in higher education, academic integrity, authentic assessment, assessment-for-learning (AfL), feedback literacy, and socio-technical governance.

Conceptual synthesis proceeded through thematic coding around recurrent assessment tensions (e.g., product versus process evidence; surveillance versus trust; automation versus professional judgement; equity versus standardisation), followed by integrative model building. The development of the AI-Resilient Authentic AfL (ARAA) framework followed Jabareen's (2009) eight-phase conceptual framework analysis, complemented by published 'how-to' guidance on designing coherent conceptual frameworks (Ayoubi et al., 2018; van der Waldt, 2020). This methodological combination provided both a transparent procedural logic for concept synthesis and an explicit set of quality criteria (conceptual clarity, relationship specification, parsimony, and applicability) for iterative refinement.

The synthesis was design-oriented because the intended output was not simply a taxonomy of themes. It was a model that could support diagnosis, redesign, implementation, and evaluation. The analysis therefore moved repeatedly between literature-derived concepts and assessment scenarios, asking whether each construct clarified a design decision, specified observable evidence, or identified a governance obligation. Concepts that did not alter a design judgement were treated as contextual rather than core components.

Research design

ARAA is advanced as a conceptual model for assessment redesign in AI-rich higher education, not as a claim about the prevalence of particular student behaviours or institutional practices. Accordingly, the chapter follows conventions for conceptual research in which the primary 'data' are scholarly arguments, constructs, and documented empirical findings that can be synthesised into a coherent explanatory and design-oriented architecture.

The intended contribution is twofold: (a) conceptual—by integrating authentic assessment and AfL as mutually reinforcing integrity infrastructures in the GenAI era; and (b) practical—by translating the synthesis into design principles and assessment patterns that can be implemented and governed. This approach aligns with guidance for conceptual articles that emphasises explicit concept definition, relationship specification, and a clear account of the authorial reasoning process by which a model is derived (Jaakkola, 2020).

The unit of analysis was the conceptual relationship among assessment purpose, task structure, evidence generation, feedback activity, disciplinary judgement, GenAI mediation, and governance. The chapter does not estimate prevalence or effect size and does not treat illustrative cases as empirical validation. Its claims are propositional: if assessment evidence is distributed across authentic task performance, visible process, and defensible judgement, then the inference from submitted work to student learning should be more credible than it is under product-only assessment. This proposition remains open to empirical testing.

Evidence identification and selection

Evidence identification was conducted as a targeted scoping search and iterative citation-chaining exercise. Initial keyword combinations were organised around five intersecting streams, namely scholarship on generative AI and higher education assessment and policy; academic integrity, misconduct, and the limitations of detection-based approaches; authentic assessment and work-integrated assessment; assessment-for-learning, formative assessment, and feedback literacy; and socio-technical governance, fairness, and quality assurance. Searches were complemented by backward citation searching (reviewing reference lists of highly relevant papers) and forward citation searching (identifying later studies that cited key anchor texts) to ensure conceptual coverage across disciplines and geographic contexts.

The original inclusion logic was refined during revision. Peer-reviewed, open-access publications with DOIs were prioritised because they maximise accessibility and verifiability. Authoritative policy reports from UNESCO and the OECD were included where they provided global governance guidance not available in journal articles, and foundational conceptual sources were retained where necessary to define feedback literacy or framework-development methodology. This approach is more accurately described as a targeted scoping synthesis with purposive inclusion than as a systematic review.

The final evidence base covered seven intersecting streams: GenAI capabilities and educational use; academic integrity and detection; authentic and hybrid assessment; assessment for learning and feedback literacy; student perspectives; faculty AI literacy and organisational readiness; and socio-technical governance, privacy, equity, and quality assurance. Backward and forward citation chaining were used to connect foundational concepts with recent empirical and policy work. Recent sources were checked against publisher or institutional records, and publication-year discrepancies were resolved in favour of the version of record.

Analytic procedure

The analytic core of the methodology was Jabareen's (2009) conceptual framework analysis (CFA), which conceptualises framework development as an iterative, interpretive process for integrating constructs from heterogeneous literatures into a coherent explanatory and design-oriented architecture. In the present chapter, CFA was implemented in a sequential yet recursive manner, moving from delimiting the conceptual perimeter of ARAA to specifying relationships between constructs that can guide assessment redesign in AI-rich contexts.

Accordingly, the work began by mapping the relevant knowledge domains—authentic assessment, AfL and feedback, academic integrity and misconduct, GenAI capabilities and institutional responses, and socio-technical governance—to ensure coverage of both pedagogical and regulatory dimensions. The resulting corpus was then read iteratively and organised into analytic memos and concept matrices so that convergences and tensions (for example, competing meanings of 'authenticity' as real-world resemblance versus epistemic agency) could be made explicit.

On that basis, candidate constructs and mechanisms were identified and named through definitional comparison, before being deconstructed into attributes, boundary conditions, and design implications. These deconstructed constructs were then integrated by specifying their relationships—most centrally, how task, process, and epistemic authenticity interact with AfL cycles and governance obligations to make learning visible and to sustain accountable GenAI use.

The integrated account was synthesised into the ARAA framework and its visual representation, and subsequently subjected to conceptual validation through stress-testing against established critiques of detection-centred integrity governance and documented equity risks (including detector bias), as well as against a range of assessment genres. Finally, the framework was iteratively refined to improve parsimony, explanatory reach, and feasibility across high- and low-resource institutional contexts.

Two further methodological resources informed this procedure. First, van der Waldt (2020) offers an open-access 'how-to' account of constructing conceptual frameworks, emphasising that conceptual frameworks should be simultaneously visual (to provide an organising map) and narrative (to justify presumed relationships). Second, Ayoubi et al. (2018) provide design guidelines for conceptual frameworks that highlight the importance of articulating assumptions, specifying causal or enabling relationships where appropriate, and iterating the framework until it functions as a usable decision-support artefact. These contributions were used as complementary quality checks throughout model development.

The procedure was documented through a concept matrix containing definitions, attributes, mechanisms, boundary conditions, and design implications. Candidate relationships were retained only when they could be stated in operational terms. For example, process authenticity was not retained merely as a normative preference for "showing the process"; it was specified through staged artefacts, revision evidence, feedback-response records, and selective dialogic checks. The same test was applied to equity and governance so that each principle corresponded to a decision, safeguard, or form of evidence.

Model specification and conceptual stress-testing

Following concept identification and deconstruction, the three authenticity dimensions were specified as the organising spine of ARAA: task authenticity (alignment to disciplinary and real-world practices), process authenticity (traceable, iterative learning activity), and epistemic authenticity (disciplinary reasoning, judgement, and justification). These dimensions were then linked to AfL processes by mapping how evidence of learning can be generated and interpreted across an assessment lifecycle: initial task interpretation, formative feedback loops, revision and resubmission, and summative judgement.

The model operationalises GenAI as a socio-technical mediator that can (a) support formative feedback and iterative improvement when bounded by transparency and accountability, but (b) also mask learning processes when used as an unacknowledged proxy author. Translating the model into assessment patterns (e.g., staged submissions, oral defences, portfolios, reflective AI disclosure, and multi-source feedback ecologies) constitutes a core part of the methodological design contribution of the chapter.

Stress-testing used five families of scenarios: text-dominant assignments, quantitative or coding tasks, professional design tasks, high-stakes judgement tasks, and large-enrolment assessments. The model was challenged with plausible failure conditions, including fabricated citations, plausible but decontextualised outputs, undisclosed proxy authorship, superficial revision, inaccessible premium tools, confidential data entered into public systems, excessive staff workload, and false-positive detector claims. Revisions were made where the framework did not provide a proportionate response to these conditions.

Trustworthiness, limitations, and ethical considerations

Because this chapter is non-empirical, trustworthiness is addressed through transparency of the model-building procedure, breadth of conceptual coverage, and explicit reporting of inclusion criteria for evidence. Nevertheless, the methodology has limitations: it does not constitute a full systematic review, and it cannot estimate effect sizes or causal impacts of GenAI on learning outcomes. Rather, ARAA should be treated as a defensible conceptual hypothesis and design heuristic set that requires further empirical testing through design-based research, evaluation studies, and equity-focused validation in both Global North and Global South contexts.

No human participants were involved and no primary data were collected; therefore, formal ethical approval was not required. Ethical attention in the chapter is directed instead to normative questions of assessment fairness, transparency, and accountability that arise when GenAI is used within students' academic work and within institutional feedback and quality assurance processes.

Trustworthiness is strengthened through an explicit evidence boundary, transparent model-building steps, comparison with adjacent frameworks, and the translation of constructs into observable design moves. Nevertheless, the selection process was purposive and cannot guarantee exhaustive coverage. The literature is also changing rapidly, and several empirical studies are context-specific. ARAA should therefore be treated as a defensible conceptual hypothesis and design heuristic, not as a validated universal standard.

Ethical responsibility also applies to the production of the chapter. No human participant data were collected for this work. Sources were verified against accessible publication records, claims were limited to the evidence reviewed, and illustrative examples are clearly identified as design scenarios. A generative-AI disclosure appears before the references so that the use of AI-assisted editorial and document-production support is transparent.

PROPOSED CONCEPTUAL MODEL

Purpose and scope of ARAA

AI-Resilient Authentic AfL (ARAA) is a conceptual framework for redesigning higher education assessment to maintain quality and integrity in GenAI-rich contexts. ARAA is designed to be actionable. Specifically, it supports educators and institutions in diagnosing where an assessment is vulnerable to inappropriate AI substitution; redesigning tasks and evidence structures so that learning processes and disciplinary reasoning become visible and assessable; and aligning these design moves with governance commitments to transparency, contestability, and equity.

ARAA conceptualises GenAI as a socio-technical mediator within the assessment ecology—supporting drafting, feedback, analysis, and ideation—rather than as an external threat. This aligns with open-access scholarship arguing that authenticity and integrity should be anchored in design rather than detection, particularly given documented detection bias and fundamental limits to perfect identification (Kickbusch et al., 2025; Liang et al., 2023; Májovský et al., 2024).

The framework is not intended to eliminate GenAI from learning. Instead, it provides a structured approach for determining when and how GenAI may be used, what must be disclosed, and which forms of evidence are required so that assessment remains a credible indicator of learning. ARAA is therefore compatible with both "AI-restricted" and "AI-integrated" assessment regimes, provided that accountability requirements are explicit and feasible (Elshall & Badir, 2025; Ilieva et al., 2025).

ARAA is not a detector replacement and does not promise to make inappropriate assistance impossible. Its purpose is to improve the quality of the evidence on which educational judgements are based. The framework is therefore compatible with different institutional positions on AI, but it rejects ambiguity: students should know what is permitted, what must be disclosed, what evidence will be assessed, how concerns will be investigated, and what alternatives exist when a tool is inaccessible or inappropriate.

Model architecture

ARAA is organised around three interlocking authenticities—task authenticity, process authenticity, and epistemic authenticity—embedded within an AfL cycle and surrounded by a governance envelope (Figure 1). The model proposes that assessment resilience in AI-rich environments is not primarily a technical problem; it is achieved by rebalancing what is assessed (the object of assessment), how evidence is generated (the evidentiary chain), and how judgements are governed (the conditions of fairness and accountability).

Figure 1 represents this architecture. The triangle identifies the ARAA core: task authenticity, process authenticity, and epistemic authenticity. The circular layer represents the assessment-for-learning cycle through which goals are clarified, evidence is elicited, feedback dialogue occurs, and students act on feedback. The outer governance envelope specifies the institutional conditions under which the model remains legitimate: transparency, contestability, privacy and data protection, equity and access, and capacity-sensitive implementation. GenAI appears as a socio-technical mediator because it can support or distort learning depending on how its role is designed and governed.

Figure 1. AI-Resilient Authentic Assessment-for-Learning (ARAA)

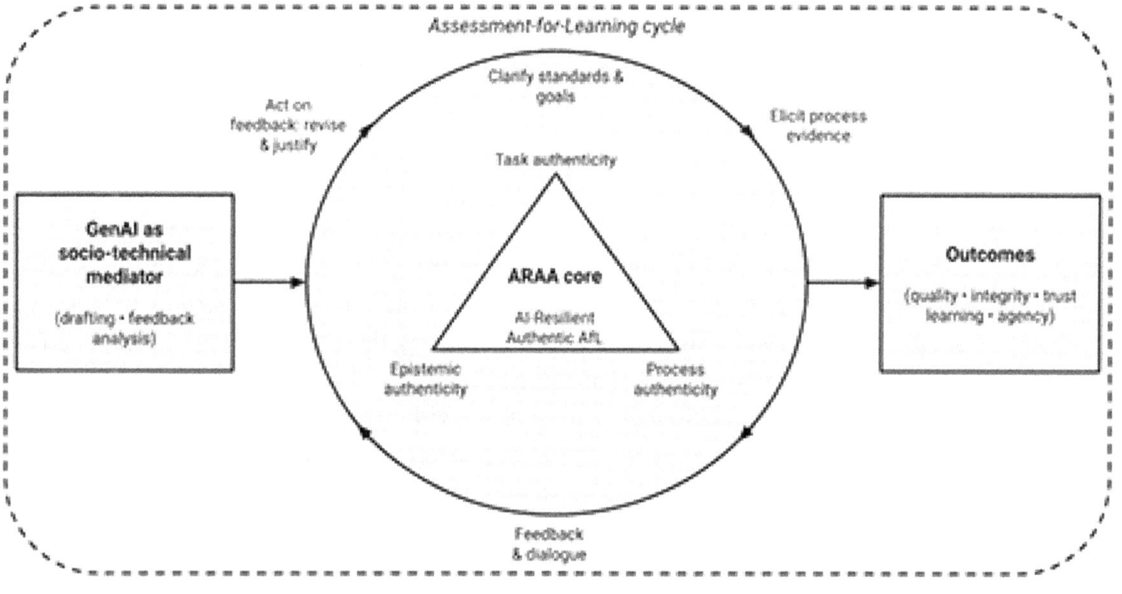

(Source: the authors)

Core propositions

ARAA is underpinned by five linked propositions that together articulate an integrity-by-design stance. First, it assumes that academic integrity is strengthened when assessment evidence extends beyond final products and makes learning processes and disciplinary judgement visible, thereby reducing the overreliance on output-only evaluation. Second, it treats authenticity as multidimensional in AI-mediated contexts, encompassing the realism and disciplinary alignment of tasks as well as the authenticity of learning processes and of epistemic justification (Vlachopoulos & Makri, 2024; Kickbusch et al., 2025).

Third, it recognises that GenAI can productively support AfL by expanding formative feedback and scaffolding self-regulated learning, but only where feedback literacy and critical evaluation are explicitly taught and assessed (Hopfenbeck et al., 2023; Gu et al., 2026; Urzúa et al., 2025). Fourth, it argues that detection-first strategies are insufficient for high-stakes decision-making because they are constrained by technical limitations and inequitable error patterns; consequently, detector outputs—if used at all—must never function as stand-alone evidence (Liang et al., 2023; Májovský et al., 2024). Finally, it positions quality assurance for AI-powered assessment as a socio-technical governance challenge that requires explicit rules, due process, and mitigation of access inequities (Jin et al., 2025; Ilieva et al., 2025).

These propositions imply a sixth operational principle: the allocation of cognitive work between learner and tool must be explicit. Permission alone is insufficient because the same tool use may be appropriate in one task and destructive in another. A brainstorming prompt can support idea generation when synthesis and evaluation remain the target; the same prompt can invalidate an assessment if idea generation is the target. ARAA therefore requires educators to state what may be delegated, what may be supported, and what must be demonstrated independently.

Task authenticity

Task authenticity refers to the degree to which an assessment requires learners to engage in meaningful disciplinary activity and/or real-world problem framing—characterised by context, constraints, ambiguity, evidence use, and stakeholder considerations. While authentic assessment has long been associated with real-world relevance, open-access synthesis indicates that authenticity also supports higher-order capability development when tasks require judgement and complex problem-solving rather than reproduction of content (Vlachopoulos & Makri, 2024).

In operational terms, ARAA treats task authenticity as a composite of disciplinary fidelity, contextual specificity, consequentiality (including audience), and constraint-based reasoning. Disciplinary fidelity requires students to employ the methods, concepts, and representational practices of the field, whereas contextual specificity anchors the task in localised cases, datasets, or briefs that demand adaptation and verification rather than generic reproduction. Consequentiality and audience further increase the need for coherence and ethical responsibility by framing outputs for plausible stakeholders beyond the marker, while constraint-based reasoning foregrounds trade-offs under limits of time, resources, data quality, and professional ethics. Taken together, these features shift assessment away from generic text production and toward situated problem framing, where performance depends on accountable judgement.

In GenAI contexts, task authenticity reduces vulnerability by lowering the value of generic, decontextualised outputs: GenAI may generate a plausible narrative, but students must still adapt it to situated constraints and produce defensible, evidence-aligned recommendations. Kickbusch et al. (2025) exemplify this approach by proposing tasks where students interrogate and improve chatbot-generated analyses through contextual critique and verification.

Task authenticity is not synonymous with workplace simulation. A task may be authentic because it reproduces a professional genre, because it requires disciplinary inquiry, because it has a consequential audience, or because it confronts the learner with uncertainty and trade-offs. The design test is whether success requires situated interpretation rather than generic production. A local dataset, stakeholder brief, case history, curriculum specification, ethical constraint, or incomplete evidence base can create this requirement without making the task unnecessarily elaborate.

Task authenticity also protects against false personalisation. Requiring students to insert autobiographical details does not necessarily create meaningful learning and may raise privacy concerns. The stronger strategy is contextual specificity that is educationally relevant: students should work with cases, data, constraints, or audiences that demand adaptation, verification, and professional responsibility. The task should be difficult to complete well through unexamined generic output, but it should not depend on hidden information or arbitrary obstacles.

Process authenticity

Process authenticity refers to the degree to which an assessment captures and values a traceable learning trajectory—planning, drafting, feedback engagement, revision, and decision-making—through explicit evidence. Process authenticity is central to ARAA because GenAI can compress product generation time, making final outputs weaker indicators of learning participation. Process-focused evidence responds to this by distributing assessment value across learning-in-action rather than end-state performance (Kickbusch et al., 2025).

ARAA operationalises process authenticity by requiring evidence that the student's work has evolved through time, interaction, and revision. Traceability is ensured through staged artefacts that allow reviewers to see how ideas, sources, and analytic choices develop, while iterativity is built in by requiring at least one substantive revision cycle in which changes are justified rather than cosmetic. Moreover, feedback uptake becomes assessable through a brief response-to-feedback memo that explains what feedback was acted upon, what was rejected, and the rationale for those decisions (Urzúa et al., 2025). Finally, where GenAI is permitted, tool transparency is normalised through a concise AI-use statement describing how tools were used and what quality-control checks were applied, positioning disclosure as accountable scholarship rather than confession.

Process authenticity also enables capacity-sensitive integrity assurance: rather than relying on continuous surveillance, educators can implement selective checkpoints (e.g., brief in-class progress reviews, targeted micro-vivas, or portfolio audits) to confirm ownership and understanding while maintaining a trust-based assessment culture (Tan & Maravilla, 2024).

Process evidence should be proportionate and purposeful. Requiring complete prompt transcripts or continuous screen recording can create privacy, workload, and performative-compliance problems. ARAA instead favours concise evidence tied to learning: an annotated draft, a decision log, a response-to-feedback memo, a source-verification record, or a summary of significant AI interactions. The evidentiary question is not whether every keystroke can be reconstructed, but whether the trajectory of learning and the student's consequential decisions are visible enough to support judgement.

Authentic process evidence must also have assessment value. When drafts and logs are collected but ignored, students experience them as surveillance artefacts rather than learning resources. Rubrics should therefore allocate credit to revision quality, feedback uptake, methodological decision-making, or critical disclosure. This creates an incentive to use process documentation as a reflective scholarly practice and reduces the temptation to fabricate a compliant record after the final product has been produced.

Epistemic authenticity

Epistemic authenticity refers to the degree to which assessment elicits and evaluates disciplinary ways of knowing: reasoning, evaluation of evidence, judgement, and justification. In the GenAI era, epistemic authenticity is the most direct safeguard of epistemic agency: students must be able to defend claims, explain methodological choices, and critique alternative outputs (including AI-generated outputs). This aligns with integrity scholarship arguing that AI does not have to undermine education when the assessment object shifts toward ethical judgement and accountable reasoning (Tan & Maravilla, 2024).

ARAA operationalises epistemic authenticity by assessing students' capacity to reason and justify in ways that are recognisably disciplinary. This begins with explicit claim–evidence alignment, in which students connect their claims to evidence while acknowledging uncertainty and limitations. It also requires methodological justification, such that students can explain why particular approaches, sources, or analytic steps were adopted and why plausible alternatives were not pursued.

Where GenAI is used, epistemic authenticity is further enacted through critical evaluation of AI outputs, including identification of potential errors, bias, hallucinations, or missing context, together with documentation of verification steps (Kolade et al., 2024). Finally, reflective judgement and dialogic accountability are cultivated through reflective accounts of what changed across drafts and why, alongside brief oral defences or structured Q&A that require students to articulate and defend pivotal decisions.

Epistemic authenticity is especially important in disciplines where professional work requires high-stakes judgement (e.g., education, health, engineering, policy). In such contexts, the integrity question becomes: can the student responsibly exercise judgement with tools, not merely produce an answer with tools? This is compatible with assessment designs that combine AI-assisted tasks with non-AI components in a balanced regime, as demonstrated in the FACT assessment framework implemented in environmental data science education (Elshall & Badir, 2025).

Epistemic authenticity is the model's strongest response to fluent but unreliable output. Students must demonstrate how they know, not only what they conclude. Appropriate evidence may include claim-evidence maps, annotated calculations, methodological rationales, uncertainty statements, source-quality judgements, critique of alternative interpretations, or a short oral defence. These requirements are not punitive additions. They are direct assessments of disciplinary knowing and are often more educationally valuable than additional prose.

Dialogic accountability should be used selectively. A micro-viva can confirm ownership and understanding, but poorly designed oral checks may disadvantage multilingual students, students with disabilities, or students unfamiliar with oral examination. Institutions should publish criteria, provide reasonable preparation, allow accessible formats, and focus questions on pivotal decisions already represented in the submitted work. The purpose is to elicit judgement, not to surprise or intimidate the student.

The feedback ecology

The ARAA feedback ecology assigns complementary functions to teacher, peer, self, and AI feedback. Teacher feedback is prioritised where disciplinary judgement, relational knowledge, or high-stakes correction is required. Peer feedback supports comparison, audience awareness, and evaluative judgement. Self-assessment requires learners to apply criteria to their own work. AI feedback can offer rapid rehearsal, alternative explanations, surface-level checking, or provisional critique. The ecology is effective only when students understand the authority and limitations of each source (Carless & Boud, 2018; Hopfenbeck et al., 2023).

Feedback orchestration also requires timing. AI feedback is most defensible before summative submission, when it can support experimentation and revision, and least defensible when it directly supplies the final judgement or replaces the learner's explanation. ARAA therefore separates formative assistance from summative evidence. Students may use AI to test a draft or generate counterarguments, but the submission must show how that feedback was evaluated and how the resulting changes align with disciplinary standards (Gu et al., 2026; Urzúa et al., 2025).

The governance envelope

Transparency requires more than an integrity statement. Each assessment should specify permitted uses, prohibited uses, disclosure expectations, data restrictions, the status of detector or provenance evidence, and the procedure followed when concerns arise. Requirements should be written in task-specific language because a generic institutional policy cannot anticipate the learning outcomes of every discipline. Where a task prohibits AI, the educational reason should be stated; where it permits AI, the boundaries and quality-control responsibilities should be equally explicit.

Contestability protects students and staff from opaque or disproportionate decisions. A concern about AI use should be documented, evaluated against multiple evidence sources, and communicated to the student, who must have a meaningful opportunity to explain the work. Detector scores should not be treated as proof. The institution should distinguish academic-development conversations, assessment-validity checks, and formal misconduct processes so that a request for clarification does not automatically function as an accusation (Liang et al., 2023; Otterbacher, 2023).

Privacy and data protection require data minimisation, approved-tool guidance, and alternatives. Students should be instructed not to enter personal, confidential, proprietary, or unpublished information into public systems. Where the institution mandates a platform, it assumes responsibility for procurement, contractual safeguards, accessibility, and communication. Where the tool is optional, non-use must not reduce the opportunity to meet the learning outcomes. These principles align with UNESCO's human-centred guidance and global policy concerns identified by Jin et al. (2025) and Miao and Holmes (2023).

Equity and access require attention to language, disability, connectivity, device ownership, paid features, and differential AI literacy. Identical access to a tool does not guarantee equivalent benefit because prompt literacy, disciplinary knowledge, and language support shape outcomes. ARAA therefore combines access provision with instructional support and alternative evidence routes. Capacity-sensitive implementation adds a further constraint: a theoretically robust design that staff cannot administer reliably is not a fair design.

Mechanisms of AI resilience

ARAA achieves AI-resilience through mechanisms that operate across task design, evidentiary structure, pedagogy, and governance. At the task level, contextual constraints and discipline-specific artefacts increase substitution resistance by reducing the adequacy of generic GenAI outputs. At the evidentiary level, staged submissions and revision traces enhance trajectory visibility, making learning participation assessable and supporting formative development. At the epistemic level, justification requirements, critique tasks, and dialogic checks support agency verification by establishing that students can explain and defend their claims and decisions.

Importantly, these mechanisms are sustained by feedback ecology orchestration: AfL cycles combine teacher, peer, and AI-supported formative feedback with explicit roles, while also building students' feedback literacy and evaluative judgement (Gu et al., 2026; Urzúa et al., 2025). Finally, governance alignment—through transparent expectations, contestability, and equity safeguards—protects students from unjust accusation and creates predictable accountability conditions, particularly salient given documented detector bias (Liang et al., 2023; Jin et al., 2025).

These mechanisms can be summarised as substitution resistance, trajectory visibility, agency verification, feedback literacy, and governance legitimacy. Substitution resistance reduces the adequacy of generic output. Trajectory visibility distributes evidence over time. Agency verification requires students to explain consequential decisions. Feedback literacy makes the use of support assessable. Governance legitimacy ensures that expectations and investigations are transparent, proportionate, and equitable. No single mechanism is sufficient; resilience emerges from their combination.

Managing productive support and dependency

ARAA manages dependency through three questions. First, does the tool perform an operation that is itself a learning outcome? If so, independent performance or a non-AI component is needed. Second, does the tool support but not replace the learning outcome? If so, guided use and reflective evidence may be appropriate. Third, is the operation peripheral to the outcome? If so, automation may be permitted with minimal disclosure. This outcome-level analysis is more precise than a universal rule about particular tools because tool capabilities change and the same feature has different meanings across disciplines.

The dependency test also considers transfer. A student who can produce a strong result with AI but cannot explain, adapt, or reproduce the underlying judgement in a new context has demonstrated assisted performance rather than durable competence. Assessment should therefore include at least one transfer or defence opportunity where pivotal knowledge is applied under altered conditions. This does not require a closed-book examination in every case; a short scenario variation, data perturbation, counterargument, or oral follow-up may provide the necessary evidence.

ARAA AS A DESIGN WORKFLOW

To support adoption, ARAA can be enacted through a practical redesign workflow that progresses from outcomes to evidence to governance. The process begins by clarifying the intended learning outcomes and the level of judgement required, and then diagnosing where GenAI could inappropriately substitute for learning (and, conversely, where it could legitimately support learning through formative guidance).

On this basis, educators design for task authenticity by selecting authentic genres, contextualised problem framings, and constraints that require adaptation and evidence-based decision-making (Vlachopoulos & Makri, 2024; Kickbusch et al., 2025). They then design for process authenticity by building staged submissions and revision artefacts, and for epistemic authenticity by embedding explicit justification requirements and dialogic accountability opportunities (Tan & Maravilla, 2024).

The workflow continues by deliberately orchestrating the feedback ecology—combining teacher, peer, and AI-supported feedback while cultivating feedback literacy (Hopfenbeck et al., 2023; Gu et al., 2026)—and culminates in governance checks that make AI-use expectations transparent, ensure contestability and due process, and mitigate inequities where tool access differs (Jin et al., 2025; Ilieva et al., 2025). Although presented sequentially, the workflow is inherently iterative: insights from implementation and student work samples should inform ongoing refinement of tasks, evidence requirements, and support structures.

Figure 2 converts the framework into an eight-stage workflow. The sequence begins with learning outcomes rather than tool capability and concludes with evidence-based refinement. Although the stages are displayed sequentially, redesign is iterative: implementation evidence may reveal that an apparently authentic task is too burdensome, that disclosure requirements are unclear, or that oral checks introduce inequity. The workflow therefore includes an explicit feedback loop from evaluation to the next design cycle.

Figure 2. ARAA assessment-redesign workflow

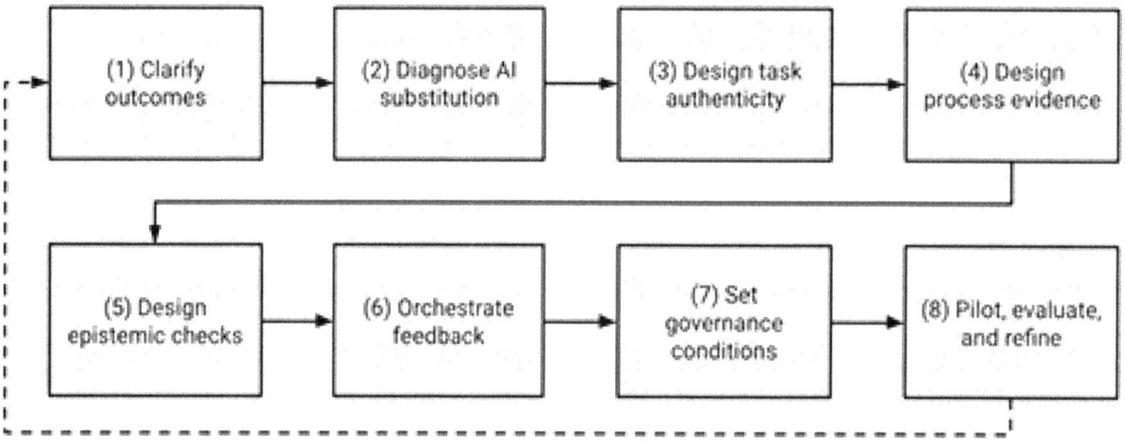

(Source: the authors)

The ARAA Canvas

The ARAA Canvas in Table 3 is a compact planning record. It can be completed at module, programme, or institutional-review level and should be retained with the assessment brief and rubric. Its value lies in forcing alignment: each design claim is linked to evidence, AI-use conditions, and a governance check. A canvas that cannot identify observable evidence or an implementable safeguard signals that the design remains aspirational rather than operational.

Table 3. ARAA Canvas for assessment planning

ARAA component	Key design question	Evidence required	AI-use and governance checks
Task authenticity	What makes the task disciplinary, contextual, consequential, and constraint-based?	Authentic genre, local case or data, stakeholder audience, documented trade-offs.	State permitted AI roles, verification duties, access assumptions, and equivalent alternatives.
Process authenticity	How will learning-in-progress and consequential decisions become visible?	Staged artefacts, annotated drafts, revision mapping, decision log, response-to-feedback memo.	Use concise disclosure; avoid compulsory surveillance or unnecessary prompt capture.
Epistemic authenticity	How will students justify claims, methods, evidence, uncertainty, and alternatives?	Rationale statement, claim-evidence map, critique, uncertainty analysis, micro-viva or Q&A.	Publish criteria, ensure accessible defence formats, and use multiple evidence sources.
Feedback ecology	Who provides feedback, when, for what purpose, and how will uptake be demonstrated?	Teacher and peer records, AI-feedback summary, action plan, reflection on accepted and rejected advice.	Teach feedback literacy and distinguish formative assistance from summative judgement.
Human-AI division of labour	Which operations may be automated, augmented, or must remain demonstrably human?	Independent component, transfer task, verification note, or explanation of retained human judgement.	Align tool permission with outcomes rather than with a blanket institutional rule.
Governance envelope	What protects transparency, privacy, equity, contestability, and feasibility?	Published guidance, approved-tool advice, audit trail, alternative route, workload and accessibility plan.	Define due process; detector outputs cannot function as stand-alone evidence.

WORKED EXAMPLES AND DISCIPLINE-SPECIFIC CHALLENGES

The following examples are design patterns rather than validated interventions. They illustrate how the same architecture can be instantiated differently across disciplines, class sizes, and resource conditions. Each pattern aligns task, process, and epistemic authenticity with feedback activity and transparent rules for GenAI use (*see* Table 4).

Teacher education: AI-supported lesson design with an inclusive-pedagogy audit

Pre-service teachers develop a lesson plan and assessment sequence for a specific cohort (e.g., multilingual learners in a local school context) with explicit constraints (time, curriculum standards, accessibility requirements). Students may use GenAI to propose activity ideas or differentiation strategies, but must adapt outputs to local policy and learner needs. This aligns with design-led arguments that authenticity in an AI-mediated world is achieved through critique, adaptation, and ethical judgement (Kickbusch et al., 2025).

Process authenticity is supported through staged artefacts. Students submit a concept note that frames the lesson design problem, followed by a draft plan with annotations; they then engage with peer feedback and produce a short action plan, before submitting a revised final plan accompanied by a response-to-feedback memo and an AI-use statement. This staging ensures traceability and creates multiple points for formative intervention.

Students complete a brief oral defence (micro-viva) focusing on why chosen pedagogical moves are appropriate for the specified learner cohort, how evidence informed differentiation, and what risks (bias, stereotyping, misinformation) were mitigated when using GenAI. Integrity is verified through disciplinary justification rather than detector outputs.

A resource-constrained version can use a paper or LMS template rather than a specialised portfolio platform. Peer review can be organised through small groups, and the micro-viva can be sampled or completed as a two-minute recorded explanation. The key evidence is not the quantity of documentation but the student's ability to connect curriculum requirements, learner needs, evidence, and ethical decisions.

Data analytics: AI-assisted coding with defensible modelling decisions

Students analyse a localised dataset (e.g., institutional retention data or publicly available municipal data) to answer a stakeholder-driven question. They produce an analytic notebook and a policy-style findings brief. Where AI coding assistants are permitted, students must still address data quality, assumptions, and interpretation limits.

Students submit versioned notebooks at two checkpoints and complete a model-decision log (what features were engineered, what models were tried, and why). A response-to-feedback memo explains revisions between checkpoints. This process mirrors the structured balance between AI-assisted and non-AI assessment components demonstrated in the FACT assessment framework for environmental data science (Elshall & Badir, 2025).

Students defend two pivotal modelling decisions (e.g., why a model was selected, how overfitting was addressed, what fairness checks were considered) and critique at least one AI-suggested approach they rejected. This foregrounds evaluative judgement and accountability.

To manage dependency, the task includes a small non-AI component in which students interpret unfamiliar output or modify a model under changed assumptions. This tests transfer without denying access to professional tools. Privacy is addressed by using public, synthetic, or de-identified data and by prohibiting the upload of restricted institutional datasets to public coding assistants. The design preserves the FACT principle of balancing AI-assisted application with independent conceptual evidence (Elshall & Badir, 2025).

Business and management: auditing an AI-generated market analysis

Students receive a client brief for a specific market entry scenario and must produce a strategic recommendation. They are provided with an AI-generated market analysis (or asked to generate one) and must evaluate its claims against credible sources, local constraints, and ethical considerations. This mirrors design patterns emphasised in open-access scholarship: students interrogate, adapt, and verify AI outputs rather than submit them uncritically (Kickbusch et al., 2025).

Students submit an 'evidence trail' documenting sources used to verify or refute AI claims, plus an annotated revision trail showing how the recommendation evolved. Peer feedback focuses on the credibility of evidence and argument coherence.

Assessment criteria reward the quality of justification (why certain evidence was weighted, how uncertainty was handled), and include a short viva or timed in-class critique where students respond to counterarguments and defend trade-offs.

The principal implementation challenge is source quality. Students may mistake confident synthesis for market evidence, particularly where local or emerging-market data are sparse. The rubric therefore separates strategic coherence from evidentiary credibility and rewards explicit treatment of uncertainty. A low-cost implementation can provide the same AI-generated baseline to all students, avoiding inequity in access to premium tools while preserving the critique and verification task.

Academic writing and EAP: GenAI-supported feedback with feedback-literacy scaffolding

Students produce a research-based paper in an academic genre relevant to their programme. GenAI may be used for formative feedback on clarity and structure, but students must demonstrate disciplinary synthesis and evidence use.

The assessment is staged: outline → annotated draft → revision plan → final paper + reflective commentary. Students attach a concise AI-feedback log summarising feedback received, what was adopted, what was rejected, and why.

Students critique AI feedback quality by identifying at least two instances where feedback was unhelpful, incorrect, or misaligned with disciplinary conventions, and justify how they corrected course. This approach aligns with evidence that AI-assisted feedback can support writing development but should be integrated to foster higher-order thinking and feedback literacy, not to replace human judgement (Urzúa et al., 2025; Gu et al., 2026).

This design is particularly relevant for multilingual writers because detector bias can create disproportionate risk while language-support tools can provide legitimate assistance. The policy should distinguish language-level support from unacknowledged substantive authorship, and the assessment should reward synthesis, source use, disciplinary positioning, and revision decisions. Students should never be required to submit work to an AI detector as a condition of demonstrating integrity (Liang et al., 2023).

Health professions: clinical reasoning with a simulated AI consultation

Students receive a de-identified clinical or professional case and an AI-generated provisional response. Their task is to identify unsafe assumptions, missing evidence, uncertainty, and context-specific considerations before producing a reasoned plan. Task authenticity is created by incomplete information and professional constraints. Process authenticity is evidenced through an annotated critique and revision record. Epistemic authenticity is assessed through justification of risk, evidence, and escalation decisions. Because professional judgement is high-stakes, the final component includes a structured oral or written defence.

Privacy safeguards are non-negotiable. No identifiable patient or client information is entered into public systems, and the AI output is generated from a synthetic case or supplied by the instructor. The task assesses responsible judgement with tools rather than the ability to obtain an answer from a tool. It also exposes a core limitation of fluent output: plausible language can conceal clinically or ethically consequential omissions.

Large-enrolment general education: evidence-based position brief

In a large introductory module, students produce a short position brief on a contested local issue using a common source pack. AI may be used for brainstorming or formative critique, but students submit a claim-evidence map, a brief verification note, and a response-to-feedback paragraph. Ownership checks are sampled rather than universal. Automated administrative processes may support submission, but summative judgement remains grounded in the student's argument, evidence alignment, and capacity to respond to a targeted follow-up question.

This pattern demonstrates capacity sensitivity. It does not require extensive portfolios or individual vivas for every student. Instead, it uses short structured artefacts, common materials, rubric calibration, and risk-based sampling. Students selected for follow-up are chosen through transparent sampling or evidence-based concerns, and the procedure is framed as validity assurance rather than presumption of misconduct.

Table 4. Discipline-specific ARAA patterns, risks, and mitigations

Discipline	Task authenticity	Process and epistemic evidence	Primary risk and mitigation
Teacher education	Local cohort, curriculum, inclusion, and lesson-design constraints.	Concept note, annotated draft, peer response, inclusive-pedagogy audit, micro-viva.	Stereotyping or generic pedagogy; mitigate through local evidence and learner-specific justification.
Data analytics	Local or public dataset and stakeholder question.	Versioned notebook, model-decision log, critique of rejected AI suggestion, transfer task.	Overreliance or data leakage; use de-identified data and retain an independent conceptual component.
Business / management	Specific client, market, regulation, and strategic trade-offs.	Source-verification trail, annotated recommendation, counterargument defence.	Fabricated or weak market evidence; separate evidence credibility from rhetorical polish.
Academic writing / EAP	Disciplinary genre, source synthesis, audience, and voice.	Outline, annotated draft, revision plan, AI-feedback log, reflective commentary.	Language support confused with authorship; define boundaries and assess synthesis and revision.
Health professions	Synthetic high-stakes case with uncertainty and ethical constraints.	Annotated AI critique, risk analysis, reasoned plan, structured defence.	Unsafe advice or privacy breach; prohibit identifiable data and assess escalation judgement.
Large-enrolment modules	Common source pack and local contested issue.	Claim-evidence map, verification note, response to feedback, sampled follow-up.	Unsustainable workload; use short templates, calibrated rubrics, and transparent sampling.

IMPLEMENTATION AND EVALUATION

Capacity-sensitive deployment

ARAA is intended to be feasible under resource constraints. Institutions can scale it through structured templates (AI-use statements, response-to-feedback memos), selective dialogic checks (sampling micro-vivas in high-stakes units), and low-cost portfolio approaches using existing learning management systems. Policy analysis indicates that institutional adoption varies globally and that capacity and equity conditions are decisive; therefore, ARAA should be implemented with explicit attention to tool access, staff development, and proportional enforcement (Jin et al., 2025).

A staged rollout is preferable to immediate institution-wide standardisation. Institutions can begin with a small set of high-enrolment, high-stakes, or visibly vulnerable assessments and support redesign teams with exemplars and facilitation. Early implementation should test administrative workload, student understanding, accessibility, and the quality of evidence produced. Policies and templates are then revised before wider adoption. This sequence treats implementation as organisational learning rather than compliance dissemination.

Low-cost implementation tools include one-page AI-use statements, response-to-feedback memos, decision logs, common source-verification templates, and brief recorded explanations. Existing learning-management systems can store staged submissions and feedback records. Micro-vivas can be sampled, conducted in groups, or replaced with structured written responses where accessibility or scale requires. These choices preserve the framework's evidentiary logic while respecting local capacity.

Student partnership and communication

Students should participate in the interpretation and refinement of AI-use rules. Chan (2023) explicitly identifies an active student role in policy development, and student-perception research shows that learners recognise both benefits and risks (Chan & Hu, 2023). Programme teams can use student panels, task walkthroughs, pilot feedback, and examples of acceptable disclosure to identify ambiguity before high-stakes use. Co-design does not transfer responsibility for standards to students; it improves the intelligibility and legitimacy of those standards.

Communication should occur at three levels. Institutional policy states common principles and due process. Programme guidance defines disciplinary expectations and approved practices. The assessment brief specifies task-level permissions, evidence, and consequences. Contradictions among these levels undermine trust and expose students to accidental non-compliance. ARAA therefore treats policy coherence as part of assessment quality assurance.

Faculty readiness, calibration, and workload

Staff development should move beyond generic demonstrations of GenAI tools. Educators need structured opportunities to diagnose substitution risk, design evidence chains, write task-specific AI guidance, calibrate judgement of process artefacts, conduct proportionate oral checks, and respond to suspected misuse. Communities of practice can reduce duplication by sharing discipline-specific patterns and annotated examples. These supports reflect the factors associated with educator AI literacy identified by Ayyoub et al. (2025).

Workload must be estimated before implementation. Process evidence can increase marking demands if every draft, prompt, and reflection is assessed in full. ARAA recommends selective evidence: identify the artefacts that most directly support validity, use concise templates, sample low-risk components, and reserve intensive review for high-stakes decisions or specific concerns. Workload data should be included in pilot evaluation because an under-resourced design will be implemented inconsistently and may become inequitable.

Privacy, equity, and approved alternatives

Institutions should publish a data-classification rule for GenAI use. Public or synthetic data may be acceptable; confidential, personal, proprietary, or restricted data should not be entered into public tools. Tool guidance should address retention, model training, account requirements, age restrictions where relevant, and the availability of institutional contracts. When these assurances cannot be provided, the assessment must offer a non-AI route that meets the same learning outcomes (Miao & Holmes, 2023).

Equity review should ask whether students have comparable opportunities to practise, obtain support, and demonstrate learning. Premium features, high-bandwidth access, advanced devices, English-dominant interfaces, and inaccessible interaction modes may advantage some groups. Mitigations include campus access, shared institutional licences, low-bandwidth alternatives, multilingual guidance, accessible formats, and assessment designs that do not reward tool sophistication in place of disciplinary competence. Global policy evidence makes clear that access and readiness remain uneven (Jin et al., 2025).

Evaluation indicators

Evaluation of ARAA implementation should prioritise educational validity rather than merely counting misconduct cases. In practice, this can be evidenced through students' ability to articulate and justify decisions in defences, through cohort-level evidence of substantive revision and feedback uptake, through student perceptions of fairness and transparency, and through patterns of tool-use disclosure. Such evaluation also supports quality assurance bodies seeking demonstrable alignment between intended learning outcomes, assessment evidence, and integrity safeguards (Ilieva et al., 2025).

Evaluation should examine educational validity, learning, fairness, and feasibility rather than using the number of misconduct cases as the primary outcome. A reduction in cases may reflect clearer guidance, but it may also reflect under-reporting or weaker enforcement. Conversely, an initial increase in disclosures may indicate improved transparency rather than increased misuse. Table 5 therefore combines multiple indicators and evidence sources.

Table 5. Indicative evaluation framework for ARAA implementation

Evaluation domain	Key question	Evidence source	Decision use
Assessment validity	Can students explain and transfer pivotal knowledge and decisions?	Rubric evidence, transfer tasks, micro-viva records, moderation samples.	Revise task or evidence requirements when polished products are not supported by understanding.
Learning and revision	Do drafts show substantive development and action on feedback?	Version comparison, response-to-feedback memos, portfolio samples.	Strengthen staging or feedback literacy when changes are superficial.
Feedback literacy	Can students evaluate, select, and justify use of teacher, peer, and AI feedback?	Feedback logs, reflective commentary, evaluative-judgement tasks.	Clarify source roles and provide guided practice.
Equity and access	Do outcomes, participation, or burden differ by access, language, disability, or tool choice?	Student surveys, differential outcomes, accessibility reports, alternative-route uptake.	Provide equivalent routes and remove avoidable tool-dependent advantage.

continued on following page

Table 5. Continued

Evaluation domain	Key question	Evidence source	Decision use
Trust and transparency	Do students and staff understand rules and regard procedures as fair?	Policy-comprehension checks, surveys, appeals, focus groups.	Rewrite guidance and strengthen contestability where ambiguity or mistrust persists.
Staff workload and consistency	Can the design be delivered reliably within available time and expertise?	Marking-time logs, moderation variance, staff feedback, support requests.	Simplify evidence, improve calibration, or phase implementation.
Governance and privacy	Are data handling, investigations, and decisions documented and proportionate?	Audit trail, incident review, approved-tool records, appeal outcomes.	Change procurement, data rules, or due-process procedures.

Empirical validation agenda

ARAA requires empirical evaluation across disciplines, cultural contexts, and institutional resource levels. Design-based research can test whether the framework improves the alignment among learning outcomes, assessment evidence, and student understanding. Quasi-experimental and longitudinal studies can compare revision quality, transfer, feedback literacy, and perceptions of fairness across redesigned and conventional tasks. Qualitative work can examine how students and staff interpret disclosure, ownership, trust, and the human-AI division of labour.

Equity-focused validation is especially important. Research should test whether process evidence and oral defence reduce or reproduce disadvantage, whether alternative routes are genuinely equivalent, and whether detector-free investigations improve due process. Studies in Global South and resource-constrained institutions should examine implementation costs, access patterns, language conditions, and the feasibility of low-bandwidth evidence practices. ARAA's value will depend on its capacity to travel without assuming uniform infrastructure or institutional power.

DISCUSSION

ARAA strengthens assessment quality by shifting validity arguments away from the assumption that the submitted artefact equals student competence, toward a richer evidentiary chain including product, process, and epistemic demonstrations. In GenAI conditions, final products become weaker proxies for learning because generative systems can produce surface-level plausibility. ARAA responds by designing tasks that require contextualised practice, visible trajectories, and defensible judgement (Kickbusch et al., 2025; Kolade et al., 2024).

The framework's first conceptual contribution is to separate three forms of authenticity that are often collapsed. Task authenticity concerns the work students are asked to undertake; process authenticity concerns the trajectory through which the work develops; epistemic authenticity concerns the quality of reasoning and justification. A task can resemble professional practice yet remain vulnerable if only the final product is assessed. Conversely, a detailed process log is not sufficient if the student cannot defend the disciplinary basis of key decisions. Resilience depends on coherence among all three dimensions.

Detector-centric strategies create governance risks that are both epistemic and ethical. Detectors are probabilistic and sensitive to domain and model changes, while evidence suggests bias against non-native English writers (Liang et al., 2023). Consequently, institutions should prioritise transparency, contestability, and redesign strategies that elicit process and epistemic evidence rather than relying on uncertain technical attribution (Májovský et al., 2024; Otterbacher, 2023).

The second contribution is to position integrity as a property of assessment and governance rather than solely of individual conduct. Students remain responsible for honest representation, but institutions are responsible for creating tasks whose evidentiary logic is credible, rules that are intelligible, data practices that are safe, and procedures that are contestable. This shared-responsibility position avoids the false choice between permissiveness and surveillance. It supports accountable tool use while retaining proportionate responses to misrepresentation.

GenAI enables scalable formative support, but effective integration requires feedback literacy and self-regulated engagement. Evidence indicates that students' self-regulated interactions with GenAI and peer feedback can influence feedback literacy development, and that GenAI feedback does not fully replicate human interaction dynamics (Gu et al., 2026). Accordingly, ARAA positions GenAI as a drafting partner and feedback scaffold whose outputs are evaluated rather than obeyed, with clear role definitions in feedback ecologies (Hopfenbeck et al., 2023; Urzúa et al., 2025).

The third contribution is the integration of feedback literacy with AI resilience. Rapid machine feedback can increase the volume of comments without improving learning if students lack criteria, judgement, or motivation to act. ARAA therefore treats the evaluation and use of feedback as visible learning. This interpretation extends assessment for learning into the GenAI context: the formative cycle does not end when feedback is generated; it continues through comparison, decision, revision, and justification.

ARAA implies that quality assurance must incorporate socio-technical governance. Core commitments include transparency standards (clear permissible AI uses and disclosure expectations), contestability and due process (especially given detector bias), equity safeguards (multiple pathways to evidence learning), and proportional enforcement. Governance should treat technical provenance tools as, at most, complementary signals rather than definitive proof (Liang et al., 2023; Májovský et al., 2024; Ilieva et al., 2025).

Compared with adjacent frameworks, ARAA is less a permission scale than an evidence architecture. The AIAS provides a powerful language for specifying levels of use, Chan's framework clarifies institutional policy dimensions, FACT demonstrates a hybrid disciplinary design, and Kickbusch et al. (2025) establish the case for authenticity beyond detection. ARAA connects these insights by asking how permission, evidence, feedback, judgement, and governance interact over the full assessment lifecycle. Its distinctiveness lies in this integration rather than in claiming that each component is individually new.

For resource-constrained contexts, ARAA emphasises low-cost process evidence (structured templates, lightweight portfolios), selective dialogic checks (sampling micro-vivas in high-stakes tasks), equitable access communication (and alternatives where tool access is uneven), and staff development as a governance priority. Institutional policy analysis suggests uneven readiness and highlights the need for implementation pathways that align with local resource realities (Jin et al., 2025).

Capacity sensitivity is therefore not a secondary implementation issue. An assessment design that depends on extensive oral examination, commercial platforms, or continuous monitoring may be invalid in contexts where these resources are unavailable or unevenly distributed. ARAA responds through modularity: institutions can use the same conceptual architecture with different evidence intensities. A high-resource professional programme may use detailed portfolios and individual defences, while a large or under-resourced module may use common source packs, concise logs, sampled checks, and existing LMS infrastructure.

As a conceptual synthesis, ARAA requires empirical evaluation across disciplines and cultures. Priority research includes measuring learning effects of process-authentic designs, examining student trust and perceived fairness, evaluating feedback literacy interventions for GenAI-supported feedback, and studying institutional implementation of transparency and contestability mechanisms (Hopfenbeck et al., 2023; Gu et al., 2026).

Several limitations remain. ARAA is a conceptual synthesis, not a systematic review, psychometric model, or validated intervention. The framework may also create new forms of performativity if process artefacts become formulaic or if students learn to simulate disclosure. Oral checks may introduce linguistic or accessibility bias; contextualised tasks may increase staff workload; and institutional policies may lag behind rapid changes in tools. These risks reinforce the need for empirical evaluation, student partnership, moderation, and iterative redesign rather than weakening the case for the framework.

The most important future question is not whether GenAI can be excluded from assessment. It is whether institutions can construct credible evidence of learning while students operate in environments where powerful tools are routinely available. ARAA offers one answer: make the target learning explicit, design contextual and consequential tasks, value the trajectory of revision, elicit disciplinary justification, teach feedback literacy, specify the human-AI division of labour, and govern the process transparently. The framework is successful only when these elements improve learning and fairness, not merely when they make misuse harder.

CONCLUSION

GenAI has destabilised conventional assessment by changing what can be produced, how quickly, and with what kinds of tool-mediated support. Detector-first and prohibition-heavy responses are increasingly exposed as insufficient and potentially inequitable. This chapter re-centres authentic assessment and AfL as complementary foundations for quality and integrity and proposes the ARAA framework—task, process, and epistemic authenticity embedded in an AfL cycle and governance envelope—as an implementable pathway to AI-resilient assessment. ARAA shifts attention from 'catching AI use' to designing assessment that makes learning visible, preserves epistemic agency, and sustains trust.

ARAA reframes assessment resilience as an educational and governance achievement. Task authenticity reduces the adequacy of generic substitution; process authenticity makes learning-in-action visible; epistemic authenticity requires defensible disciplinary judgement; the assessment-for-learning cycle turns feedback into revision; and the governance envelope protects transparency, privacy, equity, contestability, and feasibility. Together, these elements shift integrity from a reactive search for machine authorship towards a proactive design of credible evidence.

The framework does not eliminate uncertainty, nor does it prescribe a single institutional stance on AI. It provides a disciplined way to decide what tools may do, what learners must demonstrate, what evidence assessors need, and what safeguards legitimate the resulting judgement. Its next stage is empirical: implementation studies should test learning, workload, equity, trust, and transfer across disciplines and resource contexts. Until then, ARAA should be used as a transparent design hypothesis and a practical basis for collective assessment review.

REFERENCES

Ayoubi, M., Mehrabanfar, E., & Banaitis, A. (2018). Guidelines on designing conceptual framework for strategic management with application to the energy industry. *Administrative Sciences*, *8*(3), 27. Advance online publication. DOI: 10.3390/admsci8030027

Ayyoub, A. M., Khlaif, Z. N., Shamali, M., Abu Eideh, B., Assali, A., Hattab, M. K., Barham, K. A., & Bsharat, T. R. K. (2025). Advancing higher education with GenAI: Factors influencing educator AI literacy. *Frontiers in Education*, *10*, 1530721. Advance online publication. DOI: 10.3389/feduc.2025.1530721

Bittle, K., & El-Gayar, O. (2025). Generative AI and academic integrity in higher education. *Information (Basel)*, *16*(4), 296. Advance online publication. DOI: 10.3390/info16040296

Carless, D., & Boud, D. (2018). The development of student feedback literacy: Enabling uptake of feedback. *Assessment & Evaluation in Higher Education*, *43*(8), 1315–1325. DOI: 10.1080/02602938.2018.1463354

Chan, C. K. Y. (2023). A comprehensive AI policy education framework for university teaching and learning. *International Journal of Educational Technology in Higher Education*, *20*(1), 38. Advance online publication. DOI: 10.1186/s41239-023-00408-3

Chan, C. K. Y., & Hu, W. (2023). Students' voices on generative AI: Perceptions, benefits, and challenges in higher education. *International Journal of Educational Technology in Higher Education*, *20*(1), 43. Advance online publication. DOI: 10.1186/s41239-023-00411-8

Charles, T., & Alshamsi, A. (2025). Navigating challenges in technology integration for inclusive classrooms: Insights for pre-service teachers. In Ajani, O. A. (Ed.), *Empowering pre-service teachers to enhance inclusive education through technology* (pp. 87–126). IGI Global Scientific Publishing., DOI: 10.4018/979-8-3693-8759-7.ch004

Charles, T., & Hill, C. (Eds.). (2026). *Integrity, assessment, and collaboration in the AI classroom*. IGI Global Scientific Publishing., DOI: 10.4018/979-8-2600-0328-2

Charles, T., & Papadaki, M. (2025). Ethical leadership in technology integration and digital education. In Soles, B., & Meyerott, T. (Eds.), *Diverse leadership perspectives in education: From K–12 to higher education* (pp. 437–454). IGI Global Scientific Publishing., DOI: 10.4018/979-8-3693-6115-3.ch016

Elshall, A. S., & Badir, A. (2025). Balancing AI-assisted learning and traditional assessment: The FACT assessment in environmental data science education. *Frontiers in Education*, *10*, 1596462. Advance online publication. DOI: 10.3389/feduc.2025.1596462

Foung, D., Lin, L., & Chen, J. (2024). Reinventing assessments with ChatGPT and other online tools: Opportunities for GenAI-empowered assessment practices. *Computers and Education: Artificial Intelligence*, *6*, 100250. Advance online publication. DOI: 10.1016/j.caeai.2024.100250

Furze, L., Perkins, M., Roe, J., & MacVaugh, J. (2024). The AI Assessment Scale (AIAS) in action: A pilot implementation of GenAI-supported assessment. *Australasian Journal of Educational Technology*, *40*(4), 38–55. DOI: 10.14742/ajet.9434

Gu, J., Chen, J., & Yan, Z. (2026). Fostering feedback literacy by scaffolding self-regulated feedback: A comparative study of GenAI and human peers. *Frontiers in Education, 10*, 1736446. Advance online publication. DOI: 10.3389/feduc.2025.1736446

Hopfenbeck, T. N., Zhang, Z., Sun, S. Z., Robertson, P., & McGrane, J. A. (2023). Challenges and opportunities for classroom-based formative assessment and AI: A perspective article. *Frontiers in Education, 8*, 1270700. Advance online publication. DOI: 10.3389/feduc.2023.1270700

Ilieva, G., Yankova, T., Ruseva, M., & Kabaivanov, S. (2025). A framework for generative AI-driven assessment in higher education. *Information (Basel), 16*(6), 472. Advance online publication. DOI: 10.3390/info16060472

Jaakkola, E. (2020). Designing conceptual articles: Four approaches. *AMS Review, 10*(1-2), 18–26. DOI: 10.1007/s13162-020-00161-0

Jabareen, Y. (2009). Building a conceptual framework: Philosophy, definitions, and procedure. *International Journal of Qualitative Methods, 8*(4), 49–62. DOI: 10.1177/160940690900800406

Jin, Y., Yan, L., Echeverria, V., Gašević, D., & Martinez-Maldonado, R. (2025). Generative AI in higher education: A global perspective of institutional adoption policies and guidelines. *Computers and Education: Artificial Intelligence, 8*, 100348. Advance online publication. DOI: 10.1016/j.caeai.2024.100348

Kickbusch, S., Ashford-Rowe, K., Kemp, A., Boreland, J., & Huijser, H. (2025). Beyond detection: Redesigning authentic assessment in an AI-mediated world. *Education Sciences, 15*(11), 1537. Advance online publication. DOI: 10.3390/educsci15111537

Kolade, O., Owoseni, A., & Egbetokun, A. (2024). Is AI changing learning and assessment as we know it? Evidence from a ChatGPT experiment and a conceptual framework. *Heliyon, 10*(4), e25953. Advance online publication. DOI: 10.1016/j.heliyon.2024.e25953 PMID: 38379960

Liang, W., Yuksekgonul, M., Mao, Y., Wu, E., & Zou, J. (2023). GPT detectors are biased against non-native English writers. *Patterns (New York, N.Y.), 4*(7), 100779. Advance online publication. DOI: 10.1016/j.patter.2023.100779 PMID: 37521038

Luft, J. A., Jeong, S., Idsardi, R., & Gardner, G. (2022). Literature reviews, theoretical frameworks, and conceptual frameworks: An introduction for new biology education researchers. *CBE Life Sciences Education, 21*(3), rm33. Advance online publication. DOI: 10.1187/cbe.21-05-0134 PMID: 35759629

Májovský, M., Černý, M., Netuka, D., & Mikolov, T. (2024). Perfect detection of computer-generated text faces fundamental challenges. *Cell Reports. Physical Science, 5*(1), 101769. Advance online publication. DOI: 10.1016/j.xcrp.2023.101769

Miao, F., & Holmes, W. (2023). *Guidance for generative AI in education and research.* UNESCO., DOI: 10.54675/EWZM9535

OECD. (2026). *OECD Digital Education Outlook 2026: Exploring effective uses of generative AI in education.* OECD Publishing., DOI: 10.1787/062a7394-

Otterbacher, J. (2023). Why technical solutions for detecting AI-generated content in research and education are insufficient. *Patterns (New York, N.Y.)*, *4*(7), 100796. Advance online publication. DOI: 10.1016/j.patter.2023.100796 PMID: 37521044

Perkins, M., Furze, L., Roe, J., & MacVaugh, J. (2024). The Artificial Intelligence Assessment Scale (AIAS): A framework for ethical integration of generative AI in educational assessment. *Journal of University Teaching & Learning Practice*, *21*(6), 06. Advance online publication. DOI: 10.53761/q3azde36

Tan, M. J. T., & Maravilla, N. M. A. T. (2024). Shaping integrity: Why generative artificial intelligence does not have to undermine education. *Frontiers in Artificial Intelligence*, *7*, 1471224. Advance online publication. DOI: 10.3389/frai.2024.1471224 PMID: 39512399

Tlili, A., Shehata, B., Adarkwah, M. A., Bozkurt, A., Hickey, D. T., Huang, R., & Agyemang, B. (2023). What if the devil is my guardian angel: ChatGPT as a case study of using chatbots in education. *Smart Learning Environments*, *10*(1), 15. Advance online publication. DOI: 10.1186/s40561-023-00237-x

Urzúa, C. A. C., Ranjan, R., Saavedra, E. E. M., Badilla-Quintana, M. G., Lepe-Martínez, N., & Philominraj, A. (2025). Effects of AI-assisted feedback via generative chat on academic writing in higher education students: A systematic review of the literature. *Education Sciences*, *15*(10), 1396. Advance online publication. DOI: 10.3390/educsci15101396

van der Waldt, G. (2020). Constructing conceptual frameworks in social science research. *The Journal for Transdisciplinary Research in Southern Africa*, *16*(1), a758. Advance online publication. DOI: 10.4102/td.v16i1.758

Vlachopoulos, D., & Makri, A. (2024). A systematic literature review on authentic assessment in higher education: Best practices for the development of 21st century skills, and policy considerations. *Studies in Educational Evaluation*, *83*, 101425. Advance online publication. DOI: 10.1016/j.stueduc.2024.101425

Yan, L., Sha, L., Zhao, L., Li, Y., Martinez-Maldonado, R., Chen, G., Li, X., Jin, Y., & Gašević, D. (2024). Practical and ethical challenges of large language models in education: A systematic scoping review. *British Journal of Educational Technology*, *55*(1), 90–112. DOI: 10.1111/bjet.13370

KEY TERMS AND DEFINITIONS

AI-Resilient Authentic Assessment-for-Learning (ARAA): A design framework that integrates task, process, and epistemic authenticity within an assessment-for-learning cycle and a governance envelope.

Assessment for Learning (AfL): Assessment activity that clarifies goals, elicits evidence, generates feedback, and supports learners to take action that improves subsequent performance.

Authentic Assessment: Assessment that requires meaningful application of disciplinary knowledge, practices, judgement, and communication in contextually credible tasks.

Epistemic Authenticity: The extent to which assessment elicits disciplinary reasoning, evidence evaluation, methodological justification, uncertainty, and defensible judgement.

Feedback Literacy: The capacities needed to understand the purpose of feedback, judge its quality, manage responses, and take informed action.

Generative Artificial Intelligence (GenAI): Computational systems capable of generating new content, such as text, images, code, audio, or feedback, in response to user instructions and contextual input.

Governance Envelope: The institutional conditions that make assessment legitimate, including transparency, privacy, equity, contestability, accountability, and feasible implementation.

Process Authenticity: The extent to which assessment captures and values a traceable learning trajectory involving planning, drafting, feedback engagement, revision, and consequential decision-making.

Task Authenticity: The extent to which an assessment reflects meaningful disciplinary activity through context, constraints, evidence, audience, ambiguity, and trade-offs.

Tool Transparency: A concise, accountable explanation of how digital or AI tools contributed to a submission and what verification, revision, and quality-control decisions were made.

Chapter 7

Reframing Academic Integrity in the Age of AI Using a Socio-Pedagogical Framework for Quality and Trust in Higher Education Assessment

J. Viji Gripsy
http://orcid.org/0000-0002-6599-3010
PSGR Krishnammal College for Women, India

M. Sasikala
http://orcid.org/0000-0003-4342-3348
PSGR Krishnammal College for Women, India

M. Hemalatha
http://orcid.org/0000-0001-5345-2375
PG & Research Department of Computer Science, Sri Ramakrishna College of Arts and Science, Coimbatore, India

ABSTRACT

The rapid integration of AI into higher education assessment is reshaping academic integrity, quality assurance, and trust. While AI offers efficiency, scalability, and personalized feedback, it also raises ethical and equity concerns such as bias, surveillance, and inequity. This chapter argues that academic integrity cannot be ensured through technology alone, but must be treated as a socio-pedagogical practice shaped by institutional culture and global contexts. It proposes a Socio-Pedagogical Integrity Framework (SPIF) comprising pedagogical design, ethical AI use, assessment literacy, and contextual equitability. The framework promotes a shift from surveillance-based compliance to trust-based, learning-focused assessment practices.

DOI: 10.4018/979-8-3373-8939-4.ch007

1. INTRODUCTION

The development and adoption of AI Technologies in Higher Education Institutions has had a major effect on how assessments are run, requiring an examination of existing paradigms regarding the components of Academic Integrity, Quality Assurance, and to a lesser degree, TRUST. Many of these AI technologies have been developed with the purpose of increasing the efficiency of the assessment process, allowing institutions to scale and provide more personalized feedback to students through services like automated grading systems, anti-plagiarism tools, learning analytics systems and generative AI applications. Despite the numerous pedagogical opportunities that AI tools provide, several ethical and pedagogical concerns (e.g., fairness, transparency, surveillance, and agency) have emerged from the deployment of these tools.

Historically, academic integrity has been framed as a personal, moral obligation on the part of the individual student and has been put into practice through institutional policies to create means to prevent any misconduct such as cheating and/or plagiarism. However, as more assessments are mediated by AI technology, an over-reliance on compliance-based or cyber-surveillance practices as the means to uphold academic integrity, will have the effect of creating punitive atmospheres that lower trust levels between faculty members and students and limit student learning and development. Also, compliance-based approaches to academic integrity do not take into account issues of inequity in the context of where students are located; for example, in areas of the Global South where a majority of higher education institutions lack adequate access to the resources and infrastructure needed to use AI technology, and are limited in the level of support provided to students in terms of digital literacy and in their governance structures.

The chapter contends that instead of viewing academic integrity solely through the lens of technology or regulation, it should also be seen as a social pedagogical practice in the era of AI Integrating evidence and information from Critical Assessment Theory and academic integrity literature, the author presents the Socio-Pedagogical Integrity Framework (SPIF) for promoting responsible use of Artificial Intelligence in the assessment systems of institutions of Higher Education. Using examples from the theoretical literature, normative International Policies, and an early 20th century case study from a resource-constrained higher education context, India, the author outlines how using AI as a tool for creating assessments that promote trust and learning can lead an institution to build its integrity-oriented assessment practice around the principles of Quality, Fairness, and Contextual Equity. In addition, this chapter takes reference from the higher education scenario of India to show how contextual applicability can be achieved in different institutional and socio-economic situations.

2. LITERATURE REVIEW: ACADEMIC INTEGRITY AS A SOCIO-PEDAGOGICAL PRACTICE

2.1 Academic Integrity -An Overview

The definition of Academic Integrity by the definition by ICAI, defines Academic Integrity as the commitment to values such as honesty, trust, fairness, respect, and responsibility. Academic Integrity Frameworks focus on an individual's responsibility and how an academic institution's code of conduct/ enforcement can enforce Codes of Conduct through disciplinary actions. Academics have noted that the narrow focus of Academic Integrity Frameworks has neglected the cultural, pedagogical, and structural aspects of integrity (Bretag, 2013; Bretag et al., 2019).

Recent Academic Integrity Scholarship has explored Academic Integrity as a collective and contextually based concept influenced by the methods of assessment, the nature of the Learning Environment, and the Power Relationships within the Academic Institution in which the Learning takes place. Academic Integrity Violations by students are not simply viewed as a moral failure but are also indicative of Assessment Practices that are Out of Sync Between Students/Affordable (Too much pressure), and an Unequal Learning Environment.

2.2 Assessment, Trust and Power

Assessment is critical to how students behave and deal with learning (Brown et al., 2013). Research demonstrates that a high-stakes summative assessment, with little or no feedback, creates relationships to support surface-level learning approaches and increases the opportunity for academic dishonesty. On the flip side, formative, authentic, and feedback plentiful assessment have been demonstrated to foster intrinsic motivation and ethical engagement in students (Watson & Sottile, 2010).

One key yet little studied aspect of assessment is Trust. The increase use of surveillance-driven assessment methods was augmented due to the development of artificial intelligence (Coghlan et al., 2021). Proctoring and plagiarism detection systems have arisen based on the premise that students are inherently dishonest and therefore diminish the confidence that students have in the institution. Some critical theorists believe these practices represent a growing trend toward the neoliberalization of higher education systems in which accountability and control supersede care and education.

The concept of trust in assessment does not merely mean that assessment is credible from a technical point of view but also has to do with factors such as openness and fairness, communication, and the way authority is shared among educational institutions, faculty, and students. With AI-enhanced assessment, the deployment of automated detection and analytical tools and decision-making processes can influence the interaction between the above parties, as assessment authority is transferred to technology. The SPIF approach looks at trust and power as interrelated concepts because transparent governance, adequate oversight, open communication, and just assessment practices will inhibit technology from transforming into the means of institutional control. In this respect, academic integrity is viewed as a matter of relations and institutions rather than students.

2.3 AI, Ethics and Educational Governance

Artificial Intelligence (AI) is used in education but also creates new challenges for Educational Governance (Roll & Wylie, 2016). It presents challenges of Algorithmic Bias, Opacity, Data Privacy, and Accountability (UNESCO, 2023). The latest recommendations on broad use of generative AI in education underlines importance of human surveillance, openness, ethics in data use, fair treatment, and the protection of students' rights. All these reflect governance aspect envisaged in SPIF. If Automated Assessment and Analytics Systems utilize datasets that are biased in their training, then the algorithm will also reflect pre-existing Social Inequalities (Buckingham Shum et al., 2019). And if there is no transparency around how an Automated Assessment System works, the result could be furthering an existing Inequality (Williamson & Eynon, 2020; Yazici, 2026). While there has been an increasing number of Ethical AI Frameworks that promote Human-Centred Design, Explainability, and Participatory

Governance, there remains a lack of consistency in how these principles are being Operationalised across Higher Education Systems (Selwyn, 2019). In Global South Regions, the Infrastructural Restrictions and Regulatory Vacuums, and the Digital Divide create additional barriers to the adoption of AI. Research has shown that in the case of imported AI tools, it is often the case that too little attention is given to the local Pedagogical Needs or the Ethical Implications of deploying these technologies.

Cross-cultural research shows that we cannot understand the ethics and education related to AI without considering local cultures, languages, institutions, and socioeconomic conditions. Therefore, different conditions highlight the necessity of the regionally-oriented governance and evaluation of AI in higher education systems.

3. METHODOLOGY

The methodology used in this research is based on the two frameworks that make up the Socio-Pedagogical/Socio-Technical Basis of Academic Integrity. The socio-pedagogical framework allows for a better understanding of the dynamic interaction of pedagogical design, institutional governance structures, learner behaviours and context, which ultimately creates a framework for understanding how academic integrity develops over time. In addition to examining the development of academic integrity as related to the individual or as a compliance-based practice, it is viewed from a socio-political perspective as a culturally specific educational practice with an influence from surrounding societal structures. As such, it is influenced by dominant power structures, how assessments are designed, and how their use affects the academic community at large. The focus on socio-political influences extends to all types of assessments, especially in AI-mediated assessment environments, and serves as the basis for understanding the development of academic integrity over time.

Simultaneously, to identify the conceptual, ethical, and policy-related aspects of utilizing AI for evaluation practices, this study conducts a primarily qualitative-dominant research methodology and synthesizes the pertinent theoretical constructs from education, ethics, and technology studies, while critically analyzing existing institutional, national, or international policies that govern AI and academic integrity. This analytical model illustrates how pedagogy, governance, learner agency, and technological systems are related, and how they relate to each other to ultimately influence the reliability and trustworthiness of assessment practices.

The methodology includes an example of how to develop a basic AI assessment framework through a contextualised example. The example also examines how pedagogical design choices influence ethical and fair AI assessment. The structure of the chapter enables the research to better demonstrate how the factors of academic integrity develop as part of the dynamic interactions among individuals and groups in their respective contexts. This allows the research to move beyond a strictly punitive view of academic integrity and toward a view of academic integrity as a dynamic and continuous learning process within a broad, sustainable framework for collegiate academia.

The approach used in this chapter is conceptual and qualitative dominant, working on combining and analyzing available theoretical, research, and policy evidence rather than gathering novel empirical information. The process of analysis consists of thematic synthesis of the relevant literature, interpretive analysis of the policies of AI and academic honesty, and comprehensive interpretations of the examples. These processes help to analyze the relationships between educational design, governance in AI, assessment and literacy in AI, and equity in context. The resulting SPIF model is presented as a theoretically informed and context-sensitive model, which can be used for the empirical proof.

3.1 Overall Research Design

With a staged and iterative process, this research model builds each stage on the last in a systematic manner, leading to the development and contextualization of the Socio-Pedagogical Integrity Framework (SPIF). By taking a structured approach to this progression, the SPIF can provide both rigor and relevance in addressing the issue of academic integrity within AI-enabled forms of assessment.

The first stage of this process synthesizes important concepts based on an extensive literature review in the themes of academic integrity, Assessment for Learning (A4L) theory, ethical and responsible Artificial Intelligence (AI) developments and applications. This stage will identify the main concepts/dimensions/principles that are central to current academic integrity in higher education, particularly where technology has mediated the assessment process. The results of stage one will provide the basis or foundation for further analytical and methodological stages, as well as providing an understanding of what concepts and elements are relevant for SPIF to analyze.

Stage 2 studies how existing policies and governance systems dictate what is acceptable behavior in the use of Artificial Intelligence when performing assessments. Using a governance or policy analysis approach, Stage 2 explores how current policies at all levels (institutional, national and international) view the concepts of Academic Integrity, Accountability, Transparency, and Fairness regarding the use of AI to create assessments. Stage 2 also identifies regulatory shortcomings, inconsistencies and contextual factors that hinder the ability of Integrity-focused assessment systems to work effectively.

Stage 3 focuses on creating an analytical/algorithmic model that represents the interactions between AI technology, pedagogical design and Academic Integrity Qualifications. This model provides a visual aid to see how assessment design choices, learner engagement and algorithmic decision-making interactively produce assessment outcomes and create integrity risks. By bringing together Social Pedagogical and Social Technical approaches, Stage 3 establishes a method for systematically analysing and assessing AI-enabled assessments.

In Stage 4 of the research project, the SPIF has been introduced into a "real" educational context through a contextualized case study drawn from a resource-constrained higher education institution. In this stage, the Researcher will explore the impact of the socio-cultural, physical and institutional environments on using Artificial Intelligence (AI) to assess students. The Case Study will also allow the Validation and Refinement of the SPIF, providing confidence that it is built upon, and sensitive to, the local realities yet will have the potential to apply more broadly.

This staged research model will develop a theoretical and empirical foundation to validate the SPIF while ensuring the framework is grounded in its socio-contextual environment.

3.2 Data Sources and Analytical Procedures

The data sources for this research consisted of peer-reviewed articles published from 2015 to 2024, international and national policy documents, and exemplary cases of assessment based on the practice of assessment within a resource-constrained higher education context. Literature was analyzed by means of a thematic synthesis that explored similarities and differences in patterns of integrity, trust, Assessment Design, and Artificial Intelligence governance as shown across literature.

Policy documents were analyzed through the perspective of interpretive policy analysis to determine whether integrity in assessment was represented mainly through compliance, surveillance or as a pedagogical and ethical responsibility. Case studies were analyzed through a contextual interpretation and linked to how each institution managed their testing and assessment practices according to the dimensions outlined in this new framework.

The mathematical representations outlined in this part of the paper serve as conceptual operationalization's of the SPIF framework and are not distinct analytical models. Equations (1)-(6) provide the four dimensions of the SPIF framework with illustrative relationships to demonstrate how instructional design, ethical governance, evaluation and AI literacy, and contextual equity might only affect academic integrity. The purpose of the mathematical representations is to suggest a framework for interpreting the SPIF framework and indicate the future empirical testing directions.

Given that this section is principally theoretical and qualitative in nature, the trustworthiness indicator was maintained through comparative analysis of the relevant literature, policy documents, and contextual examples. Applicable outcomes were evaluated against the four components of the SPIF model for the sake of consistency. Interpretation is essentially self-reflective since the model embodies a theoretical interpretation of existing evidence rather than original data. Future empirical research should aim for establishing its validity and reliability through systematic data collection and independent verification.

3.3 Analytical Model of Academic Integrity

The equations that are present in this section are meant to serve as conceptual and heuristic representations of the relations among the four dimensions of the SPIF and are not meant to be statistical models or models that have empirical evidence.

Academic integrity in AI-mediated assessment is conceptualized as a latent construct influenced by four interdependent dimensions. The relationship is expressed as:

$$AI_g = f(P_d, G_e, L_a, E_c) \quad (1)$$

where AI_g represents academic integrity, P_d denotes pedagogical design quality, G_e ethical AI governance, L_a assessment and AI literacy, and E_c contextual equity.

3.3.1 Pedagogical Design Dimension

Pedagogical design quality reflects the extent to which assessments promote authentic learning and reduce incentives for unethical AI use. It is modelled as:

$$P_d = \alpha_1 A_u + \alpha_2 F_f + \alpha_3 R_p \quad (2)$$

where A_u represents authenticity and real-world relevance of tasks, F_f the quality of formative feedback, and R_p reflective and process-oriented components. The coefficients $\alpha_1, \alpha_2, \alpha_3$ indicate the relative emphasis placed on each pedagogical feature.

Higher values of P_d correspond to assessment designs that prioritize learning processes over product submission, thereby strengthening integrity.

3.3.2 Ethical AI Governance Dimension

This Ethical AI governance rationalizes such institutional mechanisms that regulate the ongoing use of AI transparently and fairly. Thus, this dimension is represented by:

$$G_e = \beta_1 T_r + \beta_2 A_c + \beta_3 D_p \quad (3)$$

In this equation, T_r refers to the transparency of AI systems, A_c to algorithmic accountability, and D_p to practices regarding data privacy and consent. Strong governance structures alleviate fear, uncertainty, and conflict between learners and institutions.

3.3.3 Assessment and AI Literacy Dimension

Assessment and AI literacy is referred to as the ability of students and faculty to characterize the purposes of the assessment, AI affordances, and the limits of ethicality. This is modeled as:

$$L_a = \gamma_1 S_l + \gamma_2 F_l + \gamma_3 I_c \quad (4)$$

where, S_l denotes student literacy, F_l denotes faculty competency, and I_c denotes institutional capacity-building initiatives. Development of this dimension varies with degree. More often than not, lack in this dimension manifests as unintentional misconduct or misinterpretation of the given policies on integrity based on honesty and genuine intent or truthfulness.

3.3.4 Contextual Equity Dimension

As most of the measures of Contextual Equity are related to the differences in the level of socio-economic and infrastructure development between different parts of the world (most particularly in the Global South), they will be expressed in the following formula:

$$E_c = \delta_1 A_i + \delta_2 S_e + \delta_3 L_d \quad (5)$$

Where A_i is the level of Access to Digital Infrastructure, S_e is the level of Socio-Economic Support, and L_d is the level of Linguistic and Cultural Inclusivity, with the Integrity level being diminished if the Assessor assumes equal access and readiness to participate in assessments.

3.3.5 Composite Integrity Index

To represent the overall level of Integrity, the Composite Socio-Pedagogical Integrity Index (SPII) will be calculated as follows:

$$SPII = \sum_{i=1}^{4} w_i D_i \text{ where } \sum w_i = 1 \quad (6)$$

The higher the SPII value, the more a given assessment environment supports Levels of Trust, Equity and Learning-Centric Use of Artificial Intelligence.

3.4 Algorithmic Procedure for Integrity-Oriented AI Assessment

Figure 1. Algorithmic flow for Socio-Pedagogical Integrity

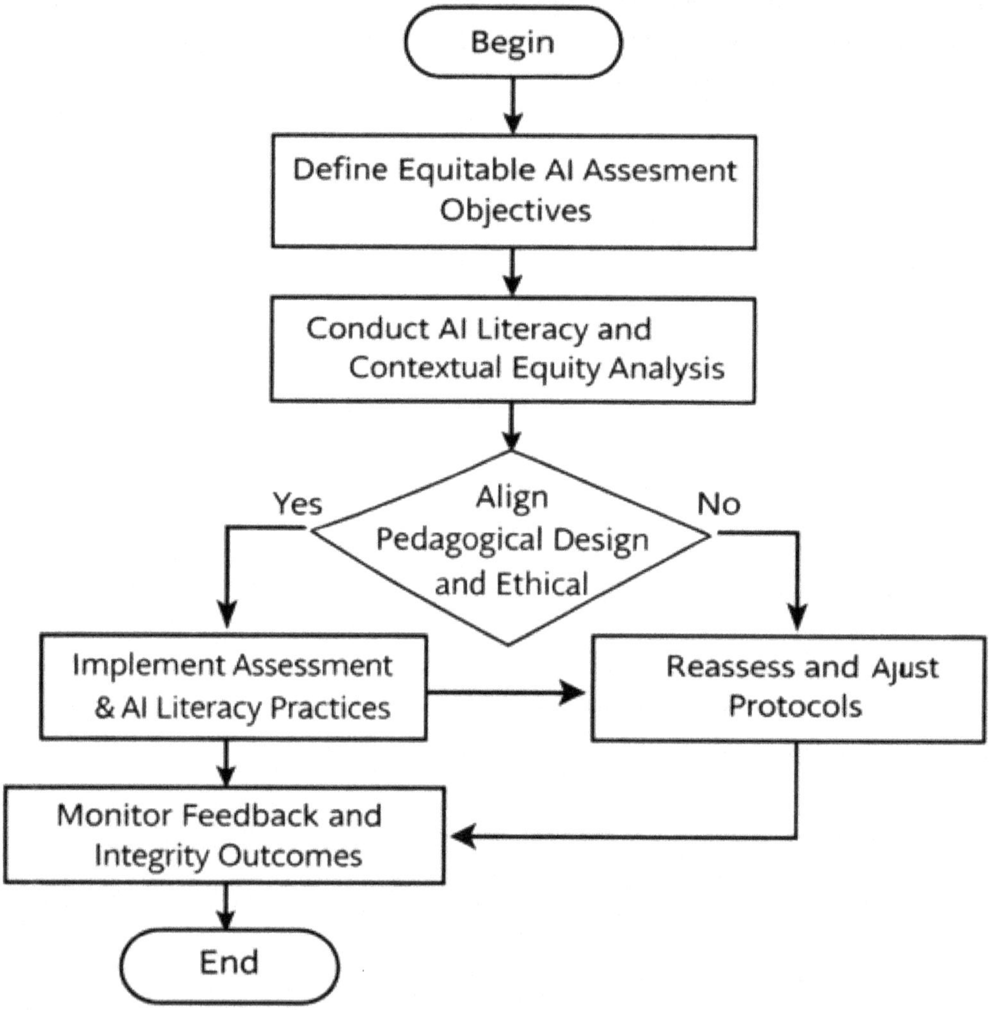

4. THE SOCIO-PEDAGOGICAL INTEGRITY FRAMEWORK (SPIF)

4.1 Reason for Developing the Framework

The integration of artificial intelligence (AI) within Higher Education Assessment practices has demonstrated that traditional academic integrity models, which utilize rule-based methods, do not adequately support students who use AI. Current models largely focus on detecting, enforcing, and sanctioning academic integrity violations through the use of surveillance technology and punitive measures. While the implementation of monitoring systems and punitive measures may be effective in deterring obvious violations of Academic Integrity Policies, they do not provide support for the drivers of Academic Integrity and/or Academic Misconduct (i.e., Pedagogical Practice, Pedagogical Beliefs, Governance, Literacy, and Equity) for students in the AI-enhanced assessment contexts.

Figure 2. Mapping AI-mediated assessment practices to the Socio- Pedagogical Integrity Framework (SPIF)

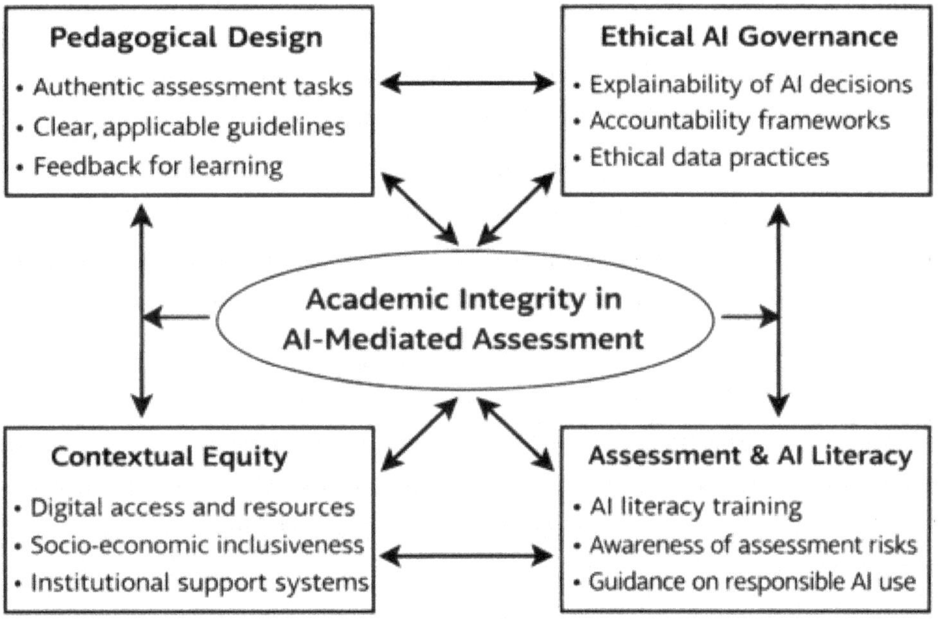

In light of these challenges, the Socio-Pedagogical Integrity Framework has been developed to provide a new understanding of how to conceptualise Academic Integrity as an Emergent Practice resulting from the Interaction between the above-mentioned components. SPIF Emergent Conceptual Framework represents a shift away from the focus of "prevention of Cheating" toward Cultivating an Environment of Trust, Accountability and Quality in Assessment.

4.2 SPIF's Theoretical Foundations

SPIF is based upon three interconnected theories. The first theory is assessment for learning, which advocates that students' learning experiences and knowledge acquisition are influenced by assessments and that integrity is enhanced through assessments that promote active engagement, thoughtful consideration, and meaning-making among learners. Second, integrity scholarship of a critical nature emphasises the role of power and institutional culture and policy in establishing the boundaries of 'acceptable' academic behaviour. Third, ethical AI and socio-technical systems theory illustrate the idea that AI systems are not simply technological artefacts without bias but rather are created and developed through the influence of social values, governance structures, and inequities inherent in our society.

As such, integrity is understood as being a collective responsibility shared by students, teachers, institutions, and creators of technology.

4.3 Overview of the SPIF Structure

The SPIF (Socio-Pedagogical Integrity Framework) contains 4 interdependent areas of consideration:

1. The Design and Assessment of Engagement and Learning
2. Ethical/Social/Accountability for AI Governance
3. An Assessment of both Staff and Students with regard to AI Literacy
4. Creating a Conducive and Inclusive Context for All

These areas of consideration are not separate from each other; they interact in a way that a weakness in any of the 4 areas of consideration can compromise the integrity of the Assessment Ecosystem as a whole.

4.4 Pedagogical Design and Assessment for Learning

Pedagogic design underpins integrity-focused assessment at SPIF. SPIF asserts that assessments that promote and support student learning provide the best opportunity to develop an environment of academic integrity, whereas traditional assessments (which focus on memorising information, and/or time constraints) and inappropriate and out-of-context tasks are most likely to be misused by unethical artificial intelligence (AI) users (Lodge et al., 2023).

Integrity-focused Pedagogy at your institution is characterised by authentic assessments, process-based assessments and formative feedback as part of the assignment process (Andrade & Du, 2005). According to SPIF, authentic assessments provide opportunities for students to demonstrate their ability to apply their knowledge (e.g. theory, research or theory in practice, etc.) to real-world scenarios or issues that are relevant to a discipline, so that generic responses generated by artificial intelligence will not suffice.

Process-based assessments are tasks where a student generates drafts or reflections on their learning, and can create, through critical thinking and reflection, a learning journal that captures how the student has grown as a result of this process, and reduces pressure on students to submit only final products (Felder & Brent, 2016).

Formative feedback is feedback that provides ongoing support to a student by assessing their abilities throughout the assignment process, and using unethical AI tools will be difficult when ethical, formative feedback is used within your institution.

4.5 Ethical and Transparent AI Governance

The second dimension of SPIF is related to ethical governance. Ethical governance establishes the framework of how institutions select, implement and create regulations for AI tools within assessment systems. Institutions often adopt AI technology to support their assessment processes without clearly disclosing how the algorithms work, what data they utilise, or the basis for making decisions. A lack of transparency leads to distrust and reinforces fears of being monitored and controlled.

SPIF incorporates principles of ethical governance; namely, transparency, accountability, proportionality and human oversight. Transparency requires organisations to communicate clearly their purpose, scope and limitation of AI-based assessment tools. Accountability means decision-making authority for assessing students should always rest with a human being (educators) and not be delegated to an AI system. Proportionality places limits on how much monitoring should be done; especially for low-stakes assessments. Finally, human oversight ensures that the results of AI systems are considered in the context of real-world situations and produced in accordance with ethical standards.

Ethical governance through SPIF does not only require compliance with data protection laws. Additionally, aligning AI technology with the values of education and integrity is essential.

4.6 Assessment and AI Literacy for Staff and Students

Assessment and AI literacy are two parts of SPIF's three pillars. In terms of literacy, this does not only mean being able to use any technology; it also means understanding ethical implications, having a critical awareness of assessment and its purpose as well as sharing a common understanding with others. In an environment where AI tools are available, there is often a great deal of confusion about what behaviours are acceptable when using those tools, leading to accidental instances of academic dishonesty.

SPIF’s approach is to assisting institutions in developing both student and faculty literacy around assessment in AI is outlined. Student literacy involves knowing how to use technology and how their learning can be enhanced by the use of these tools, as well as identifying ethical boundaries. Faculty literacy involves being able to create assessments that will withstand the ways that they may be misused as well as interpreting analytics produced by AI and discussing integrity and ethical behaviours with students.

When literacy levels are not evenly distributed, institutions are often seen to be using the integrity policy as a mechanism for exclusion rather than for developing the capacity of all involved to be able to be successful. Therefore, SPIF positions literacy as a process of building capacity rather than as a lack in an individual.

4.7 Contextual Equity and The Global South

The fourth component of the SPIF relates to the need for equity within context. Therefore, when evaluating academic integrity, academic integrity cannot be isolated from the multiple socio-economic, linguistic, and infrastructural contexts in which students learn. In terms of a Global South higher education contexts, such as, disparities in digital access, institutional resources, and a student's prior experience with Artificial Intelligence (AI) affect the ways in which students are assessed.

The SPIF, therefore, does not endorse a uniform academic integrity model. Instead, the SPIF calls for context-responsive assessment methods that acknowledge and respond to the student's lived experience. For example, the SPIF provides flexibility in the timing of assessments, offers multilingual support, provides multiple pathways for assessment, and takes into consideration the additional time and connectivity demands placed on students.

By incorporating equity into the definition of academic integrity, the SPIF challenges deficit views that attribute academic misconduct to the student's behaviour, instead of considering the broader environmental factors that influence a student's ability to participate ethically. Despite this, the Global South must be understood as a heterogeneous category, where higher education systems vary greatly depending on institutional capabilities, digital infrastructure, languages, financial resources, policy environments, and adoption of AI technologies. Within the Indian context itself, there is a huge variation among the educational institutions – from those that are better resourced to those that are hindered by serious infrastructural and accessibility issues, thus resulting in various examples of local adaptation and innovation. For this reason, SPIF prefers to call certain institutions "resource-constrained."

4.8 Integrative Functioning of the SPIF

The strength of SPIF lies in its integrated functioning, the process of integrating education, technology and ethics; without ethical governance the re-design of education would become merely an instrumentalization of AI in the name of efficiencies. Without literacy in governance, compliance will occur without understanding; additional to this, when literacy exists without equity it maintains privilege. SPIF provides a means for educators to address all three of these issues through the concept of integrity as an emergent property within the entire assessment ecosystem.

Within this context, AI is a tool for mediation rather than control. Integrity will be created by trust, conversation and shared accountability, and assessment practices will reflect the broader educational purpose of higher education.

4.9 Contribution of SPIF to Assessment Quality and Trust

The SPIF Framework brings together the principles of Social Justice, Transparency and Collaboration to enhance the quality of assessments conducted using Artificial Intelligence (AI). The SPIF Framework allows individuals, including educators, administrators, and government officials across all levels of education to evaluate and determine how well an AI is performing beyond merely its technical effectiveness. In addition to its technical capabilities, the SPIF Framework allows for a new way of looking at the way we assess academic integrity; integrity is now viewed as being an indicator of the "healthy" ethical culture of institutions.

Through incorporating academic integrity into governance, pedagogy, literacy and equity, the SPIF Framework supports creating a more sustainable, inclusive, trustworthy future for assessment processes in AI-enhanced higher education.

5. CASE STUDY: AI-MEDIATED ASSESSMENT PRACTICES IN RESOURCE-CONSTRAINED HIGHER EDUCATION CONTEXT

The higher education landscape in India can be informative in terms of understanding the opportunities and challenges presented by AI-enabled assessment in low-resource contexts. One of the major strengths of the Indian landscape is the diverse types of Indian higher education institutions, different levels of technological infrastructure, AI proficiency, as well as diverse languages and socio-economic status, which makes it a valuable place in terms of applying the principles established and articulated in the SPIF framework. The Indian landscape thus showcases how the implementation of AI-mediated assessment must be guided by local educational needs and institutions' capacity, ethical frameworks, and equalitarian principles, rather than vice versa, leading to a uniform, tech-oriented approach. Within the Global South, resource-constrained higher education context presents an appropriate context for investigating academic integrity within the realm of AI-mediated Assessment as there is a high level and diversity of Higher Education providers within the State. Over the past few years, South resource-constrained higher education context institutions have started to adopt artificial intelligence enabled assessment tools such as plagiarism detection software, LMS-based automated grading and analytical learning tools. Therefore, this adoption has taken place as a result of both licensure (accreditation) obligations and improving the efficiency of administration by streamlining operations; however, in many cases, these AI tools have been adopted without a concurrent re-design of the pedagogical approach or development of a framework to support ethical governance.

The case presented in India in this part is more illustrative and conceptual and is not meant to represent an empirical study based on primary data. It is aimed at showing how institutions can utilize the SPIF framework to explain specific problems faced in AI-assisted testing environment in higher education. Thus, the examples and patterns presented here have been chosen to demonstrate possible facts rather than to present empirical or statistically proven results.

5.1 AI Use in Assessment

AI applications in the institutions examined are primarily used to support assessment administration rather than learning-centred evaluation. Plagiarism detection systems are routinely employed for assignments and dissertations, while automated grading is common for objective-type internal assessments. Limited use of AI-based feedback tools was observed, mainly in formative contexts.

Table 1. AI Applications in Assessment Practices

AI Application	Primary Purpose	Integrity Orientation
Plagiarism detection	Similarity checking	Compliance-focused
Automated grading	Efficiency	Neutral
Learning analytics	Monitoring	Surveillance-prone
AI feedback tools	Draft improvement	Learning-oriented

5.2 Integrity-Related Challenges

A consistent challenge across the board with regard to integrity issues was the use of similarity scoring as a primary measure of academic integrity and thus supported the mentality of a surveillance-based assessment culture. The reliance on memory-based assessments with high stakes has also created an increased likelihood of the misuse of artificial intelligence (AI) in relation to assessment processes. Finally, due to the digital divide between students in rural and low-income areas, enforcing equity in the enforcement of integrity issues is more difficult for institutions of higher education. These challenges are mapped to SPIF dimensions in Table 2.

Table 2. Integrity Challenges Mapped to SPIF

SPIF Dimension	Key Challenge	Impact
Pedagogical design	Reproductive assessments	High misuse risk
Ethical governance	Opaque AI policies	Reduced trust
Assessment literacy	Unclear AI guidelines	Unintentional misconduct
Contextual equity	Digital divide	Structural disadvantage

5.3 Emerging Good Practices

While there are still many challenges ahead, Some Institutions displayed integrity-aligned practices that are aligned with the SPIF. These innovative approaches included such things as redesigning assignment formats to include local case analyses, reflective components and other aspects within an assignment, issuing guidelines that outlined where AI is acceptable and how it can be used most effectively, and using AI as a tool for formative feedback rather than as a punitive measure. Faculty development initiatives focused on assessment literacy improved the level of clarity and trust that faculty members had with their students.

In summary, the illustrative case study provides evidence that the academic integrity outcome of an institution is affected more by how academic integrity educational practices are designed, governed and implemented than by the presence of AI in those Government and corporate educational institutions in higher education context. The findings support the continued use of the SPIF framework as a flexible and context-sensitive framework for assisting in the establishment of an ethical and integrity-oriented AI response to assessment in higher education.

6. RESULTS AND DISCUSSION

The research highlighted that the way integrity is enforced by AI in tertiary education institutions in a resource-constrained higher education context is primarily by control, rather than through ethical or pedagogical practices. AI has helped educational institutions improve their administrative functions and enhance assessment feedback return windows, but has not uniformly improved the integrity and reliance placed on AI. The subsequent sections will outline this finding in the context of SPIF's four dimensions.

6.1 Pedagogical Design and Integrity Outcomes

The findings of the research support that assessment design will yield different results in terms of integrity. Tertiary institutions, which rely heavily on traditional, high-stakes, content-recall assessments, have been reported to experience greater instances of misuse of AI for written assignments and online exams. Conversely, departments that have adopted authentic, process oriented assessments have reported less reliance on generative AI to commit acts of dishonesty.

This relationship is summarised in **Table 3**.

Table 3. Assessment Design and Observed Integrity Outcomes

Assessment Design Type	AI Misuse Risk	Student Engagement	Integrity Alignment
Memory-based exams	High	Low	Weak
Standard written assignments	Moderate	Moderate	Limited
Authentic, contextual tasks	Low	High	Strong
Reflective and process-based tasks	Very low	High	Very strong

Through examining Table 3's results, it is clear that when an assessment/building approach provides greater attention to Learning Processes than Outputs, the integrity level of these assessments improves. Hence, the results from this study support assessment-for-learning theory, which supports the role of assessment in forming ethical behaviour.

6.2 Ethical AI Governance and Trust

The most important finding relates to how a perceived lack of information affects students willingness to engage with AI Systems for Assessment purposes. In those Institutions that have implemented Plagiarism detection and Analytics Tools without giving reasons as to their Purpose, Students felt anxiety and confusion, and had distrust of AI; Their Academic Faculty members are also uncertain on how to interpret AI Reports to determine whether their Students have shown compliance with their integrity policy. Figure 3 illustrates the relationship between AI governance transparency and student trust.

Figure 3. Relationship Between AI Governance Transparency and Student Trust

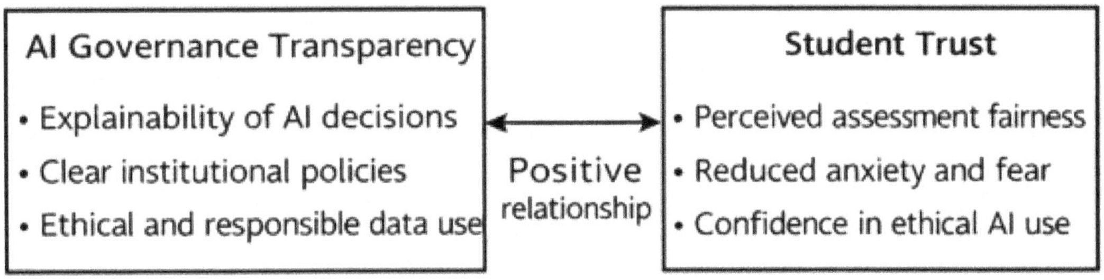

These findings align with ethical AI literature, which argues that trust is not produced by surveillance but by clarity, accountability, and human oversight.

6.3 Assessment and AI Literacy Effects

During the research, both assessments and AI literacy were identified as key moderators of the relationship between student use of AI and student academic integrity. When students were provided with clear direction regarding the acceptable use of AI (e.g., how to appropriately disclose the use of AI when completing an assignment and the ethical implications associated with using AI to draft papers) there were significant decreases in incidents of unintentional misconduct of example. Table 4 presents the relationship between literacy levels and integrity outcomes.

Table 4. Assessment and AI Literacy and Integrity Outcomes

Literacy Level	Clarity of AI Use	Misconduct Incidence	Integrity Culture
Low	Poor	High	Punitive
Moderate	Partial	Moderate	Compliance-based
High	Clear	Low	Trust-oriented

As seen in Table 4, with the increase in literacy around AI use, the culture of academic integrity transitioned from being punitive to being founded on trust and SABAI's assertion of capacity-building versus control.

6.4 Contextual Equity and Integrity

Elements of contextual equity had a substantial impact on how well students could comply with the institution's integrity expectations. Students living in rural and economically challenged areas faced numerous challenges concerning access to devices, stable internet access, and also lacked familiarity with AI-related tools. Because of this, structural constraints caused integrity violations as opposed to students intentionally committing acts of dishonesty. Figure 4 conceptualises the impact of contextual equity on integrity outcomes.

Figure 4. Impact of Contextual Equity on Academic Integrity

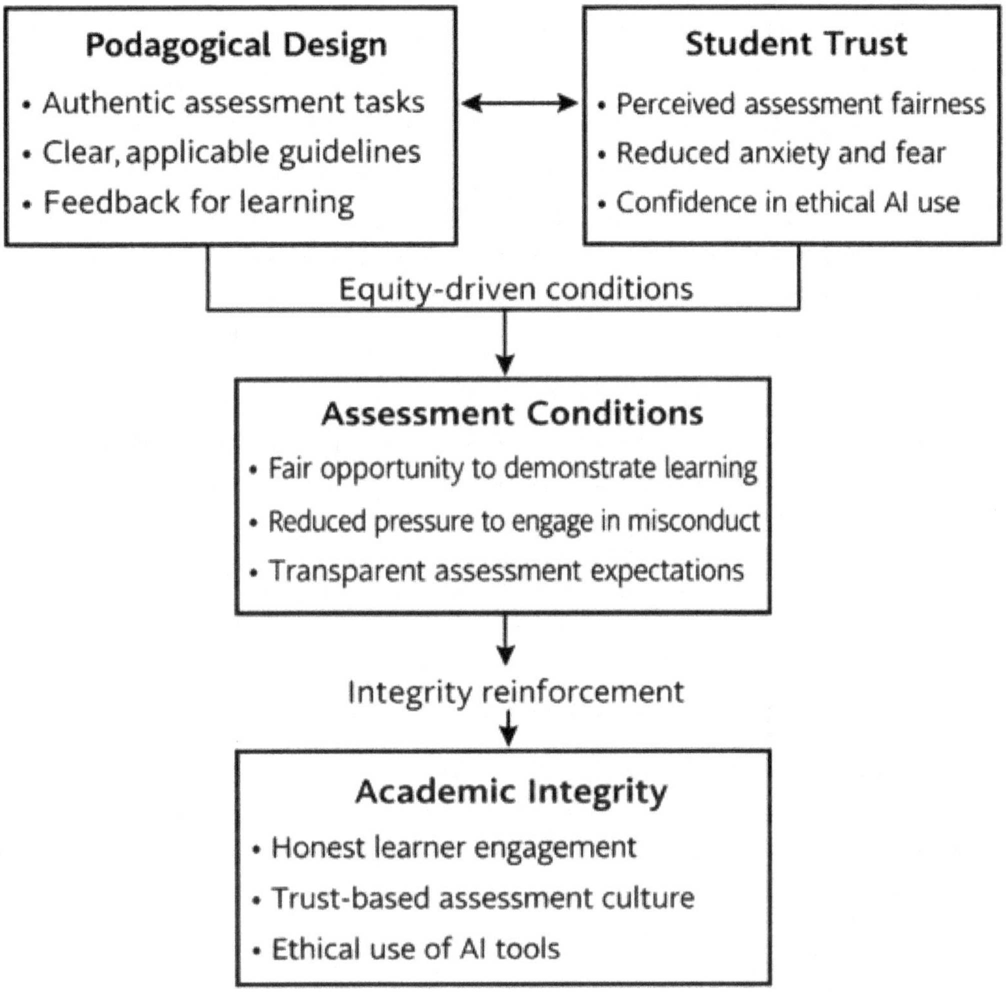

Therefore, this finding indicates that treating equity as one of the main integrity values is critical in developing countries (Global South).

6.6 Integrative Discussion of SPIF

The holistic analysis of academic integrity in AI mediated assessment using SPIF presents strong academic integrity for AI mediated assessments, when all four dimensions are balanced (at a reasonable degree). Higher reliance on detection tools only, without redesigning the pedagogy (i.e. creating a new way to do the same assignment, which is integrative), or developing student literacies, results in augmented fragmented outcomes for academic integrity and greater resistance from students regarding academic integrity policies. Conversely, the synergistic effects of integrity focused institutions can be maximised through authentic assessment design (decrease in misuse incentives), transparent governance structures (foster trust) and creating literate student expectations (creating clarity around expectations), as well as equity sensitive practices (ensuring fairness). Therefore, SPIF provides a solid analytic framework for understanding and analysing the nature of academic integrity in complex, AI enabled assessment environments.

6.7 Implications for Theory and Practice

It extends current theoretical understandings around academic integrity by identifying some system-wide influences on behaviours relating to academic integrity and moving beyond a focus on individuals to include the influence of institutional and systemic factors.

The findings from this study also indicate that metrics of integrity need to include indicators of assessment diversity, degree of student engagement, and degree of trust in addition to similarity scores.

Policymakers and quality assurance agencies are encouraged to consider how artificial intelligence may be used in assessments, not just whether or not AI is being used in assessment practices.

The case study of resource-constrained higher education context shows that artificial intelligence may be compatible with academic integrity. However, how successful AI is in providing academic integrity to learners depends upon socio-pedagogical contexts in which AI is being utilised. The SPIF framework enables practitioners to articulate alignment between educational values, quality assurance and trust.

7. IMPLICATIONS FOR POLICY, PRACTICE AND QUALITY ASSURANCE

7.1 Institutional Policy Implications

The result of the resource-constrained higher education context case study combined with the larger SPIF framework indicates that institutional policies regarding academic integrity need to be transformed from a punitive method to one based on the transparency of academic integrity. Thus, institutional policies will clearly define ethical usage of AI Tools as well as define the expected behaviours of students and faculty members in relation to AI-based assessment. Specifically, the policies will: (1) provide clarity regarding the type of AI tools that may be used in student assignments, projects and/or exams and that must be explicitly disclosed by students in their submissions, (2) create an operational governance framework which includes an effective process for ensuring the transparency, accountability, and appropriate level of human oversight of AI-mediated assessment systems, and (3) create an environment that integrates principles of academic integrity across teaching and learning strategies, rather than treating allegations of misconduct solely as an "academic compliance" issue.

By creating institutional policies that purposely establish integrity as a pedagogical and institutional priority rather than merely a regulatory issue, institutional policies foster an environment in which individuals share responsibility for developing an atmosphere of trust and responsibility regarding academic integrity.

7.2 Pedagogical Practice Implications

According to SPIF, designing assessments is the greatest influence on developing integrity in AI-embedded educational settings. Educators must implement authentic, process-based assessments and reflective assignments to limit opportunities and motivations for students to unethically use AI. Educators can establish these assessment designs by:

1. Creating assignments or examinations that evaluate critical-thinking skills, problem solving capabilities and applicable knowledge in real-world situations.
2. Including iterative feedback mechanisms and reflective aspects to ensure that student work is developed through an iterative process rather than being considered a final product.
3. Utilizing AI as a method for providing formative feedback to students via draft submission feedback or to produce learning analytics regarding student engagement rather than through surveillance of student activity.

While these pedagogical approaches improve student integrity, they also improve student engagement, academic performance, and the college-student relationship.

7.3 Assessment and AI Literacy Development

AI has been shown to be a contributor to unintentional integrity breaches as a result of students' and faculty's lack of understanding of AI's capabilities and assessments (Dogan et al., 2025). Institutions should therefore create structured capacity-building programs for stakeholders through:

1. Educating student users on the ethical use of AI technology, including how to properly disclose any use of AI to complete assignments.
2. Supporting faculty with interpreting AI-generated results, developing pedagogical methods that utilize AI for teaching purposes, and developing assessment methods that will provide them with a means of assessing student learning that is immune to AI-generated responses.
3. Incorporating AI literacy into the professional development of all faculty, into faculty orientation programmes, and into the faculty assessment guide.
4. Improved AI literacy will shift the focus of the integrity risk of AI to the possibilities it has created for supporting students through trust-building educational resources.

SPIF does not require that all summative or high-stakes assessments be substituted with formative approaches by institutions. Wherever assessments (examinations) and other summative demands are specified by either a professional or institutional agreement, SPIF can be implemented step-by-step with the help of explicit AI-use policies, authentic elements related to the assessment process, reflective practices and human monitoring.

7.4 Contextual Equity Considerations

Resource-constrained higher education contexts illustrate how equity-related constraints, including limited access to digital devices, inadequate connectivity and limited access to AI tools, create structural impediments to integrity. The need for meaningful quality assurance and policy is to address the contextual disparity between access and the ability of disadvantaged students to succeed. For instance:

1. Ensure that equitable access is provided for all students through AI-enabled learning resources, including digital infrastructure; and
2. Implement assessment methodologies that are responsive to a diverse range of socio-economic and linguistic backgrounds; and
3. Regularly monitor and mitigate against the likelihood of unintentional biases or exclusions that may arise in relation to AI-driven assessment analytics.

By embedding equity into the definition and understanding of integrity, we can ensure that policies do not unintentionally penalise disadvantaged students.

7.5 Implications for Quality Assurance and Accreditation

Quality assurance agencies and accreditation bodies must include integrity-based metrics while evaluating AI-mediated assessment approaches (Gautam, 2024), including:

1. Examining how well the AI use adheres to the SPIF dimensions of Pedagogical Design, Governance, Literacy and Equity.
2. Assessing the level of transparency and accountability in an institution's AI governance mechanisms.
3. Determining the extent to which AI adoption positively impacts Learning-centred outcomes rather than only improving Administrative Efficiency.

Embedding integrity-based indicators into accreditation frameworks affirms the belief that academic integrity is not simply a Compliance Requirement, but rather, it is an integral Quality dimension.

8. CONCLUSION

The integration of artificial intelligence in Higher Education assessment has dramatically impacted how we view and implement academic integrity, quality assurance and trust. The application of AI technologies provides several benefits with respect to scalability, efficiency and the ability to provide learner-centred feedback; however, artificial intelligence technologies also call into question existing Integrity frameworks that were created in pre-artificial intelligence environments. This chapter posits that although technological methods, such as surveillance or misconduct detection systems, can be used to protect academic integrity; they do not fully address what is needed to support academic integrity under conditions of artificial intelligence use. The chapter goes on to suggest a new way of thinking about academic integrity by proposing it as a Socio-Pedagogical Practice.

Through the introduction of the Socio-Pedagogical Integrity Framework (SPIF) as a mechanism to support an overall, holistic approach to AI mediated assessment, this chapter provides an inclusive approach to developing integrity. The SPIF identifies four interrelated dimensions: pedagogical design, ethical governance of AI, assessment literacy and equity within the context. Within the scope of this framework, it is clear that a learner's experience will promote integrity by aligning the values of the institution with the values of the education that is being delivered to the learner.

This Chapter contributes to the conversation surrounding algorithmic systems, specifically regarding AIs misconduct. Students will lose their trust in systems that rely too heavily on systems that use automation, such as proctored testing services, and the use of plagiarism checks and behavioral tracking technologies, causing an increase in the power or imbalance between students and institutions, resulting in significant levels of anxiety or stress for students, mainly in resource-limited areas or Global South. An alternative to this is Integrity Assessment Design (IA) which places integrity as the primary focus of assessment and assessment process with authentic, transparent, and supported by learner agency. IA decreases the student's desire for and opportunity for misconduct while facilitating meaningful learning. Case illustrative evidence from a resource-constrained higher education context illustrates how, even with little to no access to technological infrastructure, Integrity can still be increased through communication, building out an assessment task, and ethical guidelines.

Additionally, this Chapter emphasizes the critical role that ethical frameworks and governance over AIs have on academic integrity. Explainability, accountability, and responsible data use are not just supplements to support an institution's artificial intelligence-based assessment process, but they are the fundamental foundations for developing and building trust in an institution's AI-based or evidence assessment systems. An institution will develop trust and improve student perceptions of the fairness of an AI-supported assessment system as they educate their students and their educators on how AI systems operate, application of data, and the reasoning behind the decisions made. This information will support institutions in navigating through regulatory uncertainty and rapid AI adoption.

The concept of contextual equity is equally important. AI-mediated assessments do not exist in a vacuum; they are influenced by socio-economic circumstances and digital access, as well as through the institution's capacity to utilise AI technologies. If we do not consider these contextual factors, we risk perpetuating the inequalities already present in our academic systems while at the same time giving the appearance of being technologically innovative. By incorporating equity explicitly into the SPIF model, this chapter widens the scope of discussion on AI and higher education and takes into account the different institutional realities that exist. It also places value on ethical responsibility rather than on being technologically determinist.

Ultimately, this chapter argues that AI does not represent a threat to academic integrity; rather, it is a catalyst to rethink our cultural approach to assessment. Through the lens of socio-pedagogical principles, AI can help to enhance quality, assist in developing trusting relationships and facilitate greater sustainability within the assessment process. Therefore, higher education institutions must now determine how best to employ AI in ways that reflect their educational values, protect learners' dignity, and cultivate trust and long-standing integrity.

8.1 Limitations of the Framework

The framework comprises a number of limitations that it is important to consider. First, the framework is theoretical and has not been tested in terms of the proposed interactions among the framework elements in various institutional, disciplinary and educational contexts. Second, the application of the framework may be restricted by the disparities in institutional resources, human capacity, infrastructure, policy constraints and levels of AI literacy. Third, there is a risk that the principles of transparency, monitoring or integrity may be applied in too much of a procedural or punitive way, which basically happens in the absence of meaningful human oversight in administering the framework. Finally, the framework may require contextualization as the four dimensions of it may operate differently in various socio-economic, cultural, linguistic and institutional circumstances. These limitations confirm the need for future empirical studies to test and adjust the framework.

9. FUTURE RESEARCH DIRECTIONS

This chapter provides a foundation to guide future research into an integrity-oriented evaluation of AI. While this foundation is conceptual and illustrative, additional opportunities exist for future research based on empirical evidence. For example, validation of the SPIF framework through empirical research in multiple disciplines, cultures and institutions is needed, as well as longitudinal studies to assess the effect on student learning, behaviour and trust when using assessment methods aligned with SPIF.

Future research efforts should also examine the assessment literacy of students and faculty in AI-related environments. Understanding how various stakeholder groups interpret the use of AI feedback, the process of automated grading, and the use of AI for decision-making will enable the development of effective professional development and curriculum resources to support increased understanding and use of AI by students, faculty and administrators in educational settings, particularly when examining these differences across Global North versus Global South institutions. There needs to continue to be more research into how ethics can be governed with respect to transparency, accountability, and regulation mechanisms that pertain to AI's role in assessing learners' knowledge. Researchers from education, computing and ethics should work together to develop models of governance that strike a balance between technological advancement and ethical practices.

The need for governance research, particularly ethics-based governance related to transparency mechanisms, accountability models, and regulatory frameworks related to the use of AI in assessment, is the third component of a larger movement to improve the use of AI in higher education. In addition, future studies should focus on the possibilities of AI supported alternative assessment paradigms, including formative analytics driven feedback, reflective assessments, and collaborative knowledge creation. The direction in which research should be progressing is to investigate how AI will help design for integrity (i.e., produce environment where integrity becomes the norm) instead of investigating how AI detects dishonest behavior (i.e. misconduct).

Through advocacy for these areas of research in future scholarship, the groundwork laid in this chapter will result in more equitable, trustworthy and pedagogically appropriate AI mediated assessments for global higher education. Future empirical studies on the application of SPIF should fulfill essential requirements pertaining to ethical considerations, including obtaining informed consent, ensuring privacy of research participants, taking measures of secure storage and processing of assessment data and complying with any other relevant obligations determined by data protection regulations. Implementing those measures will play an important role in preserving the dignity of students and trust in institutions regarding the collection and analysis of AI-processed assessment materials.

REFERENCES

Andrade, H., & Du, Y. (2005). Student perspectives on rubric-referenced assessment. *Practical Assessment, Research & Evaluation, 10*(1), 3. DOI: 10.7275/g367-ye94

Bretag, T. (2013). Challenges in addressing plagiarism in education. *PLoS Medicine, 10*(12), e1001574. DOI: 10.1371/journal.pmed.1001574 PMID: 24391477

Bretag, T., Harper, R., Burton, M., Ellis, C., Newton, P., Rozenberg, P., Saddiqui, S., & van Haeringen, K. (2019). Contract cheating: A survey of Australian university students. *Studies in Higher Education, 44*(11), 1837–1856. DOI: 10.1080/03075079.2018.1462788

Brown, G., Bull, J., & Pendlebury, M. (2013). *Assessing student learning in higher education* (2nd ed.). Routledge. DOI: 10.4324/9781315004914

Buckingham Shum, S., Ferguson, R., & Martinez-Maldonado, R. (2019). Human-centred learning analytics. *Journal of Learning Analytics, 6*(2), 1–9. DOI: 10.18608/jla.2019.62.1

Coghlan, S., Miller, T., & Paterson, J. (2021). Good proctor or "big brother"? Ethics of online exam supervision technologies. *Philosophy & Technology, 34*(4), 1581–1606. DOI: 10.1007/s13347-021-00476-1 PMID: 34485025

Dogan, S., Nalbantoglu, U. Y., Celik, I., & Agacli Dogan, N. (2025). Artificial intelligence professional development: A systematic review of TPACK, designs, and effects for teacher learning. *Professional Development in Education, 51*(3), 519–546. DOI: 10.1080/19415257.2025.2454457

Felder, R. M., & Brent, R. (2016). *Teaching and learning STEM: A practical guide*. Jossey-Bass.

Gautam, D. A. S. (2024). Impact of National Assessment and Accreditation Council (NAAC) on Higher Education Institutions (HEIs) in India. *International Journal of All Research Education and Scientific Methods, 12*(8). Advance online publication. DOI: 10.2139/ssrn.4932646

Lodge, J. M., Howard, S., Bearman, M. L., Dawson, P., Agostinho, S., Buckingham Shum, S., Deneen, C., Ellis, C., Fawns, T., Gniel, H., Harper, R., Henderson, M., Liu, D. Y. T., Markauskaite, L., McLean, J., Perrotta, C., Schuwirth, L., & Slade, C. (2023). Assessment reform for the age of artificial intelligence. Tertiary Education Quality and Standards Agency. https://www.teqsa.gov.au/sites/default/files/2023-09/assessment-reform-age-artificial-intelligence-discussion-paper.pdf

Roll, I., & Wylie, R. (2016). Evolution and revolution in artificial intelligence in education. *International Journal of Artificial Intelligence in Education, 26*(2), 582–599. DOI: 10.1007/s40593-016-0110-3

Selwyn, N. (2019). *Should robots replace teachers? AI and the future of education*. John Wiley & Sons.

UNESCO. (2023). *Guidance for generative AI in education and research*. UNESCO Publishing. https://www.unesco.org

Watson, G., & Sottile, J. (2010). Cheating in the digital age: Do students cheat more in online courses? *Online Journal of Distance Learning Administration, 13*(1), 1–10.

Williamson, B., & Eynon, R. (2020). Historical threads, missing links, and future directions in AI in education. *Learning, Media and Technology*, *45*(3), 223–235. DOI: 10.1080/17439884.2020.1798995

Yazici, T. (2026). Artificial Intelligence Ethics in Communication: Challenges and Future Perspectives. Navigating Modern Digital Communication Ethics and Law, 33-74.

Chapter 8
Assessing Trust Quality, Integrity, and Power in AI-Mediated Higher Education Assessment

Salam Al E'mari
http://orcid.org/0000-0002-2134-4158
University of Petra, Jordan

Yousef Sanjalawe
http://orcid.org/0000-0002-4442-1865
University of Jordan, Jordan

Fadi Fataftah
http://orcid.org/0000-0002-3299-0972
University Canada West, Canada

ABSTRACT

Artificial intelligence (AI) is increasingly shaping assessment practices in higher education through tools such as automated grading systems, AI-generated feedback, learning analytics, and technologies designed to detect academic dishonesty. While these innovations promise greater efficiency, scalability, and consistency in evaluating student performance, they also introduce significant challenges related to fairness, transparency, academic integrity, and institutional governance. This chapter argues that the central challenge of AI-mediated assessment is not purely technological but lies in the governance of trust within assessment systems. Furthermore, it examines how AI reshapes power relations among educators, students, institutions, and technological systems, while highlighting issues such as algorithmic bias, surveillance-oriented integrity technologies, and unequal global adoption of AI.

DOI: 10.4018/979-8-3373-8939-4.ch008

1. INTRODUCTION: ARTIFICIAL INTELLIGENCE, ASSESSMENT, AND THE QUESTION OF TRUST

Artificial Intelligence has been transforming higher education at a very rapid pace and changing the very face of how we approach the processes of teaching, learning, and assessment within our institutions of higher learning. This is because of the expanding face of higher education systems that has been accompanied by an increase in the number of students seeking higher education and the need to provide timely and personalized feedback to students while ensuring quality and uniformity within the assessment process (Holmes et al., 2019; Fadlelmula & Qadhi, 2024). As technology becomes more sophisticated in terms of infrastructure, AI tools are increasingly being used within learning management systems to enable the collection of vast amounts of educational data.

Significant benefits can be realized from the adoption of AI-based technologies in the context of higher learning institutions. For instance, in the context of automated essay scoring tools, the tools can identify the linguistic features and structural patterns in the essays written by students. In another sense, generative AI-based tools can provide formative feedback to students on their assignments related to coding, problem-solving, and essays. This would allow students to receive instant feedback on their assignments that would otherwise require a lot of time from the teachers or instructors. Learning analytics tools can provide even greater benefits to students as the tools can identify patterns in students' performance data to predict potential academic risks. This would allow institutions to provide interventions that can improve students' success (Ifenthaler & Schumacher, 2016; Holmes et al., 2019). From the perspective of the institution, the benefits of AI-based tools can be realized as a way to improve efficiency in the institution.

Despite these potential benefits, there are ethical, pedagogical, and governance issues surrounding the integration of AI with assessment practices. Assessment is a fundamental practice in higher education institutions since not only do assessment outcomes measure the learning outcomes of the students, but they also shape the way the students relate to their learning and the way knowledge is valued. Establishing the grades of the students is a crucial practice with far-reaching implications for the future academic or professional prospects of the students. Traditionally, assessment has been based on professional judgment by those who understand the work of the students from a disciplinary or pedagogical perspective (Boud, 2008; Sadler, 1989). The integration of AI with assessment challenges traditional notions about the role of expertise in evaluating the learning outcomes of the students.

In this context, the locus of judgment is shared by human educators and technological algorithms. Automated essay scoring, plagiarism detection, and predictive analytics are examples of technological algorithms that play a role in the assessment infrastructure. However, there is a concern that the use of such algorithms may limit the capacity of the algorithms to address the complexities of students' learning and the contextual dimensions of students' work (Selwyn, 2019). For example, there is a concern that the decision-making process of the algorithms is opaque, such that educators and students may not be able to understand the decision-making process.

However, recent studies highlight that the major challenges linked to AI applications in education are not technological but socio institutional. Indeed, educational technologies are part of a larger socio-technical system that comprises institutional policies, pedagogical values, and cultural values related to assessment and knowledge creation (Selwyn, 2019; Williamson & Eynon, 2020). In that sense, AI-based assessment can no longer be considered a technological innovation but a change in assessment processes that impacts relationships between students, teachers, institutions, and technological infrastructures.

However, a major issue linked to assessment processes in higher education institutions is trust. Trust is considered a fundamental aspect of higher education assessment systems. Indeed, students must trust that the assessment process is fair and transparent, teachers must trust that the institutional assessment system is supportive of academic values, and employers and society must trust that academic credentials accurately represent students' competencies and learning outcomes (Tierney & Sabharwal, 2017). When AI technologies are used to make assessment decisions, the nature of that trust may change. Indeed, AI technologies can be considered "black boxes" that make it hard to understand how a given decision was made or how potential errors or biases may occur during the assessment process (Mateen, 2018).

Furthermore, concerns surrounding algorithmic bias and fairness add another dimension of complexity to the use of AI in assessment contexts. Machine learning algorithms are trained on data sets, which may have been collected in a manner that maintains existing inequalities and biases in society. Algorithmic systems, when they are biased, may perpetuate existing inequalities in academic outcomes (Noble, 2018; Mateen, 2018). For example, in essay marking systems, linguistic biases may favor linguistic styles more commonly represented in dominant academic cultures.

In addition to these challenges surrounding algorithmic bias, the pace of change in generative AI technologies has also raised questions of academic integrity in recent years. New technologies in essay composition, complex problem-solving, and computer code creation have blurred the line between legitimate academic support and academic dishonesty in many institutions around the world (Xia et al., 2024; Cotton et al., 2024). It is in this context that a larger question of academic integrity in modern higher education must be considered: modern AI technologies are pushing against existing boundaries in academic assessment even as they create opportunities for innovation in those processes.

This chapter will argue that the main problem in AI-mediated assessment is not the performance of the technology itself but rather the governance of trust in the assessment systems increasingly mediated by AI. Although the existing literature has primarily focused on the technical performance of AI systems in assessments such as their accuracy or their efficiency—there has been little emphasis on the ways in which AI systems affect the authority, accountability, and relationships in education. A proper understanding of AI in the assessment process necessitates a shift from the technical to the broader assessment process as a socio-pedagogical practice.

From the perspective of a socio-pedagogical approach to the assessment process, the assessment process is not only the technical process of measuring the outcomes of the educational process but rather a socio-pedagogical practice embedded in the values of education as well as the power structures of the educational system (Boud, 2008; Black & Wiliam, 2018). The introduction of AI systems to the assessment process changes the dynamics of the authority of the educators, the students, the educational system itself, as well as the technology itself in the higher education assessment process.

The remainder of this chapter will explore these issues through a multidisciplinary approach that draws on the fields of higher education studies, assessment theory, and the sociology of technology. The following section will consider the expanding scope of AI technologies in the assessment processes of higher education institutions. The chapter will then consider the concept of assessment as a form of socio-pedagogical practice. Next, the chapter will consider the impact of AI-mediated assessment on the power dynamics within higher education institutions. Finally, the chapter will consider the emerging risks associated with algorithmic assessment and propose a framework for trust-centered AI assessment that takes into account the concepts of transparency, contextual understanding, assessment literacy, and human oversight. By centering the concept of trust as a key governance issue in the adoption of AI technologies in higher education institutions, the chapter will contribute to the broader debates on the responsible adoption of AI technologies. The construction, maintenance, and potential subversion of trust within the assessment processes of higher education institutions are critical to the continued development of the pedagogical foundations of higher education institutions.

2. THE RISE OF ARTIFICIAL INTELLIGENCE IN HIGHER EDUCATION ASSESSMENT

Significantly, the rapid evolution of Artificial Intelligence technologies has led to a widening scope of tools that can be used to assess students' learning in higher learning institutions. For instance, over the last decade or so, there has been a growing trend in the adoption of Artificial Intelligence-based tools to support the assessment of students' learning in higher learning institutions. This can be attributed to the broader trends of digitalization and data-based decision-making in higher learning institutions (Fadlelmula & Qadhi, 2024; Holmes et al., 2019). As the number of students continues to rise in higher learning institutions, Artificial Intelligence-based tools for assessing students' learning are being advocated as a means of improving efficiency while at the same time ensuring quality learning.

AI-mediated assessment covers a broad range of technologies, which are intended for supporting or facilitating the evaluation process. Such technologies are employed at different stages of the assessment process, such as grading, feedback creation, integrity detection, and performance prediction. Although each category of the application of artificial intelligence technology solves particular issues for the institution, it is important to note that the combination of the technologies represents a major shift from the manner in which assessment systems function in the environment.

2.1 Automated Grading and Evaluation Systems

One of the first and most popular applications of AI technology in the assessment area of education is the use of automated grading. Automated essay scoring systems involve the application of natural language processing techniques to the analysis of the grammatical properties of written texts produced by the student. These systems provide a score to the essay based on the patterns learned from the training set of already graded assignments (Shermis & Burstein, 2013).

Automated grading systems were first developed for the testing environment but are also increasingly used in the higher education sector. Recent advancements in generative AI technologies have enabled the evaluation systems to go beyond the grading of assignments. These systems can be used to evaluate the performance of the student on various assignments like essays, coding assignments, etc. (Kasneci et al., 2023). Apart from the grading of assignments, AI technologies also provide an explanation for the improvement of the assignments by the students.

Advocates of this technology propose that it could help overcome some of the challenges faced by managing large classes and limited resources in instruction. For example, it could help educators save more time in grading tasks, thus enabling them to focus more on mentoring and curriculum design (Holmes et al., 2019). Nevertheless, it is also argued that automated grading systems may not be able to fully account for some of the complex aspects of students' work, such as creativity, critical thinking, and understanding of different subjects. As such, some researchers stress the need to ensure human input in the grading processes (Selwyn, 2019).

2.2 AI-Generated Feedback and Personalized Learning Support

Besides grading, AI technologies are also being utilized to offer formative feedback on students' performance. Feedback is an important factor in learning as it allows students to understand the gap between their existing performance and the expected learning outcomes (Sadler, 1989). Nevertheless, offering feedback is considered one of the resource-demanding aspects of teaching in higher learning institutions.

AI feedback technologies aim to solve the problem of feedback by analyzing students' performance and offering suggestions on how to improve their performance. For example, writing feedback technologies can recognize grammatical mistakes, offer suggestions on how to improve the writing style, as well as provide feedback on how to improve the argumentation structure. Advanced feedback technologies incorporate adaptive learning technologies that offer feedback depending on students' learning patterns and progress (Holmes et al., 2019).

Significantly, the advent of generative AI technologies like large language models has greatly expanded the possibilities for automated feedback. These technologies can be used to generate elaborate explanations, summaries, or even suggestions for improvement based on the input provided by the students. However, there are also apprehensions about the validity or appropriateness of the AI-generated feedback. Some researchers have argued that overdependence on automated feedback technologies could undermine the scope for dialogue between the students and the educator, thereby limiting the relational dimensions of teaching-learning (Xia et al., 2024).

2.3 AI and Academic Integrity Detection

One of the areas that has been a focal point within the realm of academic integrity has been highlighted with the advent of AI-mediated assessment tools. One of the most established areas of academic integrity with regards to the use of AI tools has been plagiarism detection systems. This has been particularly prevalent within the realm of higher education institutions and has been based on the comparison of assignments with extensive databases of academic publications, web-based material, and assignments to identify similarities with the work of students (Lancaster & Clarke, 2016). However, the efficacy of plagiarism detection tools has been a topic of discussion with regards to false positives and the ability to identify similarities between assignments.

The advent of generative AI has further complicated the issue of academic integrity. This is because the use of AI technology for the production of high-level written responses has challenged the long-held assumptions regarding authorship and originality of work. As such, there has been the development of AI detection technology for the identification of such responses. However, there is a possibility that the results obtained from such technology may be inconsistent, thereby creating concerns regarding fairness in the handling of academic integrity cases (Cotton et al., 2024).

In addition, there has been the use of AI technology for the proctoring of online examinations during the COVID-19 pandemic. This has been done for the purpose of maintaining academic integrity among students. As such, there has been the use of video recordings, screen, and biometric monitoring for the identification of suspicious behavior. However, there is a possibility that the use of such technology may lead to the development of surveillance-based learning environments, thereby creating concerns regarding the trust of students (Williamson & Eynon, 2020).

2.4 Learning Analytics and Predictive Assessment

Another key area of AI application in the assessment of higher learning institutions involves learning analytics. Learning analytics can be defined as the analysis of educational data to improve learning processes (Siemens & Baker, 2012). This form of analysis can be carried out through the use of AI to analyze large amounts of educational data collected from various online learning platforms.

Predictive models can be defined as a form of analysis that uses the data collected to identify patterns that can be linked to academic success or failure. For instance, a predictive model can be used to identify patterns that can be linked to a student's failure to succeed in a particular course. This can be done through the analysis of the patterns of a student's participation in the learning process (Ifenthaler & Schumacher, 2016).

In terms of assessment settings, predictive analytics may also impact on how institutions develop their assessment strategies or distribute their academic support services. However, there are ethical concerns that emerge with the use of predictive analytics, particularly with regards to data privacy and the risk of perpetuating inequality among students. Some argue that predictive analytics may inadvertently profile students that may hinder their opportunities or may perpetuate bias within institutions (Mateen, 2018).

2.5 Expanding AI Assessment Ecosystems

Automated grading systems, tools for feedback based on artificial intelligence, integrity detection tools, and predictive learning analytics are some examples that highlight the complexity of the new environment in which artificial intelligence is being evaluated. Instead of being used as standalone products, they are increasingly part of an interconnected infrastructure that includes learning management systems, analytics tools, and databases.

This is part of a larger trend toward more data-intensive educational environments, where large amounts of information are being collected and analyzed. While this may provide new possibilities for improving learning outcomes, it raises important issues regarding the role of human judgment in the assessment environment.

As these technologies become more embedded in assessment infrastructures, it is also critical to think through how these systems are impacting pedagogy and power dynamics in institutions. To do this, it is necessary to move beyond a technical discussion of these systems and into a more socio-pedagogical approach to thinking through the concept of assessment. Figure 1 presents the AI-mediated assessment ecosystem in higher education.

Figure 1. AI-Mediated Assessment Ecosystem in Higher Education.

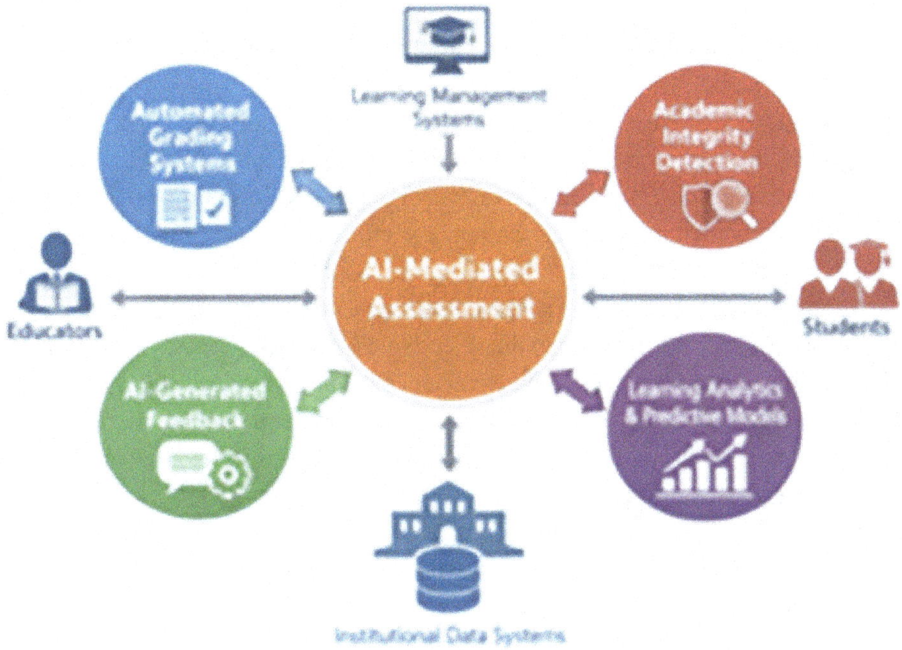

In the following section, we will discuss a socio-pedagogical approach to thinking through the concept of assessment and how it is being impacted by AI-mediated systems of assessment.

3. ASSESSMENT AS A SOCIO-PEDAGOGICAL PRACTICE: JUDGMENT, EXPERTISE, AND ALGORITHMIC AUTHORITY

In discussions around AI and educational assessment, there is often a tendency to focus on the technical capabilities of the algorithm or software used, how well it can score assignments, or how well it can identify instances of academic dishonesty or predict academic outcomes. Although these are obviously pertinent questions, they also have the potential to give the impression that the assessment process is purely a technical affair. However, the assessment process within the higher education sector is frequently very much integrated into the social, pedagogical, and institutional context. It is a process of interpretation and negotiation with a range of stakeholders. It is necessary to conceptualize the assessment process as a socio-pedagogical rather than a purely technical process if the implications of the AI-mediated assessment process are to be grasped (Boud, 2008; Black & Wiliam, 2018).

In this context, the role of assessment is not merely to evaluate the learning outcomes of the students but a very sophisticated process through which academic communities articulate their knowledge standards, make judgments about the performance of the students, and validate the outcomes of education. Grades, feedback, and assessment results can greatly affect the learning styles of the students as well as the very meaning of knowledge within the academic disciplines (Sadler, 1989). Once AI technologies become part of the assessment process, they can go beyond the scope of assisting the academic communities with the tasks to the extent of reshaping the very meaning of academic judgment and power.

3.1 Assessment and the Role of Professional Judgment

One of the major characteristics of assessment within the higher education setting is the use of professional judgment that educators apply to their students. This is different from standardized testing settings that place a great emphasis on objective scoring systems. In the higher education setting, assessment often involves evaluating students' complex performances, such as essays, designs, research papers, and creative works.

According to experts on assessment, the judgment that educators apply to their students' performances is more of an interpretive process rather than an objective assessment process. Educators use their tacit knowledge of their discipline and pedagogical experience to make sense of the students' performances that they evaluate (Sadler, 1989). This interpretive process allows educators to identify students' unique qualities that may not be quantifiable using objective assessment processes, such as originality, critical thinking ability, and understanding concepts.

Furthermore, assessment is linked to feedback processes that facilitate learning for the student. Feedback helps the student to understand the discrepancy between the current and desired learning outcomes and provides guidance on the improvement of the same (Black & Wiliam, 2018). Feedback processes are often relational and involve dialogue between the student and the instructor to facilitate learning.

The inclusion of AI systems into the assessment process disrupts the aforementioned model by incorporating computational processes to mimic some of the processes involved in the evaluative judgments of the instructor. It includes the use of automated systems to grade and provide feedback to the students, which are informed by statistical patterns derived from the data provided to the system. Although the systems are useful in identifying some of the structures involved in the work of the student, they are not able to mimic the contextual reasoning involved in the academic judgments of the instructor.

3.2 Sociotechnical Perspectives on Educational Technologies

To gain a better understanding of the effects of AI-based assessment, it is necessary to use the concept of sociotechnical approaches from the sociology of technology. These approaches highlight the fact that technology is never neutral in its effects. Rather, it is always part of a social system that affects the way in which technology is used. Technologies have a significant impact on the way in which institutions operate, as well as the way in which power is exercised. These approaches have been supported by various researchers in the field of sociology of technology.

Digital technologies have played a significant role in the field of higher education. These technologies have often been used as infrastructures to organize teaching, learning, and assessment processes. Learning management systems, analytics tools, and assessment tools have often been used to organize the way in which educators engage with students. AI systems have extended the infrastructures used in the field of higher education by incorporating decision-making processes.

From a sociotechnical perspective, AI-mediated assessment can be conceptualized as part of a larger transformation in the governance of education. Algorithmic systems have the capacity to collect and analyze vast amounts of data, providing insights that inform decision-making processes in educational institutions. These data-driven approaches have the potential to extend beyond the assessment of individual students to inform institutional policies in various areas of education (Williamson & Eynon, 2020).

However, the sociotechnical perspective is crucial in highlighting the fact that algorithmic systems have the capacity to reallocate power among various stakeholders in the education system. Decisions that were previously made by educators in the education system may now be partially influenced by the outputs of algorithmic systems that use AI. For example, grading systems may use AI to generate grades that are used by educators as a basis of review, or predictive analytics may use AI to identify students who may fail in a particular course.

Such changes raise important questions of accountability and responsibility within AI-mediated assessment contexts. In fact, when algorithmic systems play a role in evaluation processes, it may not always be clear who or what is responsible for the outcomes—software developers, administrators, or educators who make use of algorithmic recommendations.

3.3 Algorithmic Authority and Educational Governance

At the same time, the growing use of algorithmic systems in evaluation processes is creating new forms of authority in higher education. Researchers who have examined the concept of algorithmic authority in the study of algorithmic governance have noted that computational systems tend to have a form of authority where the outputs of the system are considered to be objective or true, even though the processes of the system itself cannot be completely understood (Mateen, 2018).

In the educational sphere, the concept of algorithmic authority could manifest itself in the use of AI-generated outputs as neutral or true reflections of the ability of students. However, in the process, the actual processes of the algorithmic system could have embedded biases or weaknesses that remain undetected.

Concerns about algorithmic bias have been widely documented across various domains of data-driven decision-making. For example, machine learning algorithms may perpetuate existing inequalities if the training data contains biases. As such, it is possible for such algorithms to perpetuate inequalities, especially if the training data contains biases. In the context of educational assessment, this may occur through, for example, the use of algorithms to score essays, where the algorithms may prefer certain linguistic styles that are more commonly used by dominant groups.

In addition to the potential for algorithms to be biased, there is the issue of the authority of algorithms. In the context of assessment, trust is based upon the professional standing of educators. However, the use of algorithms may lead to difficulties for stakeholders seeking to understand the decision-making processes, potentially creating a crisis of trust. In recent debates about AI in education, the focus has been on the need to maintain the significance of human oversight in the AI decision-making processes. AI systems should not replace the educator but rather be seen as a tool to support the educator's judgment while also maintaining the educator's responsibility for the evaluation (Xia et al., 2024).

3.4 Reconfiguring Authority in AI-Mediated Assessment

Lastly, the incorporation of AI systems into the assessment infrastructure alters the dynamics of power and authority between the teacher, the educational institution, the student, and the technology. To the teacher, the incorporation of AI systems into the assessment infrastructure could be the application of algorithms to aid the teacher in the grading of the student's performance, while to the educational institution's administrators, the incorporation of AI systems into the assessment infrastructure could be the application of data analysis systems to track the academic progress of the student and identify patterns from the academic achievements.

However, there is a concern that the expansion of algorithmic infrastructures may lead to the centralization of power within educational systems. For instance, technology giants offer AI-based educational infrastructures and analytics tools to educational institutions. This has been argued to represent a broader move towards the "datafication" of education, whereby students' learning processes are increasingly represented as data to be analyzed and governed (Williamson & Eynon, 2020).

These processes demonstrate the need to explore the processes of designing and implementing AI-mediated assessment systems to avoid the potential of perpetuating inequality and the loss of transparency and values in education. Figure 2 demonstrates the distribution of power and authority in AI-mediated assessment.

Figure 2. Power and Authority in AI-Mediated Assessment.

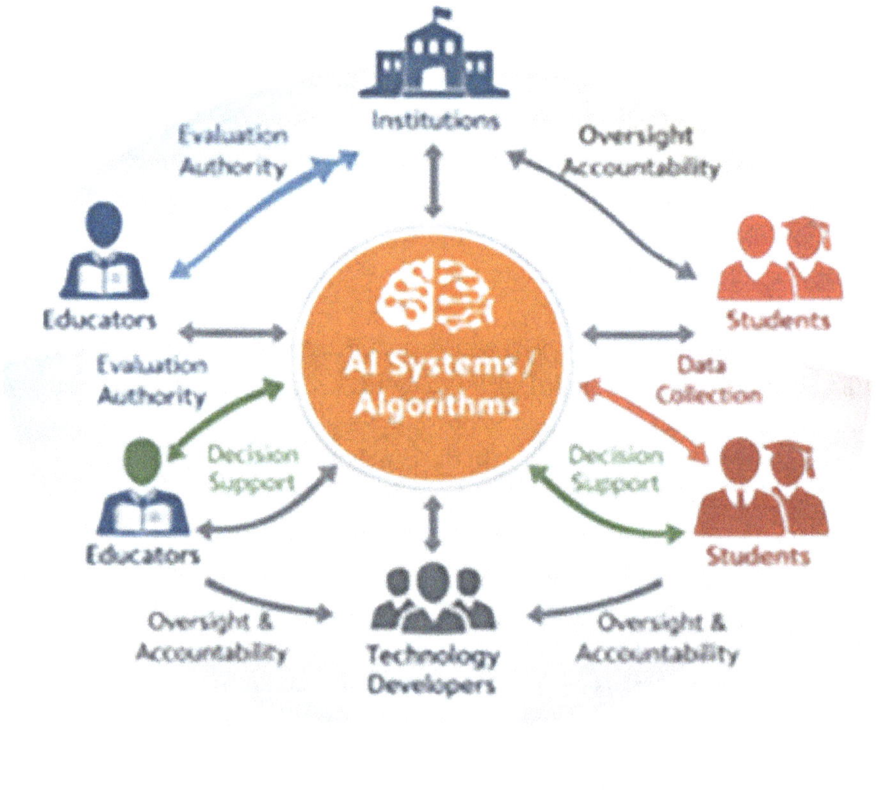

It is within this context that the challenge facing higher education institutions is no longer how to use AI technologies but how to use AI technologies while maintaining the integrity and legitimacy of assessment processes. This requires that there is a better understanding of the ethical implications of AI-mediated assessment processes. The next section of the discussion focuses on the risks associated with

AI-mediated assessment processes, including algorithm bias, surveillance integrity technologies, and the differential global infrastructure that affects AI technology uptake in higher education institutions.

4. POWER, BIAS, AND SURVEILLANCE IN AI-MEDIATED ASSESSMENT

In fact, the integration of artificial intelligence within higher education assessment has attracted considerable attention and interest because of the potential to improve efficiency and scalability within the assessment process. However, the integration of AI has also introduced new forms of power and control within the educational environment. In fact, AI-mediated assessment systems can impact the assessment of students' performance, academic integrity, and institutional decisions related to learning outcomes. In recent times, the integration of AI within assessment has been considered a critical issue that needs to be analyzed from ethical, political, and sociological perspectives as well (Selwyn, 2019; Williamson & Eynon, 2020). There are three major concerns that have been considered critical to the assessment of AI-mediated assessment systems:

- Algorithmic bias
- Surveillance-oriented integrity technologies
- Technological resources and their distribution within the global higher education system.

4.1 Algorithmic Bias and Fairness in Automated Assessment

One of the most commonly mentioned risks when discussing AI systems is algorithmic bias. Machine learning models use data to make predictions or classify information. When the data used to make these predictions contains social inequality or bias, the algorithm may replicate or enhance these characteristics (Mateen, 2018). In the field of education, algorithmic bias may impact the fairness and accuracy of AI systems.

One of the best examples of algorithmic bias can be seen with automated essay scoring systems. These systems score students' essays based on linguistic characteristics like vocabulary use, grammatical complexity, and composition structure. These characteristics may or may not impact the quality of the essay but may represent the dominant academic culture or tradition used by students. International or multicultural students may experience bias when their writing style differs from the dominant style used by the algorithm to score the essay (Shermis & Burstein, 2013).

Research on algorithmic fairness has indicated that a seemingly unbiased computational model can contain underlying biases that are a product of the data or the processes that the model was originally exposed to. In the assessment of students in higher learning institutions, this can be evidenced through various underlying biases that may favor certain styles of rhetoric or argumentation. This can mean that the algorithmic assessment tools may end up favoring certain students over others. Another argument that has been raised by various authors in the field of algorithmic assessment is that the underlying biases in the algorithms are hard to identify. This is because algorithms can be complex statistical tools that are hard to understand. This can make it hard to assess the fairness of the algorithmic assessment results or to challenge the algorithmic assessment results that may be unfavorable to certain students (Noble, 2018).

This concern points to the significance of ensuring a transparent and accountable approach in designing and using AI-based systems in assessment contexts. There is a risk of using an assessment technology that is not in line with equity and academic fairness principles if there are no mechanisms in place to audit decisions made by algorithms and assess any potential biases in these decisions.

4.2 Surveillance and Academic Integrity Technologies

The second area of concern is the increased reliance on AI-based surveillance technologies in academic integrity research. Digital learning environments provide more opportunities for academic dishonesty, including plagiarism, contract cheating, and academic collaboration without authorization. As a result, academic institutions are increasingly using technological tools to help prevent academic dishonesty.

Software programs aimed at detecting plagiarism are among the most used technologies in academic integrity research. These technologies compare students' essays with large databases of academic publications and online sources to find similarities that may indicate plagiarism (Lancaster & Clarke, 2016). Even as these technologies help teachers detect academic dishonesty, they have also been criticized as promoting a compliance-based approach to academic integrity that is focused on detection rather than educational support.

The move towards online learning during the COVID-19 pandemic has fueled the use of AI-based proctoring tools to monitor students during online examinations. These tools generally use camera feed, screen activity, and physiological data to identify suspicious patterns based on their algorithm. For instance, proctoring tools may identify students who are not looking at their screen, making unusual movements, or having their environment disturbed.

However, AI-based proctoring tools have been a major point of controversy as they may create a highly surveilled learning environment that may negatively impact the relationship between students and their learning institutions. The constant surveillance of students' physical environments may create concerns around their privacy and autonomy while learning, as surveillance becomes a normal practice in learning settings (Williamson & Eynon, 2020).

Besides the issue of privacy, other problems have been raised against the application of AI-based proctoring systems, particularly with regards to the technical limitations that could have a greater impact on some groups of students. To illustrate this, the accuracy rate of some AI-based systems, particularly with regards to the identification of individuals through the application of facial recognition, has proven to have lower accuracy rates for individuals with darker skin tones, as discussed by Buolamwini and Gebru (2018). This problem, among others, has raised pertinent questions with regards to the application of surveillance-based systems. In addition to this, the application of surveillance-based systems could have a profound impact on the relationship between the academic institution and the student. Unlike the conventional approach to academic integrity, which seeks to develop a culture of academic honesty through mutual responsibility and dialogue, the application of surveillance-based systems could have a profound impact on the values of higher education.

4.3 Global Inequalities in AI Adoption

A third critical aspect of AI-mediated assessment relates to the differential distribution of technological resources within the global higher education landscape. In that regard, there is a differential distribution of resources among higher education institutions around the world with regard to their technological infrastructure, financial resources, and policy frameworks that regulate the use of technology in education.

In the context of that differential distribution of resources, higher education institutions that are well resourced, particularly those based in the Global North, may seek to develop or procure sophisticated AI technologies that form part of a larger digital learning infrastructure.

In contrast, institutions based in less resourced contexts may experience challenges with regard to the implementation of AI-based assessment technologies due to limited access to digital infrastructure, limited technological expertise, and limited financial resources to support the procurement and implementation of AI technologies. In that sense, the benefits of AI-based educational innovation may not accrue uniformly within the global higher education landscape.

This has raised concerns that there may be the creation of a new form of digital inequality in education. This is because institutions may become dependent on external vendors when they adopt AI technology that was developed by other organizations. This may create an uneven relationship whereby technological infrastructure that was developed with reference to one context is transferred to another context that has a different form of education and governance.

Additionally, the creation of AI technology may be based on assumptions that may not be effective when transferred to another context. This is because the assumptions that are made may only apply to a given context and may not apply to another context. This may create inequality among people at the global level.

These concerns emphasize the need to consider diversity at the global level when creating AI technology that is used as a form of assessment tool in higher education institutions. The effective use of AI technology in higher education institutions requires that there is consideration of the context within which the technology is used.

4.4 Implications for Trust and Governance

The issues of algorithmic bias, surveillance-based integrity measures, and global inequality are some of the ways in which AI-mediated assessments affect power relations in higher learning institutions. Algorithmic systems affect how students are evaluated, how misconduct is monitored, and how decisions are made in institutions of higher learning. This affects the level of trust in institutions and the processes involved in assessments.

Trust in an assessment system is built on perceptions of fairness, transparency, and accountability. In the case where an algorithmic system is involved in an evaluation process, it is important to ensure that the system is aligned with principles that enhance and do not destroy perceptions of fairness, transparency, and accountability.

Therefore, the following section proposes a framework for trust-centered AI assessments and identifies some of the principles that can be followed by institutions to enhance the quality and integrity of AI technologies in higher learning institutions without compromising the values that guide higher learning institutions.

5. A TRUST-CENTERED FRAMEWORK FOR AI-MEDIATED ASSESSMENT: QUALITY, INTEGRITY, AND GOVERNANCE

However, the increasing use of AI in the assessment of students in higher education settings necessitates the rethinking of the maintenance of trust, quality, and academic integrity in the evaluation process. As mentioned in the previous sections of the essay, AI systems have the potential to improve the quality of the evaluation process through increased efficiency. Nevertheless, the use of AI in the evaluation of students is characterized by various challenges, including bias, surveillance, and infrastructure divide. These issues necessitate the development of appropriate systems for the governance of AI systems in the evaluation of students. Figure 3 presents the proposed trust-centered framework for AI-mediated assessment.

Figure 3. Trust-Centered Framework for AI-Mediated Assessment.

Trust is an important factor in the evaluation of students in the context of higher learning institutions. This is because trust is the foundation upon which the legitimacy of academic evaluation is built. In addition, trust is an important factor in the evaluation of students in the context of higher learning institutions in the sense that students should trust the evaluation process, educators should trust the technology used in the learning institutions, and society should trust the academic credentials of the students (Tierney & Sabharwal, 2017). The use of AI systems in the evaluation of students complicates the issue of trust in the evaluation process since the decision-making process is involved.

In addressing the above challenges in the evaluation process using AI systems, this chapter proposes a trust-centered model that is comprised of three important aspects: quality assurance, academic integrity, and ethical governance. This is achieved through the following four important principles: transparency, contextual sensitivity, assessment literacy, and human oversight. These four principles provide the foundation upon which AI-assisted systems can be developed to provide quality education with considerations of fairness and accountability.

5.1 Transparency and Explainability

Another key factor that could potentially result in the development of trust among the stakeholders with regard to the AI-based assessment systems could be the transparency of the systems. This could especially be the case considering the complexity of the statistical processes involved in the AI models. It could, therefore, not be possible for the stakeholders to understand the processes through which the assessment results are generated unless the transparency of the processes through which the AI systems operate is provided.

As derived from the various studies carried out by different scholars on the issue of the governance of the AI systems, the issue of transparency could play a crucial role with regard to the decision-making processes of the AI systems. It could, therefore, be possible to define the concept of explainable AI as a set of approaches through which the outputs generated by the computational processes could easily be understood by the stakeholders (Floridi et al., 2018). With regard to the educational sector, the concept of transparency could be derived as the provision of adequate documentation on the processes through which the assessment results are generated.

Another part of this dimension includes the transparency of the institution with regards to the communication of the use of AI to the students during the assessment process. It is important to inform the students about the time they are being assessed by the AI systems and provide them with avenues through which they are able to ask questions about the assessment carried out by the systems. These processes are what guarantee the non-independence of AI systems from the educational community.

5.2 Contextual Sensitivity and Pedagogical Alignment

A second key principle of trust-centered AI assessment is contextual sensitivity. Assessment practices vary significantly across disciplines, institutions, and cultural contexts. Effective assessment systems, therefore, require alignment with pedagogical goals, discipline-specific practices, and institutional values (Boud, 2008). AI technologies, which are designed for use in a particular educational context, may not work well if the context is different. For example, it is possible that the technology, which is designed for the purpose of assessing essays, may not work well for students from different linguistic or cultural backgrounds. Without appropriate adaptation, there is a possibility that the technology may exacerbate existing inequalities in the evaluation of students.

In this regard, the importance of contextual sensitivity is that it necessitates the critical evaluation of the extent to which the use of AI tools is consistent with the pedagogical goals of the institution. Thus, instead of the university adopting universal technological tools, it is essential that the use of AI assessment tools is such that it is consistent with the diversity of learning environments in the context of higher education.

This is more important for the global higher education sector, which is marked by large differences in technological infrastructure and the capacity for effective regulation. Higher education institutions may be based in different parts of the globe, where the challenges may differ with regard to technological infrastructure, linguistic diversity, and the capacity for effective regulation.

5.3 Assessment Literacy for Educators and Students

Another important aspect of trust-centered AI assessment is assessment literacy. Assessment literacy has been defined as "the knowledge and skills necessary to understand, interpret, and use assessment processes effectively" (Black & Wiliam, 2018). In AI-based assessment environments, assessment literacy needs to be developed among both teachers and students.

Teachers need to possess the ability to critically evaluate AI-based output, including graded assignments, AI-based predictions, and algorithm-based recommendations. Teachers may either overuse or underutilize AI-based tools if they lack adequate understanding of how AI tools work. It is therefore important to build teachers' assessment literacy to ensure that AI tools are used to enhance rather than replace their capabilities.

Furthermore, students need to have a degree of assessment literacy in order to meaningfully engage with AI feedback systems. Knowledge of the processes by which AI feedback is created and how to make sense of AI feedback can allow students to better use AI systems as a resource for their learning. Moreover, students can have informed perspectives on the use of AI systems in education as a result of being made aware of the processes by which AI systems operate. Universities can provide students with assessment literacy in AI systems through professional development initiatives for their academic staff, as well as curriculum development initiatives.

5.4 Meaningful Human Oversight

Although AI systems have the potential to assist with various aspects of the assessment process, it remains crucial to maintain meaningful levels of human oversight to ensure the legitimacy and ethical integrity of the assessment process.

It has been emphasized by various scholars that AI systems must operate as tools to support and enhance, rather than replace, levels of human judgment (Holmes et al., 2019). Although the role of automated systems for assessment might be to provide initial levels of assessment and/or to identify patterns within student performance, the overall assessment process must remain within the remit of qualified educators. Human oversight must also remain to deal with circumstances whereby the assessment process might operate incorrectly through the use of algorithms. Educators must have the ability to override the assessment process and provide the means to contest the assessment algorithms.

Developing the process to contest the assessment algorithms must remain an important part of the overall AI assessment process within higher education settings.

Moreover, the involvement of humans ensures the maintenance of the relational aspects of teaching and learning that are crucial for effective education. Feedback mechanisms and evaluation processes do not only involve technical aspects but also involve dialogue between the learners and the instructor. These human relationships need to be maintained for effective trust to be achieved.

5.5 Toward Responsible AI Assessment Systems

The trust-centered framework that has been described above highlights the importance of considering ethical as well as pedagogical issues while developing AI-mediated assessment systems. Rather than depending on the technological potential of the AI system, it is important to think about the implications of the AI system on the relationship between educators, learners, and educational institutions.

For the successful implementation of the trust-centered framework for AI-mediated assessment systems, it is important to ensure the cooperation of different stakeholders at different levels of the higher education system. First of all, educational institutions need to be able to develop policies to address issues such as data protection, algorithmic accountability, as well as the rights of learners. Educators need to be able to critically interact with the AI-assisted assessment systems. Technology developers need to be able to develop AI systems that focus on aspects such as transparency, fairness, as well as pedagogy.

Additionally, different international institutions and policy-making entities have also highlighted the importance of focusing on the ethical aspects of AI-assisted education. UNESCO's guidelines on AI and education highlight the importance of incorporating aspects like transparency, accountability, and the need to develop a human-centered AI system while developing AI systems in education institutions (Miao & Holmes, 2021).

Finally, the process of developing a trust-centered AI assessment process involves striking a balance between technological innovation and the pedagogical values that are at the heart of higher education institutions. AI technologies provide tremendous opportunities to enhance the quality of learning processes and the overall assessment process. There is also a possibility that AI technologies may bring new types of inequality and opaqueness into the overall process.

By developing transparency, contextual understanding, assessment literacy, and human oversight in the overall infrastructure of the AI-based assessment process, higher education institutions can capitalize on the opportunities offered by AI technologies while maintaining the integrity and legitimacy of the process. The implications of trust-centered AI assessment on the future of higher education globally, with a focus on equity, diversity, and technology governance, will be the focus of the concluding section of this chapter.

6. IMPLICATIONS FOR GLOBAL HIGHER EDUCATION AND CONCLUSION

The rapid development of the field of artificial intelligence in the assessment processes of higher educational institutions signifies a major change in the assessment processes of educational institutions. This change affects the social relationships between institutions while assessing the learning processes. This can only be comprehended by moving beyond the technical performance of technology. This chapter has established that the major challenge in the assessment processes mediated through artificial intelligence lies not within the technical performance of the technology. Rather, the major challenge lies within the governance of trust within the educational institution. This chapter has established that the assessment processes play a major role in the field of higher educational institutions. This is because the assessment processes determine the knowledge that the students acquire. Furthermore, the assessment processes determine the academic progress of the students. Finally, the assessment processes determine the legitimacy of the students within society. When the assessment processes are mediated through technology, the educational institutions must ensure that the technological innovations do not compromise the assessment processes.

One of the main implications of this concept of AI-mediated assessment is related to the educators themselves. It is suggested that, instead of replacing human judgment, AI technologies should be seen as tools to aid educators in their professional judgment. While educators may use automated grading systems, analytics tools, and even AI-generated feedback tools to help manage student work and learning patterns, it is suggested that any decisions regarding student assessment outcomes should be grounded in human judgment (Holmes et al., 2019).

Another implication of the concept of AI-mediated assessment is the governance of higher education institutions. It is suggested that higher education institutions have started to use complex infrastructures of technology to collect educational data in huge amounts. It is therefore suggested that higher education institutions must also have a system of governance in relation to issues of algorithmic accountability, transparency, and data protection (Williamson & Eynon, 2020). If this is not done, it is suggested that a new system of opacity and power could emerge in higher education institutions. This would run contrary to the traditional notions of academic autonomy and responsibility.

The diversity of the higher educational systems in the world is another factor that adds to the complexity of the adoption of AI-based assessment technologies. This diversity ranges from the technological capabilities to the regulations of the educational systems. While a higher educational institution in a well-resourced nation could have the capabilities to adopt the most advanced form of AI technology and sophisticated online tools of learning, the same may not be true for a resource-constrained nation. This could therefore give rise to a new type of inequality in the global higher educational systems (Selwyn, 2019).

In addition, it should be noted that the current state of AI technology, which is being applied in the educational system, was developed by technology companies that operate in a given cultural context. If this technology is applied in a diverse educational system, it could potentially operate within the cultural contexts in which these technology companies operate. This could be a challenge in the adoption of AI technology in the educational system.

This challenge points to a move towards a more trust-centered approach in AI technology in the educational system. This approach has been suggested to entail a set of principles such as transparency, contextual sensitivity, assessment literacy, and human oversight. It is suggested that these principles underscore the significance of AI technologies being accountable to the educational community, as opposed to being unaccountable forces in shaping educational practices in a way in which they are not adequately scrutinized.

Transparency ensures that the students and the teachers are aware of the role of AI technologies in the assessment processes. Contextual sensitivity recognizes the need to be sensitive to the values of a particular discipline or institution. Assessment literacy ensures that the teachers and the students interact with the AI technologies used in the assessment processes critically. Lastly, human oversight ensures that the role of the human mind is not ignored with appropriate checks to challenge the AI technologies.

Overall, the above-mentioned principles form a foundation for the effective implementation of a responsible AI governance framework for the assessment processes in higher education institutions. However, it is worth noting that the implementation of the above-mentioned frameworks requires collaboration and cooperation between various stakeholders in the education sector for the effective implementation of the frameworks with due consideration to the ethical guidelines and regulatory frameworks that are responsive to technological advancements.

Future studies should also focus on continued exploration of social and institutional implications of using AI in assessment processes. While existing studies have focused on technical performance and ethical concerns of using AI in higher education institutions, it is also worth pointing out that future studies should focus on continued exploration of how these technologies are impacting learning processes in various contexts of learning. Comparative studies on using AI in various regions could provide useful insights into how trust in algorithmic systems is constructed in various contexts of learning.

In conclusion, it is important to note that there is a possibility for artificial intelligence to affect the assessment process in a manner that is more efficient, especially in the context of higher learning institutions. However, it is important to note that there is an ethical dilemma that is likely to be posed by the introduction of artificial intelligence systems. By emphasizing the importance of the concept of trust as the central issue in the process of governance, the chapter emphasized the importance of creating artificial intelligence systems that enhance the quality of education, especially in the context of the diverse settings in which the process of higher learning is conducted. Thus, the capacity of artificial intelligence technologies to enhance or undermine the foundation of higher learning will depend on the capacity of the institution to combine technological innovation with human judgment and commitment to equitable educational practices.

REFERENCES

Black, P., & Wiliam, D. (2018). Classroom assessment and pedagogy. *Assessment in Education: Principles, Policy & Practice*, *25*(6), 551–575. DOI: 10.1080/0969594X.2018.1441807

Boud, D. (2008). How can practice reshape assessment? In *Assessment, learning and judgement in higher education* (pp. 1–15). Springer Netherlands., DOI: 10.1007/978-1-4020-8905-3_3

Buolamwini, J., & Gebru, T. (2018). Gender shades: Intersectional accuracy disparities in commercial gender classification. In *Conference on fairness, accountability and transparency* (pp. 77-91). PMLR. Available on https://proceedings.mlr.press/v81/buolamwini18a.html

Cotton, D. R., Cotton, P. A., & Shipway, J. R. (2024). Chatting and cheating: Ensuring academic integrity in the era of ChatGPT. *Innovations in Education and Teaching International*, *61*(2), 228–239. DOI: 10.1080/14703297.2023.2190148

Fadlelmula, F. K., & Qadhi, S. M. (2024). A systematic review of research on artificial intelligence in higher education: Practice, gaps, and future directions in the GCC. *Journal of University Teaching & Learning Practice*, *21*(6), 146–173. DOI: 10.53761/pswgbw82

Floridi, L., Cowls, J., Beltrametti, M., Chatila, R., Chazerand, P., Dignum, V., Luetge, C., Madelin, R., Pagallo, U., Rossi, F., Schafer, B., Valcke, P., & Vayena, E. (2018). AI4People—An ethical framework for a good AI society: Opportunities, risks, principles, and recommendations. *Minds and Machines*, *28*(4), 689–707. DOI: 10.1007/s11023-018-9482-5 PMID: 30930541

Holmes, W., Bialik, M., & Fadel, C. (2019). *Artificial intelligence in education promises and implications for teaching and learning*. Center for Curriculum Redesign. https://discovery.ucl.ac.uk/id/eprint/10139722/

Ifenthaler, D., & Schumacher, C. (2016). Student perceptions of privacy principles for learning analytics. *Educational Technology Research and Development*, *64*(5), 923–938. DOI: 10.1007/s11423-016-9477-y

Kasneci, E., Seßler, K., Küchemann, S., Bannert, M., Dementieva, D., Fischer, F., Gasser, U., Groh, G., Günnemann, S., Hüllermeier, E., Krusche, S., Kutyniok, G., Michaeli, T., Nerdel, C., Pfeffer, J., Poquet, O., Sailer, M., Schmidt, A., Seidel, T., & Kasneci, G. (2023). ChatGPT for good? On opportunities and challenges of large language models for education. *Learning and Individual Differences*, *103*, 102274. DOI: 10.1016/j.lindif.2023.102274

Lancaster, T., & Clarke, R. (2016). Contract cheating: The outsourcing of assessed student work. *Handbook of academic integrity*, 639-654. https://doi.org/DOI: 10.1007/978-981-287-098-8_17

Mateen, H. (2018). Weapons of math destruction: How big data increases inequality and threatens democracy. *Berkeley Journal of Employment and Labor Law*, *39*(1), 285–292. https://www.jstor.org/stable/26732553

Miao, F., & Holmes, W. (2021). Artificial intelligence and education. Guidance for policy-makers. https://unesdoc.unesco.org/ark:/48223/pf0000376709

Noble, S. U. (2018). Algorithms of oppression: How search engines reinforce racism. In *Algorithms of oppression*. New York university press., DOI: 10.18574/nyu/9781479833641.001.0001

Sadler, D. R. (1989). Formative assessment and the design of instructional systems. *Instructional Science, 18*(2), 119–144. DOI: 10.1007/BF00117714

Selwyn, N. (2019). *Should robots replace teachers? AI and the future of education.* Polity Press. https://research.monash.edu/en/publications/should-robots-replace-teachers-ai-and-the-future-of-education/

Shermis, M. D., & Burstein, J. (2013). *Handbook of automated essay evaluation.* Routledge., https://psycnet.apa.org/record/2013-15323-000 DOI: 10.4324/9780203122761

Siemens, G., & Baker, R. S. D. (2012). Learning analytics and educational data mining: towards communication and collaboration. In *Proceedings of the 2nd international conference on learning analytics and knowledge* (pp. 252-254). https://doi.org/DOI: 10.1145/2330601.2330661

Tierney, W. G., & Sabharwal, N. S. (2017). Academic corruption: Culture and trust in Indian higher education. *International Journal of Educational Development, 55*, 30–40. DOI: 10.1016/j.ijedudev.2017.05.003

Williamson, B., & Eynon, R. (2020). Historical threads, missing links, and future directions in AI in education. *Learning, Media and Technology, 45*(3), 223–235. DOI: 10.1080/17439884.2020.1798995

Xia, Q., Weng, X., Ouyang, F., Lin, T. J., & Chiu, T. K. (2024). A scoping review on how generative artificial intelligence transforms assessment in higher education. *International Journal of Educational Technology in Higher Education, 21*(1), 40. DOI: 10.1186/s41239-024-00468-z

Chapter 9

Beyond Efficiency:

Reimagining Assessment as an Ethical AI Practice in Higher Education

Siyacela Thandazani Nzuza
http://orcid.org/0000-0002-3521-7627
University of Zululand, South Africa

ABSTRACT

Artificial Intelligence (AI) is reshaping assessment in higher education by enhancing efficiency, scalability, and personalized feedback. However, its growing use raises critical ethical concerns regarding academic integrity, fairness, transparency, accountability, privacy, and trust. This chapter explores how AI can be integrated into assessment while maintaining educational values. Drawing on the Responsible Innovation (RI) framework, it reframes AI-mediated assessment as an ethical governance challenge rather than a purely technological issue. An integrative literature review synthesizes current scholarship on AI in assessment, highlighting both opportunities and risks. Findings highlight the importance of robust governance, human oversight, stakeholder engagement, transparent policies, and continuous evaluation of algorithmic impacts. The chapter argues that responsible AI adoption is essential for promoting fair, inclusive, and trustworthy assessment practices in higher education.

1. INTRODUCTION AND BACKGROUND

In the past, higher education institutions primarily administered assessments through conventional methods, and the same applied to students in undertaking assessment tasks. These traditional systems posed minimal threats to the quality and integrity of assessment outcomes. However, a few decades later, with technological developments at a fast pace, higher education institutions around the world are experiencing rapid transformation and are bound to keep abreast of technological innovation and the expanding digital environment (Maluleke, 2025). This places them in a position to ensure that comprehensible policies, strategies, and frameworks are put in place to provide a uniform directive to their staff members and students on how AI should be adopted while upholding the quality and integrity of both formative and summative assessment outcomes (Muringa, 2025). To date, there have been many discussions and debates around the use of AI within the context of higher education, with conflicting opinions as some are applauding it, while others are disapproving it, and with all views justified from different perspectives

DOI: 10.4018/979-8-3373-8939-4.ch009

(Buele & Llerena-Aguirre, 2025; Sellnow, 2025). Nevertheless, many higher education institutions have acknowledged the inevitability of AI. Although AI in education is a universal topic, up to this point, there have been no collective procedures among the global and continental institutions of higher education on how its prevailing presence should be approached in an ethical manner (Muringa, 2025).

Although a growing body of scholarship has examined artificial intelligence in higher education, existing research remains fragmented across issues such as academic integrity, bias, transparency, privacy, governance and student autonomy. Most studies examine these concerns independently, with limited attention given to how they can be integrated into a coherent ethical approach for assessment practice. Furthermore, while several reviews discuss the opportunities and challenges of AI adoption, there is insufficient analysis of how institutions can operationalize ethical principles through a structured governance perspective. As a result, a gap remains in the literature regarding the application of Responsible Innovation as a comprehensive lens for guiding ethical AI-supported assessment in higher education. This chapter addresses that gap by synthesizing contemporary scholarship through the Responsible Innovation framework. Instead of simply reviewing ethical concerns, the chapter demonstrates how the dimensions of anticipation, reflexivity, inclusion and responsiveness can guide the design, implementation, monitoring and governance of AI-enabled assessment. In doing so, the chapter advances current knowledge by repositioning assessment as an ethical governance practice rather than merely a technological or regulatory challenge.

Within this chapter, reimagining assessment as an ethical AI practice means moving beyond institutional attempts to only regulate AI use toward designing, implementing, evaluating, and governing assessment through clear ethical principles. Rather than treating AI as a problem requiring control, an ethical AI practice positions assessment as a participatory and values-based process shaped by fairness, transparency, accountability, inclusion, and trust. Through the Responsible Innovation framework, the chapter argues that ethical assessment requires institutions to anticipate risks, critically reflect on implementation, include stakeholders in decision-making, and remain responsive to emerging challenges. The chapter makes three contributions to the literature. First, it synthesizes contemporary scholarship on ethical AI in higher education assessment through the Responsible Innovation framework. Second, it critically examines how the dimensions of anticipation, reflexivity, inclusion and responsiveness address major ethical challenges including fairness, transparency, accountability and trust. Third, it provides a governance-oriented perspective that can inform institutional policy, assessment practice and future research.

The chapter is guided throughout by the Responsible Innovation framework. The dimensions of anticipation, reflexivity, inclusion, and responsiveness are adopted to interpret the literature, analyze ethical challenges, and inform recommendations for assessment governance. Accordingly, the literature review, discussion, and implications are examined through these elements to ensure a consistent theoretical perspective

In response to the identified research gap and the growing need for governance-oriented approaches to AI-supported assessment, the following research questions guide the chapter:

- How can higher education institutions integrate AI into assessment practices while safeguarding academic integrity, fairness and trust?
- What ethical challenges and risks emerge from AI-mediated assessment, and how can institutions develop policies and frameworks to mitigate them?

- In what ways do global and context-specific factors, particularly in resource-constrained environments, shape the ethical adoption of AI in higher education assessment?

2. DEFINING ETHICAL AI IN HIGHER EDUCATION ASSESSMENT

In the context of higher education, ethical AI practice refers to the careful and responsible use of artificial intelligence by both students and staff across all key aspects of assessment. This includes the design and administration of tests, assignments and examinations, as well as the processes of marking, providing feedback and detecting academic misconduct or inappropriate use of AI (Cruvinel et al., 2026). The concept emphasizes upholding ethical values and principles to the highest possible standard whenever AI is employed as an assistive tool, whether to generate responses and solutions or to evaluate student performance (Zawacki-Richter et al., 2019). The primary aim is to ensure that assessment outcomes remain fair, reliable and trustworthy, therefore reinforcing confidence in their quality and integrity (Holmes et al., 2019; Selwyn & Szili, 2025).

3. PROBLEM STATEMENT

The use of artificial intelligence (AI) in assessment activities has gained significant momentum and become increasingly widespread. This practice is not confined to a few higher education institutions but has become rife across institutions of higher learning worldwide (Selwyn & Szili, 2025; Zawacki-Richter et al., 2019), creating new opportunities and challenges for assessment practice. (Holmes et al., 2019). Academic staff are also increasingly engaging with AI, employing it to design and administer assessments, mark student work, provide feedback and detect instances of AI use in student submissions (Cruvinel et al., 2026).

While AI offers undeniable efficiency in assessment processes, it simultaneously poses serious threats to the quality and integrity of assessment outcomes. Results produced with extensive AI assistance may not always be regarded as accurate reflections of students' genuine strengths or weaknesses, hence undermining the development of graduate attributes (Luckin, 2018; Selwyn & Szili, 2025). This challenge is global in scope, as the integration of AI into education is a worldwide phenomenon (Zawacki-Richter et al., 2019). However, despite its extensive implications, higher education institutions have yet to establish consistent and uniform policies to regulate AI use. In Africa for example, institutions often rely on individual discretion (Muringa, 2025).

4. LITERATURE REVIEW

The purpose of this section is to review and synthesize literature relevant to the phenomenon under discussion in this chapter. It aims to explore and gather diverse perspectives from around the world on ethical AI practices in higher education assessment. The literature is organized into themes that directly correspond to the research questions guiding this chapter, namely integrating AI in assessment while safeguarding integrity and fairness; ethical challenges and policy frameworks for technology-mediated assessment; and the global and context-specific factors shaping ethical AI adoption in higher education.

4.1 Integrating AI in Assessment While Safeguarding Integrity and Fairness

The incorporation of artificial intelligence into higher education assessment has become the center of discussion in current educational research, particularly as institutions grapple with welcoming innovation while preserving ethical responsibility. Studies consistently highlight that while AI provides opportunities to improve efficiency, personalization and adaptability in assessment practices, its utilization must be rigorously managed to maintain academic integrity, fairness and trust. According to Mosha et al. (2026), AI-enabled grading methods can ease staff workload and provide students with prompt and individualized feedback. This efficiency benefit is particularly significant in large classes where traditional assessment techniques are often constrained by time and resources. However, Mosha et al. (2026) also caution that the promise of efficiency cannot be separated from the ethical responsibility to ensure fairness, as students may understand AI systems as biased or unclear if their functioning is not transparent.

On the other hand, Ragolane and Patel (2024), coming from a South African point of view, indicate that students frequently express uncertainty about whether AI systems can fairly assess diverse linguistic and cultural expressions. Their case study establishes that while AI can simplify assessment processes, it risks weakening trust if students feel that their distinctive contexts are not sufficiently recognized. This concern resonates globally, as fairness in assessment is not only a technical issue but also a socio-cultural one. García-López and Trujillo-Liñán (2025) contend that fairness requires entrenching explainability into AI models, assisting both students and staff to understand how grading conclusions are reached. They propose that institutions adopt hybrid models where AI is a supporting tool but does not replace human assessors, in that way, ensuring that human judgment remains pivotal to the assessment process.

The literature also stresses the importance of transparency in maintaining integrity. Ilieva et al. (2025) presents a framework for generative AI-driven assessment that includes audit trails and fairness metrics, enabling institutions to monitor and evaluate the performance of AI systems. Such systems are integral for building trust, as they provide evidence that AI systems are functioning as anticipated and not perpetuating hidden biases. Cruvinel et al. (2026) assert that unclear processes can erode confidence in assessment outcomes, especially when students and staff are unable to understand or challenge AI outcomes. Transparency, therefore, is not merely a technical feature but a major ethical requirement.

Another element of integrity relates to plagiarism and academic misconduct. AI tools can both detect and unconsciously promote plagiarism, creating a contradiction for institutions. On one hand, AI-powered plagiarism detection systems have become more advanced, enabling academic staff to identify instances of academic cheating with greater accuracy. On the other hand, generative AI tools such as large language models can be misused by students to generate assignments that escape detection. Scholars such as García-López and Trujillo-Liñán (2025) propose that institutions must develop clear policies on the ethical use of AI, ensuring that students understand the restrictions between legitimate support and misconduct. This requires not only technical measures but also educational initiatives that promote a culture of integrity.

Fairness in AI-mediated assessment also implies addressing issues of accessibility and inclusivity. Mosha et al. (2026) state that AI systems often rely on large datasets that may not adequately correspond to diverse student populations, leading to biased outcomes. For instance, students from disadvantaged backgrounds may be unfairly penalized if AI systems fail to account for linguistic diversity or complementary modes of expression. Maimela and Mbonde (2025) reiterate that in resource-constrained environments, inequities in access to technology can further intensify these challenges. Institutions must therefore ensure that AI systems are designed and implemented in ways that advance inclusivity, rather than reinforcing existing inequalities.

Trust is another persistent theme in the literature. Students and staff must believe that AI systems are trustworthy, fair and aligned with educational values. Cruvinel et al. (2026) argue that trust can only be developed through consistent communication and engagement with stakeholders. Institutions should involve students and staff in the design and implementation of AI systems, ensuring that their views are considered and their concerns are addressed. This participatory approach helps not only to improve trust but also to ensure that AI systems are responsive to the needs of the academic community. Evidence from the reviewed studies suggests the role of human oversight in safeguarding integrity. García-López and Trujillo-Liñán (2025) recommend that AI should be used to support, rather than replace humans as assessors. Human oversight ensures that AI decisions are contextualized and that mistakes or biases can be identified and corrected. This hybrid model aligns with the principle that AI should complement human judgment, rather than substitute it. Likewise, Mosha et al. (2026) stress that human oversight is vital for sustaining accountability, as it ensures that institutions remain responsible for assessment outcomes.

In addition to technical and institutional safeguards, ethical integration of AI requires developing digital literacy among students and staff. Ilieva et al. (2025) argue that transparency and fairness cannot be achieved if stakeholders lack the knowledge to understand and critically engage with AI systems. Institutions must therefore invest in training programs that equip students and staff with the skills to handle AI-supported assessment. Such initiatives not only enhance fairness but also vest stakeholders to hold institutions accountable.

Ethical AI adoption involves balancing efficiency gains with fairness, transparency, and trust. Institutions must therefore approach AI-enabled assessment as a governance challenge requiring safeguards for equity, accountability, and academic integrity.

Viewed through the Responsible Innovation framework, these findings emphasize the importance of anticipation, inclusion, and responsiveness in ensuring that technological efficiency does not compromise educational values. Institutions must therefore proactively identify risks, involve stakeholders, and continuously monitor AI systems throughout the assessment lifecycle.

While this theme demonstrates that AI can enhance efficiency, personalization, and scalability, these benefits simultaneously create complex ethical concerns that extend beyond assessment design and delivery. Consequently, the next theme examines the broader governance challenges associated with privacy, bias, autonomy, accountability, and policy development within AI-mediated assessment environments.

4.2 Ethical Challenges and Policy Frameworks for AI-Mediated Assessment

The ethical challenges linked with artificial intelligence in higher education assessment have become increasingly important in recent scholarship, as institutions are making efforts to cope with the complex relationship between technological innovation and the values of equity, accountability and student autonomy. A persistent concern in the literature is the issue of data privacy. AI systems often rely on widespread datasets to function effectively, drawing on student submissions, performance records and even behavioral data. Mosha et al. (2026) indicate that while such data can improve predictive accuracy and allow for more personalized feedback, at the same time it raises questions about consent and surveillance. Students may not fully understand how their data is being collected, stored or used, and institutions often lack clear policies to attend to these concerns. Cruvinel et al. (2026) caution that without strong governance structures, the normalization of data collection could lead to a culture of surveillance in higher education, damaging trust between students and institutions.

Systematic bias represents another major ethical challenge. García-López and Trujillo-Liñán (2025) reveal that there are cases where AI grading systems excessively penalized students from disadvantaged backgrounds, particularly those whose linguistic or cultural expressions differed from the dominant norms embedded in training datasets. The meta-review by Wickramasinghe et al. (2026) which synthesized evidence across thirteen studies, found that bias in AI systems is not merely a technical flaw but a reflection of broader socio-cultural inequities. This finding emphasizes the need for institutions to critically analyze the datasets and systems they employ, ensuring that they do not accidentally reproduce systemic inequalities. Bias in technology-mediated assessment is particularly concerning because it can perpetuate educational disadvantage under the excuse of objectivity, hence eroding the principle of fairness which is extremely important within the context of higher education.

Beyond privacy and bias, studies also highlight the ethical implications of autonomy and agency in AI-assisted evaluation. Bouakaz and Khalid (2025) note that students may feel marginalized when assessment decisions are made by opaque algorithms, particularly if they lack the ability to challenge or appeal those decisions. This concern is amplified in contexts where AI systems are implemented without adequate explanation or transparency. García-López and Trujillo-Liñán (2025) contend that respecting student autonomy requires institutions to provide clear information about how AI systems function and to ensure that students retain meaningful channels for contesting outcomes. The literature suggests that autonomy is not only an individual right but also a collective value that influences the integrity of assessment practices.

Policy frameworks have appeared as a critical response to these ethical challenges, with scholars emphasizing the need for proactive governance rather than reactive measures. Bouakaz and Khalid (2025) propose that institutions form dedicated AI ethics committees to oversee assessment practices, ensuring that ethical considerations are integrated into decision-making processes. Such committees can serve as forums for dialogue between academic staff, students and administrators, promoting a culture of accountability and transparency. Wickramasinghe et al. (2026) advocate embedding ethical principles such as justice, beneficence and respect for autonomy into institutional guidelines, hence, ensuring that AI practices align with broader educational values. These principles provide a regulating foundation for policy development, warranting that technological innovation does not come at the expense of ethical responsibility.

The literature also emphasizes the importance of training and capacity-building as integral components of ethical policy frameworks. Ilieva et al. (2025) maintain that technical safeguards alone are insufficient if staff and students lack the knowledge to critically engage with AI systems. Institutions must therefore invest in digital literacy programs that equip stakeholders with the skills to understand, evaluate and challenge AI-mediated assessment. Such programs not only improve transparency but also empower stakeholders to hold institutions accountable. Cruvinel et al. (2026) highlight that training programs can alleviate risks of misuse, ensuring that AI systems are deployed in ways that align with ethical standards. Another dimension of policy development relates to accountability mechanisms. Mosha et al. (2026) note that institutions must establish clear procedures for addressing errors or disputes in AI-supported assessment. Without such mechanisms, students may feel powerless to contest outcomes, undermining trust in the system. García-López and Trujillo-Liñán (2025) propose that institutions adopt hybrid models where AI supports but does not replace human assessors, as a result, ensuring that accountability remains with staff rather than automated systems. This approach aligns with the broader principle that AI should augment human judgment rather than substitute it.

International perspectives further enrich the discussion of ethical challenges and policy frameworks. This suggests that ethical governance must be responsive to diverse cultural and regulatory contexts. For example, institutions in Europe may prioritize compliance with data protection regulations such as the General Data Protection Regulation (GDPR), while those in other regions may face different legal and cultural imperatives. The literature recommends that while global principles can provide a common foundation, policy frameworks must be designed to fit local realities. This adaptability ensures that ethical governance is both contextually relevant and globally informed.

The concerns raised within this theme align closely with the Responsible Innovation dimensions of reflexivity and responsiveness. Institutions must critically evaluate the assumptions embedded within AI systems and continuously adapt governance structures as new ethical challenges emerge. A further tension exists between transparency and commercial protection. Although ethical governance requires explainability, many AI systems operate through proprietary algorithms that limit institutional oversight. This creates challenges for accountability and informed decision-making

Recent international policy developments further reinforce the importance of ethical AI governance in education. UNESCO's (2024) AI Competency Framework for Teachers emphasizes responsible, human-centered, and context-sensitive AI use while promoting critical engagement with emerging technologies. These principles align strongly with the Responsible Innovation dimensions of inclusion, reflexivity, and responsiveness and provide additional guidance for institutions seeking to implement ethical AI assessment practices. Similarly, the OECD (2019) AI Principles call for transparency, accountability, fairness, robustness, and inclusive growth in the development and use of AI systems. These principles provide a valuable international governance reference for higher education institutions seeking to establish responsible assessment practices supported by AI technologies. The European Union AI Act (2024) further strengthens regulatory oversight through a risk-based approach to AI governance. Although developed within a European context, its emphasis on accountability, transparency, human oversight, and risk management provides useful lessons for higher education institutions globally when adopting AI-enabled assessment systems.

Collectively, the reviewed literature suggests that privacy, bias, autonomy, and accountability are interconnected governance challenges rather than isolated ethical issues. Addressing these concerns requires institutions to move beyond technical solutions and adopt comprehensive governance structures that support ongoing monitoring, stakeholder engagement, and policy adaptation. From a Responsible Innovation perspective, these findings emphasize the importance of reflexivity and responsiveness in institutional decision-making.

Although governance frameworks are essential for managing ethical risks, their effectiveness is heavily influenced by institutional and societal contexts. Ethical principles may be universally desirable, but the conditions under which institutions implement them vary considerably across regions. For this reason, the next theme examines how contextual realities shape ethical AI adoption.

4.3 Global and Context-Specific Factors Shaping Ethical AI Adoption in Higher Education

The acceptance of artificial intelligence in higher education assessment is not a uniform process but one that is deeply informed by global and context-specific factors. Recent literature place an emphasis that gaps in resources, infrastructure and cultural attitudes extensively influence how institutions integrate AI ethically into their assessment practices. This unequal distribution of resources raises critical ethical questions about equity, as students in resource-constrained environments may be deprived by the inability of their institutions to adopt AI tools responsibly. This suggests that ethical AI adoption cannot be understood solely through technological capability. Rather, institutional readiness, resource availability, and local conditions become critical determinants of whether AI can be implemented responsibly and equitably.

Maimela and Mbonde (2025) provide a South African perspective, indicating that infrastructural limitations such as unreliable internet connectivity and restrained access to advanced technologies complicate the ethical integration of AI in assessment. Their study highlights that the introduction of AI without adequate safeguards may exacerbate rather than alleviate existing disadvantages, as inequities in access to technology risk worsening existing educational divides. In contexts where students already face challenges related to poverty and inequality, the introduction of AI without adequate safeguards may strengthen rather than alleviate disadvantage. This finding is in line with broader debates in the literature, which give emphasis to that ethical AI adoption must be sensitive to local contexts and desist from imposing one-size-fits-all solutions.

Cultural attitudes toward surveillance, autonomy and trust in technology also play a considerable role in shaping the ethical adoption of AI. Bouakaz and Khalid (2025) note that in societies where surveillance is viewed with suspicion, students may reject AI systems that collect extensive data or monitor behaviour. On the contrary, in contexts where technological innovation is incorporated as a marker of progress, AI adoption may be more readily accepted. García-López and Trujillo-Liñán (2025) record resistance in Latin American institutions where AI systems were recognized as undermining student agency, suggesting that ethical adoption must account for cultural values and expectations. These findings imply that ethical AI adoption is not merely a technical or institutional issue but also a cultural one, requiring sensitivity to the diverse ways in which students and staff understand and engage with technology.

Governing environments further shape the ethical adoption of AI in higher education assessment. In Europe, institutions must observe the General Data Protection Regulation (GDPR), which insists on strict requirements on data collection, storage and use. This regulatory framework provides a strong foundation for ethical governance, ensuring that student privacy is protected and that institutions remain accountable for their use of AI. In contrast, institutions in regions with weaker regulatory frameworks may struggle to establish clear policies, leaving students vulnerable to exploitation. This emphasizes that while global principles can offer a common foundation, policy frameworks must be designed to fit local legal and cultural contexts. This adaptability ensures that ethical governance is both contextually relevant and globally informed. International partnership emerges as a key strategy for addressing inequalities in resources and expertise. Wickramasinghe et al. (2026) argue that collaborations between institutions in different contexts can facilitate the sharing of best practices while acknowledging local realities. For example, universities in resource-constrained environments can benefit from technical support and ethical guidance provided by institutions in more developed contexts. Such relationships not only improve capacity but also promote equity, ensuring that students in diverse contexts have access to ethical AI-mediated assessment. Cruvinel et al. (2026) highlight that international networks of scholars and practitioners can play a crucial role in advancing dialogue and developing context-sensitive frameworks.

The literature also emphasizes the importance of adaptability in ethical frameworks. Mosha et al. (2026) note that global frameworks must be flexible enough to accommodate local realities, particularly in resource-constrained environments. For example, while institutions in Europe may prioritize compliance with data protection regulations, those in Africa may need to focus on addressing infrastructural limitations and ensuring unbiased access to technology. García-López and Trujillo-Liñán (2025) propose that ethical frameworks must be co-created with local stakeholders, ensuring that they represent the values and priorities of the communities they serve. This participatory approach not only enhances legitimacy but also ensures that ethical adoption is responsive to local needs.

Another component of global and context-specific factors relates to the digital divide. Maimela and Mbonde (2025) emphasize that inequities in access to technology can substantially impact on the ethical adoption of AI in assessment. Students in resource-constrained environments may lack access to reliable internet or advanced devices, limiting their ability to engage with AI-supported assessment. This digital divide raises ethical questions about fairness, as students in more privileged contexts may benefit from the advantages of AI while others are left behind. Scholars argue that addressing the digital divide requires not only technical solutions but also broader socio-economic interventions, such as investment in infrastructure and policies that promote equitable access to technology.

Global perspectives also highlight the role of cultural diversity in shaping ethical AI adoption. Bouakaz and Khalid (2025) note that cultural attitudes toward autonomy and agency have an impact on how students view AI systems. In some contexts, students may perceive AI as a tool that improves learning and provides valuable feedback, while in others, they may see it as a threat to their agency. García-López and Trujillo-Liñán (2025) emphasize that ethical adoption must be sensitive to these cultural differences, ensuring that AI systems are designed and implemented in ways that recognize diverse values and expectations. This cultural sensitivity is particularly important in higher education, where students come from diverse backgrounds and bring a wide range of perspectives to the learning process.

The reviewed literature indicates that ethical AI adoption is shaped as much by contextual realities as by technological capability. This finding challenges assumptions that ethical AI solutions can be universally applied across institutions. Instead, it highlights the importance of adapting governance approaches to local socioeconomic conditions, cultural expectations and regulatory environments. Consequently, institutional readiness may be a more significant determinant of ethical AI adoption than the sophistication of the technology itself.

5. THEORETICAL FRAMEWORK

This chapter is framed by the Responsible Innovation (RI) framework, proposed collectively by Owen, Stilgoe, Macnaghten, Gorman, Fisher and Guston (2013) in partnership with the UK Engineering and Physical Sciences Research Council (EPSRC). The RI framework stresses the need to balance technological progress with ethical responsibility, integrating components of policy, governance and stakeholder engagement. It is designed to be adaptable across global and local contexts, ensuring that innovation remains responsive to societal values. Key to RI are four major components, namely anticipation, reflexivity, inclusion and responsiveness, which provide a structured approach for enhancing ethical considerations into innovation processes (Owen et al. 2013).

Applied to the context of higher education assessment, the RI framework underpins the chapter's key argument that artificial intelligence must move beyond efficiency to prioritize fairness, integrity and trust. It provides a lens through which institutions can embed values such as transparency, inclusivity and fairness into AI adoption, while protecting academic integrity. By encouraging stakeholder participation, RI ensures that both staff and students are actively involved in shaping assessment practices, therefore strengthening legitimacy and trust. This makes RI the most suitable theoretical foundation for guiding ethical AI integration in higher education assessment, as it links technological adoption directly to ethical governance and values-based responsibility (Stilgoe et al., 2020; von Schomberg, 2013). The framework therefore serves not only as a conceptual foundation but also as an analytical lens through which the findings of the literature review and subsequent discussion are interpreted.

The contribution of this chapter continues beyond adopting Responsible Innovation as a theoretical lens. The framework is used analytically to reinterpret the ethical challenges of AI-enabled assessment and to demonstrate how its four dimensions can be translated into institutional assessment practices. Specifically, anticipation informs risk identification before AI deployment; reflexivity encourages continuous evaluation of assumptions and outcomes; inclusion promotes stakeholder participation in assessment governance; and responsiveness supports ongoing adaptation of policies and practices. This application provides a structured approach for understanding ethical AI adoption in assessment and offers a practical interpretation of Responsible Innovation within higher education contexts.

Figure 1. Illustration of Responsible Innovation framework

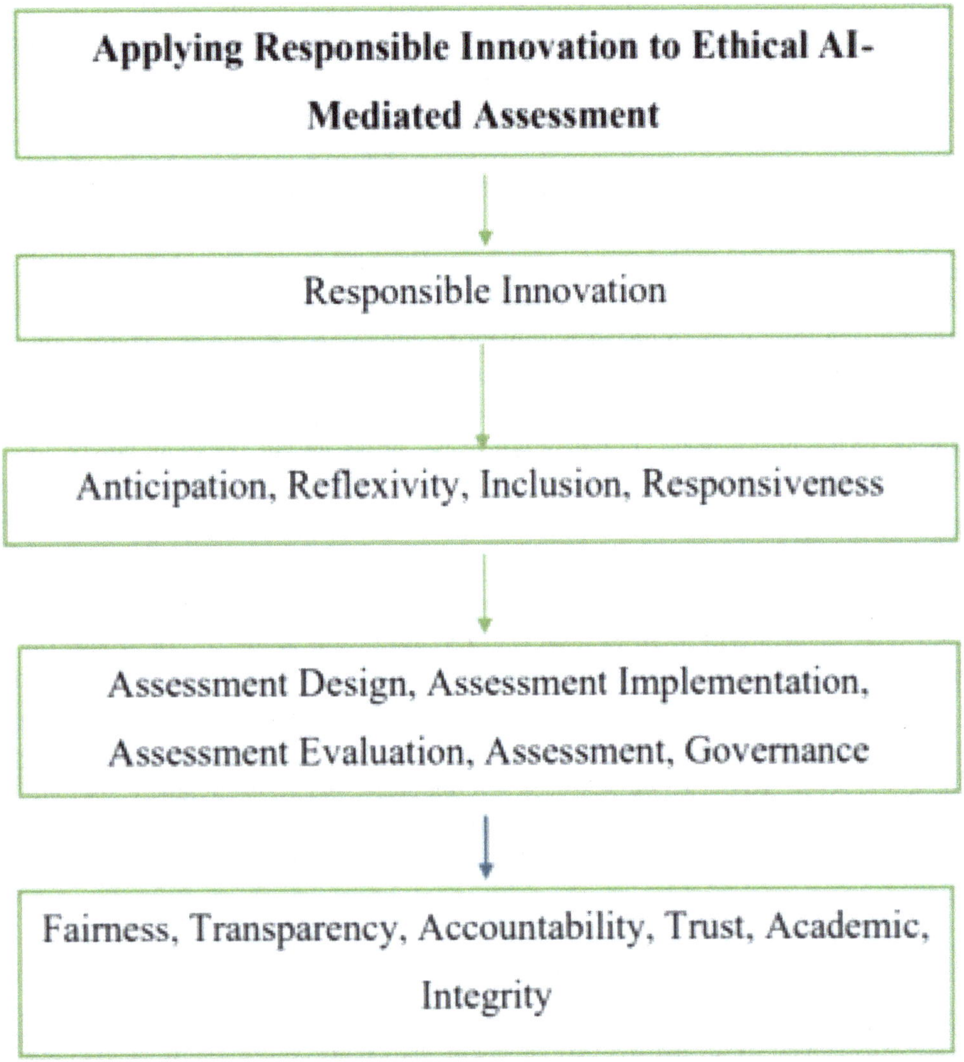

Figure 1 demonstrates how the four dimensions of Responsible Innovation can be operationalized across assessment processes to achieve ethical assessment outcomes.

6. METHODOLOGY

This chapter employed an integrative literature review to identify, analyze, evaluate, and synthesize literature relating to ethical artificial intelligence (AI) practices in higher education assessment. The integrative review approach was selected because it allows for the inclusion of diverse forms of evidence, including conceptual, theoretical, empirical, governance-oriented, and policy-related studies (Whittemore

& Knafl, 2005). Given the complex nature of AI-mediated assessment and its intersections with educational practice, ethics, technology, governance, and policy, this approach was considered appropriate for developing a comprehensive understanding of the phenomenon under investigation (Snyder, 2019). The review was conducted systematically through literature identification, screening, selection, quality assessment, and thematic synthesis, with the findings interpreted through the Responsible Innovation framework.

6.1 Rationale for the Integrative Literature Review Approach

An integrative literature review was adopted because the study sought to explore ethical AI practices from multiple perspectives rather than evaluate a narrowly defined empirical issue. The approach enabled the synthesis of scholarship addressing academic integrity, fairness, transparency, accountability, privacy, inclusivity, governance, and policy development within higher education assessment. Furthermore, it facilitated the integration of diverse forms of evidence and supported the development of broader theoretical and practical insights regarding the ethical adoption and governance of AI in assessment contexts.

6.2 Search Strategy

The literature search was conducted using four major academic databases: DOAJ, ERIC, Scopus, and Web of Science. These databases were selected because they provide extensive coverage of research in higher education, educational technology, artificial intelligence, ethics, and policy. Search terms included combinations of "artificial intelligence," "AI ethics," "higher education," "assessment," "academic integrity," "fairness," "transparency," "accountability," "Responsible Innovation," and "AI governance." Boolean operators such as AND and OR were used to refine search results and improve relevance. Priority was given to studies published within the last six years to ensure that the review reflected contemporary developments in AI-mediated assessment. However, seminal publications that continue to provide significant theoretical and conceptual foundations were also retained where necessary.

6.3 Inclusion and Exclusion Criteria

The review was guided by clearly defined inclusion and exclusion criteria to ensure relevance and academic rigor. Studies were included if they focused on the ethical use of AI within higher education and addressed assessment-related practices such as assessment design, examinations, assignments, grading, feedback, plagiarism detection, academic integrity, governance, transparency, fairness, accountability, privacy, autonomy, or human oversight. Only peer-reviewed journal articles, scholarly books, book chapters, and conference proceedings published in English were considered. Studies were excluded if they focused primarily on educational contexts outside higher education, discussed AI without direct relevance to assessment practices, or consisted of non-scholarly sources such as editorials, blogs, and news articles. Duplicate records identified during the review process were also removed.

6.4 Study Screening and Selection

Following the database searches, all retrieved records were compiled and screened for relevance. Initial screening involved reviewing article titles, followed by an assessment of abstracts against the study objectives and research questions. Articles that demonstrated relevance progressed to full-text review, where each study was evaluated according to its contribution to understanding ethical AI adoption in higher education assessment. Particular attention was given to literature addressing fairness, transparency, accountability, privacy, trust, inclusivity, academic integrity, governance, and Responsible Innovation. This systematic screening process ensured that only studies making a substantive contribution to the phenomenon under investigation were included in the final review.

6.5 Quality Assessment and Data Synthesis

To enhance the credibility of the review, studies included in the full-text stage were evaluated according to their relevance, methodological rigor, clarity of purpose, quality of evidence, and overall contribution to the literature. Preference was given to publications appearing in reputable peer-reviewed sources and those providing meaningful empirical, theoretical, governance, or policy-related insights. Following quality assessment, the selected studies were synthesized thematically according to the chapter's research questions. The resulting themes were subsequently interpreted through the Responsible Innovation dimensions of anticipation, reflexivity, inclusion, and responsiveness, providing a governance-oriented lens for understanding how ethical principles can guide the design, implementation, evaluation, and governance of AI-mediated assessment in higher education.

During the interpretive phase of analysis, the synthesized themes were further examined through the Responsible Innovation dimensions of anticipation, reflexivity, inclusion, and responsiveness. These dimensions functioned as analytical categories for understanding how ethical AI assessment practices can be governed within higher education settings.

7. DISCUSSION AND KEY FINDINGS

This section presents and discusses the key findings derived from the literature review. The findings are organized into three major themes, which reflect the reviewed scholarship and correspond directly to the research questions guiding this chapter.

7.1 Theme 1: Integrating AI in Assessment While Safeguarding Integrity and Fairness

The emergence of artificial intelligence (AI) in higher education assessment represents both a transformative opportunity and a significant ethical challenge. Recent studies show that AI-powered grading and feedback methods can extensively lower staff workload and give students timely and individualized responses (Mosha et al., 2026). This efficiency is particularly valuable in large classes where traditional assessment methods are disadvantaged by time and resources. However, the findings indicate that efficiency alone cannot justify adoption; fairness, transparency and integrity must remain central to assessment practices. The Responsible Innovation (RI) framework provides a useful lens in this chapter, specifically through its elements of anticipation and reflexivity. Anticipation requires institutions to be proactive to possible risks such as bias, inequity or erosion of trust before employing AI systems (Owen et al., 2013). Reflexivity calls for institutions to critically inspect their assumptions about objectivity and fairness in AI-assisted evaluation. For instance, Maimela and Mbonde (2025) discovered that

South African students stated concerns about whether AI systems could fairly assess diverse linguistic and cultural articulations. This emphasizes the need for reflexive practices that recognize sociocultural diversity as essential to fairness.

The prominence of efficiency benefits across the reviewed studies suggests that higher education institutions increasingly view AI as a solution to assessment scalability challenges. However, the findings also show that efficiency cannot be regarded as a sufficient justification for adoption. Instead, ethical considerations emerge as critical determinants of whether AI-supported assessment enhances or undermines educational quality. This signifies that institutions must evaluate AI not only according to operational performance but also according to its broader impact on fairness, inclusivity and trust.

Transparency is another vital dimension. Ilieva et al. (2025) propose frameworks for generative AI-driven assessment that comprise audit trails and fairness metrics, allowing institutions to monitor system performance. Such structures align with RI's principle of responsiveness, ensuring that institutions can adapt policies when unintended consequences occur. Without transparency, students and staff may perceive AI systems as "black boxes," eroding confidence in outcomes (Cruvinel et al., 2026). Issues of plagiarism and academic misconduct further complicate efforts to maintain academic integrity. While AI-powered plagiarism detection tools have improved accuracy, at the same time, the generative AI systems allow students to produce untraceable assignments. This paradox stresses the importance of inclusion within RI: institutions must engage students in discussions about legitimate versus illegitimate AI use, promoting a culture of integrity rather than relying solely on scrutiny.

Beyond its technical function, transparency serves as a mechanism for maintaining legitimacy within assessment systems. The findings indicate that students are more likely to trust AI-enabled assessment when institutional processes are understandable and open to scrutiny. This highlights a broader relationship between transparency and assessment credibility, particularly in contexts where automated decision-making influences academic outcomes.

Accessibility and inclusivity also shape fairness. Mosha et al., (2026) caution that AI systems often rely on datasets that fail to represent diverse student populations, leading to biased outcomes. In resource-constrained environments, inequities in access to technology worsen these challenges (Maimela & Mbonde, 2025). The RI framework's weight on inclusion requires institutions to design AI systems that account for diverse contexts, ensuring that deprived students are not unfairly punished. Trust emerged as a recurring theme throughout the reviewed literature. Cruvinel et al. (2026) argue that trust can only be cultivated through consistent communication and stakeholder engagement. This aligns with RI's participatory philosophy, which maintains that innovation must be co-created with those affected. Involving students and staff in AI system design and implementation not only enhances legitimacy but also ensures sensitivity to community needs. The recurrence of trust across multiple studies suggests that stakeholder confidence may be the most important determinant of sustainable AI adoption. Even technically sophisticated systems are unlikely to succeed if students and academic staff do not perceive assessment processes as fair, transparent, and accountable.

Overall, integrating AI into assessment requires a holistic approach that balances efficiency with ethical responsibility. The RI framework provides a structured route for embedding transparency, accountability, inclusivity and trust into AI systems. Institutions must ensure that AI strengthens rather than replaces human reasoning, protecting integrity and fairness while aligning assessment practices with educational values.

7.2 Theme 2: Ethical Challenges and Policy Frameworks for AI-Mediated Assessment

The ethical challenges linked to AI in higher education assessment are complex, comprising issues of privacy, bias, autonomy and accountability. Studies emphasize that these challenges cannot be solved through technical fixes alone but require strong governance frameworks. Data privacy is a pressing concern. AI systems often rely on extensive datasets, containing student submissions, performance records and behavioral data. Mosha et al. (2026) note that while such data can improve predictive accuracy, it triggers questions about consent and surveillance. Without clear policies, students may feel their privacy is compromised, leading to skepticism. Cruvinel et al. (2026) caution that unrestricted data collection risks normalizing surveillance cultures in higher education. Within the RI framework, anticipation and responsiveness are crucial: institutions must anticipate privacy risks and remain sensitive to evolving norms around data protection.

Bias denotes another major challenge. García-López and Trujillo-Liñán (2025) indicate that there are cases where AI grading systems unduly penalized students from disadvantaged backgrounds. Wickramasinghe et al. (2026) synthesized evidence across multiple studies, concluding that bias in AI systems displays broader sociocultural inequities rather than mere technical flaws. This finding aligns with RI's principle of reflexivity, which requires institutions to critically examine the datasets and assumptions underpinning AI systems. Autonomy and agency are also at stake. Bouakaz and Khalid (2025) argue that students may feel marginalized when assessment decisions are made by unclear algorithms, particularly if they lack avenues to contest outcomes. Respecting autonomy requires transparency and meaningful channels for appeal. RI's aspect of inclusion is relevant here, as it emphasizes stakeholder participation in shaping governance frameworks.

The insistence of bias across various studies suggests that ethical AI challenges cannot be fully resolved through technical improvements alone. Instead, these findings reveal that algorithmic outcomes frequently reflect broader social, cultural and institutional inequalities. This interpretation shifts the discussion from technological correction toward governance responsibility, emphasizing the need for ongoing oversight and critical evaluation of AI systems.

Policy frameworks have emerged as critical responses. Studies advocate for dedicated AI ethics committees to oversee assessment practices, ensuring accountability and transparency. Wickramasinghe et al. (2026) recommend embedding ethical principles such as justice, beneficence and respect for autonomy into institutional guidelines. These principles align with RI's anticipatory and reflexive dimensions, ensuring that innovation remains ethically grounded. Capacity-building is equally important. Ilieva et al. (2025) stress that technical protections are inadequate if staff and students lack the knowledge to critically engage with AI systems. Digital literacy programs equip stakeholders to evaluate and challenge technology-mediated assessment, advancing accountability. This reflects RI's participatory ethos, which insists that innovation must be co-created with those affected. Accountability methods are vital. Mosha et al. (2026) highlight the need for clear procedures to address errors or disputes in AI-assisted evaluation. García-López and Trujillo-Liñán (2025) recommend hybrid models where AI supports but does not replace human assessors, ensuring accountability remains with staff. This aligns with RI's principle of responsiveness, as institutions must adapt to unforeseen challenges while maintaining human oversight.

These findings indicate that institutional policy should be viewed as an active governance tool rather than merely a regulatory requirement. Effective policies create structures through which ethical principles become embedded in everyday assessment practice. Consequently, governance frameworks play a central role in translating ethical intentions into operational realities.

International perspectives further enhance the discussion. Institutions in Europe prioritize compliance with data protection regulations such as GDPR, while those in Africa face different legal and cultural imperatives (Muringa, 2025). RI's adaptability across contexts ensures that governance frameworks remain globally informed yet locally related. In conclusion, ethical challenges in AI-mediated assessment require holistic policy frameworks that integrate privacy, bias, autonomy and accountability. The RI framework provides a structured approach for embedding ethical principles into governance, ensuring that AI enhances rather than undermines higher education values.

7.3 Theme 3: Global and Context-Specific Factors Shaping Ethical AI Adoption in Higher Education

The adoption of AI in higher education assessment is greatly influenced by global and context-specific factors, including resource availability, cultural attitudes, regulatory environments and the digital divide. Resource inequalities are particularly significant. Maimela and Mbonde (2025) note that disparities in funding, digital infrastructure, and technological capacity create uneven opportunities for AI adoption across higher education institutions, with resource-constrained universities facing greater challenges in implementing AI systems responsibly and effectively. Maluleke (2025) notes that African institutions face challenges such as unreliable internet connectivity and restricted access to advanced technologies, complicating ethical integration. Within the RI framework, anticipation requires institutions to foresee how resource constraints may worsen inequities, while responsiveness demands adaptive strategies that account for local realities.

A key implication of these findings is that ethical AI adoption cannot be separated from issues of educational equity. Institutions with limited resources may face greater challenges in implementing ethical safeguards, therefore increasing the risk of unequal educational experiences. This implies that discussions of AI ethics should extend beyond technological concerns to include broader questions of access, capacity and institutional readiness.

Cultural attitudes also shape adoption. Bouakaz and Khalid (2025) highlight that in societies where surveillance is seen with suspicion, students may resist AI systems that collect extensive data. On the contrary, in contexts where technological innovation is celebrated, AI adoption may be more readily accepted. García-López and Trujillo-Liñán (2025) document resistance in Latin American institutions where AI was perceived as undermining student agency. RI's principle of inclusion is vital here, as it emphasizes sensitivity to cultural diversity and stakeholder participation in shaping ethical frameworks. Regulatory environments further influence adoption. European institutions must comply with GDPR, which enforces strict requirements on data collection and use. In contrast, institutions in regions with weaker regulatory frameworks may find it difficult to establish clear policies, leaving students at risk (Muringa, 2025). RI's adaptability ensures that governance frameworks remain globally informed yet locally relevant, balancing universal principles with contextual realities.

International collaboration arises as a key strategy. Wickramasinghe et al. (2026) argue that partnerships between institutions in different contexts can facilitate the sharing of best practices while acknowledging local realities. This finding indicates that ethical AI adoption should be viewed as a shared global challenge rather than an isolated institutional issue. Collaborative approaches can help reduce disparities in expertise, resources, and governance capacity across different higher education systems.

Overall, the reviewed literature demonstrates that ethical AI adoption is shaped not only by technological innovation but also by social, economic, cultural, and regulatory realities. These findings reinforce the Responsible Innovation principle of responsiveness, emphasizing that ethical governance frameworks must remain adaptable to diverse institutional environments. Consequently, successful AI integration depends as much on institutional readiness and contextual awareness as on technological sophistication.

While the preceding discussion identifies broad ethical and governance principles, higher education institutions require practical mechanisms for translating these principles into everyday assessment practice. The following scenarios illustrate how Responsible Innovation can be operationalized within different assessment settings.

8. INSTITUTIONAL APPLICATION SCENARIOS

The practical application of the Responsible Innovation (RI) framework can be illustrated through various assessment contexts in higher education. For example, a university implementing AI-assisted formative feedback could apply the framework by anticipating potential ethical risks before application, actively involving academic staff and students in decision-making processes, monitoring the impact of the technology on learning and assessment outcomes, and continuously refining practices based on stakeholder feedback. Similarly, an institution adopting AI-supported plagiarism detection could operationalize RI principles by ensuring transparency in how the system functions, providing students with opportunities to appeal assessment decisions, maintaining meaningful human oversight of AI-generated outcomes, and regularly evaluating the fairness and accuracy of the system across diverse student populations. These scenarios demonstrate how the dimensions of anticipation, reflexivity, inclusion, and responsiveness can guide the ethical implementation and governance of AI-mediated assessment practices in higher education.

9. THEORETICAL IMPLICATIONS

The findings indicate that ethical AI adoption should be understood as a socio-technical governance process rather than a purely technological phenomenon. Viewed through a lens of Responsible Innovation framework, challenges relating to fairness, transparency, accountability and trust emerge not as isolated technical issues but as interconnected governance concerns requiring continuous institutional engagement. This interpretation extends the application of Responsible Innovation within higher education assessment by demonstrating how its dimensions can inform both policy development and assessment practice.

10. POLICY IMPLICATIONS

The findings of this review indicate that institutions can no longer rely on reactive approaches to AI governance. As AI becomes increasingly integrated into assessment processes, policy development must move beyond regulating misconduct and toward establishing proactive governance mechanisms that promote fairness, accountability and trust. This shift represents a fundamental change in how higher education institutions approach assessment in AI-mediated environments.

The chapter's findings highlight the urgent need for higher education institutions to launch coherent and context-sensitive policy frameworks for AI adoption in assessment. Current practices remain fragmented, with institutions often relying on individual judgment, which weakens consistency and fairness (Selwyn & Szili, 2025). Policy implications include the necessity of entrenching ethical principles such as justice, beneficence, transparency and respect for autonomy into institutional guidelines, while ensuring compliance with broader regulatory frameworks like General Data Protection Regulation GDPR in Europe or comparable local policies elsewhere (Floridi & Cowls, 2022). The RI framework emphasizes stakeholder participation, proposing that policies should be co-created with students, staff and administrators to boost legitimacy and trust (Owen et al., 2013). Moreover, policies must address capacity-building by investing in digital literacy programs, accountability mechanisms and transparent procedures for contesting AI-mediated outcomes (Cruvinel et al., 2026; Zawacki-Richter et al., 2019). Jointly, these measures ensure that AI enhance rather than erode the values of higher education (Holmes et al., 2019).

11. RECOMMENDATIONS

Based on the findings of this study, the recommendations are extended to stakeholders in education, particularly to global higher education institutions. Higher education institutions should develop clear and comprehensive policies on ethical AI use while aligning them with internationally recognized principles and adapting them to local institutional contexts. Furthermore, policies and practices must integrate RI's dimensions of anticipation, reflexivity, inclusion and responsiveness to balance efficiency with fairness, integrity and trust. In addition, institutions should adopt AI systems with audit trails, fairness metrics and explainable algorithms to build confidence among students and staff. While embracing AI technologies, AI should support rather than replace human judgment, with staff retaining accountability for final assessment outcomes. Moreover, clear guidelines must distinguish between legitimate AI support and misconduct, supported by awareness campaigns and advanced plagiarism detection tools.

Equally important, AI systems should be designed to recognize diverse linguistic, cultural and socio-economic contexts, ensuring equitable treatment of all students. To promote responsible engagement, institutions should invest in training for staff and students to critically engage with AI systems, encouraging accountability and informed use. Likewise, clear procedures should be in place for contesting AI-mediated outcomes addressing errors and ensuring fairness in dispute resolution. At the governance level, governance frameworks should align with global ethical principles while remaining sensitive to local realities, particularly in resource-constrained environments. Finally, partnerships across institutions and regions should be encouraged to share best practices, address inequalities and co-create context-sensitive ethical frameworks.

12. FUTURE RESEARCH DIRECTIONS

Future research should investigate how the RI framework can be applied across diverse educational contexts, especially in resource-constrained environments where infrastructural limitations and digital divides pose major challenges (Stilgoe et al., 2020; Zawacki-Richter et al., 2019). Comparative studies across regions would provide insights into how cultural attitudes, regulatory environments and socioeconomic realities shape ethical AI adoption in assessment (Selwyn & Szili, 2025). Longitudinal research study is also needed to examine the evolving impact of AI on student autonomy, trust and graduate attributes over time. In addition, empirical research studies into hybrid models, where AI supports but does not replace human assessors, could provide clear lens on how institutions can balance efficiency with accountability (Luckin, 2018). In conclusion, interdisciplinary research that combines perspectives from education, computer science, ethics and policy studies would reinforce the development of holistic frameworks, ensuring that AI adoption in higher education assessment remains aligned with fairness, integrity and inclusivity (Floridi & Cowls, 2022).

13. CONCLUSION

This chapter has emphasized that while artificial intelligence provides unquestionable efficiency and adaptability in higher education assessment, its implementation must be informed by ethical responsibility, fairness and integrity. A key contribution of the chapter is the demonstration of how Responsible Innovation can be operationalized within higher education assessment. By synthesizing current ethical debates through the dimensions of anticipation, reflexivity, inclusion and responsiveness, the chapter provides a structured perspective for understanding assessment governance in AI-mediated environments. This contribution extends existing literature, which often discusses ethical concerns separately, by illustrating how these concerns can be interpreted collectively through a single governance-oriented lens. The integrative literature review revealed that challenges such as bias, privacy, autonomy, inclusivity and trust are deeply embedded in the socio-technical fabric of education, requiring institutions to move beyond efficiency-driven approaches. The Responsible Innovation (RI) framework provided a constructive lens for balancing innovation with ethical governance, emphasizing anticipation, reflexivity, inclusion and responsiveness as essential components for sustainable adoption. More importantly, the review demonstrates that the future of AI-supported assessment will be determined less by technological capability and more by the capacity of institutions to govern AI responsibly. The long-term success of AI in higher education therefore depends on the ability of institutions to embed ethical considerations within assessment design, implementation and decision-making processes. Overall, the findings indicate that higher education institutions must embed transparency, accountability and human oversight into AI-powered assessment, while remaining responsive to diverse cultural and infrastructural realities. To conclude, reimagining assessment as an ethical AI practice requires higher education institutions to move beyond viewing AI as a tool for efficiency and instead govern it as a socio-technical innovation grounded in fairness, accountability, transparency, inclusion, and trust. The future success of AI-mediated assessment will therefore depend less on technological capability and more on institutions' ability to govern AI responsibly through values-based and context-sensitive approaches.

14. TERMS AND DEFINITIONS

The purpose of this section is to define the key terms employed throughout the chapter. This is to ensure that readers are provided with clarity to deepen their understanding of the major concepts used.

14.1 Artificial Intelligence (AI)

Artificial Intelligence refers to a branch of computer science that advances systems that are able to perform tasks that typically require human intelligence, such as problem-solving, learning and decision-making. In higher education assessment, AI is used by students for completing assessment tasks, and by institutions for grading, feedback, plagiarism detection and exam administration.

14.2 Ethical AI in Higher Education Assessment

Ethical AI in higher education assessment is described as the responsible and values-based use of AI tools in designing, administering and evaluating student assessments. It puts emphasis on fairness, transparency, inclusivity, accountability and trust to ensure that outcomes remain reliable and maintain academic integrity.

14.3 Academic Integrity

Academic integrity is the commitment to honesty, fairness and responsibility in academic work. Within AI-enabled assessment, it refers to safeguarding against misconduct such as plagiarism or unauthorized AI use, while ensuring that student performance reflects genuine ability.

14.4 Fairness

Fairness is the principle that all students should be assessed equitably, without bias or disadvantage due to linguistic, cultural or socioeconomic differences. Fairness in AI systems requires explainability, inclusivity and sensitivity to diverse contexts.

14.5 Transparency

Transparency is the clarity with which AI systems operate, including the ability to explain how decisions are made. Transparency involves audit trails, fairness metrics and accessible explanations that allow students and staff to understand and challenge AI decisions.

14.6 Trust

The confidence that students and staff place in AI systems to produce fair, reliable and ethical assessment outcomes. Trust is cultivated through stakeholder engagement, clear communication and participatory design of AI tools.

14.7 Human Oversight

Human oversight refers to the continued involvement of academic staff in supervising and validating technology-mediated assessment processes. Human oversight ensures accountability, contextual judgment and correction of errors or biases that AI systems may produce.

14.8 Plagiarism and Academic Misconduct

The unethical practice of presenting work generated by others or by AI systems as one's own. AI complicates this issue by both enabling detection of misconduct and providing tools that can be misused by students to escape detection.

14.9 Responsible Innovation (RI) Framework

A theoretical model developed by Owen, Stilgoe, Macnaghten and colleagues, emphasizing anticipation, reflexivity, inclusion and responsiveness in innovation. In this chapter, RI provides the lens for balancing technological efficiency with ethical responsibility in AI adoption.

14.10 Digital Literacy

Digital literacy refers to the ability of students and staff to critically understand, evaluate and engage with digital and AI technologies. Digital literacy is vital for navigating AI-assisted evaluation responsibly and holding institutions accountable.

14.11 Global and Context-Specific Factors

The diverse cultural, regulatory, infrastructural and socioeconomic conditions that influence how AI is adopted in higher education. These factors highlight the need for adaptable ethical frameworks that balance universal principles with local realities.

REFERENCES

Act, E. A. I. (2024). The EU artificial intelligence act. *European Union.*

Bouakaz, L., & Khalid, S. (2025). AI in education: A sociological exploration of technology in learning environments. *Frontiers in Education, 10*, 1700876. Advance online publication. DOI: 10.3389/feduc.2025.1700876

Buele, J., & Llerena-Aguirre, L. (2025). Transformations in academic work and faculty perceptions of artificial intelligence in higher education. In *Frontiers in Education* (Vol. 10, p. 1603763). Frontiers Media SA. https://doi.org/DOI: 10.3389/feduc.2025.1603763

Cruvinel, L., Ascama, O. H., & Silva, M. M. (2026). *AI ethics in higher education: A review of ethical challenges*. Springer., DOI: 10.1007/978-3-032-01429-0_17

Floridi, L., & Cowls, J. (2022). A unified framework of five principles for AI in society. *Machine learning and the city: Applications in architecture and urban design*, 535-545. https://doi.org/DOI: 10.1002/9781119815075

García-López, I. M., & Trujillo-Liñán, L. (2025). Ethical and regulatory challenges of generative AI in education: A systematic review. *Frontiers in Education, 10*(2), 115–130. DOI: 10.3389/feduc.2025.1565938

Holmes, W., Bialik, M., & Fadel, C. (2019). *Artificial intelligence in education promises and implications for teaching and learning*. Center for Curriculum Redesign. https://discovery.ucl.ac.uk/id/eprint/10139722

Ilieva, G., Yankova, T., Ruseva, M., & Kabaivanov, S. (2025). A framework for generative AI-driven assessment in higher education. *Information (Basel), 16*(6), 472. DOI: 10.3390/info16060472

Instruments, O. L. (2019). *Recommendation of the council on artificial intelligence*. Organization for Economic Cooperation and Development.

Luckin, R. (2018). *Machine Learning and Human Intelligence. The future of education for the 21st century*. UCL institute of education press.

Maimela, C., & Mbonde, P. (2025). Artificial intelligence in South African universities: Curriculum transformation and decolonisation—aid or obstacle? *Frontiers in Sociology, 10*, 1543471. DOI: 10.3389/fsoc.2025.1543471 PMID: 40697567

Maluleke, A. F. (2025). AI adoption in African higher education: A systematic review of benefits and ethical implications. *Interdisciplinary Journal of Education Research, 7*(2), a05–a05. DOI: 10.38140/ijer-2025.vol7.2.05

Mosha, N. F. V., Chigwada, J., Ketchiwou, G. F., & Ngulube, P. (2026). A systematic review of artificial intelligence in higher education institutions (HEIs): Functionalities, challenges, and best practices. *Education Sciences, 16*(2), 185. DOI: 10.3390/educsci16020185

Muringa, T. P. (2025). Exploring ethical dilemmas and institutional challenges in AI adoption: A study of South African universities. *Frontiers in Education, 10*, 1628019. DOI: 10.3389/feduc.2025.1628019

Owen, R., Stilgoe, J., Macnaghten, P., Gorman, M., Fisher, E., & Guston, D. (2013). A framework for responsible innovation. *Responsible innovation: managing the responsible emergence of science and innovation in society*, 27-50. https://doi.org/DOI: 10.1002/9781118551424

Ragolane, M., & Patel, S. (2024). Transforming Educ-AI-tion in South Africa: Can AI-Driven grading transform the future of higher education. *Journal of Education and Teaching Methods*, *3*(1), 26–51. DOI: 10.58425/jetm.v3i1.267

Sellnow, D. D. (2025). Reflection-AI: Exploring the challenges and opportunities of artificial intelligence in higher education. *Frontiers in Communication*, *10*, 1615040. DOI: 10.3389/fcomm.2025.1615040

Selwyn, N., & Szili, A. (2025). The role of 'AI advocate'teachers in mediating technological change across Australian schools. *Teachers and Teaching*, •••, 1–16. DOI: 10.1080/13540602.2025.2596832

Snyder, H. (2019). Literature review as a research methodology: An overview and guidelines. *Journal of Business Research*, *104*, 333–339. DOI: 10.1016/j.jbusres.2019.07.039

Stilgoe, J., Owen, R., & Macnaghten, P. (2020). Developing a framework for responsible innovation. In Krimsky, S. F., & Powell, K. C. (Eds.), *The ethics of nanotechnology, geoengineering, and clean energy* (pp. 347–359). Routledge., DOI: 10.4324/9781003075028-22

UNESCO. (2024). *AI competency framework for teachers*. United Nations Educational, Scientific and Cultural Organization., DOI: 10.54675/ZJTE2084

Von Schomberg, R. (2013). A vision of responsible research and innovation. In Owen, R., Bessant, J., & Heintz, M. (Eds.), *Responsible innovation: Managing the responsible emergence of science and innovation in society* (pp. 51–74). Wiley., DOI: 10.1002/9781118551424.ch3

Whittemore, R., & Knafl, K. (2005). The integrative review: Updated methodology. *Journal of Advanced Nursing*, *52*(5), 546–553. DOI: 10.1111/j.1365-2648.2005.03621.x PMID: 16268861

Wickramasinghe, M., Gunawardena, L., & Padukkage, A. (2026). Ethical principles for artificial intelligence in education: A meta-review approach. *AI and Ethics*, *6*(1), 63–75. DOI: 10.1007/s43681-025-00878-3

Zawacki-Richter, O., Marín, V. I., Bond, M., & Gouverneur, F. (2019). Systematic review of research on artificial intelligence applications in higher education – where are the educators? *International Journal of Educational Technology in Higher Education*, *16*(1), 1–27. DOI: 10.1186/s41239-019-0171-0

Chapter 10
From Cheating Prevention to Integrity Innovation in AI-Based Assessment:
From Surveillance to Systemic Integrity

Naveen Nandal
http://orcid.org/0009-0007-2272-7437
DIHE, India

Deepak Chahal
Jagan Institute of Management Studies, India

Rajesh Dhaka
Jagannath University, India

Raman Joshi
Jagannath University, India

Suraj Yadav
Jagannath University, India

ABSTRACT

The rapid adoption of artificial intelligence in higher education assessment has exposed the limits of surveillance- and compliance-based approaches to academic integrity. Institutional responses have largely focused on cheating detection and control, framing integrity as an individual behavioral problem rather than a systemic educational outcome. This chapter argues that such approaches are inadequate in AI-mediated assessment contexts. Drawing on academic integrity research, assessment theory, higher education governance, and AI ethics, it introduces integrity innovation as an alternative framework. Integrity innovation conceptualizes integrity as an outcome of alignment across assessment design, governance, and institutional culture. The chapter shows how AI-based assessment redistributes agency, challenges authorship and originality, and risks deepening global inequities. It positions assessment design and shared responsibility as central to sustaining trust, legitimacy, and the educational mission of higher education in the AI era.

DOI: 10.4018/979-8-3373-8939-4.ch010

1. INTRODUCTION

The Integrity Crisis in AI-Based Assessment

AI has become a part of the education assessment system. Grading, algorithmic proctoring, learning analytics, and adaptive feed-forward are commonplace in higher education, and generative tools can generate essay-like answers to virtually any assessment task with a moment's notice. The use of generative AI has brought assessment in higher education to the forefront of the educational agenda as a crisis, which was highlighted by Boud and Falchikov (2007) when they asserted that assessment in higher education was becoming "drifting away from institutional values and longer term learning objectives. The institutional response to AI has been broadly cross-sectoral, seeing it as a detection and control issue (more observations, more aggressive observations, more consistent observations). However, the progress of AI challenges the seemingly indestructible walls of the integrity boundaries that current integrity frameworks rely upon, such as between "assistance" and "misconduct," "original work" and "copy," and "student" and "institution" (McCabe, Butterfield, & Trevino, 2012). When grading, feedback and invigilation are partially automated, the integrity of whole systems of assessment is more than just a matter of individual acts (Perrotta & Selwyn, 2020; Prinsloo & Slade, 2017).

Empirical research in recent years has demonstrated the extent to which the detection paradigm has already failed. In the UK, after placing 100% AI-generated responses on a legitimate university exam platform, Scarfe, Watcham, Clarke and Roesch (2024) discovered that 94% of the answers were not identified as AI-generated, and the average AI score was higher than the average score of real test takers. To test the effectiveness of the scripts' answers, experienced university teachers, blinded to the authorship of the machines, gave passing grades to a significant proportion of the scripts and were very unlikely to suspect their machine origin (Farazouli, Cerratto-Pargman, Bolander-Laksov, & McGrath, 2024). An integrity strategy that depends on the identification of individual offenders, based on trained assessors' ability to distinguish AI-generated content from students' work, is not sound.

Insisting that the misuses made by students are a personal moral failing is a mistake, framing the issue as one of personal responsibility rather than a governance issue. It blames students instead of institutions and technologies for students' problems and sees students as "risk subjects" instead of ethical professionals. It also enables black-box systems to be opaque and to breed compliance, anxiety, and doubt about the fairness of assessment. When viewed systemically, AI restructures academic judgment: algorithms judge only what they can, in a context-free, nuance-free, and pedagogy-free way. A limited view of student behavior distracts from the broader integrity issues that stem from institutional incentives, assessment design, and the power dynamics these incentives and designs create for and between students, across trust, learning, and equity around the world. This chapter builds on this, explaining an alternative approach, an Integrity Innovation: an approach that makes integrity the result of the design of assessments, the governance of them, and the institutional culture in which they exist, and situates responsibility within the entire assessment ecosystem, not just in individual integrity. That way, it honors the variety of assessment contexts around the world and calls for a new and different approach to systems thinking.

2. ACADEMIC INTEGRITY BEFORE AI: ASSUMPTIONS AND CONSTRAINTS

The issue of integrity is a major concern in debates about the use of AI in assessment that are currently underway. Indeed, many of the tensions which are now apparent are the result of inherited structures based on assumptions that are no longer valid. These are not conceptually inconsistent frameworks, but rather contextually incongruous ones, as they stem from conditions that are very different to those of AI-mediated assessment, both institutional, pedagogical, and technological. Traditional integrity systems were based on the notion of violation of rules, with similarity or copying being the evidence of the violation, and sanctions being the deterring mechanism. They had ideas of education, but they were guided by ideas of compliance, knowing what was meant by the author and assuming what could be considered to be a passive tool. Originality was regarded as a trait of students' personality, which could be assessed using similarity scores and source matching. They are well suited to the evaluation systems that focus on the work of one author at a time, like an essay, exam, or single task. Plagiarism-detection software was seen as a neutral program that assists in enforcing plagiarism, but one that is inferior and dependent on human judgment (Sutherland-Smith, 2008).

Not everything about inheritances was negative. Honor code practices in North America had three key elements: moral development, peer accountability, and trust (McCabe & Pavela, 2004); teaching programs aimed to foster an ethical awareness by teaching and giving feedback. However, even these were based on the same significant simplifications: that boundaries could be drawn between acceptable help and wrongdoing, and that there was a clear distinction between student agency and outside help. Since it was believed that integrity judgments are personal and constant, technology change was not thought to upset them. These assumptions were undermined by the emergence of online learning, which began to make the boundaries between contributions porous and detection more difficult, prompting responses from institutions primarily in the form of increased observation and more policies, in turn strengthening the assumption that students needed to be observed/guarded to comply. (Eaton, 2020)

This is where AI-based assessment can come in and make a significant impact, revealing the shortcomings of this legacy. Academic work based on interaction with generative systems instead of individual text production undermines integrity-as-individual-compliance. Originality is difficult to identify, and responsibility is spread between humans and non-humans. This can be referred to as one of the "post-plagiarism" scenarios, as proposed by Eaton (2023); the new normal in academic writing and policing of textual similarity becomes a mix of human and AI-generated content. These distributed effects are not discussed in existing frameworks, and individualizing integrity hides the influence of institutional design on ethical behaviour. The design of assessment itself can foster cheating, as such tasks that promote quickness or standardization encourage shallow Engagement with the material (Bretag et al., 2019; Dawson, 2021). In the meantime, there is much assessment that is proprietary and uses AI that faculty do not have access to.

The earlier models of integrity were also based on the premise of transparency and contestability of institutional decision-making. Kitchin (2017) demonstrates how today's systems are hard to question with algorithmic inference, proprietary logic and data-driven decision-making. Integrity models used for student behaviour say nothing about failures in the design of the systems themselves, which are beyond any control, or failures due to outsourced infrastructure. What is required is not a loss of academic integrity, but rather a remapping of the frameworks in which academic integrity is currently being practiced: the current frameworks largely focus on rules, checks and penalties and need to be adapted to the transformations that technology brings to authorship, authority and responsibility. The aim is to take steps towards broadening integrity thinking beyond detection to systemic agency and design, not to move away from it into the past, and not into speeding up detection.

Table 1. Inherited Academic Integrity Assumptions and Their Limits in AI-Mediated Assessment

Dimension	Pre-AI Integrity Frameworks	AI-Based Assessment Context
Authorship	Individual, bounded	Hybrid, human–machine
Originality	Textual uniqueness	Processual contribution
Responsibility	Student-centered	Distributed across system
Integrity Logic	Rule compliance	Ethical alignment
Enforcement Mode	Post hoc detection	Embedded system effects

3. AI-BASED ASSESSMENT ECOSYSTEMS: TECHNOLOGIES AND POWER SHIFTS

Assessing the performance of AI in assessment demands focusing more on the systems, policies, data systems, and institutional processes and practices that influence their use and for whom they are used, rather than on a list of products. The difference with AI is that the change is not only in the assessment tool, but also it the flows of authority, influence, and control that surround the tool. Delivering an assessment technology as a networked ecosystem demonstrates power and ethical changes beyond what can be seen in a tool-by-tool analysis: Williamson (2017); Selwyn (2019); Swiecki et al. (2022). Automated essay scoring is one example: automated systems tuned for statistical uniformity might reward surface correctness over disciplinary thinking and expressive freedom (Perelman, 2014; Williamson & Eynon, 2020). Learning to write for the algorithm, not for understanding, leads to strategic compliance, not learning, with repercussions for learning and institutional integrity. Adaptive testing and learning analytics take this one step further by constantly collecting interaction data and feedback to modify the content based on the information gleaned by the system and thus shifting the evaluative power from the teacher to the algorithm (Prinsloo & Slade, 2017). The probabilistic nature and often the lack of transparency of output further render errors and biases hard to track, which puts the integrity of the assessment process at risk.

The use of generative AI has revolutionized assessment by transforming the way that assessment is taught and learned by making the line between learning support and independent work extremely fuzzy. Artificial Intelligence (AI)-based tutoring systems, automated feedback, and chatbots are improving learning but also have the potential to blur the lines between authorship and academic honesty (Luckin et al., 2016; Kasneci et al., 2023). Research indicates that ChatGPT can generate satisfactory answers in various fields, which, according to Nikolic et al. (2023), renders the assessment vulnerable to the way tasks are designed, not necessarily to the content of the assessment. Meanwhile, AI proctoring systems record behavior and biometric data, resulting in greater stress among students and unfair targeting of disadvantaged groups through false-positive detections (Kahn et al., 2022). Likewise, proprietary AI systems diminish transparency and move control and decisions from educators to technology vendors, creating accountability gaps (Eubanks, 2018; Selwyn, 2023). Thus, an ethical approach to academic integrity involves governance in addition to transparency in assessment design, not only mechanisms of surveillance for efficiency and misconduct detection.

4. SURVEILLANCE, COMPLIANCE, AND THE LIMITS OF CHEATING PREVENTION

With the increasing AI-mediated nature of assessment, there is a general institutional response to threats of integrity: surveillance. Cheating prevention and credibility certification are promised by proctoring platforms, plagiarism detection, AI text classifiers, and behavioural analytics. This diminishes academic integrity from an educational value into being a technical visibility issue, according to Lyon (2018) and Dawson, Sutherland-Smith and Harris (2019). Students put in effort to manage how they are viewed by monitoring systems instead of understanding course material, shifts burden of proof to students, and creates anxiety that impedes deep learning (Kahn et al., 2022); students put effort into how they look to students and monitoring systems instead of content of course; It is not equally applied, and impacts negatively students from marginalized groups, students with disabilities and/or students who lack access to technology (Gilliard & Culik, 2016; Swauger, 2020). Surveillance also undermines the educational relationship itself by fostering suspicion and replacing the power of the teacher with suspicion. When automatic judgement becomes the norm, professional responsibility becomes silent, and a culture of compliance replaces that of internalized norms, deliberation and reflection, which are essential to the development of professional ethics in higher education.

There are serious concerns about the reliability and fairness of academic integrity detection tools based on artificial intelligence. Academic integrity detection tools based on AI are not reliable or fair, as there are serious concerns about this. Existing AI detectors have been found to return false alarms and false negatives, especially when the text is paraphrased or written by a non-native English speaker (Weber-Wulff et al., 2023; Liang et al., 2023). Additionally, empirical evidence shows that actual cases of cheating assisted by AI are still fairly scarce, raising concerns that they are more likely to be a product of the institution than of the student, as suggested by Scarfe et al. (2024) and Lee et al. (2024). Relying too heavily on surveillance technologies, then, will risk solving perceived, not real, problems. High-stakes monitoring also does not address the root causes of academic dishonesty, which are often connected to assessment design and learning environments (Boud & Falchikov, 2007). Additionally, there are ethical issues related to privacy, informed consent, and data governance (Prinsloo & Slade, 2017). Surveillance-based practices may fail to promote academic integrity and may promote compliance based on fear of detection rather than good learning and ethical behavior.

Table 2. From Surveillance-Centric Integrity to Integrity Innovation: A Conceptual Comparison

Dimension	Surveillance-Centric Integrity	Integrity Innovation
View of students	Risk subjects	Ethical agents
Integrity focus	Detection & punishment	Design & alignment
Role of AI	Policing tool	Pedagogical support
Impact on trust	Erosion	Cultivation
Equity implications	Amplifies inequality	Context-sensitive

5. GLOBAL ADOPTION AND CONTEXTUAL INEQUALITIES

There have been growing calls for the use of AI-based assessment systems to standardise assessment and ensure consistency and fairness. However, the use of these systems in different education environments disregards national, legal, institutional, cultural, and governance differences. Highly funded universities may have the capability and resources to tailor AI tools, track their outcomes, and counteract any potential biases. Conversely, resource-limited institutions often rely on pre-existing algorithms that are commercially developed black boxes, with little understanding of the algorithm or the decision-making process. Such tools have generally been trained on culturally and linguistically specific datasets and are more likely to penalize students of different cultural and linguistic backgrounds, including disproportionately affecting the students with English as an Additional Language (EAL), who are at greater risk of being falsely identified as misbehaving by the AI (Liang et al., 2023). There is also uneven readiness for policy the implementation. Many universities did not have a formal policy regarding generative AI, and less than half of the top universities in the world published a policy on AI assessment shortly after ChatGPT was introduced, as reported by UNESCO (2023) and Moorhouse et al. (2023). In developing countries, it is even greater due to a lack of infrastructure, inadequate regulatory measures, and limited access to digital tools. Without an adaptation of the context, using AI assessment could also be reinforcing the inequalities that already exist in education. In conclusion, the implementation of AI must be transparent, considerate of cultural context and sensitive to the institution, while balancing technological innovation and ethical supervision, resulting in AI governance that respects academic integrity as a product of responsible institutional design instead of a one-size-fits-all technological solution.

6. INTEGRITY INNOVATION: A CONCEPTUAL FRAMEWORK

The analysis conducted so far indicates that the achievement of academic integrity in assessment with the help of AI is not feasible by surveillance, detection, and rule enforcement. Trying to define ethics in the individual, that is, in the student, is to locate responsibility, which is a mediated one, in the individual, but this is an individual who is a part of institutions, technologies, and governance arrangements that also shape the nature of the responsibility. Integrity issues in the use of AI in assessments should be seen as systemic misalignments in the design, governance, and culture of assessment. Integrity innovation is the framework of this chapter and considers integrity an emergent property of that three-way alignment (Figure 1). Integrity is not a policy thing, and it is not a technology thing; it is a design, governance, and culture thing, with responsibility and ethics shared.

Integrity as a Design Outcome: Assessment Architecture

The first domain in Figure 1 is an assessment architecture view of integrity. The design of the tasks influences the way that students view the tasks, their efforts to complete them, and whether shortcuts seem to make sense. Misconduct risk has been consistently associated with task design, stakes and feedback, but not with students' moral character (Boud & Falchikov, 2007; Bretag et al., 2019). Integrity-oriented design thus focuses on real tasks, reflection, and clear AI use. It eliminates the impetus for shortcuts by giving up on standardized, high-stakes formats that lead to reproducible output. When algorithmic evaluation is involved, design should take into account its well-established bias toward surface conformity over reasoning

(Perelman, 2014). Recent tools make this space operational, such as the Artificial Intelligence Assessment Scale, which allows designers to assign a graduated language to every task, rather than a blanket prohibition, while making sure that there is transparency about the level of AI use that is authorized and expected in each task (Perkins, Furze, Roe, & MacVaugh, 2024). Design-based integrity focuses on clarity of task and technology because students are unable to have ethical agency within a closed system.

Integrity as a Governance Outcome: Responsible Oversight

The second domain focuses on integrity as responsible oversight of system selection, control, and accountability. The majority of institutions regulate the use of AI tools in a centralized way that focuses on efficiency over faculty judgment and student voice (Williamson & Hogan, 2020). Rather, integrity innovation introduces the principles of accountability, transparency, and participative decision-making. AI tools and services should never be allowed to make decisions entirely on their own without faculty interpretation. Whenever grades or credentials are impacted, they should be accompanied by explanations and avenues of appeal for students (Prinsloo & Slade, 2017). Since the advent of generative AI, various policy frameworks have been created, from the multi-dimensional AI education policy framework proposed by Chan (2023), which identifies pedagogical, governance, and operational dimensions, to the three-part policy framework by the OECD (2023). All these policy frameworks are based on the same premise: governance is not an afterthought, but an integral part of integrity. Responsible institutions are still held accountable for the impact of the systems they have put in place, whether these are developed in-house or outsourced.

Integrity as a Cultural Outcome: Institutional Culture

The third domain is about integrity in institutional culture (norms, relationships and shared understandings that support ethical assessment practice). It comprises trust and dialogue, integrity education, educational community, and faculty-student partnership (Figure 1). Rather than fostering a culture of suspicion, as is the case with surveillance-heavy regimes, where students are perceived as potential offenders and faculty members become monitors, integrity innovation is about a human-centered approach to using AI in education, in accordance with the international guidance to this effect proposed by UNESCO (2023). Integrity education is not just about conveying policy; it explicitly involves students in issues of responsibility and ownership, and in deciding when it is and when it is not appropriate to use AI. This is not the only thing that faculty culture has to offer. Limiting evaluative discretion to systems that emphasize "standardized" outputs is a form of marginalization, whereas seeing faculty as co-owners of evaluation practice is another way of combating this marginalization. Raising investment in AI literacy helps teachers to interact with these systems critically, make informed decisions, and model ethical interaction for students (Selwyn, 2023). In this perspective, integrity is a product of participation and not something that is imposed.

Shared Responsibility and Ethical Alignment

Integrity failures are never solely the student's because they are the result of an interaction of assessment incentives, governance, technologies, and culture. Shared responsibility and ethical alignment are at the base of Figure 1: integrity failures are never wholly the student's, but rather the result of an interaction of assessment incentives, governance, technologies, and culture. Compliance models focus exclusively on the ethical responsibilities of the students, and do not consider institutional conditions. The innovations of integrity shift responsibilities in the ecosystem, as institutions are responsible for ethical procurement and governance, faculty members are responsible for designing assessments transparently and reflectively, students are responsible for engaging with their learning transparently and reflectively, and technology providers are responsible for embedding fairness, transparency, and accountability into the technology. Integrity cannot be established when these responsibilities are not harmonized. This differs from detection-oriented models because the innovation is not limited to merely detecting integrity issues but also to addressing them. Instead, it takes a proactive approach and creates situations in which moral involvement is the most sensible and best-supported choice; standards and consequences are still in place but in an educational rather than a policing logic. Nor is the framework a "one size fits all." As previous chapters suggest, AI-based assessment plays out in very different settings of resources, regulations, and culture and is intentionally flexible: it provides institutions with a lens through which to investigate the interactions among design, governance, and culture as they determine the integrity outcomes for institutions they live within. In the next section, the authorship, originality, and collaboration, which are most shaken by AI, are examined using this systemic understanding.

Figure 1. illustrates the integrity innovation framework, showing how alignment across assessment design, governance, and institutional culture produces ethical outcomes in AI-based assessment systems.

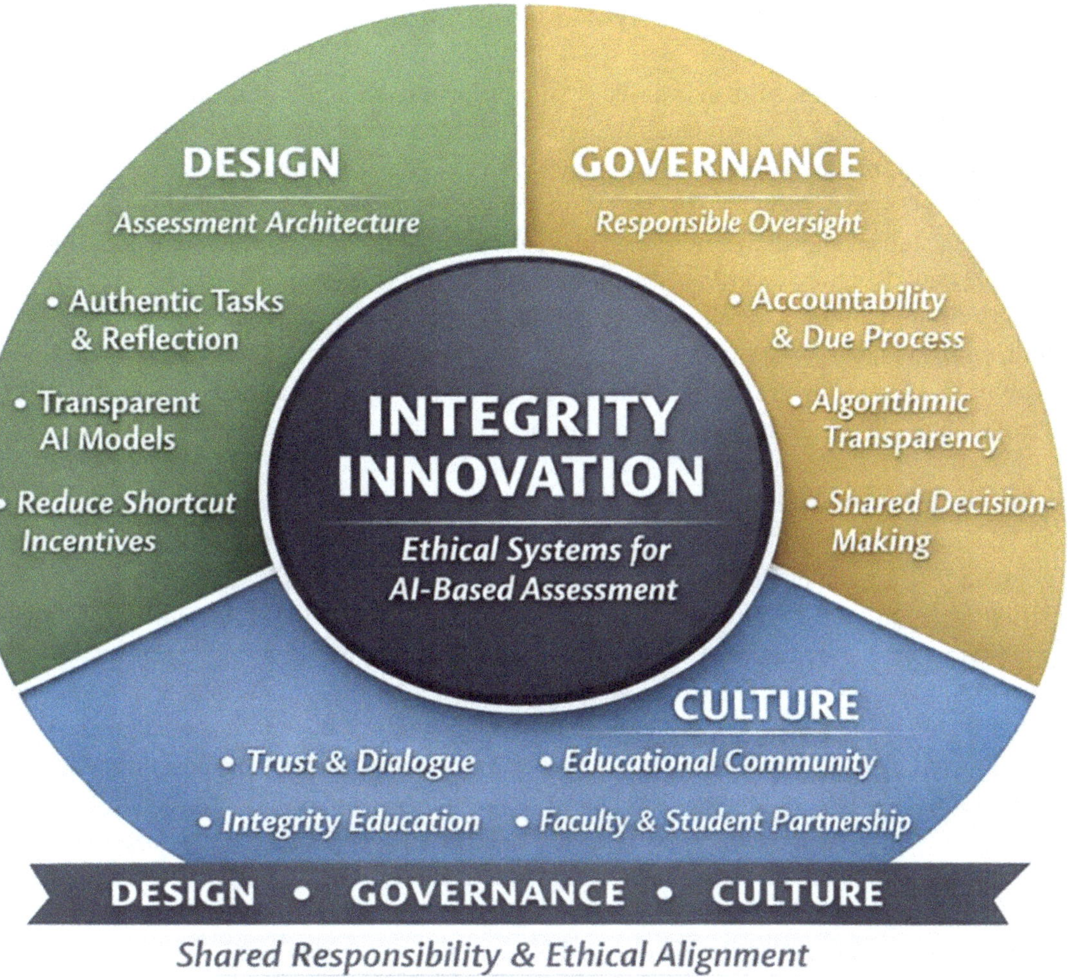

Integrity innovation is shown as an emergent institutional outcome arising from alignment across assessment design, governance, and institutional culture. The framework emphasizes shared responsibility, ethical alignment, and educational coherence over surveillance-based compliance.

7. RETHINKING AUTHORSHIP, ORIGINALITY, AND COLLABORATION IN THE AGE OF AI

An integrity innovation system can be used to rethink the notions most challenged by the current assessment: authorship, originality, and collaboration. These notions have long been the foundation of assessment rules, definitions of misconduct, and evaluative judgment. Their conventional applications become challenging in AI-mediated environments, but they should not be thrown away or set in stone.

These need to be re-interpreted in the context of hybrid knowledge production, distributed agency and changing academic practice.

From Individual Authorship to Hybrid Production

Academic integrity has assumed that it is straightforward to assign responsibility for items submitted, which is the case for individual authorship. Generative AI changes the equation by enabling hybrid authorship, meaning that students interact with systems that offer suggestions, arguments, and reorganizations (Köbis & Mossink, 2021). The opacity, immediacy, and scale of AI create challenges in distinguishing student knowledge from machine-generated work. In contrast, earlier tools did not, and Eaton (2023) says that hybrid writing is becoming more of a permanent reality than a rare occurrence in academic writing. This is not the integrity issue of getting help, but misrepresentation in the frameworks when there is no language to differentiate it. The focus changes from "Was AI used?" to "How, why, and who used AI, and how transparent was the use? Students continue to make intellectual decisions: the attribution of authorship is finally a moral decision.

Originality Beyond Novel Text

Originality has traditionally been defined in terms of novelty in the text and enforced through similarity detection. This narrow definition focuses on superficial differences rather than intellectual contributions. These limitations are revealed when using generative AI: AI can create text that is new in form but not in content, and students can generate text that may support and enhance content that they have contributed to but whose composition is not. In the review of institutional generative-AI policies that I conducted in 2024, I found that many policies rely on an unsustainable definition of originality as unaided creation of a text. I suggested that this definition needs to be reconceptualised as what constitutes students' own work. Originality in AI-mediated assessment is more recognized as intellectual contribution and epistemic responsibility (Eaton, 2020). This involves going beyond the identification of novelty and engaging with it: assessments that call for explanation, contextualization, and reflective justification will demonstrate originality that similarity metrics cannot (Boud, Ajjawi, Dawson, & Tai, 2018). The change also addresses an ongoing problem as the notion of originality is often confused with the idea of uniqueness, which unfairly buries ordinary scholarly activities like revision, synthesis, and instructed development. Integrity innovation adopts a relational and situated perspective on originality, and a cumulative and dialogic approach to knowledge, even in the presence of AI. The originality of the students is reflected in problem setting, data interpretation, and decision making.

Collaboration, Assistance, and the Collapse of Binary Categories

AI also challenges the boundary between independent work and illegitimate support on which the restrictive support rules rely.AI also blurs the line between independent work and illegitimate support on which restrictive support rules depend. The assistance it provides is similar to tutoring, editing, and brainstorming, and students and institutions are not sure where the boundaries are. Survey research similarly reveals that both students and institutions desire the use of generative tools to support learning, yet are uncertain about their boundaries (Chan & Hu, 2023). Use will proliferate in the dark in binary allow-or-ban systems, and so will cover violations of the rules. Cover violations of use will be encouraged, and more and more surveillance will be asked for, in binary allow-or-ban systems. By applying the principles approach, expectations are set about purpose, honesty, and proportionality. It decreases the need for unreliable detection technologies (Weber-Wulff et al., 2023) and promotes professional judgment that is subject to open dialogue and not prohibited.

Transparency as a Scholarly Integrity Practice

The principles of transparency are equally applicable to authorship, originality, and collaboration. Just as it is considered good academic practice to assert the originality of one's own work by citing sources and citing collaborators, it is good practice for responsible use of AI to acknowledge the contributions of the AI and identify it. Disclosure fosters trust, helps to make evaluation fairer, and facilitates maintaining students' autonomy while shifting the focus on integrity from suspicion to dialogue. Work can be evaluated in context, and students are encouraged to consider the impact of AI on their learning. The findings indicate that a supportive policy approach, as opposed to a punitive one, leads to students being more willing to be honest about the help they sought (Eaton & Turner, 2022; Chan & Hu, 2023).

Implications for Assessment Design and Governance

Delinking authorship and originality has direct implications for assessment design. With AI being widely used in production, evaluations based on the work of one person are increasingly artificial. Integrity innovation values the evaluation of reasoning and interpretation, ethical judgments, and reflective consciousness more than the evaluation of product. Governance should evolve alongside: As a governance tool, integrity policy needs to state long-term principles, not rules for a given version of a tool that will be outdated with every new tool release; graduated frameworks like the AI Assessment Scale provide one concrete approach to this (Perkins et al., 2024). The school must provide professional development for faculty to make contextual decisions, and students must also be engaged as partners to help develop norms for responsible AI use. When design, governance, and culture do not align, integrity policy becomes arbitrary, contested, and not related to learning.

Toward Responsible Academic Practice

The goal of integrity innovation is not to normalize uncritical reliance on AI, or to reduce standards, but to maintain the educational function of assessment in this new technological landscape. The reframing of authorship as agency, originality as contribution, and collaboration as ethically-bounded practice provides a way out of the prohibition and permissiveness that had characterized the field. While in the traditional assessment, integrity is the demand that students assess their work without collaboration with others, in AI-mediated assessment, it is the demand that students participate in complex socio-technical systems collaboratively, responsibly, transparently, and reflectively. This reframing immediately leads to the next part of this paper, which states that assessment design is the first place of integrity.

8. ASSESSMENT DESIGN AS THE PRIMARY SITE OF INTEGRITY INNOVATION

Integrity innovation that is not just theory requires a means of operationalization, namely in the design of assessment. Where there is the greatest ethical pressure on both students and faculty, integrity innovation must be operationalized; that is, in the design of assessment. Many of the alleged integrity issues that have been blamed on AI are instances of moral failure but are really design failures that AI amplifies, and that are more readily exploited and less readily governed by misaligned assessments. Designing assessments is thus the time when integrity is most likely to be compromised and when it is strongest when it is restored.

The Integrity Burden of High-Stakes, Standardized Assessment

The assessment in higher ed is still very high stakes, standardized, and focused on outcomes. Summative results influence grades, progression to further education, scholarships, and jobs and would predate the advent of AI and its emphasis upon surface learning and strategic compliance (Boud & Falchikov, 2007). AI tools can amplify these incentives by providing quick, plausible results at a lower cost than thought. In the case of rewards uniformity tests, the integrity failures make sense because they are the only way to get the reward, but it is not seen as an indication of design; it is seen as deviation. They are particularly vulnerable because they are comprised of standardized formats, and empirical evidence of their ability to perform on a diverse set of conventional assessment tasks, like engineering tasks and unseen examination items, indicates a structural vulnerability, as does the ability of generative models to execute a wide range of conventional exam types (Nikolic et al., 2023; Scarfe et al., 2024). Integrity strategy should instead question the standardization of formats, especially in high-stakes contexts, and not reinforce it through monitoring.

Incentive Structures and Ethical Behavior

An institution's values are expressed in the design of its assessment. Detection-based integrity systems do not address systems that focus on efficiency, correctness, and conformity, as they do not change the incentives for students to pay attention to output rather than understanding. AI adds to the equation by decreasing the price of shortcuts, particularly when it comes to writing. Pedagogically valuable shortcuts are the one answer to the design challenge, rather than difficult ones: weight process over product; reasoning over answers; interpretation over replication. However, when students are required to keep their own records, give feedback, explain changes, and explain methods, automation becomes irrelevant since AI can provide text without context and judgment. In this model, Design is an integral part of enforcing integrity; control is just the other part.

Reflection, Iteration, and Process Visibility

Traditional assessment focuses on the product, and the learning process is invisible a state in which AI-polished output is the most difficult to interpret. Integrity-oriented design makes process visible: students describe the development process, challenges encountered, and how feedback was utilized; staged drafts allow the teacher to "see" learning over time and minimize the payoff of last-minute substitutions. The structures follow formative assessment principles which are linked with deeper learning

(Boud et al., 2018). Process visibility ensures fair judgment by distinguishing true Engagement with the text and activity from compliance, and provides faculty with interpretable evidence of learning that maintains integrity.

Contextualized and Authentic Assessment Tasks

Integrity innovation is at its core the use of contexted and authentic tasks that require situating understanding in personal experience or real-world interactions. While AI can help with research and drafting, it cannot provide the judgment and lived context these require; more importantly, these tasks are more aligned to professional practice, where collaboration with AI is the norm. It is not meant to remove the need for AI, but to create tasks that incorporate its responsible and critical use in a way that is learned, and thus helping to turn the threat of AI into a learning opportunity. However, poor design in the real world leads to routinization and automatability of tasks, so authenticity is not granted as a given. The key features that maintain integrity are variety, local knowledge, and the flexibility of task design.

Dialogic and Formative Assessment

Another aspect of integrity-based design is the increased use of dialogic and formative assessment. Misunderstandings and ethical issues emerge before they become misconduct when assessment becomes a conversation through feedback loops, peer discussion, and opportunities to clarify. It is not surprising that teachers in the Farazouli et al. (2024) study found the challenge of identifying the chatbot texts difficult, and many of them determined that there should be more oral, dialogic, and in-person components in their assessment toolkit. AI can be used transparently to assist with dialogic assessment, further enhance feedback capacity, but be used as guidance instead of judgement, and retain the locus of control with the human teacher. Feedback is also a regular and timely intervention that will reduce the pressure of deadlines and the ambiguity as to what to do, as it will make the assessment more regular and timely, and reduce the conditions for breaches.

The Faculty Judgement and Autonomy in Assessment

Design that is oriented towards integrity relies on the subjective assessment of faculty, while AI-based systems tend to become more linear with templates, automated scoring and standardised processes. Integrity innovations rely on the idea that design should leave room for professional judgment: faculty are experts in their disciplines, responsible for the fairness and validity of assessment. This will take time, which institutional support is needed for, particularly at scale, as well as resources that would otherwise be used for surveillance, which can be better spent on redesigning assessments. In this sense, the decisions that people make around investments are ethical. Faculty also need to be supported to consider how AI is transforming the system of performance and evaluation in their own disciplines, such as how the disciplinary values should be thoughtfully incorporated into the design of assessment. Assessment is not being evaluated the same way now; instead, it is undergoing a process of rethinking around disciplinary values as integrity and innovation.

Assessment Design as Ethical Infrastructure

These elements combined can be seen as forms of ethical infrastructure of assessment design. Alternatively, as with the physical infrastructure, the norms of conduct are determined by conditions of assessment: assessments poorly designed will encourage and produce the very behavior they punish, and assessments well designed will cause conduct to be the natural path. This view sees violation of integrity as a sign of design, not a judgment of character. The feedback loops are faster with AI, giving designers a clearer view of design mistakes, and a greater sense of urgency to fix them.

From Policing to Pedagogy

The transition from policing to pedagogy is realised at the level of the design of the assessment. Integrity innovation does not ignore standards and consequences. However, it places them as subordinates of design: ethical assessment is not done more closely and more efficiently on students but done through designing tasks that allow students to become actively involved in their ethical evaluation and that the students can see and value. In AI-mediated environments, this is an inevitability. In the best-case scenario, surveillance will help to slow misuse of the technology, but only design will get learning back on track and help to restore trust. With assessment architecture at the heart of the integrity strategy, the institutions shift from being reactive and controlling to proactive and ethical. The subsequent section looks at the role of governance, law and accountability in the process of such redesign, considering what it means for the legitimacy and feasibility of that redesign.

9. GOVERNANCE, LAW, AND ETHICAL ACCOUNTABILITY IN AI-BASED ASSESSMENT

Proper governance, legal frameworks, and ethical accountability are necessary to promote the use of AI for improved academic assessment without compromising it. The institutional and regulatory context is key to the achievement of innovative design, which is a facilitator of learning and integrity. AI assessment systems are not standalone, but are part of a governance framework that establishes accountability, decision-making processes, and procedures for dealing with harm. Academic Integrity encompasses the responsibility of good governance, ethical oversight, and transparency. With AI, the governance functions have shifted to a central point as there is one source of assessment. Traditionally, educators were free to choose which assessments to use, but AI platforms are typically centrally ordered for standardization, efficiency, and consistency. This puts the authority of standards and integrity into the hands of compliance officers, vendors, and administrators, rather than faculty. Centralization can be more efficient, but it can also diminish the quality of educational judgment to merely follow the steps required, thereby impairing the skills of the disciplines and the discretion of teachers. One of the other difficulties is that commercial AI systems are opaque. Most tools for grading, plagiarism detection, analytics, and proctoring are built with proprietary algorithms and undisclosed data, which are used without knowing the decisions and biases. This opacity leads to a lack of accountability as institutions use these systems and vendors have no responsibility. Ethically, institutions need to ensure the transparency, explainability, and independent audit of AI. Vendors should provide information regarding the algorithms, accuracy, error rates, and decision parameters to ensure fairness and trust. Procedural fairness is extremely important in

AI evaluation, making sure that students have the information, access, and chance to challenge AI-driven decisions that impact their rights. However, the impact of AI tools on academic and professional futures can lead to false positives, particularly for linguistically diverse learners. Fairness is very important, and AI is used to provide guidance. Responsible data management is also part of ethical governance, which includes understanding what personal data is being collected, the purposes of the collection, who can access it, and for how long. Consent should be truly free and provide choices in relation to the level of intrusive surveillance. Effective data policies protect privacy, trust and student rights.

Algorithmic bias and differential exposure to risk must also be addressed in governance. Many studies have established a correlation between AI proctored systems and the disproportionate identification of students with disabilities, minority background or low socio-economic status, or limited technological access. Likewise, AI text detectors tend to make false positives when detecting texts written by non-native English speakers, putting already marginalised groups at a disadvantage. The differences are not necessarily indicative of academic dishonesty, but are instead based on the biases of training sets and system design. As a result, institutions should ask vendors to report results for a variety of demographic groups, have regular bias audits, and regularly review the results of these assessments to ensure equal treatment of all students. Finally, good governance is not just compliance with regulations but also a basis of legitimacy and trust by the public. The University is expected to demonstrate fairness, transparency and ethical responsibility and to be a leader in technological innovation. Transitioning to AI in assessment while being accountable requires proper governance structures that facilitate stakeholder involvement, the transparency of decision-making, the independence of oversight, and the regularity of monitoring. Incorporating ethical considerations, procedural justice, data privacy, and human oversight into the governance of AI systems allows higher education institutions to develop an AI assessment system that fosters academic integrity and innovation while simultaneously earning the trust of students, faculty, and society.

10. FACULTY AND STUDENT ROLES IN INTEGRITY-CENTERED AI-BASED ASSESSMENT

Integrity innovations will not happen with a policy, an assessment system, or a governance system; they happen in the day-to-day work of academics and in the process of negotiating and experiencing it. It is dependent on faculty and students' understandings of their roles and how they use judgment and interact in AI-mediated assessments. This section draws on the notion of integrity-centered assessment systems as active systems carried out not passively by faculty or students, but by faculty and students.

Faculty Between Professional Judgment and Algorithmic Authority

With AI-based assessment, faculty are now in a real dilemma, because they increasingly bear responsibility for standards and integrity and have less influence over the systems they are a part of. Selwyn (2023) notes that technology for automated marking, analysis, and identification of errors reduces teachers' freedom of choice and transforms them into participants in the production by machines. To this, integrity innovation brings back the ethical value of faculty judgment: Assessment is not purely a technical classification but an interpretation that must be grounded in context, discipline, and pedagogy. Automated scores can facilitate judgement, but not be used as a substitute for it, and uncritical acceptance of the automated scores is a threat to integrity, as evidenced in the documented error rates of AI-detection tools (Weber-Wulff et al., 2023). Institutional support is key here: faculty professional development on AI literacy is crucial to knowing how these systems work, their presumptions, and where faculty's authority stops. The decision on whether students are using AI productively to support learning is not technical but academic, and it should be made by engaged faculty.

Faculty as Designers and Ethical Stewards

The faculty also demonstrate integrity in their design. As discussed in the previous sections, the design of the assessment affects moral conduct, and teachers can design tasks that require students to engage in contextual reasoning, decision-making, and reflection. However, limited time and student resources, as well as efficiency, also limit teachers. Ethical stewardship in design involves making explicit expectations about the use of AI, engaging students in open and critical Engagement with AI, and introducing students to disciplinary norms of appropriate use with AI. Replacing surveillance technology with this design work risks the integrity, not the protection, of assessment. The process of shared development of assessment criteria increases the consistency and fairness, especially in the case of judgments related to AI across courses or programs.

Students as Ethical Agents, Not Compliance Subjects

In the past, integrity policy has assumed that students are to blame, and it has scaffolded around this assumption, making integrity an imposition. Rather than students as incapable moral actors, integrity innovation sees students as capable moral actors and expects them to make defensible decisions when they have clear expectations, transparency, and meaningful participation. In the context of AI-saturated environments, students make tough decisions about how to use tools, how to collaborate, and what constitutes "credit" for their work. The evidence of student thinking indicates that they are ready to use generative AI to learn, and they also seem to have mixed feelings about its ethical boundaries (Chan & Hu, 2023; Sullivan, Kelly, & McLaughlan, 2023). Such choices cannot be solved by rules alone; they must be explained, discussed, and reflected upon, not feared, in order to be developed in ethical competence. Students also believe they comply more with rules that they think are fair and aim at an educational objective (Eaton, 2021). Student pressure issues also must be taken into consideration, since assessment stress is a catalyst for shortcut behavior; integrity innovation does not justify misconduct; it helps to explain it; and if a student's integrity is a problem, it is necessary to pay attention to emotional and situational factors alongside the structures and rules in an effort to solve the integrity problem.

Transparency, Dialogue, and Trust-Building

Trust is the missing component of assessment in the AI era, and impenetrable systems erode trust on both sides. Integrity innovation fosters trust by communicating and engaging. Transparency is not just about publishing policies; it is about explaining the role that AI systems play in assessment, their capabilities and limitations, and how their outputs are reviewed. If students are aware of the role of AI in their assessment, they can present their concerns about error or unfairness, which lessens the pressure for faculty to take what is produced by AI on its own. Dialogue is important, too: Rules cannot exhaustively specify integrity. Planned discussions between faculty and students around the use of AI, ethical challenges, and expectations for evaluation create common understanding and foster a new understanding of integrity, moving past enforcement and prosecution to education, which is a higher education's mandate.

Students as Partners in Integrity Governance

It takes student voice to governance with Integrity innovation. The student body is the group most impacted by the use of AI-based assessment systems. It is continually marginalized from the process of deciding about and regulating its use, which undermines institutional legitimacy and the experiential knowledge of the institution. There are a wide variety of forms of partnership, such as representation on assessment committees, consultation during procurement, and involvement in policy review. Such involvement indicates that integrity is not viewed as an obligation from the top down, but rather as an institutional goal, and student voice is incorporated into decisions regarding surveillance, data use, and appeals. Partnership does not reduce standards; it recognizes that systems benefit from feedback from people who experience the consequences. Schools that are merely acting as objects are teaching compliance, and likely having their students resist; schools that are acting as allies are aligning their students' moral perspectives.

Navigating Risk Without Reverting to Control

There is a strong tendency for institutions to be concerned that giving faculty greater flexibility and discretion, and leaving it to the students to choose their own activities, would diminish enforcement. There is a difference between risk management and ethical alignment, and that is what integrity innovation is all about: control-driven approaches buy trust and learning at a high price, whereas ethically driven approaches require trust and learning to be bought at a lower price. Agency-centred approaches do not remove the standards, investigation or sanctions procedures from the way in the clear cases; they re-embed them in a wider educational logic. If faculty and students have fair, proportionate experiences of integrity processes in which shared values are involved, they are much more likely to live by them.

Collective Responsibility in Practice

The faculty and students have complementary roles in integrity-based assessment. They bring faculty experiences of discipline, design, and moral leadership; they bring students' lived experiences, experiences of context, and moral agency. The success of integrity innovation will rely on alignment and support of institutions to these roles. If faculty are involved in the process and not checked off, and if students are involved in the process and not monitored, then integrity becomes a practice in the community, not a constraint. However, AI-powered evaluation does not remove human judgment, but makes it much more important to get it right, and integrity innovation sees no threat, only an opportunity.

11. LONG-TERM IMPLICATIONS AND FUTURE RESEARCH DIRECTIONS

The use of AI in education assessment has broad and long-lasting implications for universities, not just because of technological uptake, but also because of its impact on quality of education, institutional trust, and ethics. Rather than a reaction to the new technologies, integrity innovation is seen as an ongoing institutional effort. In addition to granting degrees, universities have the role of cultivating ethical working professionals, critical thinkers, and responsible citizens. Therefore, AI-driven assessment should align with these broader learning goals, ensuring that assessments are fair, transparent, and uphold academic integrity. One of the biggest implications in the long term would be having to do with the ethical development of students. With more and more students going into the workforce with AI driving their work, what they learn in school will influence how they will apply technology at work. Integrity is more likely to be fostered if the assessment system includes reflection, responsible use of AI, and ethical decision-making components. Assessment systems that include components for reflection, responsible use of AI, and ethical decision-making are more likely to foster integrity than those that solely rely on surveillance or misconduct detection. Research is thus required to explore the impact of various AI-based assessment designs on students' ethical thinking, professional identity, and future attitudes toward responsible technology use in fields like health care, engineering, business, and education.

There are also several key research gaps. Past research has largely been concerned with the accuracy of the AI detection tools, students' views on academic dishonesty, and system accuracy. At the same time, relatively little attention has been devoted to students' perceptions of the fairness, trust, and policies of the institutions. Additional studies are needed to explore the experiences of students from different cultural, linguistic, and socioeconomic backgrounds with AI-powered assessment. Likewise, faculty views on the use of AI recommendations are worth examining, as well as faculty trust in AI recommendations, their willingness to challenge AI decisions, and the influence of governance processes on faculty autonomy. Comparative and design-based approaches to future scholarship should also be used. Cross-national research can help determine practices that help to foster fairness in distinct educational systems, and design-based research can help assess the impact of the iterative modifications of assessment design on ethical learning and responsible use of AI. In conclusion, while AI can be a valuable addition to the teaching and learning process, it should not be seen as a threat to human judgment, but rather as a tool that requires careful use, regular assessment, and a commitment to maintaining academic integrity within institutions. In an age of rapid technological advancement, universities have a vital role to play in making sure that artificial intelligence benefits, rather than undermines, higher education. As AI technology evolves, universities must promote the ethical use of AI and foster innovation grounded in evidence to ensure that this technology enhances, not detracts from, the future of higher education.

12. CONCLUSION: FROM POLICING TO SYSTEMIC INTEGRITY

Academic integrity cannot be ensured by detection and surveillance, as this is a form of covering up and concealing. Detection and surveillance are more of covering something up than ensuring academic integrity, as per the argument in this chapter. The mainstreaming of AI has thus created new challenges for both institutional framings of integrity, which have tended to focus on the individual and on technical risk, respectively, and resulted in an erosion of trust and a further increase in inequality. The concern voiced here, from never-noticed AI-generated tests to detection systems that are under fire for systematically misidentifying authentic student writing, is not so much about cheating as it is about institutional imagination. Integrity innovation answers by making integrity a systemic goal that can be designed, for which institutions, faculty, students, and technology developers are held accountable, and that grows out of coherent, transparent assessment processes, governance, and a culture of trust. Several conclusions follow. Assessment design has a greater, if not equal, influence on ethical behavior than does policy. If it is misaligned, it creates the shortcut incentives that surveillance creates without affecting them. Governance of AI-enabled assessment needs to be transparent, participative, and process-based to ensure the legitimacy of the detection instruments, especially in view of the proven unreliability and the bias of detection instruments. An integrity-centered institution fosters integrity in students and teachers, rather than assuming they are untrustworthy. Since adoption of AI is uneven across the world, approaches based on institutional responses to contextual diversity risk increasing injustice. In contrast, integrity innovation provides a common ethical grammar to which institutions can adapt their context. The return to a pre-AI academy is not an option, and its important questions are no longer about what tools are available, but who is controlling them and what are the circumstances? A strategy of restriction and more intrusive detection is unstable, does not build trust, and can eventually backfire, not to mention be unethical. I think the constructive approach is to innovate to make integrity part of the assessment process, and thus create students of integrity, rather than just seeking students who cheat.

REFERENCES

Boud, D., Ajjawi, R., Dawson, P., & Tai, J. (2018). *Developing evaluative judgement in higher education: Assessment for knowing and producing quality work*. Routledge., DOI: 10.4324/9781315109251

Boud, D., & Falchikov, N. (2007). *Rethinking assessment in higher education: Learning for the longer term*. Routledge. DOI: 10.4324/9780203964309

Bretag, T., Harper, R., Burton, M., Ellis, C., Newton, P., van Haeringen, K., Sadgrove, J., & Rozenberg, P. (2019). Contract cheating: A survey of Australian university students. *Studies in Higher Education*, *44*(11), 1837–1856. DOI: 10.1080/03075079.2018.1462788

Chan, C. K. Y. (2023). A comprehensive AI policy education framework for university teaching and learning. *International Journal of Educational Technology in Higher Education*, *20*(1), 38. Advance online publication. DOI: 10.1186/s41239-023-00408-3

Chan, C. K. Y., & Hu, W. (2023). Students' voices on generative AI: Perceptions, benefits, and challenges in higher education. *International Journal of Educational Technology in Higher Education*, *20*(1), 43. Advance online publication. DOI: 10.1186/s41239-023-00411-8

Dawson, P. (2021). *Defending assessment security in a digital world: Preventing e-cheating and supporting academic integrity in higher education*. Routledge., DOI: 10.4324/9780429324178

Dawson, P., Sutherland-Smith, W., & Harris, B. (2019). Contract cheating, artificial intelligence and assessment design. *Assessment & Evaluation in Higher Education*, *44*(6), 847–857. DOI: 10.1080/02602938.2018.1527892

Design-Based Research Collective. (2003). Design-based research: An emerging paradigm for educational inquiry. *Educational Researcher*, *32*(1), 5–8. DOI: 10.3102/0013189X032001005

Eaton, S. E. (2020). Academic integrity in online learning: What to do when students cheat. *Canadian Journal of Higher Education*, *50*(2), 1–14. DOI: 10.47678/cjhe.v50i2.188901

Eaton, S. E. (2021). *Academic integrity in Canada: An enduring and essential challenge*. Springer., DOI: 10.1007/978-3-030-83255-1

Eaton, S. E. (2023). Postplagiarism: Transdisciplinary ethics and integrity in the age of artificial intelligence and neurotechnology. *International Journal for Educational Integrity*, *19*(1), 23. Advance online publication. DOI: 10.1007/s40979-023-00144-1

Eaton, S. E., & Turner, K. L. (2022). Exploring academic integrity and artificial intelligence in higher education. *International Journal for Educational Integrity*, *18*(1), 11. Advance online publication. DOI: 10.1007/s40979-022-00110-0

Eubanks, V. (2018). *Automating inequality: How high-tech tools profile, police, and punish the poor*. St. Martin's Press.

Farazouli, A., Cerratto-Pargman, T., Bolander-Laksov, K., & McGrath, C. (2024). Hello GPT! Goodbye home examination? An exploratory study of AI chatbots' impact on university teachers' assessment practices. *Assessment & Evaluation in Higher Education*, *49*(3), 363–375. DOI: 10.1080/02602938.2023.2241676

Gilliard, C., & Culik, A. (2016). Digital redlining, access, and privacy. *Journal of Information Ethics*, *25*(2), 24–36.

Kahn, L., Everington, L., Kelm, K., Reid, I., & Watkins, F. (2022). Proctoring anxiety and digital surveillance in higher education. *Computers and Education Open*, *3*, 100068. DOI: 10.1016/j.caeo.2022.100068

Kasneci, E., Sessler, K., Küchemann, S., Bannert, M., Dementieva, D., Fischer, F., Gasser, U., Groh, G., Günnemann, S., Hüllermeier, E., Krusche, S., Kutyniok, G., Michaeli, T., Nerdel, C., Pfeffer, J., Poquet, O., Sailer, M., Schmidt, A., Seidel, T., & Kasneci, G. (2023). ChatGPT for good? On opportunities and challenges of large language models for education. *Learning and Individual Differences*, *103*, 102274. DOI: 10.1016/j.lindif.2023.102274

Kitchin, R. (2017). Thinking critically about and researching algorithms. *Information Communication and Society*, *20*(1), 14–29. DOI: 10.1080/1369118X.2016.1154087

Köbis, N., & Mossink, L. D. (2021). Artificial intelligence versus human decision-making: Accountability and responsibility in AI systems. *AI & Society*, *36*(3), 747–755. DOI: 10.1007/s00146-020-01039-x

Lee, V. R., Pope, D., Miles, S., & Zárate, R. C. (2024). Cheating in the age of generative AI: A high school survey study of cheating behaviors before and after the release of ChatGPT. *Computers and Education: Artificial Intelligence*, *7*, 100253. DOI: 10.1016/j.caeai.2024.100253

Liang, W., Yuksekgonul, M., Mao, Y., Wu, E., & Zou, J. (2023). GPT detectors are biased against non-native English writers. *Patterns (New York, N.Y.)*, *4*(7), 100779. DOI: 10.1016/j.patter.2023.100779 PMID: 37521038

Luckin, R., Holmes, W., Griffiths, M., & Forcier, L. B. (2016). *Intelligence unleashed: An argument for AI in education*. Pearson.

Lyon, D. (2018). *The culture of surveillance: Watching as a way of life*. Polity Press.

McCabe, D. L., Butterfield, K. D., & Treviño, L. K. (2012). *Cheating in college: Why students do it and what educators can do about it*. Johns Hopkins University Press.

McCabe, D. L., & Pavela, G. (2004). Ten principles of academic integrity. Change. *The Magazine of Higher Learning*, *36*(3), 10–15. DOI: 10.1080/00091380409605574

Moorhouse, B. L., Yeo, M. A., & Wan, Y. (2023). Generative AI tools and assessment: Guidelines of the world's top-ranking universities. *Computers and Education Open*, *5*, 100151. DOI: 10.1016/j.caeo.2023.100151

Nikolic, S., Daniel, S., Haque, R., Belkina, M., Hassan, G. M., Grundy, S., Lyden, S., Neal, P., & Sandison, C. (2023). ChatGPT versus engineering education assessment: A multidisciplinary and multi-institutional benchmarking and analysis of this generative artificial intelligence tool to investigate assessment integrity. *European Journal of Engineering Education*, *48*(4), 559–614. DOI: 10.1080/03043797.2023.2213169

Perelman, L. (2014). When "the state of the art" is counting words. *Assessing Writing*, *21*, 104–111. DOI: 10.1016/j.asw.2014.05.001

Perkins, M., Furze, L., Roe, J., & MacVaugh, J. (2024). The Artificial Intelligence Assessment Scale (AIAS): A framework for ethical integration of generative AI in educational assessment. *Journal of University Teaching & Learning Practice, 21*(6). Advance online publication. DOI: 10.53761/q3azde36

Perrotta, C., & Selwyn, N. (2020). Deep learning goes to school: Toward a relational understanding of AI in education. *Learning, Media and Technology, 45*(3), 251–269. DOI: 10.1080/17439884.2020.1686017

Prinsloo, P., & Slade, S. (2017). Big data, higher education and learning analytics: Beyond justice, toward an ethics of care. *British Journal of Educational Technology, 48*(1), 10–19. DOI: 10.1111/bjet.12441

Scarfe, P., Watcham, K., Clarke, A., & Roesch, E. (2024). A real-world test of artificial intelligence infiltration of a university examinations system: A "Turing Test" case study. *PLoS One, 19*(6), e0305354. DOI: 10.1371/journal.pone.0305354 PMID: 38923941

Selwyn, N. (2019). *Should robots replace teachers? AI and the future of education*. Polity Press.

Selwyn, N. (2023). *Education and technology: Key issues and debates* (3rd ed.). Bloomsbury Academic.

Sullivan, M., Kelly, A., & McLaughlan, P. (2023). ChatGPT in higher education: Considerations for academic integrity and student learning. *Journal of Applied Learning and Teaching, 6*(1), 31–40. DOI: 10.37074/jalt.2023.6.1.17

Sutherland-Smith, W. (2008). *Plagiarism, the Internet, and student learning: Improving academic integrity*. Routledge. DOI: 10.4324/9780203928370

Swauger, S. (2020). Software that monitors students during exams perpetuates inequity. *Teaching in Higher Education, 25*(1), 104–107. DOI: 10.1080/13562517.2019.1677821

Swiecki, Z., Khosravi, H., Chen, G., Martinez-Maldonado, R., Lodge, J. M., Milligan, S., Selwyn, N., & Gašević, D. (2022). Assessment in the age of artificial intelligence. *Computers and Education: Artificial Intelligence, 3*, 100075. DOI: 10.1016/j.caeai.2022.100075

UNESCO. (2023). *Guidance for generative AI in education and research*. United Nations Educational, Scientific and Cultural Organization., DOI: 10.54675/EWZM9535

Weber-Wulff, D., Anohina-Naumeca, A., Bjelobaba, S., Foltýnek, T., Guerrero-Dib, J., Popoola, O., Šigut, P., & Waddington, L. (2023). Testing of detection tools for AI-generated text. *International Journal for Educational Integrity, 19*(1), 26. Advance online publication. DOI: 10.1007/s40979-023-00146-z

Williamson, B. (2017). Big data in education: The digital future of learning, policy and practice. *Sage (Atlanta, Ga.)*. Advance online publication. DOI: 10.4135/9781529714920

Williamson, B., & Eynon, R. (2020). Historical threads, missing links, and future directions in AI in education. *Learning, Media and Technology, 45*(3), 223–235. DOI: 10.1080/17439884.2020.1798995

Williamson, B., & Hogan, A. (2020). Commercialisation and privatisation in/of education in the context of AI. *Globalisation, Societies and Education, 18*(4), 1–17. DOI: 10.1080/14767724.2020.1718754

Chapter 11
Contractual and Liability Issues in AI Educational Technologies

S. Md. Azash
http://orcid.org/0000-0001-6284-7854
Presidency University, Bangalore, India

G. M. Mamatha
Presidency University, Bangalore, India

Yusuf Hayath Md.
http://orcid.org/0009-0003-7491-0955
Presidency University, Bangalore, India

ABSTRACT

The integration of Artificial Intelligence (AI) into educational technologies has significantly transformed teaching, learning, and administrative processes within modern educational systems. AI-driven tools such as intelligent tutoring systems, automated grading platforms, and predictive learning analytics offer opportunities for personalized learning, improved efficiency, and enhanced academic outcomes. However, the increasing reliance on these technologies also raises important contractual, regulatory, and liability concerns, particularly within the evolving legal framework of the Indian education sector. This study examines the contractual governance and liability allocation associated with AI educational technologies by analyzing stakeholder perceptions of contractual clarity, regulatory compliance, ethical safeguards, and institutional support mechanisms. Using an empirical mixed-methods research design, data were collected from 300 stakeholders including AI developers, educational administrators, teachers, and students across four South Indian states.

INTRODUCTION

The rapid incorporation of Artificial Intelligence (AI) into educational technologies has reshaped the educational landscape globally, with India witnessing significant growth in this domain due to its diverse and expanding education system. AI-driven solutions provide personalized learning, automate administrative workflows, and enhance assessment accuracy, promising improved educational outcomes.

DOI: 10.4018/979-8-3373-8939-4.ch011

However, these technological advancements introduce complex contractual and liability challenges, particularly within the Indian context characterized by evolving regulatory frameworks, diverse institutional structures, and varying levels of technological maturity. This chapter examines these contractual and liability issues in AI educational technologies in India, integrating theoretical perspectives with empirical data collected from key stakeholders in the Indian education sector.

The Indian education system, being one of the largest in the world, comprises a heterogeneous mix of public and private institutions, informal coaching centers, and digital startups. This diversity creates unique challenges when integrating AI technologies, as contractual agreements must be adaptable to varied institutional capacities and governance models. Moreover, India's legal and regulatory environment is in a state of transition, with emerging data protection laws and nascent AI-specific policies that have yet to fully address the nuances of AI deployment in education. These factors necessitate a comprehensive examination of contractual clarity, liability allocation, compliance risks, and ethical considerations within the Indian context.

Artificial Intelligence based educational technologies are now widely used in schools, universities, and online learning platforms. These systems include intelligent tutoring systems, automated grading tools, predictive analytics platforms, and generative learning assistants. While they improve efficiency and personalization, they also introduce complex contractual and liability concerns among technology providers, educational institutions, instructors, and students. A conceptual framework helps explain how legal responsibility, contractual obligations, and technological risks interact within AI driven education environments.

Core Concepts of the Framework- AI Educational Technologies

The framework is built around five major constructs. These constructs interact to determine the allocation of responsibility and legal risk in AI powered education systems.

AI Educational Technologies

AI educational technologies refer to software systems that use machine learning, natural language processing, or automated decision systems to support teaching and learning. These technologies often operate through cloud services and rely on large datasets. Because they can influence grading, admissions decisions, academic feedback, and learning analytics, their operation can produce legal consequences when errors occur (Holmes, Bialik, & Fadel, 2019).

Contractual Agreements

Contracts govern the relationship between educational institutions and AI technology vendors. These agreements usually define service scope, data ownership, system reliability, intellectual property rights, and liability limitations. Institutions depend on these contracts to regulate vendor responsibility for system performance, security breaches, and misuse of student data (Edwards & Veale, 2017).

Contracts in AI education systems often include:

- Service level agreements
- Data processing agreements

- Licensing terms
- Limitation of liability clauses
- Indemnification provisions

These provisions determine which party bears responsibility if the technology causes harm or fails to perform as expected.

Data Governance and Privacy

AI systems in education rely heavily on student data such as academic records, learning behavior, and personal information. Improper data management may lead to privacy violations or regulatory breaches. Data governance policies and contractual clauses attempt to regulate how vendors collect, store, process, and share educational data (Williamson & Eynon, 2020).

Strong governance structures influence liability exposure. Weak governance increases institutional risk when AI systems misuse sensitive student data.

Algorithmic Risk and System Error

AI educational systems may produce biased outcomes, inaccurate predictions, or flawed grading decisions due to algorithmic limitations or training data bias. When such errors occur, determining legal responsibility becomes complex. Responsibility may lie with the vendor who designed the algorithm, the institution that implemented the system, or the instructor who relied on its output (Calo, 2017).

Algorithmic risk includes:

- Bias in grading or assessment
- Incorrect academic recommendations
- Discriminatory predictive analytics
- Faulty automated feedback

These risks directly influence potential legal claims such as negligence, discrimination, or breach of duty of care.

Liability Allocation

Liability allocation refers to how legal responsibility is distributed between stakeholders when harm results from AI system use. The framework assumes that liability depends on three factors:

- contractual terms
- degree of institutional oversight
- level of algorithmic autonomy

Where institutions rely heavily on automated decision making with minimal oversight, liability risks increase. Clear contractual clauses and transparent AI governance structures reduce uncertainty about responsibility.

Stakeholder Relationships

The framework identifies four primary stakeholders.

1. Technology vendors develop and maintain AI systems and usually control the algorithm design and infrastructure.
2. Educational institutions purchase or license AI technologies and integrate them into teaching and administrative systems.
3. Educators interact with the technology and may rely on its outputs in academic decision making.

Students are the primary users and data subjects whose information feeds the system.

4. Contracts regulate the relationship between vendors and institutions, while institutional policies govern interactions with educators and students. Liability may arise from any layer of this relationship network.

Structural Relationships in the Framework

The conceptual model assumes the following relationships:

1. AI educational technologies influence algorithmic risk and data governance requirements.
2. Contractual agreements regulate how technology is implemented and determine liability limitations.
3. Data governance mechanisms affect privacy protection and regulatory compliance.
4. Algorithmic risks increase the likelihood of legal disputes or liability claims.

Liability allocation is shaped jointly by contractual terms, governance structures, and system design.

In this framework, contractual governance acts as the central control mechanism that moderates risk between technology use and legal accountability.

Implications of the Framework

The framework highlights the need for clearer legal standards and more detailed contractual structures in AI education systems. Institutions must negotiate contracts that address algorithm transparency, vendor accountability, and data protection responsibilities. Technology providers must incorporate ethical AI design and risk mitigation strategies to reduce liability exposure.

By mapping the interaction between AI technologies, contractual arrangements, and legal risk, this framework provides a foundation for empirical research on regulatory governance and legal accountability in AI driven education.

REVIEW OF LITERATURE

The literature shows that AI based educational technologies are widely used to automate academic processes and analyze large volumes of student data. These systems use machine learning algorithms to identify learning patterns, recommend instructional content, and support decision making in academic environments. Researchers note that the rapid integration of AI into education has outpaced the development of adequate legal frameworks governing its use. As a result, concerns have emerged regarding transparency, fairness, and accountability in automated educational systems (Williamson & Eynon, 2020).

Studies also highlight that AI technologies rely heavily on large datasets collected from students, including academic performance, behavioral patterns, and personal information. The extensive collection and processing of this data raise concerns about privacy protection and regulatory compliance, particularly when institutions rely on external technology vendors to manage AI systems (Selwyn, 2019).

Contracts are central to managing relationships between educational institutions and technology providers that develop and maintain AI systems. These contractual agreements typically regulate service scope, intellectual property rights, system reliability, and data management practices. Scholars argue that contracts must clearly define responsibilities for system performance, maintenance, and security because AI technologies can significantly influence educational decisions (Edwards & Veale, 2017).

Service level agreements and licensing contracts often include provisions that limit vendor liability or transfer certain responsibilities to educational institutions. However, researchers note that such clauses may create legal uncertainty when AI systems produce incorrect outcomes or cause harm to students. In these cases, disputes may arise regarding whether the institution, the technology developer, or the instructor bears responsibility for the resulting damage (Calo, 2017).

Recent studies also discuss the growing role of AI in automating aspects of contract drafting and analysis. AI tools can assist organizations in generating contractual documents and identifying legal risks, which introduces new questions about contract validity, interpretation, and enforceability when automated systems participate in contractual processes (Surden, 2019).

A significant portion of the literature focuses on the difficulty of assigning liability when AI systems produce errors or harmful outcomes. Traditional legal frameworks generally assume that responsibility lies with human actors. However, AI systems often operate with a degree of autonomy and unpredictability, making it difficult to determine the exact cause of an error (Calo, 2017).

Legal scholars argue that liability may arise under several doctrines, including negligence, product liability, and contractual liability. For example, developers may be held liable if the design of an AI system contains defects or biases that produce discriminatory outcomes. Similarly, educational institutions may face liability if they deploy AI technologies without proper oversight or fail to verify the accuracy of automated decisions affecting students (Floridi et al., 2018).

The "black box" nature of many machine learning algorithms further complicates liability assessment. Because the internal logic of some AI systems is not easily interpretable, determining how a specific decision was reached may be difficult. This lack of transparency creates challenges for courts attempting to assign responsibility in cases involving AI related harm (Edwards & Veale, 2017).

Data protection represents another critical issue in the literature on AI educational technologies. AI systems depend on extensive data collection to generate accurate predictions and recommendations. However, improper handling of student data can result in privacy violations and legal disputes. Scholars emphasize that institutions must establish clear policies regarding data ownership, consent, and security when implementing AI technologies (Williamson & Eynon, 2020).

Regulatory frameworks such as data protection laws require organizations to ensure that personal data is processed transparently and securely. Educational institutions that fail to comply with these requirements may face legal penalties and reputational damage. Consequently, contractual agreements between institutions and technology vendors must clearly specify responsibilities for data protection and regulatory compliance (Selwyn, 2019).

Researchers widely acknowledge that current legal frameworks are not fully prepared to address the unique challenges posed by AI technologies. Existing liability regimes were designed for traditional technologies and may not adequately account for autonomous decision-making systems. Scholars therefore call for the development of updated legal frameworks that address issues such as algorithmic accountability, transparency, and shared responsibility among stakeholders (Floridi et al., 2018).

In the context of education, the regulatory environment remains particularly fragmented. Different jurisdictions apply varying standards regarding data protection, digital governance, and technology regulation. This lack of uniform regulation creates uncertainty for institutions that adopt AI systems in teaching and administrative processes (Williamson & Eynon, 2020).

Research Gaps

Despite the growing body of research on AI governance and liability, there remains limited scholarship specifically focusing on contractual and liability issues in AI educational technologies. Most existing studies examine AI liability in sectors such as healthcare, finance, or autonomous vehicles. Consequently, further research is needed to develop sector specific frameworks that address legal risks associated with automated grading, algorithmic decision making, and AI driven learning analytics in educational institutions.

OVERVIEW OF AI EDUCATIONAL TECHNOLOGIES IN INDIA

AI educational technologies include intelligent tutoring systems, adaptive learning platforms, automated grading tools, and virtual classrooms. In India, the adoption of these technologies has been accelerated by government initiatives such as Digital India and the National Education Policy (NEP) 2020, which emphasize the integration of technology in education to improve accessibility and quality. Despite this momentum, challenges remain in standardizing AI tools, ensuring quality assurance, and ethically deploying AI systems across heterogeneous educational institutions. The Indian market features a mix of public universities, private institutions, and informal coaching centers, each with distinct needs and capabilities, complicating uniform adoption.

Despite this momentum, the Indian market faces significant challenges. The lack of standardization across AI tools leads to variability in quality and effectiveness. Many educational institutions, especially in rural or under-resourced areas, struggle with infrastructure limitations and digital literacy gaps, impeding uniform adoption. Ethical deployment of AI remains a concern, given the potential for algorithmic biases and the sensitive nature of educational data. Furthermore, the coexistence of formal institutions and informal coaching centers complicates regulatory oversight and contractual uniformity.

ROLE AND SCOPE OF CONTRACTUAL CLARITY IN AI EDUCATIONAL TECHNOLOGIES

Defining Roles and Responsibilities

Clear contractual delineation of roles and responsibilities is foundational to effective AI integration in education. AI developers are responsible for designing, developing, and maintaining functional and secure AI systems. Educational institutions must ensure appropriate deployment, user training, and compliance with usage guidelines. End-users, including students and educators, are expected to engage with AI tools responsibly, adhering to prescribed protocols.

In India's diverse educational ecosystem, contracts must be sufficiently flexible to accommodate varying institutional models while maintaining precision to prevent accountability gaps. For example, public universities may have different operational constraints compared to private coaching centers, necessitating tailored contractual clauses. Failure to clearly define these roles can lead to disputes, operational inefficiencies, and legal ambiguities, potentially undermining trust among stakeholders.

Specifying Use Cases and Limitations

Contracts should explicitly define the intended use cases of AI technologies, detailing permissible applications and inherent limitations. This clarity safeguards against misuse and overreliance on AI outputs that may not yet meet rigorous validation standards. For instance, AI-based assessment tools may be restricted contractually to formative assessments rather than summative or high-stakes examinations, reflecting current reliability and ethical considerations.

Moreover, specifying limitations addresses issues related to AI's evolving capabilities and the dynamic nature of educational needs. Contracts may include provisions for periodic review and update of use cases to align with technological advancements and institutional requirements. This dynamic contractual approach ensures that AI tools remain fit for purpose while managing risks associated with unanticipated applications.

Data Privacy and Intellectual Property Rights

Handling sensitive student data introduces critical contractual considerations. Indian data protection frameworks, including the Information Technology Act and the forthcoming Personal Data Protection Bill, require stringent data privacy and security measures. Contracts must incorporate provisions that ensure compliance with these laws, clearly defining data ownership, usage rights, retention periods, and security protocols. Additionally, intellectual property rights related to AI algorithms and educational content must be explicitly addressed to prevent unauthorized use or infringement, protecting both developers' innovations and institutions' content assets.

Contracts must incorporate robust data privacy clauses that define data ownership, usage rights, retention periods, and security protocols. Developers and institutions should commit to compliance with applicable laws, implement encryption and anonymization where appropriate, and establish clear protocols for data breach response. Intellectual property (IP) rights related to AI algorithms, training data, and educational content also require explicit contractual articulation. Protecting developers' innovations and institutions' proprietary content prevents unauthorized use, infringement, and disputes over ownership or derivative works.

LIABILITY ALLOCATION IN AI EDUCATIONAL TECHNOLOGIES

Liability for AI Errors and Biases

AI systems inherently carry risks of errors and biases, which can adversely affect student evaluations, learning outcomes, and equity. Contractual liability clauses must clearly allocate responsibility for such inaccuracies. In India, the absence of explicit AI-specific legislation complicates liability determination, often leaving parties to navigate ambiguous legal terrain.

Contracts should anticipate potential AI errors by defining liability scopes, including scenarios of algorithmic bias, incorrect assessments, or system misclassifications. Shared liability models may be appropriate, reflecting the collaborative nature of AI deployment, where developers, institutions, and users each bear responsibility within their domain of control. Such clarity mitigates legal uncertainty and promotes proactive risk management.4.2 Liability for Software

Liability for Software Malfunctions and Data Breaches

Software malfunctions, including system downtimes, bugs, or failures, can disrupt educational processes significantly. Contracts must specify liability for such incidents, including remediation obligations and compensation mechanisms. Additionally, data breaches involving sensitive student information expose institutions to reputational damage and legal penalties.

Clear contractual provisions should allocate liability for breaches, mandate preventive security measures, and establish incident response protocols. Given the criticality of educational data, contracts may require developers and institutions to maintain cybersecurity certifications, conduct vulnerability assessments, and report breaches promptly to affected parties and regulators.

Indemnity and Accountability Balance

Indemnity clauses often protect developers and institutions from certain claims, transferring risk and limiting exposure. However, excessive indemnity may erode accountability and undermine stakeholder trust. Indian contracts must balance indemnity provisions to shield parties from unforeseeable risks while ensuring responsibility for negligence, wilful misconduct, or breach of contractual obligations.

This balance is essential in fostering a collaborative environment where parties remain incentivized to maintain high standards of performance, security, and ethical conduct. Negotiated indemnity terms should be transparent, equitable, and aligned with Indian legal principles to withstand potential judicial scrutiny.5. Compliance and Regulatory Risks

COMPLIANCE AND REGULATORY RISKS

Adherence to Educational Standards

AI educational technologies must align with academic standards prescribed by Indian regulatory authorities such as the University Grants Commission (UGC) and the All-India Council for Technical Education (AICTE). These bodies set guidelines for curriculum design, assessment methods, and quality assurance, which AI tools must respect to maintain educational integrity.

Contracts should mandate AI system compliance with these standards, including adaptability to curriculum frameworks and adherence to assessment protocols. Failure to comply risks regulatory sanctions, invalidation of assessments, and erosion of institutional credibility.

Data Protection and AI-Specific Regulations

Data protection compliance is paramount, especially with the anticipated implementation of the Personal Data Protection Bill, which will impose rigorous standards on data processing, user consent, and data subject rights. Contracts must be forward-looking, embedding provisions for transparency, data minimization, explicit consent mechanisms, and mechanisms enabling users to exercise their rights.

Additionally, emerging AI-specific guidelines, such as those proposed by the Indian government's AI task forces, emphasize explainability, fairness, and accountability. Contracts should incorporate these principles, ensuring AI deployments meet evolving regulatory expectations and ethical benchmarks.

Transparency, Explainability, and Auditability

Transparency in AI decision-making fosters trust and facilitates ethical use. Contractual clauses can mandate regular audits, documentation, and reporting of AI algorithms' functioning, enabling institutions and users to understand and verify AI outputs. Explainability provisions ensure that AI recommendations or assessments can be interpreted and challenged if necessary.

Auditability clauses may require independent third-party evaluations or institutional review boards to periodically assess AI system performance, bias, and compliance. Such governance mechanisms enhance accountability and support continuous improvement.

RISK MANAGEMENT AND MITIGATION STRATEGIES FOR USING AI EDUCATIONAL TECHNOLOGIES

Warranties, Disclaimers, and Limitations of Liability

Contracts typically include warranties guaranteeing AI technologies' performance, accuracy, and reliability. Disclaimers and limitations of liability help manage expectations and reduce litigation risks. In India, these clauses must comply with consumer protection statutes, such as the Consumer Protection Act, ensuring they are enforceable and not unconscionable.

Clear articulation of warranty scopes, duration, and remedies for breach supports risk mitigation. Limitations of liability should be reasonable, avoiding blanket exclusions that could be invalidated by courts.

Incident Response and Dispute Resolution

Effective risk management requires clearly defined incident response procedures for events such as data breaches or AI system failures. Contracts should specify dispute resolution mechanisms, favoring arbitration or mediation to enable timely, cost-effective conflict resolution, which is particularly important given the technical complexities involved.

Given the technical complexity of AI systems, dispute resolution clauses may also include expert determination or technical advisory panels to assist in resolving specialized issues.

System Updates and Corrections

AI technologies necessitate continuous updates to address bugs, security vulnerabilities, and evolving educational needs. Contracts must delineate responsibilities for system maintenance, update frequency, and timelines for implementing corrections to ensure sustained functionality and security.

Service level agreements (SLAs) can specify uptime guarantees, response times for issue resolution, and penalties for non-compliance, ensuring sustained system reliability and user satisfaction.

ETHICAL AND SOCIAL CONSIDERATIONS ISSUES IN AI EDUCATIONAL TECHNOLOGIES

Addressing Bias and Fairness

AI systems risk perpetuating or amplifying biases, adversely affecting fairness in educational assessments and opportunities. Contracts should include commitments to regular bias testing, validation, and corrective measures, ensuring AI tools promote equity and do not discriminate against any group.

These provisions may require developers to implement fairness audits, retrain models with representative data, and transparently report bias mitigation efforts. Institutions should monitor AI outputs to ensure equitable treatment of all learners.

User Consent and Data Collection

Obtaining informed consent for data collection and AI-driven interventions is both an ethical imperative and a legal requirement. Contractual provisions must ensure that users, including students and guardians, are fully informed about data usage, their rights, and consent mechanisms, safeguarding autonomy and privacy.

Consent processes should be clear, accessible, and compliant with Indian data protection norms, fostering user autonomy and trust.

Inclusivity and Accessibility

AI educational technologies must accommodate diverse learner needs, including individuals with disabilities. Contracts can mandate compliance with accessibility standards such as the Rights of Persons with Disabilities Act, 2016, and relevant international guidelines.

Ensuring AI tools are usable by all learners promotes inclusive education and aligns with India's commitment to equitable access.

Sustained reliability of AI educational technologies depends on continuous maintenance. Contracts should specify the scope, frequency, and quality standards of maintenance activities, including preventive measures and emergency response.

Regular maintenance ensures system stability, security, and adaptability to evolving educational requirements.

Successful AI integration requires comprehensive user training and ongoing support. Contracts must delineate the nature, extent, and delivery of support services for educators and students, facilitating effective adoption and maximizing the educational benefits of AI tools.

Effective support enhances user confidence, reduces resistance to adoption, and maximizes educational benefits.

STATEMENT OF THE PROBLEM

The rapid deployment of AI educational technologies in India has outpaced the development of clear contractual frameworks and liability provisions, leading to ambiguities and legal uncertainties. This gap complicates accountability for AI errors, data privacy breaches, and ethical concerns, hindering widespread adoption and trust among educational institutions, developers, and users. The lack of standardized contracts and regulatory clarity poses risks to educational quality, student rights, and institutional compliance.

IMPORTANCE AND SIGNIFICANCE OF THE STUDY

This study addresses a critical gap in understanding the contractual and liability challenges unique to AI educational technologies within the Indian context. By providing empirical insights from diverse stakeholders, it informs the development of robust contractual frameworks that balance innovation with accountability, compliance, and ethical integrity. The findings will guide policymakers, educational institutions, and technology developers in creating legally sound and ethically responsible AI deployments, thereby promoting trust and sustainable integration of AI in Indian education.

OBJECTIVES OF THE STUDY

- To identify key contractual ambiguities and liability concerns faced by stakeholders in AI educational technology adoption in India.

- To examine the regulatory and ethical challenges impacting contractual clarity and liability allocation.
- To assess the adequacy of current contractual provisions related to data privacy, intellectual property, and risk management.
- To explore stakeholder perspectives on support, training, and compliance mechanisms associated with AI educational tools.
- To propose recommendations for standardized contractual frameworks tailored to the Indian education sector.

RESEARCH QUESTIONS

1. What are the primary contractual challenges encountered by Indian educational institutions and AI developers in AI technology adoption?
2. How do stakeholders perceive liability allocation for AI errors, biases, and data breaches?
3. What regulatory uncertainties affect contractual formulations in AI educational technologies?
4. To what extent do existing contracts address ethical concerns such as bias, fairness, and user consent?
5. What support and training gaps influence effective AI integration in Indian educational settings?

HYPOTHESIS

H1: Ambiguities in contractual terms and unclear liability provisions significantly hinder the adoption of AI educational technologies in India.

H2: Stakeholders perceive current regulatory frameworks as insufficient to address the unique challenges of AI deployment in education.

H3: Enhanced contractual clarity and incorporation of ethical safeguards positively influence stakeholder trust and willingness to adopt AI technologies.

SCOPE AND LIMITATIONS OF THE STUDY

The study focuses on contractual and liability issues related to AI educational technologies within the Indian education sector, encompassing public and private institutions, AI developers, educators, and students. It examines legal, ethical, and operational dimensions through qualitative and quantitative empirical methods.

Limitations include potential variability in stakeholder responses due to regional and institutional diversity, evolving regulatory environments that may change post-study, and the exclusion of AI applications outside formal educational settings or beyond the Indian jurisdiction.

RESEARCH METHOD AND DESIGN

Research Design

The study employs a descriptive research design aimed at systematically exploring and explaining contractual and liability issues associated with AI educational technologies within the Indian education sector. This design facilitates detailed examination of stakeholder perceptions, regulatory challenges, and ethical considerations in a real-world context.

Nature of the Study

The research is empirical and mixed-methods in nature, combining quantitative data from structured surveys with qualitative insights from open-ended responses. This approach enables comprehensive understanding of both measurable trends and nuanced stakeholder experiences.

Population

The population includes AI developers, educational administrators, teachers, and students engaged with AI educational technologies across India. This diverse group represents the key actors involved in AI deployment, usage, and governance in education.

Sample Frame

The sampling frame comprises institutions and individuals from various geographic regions and institutional types, including public universities, private colleges, and informal coaching centers. This diversity ensures the sample reflects the heterogeneity of the Indian education sector.

Sample Size Determination

Sample size is calculated using Cochran's formula for estimating proportions, adjusted for finite population correction where applicable, targeting approximately 300 respondents. This size balances the need for statistical power with practical constraints of data collection.

n_0 = \frac{Z^2 p(1-p)}{e^2}

Cochran formula determines the minimum number of respondents required when estimating population proportions.

n_0 = required sample size
Z = Z score for the chosen confidence level
p = estimated population proportion
e = acceptable margin of error
Using common research parameters
Confidence level = 95 percent
Z = 1.96

Estimated proportion $p = 0.5$
Margin of error $e \approx 0.056$
Substituting the values
$n_0 = (1.96^2 \times 0.5 \times 0.5) / (0.056^2)$
$n_0 \approx 300$
Therefore, the calculated minimum sample size equals approximately 300 respondents.

Sample Size

The final sample consists of roughly 300 participants distributed across stakeholder categories to ensure representativeness and sufficient data for meaningful analysis. The total sample size is 300 respondents distributed equally across the four South Indian states: Tamil Nadu, Karnataka, Andhra Pradesh, and Telangana.

Each state contributes 75 respondents, equally divided among the four stakeholder categories: AI developers, educational administrators, teachers, and students (25 each).

Table 1. Sample Size of the study

S.No	State	Stakeholder Category	Sample Representation (Number of Respondents)	Percentage of Total Sample (%)
1	**Tamil Nadu**	AI Developers	25	8.3
		Educational Administrators	25	8.3
		Teachers	25	8.3
		Students	25	8.3
2	**Karnataka**	AI Developers	25	8.3
		Educational Administrators	25	8.3
		Teachers	25	8.3
		Students	25	8.3
3	**Andhra Pradesh**	AI Developers	25	8.3
		Educational Administrators	25	8.3
		Teachers	25	8.3
		Students	25	8.3
4	**Telangana**	AI Developers	25	8.3
		Educational Administrators	25	8.3
		Teachers	25	8.3
		Students	25	8.3
	Total		300	100

Sampling Technique

A stratified random sampling technique is employed, stratifying by stakeholder group and institutional type. This method ensures proportional representation and enhances the generalizability of results.

Geographical Area

geographical area cover under the study south Indian states such as Tamil Nadu, Karnatak, Andhra Pradesh and Telangana from each state sample representation has to take.

Sources of Data

Data sources include both primary and secondary data. Primary data is collected directly from respondents through an online survey. Secondary data comprises academic literature, government policies, legal statutes, and industry reports relevant to AI in education and contractual frameworks.

Primary and Secondary Data

Primary data captures current stakeholder experiences and perceptions, while secondary data provides contextual background, theoretical grounding, and regulatory insights.

Data Collection through Online Survey

An online survey instrument is administered to the selected sample, allowing efficient, wide-reaching data collection across diverse regions and institutions.

Pilot Study

A pilot study involving 30 participants from each stakeholder group is conducted to test the survey's clarity, reliability, and validity. Feedback from this pilot informs refinement of the questionnaire to enhance contextual relevance and comprehension.

Instrument of Data Collection

The main instrument is a structured questionnaire comprising multiple sections designed to capture demographic data, contractual clarity, liability perceptions, regulatory compliance, ethical considerations, and support and training aspects.

Questionnaire and Its Sections

The questionnaire includes:

1. Demographic information (age, role, institution type)
2. Contractual clarity (items assessing understanding and satisfaction with contract terms)

3. Liability perceptions (views on responsibility allocation for AI errors and breaches)
4. Regulatory compliance (awareness and impact of legal frameworks)
5. Ethical considerations (bias, fairness, consent)
6. Support and training (availability and adequacy of user assistance)

Scale Development from Previous Studies and Review of Literature

Likert-scale items and constructs are adapted from validated scales in AI adoption, legal studies, and educational technology research. These are contextualized for the Indian educational and legal environment through a thorough literature review.

Table 2. Scale Development of the Questionnaire

S. No.	Nature of Variable	Number of Questions	Method of Development	Source of Reference
1	**Contractual Clarity**	5	Items adapted from contract governance and technology adoption literature; refined through expert review and contextualized to Indian legal and educational settings	Pasquale (2015); Kerr & Earle (2022); UGC (2020)
2	**Compliance and Regulatory Risks**	5	Items derived from regulatory compliance and data protection studies; aligned with Indian educational and data protection laws	IT Act, 2000; DPDP Act, 2023; OECD (2019)
3	**Ethical and Social Considerations**	5	Items developed from AI ethics, fairness, and inclusivity frameworks; contextualized for education and Indian social diversity	UNESCO (2021); Binns (2018); Selwyn (2019)
4	**Maintenance and Support**	5	Scale items adapted from technology support and system sustainability literature; validated through pilot testing	OECD (2019); Selwyn (2019)
5	**Stakeholder Trust**	5	Items adapted from trust and technology acceptance models; modified for AI governance and contractual assurance contexts	Gefen et al. (2003); Floridi et al. (2018)
6	**Willingness to Adopt AI Technologies**	5	Items adapted from Technology Acceptance Model (TAM) and AI adoption literature; contextualized to educational settings	Davis (1989); Venkatesh et al. (2003); Selwyn (2019)

Tools of Data Analysis

Data analysis is performed using IBM SPSS Statistics and Microsoft Excel, facilitating both descriptive and inferential statistical procedures.

Statistical Techniques Used

1. Descriptive statistics (means, frequencies, percentages) summarize respondent characteristics and perceptions.
2. Correlation and Regression analysis tests hypothesized relationships among variables.
3. Factor analysis validates the questionnaire's underlying constructs.

Identification of Variables

Independent variables: contractual clarity, regulatory compliance, ethical safeguards, support mechanisms.

Dependent variables: stakeholder trust and willingness to adopt AI technologies

Specification of Independent and Dependent Variables

Independent variables represent factors influencing adoption and trust, while dependent variables capture outcomes related to user acceptance and perceived responsibility.

Hypothesized Research Model

The model posits that enhanced contractual clarity, robust regulatory compliance, and strong ethical safeguards positively influence stakeholder trust and willingness to adopt AI educational technologies.

ANALYSIS AND DISCUSSION

Table 3. Descriptive Analysis of Contractual Clarity (N = 300)

Statement	Strongly Disagree	Disagree	Neutral	Agree	Strongly Agree	Mean
Roles and responsibilities of all parties in AI educational technology contracts are clearly defined	20	38	62	118	62	3.55
Contracts explicitly specify the intended use cases of AI tools	17	41	64	116	62	3.55
Limitations of AI technologies are clearly stated in the contracts	24	46	70	106	54	3.40
Data privacy provisions comply with Indian data protection laws	18	39	67	112	64	3.55
Intellectual property rights related to AI technologies and educational content are clearly addressed	21	44	69	108	58	3.46

The table 3 shows that the majority of respondents selected agree or strongly agree across the five statements. Mean values range from 3.40 to 3.55, indicating that respondents generally perceive a moderate level of contractual clarity in AI educational technology agreements. The highest perception is related to clearly defined roles, intended use of AI tools, and compliance with data protection laws, while slightly lower agreement appears in the statement related to clearly explaining limitations of AI technologies.

Table 4. Descriptive Analysis of Compliance and Regulatory Risks (N = 300)

Statement	Strongly Disagree	Disagree	Neutral	Agree	Strongly Agree	Mean
AI educational technologies comply with academic standards set by Indian regulatory bodies	18	40	66	116	60	3.53
Contracts include provisions that anticipate changes in data protection laws such as the Personal Data Protection Bill	22	44	70	108	56	3.44
Contracts mandate transparency and explainability of AI decision making processes	20	42	64	112	62	3.51
Regular audits of AI systems are required by contractual agreements	24	48	72	104	52	3.37
Contracts ensure AI technologies meet ethical and legal standards in India	19	39	68	114	60	3.52

The descriptive results (table 4) indicate that most respondents agree that AI educational technology contracts address regulatory and compliance requirements. Mean scores range from 3.37 to 3.53, which reflects a moderate level of agreement among the 300 respondents. The highest level of agreement appears in statements related to compliance with academic standards and ethical legal requirements, while slightly lower agreement is observed in the requirement for regular AI system audits and anticipation of future regulatory changes. Overall, the findings suggest that respondents perceive contractual provisions related to regulatory compliance and legal standards to be reasonably present but still open to improvement.

Table 5. Descriptive Analysis of Ethical Safeguards (N = 300)

Statement	Strongly Disagree	Disagree	Neutral	Agree	Strongly Agree	Mean
Contracts include provisions to regularly test and mitigate biases in AI systems	23	45	69	108	55	3.42
User consent for data collection and AI interventions is clearly obtained and documented through contracts	18	38	63	116	65	3.57
AI educational technologies are required by contract to be accessible to learners with disabilities	21	42	70	110	57	3.47
Ethical considerations are prioritized in contractual agreements for AI deployment	20	40	66	114	60	3.51
Contracts promote fairness and inclusivity in AI educational technologies	19	37	68	115	61	3.54

The descriptive analysis (table 5) shows that respondents generally perceive the presence of ethical safeguards in AI educational technology contracts. Mean values range from 3.42 to 3.57, indicating moderate agreement among the 300 respondents. The highest agreement appears in the statement related to user consent for data collection and AI interventions, suggesting that respondents recognize the importance of consent documentation in contracts. Slightly lower agreement is observed in provisions related to testing and mitigating AI bias, indicating some uncertainty regarding the effectiveness or clarity of such safeguards. Overall, the results suggest that ethical considerations, fairness, and inclusivity are moderately addressed within contractual agreements governing AI educational technologies.

Table 6. Descriptive Analysis of Support Mechanisms (N = 300)

Statement	**Strongly Disagree**	**Disagree**	**Neutral**	**Agree**	**Strongly Agree**	**Mean**
Contracts specify the scope and frequency of AI system maintenance activities	22	43	68	110	57	3.46
Adequate user training is mandated by contracts to ensure effective AI adoption	20	41	65	114	60	3.51
Contracts require ongoing technical support for educators and students using AI tools	19	39	66	116	60	3.53
Support services provided under contracts are sufficient to address user issues promptly	24	47	72	105	52	3.38
Training programs cover ethical use and data privacy related to AI educational technologies	21	40	67	112	60	3.50

The descriptive results (table 6) indicate that respondents generally perceive the presence of support mechanisms in contracts governing AI educational technologies. Mean scores range from 3.38 to 3.53, reflecting moderate agreement among the 300 respondents. The highest agreement appears in statements related to ongoing technical support and mandatory training for users, suggesting that respondents recognize the importance of institutional support for effective AI adoption. Slightly lower agreement is observed regarding the promptness and adequacy of support services, indicating that some respondents feel improvements may be required in the responsiveness of support systems. Overall, the findings suggest that maintenance activities, training programs, and technical support provisions are reasonably addressed in contractual agreements related to AI educational technologies.

Table 7. Descriptive Analysis of Stakeholder Trust (N = 300)

Statement	**Strongly Disagree**	**Disagree**	**Neutral**	**Agree**	**Strongly Agree**	**Mean**
I trust that AI educational technologies deployed in my institution operate reliably and securely	19	40	65	116	60	3.53
The contractual provisions in place make me confident in the responsible use of AI tools	21	42	68	110	59	3.48
I believe that developers and institutions are accountable for the outcomes produced by AI systems	18	37	63	118	64	3.58
Transparency in AI decision making increases my trust in these technologies	17	35	60	120	68	3.62
I feel assured that my data privacy is protected when using AI educational technologies	22	44	70	108	56	3.44

The descriptive results (table 7) show that respondents generally demonstrate a moderate level of trust in AI educational technologies used within their institutions. Mean values range from 3.44 to 3.62, indicating that most respondents tend to agree with statements related to reliability, accountability, transparency, and data protection. The highest level of agreement is observed in the statement related to transparency in AI decision making, suggesting that openness and explainability significantly influence trust. Slightly lower agreement appears in perceptions related to data privacy protection, indicating that some respondents remain cautious about how personal data is handled by AI systems. Overall, the findings suggest that stakeholder trust in AI educational technologies is reasonably positive but still dependent on clear accountability and transparency mechanisms.

CORRELATION ANALYSIS BETWEEN THE INDEPENDENT VARIABLES AND STAKEHOLDER TRUST

A correlation analysis was conducted to examine the relationship between the independent variables' contractual clarity, regulatory compliance, ethical safeguards, and support mechanisms with the dependent variable stakeholder trust. The analysis used Pearson correlation for the responses of 300 participants.

Table 8. **Correlation Analysis between the independent variables and stakeholder trust**

Variables	Contractual Clarity	Regulatory Compliance	Ethical Safeguards	Support Mechanisms	Stakeholder Trust
Contractual Clarity	1	0.54	0.48	0.51	0.63
Regulatory Compliance	0.54	1	0.57	0.49	0.60
Ethical Safeguards	0.48	0.57	1	0.46	0.58
Support Mechanisms	0.51	0.49	0.46	1	0.55
Stakeholder Trust	0.63	0.60	0.58	0.55	1

The results indicate that all independent variables show a positive correlation with stakeholder trust. Contractual clarity has the strongest relationship with stakeholder trust with a correlation coefficient of 0.63. Regulatory compliance also shows a strong positive relationship with stakeholder trust at 0.60. Ethical safeguards demonstrate a moderate positive relationship with stakeholder trust at 0.58, while support mechanisms show a correlation of 0.55.

The inter correlations among the independent variables are moderate and positive, indicating that these governance and operational factors tend to coexist within AI educational technology environments. Overall, the correlation results suggest that improvements in contractual clarity, regulatory compliance, ethical safeguards, and support mechanisms are associated with higher levels of stakeholder trust in AI educational technologies.

REGRESSION ANALYSIS

Multiple regression analysis was conducted to determine the extent to which contractual clarity, regulatory compliance, ethical safeguards, and support mechanisms predict stakeholder trust among the 300 respondents.

Table 9. The regression model for the independent variables and stakeholder trust

Model	R	R Square	Adjusted R Square	Std Error
1	0.72	0.52	0.51	0.46

The regression model shows an R value of 0.72, indicating a strong overall relationship between the independent variables and stakeholder trust. The R Square value of 0.52 suggests that 52 percent of the variation in stakeholder trust can be explained by contractual clarity, regulatory compliance, ethical safeguards, and support mechanisms.

Table 10. ANOVA test results between the independent variables and stakeholder trust

Source	Sum of Squares	df	Mean Square	F	Significance
Regression	68.40	4	17.10	81.32	0.000
Residual	63.10	295	0.21		
Total	131.50	299			

The ANOVA results show that the regression model is statistically significant with an F value of 81.32 and a significance level less than 0.001. This indicates that the independent variables collectively have a significant effect on stakeholder trust.

Table 11. Regression coefficient between the independent variables and stakeholder trust

Variable	Unstandardized B	Standard Error	Beta	t	Significance
Constant	0.84	0.18		4.67	0.000
Contractual Clarity	0.31	0.05	0.35	6.20	0.000
Regulatory Compliance	0.27	0.06	0.29	5.02	0.000
Ethical Safeguards	0.22	0.05	0.25	4.40	0.000
Support Mechanisms	0.18	0.05	0.20	3.65	0.001

The regression results indicate that all four independent variables have a positive and statistically significant effect on stakeholder trust. Contractual clarity shows the strongest influence on stakeholder trust, followed by regulatory compliance, ethical safeguards, and support mechanisms.

Overall, the regression findings suggest that improving contractual transparency, ensuring regulatory compliance, strengthening ethical safeguards, and providing effective support mechanisms significantly contribute to building stakeholder trust in AI educational technologies.

CORRELATION ANALYSIS BETWEEN THE INDEPENDENT VARIABLES AND WILLINGNESS TO ADOPT AI TECHNOLOGIES

A Pearson correlation analysis was conducted to examine the relationship between the independent variables' contractual clarity, regulatory compliance, ethical safeguards, and support mechanisms with the dependent variable willingness to adopt AI technologies. The analysis was based on responses collected from 300 participants.

Table 12. Correlation Analysis between the independent variables and willingness to adopt AI technologies

Variables	Contractual Clarity	Regulatory Compliance	Ethical Safeguards	Support Mechanisms	Willingness to Adopt AI Technologies
Contractual Clarity	1	0.52	0.47	0.50	0.61
Regulatory Compliance	0.52	1	0.55	0.48	0.59
Ethical Safeguards	0.47	0.55	1	0.46	0.56
Support Mechanisms	0.50	0.48	0.46	1	0.58
Willingness to Adopt AI Technologies	0.61	0.59	0.56	0.58	1

The correlation results indicate positive relationships between all independent variables and the dependent variable willingness to adopt AI technologies. Contractual clarity shows the strongest relationship with willingness to adopt AI technologies with a correlation coefficient of 0.61. This suggests that when contracts clearly define responsibilities, rights, and operational terms related to AI educational technologies, stakeholders are more likely to accept and adopt these technologies.

Regulatory compliance also demonstrates a strong positive relationship with willingness to adopt AI technologies with a correlation coefficient of 0.59. This indicates that adherence to academic standards and legal regulations increases stakeholder confidence in adopting AI systems.

Ethical safeguards show a moderate positive correlation with willingness to adopt AI technologies with a coefficient of 0.56. This suggests that provisions addressing fairness, bias mitigation, accessibility, and ethical use of AI play an important role in encouraging adoption.

Support mechanisms display a correlation coefficient of 0.58 with willingness to adopt AI technologies. This indicates that the availability of training, technical assistance, and maintenance support contributes to users feeling more comfortable adopting AI based educational tools.

The correlations among the independent variables are also moderate and positive, ranging between 0.46 and 0.55. This indicates that institutions that maintain clear contractual terms often also emphasize regulatory compliance, ethical safeguards, and strong support mechanisms.

Overall, the findings suggest that stronger governance structures and operational support related to AI educational technologies are associated with higher willingness among stakeholders to adopt these technologies.

REGRESSION ANALYSIS

Multiple regression analysis was conducted to examine the influence of contractual clarity, regulatory compliance, ethical safeguards, and support mechanisms on the dependent variable willingness to adopt AI technologies among 300 respondents.

Table 13. The regression model for between the independent variables and willingness to adopt AI technologies

Model	R	R Square	Adjusted R Square	Std Error of Estimate
1	0.74	0.55	0.54	0.44

The model shows a strong relationship between the independent variables and willingness to adopt AI technologies. The R value of 0.74 indicates a strong association between the predictors and the dependent variable. The R Square value of 0.55 indicates that 55 percent of the variation in willingness to adopt AI technologies is explained by contractual clarity, regulatory compliance, ethical safeguards, and support mechanisms.

Table 14. ANOVA test results between the independent variables and willingness to adopt AI technologies

Source	Sum of Squares	df	Mean Square	F	Significance
Regression	72.80	4	18.20	93.45	0.000
Residual	59.10	295	0.20		
Total	131.90	299			

The ANOVA results show that the regression model is statistically significant. The F value of 93.45 with a significance level of 0.000 indicates that the independent variables collectively have a significant effect on willingness to adopt AI technologies.

Table 15. Regression coefficient between the independent variables and willingness to adopt AI technologies

Variable	Unstandardized B	Standard Error	Beta	t	Significance
Constant	0.76	0.17		4.47	0.000
Contractual Clarity	0.33	0.05	0.36	6.58	0.000
Regulatory Compliance	0.28	0.06	0.30	5.18	0.000
Ethical Safeguards	0.21	0.05	0.24	4.36	0.000
Support Mechanisms	0.19	0.05	0.21	3.87	0.000

The regression results indicate that all four independent variables have a positive and statistically significant impact on willingness to adopt AI technologies. Contractual clarity has the strongest influence on adoption willingness, followed by regulatory compliance, ethical safeguards, and support mechanisms.

Overall, the findings indicate that clear contractual frameworks, adherence to regulatory standards, strong ethical protections, and effective support structures play an important role in increasing stakeholders' willingness to adopt AI technologies in educational environments.

FINDINGS

The study examined contractual and liability issues in AI educational technologies using responses from 300 stakeholders including AI developers, educational administrators, teachers, and students across South Indian states. The analysis reveals several important findings regarding contractual governance, regulatory compliance, ethical safeguards, support mechanisms, and their influence on stakeholder trust and willingness to adopt AI technologies.

First, the descriptive analysis indicates that stakeholders perceive a moderate level of contractual clarity in AI educational technology agreements. Respondents generally agreed that contracts define roles and responsibilities, specify intended uses of AI tools, and address data privacy and intellectual property rights. However, slightly lower agreement was observed regarding the clarity of AI system limitations. This suggests that while contractual frameworks exist, they may not fully explain the technological constraints and risks associated with AI systems.

Second, the study found that compliance with regulatory requirements is moderately recognized in existing contracts. Respondents indicated that contracts generally ensure adherence to academic standards and ethical legal requirements. However, provisions related to anticipating future regulatory changes and conducting regular AI audits received comparatively lower agreement. This reflects a need for more proactive regulatory compliance mechanisms within contractual arrangements.

Third, ethical safeguards were perceived as moderately integrated within contractual agreements. Stakeholders acknowledged the importance of obtaining user consent, promoting fairness and inclusivity, and ensuring accessibility for learners with disabilities. Nevertheless, provisions related to bias testing and mitigation were perceived as relatively weaker. This indicates that ethical governance mechanisms for AI systems require stronger contractual articulation and implementation.

Fourth, support mechanisms such as technical assistance, user training, and system maintenance were generally acknowledged by respondents. Contracts appear to mandate ongoing technical support and training programs for users. However, some respondents expressed concerns regarding the promptness and adequacy of support services, suggesting that operational support structures need improvement.

Fifth, the analysis revealed a moderate level of stakeholder trust in AI educational technologies. Respondents indicated confidence in the reliability and accountability of AI systems when transparency and clear contractual provisions are present. Transparency in AI decision making was identified as a key factor influencing trust, while concerns about data privacy protection slightly reduced overall trust levels.

Sixth, correlation analysis shows that contractual clarity, regulatory compliance, ethical safeguards, and support mechanisms are positively associated with stakeholder trust. Contractual clarity demonstrated the strongest correlation with stakeholder trust, followed by regulatory compliance, ethical safeguards, and support mechanisms.

Seventh, regression analysis confirmed that all four independent variables significantly influence stakeholder trust. Contractual clarity emerged as the most influential predictor, indicating that clearly defined contractual provisions play a crucial role in building trust among stakeholders.

Finally, similar patterns were observed in relation to willingness to adopt AI technologies. All independent variables showed positive correlations with adoption willingness. Regression analysis also demonstrated that contractual clarity, regulatory compliance, ethical safeguards, and support mechanisms significantly influence stakeholders' willingness to adopt AI technologies, with contractual clarity again showing the strongest influence.

Overall, the findings demonstrate that strong contractual governance and institutional support mechanisms significantly influence both trust and adoption of AI educational technologies in the Indian education sector.

SUGGESTIONS

Based on the findings, several measures can be recommended to strengthen contractual governance and responsible adoption of AI educational technologies.

Educational institutions and technology providers should develop standardized contractual frameworks that clearly define roles, responsibilities, and liability provisions for AI system performance. Such contracts should explicitly address algorithmic risks, system limitations, and accountability for AI errors.

Contracts should incorporate stronger data governance provisions to ensure compliance with evolving data protection regulations such as the Digital Personal Data Protection Act. Clear policies regarding data ownership, consent, storage, and breach response should be included in contractual agreements.

Institutions and developers should establish contractual provisions requiring regular auditing and monitoring of AI systems. Independent audits can help identify algorithmic bias, system errors, and compliance gaps, thereby improving transparency and accountability.

Contracts should mandate comprehensive ethical governance mechanisms. These should include bias testing, fairness assessments, accessibility standards, and explicit protections for vulnerable users such as students with disabilities.

Technology providers and institutions should strengthen support mechanisms by offering continuous user training, technical assistance, and maintenance services. Effective support structures will improve user confidence and facilitate smoother integration of AI technologies.

Regulatory bodies such as the University Grants Commission and AICTE should develop sector specific guidelines for AI deployment in education. These guidelines can support institutions in drafting legally robust and ethically responsible contracts.

IMPLICATIONS OF THE STUDY

The study has several important theoretical, practical, and policy implications.

From a theoretical perspective, the study contributes to the literature on AI governance by highlighting the importance of contractual structures in managing technological risks and liability issues in educational environments. It extends existing research by providing empirical evidence on how contractual clarity and ethical safeguards influence stakeholder trust and technology adoption.

From a practical perspective, the findings provide guidance for educational institutions and AI developers in designing effective contractual agreements. Institutions can use these insights to negotiate contracts that clearly define responsibilities, address data protection risks, and ensure accountability for AI system outcomes.

From a policy perspective, the study highlights the need for clearer regulatory frameworks governing AI technologies in education. Policymakers can use the findings to develop legal guidelines that support responsible AI deployment while protecting student rights and institutional integrity.

The study also has implications for institutional governance. Universities and educational organizations must develop internal policies and oversight mechanisms that complement contractual provisions and ensure responsible AI usage.

SCOPE FOR FUTURE RESEARCH

Although the study provides valuable insights, several opportunities remain for future research.

Future studies may examine AI contractual governance in other regions of India or compare practices across different countries to understand how regulatory environments influence AI adoption in education.

Further research can explore sector specific liability frameworks for AI systems, particularly focusing on legal doctrines such as product liability, negligence, and algorithmic accountability.

Researchers may also investigate the long-term impact of AI technologies on educational outcomes, academic decision making, and institutional governance.

Another area for future study is the role of emerging technologies such as generative AI, automated assessment systems, and predictive learning analytics in shaping new contractual and ethical challenges.

Qualitative research involving in depth interviews with policymakers, legal experts, and AI developers could also provide deeper insights into practical challenges in drafting and implementing AI related contracts.

Finally, future research could develop standardized contractual models or legal frameworks specifically tailored for AI educational technologies.

CONCLUSION

The integration of artificial intelligence into educational technologies has created significant opportunities for improving teaching, learning, and institutional efficiency. However, it has also introduced complex contractual and liability challenges that must be addressed to ensure responsible and sustainable adoption.

This study examined contractual clarity, regulatory compliance, ethical safeguards, and support mechanisms as key governance factors influencing stakeholder trust and willingness to adopt AI technologies in the Indian education sector. The findings demonstrate that these factors play a critical role in shaping stakeholder perceptions and acceptance of AI systems.

Among the examined variables, contractual clarity emerged as the most influential factor affecting both stakeholder trust and adoption willingness. Clear contractual agreements that define responsibilities, liability provisions, and operational standards significantly enhance confidence in AI technologies. Regulatory compliance, ethical safeguards, and institutional support mechanisms also contribute to building trust and encouraging adoption.

Despite these positive relationships, the study identified several gaps in existing contractual frameworks, particularly in relation to bias mitigation, AI system auditing, and data protection governance. Addressing these gaps requires stronger collaboration among educational institutions, technology developers, and regulatory authorities.

Ultimately, the responsible integration of AI in education depends on the development of transparent, legally robust, and ethically grounded contractual frameworks. By strengthening governance structures and institutional support mechanisms, stakeholders can harness the benefits of AI technologies while minimizing legal risks and protecting the interests of learners and educators.

REFERENCES

All India Council for Technical Education. (2020). *Approval process handbook*. AICTE.

Binns, R. (2018). Fairness in machine learning: Lessons from political philosophy. *Proceedings of the 2018 Conference on Fairness, Accountability and Transparency, 81*, 149–159. https://doi.org/DOI: 10.1145/3287560.3287598

Calo, R. (2017). Artificial intelligence policy: A primer and roadmap. *U.C. Davis Law Review, 51*(2), 399–435.

Consumer Protection Act, 2019, No. 35, Acts of Parliament, India.

Data Protection Board of India. (2023). *Digital Personal Data Protection Act, 2023*. Government of India.

Davis, F. D. (1989). Perceived usefulness, perceived ease of use, and user acceptance of information technology. *Management Information Systems Quarterly, 13*(3), 319–340. DOI: 10.2307/249008

Edwards, L., & Veale, M. (2017). Slave to the algorithm? Why a "right to an explanation" is probably not the remedy you are looking for. *Duke Law & Technology Review, 16*(1), 18–84. DOI: 10.31228/osf.io/97upg

European Commission. (2021). *Proposal for a regulation laying down harmonised rules on artificial intelligence*. Artificial Intelligence Act.

Floridi, L., Cowls, J., Beltrametti, M., Chatila, R., Chazerand, P., Dignum, V., Luetge, C., Madelin, R., Pagallo, U., Rossi, F., Schafer, B., Valcke, P., & Vayena, E. (2018). AI4People—An ethical framework for a good AI society. *Minds and Machines, 28*(4), 689–707. DOI: 10.1007/s11023-018-9482-5 PMID: 30930541

Gefen, D., Karahanna, E., & Straub, D. W. (2003). Trust and TAM in online shopping: An integrated model. *Management Information Systems Quarterly, 27*(1), 51–90. DOI: 10.2307/30036519

Government of India. (2020). National [Ministry of Education.]. *Educational Policy*, •••, 2020.

Holmes, W., Bialik, M., & Fadel, C. (2019). *Artificial intelligence in education: Promises and implications for teaching and learning*. Center for Curriculum Redesign.

Information Technology Act, 2000, No. 21, Acts of Parliament, India.

Kerr, I., & Earle, J. (2022). Prediction, preemption, and policy: Artificial intelligence and the challenges of accountability. *Law, Innovation and Technology, 14*(1), 1–26. DOI: 10.1080/17579961.2022.2036955

Organisation for Economic Co-operation and Development. (2019). *OECD principles on artificial intelligence*.

Pasquale, F. (2015). *The black box society: The secret algorithms that control money and information*. Harvard University Press. DOI: 10.4159/harvard.9780674736061

Selwyn, N. (2019). *Should robots replace teachers? Artificial intelligence and the future of education*. Polity Press.

Surden, H. (2019). Artificial intelligence and law: An overview. *Georgia State University Law Review, 35*(4), 1305–1335.

UNESCO. (2021). *Recommendation on the ethics of artificial intelligence.*

University Grants Commission. (2020). *Guidelines on academic integrity and prevention of plagiarism.* UGC.

Venkatesh, V., Morris, M. G., Davis, G. B., & Davis, F. D. (2003). User acceptance of information technology: Toward a unified view. *Management Information Systems Quarterly, 27*(3), 425–478. DOI: 10.2307/30036540

Williamson, B., & Eynon, R. (2020). Historical threads, missing links, and future directions in AI in education. *Learning, Media and Technology, 45*(3), 223–235. DOI: 10.1080/17439884.2020.1798995

Chapter 12
A Systematic Review of AI-Powered Assessment in the Global South:
Opportunities and Challenges in Resource-Constrained Higher Education Contexts

Nontobeko Prudence Khumalo
http://orcid.org/0000-0002-0792-8771
University of South Africa, South Africa

Ntandokamenzi Penelope Dlamini
http://orcid.org/0000-0002-6152-5607
University of South Africa, South Africa

ABSTRACT

The findings show that although AI holds considerable promise for enhancing assessment efficiency and feedback quality, its actual impact is heavily conditioned by infrastructural deficits, ethical issues, and uneven institutional capacity across the Global South. This review offers evidence-informed insights into how AI is shaping higher education assessment and underscores the importance of contextually responsive strategies that confront structural inequities. It also guides policy and institutional decision-making by foregrounding fair and sustainable approaches to integrating AI into assessment. Additionally, the study outlines key avenues for future research on AI-mediated assessment in under-resourced higher education systems.

INTRODUCTION

Assessment is widely recognised in the literature as an inseparable part of the teaching and learning process, since it is only through assessment that lecturers are able to make informed judgements about whether learning has actually taken place and the extent to which intended learning outcomes have been

DOI: 10.4018/979-8-3373-8939-4.ch012

achieved. It also provides feedback to both lecturers and students. Traditional assessment methods, such as multiple-choice questions, short-answer tasks, and essay-based examinations, have long dominated higher education assessment practices as tools for inferring student knowledge. While these methods are well-established and widely accepted, the literature consistently highlights several important limitations that call into question their continued adequacy in contemporary educational environments. These assessment approaches are often described as time-consuming and labour-intensive, particularly for lecturers already managing heavy teaching loads and multiple institutional responsibilities. The accelerated advancement of digital technologies has transformed educational practices, with Artificial Intelligence (AI) emerging as a vital innovation in contemporary teaching and learning. AI-based systems are increasingly used to facilitate personalized learning routes, foster learner engagement, and modernise or automate pedagogical and administrative processes. In the context of assessment, AI has enabled the design and implementation of innovative frameworks that provide real-time, formative feedback, adapt to individual learners' needs, and generate insights into student performance. These AI-enabled assessment mechanisms are transforming traditional assessment practices and creating new possibilities for improving learning outcomes. This study used a systematic review approach to examine the use of AI-powered assessment in higher education across the Global South.

LITERATURE REVIEW

Artificial intelligence (AI) represents a potentially transformative development in education, with the capacity not only to support but in some cases to partially automate aspects of conventional assessment practice (Cope, Kalantzis, & Searsmith, 2021). In the literature, AI is broadly defined as a branch of computer science focused on developing systems capable of performing tasks that typically require human cognition, including reasoning, decision-making, perception, and problem-solving (Mintz & Brodie, 2019; Zhang & Lu, 2021). In the educational context, this has led to the emergence of concepts such as Educational Artificial Intelligence (EAI), which refers specifically to AI applications designed to enhance teaching, learning, and administrative processes (Isafani et al., 2025). Related developments are also described as smart education or smart classrooms, in which AI technologies are integrated into educational environments to support both instructional delivery and assessment practices (Ocaña-Fernández et al., 2019). Importantly, within this body of literature, AI is often positioned not simply as a tool for efficiency, but as a systemic innovation capable of reshaping how assessment is conceptualised and implemented in higher education.

A number of studies further emphasise the functional capabilities of AI in assessment contexts, particularly its ability to automate tasks that were traditionally performed by lecturers. Cope et al. (2021) argue that AI systems can generate assessment tasks, assist in selecting peer reviewers, and automate grading processes, thereby significantly reducing the administrative burden on lecturers. Empirical evidence from different international contexts, including Turkey, Australia, and South Korea, supports this view, with findings suggesting that AI adoption in assessment has been associated with improved efficiency, reduced workload, and faster feedback cycles for students (Başar & Şahin, 2021; Yang & Kyun, 2022). The acceleration of digital transformation during the COVID-19 pandemic further intensified these developments, as institutions increasingly relied on automated and online systems to maintain continuity in teaching and assessment. However, despite these advantages, a critical reading of this literature reveals that much of the dominant discourse is strongly oriented towards efficiency and technological optimisation, with comparatively less attention given to the pedagogical, ethical, and contextual implications of AI adoption in assessment practices.

Alongside this more optimistic narrative, an alternative strand of literature adopts a more critical stance, particularly regarding the uneven adoption of AI in education across global contexts. While some regions have made measurable progress in integrating digital technologies into education systems, scholars such as Ayanwale (2023) argue that many African and other Global South contexts continue to face significant structural barriers that limit the effective implementation of AI in education. These barriers include inadequate digital infrastructure, limited access to advanced technological tools, shortages of relevant technical and pedagogical expertise, and weak or inconsistently implemented policy frameworks (Ayentimi & Burgess, 2019; Vashchenko et al., 2018). From this perspective, the literature highlights a clear imbalance in global AI discourse, where assumptions about seamless adoption often reflect conditions in well-resourced environments rather than the realities of resource-constrained educational systems. This raises important questions about the extent to which AI-enabled assessment models developed in the Global North can be meaningfully transferred to, or sustained within, Global South contexts without significant adaptation.

The literature also highlights a range of pedagogical and ethical concerns associated with the growing use of AI in assessment. Several studies suggest that AI-enabled tools have contributed to growing concerns around academic integrity, particularly as students gain access to systems capable of generating assignments, essays, and examination responses with minimal human input (Mutongoza & Olawale, 2022; Surahman & Wang, 2022). Rather than solely enhancing learning, AI is sometimes perceived as enabling new forms of academic misconduct, raising questions about the validity and credibility of AI-mediated assessment processes. At the same time, other scholars caution that increased reliance on AI may reduce both student effort and lecturer engagement, contributing to what has been described as "pedagogical deskilling," where lecturers gradually lose confidence or competence in traditional assessment practices (Ifedayo, 2025). This concern is further reinforced by arguments that overreliance on AI may undermine the development of critical thinking, creativity, and problem-solving skills, thereby weakening core educational outcomes that assessment is intended to support (Omari et al., 2022; Mikalef, 2022). In this sense, the literature reflects a clear tension between AI as a tool for improvement and AI as a potential disruptor of foundational academic practices.

This literature highlights important systemic and operational challenges that influence the successful implementation of AI-powered assessment systems, particularly in resource-constrained environments. Issues such as the high cost of internet data, unstable connectivity, and inconsistent access to digital infrastructure are repeatedly identified as significant barriers, especially for students who rely on off-campus access for learning and assessment activities (Ifedayo, 2025). In addition, concerns around data privacy and sovereignty have become increasingly prominent, as AI systems often require the collection and storage of sensitive student data, including performance metrics and behavioural information (Isafani et al., 2025). These challenges indicate the need for clear institutional policies and regulatory frameworks that govern the ethical use of AI in education. Furthermore, several studies emphasise that the successful integration of AI in assessment is highly dependent on the readiness and capacity of academic staff, with targeted training and professional development identified as essential for building confidence and competence in using these technologies effectively (Ifedayo, 2025). Despite these insights, a consistent gap in the literature is the strong emphasis on technical implementation over pedagogical integration. Systematic reviews, such as that conducted by González-Calatayud et al. (2021), indicate that much of the existing research prioritises how AI systems function rather than how they meaningfully reshape assessment practices in educational contexts. This gap is particularly evident in studies focusing on the Global South, where contextual constraints are often underexplored. It is precisely within this gap that the present study positions itself by examining not only the implementation of AI-powered assessment but also the opportunities and challenges it presents in resource-constrained higher education environments.

THEORETICAL FRAMEWORK

This study is guided by the Unified Theory of Acceptance and Use of Technology (UTAUT), developed by Venkatesh et al. (2003), which offers a well-established lens for understanding how and why individuals and institutions adopt new technologies. The model is particularly useful for this study because it moves beyond purely technical explanations of technology use and instead foregrounds the social, organisational, and perceptual factors that shape adoption. In the context of AI-powered assessment in higher education, especially within resource-constrained environments in the Global South, UTAUT provides a structured way of interpreting why some institutions and lecturers are more willing or able to integrate these tools into assessment practices, while others remain hesitant or unable to do so despite recognising their potential benefits. This makes the framework highly suitable for making sense of the uneven and often complex patterns of AI adoption that emerge in the literature on educational technology and artificial intelligence in education (Venkatesh et al., 2003; Crompton & Burke, 2023).

At the core of UTAUT are four interrelated constructs: performance expectancy, effort expectancy, social influence, and facilitating conditions. Performance expectancy refers to the extent to which users believe that using a particular technology will enhance their job performance. In this study, this is closely linked to the perceived benefits of AI-powered assessment tools, such as improving grading efficiency, reducing lecturer workload, and enhancing the speed and quality of feedback provided to students, which are widely reported advantages in AI-in-education literature (Cope et al., 2021; Crompton & Burke, 2023). Effort expectancy relates to the perceived ease of using the technology, which is particularly important in higher education contexts where academic staff may lack advanced technical training or prior experience with AI systems (Mintz & Brodie, 2019). In such cases, even highly beneficial technologies may not be adopted if they are perceived as too complex, time-consuming, or difficult to integrate into existing assessment practices, a concern that is frequently highlighted in studies on educational technology adoption (Zhang & Lu, 2021; Ifedayo, 2025). The third construct, social influence, refers to the extent to which individuals perceive that important stakeholders, such as institutional leadership, colleagues, policy frameworks, or the broader academic community, expect or encourage the use of a particular technology. In relation to AI-powered assessment, this is evident in how universities are increasingly shaping expectations around digital transformation, often positioning AI as part of broader institutional innovation agendas (Makeleni et al., 2023; Ocaña-Fernández et al., 2019). However, the literature also suggests that social influence can operate in both enabling and constraining ways. While some institutions actively promote AI integration through policy direction and strategic priorities, others express caution due to concerns around academic integrity, ethical risks, and the reliability of AI-generated outputs (Mutongoza & Olawale, 2022; Surahman & Wang, 2022). This creates an environment where adoption decisions are not purely individual, but are strongly shaped by institutional culture, governance structures, and policy expectations. The fourth construct, facilitating conditions, is particularly significant for this study because it captures the extent to which organisational and technical infrastructure exists to support the use of technology. In the context of the Global South, this includes access to stable internet connectivity, availability of digital tools and platforms, institutional funding, technical support, and staff development opportunities. The literature consistently highlights that even when there is willingness to adopt AI-powered assessment systems, these facilitating conditions are often weak or unevenly distributed, which directly affects implementation capacity (Ayanwale, 2023; Ayentimi & Burgess, 2019). As a result, facilitating conditions provide an important explanatory layer for understanding why AI adoption remains inconsistent across higher education institutions in resource-constrained settings, despite global enthusiasm for such technologies (Vashchenko et al., 2018; Ifedayo, 2025).

While UTAUT provides a strong foundation for explaining technology acceptance and use at the individual and organisational level, this study also recognises that adoption of AI-powered assessment cannot be fully understood without considering broader structural inequalities. For this reason, the model is interpreted alongside insights from digital inequality perspectives, which emphasise the uneven distribution of technological access, infrastructure, and capabilities across different regions (van Dijk, 2020; Ayanwale, 2023). In the context of the Global South, these inequalities are particularly significant, as they determine not only whether technologies are adopted but also how they are experienced and sustained in practice. Issues such as high data costs, unstable connectivity, limited institutional capacity, and unequal access to devices shape technology adoption, often more than purely pedagogical or individual choices (Ifedayo, 2025; Ayanwale, 2023). By integrating these contextual realities with UTAUT, this study provides a more nuanced explanation of AI-powered assessment adoption, one that accounts for both human perceptions and the broader systemic conditions that shape educational practice.

METHODOLOGY

Research Design

This study used a systematic review approach to examine the use of AI-powered assessment in higher education across the Global South. A systematic review is well suited to this study as it allows for a structured and transparent synthesis of existing research, helping to identify patterns, gaps, and emerging insights in a rapidly developing field. Given the uneven development of digital infrastructure and institutional capacity across the Global South, this approach also supports a more nuanced understanding of how context shapes the adoption of AI in assessment. The review is guided by the following research questions:

RQ1: How are AI-powered assessment tools currently being implemented in higher education institutions across the Global South in resource-constrained contexts?

RQ2: What opportunities do AI-powered assessment systems offer for improving assessment quality, efficiency, and student outcomes in these contexts?

RQ3: What are the key technical, pedagogical, ethical, and infrastructural challenges affecting the adoption and effectiveness of AI-powered assessment in the Global South?

The review was guided by established systematic review principles and reported in line with PRISMA (Preferred Reporting Items for Systematic Reviews and Meta-Analyses) guidelines to ensure transparency and replicability.

Eligibility Criteria

This review focused on peer-reviewed journal articles published between 2015 and 2025, reflecting the period during which AI technologies became increasingly integrated into educational practices. Only empirical studies were included in order to ensure that the findings are grounded in observed data and real-world applications of AI in higher education assessment. Empirical studies provide evidence-based insights into how AI tools are implemented, experienced, and evaluated in practice, which the authors deem important in Global South contexts, where contextual realities such as infrastructure, access, and institutional capacity influence technology adoption. Conceptual and theoretical papers were therefore excluded because they do not provide direct evidence of implementation and measurable outcomes. Only articles published in English were included to ensure consistency in analysis.

Table 1. Inclusion criteria

Criterion	Details
Type of study	Original research, empirical studies
Publication type	Peer-reviewed journal articles
Language	English
Publication date range	2015-2025
Education level	Higher education
Context	Global South
Focus	AI-powered assessment

Studies were excluded if they focused on basic education (i.e., primary and/or secondary education), did not explicitly address assessment practices, or lacked an AI component. Non-peer-reviewed sources such as conference proceedings, theses, reports, and book chapters were excluded to maintain the academic rigor of the review. In this review, the Global South is understood to include low- and middle-income countries across regions such as Africa, Asia, Latin America, and parts of Oceania. These contexts are often characterised by resource constraints, infrastructural limitations, and inequalities, which are critical factors in understanding the adoption and implementation of AI in higher education assessment.

Data Sources and Search Strategy

A literature search was conducted across three databases: the Directory of Open Access Journals (DOAJ), ERIC (Education Resources Information Center), and African Journals Online (AJOL). These databases were deliberately selected to capture internationally indexed research and regionally grounded scholarship, particularly from African contexts that are often underrepresented in global databases. The search strategy used a combination of keywords and Boolean operators to refine results. Core search terms included variations of "artificial intelligence," "AI," "machine learning," "automated assessment," and "AI-powered assessment," combined with terms such as "higher education," "university," and "tertiary education." These were further paired with context-specific terms, including "Global South," "developing countries," "resource-constrained," "Africa," "Asia," and "Latin America." This approach ensured both conceptual relevance and contextual specificity in the retrieved studies. The search process yielded a total of 346 records across the three databases, comprising 130 records from DOAJ, 113 from ERIC, and 103 from AJOL.

Screening

The retrieved studies from the three databases (DOAJ, ERIC, and AJOL) were imported into ZOTERO reference management software to facilitate systematic organisation, deduplication, and screening. Zotero was used to manage the search results, ensuring that duplicate studies across the three databases were identified and removed before screening. The screening process was done in two stages. The first involved reviewing titles and abstracts to remove studies that were irrelevant, i.e., those that did not mention artificial intelligence-powered assessments in higher education in the Global South. Such articles that did not meet the inclusion criteria were excluded at this stage. The second stage involved a full-text screening of the remaining articles to confirm whether they met the inclusion criteria. Each article was examined carefully against the predefined inclusion and exclusion criteria, with particular attention to the presence of empirical evidence, relevance to higher education assessment, and contextual alignment with Global South settings. Where uncertainties arose, studies were carefully re-examined in relation to the research questions and inclusion criteria. The screening process followed a consistent set of criteria to ensure reliability. A PRISMA flow diagram was used to document the screening process and provide a transparent account of how the final set of studies was selected.

Figure 1. PRISMA flow diagram (Page et al.,2021)

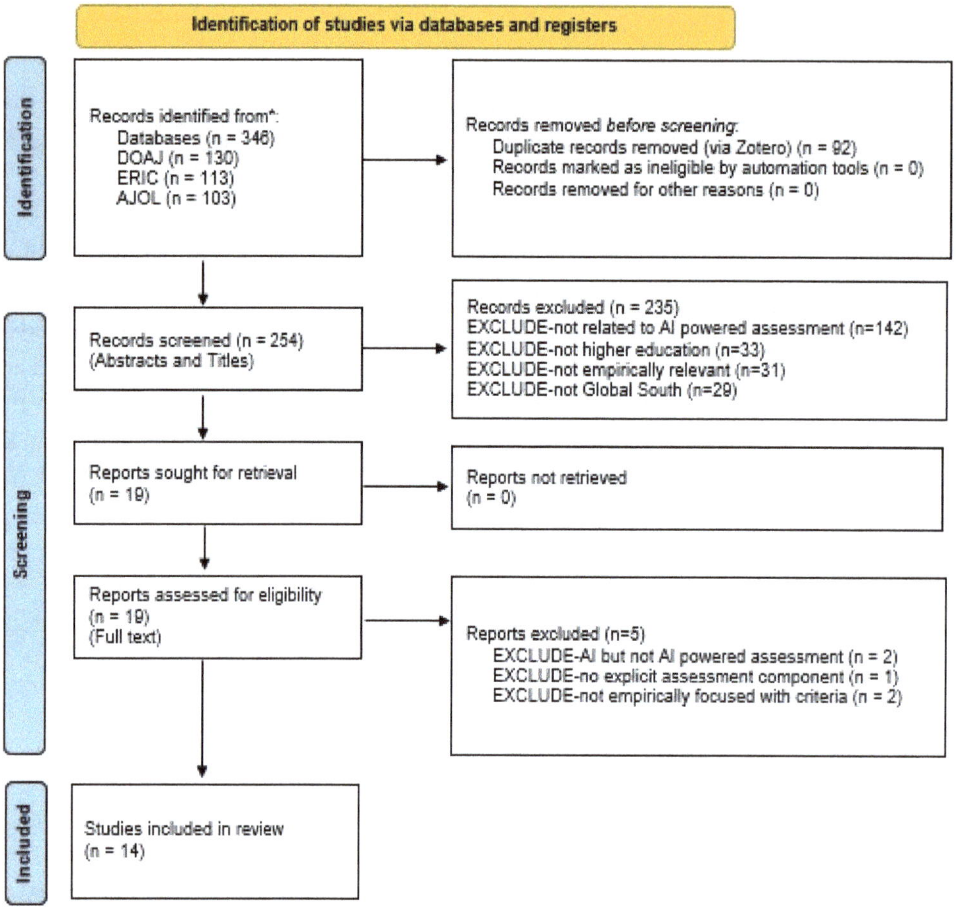

Following full-text review, 5 studies were excluded for failing to meet the inclusion criteria. Ultimately, 14 empirical studies were included in the final synthesis, as seen in Table 2 below.

Table 2. Included studies

No.	Authors	Year	Study Title	Database	Country/Region	Method/Focus
1	Twabu, K. & Nakene-Mginqi, M.	2024	Developing a design thinking AI-driven auto-marking/grading system for assessments to reduce lecturer workload	DOAJ	South Africa	System design / qualitative / AI assessment tool development
2	Muringa, T.P.	2025	Exploring ethical dilemmas and institutional challenges in AI adoption in South African universities	DOAJ	South Africa	Qualitative interviews (students)
3	Combrinck, C. & Loubser, N.	2025	Student self-reflection as a tool for managing GenAI use in large class assessment	DOAJ	South Africa	Mixed methods (MMR), AI detection + reflection
4	Ayyoub, A. et al.	2024	University teachers' views on adoption of GenAI tools for student assessment	DOAJ	Middle East	Quantitative (UTAUT model, survey)
5	Soko, J., Pete, J., & Mureithi, G.	2025	Assessing awareness and usage of AI tools among faculty and learners in Sub-Saharan Africa	ERIC	Sub-Saharan Africa	Quantitative survey
6	Anyanwu, R., Le Grange, L., & Beets, P.	2015	Climate change science: Literacy of Geography teachers in Western Cape	AJOL	South Africa	Empirical (survey/interviews)
7	Nsubuga, Y. et al.	2025	Development of teachers' pedagogical content knowledge in climate change education	AJOL	South Africa	Qualitative / CPD intervention
8	Olawumi, K.B. & Mavuso, M.P.	2024	In-service teacher training programmes for Education for Sustainable Development	AJOL	Africa	Literature review (systematic/ narrative)
9	Vogel, C. & Misser, S.	2015	Teaching and learning for climate change: curriculum and materials	AJOL	South Africa	Policy/curriculum analysis
10	Shabalala, N.P.	2025	Distributed leadership in environmental education curriculum management	AJOL	South Africa	Qualitative
11	Sikhulile, M.	2023	Climate change content and teaching methods in South African curriculum	AJOL	South Africa	Curriculum analysis
12	Bonilla-Jurado et al.	2024	Benefits of education for sustainable development in universities	AJOL	Latin America	Empirical/quantitative
13	Awuzie & Emuze	2017	Sustainable development implementation in South African higher education	AJOL	South Africa	Empirical case study
14	Nakidien, Singh & Sayed	2021	Teachers and teacher education and SDG 4 attainment	AJOL	South Africa	Qualitative/policy analysis

Coding and Data Extraction

After the screening process, the final set of included studies was systematically coded using a structured data extraction framework aligned with the study's research questions. For each article, relevant methodological and contextual information was extracted, including the author(s) and year of publication, the country or regional setting, and the research design and methodological approach used. Specific attention was given to the nature of AI-powered assessment tools discussed in each study, including whether they involved automated grading systems, generative AI applications, or broader AI-enabled assessment platforms. The extraction process also focused on substantive content relevant to the review objectives. This included key findings on how AI was implemented in assessment practices, the reported opportunities and benefits associated with its use, and the challenges and barriers identified across different higher education contexts. Particular attention was also given to issues of equity, access, infrastructure, and educational quality, given this review's emphasis on resource-constrained settings in the Global South. Where available, policy and practice recommendations reported in the original studies were also captured to support a more applied interpretation of the findings.

DATA ANALYSIS

The extracted data were analysed using a structured thematic synthesis approach appropriate for systematic literature reviews. Each included study was read repeatedly to ensure deep familiarity with both explicit findings and underlying patterns related to AI-powered assessment in higher education within resource-constrained contexts. This iterative reading process enabled systematic comparison across studies conducted in different regions of the Global South and across varying institutional and methodological contexts. An inductive coding process was used to organise the data into analytically meaningful categories. The initial coding framework was guided by the three research questions, providing a deductive structure for analysis, while inductive coding allowed additional patterns and sub-themes to emerge from the data through repeated comparisons across studies. These codes were developed progressively and refined through constant comparison across studies, ensuring that emerging patterns remained closely aligned with the study's research questions and conceptual framing through the Unified Theory of Acceptance and Use of Technology (UTAUT). Rather than applying predetermined categories, the analysis allowed themes to emerge from the data while still being sensitised by the study's theoretical lens. The final analytical themes reflected the dominant patterns identified across the included studies and were structured as follows: the implementation of AI-powered assessment practices in higher education institutions, including automated grading systems, generative AI tools, and AI-assisted feedback mechanisms; the perceived opportunities and performance benefits of AI adoption, particularly in relation to workload reduction, efficiency gains, and feedback enhancement; the technical, pedagogical, ethical, and infrastructural barriers affecting adoption and effectiveness, including issues of digital inequality, academic integrity, and limited institutional capacity; and the contextual conditions shaping adoption decisions, particularly in relation to facilitating conditions and social influence as outlined in the UTAUT framework. These themes were not treated as isolated categories but were analysed in relation to one another in order to capture the complexity of AI adoption in higher education. This approach allowed for a more nuanced interpretation of how institutional, technological, and human factors interact to shape the implementation and effectiveness of AI-powered assessment systems in the Global South.

FINDINGS

The literature search across Directory of Open Access Journals, ERIC, and African Journals Online yielded a total of 346 articles (DOAJ = 130; ERIC = 113; AJOL = 103). After removing duplicates and conducting initial screening based on titles and abstracts, a large number of studies were excluded for failing to meet the formal and content-related criteria. Following full-text assessment, 14 empirical studies were included in the final analysis. The majority of excluded articles addressed artificial intelligence in education in a general sense but did not specifically focus on assessment practices in higher education or were not situated within Global South contexts. While excluded, these studies still reflect the rapid growth of AI-related research in education, particularly around teaching, learning, and institutional adoption, rather than assessment specifically. The findings of the selected studies are presented below in relation to the research questions.

Implementation of AI-Powered Assessment in Higher Education

Across the 14 empirical studies analysed in this review, AI-powered assessment in higher education across the Global South is implemented in diverse and evolving ways, reflecting both experimentation and adaptation to resource-constrained environments. The studies collectively show that AI is not yet uniformly institutionalised, but rather introduced through a combination of formal systems, lecturer-led innovations, and student-driven practices. In many cases, implementation is shaped by contextual realities such as limited infrastructure, large class sizes, and increasing pressure on academic staff, which position AI as both a practical solution and a disruptive force within existing assessment systems (Soko et al., 2025; Twabu & Nakene-Mginqi, 2024).

A prominent pattern across the studies is the use of AI to support assessment efficiency, particularly in contexts where lecturers face heavy workloads. For instance, the development of AI-driven auto-marking systems demonstrates how institutions are leveraging machine learning tools to streamline grading processes while maintaining consistency and timeliness in feedback (Twabu & Nakene-Mginqi, 2024). Similarly, AI detection tools such as Turnitin are being incorporated into assessment workflows, often alongside pedagogical strategies such as student self-reflection, to manage the growing influence of generative AI on student submissions (Combrinck & Loubser, 2025). These approaches suggest that implementation is not purely technological, but increasingly hybrid, combining automated systems with human judgment and reflective practices to preserve academic integrity. In addition to institutionally supported tools, several studies highlight the informal, student-driven use of AI for assessment-related tasks. Students are reported to engage extensively with generative AI tools for activities such as essay writing, idea generation, and exam preparation, often without clear institutional guidelines (Muringa, 2025; Soko et al., 2025). This form of implementation operates largely outside formal assessment design, yet it significantly shapes how assessment is experienced and enacted in practice. The absence of structured policies in many institutions means that AI integration is, in some cases, reactive rather than planned, with lecturers attempting to adapt assessment methods in response to emerging student behaviours rather than through proactive design.

The role of lecturers in mediating AI adoption is also evident across the studies. Lecturers are not merely passive recipients of AI tools but active agents who interprete, adapt, and sometimes resist these technologies within their assessment practices. For example, research grounded in models such as the Unified Theory of Acceptance and Use of Technology (UTAUT) shows that factors such as perceived usefulness, ease of use, and institutional support significantly influence whether and how lecturers integrate AI into assessment (Ayyoub et al., 2024). In contexts where professional development and policy guidance are limited, implementation tends to be uneven, with early adopters experimenting with innovative approaches while others remain cautious due to concerns about reliability, ethics, and pedagogical value. Geographically, the implementation patterns show a concentration of studies in Sub-Saharan Africa, particularly South Africa, alongside contributions from the broader Global South, including the Middle East and Latin America. While these contexts differ in their infrastructure and policy environments, a common thread is the need to adapt AI tools to local conditions rather than adopt them wholesale. This includes considerations of internet access, digital literacy, class sizes, and institutional readiness. As a result, AI-powered assessment in these settings often takes the form of incremental integration rather than large-scale transformation, with institutions testing specific tools or strategies before broader adoption.

The findings indicate that AI-powered assessment in the Global South is characterised by a dynamic interaction between innovation and constraint. Implementation is shaped not only by technological possibilities but also by institutional capacity, lecturer agency, and student practices. Rather than a single, standardised model, what emerges is a fragmented yet rapidly evolving landscape in which AI is being integrated into assessment in multiple, context-sensitive ways. This indicates the importance of understanding implementation not as a fixed outcome, but as an ongoing process of negotiation between technology, pedagogy, and context.

Opportunities of AI-Powered Assessment for Improving Quality, Efficiency, and Student Outcomes

Across the studies included in this review, AI-powered assessment is consistently associated with opportunities that could transform assessment practices in higher education, particularly in resource-constrained contexts. These opportunities are largely centred on improving efficiency, enhancing the quality and consistency of assessment, and supporting student learning in more flexible and responsive ways. While the extent to which these benefits are realised varies across contexts, the literature suggests that AI is increasingly being viewed not merely as a technological tool, but as a catalyst for rethinking how assessment is designed and implemented in the Global South. One of the most prominent opportunities identified is AI systems' ability to significantly reduce the workload of academic staff, particularly in large-class settings. Automated marking and grading systems, for example, enable lecturers to process high volumes of student work more efficiently while maintaining consistency in evaluation (Twabu & Nakene-Mginqi, 2024). This is especially important in institutions where staff-to-student ratios are high and administrative burdens limit the time available for meaningful student engagement. By automating repetitive assessment tasks, AI allows lecturers to redirect their efforts toward more pedagogically valuable activities such as providing personalised feedback, mentoring students, and refining curriculum design. In this sense, AI contributes not only to operational efficiency but also to the potential improvement of teaching quality.

Related to efficiency is the opportunity for AI to enhance the quality and timeliness of feedback provided to students. Several studies highlight how AI-powered tools can generate immediate, structured, and in some cases personalised feedback, which supports ongoing learning rather than limiting assessment to summative evaluation points (Combrinck & Loubser, 2025). In contexts where delayed feedback is common due to large enrolments or limited staff capacity, this represents a significant shift toward more formative and student-centred assessment practices. The integration of tools such as AI detectors, alongside reflective activities, also encourages greater transparency in how assessments are evaluated, helping students better understand expectations and take greater responsibility for their learning processes. The literature further points to the role of AI in supporting student learning and academic performance through increased access to academic support tools. Students' use of generative AI for tasks such as idea generation, drafting, and exam preparation is associated with perceived improvements in efficiency, clarity of expression, and confidence in completing assignments (Soko et al., 2025). In resource-constrained environments, where access to academic support services may be limited, these tools can function as supplementary learning aids, helping to bridge gaps in instructional support. This is particularly relevant for students who may not have consistent access to lecturers or formal tutoring, suggesting that AI can contribute to more equitable learning opportunities when used appropriately.

Another important opportunity emerging from the studies is the potential for AI to promote more consistent and, in some cases, less biased assessment practices. Automated systems can apply predefined criteria uniformly across large cohorts, reducing variability that may arise from human subjectivity (Twabu & Nakene-Mginqi, 2024). While concerns about algorithmic bias remain (as discussed in the following section), the perceived objectivity of AI systems is seen by some lecturers as a means of enhancing fairness in grading, particularly in contexts where standardisation is difficult to achieve manually. This consistency is also valuable in ensuring that students receive comparable evaluation experiences, regardless of class size or institutional constraints. The adoption of AI-powered assessment is seen as an opportunity to stimulate pedagogical innovation and institutional development. The introduction of AI tools often prompts lecturers and institutions to reconsider traditional assessment methods and explore alternative approaches that are better aligned with digital learning environments. For example, the use of reflective assessment tasks, AI-integrated assignments, and new forms of academic integrity management indicates a shift toward more adaptive and forward-looking assessment practices (Ayyoub et al., 2024; Muringa, 2025). In this way, AI not only enhances existing systems but also creates space for reimagining assessment in ways that are more responsive to contemporary educational challenges.

The findings suggest that AI-powered assessment offers substantial opportunities to improve efficiency, enhance feedback, support student learning, and foster innovation in higher education across the Global South. However, these opportunities are closely intertwined with contextual factors and are not automatically realised. Their effectiveness depends on how AI tools are implemented, the level of institutional support available, and the extent to which lecturers and students are equipped to use them responsibly and effectively.

Challenges Affecting the Adoption and Effectiveness of AI-Powered Assessment

Despite the significant opportunities associated with AI-powered assessment, the studies included in this review reveal a complex range of challenges that shape how these technologies are adopted and experienced in higher education across the Global South. These challenges are not isolated, but rather interconnected, spanning technical, pedagogical, ethical, and infrastructural dimensions. Importantly, they highlight that the integration of AI into assessment is not simply a matter of access to technology, but involves deeper issues related to institutional readiness, capacity, and the broader educational context in which these tools are introduced. A central challenge identified across multiple studies relates to infrastructural and technical limitations, which are particularly pronounced in resource-constrained environments. Issues such as unreliable internet connectivity, limited access to digital devices, and inadequate institutional ICT infrastructure can significantly hinder the effective use of AI-powered tools (Soko et al., 2025). In such contexts, the adoption of AI is often uneven, with some institutions or student groups able to engage fully with these technologies while others are excluded. This creates disparities not only in access to AI tools but also in the benefits they offer, raising concerns about widening existing inequalities within higher education systems. Furthermore, implementing advanced AI systems often requires technical expertise and maintenance capacity that many institutions currently lack, limiting their ability to sustain long-term integration.

Linked to infrastructural challenges are pedagogical concerns regarding how AI aligns with existing assessment practices and learning objectives. Several studies point to uncertainty among lecturers about how to meaningfully integrate AI into assessment without undermining core academic skills such as critical thinking, writing, and independent problem-solving (Ayyoub et al., 2024). The increasing use of generative AI by students, particularly for completing assignments, has raised concerns that traditional assessment formats may no longer accurately reflect students' learning or effort (Muringa, 2025). As a result, lecturers face the challenge of redesigning assessment tasks in ways that both incorporate AI and preserve academic integrity. However, this requires pedagogical training and support that is not always available, leading to inconsistent and sometimes reactive approaches to AI integration. Ethical challenges also emerge prominently in the literature, particularly regarding academic integrity, data privacy, and the responsible use of AI tools. The widespread but often informal use of AI by students has created ambiguity around what constitutes acceptable practice, especially in the absence of clear institutional policies (Muringa, 2025; Soko et al., 2025). Concerns about plagiarism, over-reliance on AI-generated content, and the potential erosion of students' original thinking are frequently highlighted. At the same time, the use of AI detection tools introduces its own ethical dilemmas, including questions about accuracy, transparency, and the potential for false positives to unfairly penalise students (Combrinck & Loubser, 2025). Data privacy is another critical issue, as many AI systems require access to student data, raising concerns about how this information is stored, used, and protected, particularly in contexts where regulatory frameworks may be underdeveloped.

Another key challenge relates to the lack of institutional frameworks and policy guidance for AI adoption. Several studies emphasise that many higher education institutions in the Global South have not yet developed clear strategies or guidelines for integrating AI into teaching and assessment (Ayyoub et al., 2024; Muringa, 2025). This lack of formal direction leads to fragmented implementation, with individual lecturers or departments experimenting with AI tools without coordinated support or oversight. Consequently, practices vary widely within and across institutions, leading to inconsistencies in how assessment is conducted and how AI use is regulated. The lack of policy also contributes to uncertainty among lecturers and students alike, further complicating efforts to integrate AI in a coherent and equitable manner. Issues related to digital literacy and capacity building continue to be a barrier to effective AI adoption. Both lecturers and students may lack the necessary skills to use AI tools critically and responsibly, limiting their potential benefits (Soko et al., 2025). For lecturers, this includes not only technical proficiency but also an understanding of how to integrate AI into assessment design. For students, limited AI literacy can lead to misuse or overreliance on these tools, ultimately undermining learning outcomes. Addressing these challenges requires sustained investment in training and professional development, as well as efforts to embed AI literacy into curricula.

The findings from this review suggest that the adoption of AI-powered assessment in the Global South is constrained by structural, pedagogical, and ethical challenges. While AI offers considerable promise, its effectiveness depends on the extent to which these challenges are recognised and addressed.

Without adequate infrastructure, clear policies, and capacity-building initiatives, there is a risk that AI may reinforce existing inequalities and create new forms of educational disadvantage. As such, the successful integration of AI into assessment requires not only technological innovation but also careful attention to context, equity, and institutional support systems.

DISCUSSION

The findings of this study, when read alongside the existing literature, suggest that AI-powered assessment in higher education is increasingly positioned as both a technological solution to long-standing assessment challenges and a source of new pedagogical and ethical tensions. The literature makes it clear that assessment has always been central to teaching and learning, with its primary purpose being to determine whether learning has taken place (Swiecki et al., 2022). However, traditional assessment approaches such as essays, short-answer questions, and multiple-choice tests have been widely critiqued for being labour-intensive, time-consuming, and often unable to capture the complexity of student learning in diverse educational contexts. These limitations become even more pronounced in resource-constrained higher education systems where large class sizes, limited staffing, and administrative overload place additional pressure on lecturers. In this context, AI-powered assessment is framed as a necessary innovation rather than an optional enhancement, particularly because it promises efficiency gains, automated grading, and faster feedback cycles that can ease institutional burden. However, findings of this review suggest that this framing is not uniform across contexts, especially within the Global South. While AI is widely described in the literature as a transformative force capable of reshaping assessment practices (Cope et al., 2021; Makeleni et al., 2023), its implementation is uneven due to structural and contextual constraints. In many African and other Global South higher education systems, the adoption of AI is limited by infrastructural weaknesses, insufficient digital capacity, and inconsistent policy environments (Ayanwale, 2023; Ayentimi & Burgess, 2019). These constraints affect whether AI can be adopted, and how it is experienced by both lecturers and students. From a UTAUT perspective, these issues strongly reflect weak facilitating conditions, where even if individuals perceive AI tools as useful, the absence of reliable infrastructure and institutional support reduces actual usage and long-term sustainability.

The literature and findings further indicate that performance expectancy is among the strongest drivers of AI adoption in assessment contexts. Across the reviewed studies, AI is consistently associated with improved efficiency, reduced workload, and enhanced feedback mechanisms. For example, AI-driven tools are described as being capable of generating assessment tasks, supporting automated marking, and even assisting in peer selection for evaluation (Cope et al., 2021). Similarly, empirical studies from different contexts, including South Africa, Turkey, Australia, and South Korea, highlight that lecturers perceive AI as a time-saving tool that allows them to focus more on teaching and less on repetitive marking tasks (Başar & Şahin, 2021; Yang & Kyun, 2022). This aligns with the findings of this review, which identified efficiency and workload reduction as dominant expectations associated with AI adoption. However, what is important to note is that this perceived benefit is often balanced by concerns about validity, academic integrity, and the extent to which AI can genuinely capture meaningful learning. In other words, while performance expectancy is high, it is not uncontested, and it operates within a broader field of pedagogical doubt.

Similarly, effort expectancy plays a significant but uneven role in shaping adoption. The literature suggests that AI tools are increasingly user-friendly, particularly generative AI systems that can assist with writing, grading, and feedback generation. However, ease of use does not automatically translate into effective integration. In many cases, lecturers still struggle to understand how to meaningfully incorporate AI into assessment design, rather than simply using it as a replacement for marking or feedback. This gap between technical usability and pedagogical integration is important because it suggests that adoption is often superficial rather than transformative. In resource-constrained environments, this challenge is intensified by limited training opportunities and a lack of institutional capacity-building initiatives, which further increases the perceived effort required to use AI effectively. As a result, even when AI is considered useful, its adoption is slowed by uncertainty and lack of confidence among lecturers.

The role of social influence is also evident in the literature, particularly regarding academic integrity concerns and institutional culture. Across multiple studies, there is evidence that attitudes toward AI are shaped by peer practices, institutional expectations, and broader global narratives about technology in education. On one hand, AI is often promoted as part of the "Fourth Industrial Revolution" and associated with innovation and modernisation in higher education. On the other hand, there is growing skepticism among academics who associate AI with academic dishonesty, overreliance on technology, and reduced student effort (Makeleni et al., 2023; Mutongoza & Olawale, 2022). This tension is especially evident in assessment practices, where the use of AI-generated content and automated grading raises questions about fairness, authenticity, and trust. In many cases, lecturers' willingness to adopt AI is influenced not only by their own beliefs but also by how their peers and institutions interpret the legitimacy of AI-assisted assessment.

One of the most consistent findings across both the literature and the reviewed studies is that AI adoption in assessment is deeply constrained by facilitating conditions, particularly in the Global South. Even where there is interest in AI, structural barriers such as unreliable internet connectivity, high data costs, lack of digital infrastructure, and weak institutional policy frameworks significantly limit implementation (Ayanwale, 2023; Vashchenko et al., 2018). These constraints are not peripheral issues; they are central determinants of whether AI-powered assessment can function at all. In addition, concerns around data privacy and data sovereignty further complicate adoption, as institutions remain uncertain about how student data is collected, stored, and governed within AI systems (Isaifan et al., 2025). This creates a situation where AI is often adopted in fragmented or experimental ways rather than being fully institutionalised into assessment systems.

At the same time, the literature highlights broader pedagogical concerns that extend beyond technical implementation. Several scholars argue that while AI can enhance efficiency, it may also contribute to reduced critical thinking, diminished creativity, and what has been described as pedagogical deskilling among both lecturers and students (Ifedayo, 2025; Lubinga et al., 2023). These concerns complicate the otherwise positive narrative around AI in assessment, suggesting that technological efficiency does not automatically translate into educational quality. Instead, there is an ongoing tension between automation and meaningful learning, particularly in contexts where students may become overly dependent on AI tools for completing academic tasks. This reinforces the idea that AI adoption is not purely a technical shift but a pedagogical one that requires careful balancing between innovation and educational integrity.

CONCLUSION

It is clear that AI-powered assessment in higher education is shaped by a complex relationship of perceived usefulness, ease of use, social expectations, and enabling conditions. However, what distinguishes the Global South context is the overwhelming influence of facilitating conditions, which often determine whether adoption is even possible. While performance expectancy and effort expectancy explain why individuals may be interested in AI, and social influence explains how attitudes are shaped, it is the structural environment that ultimately constrains or enables meaningful implementation. This suggests that AI-powered assessment cannot be understood simply as a technological innovation, but must instead be viewed as a socio-technical process embedded within unequal institutional and infrastructural realities.

REFERENCES

Anyanwu, R., Le Grange, L., & Beets, P. (2015). Climate change science: The literacy of geography teachers in the Western Cape Province, South Africa. South African Journal of Education, 35(3), 1-9. Distance Education, 20(2). http://www.asianjde.com/ojs/index.php/AsianJDE/article/view/847

Ayanwale, M. (2023). Can Experience Determine the Adoption of Industrial Revolution 4.0 Skills in 21st Century Mathematics Education? *Research in Social Sciences and Technology*, *8*(1), 74–91. DOI: 10.46303/ressat.2023.6

Ayentimi, D., & Burgess, J. (2019). Is the fourth industrial revolution relevant to sub-Sahara Africa? *Technology Analysis and Strategic Management*, *31*(6), 641–652. DOI: 10.1080/09537325.2018.1542129

Başar, T., & Şahin, L. (2021). Technology integration in teaching English as a foreign language: A content analysis study. *Journal of Educational Technology & Online Learning*, *5*(1), 204–222. DOI: 10.31681/jetol.972577

Combrinck, C., & Loubser, N. (2025). Student self-reflection as a tool for managing GenAI use in large class assessment. *Discover Education, 4*(1), 72.| DOI: 10.1007/s44217-025-00461-2

Cope, B., Kalantzis, M., & Searsmith, D. (2021). Artificial intelligence for education: Knowledge and its assessment in AI-enabled learning ecologies. *Educational Philosophy and Theory*, *53*(12), 1229–1245. Advance online publication. DOI: 10.1080/00131857.2020.1728732

Crompton, H., & Burke, D. (2023). Artificial intelligence in higher education: The state of the field. *International Journal of Educational Technology in Higher Education*, *20*(1), 22. DOI: 10.1186/s41239-023-00392-8

González-Calatayud, V., Prendes-Espinosa, P., & Roig-Vila, R. (2021). Artificial intelligence for student assessment: A systematic review. *Applied Sciences (Basel, Switzerland)*, *11*(12), 5467. DOI: 10.3390/app11125467

IFEDAYO, A. E. (2025). A CRITICAL ANALYSIS OF AI-POWERED MOBILE LEARNING SYSTEMS FOR ENHANCED EDUCATIONAL OUTCOMES IN NIGERIAN UNIVERSITIES. *International Journal of Library Science and Educational Research*. DOI: 10.70382/caijlser.v9i8.042

Isaifan, R. J., Tawalbeh, A., & Hasna, M. O. (2025, October). From principles to practice: a novel matrix for evaluating AI-powered learning platforms based on the UNESCO Ethical Impact Assessment tool. In *Frontiers in Education* (Vol. 10, p. 1640780). Frontiers Media SA. https://doi:DOI: 10.3389/feduc.2025.1640780

Lubinga, S., Maramura, T. C., & Masiya, T. (2023). The fourth industrial revolution adoption: Challenges in South African higher education institutions. *Journal of Culture & Values in Education*, *6*(2), 1–17. DOI: 10.46303/jcve.2023.5

Makeleni, S., Mutongoza, B. H., & Linake, M. A. (2023). Language education and artificial intelligence: An exploration of challenges confronting academics in global south universities. *Journal of Culture and Values in Education*, *6*(2), 158–171. DOI: 10.46303/jcve.2023.14

Mikalef, P., Conboy, K., Lundström, J. E., & Popovič, A. (2022). Thinking responsibly about responsible AI and the 'dark side' of AI. *European Journal of Information Systems, 31*(3), 257–268. DOI: 10.1080/0960085X.2022.2026621

Mintz, Y., & Brodie, R. (2019). Introduction to artificial intelligence in medicine. *Minimally Invasive Therapy & Allied Technologies, 28*(2), 73–81. DOI: 10.1080/13645706.2019.1575882 PMID: 30810430

Muringa, T. P. (2025, September). Exploring ethical dilemmas and institutional challenges in AI adoption: A study of South African universities. In *Frontiers in Education* (Vol. 10, p. 1628019). Frontiers Media SA. DOI: 10.3389/feduc.2025.1628019

Mutongoza, B. H., & Olawale, B. E. (2022). Safeguarding academic integrity in the face of emergency remote teaching and learning in developing countries. *Perspectives in Education, 40*(1), 234–249. DOI: 10.18820/2519593X/pie.v40.i1.14

Nakidien, T., Singh, M., & Sayed, Y. (2021). Teachers and teacher education: Limitations and possibilities of attaining SDG 4 in South Africa. *Education Sciences, 11*(2), 66. DOI: 10.3390/educsci11020066

Ocaña-Fernández, Y., Valenzuela-Fernández, L. A., & Garro-Aburto, L. L. (2019). Inteligencia artificial y sus implicaciones en la educación superior. *Propósitos y Represent.*, *7*(2). Advance online publication. DOI: 10.20511/pyr2019.v7n2.274

Olawumi, K. B., & Mavuso, M. P. (2024). In-service teacher training programmes that promote education for sustainable development: A review of emerging literature. *Interdisciplinary Journal of Education Research, 6*, 1-20.2024: Vol 6, pp 1-20. DOI: 10.38140/ijer-2024.vol6.35

Omari, E. B., Salifu Yendork, J., & Ankrah, E. (2022). University students' perspectives on the benefits and challenges of emergency remote teaching during the Covid-19 pandemic in Ghana. *Education and Information Technologies*, **•••**, 1–21. DOI: 10.1007/s10639-022-11401-0 PMID: 36406783

Shabalala, N. P., & Gumbo, M. (2023). Africanising distributed leadership in environmental education curriculum management. *Southern African Journal of Environmental Education, 39*. Advance online publication. DOI: 10.4314/sajee.v39.11

Surahman, E., & Wang, T. H. (2022). Academic dishonesty and trustworthy assessment in online learning: A systematic literature review. *Journal of Computer Assisted Learning, 38*(6), 1535–1553. DOI: 10.1111/jcal.12708

Swiecki, Z., Khosravi, H., Chen, G., Martinez-Maldonado, R., Lodge, J. M., Milligan, S., Selwyn, N., & Gašević, D. (2022). Assessment in the age of artificial intelligence. *Computers and Education: Artificial Intelligence, 3*, 100075. DOI: 10.1016/j.caeai.2022.100075

Tehzeeb, N., & Raza, A. (2022). Understanding social and ethical implications of artificial intelligence. *Pakistan Journal of Social Research, 4*(4), 708–716. DOI: 10.52567/pjsr.v4i04.884

Twabu, K., & Nakene-Mginqi, M. (2024, December). Developing a design thinking artificial intelligence driven auto-marking/grading system for assessments to reduce the workload of lecturers at a higher learning institution in South Africa. In *Frontiers in Education* (Vol. 9, p. 1512569). Frontiers Media SA. https://doi.DOI: 10.3389/feduc.2024.1512569

Vashchenko, M., Taraniuk, L., Danko, Y., & Taraniuk, K. (2018). Assessment of the technological readiness of the countries of the world for the radical innovations. *Marketing & Management of Innovations*, *4*, 86–97. DOI: 10.21272/mmi.2018.4-08

Vogel, C., Schwaibold, U., & Misser, S. (2015). 'Teaching and Learning for Climate Change'–The Role of Teacher Materials and Curriculum Design in South Africa. *Southern African Journal of Environmental Education*, *31*, 78–97.

Yalçin-Incik, E., & Incik, T. (2022). Generation Z students' views on technology in education: What they want what they get. *Malaysian Online Journal of Educational Technology*, *10*(2), 109–124. DOI: 10.52380/mojet.2022.10.2.275

Yang, H., & Kyun, S. (2022). The current research trend of artificial intelligence in language learning: A systematic empirical literature review from an activity theory perspective. *Australasian Journal of Educational Technology*, *38*(5), 180–210. DOI: 10.14742/ajet.7492

Zhang, C., & Lu, Y. (2021). Study on artificial intelligence: The state of the art and future prospects. *Journal of Industrial Information Integration*, *23*, 100224. DOI: 10.1016/j.jii.2021.100224

Chapter 13
AI and Assessment in Global South, Rural, and Resource-Constrained Higher Education Contexts

Michael Oyedele Oyenuga
http://orcid.org/0000-0001-9921-5711
Woxsen University, Hyderabad, India

ABSTRACT

A combination of pressure points that question traditional approaches to evaluation is experienced in the Global South and low-density rural higher education contexts. The chapter explores the AI-enabled assessment for the Global South, rural and resource-constrained higher education. It draws together cross-sectional evidence about approaches to architecture, governance, pedagogy and equity in order to explore how AI can support assessment whilst respecting local goals and limitations. The Principal Analysis spots four design levers, namely: lightweight and offline-capable assessment tools; governance and data sovereignty-based data collection; modular architectures through capacity building and evidence across domains. But there will be growing dangers in relation to data privacy, algorithmic bias, inequalities in language and culture, as well as dependency on suppliers. The chapter ends with policy, university governance and sustainable scaling implications focused on learner rights and educational justice that is locally stewarded.

1. INTRODUCTION

The Global South, rural, and resource-constrained higher education contexts experience an intersection of pressure points that push the boundaries of traditional assessment frameworks. In each of these contexts, students are navigating uneven access to infrastructure, differences in digital literacy, and wide-ranging gaps in equity as learning opportunities differ widely – including how knowledge is assessed, validated and credentialized. AI has the potential to transform assessment in these contexts by providing scalable, data-informed avenues for personalised feedback, adaptive testing and high-stakes and formative evaluation moderation(Apata & Oyedele, 2025). But the same technologies that open up

DOI: 10.4018/979-8-3373-8939-4.ch013

new paths for measurement also run the risk of enshrining inequities when deployments replicate existing advantages of certain populations, languages or infrastructures. Accordingly, an optimistic but cautious evidence-informed discourse of AI and assessment in the Global South should attend carefully to issues of context, governance and sustainability (Saleem et al., 2025; Chen, 2025; Makeleni et al., 2023).

Resource constraints, bandwidth, electricity outages and device access are not equal for all of us. For many rural and underserved areas in higher education, assessments are not just about measuring learning; they work as systems for social mobility, professional readiness, and public accountability. The use of artificial intelligence (AI) can be harnessed in a variety of assessments to provide unique, continuous, and criterion-referenced feedback, scalability for manual calibration assessment tasks with large cohorts, and enhance integrity and fairness via scalable proctoring analytics (Oyenuga et al., 2026). Moreover, the perspectives that will translate into practice and recommendations are quite pronounced because of the different languages, educational cultures and aspects related to disciplines in a Global South context.

An increasing volume of literature in educational settings, particularly from rural and global south contexts, show that AI can improve teaching effectiveness and student learning when informed by sound pedagogy, teacher preparedness, and culturally responsive design; risks appear when digital tools mismatch local needs or remain unimplemented due to persistent infrastructure gaps(Kundu & Bej, 2025; Oyenuga et al., 2024).

In this context, several core commitments guide the present chapter. It does this by: (i) foregrounding assessment as a social and educational practice phenomenon, which needs to be aligned with local ends rather than treating it as a technical fix that can be applied globally. Second, it asks how AI-enabled assessment can be intentionally designed in ways that foster equity, accommodate scarce infrastructure, and support resourced sustainable learning in rural and resource-poor institutions. Third, it advocates for governance frameworks, data stewardship and capacity-building that consider the ethical/ legal/ cultural aspects of AI in education. Finally, it examines feasible configurations—going from "thin" offline-supported assessment applications and frugal information assemblages to cloud-enabled analytics that meet local data sovereignty needs—that could work in the Global South and similar contexts.

This synthesis, therefore, grounds these discussions with evidence from four domains in which AI intersects with assessment within resource-limited higher education: (1) AI-assisted feedback and adaptive testing; (2) automated scoring and moderation; (3) integrity and plagiarism detection, with privacy-protecting measures applied; and (4) analytics to elucidate learning progressions without adding the burden of additional accountability for already overstretched instructors. Importantly, this synthesis also recognizes the heterogeneity of resource-poor settings, rural campuses in sub-Saharan Africa & South Asia; peri-urban institutions in other emerging economies, where contextual determinants (framework)including electricity availability, internet connection, devices accessible and languages spoken by students and academic staff as well as professional development needs for faculty will influence what is possible in terms of AI-enabled assessment and appropriate governance measures to accompany it (Saleem et al., 2025).

Although the literature on AI in education has expanded rapidly, existing reviews predominantly examine technologically advanced educational systems or focus on isolated dimensions such as automated grading, learning analytics, or academic integrity. Comparatively little synthesis has examined AI-enabled assessment through the combined lenses of infrastructure constraints, governance, equity, data sovereignty, and contextual pedagogy within Global South, rural, and resource-constrained higher education environments. Existing reviews also rarely translate evidence into implementation-oriented design principles suitable for institutions operating under severe infrastructural and policy limitations.

This chapter addresses these gaps by synthesising evidence across multiple disciplines to develop an integrated evidence-informed perspective centred on four interrelated design levers:

a. context-sensitive infrastructure,
b. governance and data stewardship,
c. modular assessment architecture,
d. sustainable institutional capacity-building.

Rather than reviewing technologies in isolation, the chapter proposes an integrated implementation perspective that connects pedagogical, technological, governance, and policy considerations into a coherent framework for equitable AI-enabled assessment.

The chapter delineates a framework for understanding AI and assessment in these contexts, proposes design principles for equitable and resilient AI-enabled assessment architectures, and illustrates via case-informed scenarios how universities and policymakers can navigate the trade-offs between innovation and inclusion. In doing so, this chapter emphasises that the value of AI in assessment emerges not simply from technological novelty but from its integration with pedagogical intent, local expertise, and robust governance that centres learner needs and educational justice. The chapter develops an evidence-informed synthesis that progresses from conceptual foundations to implementation configurations, case-informed scenarios, policy pathways, and future research priorities for AI-enabled assessment in Global South and resource-constrained higher education.

2. METHODOLOGY

This chapter adopts a narrative evidence-synthesis approach to examine the evolving literature on AI-enabled assessment within Global South, rural, and resource-constrained higher education contexts. Rather than undertaking a systematic review or meta-analysis, the chapter draws upon contemporary peer-reviewed research, policy documents, and conceptual studies to develop an integrated understanding of current knowledge, emerging themes, and implementation considerations.

The chapter synthesises evidence across four recurring analytical domains identified in the literature: (i) infrastructure and technological readiness, (ii) pedagogy and assessment design, (iii) governance, ethics and data sovereignty, and (iv) sustainability and institutional capacity. These domains provide the organising structure for the subsequent discussion and enable comparison of evidence from diverse educational contexts.

While the introduction establishes the need for AI-enabled assessment in Global South and resource-constrained higher education, understanding how these technologies should be implemented requires a stronger conceptual grounding. The following section therefore examines the theoretical foundations that frame assessment as a socially situated practice while positioning AI within broader debates on governance, equity, culture, and educational justice. These concepts provide the analytical lens through which the subsequent discussion is organised.

3. CONCEPTUAL FOUNDATIONS

3.1 Assessment as Social Practice and Credentialing in Context

Assessment is understood, within higher education, as more than just a measurement of learning outcomes: rather, it is a social practice that reinforces and legitimises community values, knowledge claims and professional norms in context. Assessments operate as engines of social mobility and workforce development in resource-scarce and Global South contexts, determining who is granted access to opportunities and the validation of knowledge (Kundu & Bej, 2025; Li & Gao, 2025). The sociopolitical model of assessment posits that validity is not limited to items being reliable but also includes considerations such as cultural relevance and language access, as well as relevance to local educational goals and epistemologies (such as Afrocentric or other context-driven knowledge systems) (Kundu & Bej, 2025). As non-universal technical fixes, mega-optimising assessments cannot rely on or assume the consistency of context in terms of contextual legitimacy, learner agency and local governance structures to guide their design.

3.2 AI in Education: Capabilities, Limitations, and Governance Considerations

AI in education embraces a wide range of technologies, adaptive feedback systems, automated scoring, learning analytics, intelligent tutoring and content generation, that can enhance teaching and assessment if they are designed and governed with care. AI has potential for scalable feedback, formative progress monitoring and moderation of large cohorts in contexts with little existing infrastructure; however, whether these benefits materialise depends on data quality, representativeness and governance capable of mitigating the aggravation of existing inequities or weakening learner autonomy (Mhlanga et al., 2022; Maina, 2025). Governance concerns ethics in the usage of data, privacy, algorithmic injustice and bias, interpretability, as well as local data sovereignty and stewardship arrangements on language and culture.

3.3 Equity, Access, Culture, and Language in AI-Enabled Assessment

In order to ensure equity in AI-enabled assessment, it is therefore imperative to design an ecosystem that can address such disparities within electricity reliability, internet connectivity, device access, language diversity and digital literacy. What is especially salient in multilingual contexts typical of Global South institutions, where language inclusivity assessment tools (or lack thereof), feedback language, and even AI-powered analytics may favour dominant languages at the expense of minority language speakers. Culturally responsive design and a participatory development process can potentially minimise biases such as these by ensuring that AI tools recognise local discourse patterns, disciplinary practices, and the conventions of assessment (Siyi et al., 2023; Mangubat & Mangubat, 2025; Zhang & Wu, 2025).

The conceptual foundations demonstrate that AI-enabled assessment is shaped by educational, ethical, and governance considerations rather than technology alone. Building on these principles, the next section examines how contextual resource limitations influence the practical design choices available to higher education institutions operating in Global South and resource-constrained environments.

4. RESOURCE CONSTRAINTS AND DESIGN IMPERATIVES

The Global South, rural, and resource-constrained higher education contexts demand a deliberate, context-sensitive approach to the design and deployment of AI-enabled assessment(Table 1). Drawing on the multi-domain evidence summarised in the introduction, this section emphasises infrastructure realities, pedagogical alignment, data governance, and long-term capacity-building as interdependent design levers.

4.1 Infrastructure: Bandwidth, Electricity, Devices, and Offline Capabilities

Data-scarce situations are often characterised by frequent power cuts, limited or high-priced bandwidth and varying device penetration. These limitations impose direct constraints on in-cloud-only AI testing solutions, prompting the use of either offline or hybrid architectures. Previous syntheses across contexts in education in LMICs consistently show that network availability, supply of electricity, and hardware quality are critical for the successful scaling of any digital tools, including AI-enabled assessment and analytics (Oyenuga & Omale, 2024).

4.2 Pedagogy and Learning Design Aligned With Local Aims

Assessment design is a product of local aims, disciplinary practices and pedagogical values likely requiring the adaptation or re-framing of imported models for an unknown post-qualification setting. Your introduction emphasised that assessment functions as a social practice intertwined with social mobility, job readiness, and community goals; thus, AI-enabled assessment needs to enhance, rather than detract from, locally valued learning outcomes. A recent review of Global South EFL classrooms, focusing on rural China and other rural LMICs, suggests that AI can improve instructional quality when leveraged with a careful pedagogy, teacher capacity and culturally congruent design, but risks associated with ill-aligned tools to local needs or an incorrect leverage point only deepen these existing disparities (Kundu & Bej, 2025).

4.3 Data Governance, Privacy, and Local Data Sovereignty

Given that regulatory frameworks are still evolving, data literacy is not uniform, and the potential for privacy violations or misuse is pronounced, governance is essential to confirm that AI deployment and integration are ethical. Results show how the introduction flags current governance gaps, ethical challenges, and local data stewardship to avoid reproducing inequities and eroding learner rights (Berkel et al., 2020; Chand et al., 2020; Diallo et al., 2025). While the above is a general governance principle, resource-constrained environments introduce additional complications that can only be addressed with context-sensitive responses. A major focus area is data minimisation and purpose-limited collection, where only the data required for assessment validity and fairness is collected; implemented pruning and lifecycle management controls help to limit risk exposure. Closely related is the principle of local data sovereignty, i.e., that data should be stored and processed – as far as possible – in the country or institution concerned, with clear rules of data sharing under which host countries (often) define legal frameworks with due consideration to cultural practices.

Importantly, this should be accompanied by transparency and explainability in that AI-based scoring or feedback mechanisms are communicated to learners as well as to instructors in such ways that can facilitate accountability (Berkel et al., 2020). This should go hand-in-hand with a privacy-by-design mindset, ensuring that protections around privacy are integrated from the beginning of system development, such as culturally acceptable informed consent processes and clear risk/benefit statements (Berkel et al., 2020). Finally, strong audit and accountability mechanisms are critical in establishing continuous oversight of algorithms, which perform biased audits to identify misalignment of outcomes across linguistic classes, gender expressions, rural–urban divides, and differential access to input-based resources.

4.4 Sustainability, Capacity-Building, and Local Ownership

The international literature shows that the success of technology-driven innovation in LMICs can be undermined if funding, local capacity and a sense of ownership to ensure long-term results beyond pilot projects are not secured. Several scholars consistently stress the need for capacity-building in digital literacy, data governance and AI literacy among faculty and administrators, while also emphasising that sustainable funding models are needed alongside strong local partnerships to prop up the newly developing assessment ecosystems enabled by AI. This process leads to several design imperatives that are important if lasting, locally managed outcomes are to be secured. To begin with, the planned capacity-building pipelines are long-term and need to integrate continuous professional development for instructors, assessors and IT staff supported by timelines, measurable outcomes and incentives that retain engagement beyond initial implementation windows.

Second, individual governance structures, including a co-governance body with students, faculty, administrators and community stakeholders. Being as inclusive in such arrangements as possible helps ensure that AI-enabled assessment initiatives continue to match local priorities but also promote fair and context-sensitive decision-making using AI-based approaches (Wang et al., 2023). Third, it endorses an incremental and modular deployment method where systems are fielded in scaffolded components, for example, offline-capable apps, modular analytics, and scoring rubrics that allow portability, which can be upgraded or replaced as institutional capability matures, thereby lessening the implementation risk and facilitating iteration. Simultaneously, sustainable funding also needs to be in place to ensure long-term viability, achieving a balance of public funding with institutional resources and targeted philanthropic or multilateral support to cover infrastructure, maintenance, training and software licensing. Open standards and open-source tools reduce the total cost of ownership and improve accessibility. Lastly, North–South and South–South collaborations are extremely important for knowledge exchange, resource sharing,3 and the dissemination of best practices while maintaining preservation of context-specific adaptation and avoiding overdependence on external providers (Mariyono & Mistar, 2025).

Table 1. Resource constraints and design imperatives

Design Dimension	Key Challenges in Resource-Constrained Contexts	Design Imperatives / Recommended Responses
Infrastructure: Bandwidth, Electricity, Devices, and Offline Capabilities	Unreliable electricity supply, limited internet connectivity, expensive bandwidth, and unequal device access constrain cloud-dependent AI assessment systems.	Adopt offline-capable or hybrid architectures, edge computing, frugal data pipelines, local processing, backup power solutions, and low-bandwidth assessment platforms.
Pedagogy and Learning Design Aligned with Local Needs	Imported AI assessment models may not align with local educational goals, cultural contexts, workforce expectations, or disciplinary practices.	Design AI-enabled assessment around locally valued learning outcomes, contextual realities, teacher capacity, cultural relevance, and community priorities. Ensure AI supports rather than replaces meaningful learning.
Data Governance, Privacy, and Local Data Sovereignty	Weak regulatory environments, uneven data literacy, privacy risks, algorithmic bias, and external control of educational data may undermine trust and equity.	Implement data minimization, purpose-limited data collection, privacy-by-design principles, local data sovereignty, transparency, explainability, informed consent procedures, and continuous algorithm audits.
Sustainability, Capacity-Building, and Local Ownership	Short-term funding, limited institutional capacity, dependence on external providers, and lack of local ownership threaten long-term sustainability.	Establish continuous AI literacy and professional development programmes, inclusive governance structures, modular deployment approaches, sustainable funding mechanisms, open-source solutions, and North–South/South–South partnerships that support contextual adaptation.

Callout: The effectiveness of AI-enabled assessment in resource-constrained higher education settings depends less on technological sophistication and more on contextual appropriateness. Sustainable implementation requires the alignment of infrastructure realities, pedagogical priorities, data governance frameworks, and long-term capacity-building strategies to ensure equitable and meaningful educational outcomes.

Having established the principal design imperatives for AI-enabled assessment, the discussion now evaluates how these principles are reflected across the existing evidence base. Rather than considering technological applications in isolation, the following synthesis critically examines where current evidence converges, diverges, and remains incomplete across the major domains of AI-enabled assessment.

5. EVIDENCE BASE ACROSS DOMAINS

This section synthesises evidence on AI-enabled assessment in resource-constrained higher education contexts, drawing on studies of AI-assisted feedback, adaptive testing, learner analytics, automated scoring and integrity safeguards, privacy and fairness considerations, and case-informed insights from rural and Global South settings (Figure. 1). The aim is to move beyond isolated findings to a cohesive understanding of what works, for whom, and under what conditions, acknowledging tensions and gaps where they arise in the literature (Li & Gao, 2025; Siyi et al., 2023; Jafar et al., 2025).

Although studies consistently acknowledge the educational potential of AI-enabled assessment, they differ considerably in explaining the conditions under which successful implementation occurs. For example, Chen (2025) primarily attributes positive outcomes to pedagogical integration, whereas Saleem et al. (2025) emphasise faculty preparedness and institutional support. Altogether, these studies suggest that implementation success depends on the interaction of pedagogical, technological, and governance factors rather than any single dimension.

5.1 AI-Assisted Feedback, Adaptive Testing, and Learner Analytics

Feedback enabled by AI and adaptive testing has potential for scalability, formative assessment in larger cohorts characteristic of the resource-constrained higher education sector, mainly where they are designed to supplement rather than supplant instructor input. AI-assisted feedback can thus speed up the provision of actionable guidance, strengthen vocabularies and writing across variations in infrastructure in rural and Global South contexts as well. Adaptive testing methods can match item difficulty to individual student progress, and they hold potential for reducing test anxiety and enhancing item validity with heterogeneous student populations if data mirror local epistemologies and language practices (Kundu & Bej, 2025; Li & Gao, 2025).

5.2 Automated Scoring, Moderation, and Integrity Safeguards

Automated websites provide throughput advantages for large enrollments and specialisation capabilities in assessment, driving consistency of quality. Automated scoring and integrity safeguards both serve unique purposes in the grading workflow: automated scoring to lessen instructor burden and provide scalable moderation, while integrity safeguards seek to maintain fairness and limit cheating risk even in resource-constrained contexts. Yet, issues related to validity, bias and transparency are still swept under the carpet, especially when models are trained on well-resourced context datasets or in cases of large language diversity.

5.3 Privacy, Fairness, and Bias Considerations in Low-Resource Settings

Privacy, fairness and bias have to be core issues with regard to deployed AI technologies in the Global South context. The literature repeatedly highlights the urgency for data governance to be locally grounded, contextually located and able to protect learner rights whilst allowing analytics on their behalf that may be beneficial. Data sovereignty and fair data sharing are highlighted as tactical targets to avert digital colonialism in the Global South literature, emphasising local community-directed benefits (Berkel et al., 2020; Chand et al., 2020).

5.4 Case-Informed Insights From Rural and Global South Contexts

Across contexts in rural and Global South locales, qualitative studies and systematic reviews on the overall use of AI-enabled assessment systems offer a number of common themes. AI has the capacity to augment education quality and make assessment more efficient, but its immediate potential depends greatly on context-sensitive design. Infrastructure, heterogeneity of languages spoken, and lack of faculty development are strong determinants of outcomes across these contexts. Case-based evidence from ESL contexts in LMICs, including Pakistan and rural China, highlights both opportunities (and dangers), underpinning the role of tailored instructional design, robust offline or edge-enabled technological modalities and stakeholder governance across a spectrum of scalable but sustainable and equitable impact (Kundu & Bej 2025).

By implication, the literature review reinforces claims that AI tools need to be aligned with rural and sub-Saharan contexts if they are ultimately to deliver maximum benefit, ruling out local epistemologies, multi-lingual realities and discipline-specific practices. These benefits, however, are highly contingent upon effective teacher preparation and sustained professional support. Furthermore, cross-border partnerships, especially South–South collaborations, are important conduits for knowledge exchange and data sharing, allowing datasets/tools to be used across geographic boundaries without the threat of dependence on Northern-centric data infrastructures, if governance mechanisms preserve data sovereignty (Li & Gao 2025). Similarly, parallel to the transformations in technologies, it has been documented that ethical and governance frameworks need to grow along with them to solve for transparency, accountability and access-to-redress issues for the learners affected by these (Moon, 2023).

While there is consensus that AI can add value in these contexts, the literature also highlights important nuances and disagreements of magnitude. Some scholars recommend rapid AI-scaling as a tool for closing equity gaps and speeding up the inclusion of marginalised people in education, while others issue a warning that if we previously deployed technologies early, especially without adequate governance mechanisms and local capacity, we may reignite similar inequalities with insufficiently tested development scale. An emerging synthesis offers a balanced perspective suggesting the need for contextualised design, ongoing capacity-building and robust policy frameworks as necessary preconditions for scaleable impact, equity (Chand et al., 2020).

Analysis of the four subsections converges towards a common theme, that AI-enabled assessment in the Global South, as well as rural and resource-constrained higher education contexts, can make an important contribution to improving matters of increasing quality in feedback provision, boosting operational efficiency and obtaining better learner outcomes. But this promise can only be fulfilled when implementation is based on national priorities, backed by effective governance mechanisms, and explicitly designed to promote equity through linguistic and cultural inclusion, along with learner agency. The variations in outcomes of the studies, however, are to a large extent reflective of unique infrastructure, data quality, faculty readiness and policy environments. The literature also points to unresolved issues, particularly in terms of tradeoffs with respect to edge and cloud computing; the degree of automation in assessment and moderation; and best governance models for ensuring that AI educational systems do not serve to compound existing inequities but rather promote educational justice.

Figure 1. Evidence Base Across Domains (AI-Enabled Assessment)

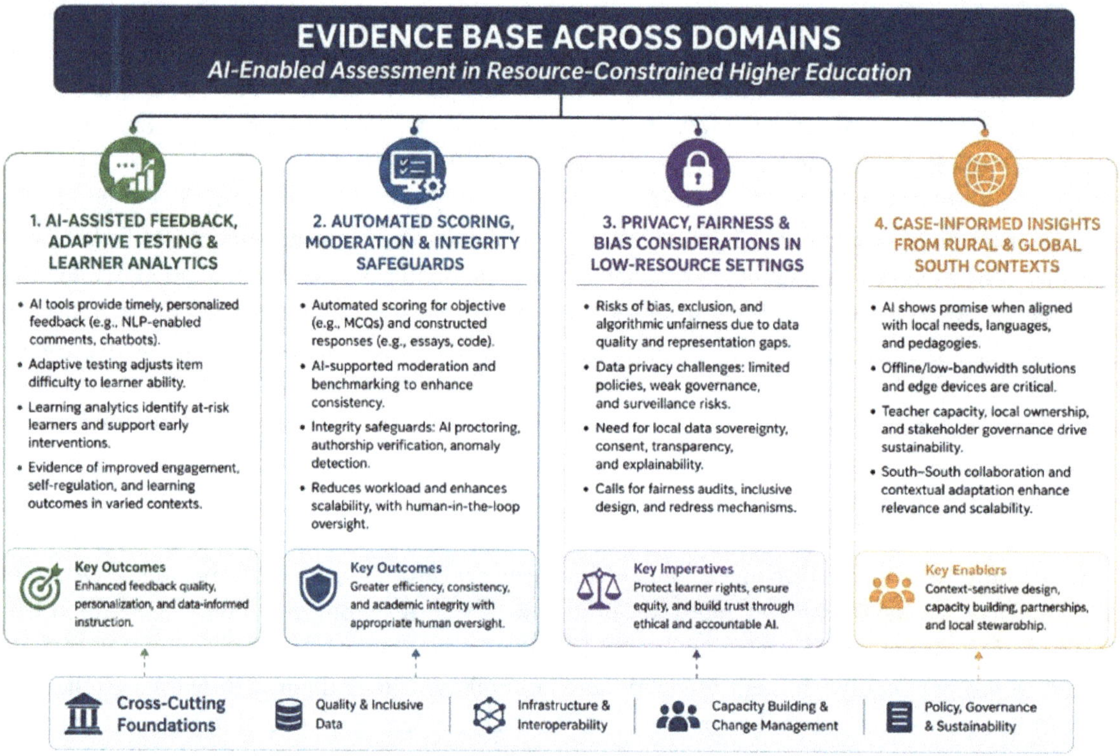

Callout: The value of AI-enabled assessment does not lie in technology alone, but in the alignment of pedagogical innovation, ethical governance, and contextual relevance. Effective deployment emerges at the intersection of intelligent feedback systems, robust assessment integrity, equitable data practices, and deep sensitivity to local realities, particularly in resource-constrained and Global South contexts.

The preceding evidence demonstrates that successful AI-enabled assessment depends not only on technological capability but also on institutional context, governance, and educational priorities. Building upon these findings, this section translates the evidence into practical implementation configurations that institutions can adapt according to their own resource environments.

6. PRACTICAL CONFIGURATIONS FOR VIABLE DEPLOYMENTS

Deploying AI-enabled assessment in Global South, rural, and resource-constrained higher education contexts requires configurations that are both technically feasible and socio-culturally appropriate. The four configurations presented in this section collectively constitute an implementation model for AI-enabled assessment in resource-constrained higher education. Rather than prescribing a single technological solution, the model illustrates how infrastructure, governance, modular system design, and stakeholder collaboration interact to support context-sensitive institutional adoption. Drawing on evidence across healthcare, education, and digital infrastructure in low-resource settings, this section outlines four practical configurations that can support viable deployments: (6.1) lightweight, offline-capable assessment apps and frugal data pipelines; (6.2) cloud-enabled analytics with local data stewardship; (6.3) modular assessment architectures for diverse disciplines; and (6.4) defined stakeholder roles spanning instructors, administrators, policymakers, and communities (Figure 2). These configurations reflect a design orientation that prioritises resilience, equity, and sustainability while acknowledging contextual trade-offs and governance needs.

6.1 Lightweight, Offline-Capable Assessment Apps and Frugal Data Pipelines

In settings characterised by intermittent connectivity and limited bandwidth, offline-capable assessment apps paired with frugal data pipelines are essential for maintaining continuity of assessment activities and learner feedback. The empirical synthesis from low-middle-income country (LMIC) health and education contexts identifies edge computing, on-device inference via machine learning, and asynchronous data sync as core elements to mitigate outages while preserving data sovereignty. On the practical side, lightweight mobile or desktop apps must enable local storage of submissions, offline rubrics, and offline plagiarism checks, with secure (batched) synchronisation when connectivity gets better. Frugal data pipelines dramatically reduce bandwidth by sending only select features or metadata so analytics can be performed on time with minimal impact on network resources (Wang et al., 2023). Energy concerns call for energy-efficient hardware and, whenever possible, solar-powered solutions to avoid outages that may interrupt assessment cycles. To make sure that these delivery channels can deliver continued continuity during outages, data such as printable rubrics and low-bandwidth interfaces help. These approaches are part of a broader necessity to protect learner participation and preserve the integrity of assessment in resource-sparse contexts (Kundu & Bej, 2025).

Figure 2. Viability Through Alignment

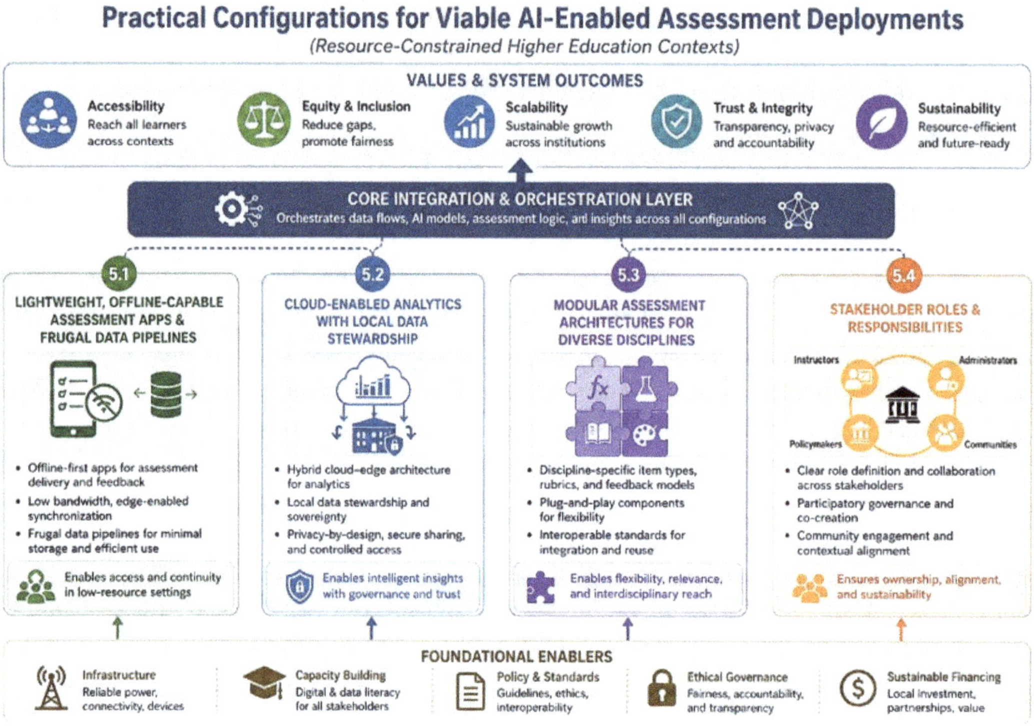

Callout: Viable AI-enabled assessment systems emerge not from technology alone, but from the alignment of lightweight infrastructure, responsible data governance, modular design, and inclusive stakeholder engagement. When these elements operate in synergy, they enable equitable, scalable, and sustainable learning outcomes in resource-constrained contexts.

6.2 Cloud-Enabled Analytics With Local Data Stewardship

Cloud-powered analytics provide impressive yet under-utilised learning analytics and scoring that are particularly relevant to large cohorts, but need to be deployed with care because they may breach data sovereignty and privacy in contexts where regulatory maturity is uneven. A governance-savvy configuration connects cloud analytics with strong local data stewardship that encompasses data localisation and transparent data use policies coupled with adequate consent practices based on local customs (Berkel et al., 2020; Tidjon & Khomh, 2022). Federated or edge-enabled analytics may find a sweet spot between analytic power vs locality/privacy. Unless existing legislation and regulatory environments are permissive, multilateral or regional data-sharing arrangements would be needed to support benchmarking as well as cross-institutional fairness audits, at an institution-specific level where governance standards are harmonised, and appropriate stakeholder voices heard in the decision-making process (Kundu & Bej, 2025). Analytics should be formative in nature, tracking paths of both learning and teaching to provide timely feedback from instructors to guide focused intervention; however, analytics can also be used for high-stakes decisions, undermining agency in the learner.

6.3 Modular Assessment Architectures for Diverse Disciplines

A modular architecture allows reconfigurable assessment components to be added, combined or substituted without needing to rebuild the entire modular system and supports diverse disciplinary needs across varying institution capacities. Configurable assets like discipline-agnostic rubrics and language considerations can be integral to modules addressing core functions like AI-assisted feedback, automated scoring, integrity safeguards and learning analytics. In practice, a modular approach enables embeddable (offline) modules for content delivery and formative assessment; cloud-enabled modules for advanced analytics or large-scale moderation; and discipline-specific scoring rubrics that are co-designed with local faculty to ensure epistemic alignment and cultural reciprocity (Kundu & Bej, 2025). Heterodonty is especially important in rural and Global South contexts where disciplinary practices and resource availability vary widely: modularity allows for differences while enabling scalability and rapid iterative improvement. Governance should guarantee that modules are piloted with representative student populations and local capacity-building accompanies module adoption to ensure quality and equity across disciplines.

6.4 Stakeholder Roles: Instructors, Administrators, Policymakers, Community

A responsible deployment must define roles for stakeholders and require collaborative governance to anchor AI in meeting educational goals and learners' rights. Faculty still play a key role in pedagogical judgement, by interpreting AI feedback, confirming automated scoring, and protecting the integrity of their discipline. Administrators organise deployment, assess the adequacy of infrastructure and fundamentals, manage funding, and oversee compliance with data governance and ethical standards. Policymakers oversee the guardrails for all of this regulation, promoting cross-institutional collaboration and linking funding streams to national or regional educational justice objectives. Participation of community representatives and student bodies in governance must be emphasised as a safeguard to ensure transparency, accountability, and culturally responsive design that minimises the chances for bias by ensuring assessments track what counts as legitimate local values and languages. Evidence from a diversity of South–South and Global South contexts suggests the need for participatory governance where stakeholders co-design AI tools, build consent and redress mechanisms, and monitor fairness and impact over time. On an operational level, governance structures should incorporate simple ethics checklists during the project scoping, recurring bias audits and transparent reporting on AI performance and shortcomings to all stakeholders. Roles aligned with local capacity-building initiatives, like faculty development, training in data literacy and IT skills, not only promote sustainability and local ownership but also limit dependence on external providers for improvements that often do not endure beyond pilot projects.

In sum, viable deployments in resource-constrained higher education settings require a triad of strategies (Figure 3): (i) technical configurations that prioritise offline functionality, data frugality, and resilience; (ii) governance and data stewardship that safeguard privacy, local sovereignty, and transparency; and (iii) a modular, discipline-sensitive architecture underpinned by authentic stakeholder engagement and capacity-building. When implemented with attention to local aims, language and culture, and equitable governance, these configurations can yield AI-enabled assessments that are both impactful and sustainable in the Global South, rural, and resource-constrained higher education contexts.

Figure 3. The Triad of Viability

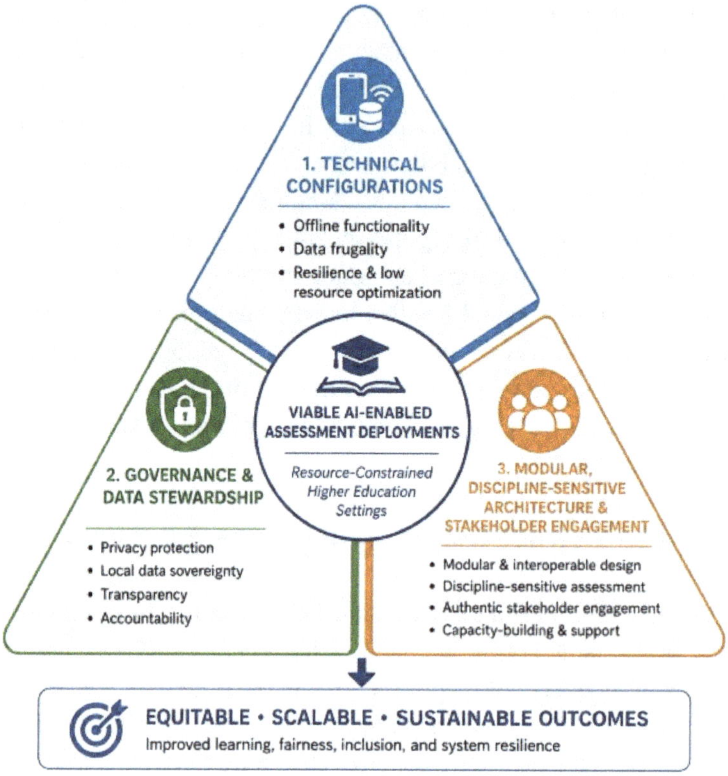

Callout: Sustainable AI-enabled assessment in resource-constrained higher education emerges at the intersection of technical resilience, ethical governance, and modular, stakeholder-driven design. When these three elements are aligned, they enable systems that are not only functional but also equitable, scalable, and contextually grounded.

The implementation configurations proposed above provide general guidance for institutional deployment. Their practical relevance becomes clearer, however, when considered within representative institutional scenarios that illustrate how different contextual conditions shape implementation choices.

7. CASE STUDIES AND SCENARIOS

To illustrate how the conceptual principles and implementation configurations discussed in earlier sections translate into practice, this section presents case-informed scenarios drawn from evidence reported across Global South and resource-constrained higher education contexts. Rather than describing isolated institutional experiences, these scenarios synthesise recurring implementation patterns, governance challenges, and contextual adaptations observed across the literature.

7.1 Rural Campus Implementation in Sub-Saharan Africa and South Asia

Case evidence from rural campuses in sub-Saharan Africa and South Asia highlights the importance of context-sensitive deployment; feasibility and impact are mediated by capacity limitations, language diversity, and faculty development. Offline-capable AI-enabled assessment tools and edge or hybrid architectures become so fundamental in discontinuous electricity and limited bandwidth environments, ensuring that frequent assessment cycles are enabled with timely feedback despite connectivity gaps. In resource-constrained environments, co-designing local assessment tasks with faculty and communities maintains relevance through epistemological and disciplinary alignment while protecting the agency of learner. Governance mechanisms, where transparently, data practices share how consent is used and how ongoing bias monitoring will continue to be measured, are vital for trust and ensuring that learners are treated equitably across languages and local livelihoods (Berkel et al., 2020). Cross-case evidence also highlights the importance of scalable, repeatable, modular components that can be iteratively refined as capacity in solution-providing rural campuses grows with focused attention on building individual and institutional capabilities while maximising local ownership and South–South support to avoid creating a reliance on external providers and specifying guidance tools according to regional requirements (Li & Gao, 2025; Zhang & Wu, 2025).

7.2 Peri-Urban and LMIC Institutions: Governance and Sustainability

Peri-urban and LMIC contexts also present a unique confluence of opportunities and challenges, with changing regulatory environments, variable infrastructure, and severe budgetary constraints. In these contexts, viable deployments focus on governance and sustainability as key principles of design: data sovereignty and privacy-by-design, minimal ethics review processes, and stakeholder-inclusive governance comprising students, faculty, and community voices in decision-making (Kundu & Bej, 2025). In practice, this translates to cloud analytics balanced by local data stewardship; federated or edge-enabled analytics respecting sovereignty and fiscal realities; modular deployment strategies fitting budgeting constraints and maintenance capacity (Wang et al. 2023). The literature highlights the need for building local capacity, digital literacy for faculty and administrators, ongoing technical support, and pathways to maintenance and upgrades, to ensure initial pilots can be institutionalised as lasting, scalable practices rather than temporary experiments. Partnerships across institutions, including South–South partnerships, provide mechanisms to exchange or share data/ tooling/ knowledge while maintaining a local control mindset and context sensitivity, elements that ground sustainability enhancement in a more legitimate governance (Tidjon & Khomh, 2022).

7.3 Cross-Institutional Partnerships and North-South Collaboration

Collaborative cross-institutional partnerships–North-South, South-South, and intra-regional collaborations-are characterised in the literature as necessary for effective scaling of AI-enabled assessment in Global South sites, so long as they are built on mutual benefit, equity, and strong governance. While North–South collaborations can open up powerful digital tools and datasets, they also have the potential for solar colonialism unless true local data sovereignty, contextualization, and genuine participatory governance are rigorously pursued (Sampath et al., 2021). South–South partnerships are touted to offer a possible solution for geopolitically significant eastern and southern data sharing, open-source tooling, and best practices whilst reducing dependency upon Northern providers; however, they need governance frameworks that ensure equitable decision-making, capacity-building and transparent accountability (Zhang & Wu, 2025). It is also argued that success in AI adoption hinges on close co-design of competencies, research agendas and capacity-building programs (Berkel et al., 2020), with special care applied to embedding ethical reasoning, consent, and opportunities for redress when learners are directly affected by an AI-driven decision-making process (Kundu & Bej, 2025). These collaborations are usually most effective when grounded in open standards, shared data governance agreements, and a firm expression of advantages to all participating partners, including students and frontline faculty (Mariyono & Mistar, 2025).

7.4 Scenario Planning: Envisioning Equitable AI-Enhanced Assessment Trajectories

Scenario planning in this context helps illuminate the future of AI-enhanced assessment in higher education, grade aids combined with course validation constraint points that help tease out vital leverage points regarding equity, governance and sustainability. A potential path is the conservative-growth scenario, with deployments favouring offline-capable and easily modifiable systems backed by robust local governance structures, limited reliance on cloud-based analytics, and tight ethical controls. This pathway promotes equity through strategic language supports, culturally responsive assessment rubrics, and long-term capacity-building support. But yes, it removes some risk and fits nicely into context; this comes at the cost of scalability and a much slower rate of cross-institution learning (due to having less data shared).

The second trajectory is the inclusive-acceleration scenario, where federated and edge-enabled analytics drive rapid scaling of AI-enabled assessment in partnership across institutions and regions. It fuses technological expansion with all- encompassing capacity-overtaking and participatory governance to ensure that stakeholders are deeply involved in determining implementation. The returns derived include improved feedback quality at a faster pace, richer learner analytics, and system-level impact. Simultaneously, this scenario prioritises a robust data property rights structure while protecting against privacy violation and enforcing an accountability mechanism for all processes, avoiding the internal reinforcement of existing inequalities as scale increases.

The third scenario is an uneven-advancement trajectory where improvements have not been across the board or at all institutions. Because sophisticated infrastructure and governance unlock fruitful potential for significant growth at some institutions, it is regarding to observe areas where applicable action resources are underutilised because of constraints that stem from limited financial capital, weak governance frameworks or institutional disaggregation. This schism could deepen the equity gap, creating a widening disparity between institutions and learner populations. This underscores the need for purposeful bridge-building efforts, standards-setting and focused investment to promote a more balanced advancement across the higher ed ecosystem.

Core design principles remain consistent across these trajectories: Assessments must be grounded in local objectives and epistemologies; privacy, fairness, and cultural responsiveness must drive decisions at every stage; configurations that prefer edge-first and offline-capable implementations can safeguard equity of access over time; systems should exhibit governance and capacity-building that distributes ownership between instructors, administrators, policymakers, and communities. The literature consistently warns against uncontextualized capacities to produce AI, although it also reports the considerable potential for AI-enabled diagnosis to enhance learning, equity and social mobility in rural and LMIC higher education under these conditions.

The preceding case-informed scenarios illustrate both the opportunities and constraints associated with AI-enabled assessment. The final analytical step is therefore to translate these lessons into actionable implications for universities, policymakers, funding agencies, and institutional leaders responsible for future implementation.

8. IMPLICATIONS FOR POLICY AND PRACTICE

8.1 Implications for University Governance and Accreditation

To successfully implement AI-enabled assessment in low-and-middle-income contexts, universities must build mechanisms for governance that both preserve students' rights whilst preserving the relevance of assessing within local contexts as innovation flourishes. Governance needs to align with accreditation expectations by clearly delineating the place of AI in assessment, making scoring and feedback transparent across programs, and creating redress pathways for learners adversely impacted by algorithmic decisions (Berkel et al., 2020). Formal AI governance policies are needed to fill the gaps that arise as institutions adopt AI across faculties and programs (Cudjoe, 2025; Diallo et al., 2025). Context-appropriate, modular and offline-capable configurations unlikely to meet the cloud-only model privileged by many accreditation bodies in rural LMIC settings may need to revise their criteria. To sustain the quality and equity of AI-enabled assessments, universities must embed capacity-building programs for faculty and assessment staff in data literacy, management of algorithmic accountability, and feedback, scoring rubric design.

8.2 Policy Recommendations for Government and Funding Agencies

Policy makers and funders could thus be in a position to shape the enabling environment for equitable AI-enabled assessment in the Global South. Recommendations include: (a) develop a national or regional AI governance framework for education that clearly addresses the issues of privacy, data sovereignty, bias monitoring and redress mechanisms with assignments of accountability to bodies and timelines available for policy maturation. Funding the development of sustainable, modular architectures that support offline capabilities and open standards to incentivize capacity-building and local ownership (b) promote cross-institutional and cross-country data governance arrangements that can reconcile competing pressures for data sharing and sovereignty; ensuring datasets used for AI in education reflect local languages, epistemologies, and disciplinary practices (c) bind funding and require impact assessment and continuous auditing (includes: bias audits, privacy impact assessments, public reporting of AI performance/limitations/corrective actions); (Mariyono & Mistar 2025); and (d) promote South–South as well North–South collaboration based on sharing governance principles to ensure more equitable benefits, mutual benefit and capacity-building while sidestepping the digital colonialism or unintentional dependency on Northern vendors (Tidjon & Khomh, 2022). Likewise, wherever possible, funders should support work on open-source tooling and open data practices to help decrease the total cost of ownership and improve transparency and reproducibility.

8.3 Pathways to Scale While Preserving Inclusion and Learner Agency

Scaling up AI-enabled assessment in resource-constrained higher education has to be undertaken with care and reference to inclusion and learner agency. Broadly, key pathways comprise: (a) edge-first and offline-capable architectures to enable continuous assessment and feedback across unreliable connectivity, with modular analytics built for low-bandwidth; (b) iterative co-design procedures that engage students, faculty, and communities in producing locally-meaningful tasks, multilingual rubrics, and culturally situated feedback to render assessments both legitimate (Wang et al., 2025) (c) strategy for data sovereignty-leading with local storage and processing where appropriate,36 then federated or edge-enabled analytic production to balance power, privacy and analytic utility (Berkel et al.,2020); (4) existing infrastructure, long-term collaboration with on-the-ground organizations; (d) useable evaluation frameworks which link learning outcomes to equity metrics, supporting evidence-informed scaling that narrows gaps in language in rural and resource-poor settings (Li & Gao, 2025). Institutional collaborations must integrate open standards, competencies and capacity building programs to scale-up, but in a context-sensitive manner where local governance is respected (Mariyono & Mistar, 2025).

In essence, the journey towards scaling can only be paved through a careful blending of technical feasibility with principles of good governance and unyielding commitments to learner rights, culture and justice in education, ensuring that AI-enabled assessment is deployed as an enabler for equitable high-quality teaching and learning in disadvantaged higher education contexts (Kundu & Bej, 2025).

Drawing together the conceptual discussion, evidence synthesis, implementation configurations, and policy implications presented throughout the chapter, the conclusion highlights the central lessons emerging from the literature and identifies priorities for future AI-enabled assessment in resource-constrained higher education.

9. FUTURE RESEARCH DIRECTIONS

The synthesis presented in this chapter demonstrates that AI-enabled assessment has considerable potential to transform higher education in Global South, rural, and resource-constrained contexts. However, the current evidence base remains fragmented, with important conceptual, methodological, and practical gaps that warrant further investigation.

First, there is a need for longitudinal research examining the sustained impact of AI-enabled assessment on student learning, assessment quality, academic integrity, and graduate outcomes. Most existing studies evaluate pilot implementations or short-term interventions, providing limited evidence regarding institutional sustainability or the long-term educational consequences of AI adoption. Future research should therefore examine how AI-enabled assessment evolves across multiple academic cycles and institutional contexts.

Second, comparative studies across Global South regions are required. Although the literature increasingly recognises that resource-constrained contexts are highly heterogeneous, relatively few studies compare implementation experiences across Africa, South Asia, Southeast Asia, Latin America, and other developing regions. Comparative investigations would improve understanding of how differences in infrastructure, governance, language diversity, educational policy, and institutional capacity influence AI adoption and assessment outcomes.

Third, further research is needed to develop and validate context-sensitive implementation and governance frameworks for AI-enabled assessment. Existing governance models are largely derived from technologically advanced educational systems and often assume levels of digital infrastructure, regulatory maturity, and institutional capacity that are not universally available. Future studies should therefore investigate governance approaches that reflect local policy environments, institutional realities, and cultural expectations while protecting learner rights, data sovereignty, transparency, and accountability.

A fourth priority concerns equity, language, and cultural inclusivity. Current AI assessment systems frequently rely on datasets and language models developed for dominant global languages, creating risks of algorithmic bias and unequal educational opportunities. Future research should explore multilingual assessment models, culturally responsive AI systems, and evaluation approaches capable of recognising diverse epistemologies, disciplinary traditions, and local knowledge systems within higher education.

Fifth, there is considerable scope for research examining low-resource technological architectures. While this chapter highlights the importance of offline-capable applications, edge computing, modular assessment systems, and frugal data infrastructures, empirical evidence evaluating their educational effectiveness remains limited. Comparative studies examining different technological configurations under varying levels of infrastructure availability would provide valuable guidance for institutional decision-makers.

Finally, future scholarship should move beyond evaluating technological performance alone and examine the broader institutional transformation associated with AI-enabled assessment. This includes faculty readiness, organisational change, policy implementation, professional development, stakeholder participation, learner trust, and institutional governance. Mixed-methods and interdisciplinary research capable of integrating technological, pedagogical, organisational, and policy perspectives will be particularly valuable in generating evidence that supports equitable and sustainable AI adoption.

These research priorities suggest that the future of AI-enabled assessment lies not simply in developing increasingly sophisticated technologies, but in understanding how technological innovation can be aligned with pedagogical purpose, institutional governance, cultural diversity, and educational justice. Advancing this agenda will require collaborative research involving educators, policymakers, technologists, and local communities to ensure that AI-enabled assessment contributes meaningfully to inclusive and contextually responsive higher education.

10. CONCLUSION

Altogether, the evidence suggests AI-driven assessment has potential for significant improvements in timely feedback, instructional quality and scalable moderation in resource-constrained higher education, but only if deployments are contextualised by local aims, underpinned by strong governance, and designed inclusively. Important design imperatives include offline-first and edge-enabled configurations to progress narrower ranges of unreliable connectivity, uncertain vitality, modular architectures that can adapt to self-determination diversity and changing capacity trades, and data governance set up locally sovereign baseline functionality with transparency mechanisms and continual auditing for bias. It should involve consent, redress mechanisms, and participatory decision-making that engages students, faculty, administrators, and community representatives to validate the cultural relevance of human expertise as a bulwark of learner agency. Capacity-building, which homes in on continuous professional development in AI literacy, data governance, and ethical design, appears necessary to support sustainability beyond pilot projects. Cross-institutional collaboration, especially South–South partnerships, represents a practical means for sharing tools and datasets (especially context-sensitive learning as opposed to export-based learning) while reducing dependence on more Northern-led providers. When AI is implemented with due care and caution, the returns on investment in terms of pathways to learning, equitable access, and increased social mobility can be extraordinarily high, helping ensure more inclusive and robust higher education systems in the Global South and similar resource-limited environments globally. This synthesis argues that an effective balance among potential, principles, governance, pedagogy, and rootedness is required if AI-assisted assessment promotes equity in education rather than undermining it.

REFERENCES

Apata, A. O., & Oyedele, M. O. (2025). Undergraduates' Application of ChatGPT in Academic Writing: Perceptions, Problems and Prospects. *International Journal of Social Sciences and Management Review*, *8*(3), 201–218. DOI: 10.37602/IJSSMR.2025.8312

Berkel, N. van, Papachristos, E., Giachanou, A., Hosio, S., & Skov, M. B. (2020). A Systematic Assessment of National Artificial Intelligence Policies: Perspectives from the Nordics and Beyond. 1–12. DOI: 10.1145/3419249.3420106

Chand, V. S., Kostić, S., & Reis, A. (2020). Taxing Artificial Intelligence and Robots: Critical Assessment of Potential Policy Solutions and Recommendation for Alternative Approaches. *World Tax J.*, *12*(4). Advance online publication. DOI: 10.59403/2sjxe4d

Chen, R., Wu, Y., Chen, Z., & Zhou, P. (2025). Advancing educational equity in rural China: The impact of AI devices on teaching quality and learning outcomes for sustainable development. *Frontiers in Psychology*, *16*, 1588047. Advance online publication. DOI: 10.3389/fpsyg.2025.1588047 PMID: 41267767

Cudjoe, E. K., & Adebayo, J. O. (2025). Investigating the Existence of AI Policy in Higher Education Institutions in Sub-Saharan Africa. *Proceedings of the Association for Information Science and Technology*, *62*(1), 1414–1417. DOI: 10.1002/pra2.1421

Diallo, K., Smith, J. W., Okolo, C. T., Nyamwaya, D., Kgomo, J., & Ngamita, R. (2025). Case studies of AI policy development in Africa. *Data & Policy*, *7*, e15. Advance online publication. DOI: 10.1017/dap.2024.71

Jafar, S. H., Oyedele, O. M., Nawaah, D., & Bolanle, A. S. (2025). Exploring Leadership Challenges for Adoption of Digital Innovation and Sustainability, Singh, R., Corvello, V., Coniglio, I.M. and Khan, S. (Ed.) *Innovation Ecosystems and Sustainable Technologies* (*Emerald Studies in Sustainable Innovation Management*), Emerald Publishing Limited, Leeds, pp. 253-269. DOI: 10.1108/978-1-83662-368-720251012

Kundu, A., & Bej, T. (2025). Empowering Students' Autonomy in EFL Learning: AI Innovations in Schools of the Global South. *The Electronic Journal on Information Systems in Developing Countries*, *91*(6), e70041. Advance online publication. DOI: 10.1002/isd2.70041

Li, M., & Gao, W. (2025). Exploring How Human Capital Development Promotes Economic Transformation. *Journal of Organizational and End User Computing*, *37*(1), 1–22. DOI: 10.4018/JOEUC.388939

Maina, M. F. (2025). *Enhancing personalized formative feedback in higher education: A GenAI-powered tool design and implementation.* In *Proceedings of the EDEN Annual Conference 2025: Shaping the Future of Education in the Age of AI.*

Makeleni, S., Mutongoza, B. H., & Linake, M. A. (2023). Language Education and Artificial Intelligence: An Exploration of Challenges Confronting Academics in Global South Universities. *Journal of Culture and Values in Education*, *6*(2), 158–171. DOI: 10.46303/jcve.2023.14

Mangubat, F. M., & Mangubat, F. (2025). Consequences, Trends, and Future Directions in Using AI in Science Education: Is it a Boon or a Bane? *Research Square*. DOI: 10.21203/rs.3.rs-7708506/v1

Mariyono, D., & Mistar, J. (2025). Digital Education Strategies in Anaesthesiology: A Systematic Review and SWOT Analysis. DOI: 10.21203/rs.3.rs-7476309/v1

Mhlanga, D., Denhere, V., & Moloi, T. (2022). COVID-19 and the Key Digital Transformation Lessons for Higher Education Institutions in South Africa. *Education Sciences*, *12*(7), 464. DOI: 10.3390/educsci12070464

Moon, M. J. (2023). Searching for inclusive artificial intelligence for social good: Participatory governance and policy recommendations for making AI more inclusive and benign for society. *Public Administration Review*, *83*(6), 1496–1505. DOI: 10.1111/puar.13648

Oyenuga, M. O., Andah, R. A., & Apata, S. B. (2026). AI and Assessment: Generating and Grading Foreign Language Assignments Automatically. In Dehghan, F. (Ed.), *Harnessing AI-Generated Content in Language Education* (pp. 123–152). IGI Global Scientific Publishing., DOI: 10.4018/979-8-3373-2721-1.ch006

Oyenuga, M. O., Apata, S. B., & Sulaiman, M. M. (2024). Pre-Service Teachers' Perceptions and Utilisation of Chatgpt in Higher Institutions using UTAUT Theory: Evidence from an Emerging Economy. *British Journal of Contemporary Education*, *4*(2), 28–42. DOI: 10.52589/BJCE-DBIT7S4T

Oyenuga, M. O., & Omale, S. A. (2024). Is Africa Jinxed? Exploring the Challenges of Technology Access and Adoption in Africa. *African Journal of Economic and Sustainable Development*, *7*(4), 142–161. DOI: 10.52589/AJESD-ULN1LRNF

Saleem, T., Saleem, A., & Aslam, D. M. (2025). Integrating AI in Pakistani ESL classrooms: Teachers' practices, perspectives, and impact on student performance. *PLoS One*, *20*(9), e0333352. DOI: 10.1371/journal.pone.0333352 PMID: 41026767

Sampath, P. G. (2021). Governing Artificial Intelligence in an Age of Inequality. *Global Policy*, *12*(S6), 21–31. DOI: 10.1111/1758-5899.12940

Siyi, C., Yu, Q., & Al-Samawi, A. (2023). Effects of digital education on human resource development. *Human Systems Management*, *42*(6), 691–706. DOI: 10.3233/HSM-230111

Tidjon, L. N., & Khomh, F. (2022). The Different Faces of AI Ethics Across the World: A Principle-Implementation Gap Analysis. /arxiv.2206.03225DOI: 10.48550

Wang, X., Sanders, H. M., Liu, Y., Seang, K., Tran, B. X., Atanasov, A. G., Qiu, Y., Tang, S., Car, J., Wang, Y. X., Wong, T. Y., Tham, Y. C., & Chung, K. C. (2023). ChatGPT: Promise and challenges for deployment in low- and middle-income countries. *The Lancet Regional Health. Western Pacific*, *41*, 100905. DOI: 10.1016/j.lanwpc.2023.100905 PMID: 37731897

Zhang, J., & Wu, H. (2025). Reimagining South–South Higher Education Interactions Under "Triple Disruptions.". *Ecnu Review of Education*, *8*(3), 638–657. DOI: 10.1177/20965311251335986

Chapter 14
Generative Artificial Intelligence in South African Higher Education:
Ethical Challenges, Misuse, and Implications for Assessment Outcomes and Academics

Patrick Alpheous Nyathi
http://orcid.org/0000-0002-3473-7743
University of South Africa, South Africa

Nokuthula Diborah Nkosi
http://orcid.org/0000-0002-0586-6466
University of South Africa, South Africa

ABSTRACT

This chapter examines the implications of generative artificial intelligence for assessment practices, academic integrity and quality assurance in South African higher education institutions. As AI-powered tools such as ChatGPT, SciSpace, Gemini, and Copilot become embedded in teaching, learning and assessment, they offer opportunities to enhance efficiency, feedback and assessment design while raising ethical concerns about misconduct, authorship, transparency and assessment validity. Drawing on the Theory of Planned Behaviour and the Utilitarian Theory of Ethics, the chapter adopts a conceptual and critical approach to analyse how the literature portrays academics' and students' perceptions, adoption and justification of the ethical or unethical use of generative artificial intelligence in assessment contexts. Particular attention is given to challenges surrounding originality, intellectual property, and authenticity, which, in turn, have implications for assessment outcomes.

DOI: 10.4018/979-8-3373-8939-4.ch014

INTRODUCTION

The concept of artificial intelligence (AI) is not new. It was coined by McCarthy in 1956 and the field is now approaching seven decades old. This concept holds different meanings for individuals across various fields and is experiencing rapid growth worldwide (Hutson et al., 2022). This reality necessitates a rethinking and reimagining of the future of higher education, where Generative Artificial Intelligence (GenAI) is understood not merely as a disruptive force but as an embedded and enduring feature of academic life. AI is now poised to drive significant disruption and transformation across various aspects of human life. The rapid expansion of AI-powered applications is evident, with their presence growing across key industries, including healthcare, aerospace, education, law, manufacturing, agriculture and transportation (Dhawan & Batra, 2020). It has grown and changed since 1956 as significant technological advancements have occurred (Crompton & Burke, 2023). Since then, AI has become integral to many aspects of human life (Gnambs et al., 2025), including the global higher education landscape.

The emergence of generative artificial intelligence (GenAI) in academic spaces has elicited mixed emotions among academics, administrators and university management personnel. It is one of the most widely discussed and analysed technological developments of the modern era. While some scholars caution against its widespread use, arguing that GenAI compromises academic integrity and diminishes students' intellectual engagement (see Pisica et al., 2023), others advocate for its ethical adoption, emphasising its potential to enhance teaching, learning and assessment when appropriately regulated (see Mhlanga, 2023). These divergent perspectives underscore the need for nuanced, context-sensitive analyses that move beyond binary positions of acceptance or rejection.

Within higher education, assessment has emerged as one of the most contested and high-stakes domains of GenAI adoption. AI-powered tools are increasingly used by students to generate assignments and by academics to design assessments, produce feedback and evaluate student work. While these practices offer potential efficiency gains and pedagogical benefits, they simultaneously raise profound ethical concerns regarding academic integrity, assessment validity, authorship, transparency and quality assurance. As a result, assessment has become a critical site where the tensions between innovation and integrity, efficiency and equity and opportunity and risk are most sharply visible and where institutional responses to GenAI are most urgently required.

The chapter acknowledges the divergent views and concerns revolving around the ethical and unethical use of GenAI and argues that higher education institutions should neither uncritically resist nor unconditionally embrace these technologies. Instead, it contends that GenAI is not a temporary phenomenon but a permanent feature of contemporary academic practice that requires thoughtful governance and ethical stewardship. This chapter employs a conceptual and critical approach to explore the ethical and unethical use of GenAI in Higher Education Institutions (HEIs) through the lens of the Theory of Planned Behaviour (TPB). It draws on existing scholarship and policy-oriented debates to examine how attitudes, subjective norms and perceived behavioural control shape AI-related decision-making among students and academics, particularly in relation to assessment practices. In doing so, the chapter provides insight into the motivations that underpin both responsible and irresponsible engagement with GenAI in academic contexts.

To complement this behavioural analysis, the potential benefits and harms of GenAI are examined through the Utilitarian Theory of Ethics, which evaluates ethical action based on its consequences for collective well-being. This dual-theoretical framing enables a balanced interrogation of GenAI's role in higher education assessment, weighing efficiency, innovation and access against risks to integrity, fairness and educational quality. In this way, the chapter advocates the ethical adoption of GenAI as a potentially positive educational tool, while emphasising the need for regulation, assessment redesign, and institutional safeguards to ensure that learning outcomes, research quality and academic standards are not compromised by misuse or opacity.

This chapter contributes to the ongoing discourse on GenAI in higher education by offering theoretically grounded insights into how assessment practices can be reimagined in the age of AI without sacrificing academic integrity or quality assurance, ultimately informing educators, policymakers and institutional leaders seeking responsible pathways for AI integration in higher education.

PROBLEM STATEMENT

Generative Artificial Intelligence (GenAI) is rapidly reshaping assessment practices in higher education, offering new possibilities for efficiency, feedback and assessment design. At the same time, its growing use in assessment contexts has raised significant ethical, pedagogical, and quality-assurance concerns, particularly regarding academic integrity, authorship, and the validity of student learning outcomes. While some scholars advocate for the responsible integration of GenAI into assessment, others caution that its misuse may undermine authentic assessment and compromise the credibility of higher education qualifications. In South Africa, where higher education institutions operate within complex socio-economic and infrastructural conditions, the literature offers limited synthesis on how students and academics are reported to perceive, adopt, and justify the use of generative artificial intelligence in assessment practices. In particular, there is insufficient insight into the motivations, norms, and institutional conditions that shape ethical and unethical uses of AI-powered assessment tools. This gap constrains universities' ability to design assessment policies, quality assurance mechanisms, and pedagogical responses that safeguard academic integrity while harnessing the potential of GenAI. Addressing this problem is critical for informing ethical frameworks and assessment reforms that support quality and integrity in South African higher education.

RESEARCH AIM

This chapter aims to critically examine the use and potential abuse of Generative Artificial Intelligence (GenAI) in South African higher education institutions, with special focus on assessment, assessment outcomes and academic integrity. Grounded in the Theory of Planned Behaviour and the Utilitarian Theory of Ethics, the chapter examines how the literature portrays students' and academics' perceptions, adoption and justification of generative AI use. It interrogates the ethical and pedagogical implications of such practices for assessment design, submission, feedback and the evaluation process in Higher Education. It draws on existing scholarship and policy debates to illuminate the tensions between innovation and integrity, efficiency and equity and individual intentions and collective consequences, ultimately offering insights into how GenAI might be ethically and responsibly integrated into teaching, learning and assessment to safeguard quality and integrity.

RESEARCH QUESTIONS

The following research questions have been formulated to guide this chapter on the ethical and potential misuse of Generative Artificial Intelligence (GenAI) in assessment, academic practices and teaching and learning processes within South African higher education institutions:

- What does the existing literature reveal about how students and academics perceive the use of generative artificial intelligence in teaching, learning and particularly in assessment activities such as assignments, feedback and evaluation?
- What behavioural, social and institutional factors influence the ethical and unethical use of GenAI in assessment, as understood through the Theory of Planned Behaviour?
- How does the literature portray the ways students and academics justify the use or misuse of generative artificial intelligence in assessment and scholarly work from a utilitarian ethical perspective?
- What strategies can higher education institutions employ to ensure the responsible and ethical integration of GenAI into teaching, learning, assessment, and research, thereby upholding academic integrity and quality assurance?

KEY CONCEPTS AND WORKING DEFINITIONS

For clarity and consistency, this chapter uses the following working definitions, developed for the purposes of this discussion rather than drawn from a single external source.

- **Use**: generative artificial intelligence applied to support legitimate academic activity, such as idea generation, drafting assistance, feedback, research support, disclosed and consistent with institutional policy and the specific assessment's requirements.
- **Misuse/abuse**: generative artificial intelligence use that breaches academic integrity, for example, submitting AI-generated content as one's own without disclosure, relying on fabricated or unverified citations or circumventing an assessment designed to test independent thought or skill.
- **Ethical use**: use that is transparent (disclosed) and whose likely consequence, judged on utilitarian grounds, supports learning, fairness and academic integrity rather than undermines them.
- **Assessment outcome**: the result of an assessment process, understood in terms of whether it is validly and fairly reflects the student's own competence, understanding and effort.
- **Quality assurance**: the institutional structure, policies and processes through which higher education institutions verify that assessment practices, credentials and academic standards remain valid, trustworthy and fair in the context of generative AI adoption.

THEORETICAL PERSPECTIVES

This chapter adopts two theories to examine the use and potential misuse of Generative Artificial Intelligence (GenAI) in South African Higher Education Institutions (HEIs). Theoretical framing is explicitly applied to assessment contexts, including assignment generation, evaluation, feedback, and institutional quality control. The Theory of Planned Behaviour is used to understand the intentions, attitudes and perceived control that influence the adoption of GenAI by students and academics. The Utilitarian Theory of Ethics guides the ethical analysis, weighing the benefits and harms of GenAI use in educational contexts. These frameworks offer insight into both behavioural motivations and ethical implications, particularly as they relate to assessment integrity, quality assurance and responsible AI adoption in higher education.

The Theory of Planned Behaviour (TPB)

Since its introduction, the Theory of Planned Behaviour (TPB) has become one of the most frequently cited and influential models for predicting human social behaviour (Ajzen, 2011; Armitage, 2001). According to Armitage (2001), this theory is essentially an extension of the Theory of Reasoned Action (TRA), which includes measures of control, belief and perceived behavioural control. Despite its popularity, TPB has been widely criticised and has sparked debate. While other researchers embrace it, others have rejected it outright as an adequate explanation of human social behaviour (Ajzen, 2011). These critics overlook the significance of consciousness as a causal agent of human social behaviour (Ajzen, 2011). The Theory of Planned Behaviour (TPB) is not inherently a theory of behaviour change but rather a framework for explaining and predicting individuals' intentions and actions. However, it can still effectively design interventions to influence behaviour (Ajzen, 2014). Numerous factors drive human social behaviours, some intentional, others unintentional.

In the context of GenAI in HEIs, TPB provides a valuable lens for understanding the intentions behind both the ethical use and misuse (abuse) of GenAI by students and academics, particularly in assessment-related tasks such as assignment writing, feedback and evaluation. It also helps understand the attitudes, subjective norms and perceived behavioural control that shape the intention to use AI ethically or unethically. this framework thus explains why some users adopt responsible GenAI practices in assessment, while others exploit GenAI for academic dishonesty or manipulation of learning outcomes.

Figure 1. **The Theory of Planned Behaviour.** *This diagram illustrates how attitude, subjective norms and perceived behavioural control influence an individual's intention and, ultimately, their behaviour. Perceived behavioural control may also have a direct effect on behaviour (source: Ajzen, 1991)*

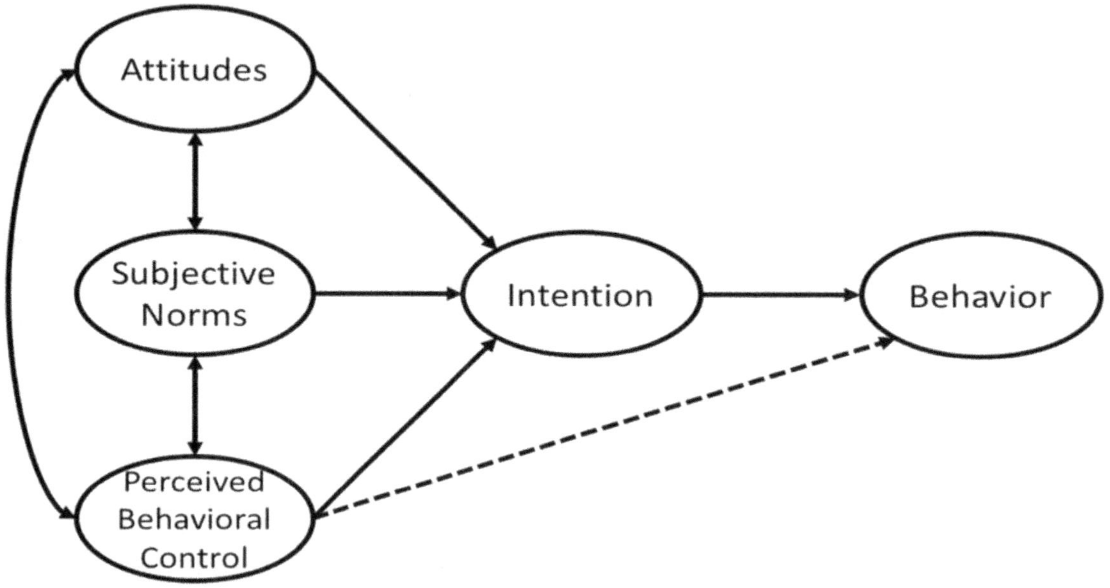

Utilitarian Theory of Ethics

Utilitarianism holds that the ethical value of an action is determined solely by its consequences. It is essential to emphasise that only the outcomes, both positive and negative, determine whether an action is morally right or wrong. Ethical actions yield beneficial consequences, whereas unethical actions result in harmful outcomes (Quiambao, 2022).

In evaluating GenAI in Higher Education, the *Utilitarian Theory of Ethics* provides a pragmatic framework for understanding institutional choices and decisions related to assessment design, academic work and institutional policies. Rooted in the principle of promoting the greatest good for the greatest number, this ethical lens guides the argument that the morality of AI use in HEIs should be judged by its outcomes, specifically, the extent to which it maximises benefits while minimising harm for key stakeholders, including students, academics, administrative staff and society at large.

Rather than demonising AI technologies, a utilitarian perspective encourages responsible adoption where they demonstrably enhance teaching, learning, research and institutional efficiency. This theory advocates for a cost-benefit analysis of AI implementation, weighing the educational advantages, such as personalised learning, automated feedback and improved access, against potential risks, including academic dishonesty, dependency, bias or the erosion of critical thinking. As Schlagwein and Willcocks (2023) argue, the ethical standing of AI is not inherent in the tool itself but is defined by its consequences: how it is used, by whom and to what effect.

Using the utilitarian theory, the ethical use of GenAI is guided by its ability to improve assessment outcomes, support responsible teaching and learning practices, promote educational equity, enhance learner outcomes, support faculty productivity, and advance institutional quality assurance goals. The technology is morally justified when it leads to broader societal benefits, such as widening access to quality education, reducing administrative burdens and fostering innovation in pedagogy and strengthening assessment integrity and reliability (Hassan, 2025).

The diagram below illustrates how Utilitarian Theory evaluates actions based on their capacity to produce the greatest good for the largest number of stakeholders, including students, academics, administrative staff, and society as a whole. Decisions that enhance collective well-being are considered "right," while those that cause widespread harm or limit benefit are "wrong." In the case of GenAI, ethical use is judged by its capacity to support academic integrity, improve assessment quality and contribute positively to the higher education community and beyond.

Figure 2. Decision flowchart depicting Utilitarian Theory. It demonstrates that actions are assessed by their consequences, prioritising those that maximise happiness and overall well-being for most people (adapted from utilitarian principles in Mill, 1863/2016).

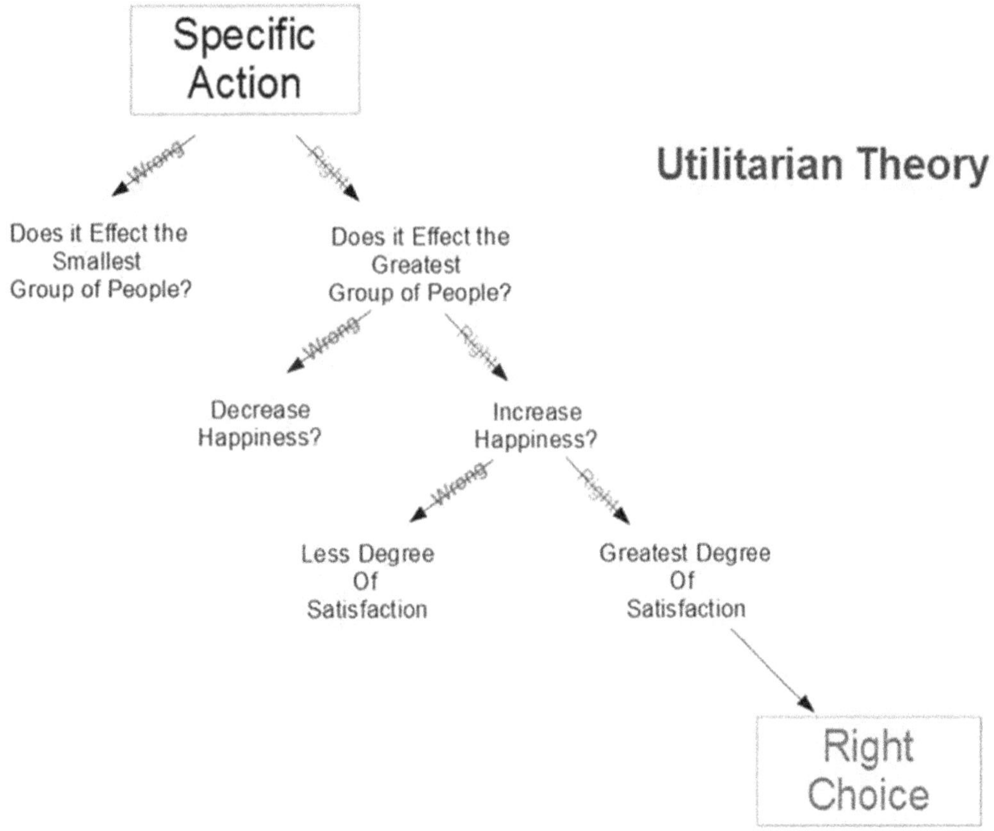

METHODOLOGICAL APPROACH

Research Design

This chapter is conceptual and critical in nature. Rather than collecting or analysing primary data, it develops a theoretically grounded argument about the use and potential misuse of generative artificial intelligence in South Africa's higher education assessment by critically engaging with existing scholarship, policy documents, and institutional reports. The Theory of Planned Behaviour (Ajzen, 1991) and the utilitarian theory of ethics (Mill, 1863/2016) serve as interpretive lenses that structure this engagement. The former organises the discussion of why students and academics might adopt or resist generative artificial intelligence, and the latter organises the discussion of when such adoption is ethically defensible. This approach does not constitute a systematic or scoping review, and the chapter makes no claim to exhaustive or reproducible coverage of the literature. Its contribution lies in the theoretically informed argument it builds, rather than in a document search protocol.

Scope of the Literature Reviewed

This chapter does not involve human participants and reports no primary data. It draws instead on peer-reviewed scholarly literature, policy documents and institutional reports relevant to higher education, artificial intelligence, ethics in technology and academic and student practices around assessment, academic integrity and quality assurance.

Literature was selected purposively rather than through a documented systematic search. Sources were included where they addressed higher education, artificial intelligence, ethics in technology or academic integrity, drawing on both South African and international scholarship to situate the South African context within broader global debates. Sources focused exclusively on AI in industry or non-tertiary education or on speculative technological discourse with no clear bearing on assessment or academic integrity were excluded. Because this selection was purposive rather than exhaustive, the claims in this chapter are best read as an argument grounded in illustrative literature rather than as a comprehensive survey of the field.

Approach to the Literature

Sources were drawn from academic databases, policy repositories and institutional publications, comprising peer-reviewed journal articles, ethical frameworks and higher education policy documents and reports addressing AI adoption, AI-powered assessment, academic integrity and related educational practices. Literature was located and screened for relevance to the chapter's focus on generative artificial intelligence in higher education assessment and for its bearing on the ethical, behavioural, and institutional dimensions of AI use. No database names, search strings, dates or record counts are reported here because this is purposive, argument-led engagement with the literature rather than a systematic or scoping review.

Analytical and Argumentative Approach

Rather than applying a formal coding procedure to a defined corpus, this chapter uses the Theory of Planned Behaviour and Utilitarian ethics as organising lenses for the argument. Recurring concerns in the literature around academic integrity, assessment validity, efficiency, equity, surveillance, and quality assurance are grouped for discussion under the broad headings of "use" and "abuse" of generative artificial intelligence, and tensions between them are examined rather than resolved. The Theory of Planned Behaviour frames the discussion of why students and academics might adopt or resist generative artificial intelligence in assessment-related activities, while the Utilitarian Theory of Ethics frames the discussion of when such use if ethically defensible, weighing likely benefits against likely harms for the stakeholders involved. This is an interpretive and argumentative strategy rather than an empirical analysis. No claim is made that these discussed were derived through a replicable coding process.

Research Ethics

Although this chapter does not involve human subjects, ethical responsibility remains a central component of the research design. It is guided by a humanising, integrity-oriented approach that takes the hopes, fears, and lived realities of students and academics seriously as they navigate a rapidly changing technological landscape, particularly in relation to assessment, academic evaluation, and quality assurance. As this chapter does not involve human participants or the collection of primary data and draws exclusively on previously published, publicly available literature, formal human-research ethics clearance was not sought. Scholarly integrity was instead addressed through attentiveness to fair and accurate representation of sources, careful verification of citations against references list and avoidance of selective or biased framing of contested debates in the literature.

The authors declare the use of Artificial Intelligence (AI) tools in writing this chapter, in line with emerging principles of transparency and responsible AI use in higher education scholarship. Five AI tools were utilised: ChatGPT, Copilot, Gemini, Meta AI (via WhatsApp), and SciSpace. These tools were used for literature exploration, idea clarification, and comparative testing of AI-generated content. The authors take full responsibility for reviewing, verifying, and editing all AI-generated material to ensure accuracy, clarity, and academic integrity, and to prevent the uncritical reproduction of AI-generated inaccuracies or bias.

As part of this ethical engagement, the chapter incorporated a demonstrative and critical comparative exercise to illustrate concerns regarding potential data misrepresentation, hallucinations, and factual inaccuracies in AI outputs. Table 1 presents verbatim responses generated by the five AI tools when asked the following question: *"In one brief paragraph of not more than 150 words, answer this question: 'What is the historical and cultural significance of the Dukuduku State Forest to the Zulu people of KwaZulu-Natal?'"* This exercise is not intended to evaluate the cultural knowledge of AI tools per se, but to illustrate broader ethical risks associated with relying on GenAI for knowledge production, assessment-related tasks, and scholarly outputs without adequate verification.

DISCUSSIONS AND IMPLICATIONS OF GENAI ON ASSESSMENT OUTCOMES AND RESEARCH

Perspectives on the Use and Potential Misuse of GenAI

The rapid integration of GenAI into academic spaces has profound implications for teaching, learning, assessment outcomes and research worldwide. Two divergent perspectives mark the discourse surrounding its adoption in the academic spaces. On the one hand, the dystopian view warns that AI is replacing human capabilities, leading to a loss of essential cognitive skills. On the other hand, the utopian perspective argues that AI is a powerful tool that enhances human productivity by automating routine tasks, thus freeing individuals to focus on higher-order intellectual and creative endeavours (Bearman et al., 2023).

Bearman et al. (2023) highlight the ongoing scholarly debate regarding the role of AI in academia. Some researchers contend that GenAI is a transformative force that significantly enhances educational outcomes. Studies indicate that AI contributes to personalised learning experiences, improves accessibility, increases student retention, reduces educational costs and accelerates degree completion (Fortuna et al., 2025; Hutson et al., 2022; Malagoudar & Karadi, 2025; Panda et al., 2022; Sakri et al., 2025). Additionally, AI-driven tools, such as automated grading systems, chatbots and virtual teaching assistants, reshape pedagogical practices. Moreover, AI-driven analytics enable faculty and researchers to process massive datasets efficiently, uncovering patterns that facilitate groundbreaking research and innovative academic insights (Hutson et al., 2022).

Despite these advancements, AI adoption in higher education remains in its early stages, particularly in developing regions. Bates et al. (2020) argue that many institutions have been slow to embrace AI, partly due to limited institutional demand and concerns over academic integrity. Related South African evidence points to causal AI adoption in organisational settings more broadly (Schoeman, 2022), in medium-sized organisations (Nkobane, 2025), and in auditing firms, although direct empirical evidence of resistance specifically within universities remains limited and would need to be established rather than assumed. However, existing research underscores that AI is not a passing trend but an enduring technological evolution that institutions must integrate strategically. Therefore, the higher education sector must shift from viewing AI as a disruptive threat to recognising it as an indispensable tool for driving knowledge production and pedagogical innovation.

A critical concern in the GenAI discourse is its ethical application in education. Popenici and Kerr (2017) emphasise that AI can extend human capabilities when used responsibly, yet they acknowledge its disruptive impact on employment. For example, AI-driven automation has replaced specific administrative and teaching roles, particularly in distance learning institutions. At some South African universities, traditional examination invigilation practices have been replaced by AI-powered proctoring tools, such as the widely used “Invigilator App.” While AI-driven efficiencies enhance institutional operations, they pose significant challenges for labour unions, which advocate for job security amidst rapid technological advancements. The Covid-19 pandemic further accelerated the digitisation of education, particularly in the Global South, demonstrating AI’s potential to sustain academic operations during crises. AI will likely play an even more integral role in higher education, especially in responding to future global disruptions.

Figure 3. Conceptual model of the use and abuse of GenAI in Higher Education Institutions. The model shows how GenAI tool characteristics influence response attributes and quality dimensions (accuracy, cultural sensitivity, completeness and consistency). These, in turn, shape user interpretation and learning outcomes, which impact the integrity of knowledge. A feedback loop highlights the risk of overreliance on GenAI, reinforcing positive and negative learning trajectories.

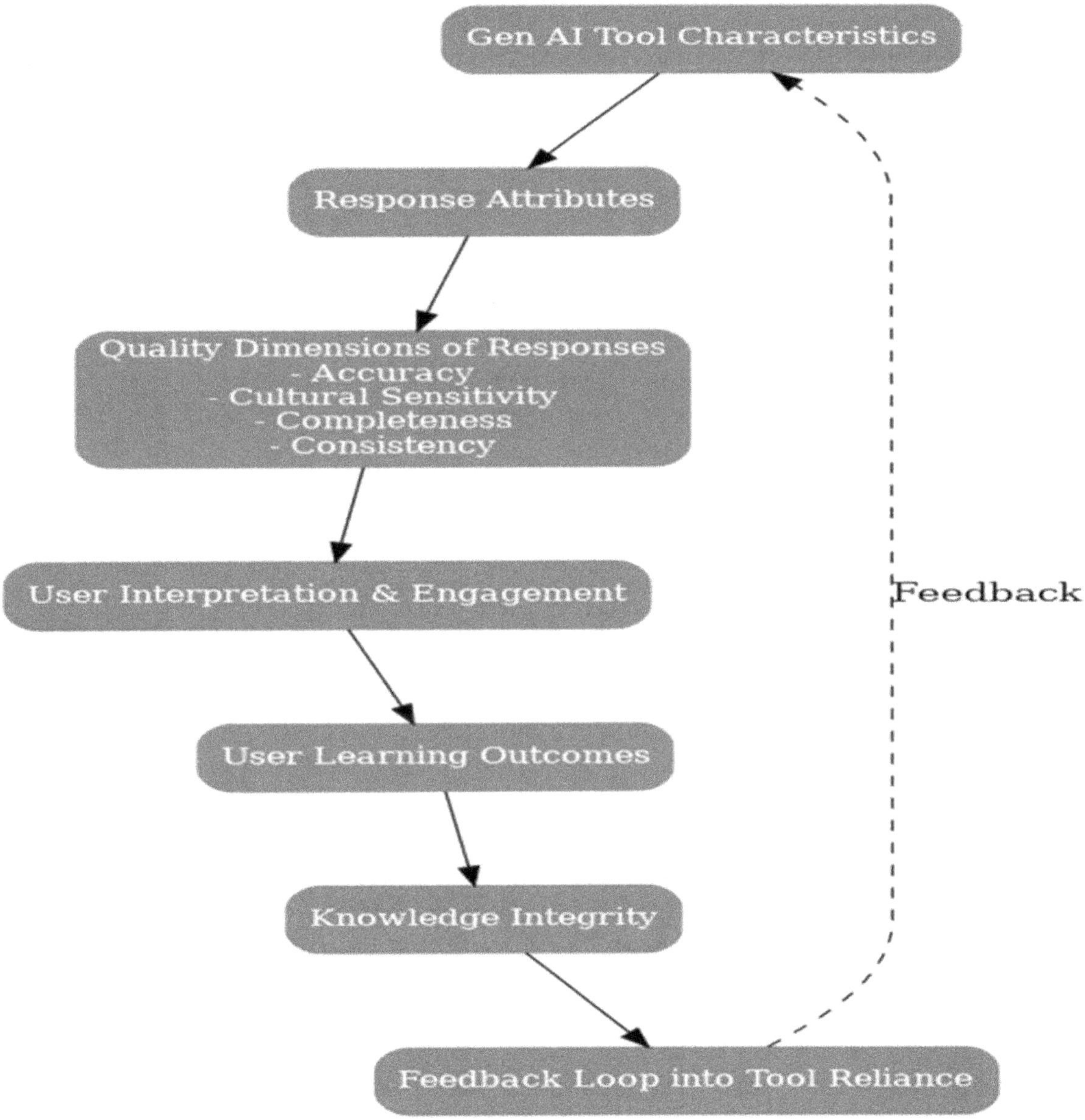

Why do Universities "fear" GenAI?

The rapid advancement of technology has led to a shift in habits among global citizens (Alsaleh, 2024; Fakunle et al., 2023; Hinojo-Lucena et al., 2019). The way AI and machine learning were presented as demons that would replace humans and cause unemployment has led to reluctance to accept this powerful tool that could transform many aspects of our lives as never before. Licht (2024) posits that various institutions and policymakers have taken different positions regarding the use of GenAI within their institutions. Some have embraced the use of AI and adopted what Licht (2024) terms a "middle-ground" approach, calling for its responsible and ethical use. These institutions have recognised that opposition to AI use would be futile.

However, some institutions accept AI use, while others have completely banned it or strongly discouraged its use (see Licht, 2024). Various factors inform universities' different positions on AI use. For instance, Licht (2024) argues that universities, especially those well under-resourced, ban or discourage the use of AI. This prohibition will result in the university having less involvement in outcomes and processes that are morally objectionable or questionable. Furthermore, it is believed that under-resourced institutions may have academics who lack sufficient knowledge about AI and are therefore unable to assist their students with AI-related matters. At the same time, well-resourced universities may efficiently train and equip their staff to address AI-related issues and possess the technological capacity to handle questionable behaviours.

Another concern about AI tools as they become more prevalent is the protection of personal information. AI systems usually require sensitive personal information, making robust data measures essential (Nguyen, 2025). AI models can significantly impact the quality of education and assessment by exacerbating inequalities, misrepresenting students' capabilities, and promoting bias. Bias algorithms may favour one demographic group over another, leading to unfair misrepresentations, evaluations and recommendations that undermine and disadvantage other social groupings (Nguyen, 2025). GenAI may be biased toward indigenous knowledge systems that are relevant to specific regions. This results in factual misrepresentations and the spreading of incorrect information. Lastly, the rise of GenAI tools in education raises significant issues, including plagiarism, intellectual property concerns and potential misuse in academic work.

The concerns regarding data misrepresentation and inaccuracy are illustrated below. The table presents responses from five GenAI tools to the question: ***In one brief paragraph of not more than 150 words, answer this question: 'What is the historical and cultural significance of the Dukuduku State Forest to the Zulu people of KwaZulu-Natal?'*** Five GenAI tools (listed alphabetically) were used to answer this question and responses are captured verbatim. Meta AI was deliberately included in this comparison due to its ease of access, particularly through WhatsApp, making it a widely available AI tool for WhatsApp users who may not have access to other tools.

This exercise was conducted in October 2025 using the free, publicly accessible versions of ChatGPT, Copilot, SciSpace, Gemini and Meta AI, the versions most realistically available to South African students and academics, many of whom may not afford the paid subscription tiers. Each tool was queried once, and the response reported is the single output generated, not a selection from repeated attempts. Specific model version numbers were not recorded at the time this exercise was carried out. Table 1 is accordingly presented as an illustrative, non-reproducible demonstration of how freely accessible generative AI tools handled a single query on a specific indigenous knowledge context at one point in time, rather than as a systematic or generalisable benchmark of AI accuracy.

Table 1. Illustrative comparison of verbatim responses from five generative artificial intelligence tools to a single prompt about the Dukuduku state forest, presented as a heuristic demonstration of response variability rather than a verified benchmark of factual accuracy.

AI Tool	Response to the question
ChatGPT	The Dukuduku State Forest holds deep historical and cultural significance for the Zulu people of KwaZulu-Natal. Traditionally, it was a source of medicinal plants, grazing land, and spiritual connection, playing a vital role in indigenous knowledge systems and livelihoods. The forest was home to various Zulu clans who maintained a harmonious relationship with the environment through customary practices and sustainable use. During apartheid and post-apartheid land reform efforts, the area became a site of contestation as communities resisted forced removals and sought to reclaim their ancestral land. Today, the Dukuduku Forest remains symbolic of both cultural resilience and the struggle for land rights, as Zulu people continue to assert their identity and heritage amid environmental conservation policies that have sometimes marginalised their access to traditional lands.
Copilot	The Dukuduku State Forest holds deep historical and cultural significance for the Zulu people of KwaZulu-Natal. Traditionally, it was home to indigenous Zulu communities who relied on the forest for sustenance, spiritual practices, and cultural identity. Over the decades, the forest became a contested space due to forced relocations and conservation efforts, disrupting local livelihoods. Despite these challenges, the Zulu people have continuously resisted displacement, asserting their ancestral connection to the land. The forest also serves as a repository of indigenous knowledge, medicinal plants, and sacred sites, reinforcing its role in Zulu heritage. Today, the struggle for land rights and sustainable coexistence remains central to the community's relationship with Dukuduku.
Gemini	The Dukuduku State Forest, historically known as KwaNcube, holds deep significance for the Zulu people, particularly the Ncube clan, who were granted the land by the Mthethwa chiefdom in the early 1800s. Serving as their ancestral home and a source of livelihood, the forest became intertwined with their cultural identity and traditional practices. However, the declaration of Dukuduku as a state forest in 1930 marked the beginning of forced removals, a traumatic experience that significantly impacted the Zulu communities living there, disrupting their way of life and severing their direct connection to this historically and culturally important land. Despite these displacements, the forest remains a symbol of their heritage and a focal point in ongoing land restitution claims.
MetaAI (WhatsApp)	The Dukuduku state forest holds significant historical and cultural importance to the Zulu people of KwaZulu-Natal. The forest is believed to be a sacred site, providing spiritual and ancestral connections. It has been a source of traditional medicine, food and shelter for generations. The forest also serves as a cultural landscape with various sites holding spiritual significance, such as ancestral graves and ritual areas. Furthermore, the forest is intertwined with Zulu folklore and mythology, featuring in stories of legends passed down through generations. The Dukuduku forest represents a vital part of the Zulu heritage, embodying their relationship with nature and their ancestors. Its preservation is crucial for maintaining cultural identity and traditional practices.
SciSpace	The Dukuduku State Forest holds profound historical and cultural significance for the Zulu people of KwaZulu-Natal, representing both a site of ancestral heritage and a focal point of land restitution struggles. Historically, the forest has been a vital resource for the Zulu, providing sustenance and materials essential for their livelihoods. However, government-sanctioned forced removals since the 1930s have disrupted their connection to this land, particularly during the apartheid era, leading to significant dispossession and cultural dislocation (Nyathi, 2024; Aardenburg & Nel, 2019). The ongoing land restitution efforts post-1994 aim to rectify these injustices, emphasising the need for a balanced approach that respects both environmental conservation and the rights of local communities (Sundnes, 2013). Conversely, some argue that prioritising conservation efforts over human habitation has led to further marginalisation of the Zulu people, complicating their claims to the land and resources they historically relied upon (Nyathi, 2024).

The responses from the five GenAI tools demonstrate a shared understanding of the Dukuduku State Forest's cultural and historical significance to the Zulu people, albeit with varying depth and emphasis. ChatGPT, Copilot and SciSpace highlight the forest as a site of traditional livelihoods, spiritual connection and resistance against forced removals, with SciSpace citing academic sources (Aardenburg & Nel, 2019; Nyathi, 2024); Sundnes, 20130 that were verified by the authors as accurate, existing scholarship on the Dukuduku area, lending SciSpace's response a level of credibility not matched by other tools assessed. Gemini offers a unique perspective by naming the Ncube clan and referencing the Mthethwa chiefdom, thereby adding historical specificity. MetaAI emphasises ancestral and spiritual ties, traditional medicine and folklore, offering a culturally rich but less historically grounded view. Collectively, the tools recognise themes of dispossession, cultural heritage and the tension between conservation and indigenous rights. However, only SciSpace and Gemini incorporate specific historical dates or references to legal and political processes, while MetaAI leans more into oral tradition and spirituality.

These variations illustrate the differing capabilities of AI models to balance factual accuracy, cultural sensitivity and historical context when addressing indigenous knowledge, thereby influencing the assessment outcomes. Therefore, students and academics should use GenAI tools as supportive aids rather than unquestioned authorities. While these tools can provide useful summaries and varying perspectives, their responses often differ in depth, accuracy and cultural sensitivity. This has far-reaching implications for assessment outcomes and their integrity. Students and academics should cross-reference outputs with credible academic sources, especially when dealing with indigenous knowledge or contested histories. It is essential to remain critical, verify information and acknowledge the limitations of AI. The responsible use of GenAI also involves transparency, declaring when GenAI has been used and ethical engagement by avoiding plagiarism, respecting intellectual property and applying AI tools in ways that uphold academic integrity.

Preparing for the Future

It is essential to equip students, teachers, preservice teachers and society at large with the knowledge of AI, as they will inevitably live in a future where AI is an integral part of daily life (Dhawan & Batra, 2020). Ignoring this reality risks deepening the divide between the Global South and developed economies, further entrenching existing inequalities. Students must begin their preparation today to compete effectively in an AI-driven future. AI-driven systems and technologies have the potential to significantly transform higher education institutions (Dhawan & Batra, 2020). However, their impact on teaching and learning has been limited thus far, as the education sector generally lags in adopting new technologies. A reluctance to take risks, resistance to innovation and insufficient funding for alternatives to traditional teaching methods have hindered the integration of AI into education, learning and development. Many academics require evidence that new technologies can genuinely enhance learning outcomes and experiences, leading to a highly cautious approach toward AI adoption (Bates et al., 2020).

Bates et al (2020) raise a crucial question: Can GenAI truly transform the higher education landscape? GenAI presents a significant opportunity to reshape academic and research practices globally, provided it is used ethically. While GenAI has the potential to enhance research and learning, its misuse could compromise the integrity of academic work and undermine the quality of research outputs. Rather than demonising GenAI, academics should embrace its ethical use, recognising that these tools are not a passing trend but a permanent feature of the educational landscape. Therefore, if GenAI is effectively implemented and aligned with human-centred objectives, the future workforce will acquire diverse skills tailored to the evolving demands of the labour market (Pisica, Edu, Zaharia and Zaharia, 2023).

Ethics, Integrity and Accountability

Ethics, integrity and accountability remain central concerns in the debate over fully embracing AI in HEIs. While GenAI can potentially transform various sectors of society, it raises significant ethical challenges, including privacy, security, bias, accountability and transparency (Akhtar et al., 2024). Universities already utilise AI extensively, from proctoring tools in examinations to plagiarism-detection software such as Turnitin. However, the rapid rise of GenAI has caught many institutions off guard, necessitating a reassessment of AI's role with a strong emphasis on ethical considerations. Dhawan and Batra (2020, p. 16) cautioned that "relying on such sensitive technology, which can easily compromise security, privacy and fairness, involves ethical dilemmas." Therefore, universities must develop robust policies to ensure the responsible and fair integration of GenAI into higher education. The responsible and ethical use of artificial intelligence in education extends beyond ensuring technical precision; it also encompasses careful consideration of the broader social and ethical implications of its deployment. These include personal privacy issues, algorithmic bias and the transformative role of AI in reshaping the educational landscape (Mhlanga, 2023).

Mhlanga (2023) argues that the ethical use of tools such as ChatGPT is a complex, multidimensional challenge that demands a nuanced, interdisciplinary approach. Nonetheless, he acknowledges that fostering ethical and responsible use of AI is central to advancing lifelong learning and the broader discourse on AI ethics. Scholars concur that integrating AI into educational contexts raises critical questions about users' ethical behaviour and accountability (Mhlanga, 2023; Kuleto et al., 2021). Pisica et al. (2023) highlight growing concerns about academic dishonesty, as students may be tempted to use highly sophisticated AI tools to complete assessments, thus challenging traditional notions of integrity. Their study revealed that academic staff are apprehensive about cheating and the potential weakening of assessment credibility due to reduced human oversight. Additionally, the question of how to effectively educate students about AI-related ethics remains underexplored, signalling the need for deeper engagement in this area. Baidoo-Anu, Asamoah, Amoako and Mahama (2024) propose a comprehensive strategy to ensure the ethical integration of AI tools, such as ChatGPT. This includes measures such as training users on responsible use, enforcing privacy protections, moderating content and integrating feedback loops for continuous oversight. When paired with strong institutional accountability, these measures can promote ethical behaviour, uphold academic integrity and optimise the educational value of AI in higher education settings.

Charting the Way Forward: What Should South African Universities do?

The use of GenAI in HEIs remains a subject of intense debate (Pisica et al., 2023). This is mainly due to the complexity and challenges of integrating GenAI across universities worldwide. Many institutions remain hesitant to fully adopt GenAI in teaching, learning, research and assessment. However, the growing presence of GenAI necessitates a redefinition of lecturers' roles to uphold higher education's core values (Popenici & Kerr, 2017) and ensure the credibility of qualifications awarded to students. To navigate GenAI-related challenges effectively, lecturers require comprehensive training that fosters faculty confidence and encourages the adoption of AI, with a special focus on research design, feedback, and safeguarding the integrity of qualifications offered at HEIS. HEIs must also invest significantly in AI and technology to remain globally competitive, as AI-driven tools are becoming the norm. Such investments will enhance the quality of education and equip students with the skills needed for an AI-driven job market.

CONCLUSION

The resistance to change is a common human trait (Darmawan & Azizah, 2020), and it is therefore unsurprising that some academics and higher education institutions (HEIs) remain cautious about embracing Generative AI (GenAI) in academic environments, particularly in high-stakes domains such as assessment and evaluation. This chapter has recognised both the transformative potential of GenAI and the complex global challenges it introduces. While GenAI offers significant opportunities for innovation in teaching, learning and research (Pisica et al., 2023; Bates et al., 2020), including enhanced feedback mechanisms, efficiency gains and new forms of assessment design, it also poses ethical, legal and academic risks that cannot be ignored (Baidoo-Anu et al., 2024; Crompton & Burke, 2023).

The chapter advocates for the responsible and ethical integration of GenAI, underpinned by transparent institutional policies and clear guidelines that explicitly address AI use in assessment, authorship, feedback and academic decision-making, in order to prevent misuse and protect the credibility of educational qualifications. To safeguard research integrity and academic standards, universities must proactively manage the implementation of GenAI through assessment redesign, capacity-building initiatives, and the cultivation of AI literacy among academics and students.

Finally, users of AI tools must remain aware that these systems are fallible; critical thinking, cross-referencing and human oversight are essential to avoid data misrepresentation and ensure accuracy. From a utilitarian ethical perspective, GenAI can only be considered morally justified when its use demonstrably enhances collective educational benefit without undermining fairness, integrity or trust in assessment outcomes. Only through a balanced, informed and principled approach can higher education fully harness the benefits of GenAI while safeguarding academic integrity, quality assurance and public confidence in higher education credentials.

Disclosure Statement

No potential conflict of interest.

Funding

This work was not supported by any funding.

Declaration

The authors declare the use of Artificial Intelligence (AI) tools in preparing this manuscript. Five AI tools were utilised: ChatGPT, Copilot, Gemini, Meta AI (via WhatsApp) and SciSpace. These tools were used for different purposes, including literature exploration and comparative testing of AI-generated content, in this chapter. The authors take full responsibility for reviewing, verifying and editing all AI-generated material to ensure accuracy, clarity and academic integrity. In particular, the chapter incorporated a comparative exercise to illustrate concerns regarding potential data misrepresentation and factual inaccuracies in AI outputs. Table 1 presents verbatim responses generated by the five AI tools when asked the following question: "In one brief paragraph of not more than 150 words, answer this question: 'What is the historical and cultural significance of the Dukuduku State Forest to the Zulu people of KwaZulu-Natal?'"

REFERENCES

Aardenburg, E., & Nel, A. (2019). Fatalism and dissidence in Dukuduku, KwaZulu-Natal, South Africa: Ongoing contestations over land, resources and identities. *Journal of Southern African Studies*, *45*(2), 393–411. DOI: 10.1080/03057070.2019.1619429

Ajzen, I. (1991). The theory of planned behavior. *Organizational Behavior and Human Decision Processes*, *50*(2), 179–211. DOI: 10.1016/0749-5978(91)90020-T

Ajzen, I. (2011). The theory of planned behaviour: Reactions and reflections. *Psychology & Health*, *26*(9), 1113–1127. DOI: 10.1080/08870446.2011.613995 PMID: 21929476

Ajzen, I. (2014). The theory of planned behaviour is alive and well and not ready to retire: A commentary on Sniehotta, Presseau, and Araújo-Soares. *Health Psychology Review*, *9*(2), 131–137. DOI: 10.1080/17437199.2014.883474 PMID: 26209198

Akhtar, M. A. K., Kumar, M., & Nayyar, A. (2024). Transparency and accountability in explainable AI: Best practices. In *Towards ethical and socially responsible explainable AI* (Vol. 551, pp. 1–18). Springer., DOI: 10.1007/978-3-031-66489-2_1

Alsaleh, A. (2024). The impact of technological advancement on culture and society. *Scientific Reports*, *14*(1), 32140. DOI: 10.1038/s41598-024-83995-z PMID: 39738478

Armitage, C. J., & Conner, M. (2001). Efficacy of the theory of planned behaviour: A meta-analytic review. *British Journal of Social Psychology*, *40*(4), 471–499. DOI: 10.1348/014466601164939 PMID: 11795063

Baidoo-Anu, D., Asamoah, D., Amoako, I., & Mahama, I. (2024). Exploring student perspectives on generative artificial intelligence in higher education learning. *Discover Education*, *3*(1), 98. DOI: 10.1007/s44217-024-00173-z

Bates, T., Cobo, C., Mariño, O., & Wheeler, S. (2020). Can artificial intelligence transform higher education? *International Journal of Educational Technology in Higher Education*, *17*(1), 42. DOI: 10.1186/s41239-020-00218-x

Bearman, M., Ryan, J., & Ajjawi, R. (2023). Discourses of artificial intelligence in higher education: A critical literature review. *Higher Education*, *86*(2), 369–385. DOI: 10.1007/s10734-022-00937-2

Crompton, H., & Burke, D. (2023). Artificial intelligence in higher education: The state of the field. *International Journal of Educational Technology in Higher Education*, *20*(1), 22. DOI: 10.1186/s41239-023-00392-8

Darmawan, A. H., & Azizah, S. (2020, January). Resistance to change: Causes and strategies as an organizational challenge. In *5th ASEAN conference on psychology, counselling, and humanities (ACPCH 2019)* (pp. 49–53). Atlantis Press. https://doi.org/DOI: 10.2991/assehr.k.200120.010

de Fine Licht, K. (2024). Generative artificial intelligence in higher education: Why the "banning approach" to student use is sometimes morally justified. *Philosophy & Technology*, *37*(3), 113. DOI: 10.1007/s13347-024-00799-9

Dhawan, S., & Batra, G. (2020). Artificial intelligence in higher education: Promises, perils, and perspective. Expanding Knowledge Horizon. OJAS, 11, 11–22. https://www.researchgate.net/publication/348910302_Artificial_Intelligence_in_Higher_Education_Promises_Perils_and_Perspective

Fakunle, S. O., Okunola, J. L., & Ajani, B. K. (2023). Technological Advancement, Globalization, and Developing Countries. In *The Palgrave Handbook of Global Social Change*. Palgrave Macmillan., DOI: 10.1007/978-3-030-87624-1_160-1

Fortuna, A., Prasetya, F., Samala, A. D., Rawas, S., Criollo-C, S., Kaya, D., Raihan, M., Andriani, W., Safitri, D., & Nabawi, R. A. (2025). Artificial intelligence in personalized learning: A global systematic review of current advancements and shaping future opportunities. *Social Sciences & Humanities Open*, *12*, 102114. DOI: 10.1016/j.ssaho.2025.102114

Gnambs, T., Stein, J. P., Appel, M., Griese, F., & Zinn, S. (2025). An economical measure of attitudes towards artificial intelligence in work, healthcare, and education (ATTARI-WHE). *Computers in Human Behavior: Artificial Humans*, *3*, 100106. DOI: 10.1016/j.chbah.2024.100106

Hassan, Z. Y. (2025). AI-Driven Horizons: Shaping the Future of Global Quality Assurance in Higher Education. *AI and Ethics, Academic Integrity and the Future of Quality Assurance in Higher Education*, 105.

Hinojo-Lucena, F. J., Aznar-Díaz, I., Cáceres-Reche, M. P., & Romero-Rodríguez, J. M. (2019). Artificial intelligence in higher education: A bibliometric study on its impact in the scientific literature. *Education Sciences*, *9*(1), 51. DOI: 10.3390/educsci9010051

Hutson, J., Jeevanjee, T., Graaf, V. V., Lively, J., Weber, J., Weir, G., Arnone, K., Carnes, G., Vosevich, K., Plate, D., Leary, M., & Edele, S. (2022). Artificial intelligence and the disruption of higher education: Strategies for integrations across disciplines. *Creative Education*, *13*(12), 3953–3980. DOI: 10.4236/ce.2022.1312253

Kuleto, V., Ilić, M., Dumangiu, M., Ranković, M., Martins, O. M., Păun, D., & Mihoreanu, L. (2021). Exploring opportunities and challenges of artificial intelligence and machine learning in higher education institutions. *Sustainability (Basel)*, *13*(18), 10424. DOI: 10.3390/su131810424

Malagoudar, A. F., & Karadi, A. A. (2025). Transforming Student Learning Through Artificial Intelligence: Evidence from Personalization, Accessibility, and Pedagogical Innovation. *International Journal for Multidisciplinary Research*, *7*(6), 1–17. https://www.ijfmr.com/papers/2025/6/65191.pdf. DOI: 10.36948/ijfmr.2025.v07i06.65191

Mhlanga, D. (2023). Open AI in Education, the Responsible and Ethical Use of ChatGPT Towards Lifelong Learning. In *FinTech and Artificial Intelligence for Sustainable Development*. Sustainable Development Goals Series. Palgrave Macmillan., DOI: 10.1007/978-3-031-37776-1_17

Mill, J. S. (2016). Utilitarianism. In *Seven masterpieces of philosophy* (pp. 329–375). Routledge.

Nguyen, K. V. (2025). The use of generative AI tools in higher education: Ethical and pedagogical principles. *Journal of Academic Ethics*, *23*(3), 1435–1455. Advance online publication. DOI: 10.1007/s10805-025-09607-1

Nkobane, J. G. (2025). Benefits and Challenges of Utilizing Automation and Artificial Intelligence in Auditing Firms in South Africa. In International Conference of Accounting & Business, 667 – 682. Springer DOI: 10.1007/978-3-031-84885-8_36

Nyathi, P. A. (2024). Exploring tensions between conservationists and African subsistence farmers in the Dukuduku forest area, KwaZulu-Natal, in the 1980s and 1990s. *IAHRW International Journal of Social Sciences Review*, *12*(1), 33–41.

Panda, M., Dehuri, S., Patra, M. R., Behera, P. K., Tsihrintzis, G. A., Cho, S. B., & Coello, C. A. C. (Eds.). (2022). Innovations in intelligent computing and communication: First international conference, ICIICC 2022, Bhubaneswar, Odisha, India, December 16–17, 2022, Proceedings. Springer Nature.

Pisica, A. I., Edu, T., Zaharia, R. M., & Zaharia, R. (2023). Implementing artificial intelligence in higher education: Pros and cons from the perspectives of academics. *Societies (Basel, Switzerland)*, *13*(5), 118. DOI: 10.3390/soc13050118

Popenici, S. A., & Kerr, S. (2017). Exploring the impact of artificial intelligence on teaching and learning in higher education. *Research and Practice in Technology Enhanced Learning*, *12*(1), 22. DOI: 10.1186/s41039-017-0062-8 PMID: 30595727

Quiambao, J. E. A. (2022). Thinking ethically: The utilitarianism approach in moral decision making. *International Journal of Multidisciplinary Research and Growth Evaluation*, *3*(3), 602–604. DOI: 10.54660/anfo.2022.3.3.30

Sakri, L. I., Kori, D. N., Joshi, S. S., Nayak, A. S., & Marigoudar, S. (2025). AI-Enabled Transformation of Online Learning through Personalization. *Journal of Engineering Education Transformations*, *39*(s1, is1), 26–33. DOI: 10.16920/jeet/2025/v39is1/25131

Schlagwein, D., & Willcocks, L. (2023). 'ChatGPT et al.': The ethics of using (generative) artificial intelligence in research and science. *Journal of Information Technology*, *38*(3), 232–238. https://doi.org/. DOI: 10.1177/02683962231200411

Schoeman, F., & Seymour, L. F. (2022). Understanding the Low Adoption of AI in South African Medium Sized Organisations. In 43rd Conference of the South African Institute of Computer Scientists and Information Technologists, SAICSIT, 257–269.

Sundnes, F. (2013). Scrubs and squatters: The coming of the Dukuduku forest, an indigenous forest in KwaZulu-Natal, South Africa. *Environmental History*, *18*(2), 277–308. DOI: 10.1093/envhis/emt003

Chapter 15

Preparing Higher Education Academics for Artificial Intelligence–Driven Assessment in South African Higher Education

Oluwatoyin Ayodele Ajani
http://orcid.org/0000-0001-6545-0203
University of KwaZulu-Natal, South Africa

ABSTRACT

The rapid adoption of generative artificial intelligence in higher education has transformed assessment faster than academic development has adapted. This conceptual chapter examines preparedness for artificial intelligence driven assessment in South African universities, where policies have expanded since 2023 but staff development remains uneven. Drawing on Technological Pedagogical Content Knowledge, the Artificial Intelligence Assessment Scale, Diffusion of Innovations Theory, and the Technology Acceptance Model, supported by emerging South African evidence, it argues that preparedness extends beyond technical competence. It proposes a four dimensional model comprising technological and pedagogical fluency, assessment design capability, academic integrity, and institutional readiness, with implications for policy, academic development, and future research. It emphasises assessment redesign, ethical practice, and institutional investment to strengthen quality and implementation now.

INTRODUCTION

Generative artificial intelligence has become one of the most consequential developments in the recent history of higher education. Artificial intelligence itself is not new to universities: intelligent tutoring systems, adaptive learning platforms and learning analytics have shaped teaching and administration for decades (Zawacki-Richter et al., 2019). What changed with the public release of ChatGPT in November 2022 was the scale and visibility of what artificial intelligence could now do in full view of students and academics alike. A single freely available application could produce a coherent essay, solve a math-

DOI: 10.4018/979-8-3373-8939-4.ch015

ematical problem, generate working computer code, summarise a body of literature, translate between languages and answer an academic question in seconds (Dwivedi et al., 2023). These capabilities went to the heart of an assumption that had underpinned university assessment for generations: that a piece of written work reliably indicates what its author knows.

The initial institutional response, in South Africa and internationally, was largely defensive. Many universities attempted to prohibit the use of ChatGPT and comparable tools, anticipating a wave of academic dishonesty and a decline in the quality of student learning (Perkins et al., 2024). Prohibition proved difficult to sustain. Generative artificial intelligence did not remain a discrete application that students visited deliberately; it became embedded within word processors, search engines and the everyday productivity software that students and academics already used. Universities were consequently pushed towards a harder question than whether to permit artificial intelligence: what assessment itself is for in an environment where instant, competent machine-generated text is simply available (Furze et al., 2024).

This question carries particular weight within South African higher education, a sector still working through the structural inequalities of its own history while responding to a global technological shift on a compressed timescale. South African universities differ markedly in digital infrastructure, technological investment, staffing and student demographics. Historically advantaged institutions tend to possess more developed digital ecosystems and can experiment with new technologies relatively quickly; historically disadvantaged institutions continue to contend with connectivity constraints, staffing shortages and limited discretionary funding (Chaka et al., 2024). These disparities do not simply slow the rollout of artificial intelligence in some places and accelerate it in others; they shape what preparedness for artificial intelligence-driven assessment can realistically mean at a given institution, a point Maimela and Mbonde (2025) demonstrate directly in their comparison of historically white and historically black South African universities, discussed further below.

South African higher education is also distinguished by an explicit, long-standing commitment to widening participation, redress and epistemic justice. Introducing artificial intelligence into assessment is, therefore, never a purely technical matter here. It raises immediate questions of fairness: students from economically disadvantaged backgrounds may have limited access to premium artificial intelligence platforms or reliable data and connectivity, and academics at less well-resourced institutions may receive far less institutional support for redesigning their assessment practices than colleagues elsewhere in the sector. At the same time, artificial intelligence offers a genuine opportunity to address problems that have long constrained South African higher education. Large class sizes make timely, individualised feedback difficult to sustain through conventional means; heavy administrative workloads leave little space for assessment innovation; and a diverse student body continually raises the need for more differentiated learning support (van den Berg & du Plessis, 2023).

Whether these opportunities are realised depends on something no piece of software can supply on its own: the preparedness of the academics who design and mark assessments. Mishra and Koehler (2006) advanced a version of this argument two decades before generative artificial intelligence existed, proposing the Technological Pedagogical Content Knowledge framework to explain why meaningful technology integration in teaching depends on the interaction of technological, pedagogical, and content knowledge rather than on technological competence in isolation. The argument has lost none of its force, and the scale and speed of generative artificial intelligence adoption have made the gap between technological availability and pedagogical readiness more visible than earlier waves of educational technology ever did.

The available evidence suggests that this gap has not closed. Many academics report continuing uncertainty about what constitutes acceptable use of artificial intelligence in assessment and how existing assignments should be redesigned (Sevnarayan, 2024). Institutional policies, where they exist, tend to offer broad ethical principles rather than practical guidance for day-to-day assessment decisions, leaving individual academics to interpret those principles largely on their own. The result is inconsistent practice across faculties, departments and even individual modules within the same institution.

The challenge facing academics is not simply technical. It requires reconsidering long-held assumptions about what assessment is meant to demonstrate. Conventional assessment in many disciplines has rewarded the accurate recall and written reproduction of information, often produced individually and outside any supervised setting. That model becomes increasingly fragile once a freely available tool can produce a fluent, broadly accurate response to almost any assignment prompt within seconds. This does not mean artificial intelligence necessarily diminishes the quality of higher education. It means universities are being forced to ask, with unusual urgency, which knowledge, skills and dispositions genuinely warrant a university education in the first place.

This chapter uses academic preparedness to mean something more specific than familiarity with artificial intelligence tools or awareness of institutional policy. It refers to the combined capability of an academic to judge, within their own discipline, when and how generative artificial intelligence use is appropriate; to translate that judgement into defensible assessment design; and to hold a workable, contextually grounded understanding of what academic integrity now requires, all within an institutional environment that either sustains or quietly undermines the effort involved. Preparedness in this sense is closer to an ongoing professional capability than a state an academic arrives at after a single workshop.

The chapter argues, and justifies through a dedicated derivation section below, that this capability rests on three interacting academic dimensions: technological and pedagogical fluency, assessment design capability, and academic integrity, situated within institutional readiness as the enabling condition that determines whether the other three can be exercised at all. The discussion draws on contemporary literature on artificial intelligence, assessment, academic development, and higher education transformation, with sustained attention to South African and wider African scholarship, including decolonial and epistemic justice perspectives that bear directly on how generative artificial intelligence should be understood in an African university context. The chapter does not treat artificial intelligence as either an unambiguous threat to educational quality or a straightforward solution to long-standing problems. Its position is that educational outcomes depend overwhelmingly on the preparedness of the academics responsible for designing meaningful learning experiences within an increasingly technology-rich environment.

BACKGROUND: GENERATIVE ARTIFICIAL INTELLIGENCE AND ASSESSMENT IN HIGHER EDUCATION

The trajectory described above is not unique to South Africa. Artificial intelligence has quietly shaped higher education for decades through intelligent tutoring systems, automated grading and learning analytics used to identify students at risk of failure (Ifenthaler & Yau, 2020; Zawacki-Richter et al., 2019). These earlier applications operated largely inside institutional systems, at some distance from the everyday work of assessment design, and most academics continued to construct assignments using familiar pedagogical assumptions without needing to reconsider them fundamentally.

Generative artificial intelligence broke that pattern because it engages directly with activities long regarded as distinctively human: producing original text, solving open-ended problems, and constructing an argument. Within weeks of ChatGPT's release, students across the world had begun using it to brainstorm ideas, summarise readings, improve the fluency of their writing and generate revision notes (Dwivedi et al., 2023). Many of these uses supported legitimate learning; others plainly did not, and universities were left with little empirical basis on which to distinguish the two in the moment.

As complete prohibition proved unworkable, institutional attention shifted from restriction towards redesign (UNESCO, 2023). Perkins et al. (2024) responded to this dilemma with the Artificial Intelligence Assessment Scale, which replaces a binary permit-or-prohibit decision with a graduated series of levels of artificial intelligence use, matched to the specific learning outcomes an assessment task is designed to serve. This reframing has become one of the more influential conceptual resources available to academics attempting to redesign assessment in a principled rather than reactive way. However, as later sections argue, it is not without its own practical limitations.

Academic integrity has occupied a particularly prominent place in this international debate. Cotton et al. (2024) argue that the arrival of generative artificial intelligence does not so much create new integrity problems as expose weaknesses already present in assessment designs that relied heavily on unsupervised written coursework. Treating the use of artificial intelligence as simply a more sophisticated form of plagiarism understates how thoroughly the technology unsettles the concept of individual authorship on which conventional integrity policy depends. Dwivedi et al. (2023), drawing together perspectives from a wide range of disciplines, reach a related conclusion: generative artificial intelligence raises questions for research, practice and policy that cut across the usual boundaries between technical, ethical and pedagogical concerns, and institutions that address these questions through any single lens are likely to find their response inadequate to the scope of the change involved. This international literature does not offer South African universities a ready-made solution, since the resource conditions under which it was largely developed differ considerably from those found across much of the South African sector. It does, however, establish that the difficulty South African institutions have experienced in moving from policy to practice is not simply a local failing; it is a feature of how generative artificial intelligence has entered higher education everywhere.

It is worth being explicit about a further tension this international literature leaves unresolved, since it recurs throughout the remainder of this chapter. Much of the early scholarship on artificial intelligence in assessment treats artificial intelligence enhancement and academic integrity as complementary goals, both achievable through sufficiently careful assessment redesign. The South African evidence reviewed in the following section suggests a less comfortable picture: for some academics, and for some categories of assessment task, the two goals are not straightforwardly compatible, and a chapter that presents them as such would understate a genuine and reasonable disagreement within the field rather than a problem that better assessment design can dissolve.

THE SOUTH AFRICAN HIGHER EDUCATION ASSESSMENT LANDSCAPE

South African higher education entered the generative artificial intelligence era from a position already shaped by long-standing structural inequality: uneven digital infrastructure, large class sizes at many institutions, and a substantial reliance on distance and open distance e-learning models to widen access. The University of South Africa, which serves several hundred thousand students through an open distance e-learning model, has produced some of the earliest South African empirical accounts of how academics and students are actually engaging with ChatGPT and comparable tools (Sevnarayan, 2024; van den Berg & du Plessis, 2023; van Wyk et al., 2023). These accounts describe a mixture of enthusiasm and apprehension. Academics recognise the potential of generative artificial intelligence to support personalised feedback and culturally responsive assessment rubrics, while expressing concern about the erosion of critical thinking, the practical difficulty of verifying authorship, and the risk of relying on tools whose training data may not reflect South African or wider African realities (van den Berg & du Plessis, 2023).

At the level of institutional policy, Chaka et al. (2024) conducted an environmental review of the generative artificial intelligence policies and guidelines published by twenty-six South African higher education institutions. Responsible use, academic integrity and risk management emerged as the most consistent points of convergence. Their analysis, however, also found that the policies were framed predominantly in defensive terms, oriented towards containing misuse rather than towards redesigning curriculum and assessment or building academic staff capability. A qualitative study of academics and teaching and learning specialists at a private South African institution reached a broadly similar conclusion: ethical concerns dominated academic thinking about generative artificial intelligence, well ahead of any settled institutional position on its pedagogical use (Pramjeeth & Ramgovind, 2024). Read together, this evidence points to a sector that has moved comparatively quickly to state ethical positions on generative artificial intelligence and comparatively slowly to translate those positions into practical support for assessment redesign.

The institutional diversity that shapes this picture is not incidental, and recent empirical work makes the resulting inequality directly visible. Applying diffusion of innovations theory to compare historically white and historically black South African universities, Maimela and Mbonde (2025) found that better funding and international collaboration allowed historically white institutions to make considerably more rapid progress in artificial intelligence integration, while historically black institutions continued to face systemic infrastructural and policy barriers to equitable access. Their analysis adds an important and largely African epistemic dimension to the concern already visible in the international literature: generative artificial intelligence systems trained predominantly on Western data risk reinforcing Western-centric knowledge production within a curriculum that South African higher education has, since the 2015 and 2016 student protests, been under sustained pressure to decolonise (Le Grange, 2016). A conceptual model of academic preparedness that ignores this diversity, treating South African higher education as a single, roughly uniform system, would misdescribe the sector it claims to explain.

Research examining how academics themselves interpret and use generative artificial intelligence complicates this picture in an instructive way. Some academics deliberately use tools such as ChatGPT and Copilot to model professional practice, reasoning that a technology already routinely used in the workplaces for which students are being prepared should also have a legitimate place in university teaching (Maistry & Singh, 2025). Others place greater weight on the university's role as custodian of a disciplinary tradition of knowledge-building, one that generative artificial intelligence risks short-circuiting, particularly where the appearance of instant, polished output discourages students from doing the slower work of developing an academic voice of their own. This tension, between generative artificial intelligence as preparation for a technologically mediated workplace and as a threat to the formation of academic identity, runs through much of the emerging South African literature. It carries a direct implication for academic development: a single, generic training intervention is unlikely to serve academics who hold such different underlying conceptions of what a university education is for.

This is also where institutional policy across the sector shows a genuine internal contradiction rather than mere inconsistency between institutions. Chaka et al. (2024) find that most South African generative artificial intelligence policies simultaneously encourage responsible pedagogical use and warn against the erosion of independent student work, without specifying how academics are meant to reconcile the two where they conflict for a given assessment task. A policy document can affirm both commitments in the same paragraph without contradiction at the level of principle; it is only at the level of a specific assessment decision, whether a first-year essay may draw on generative artificial intelligence assistance, for example, that the tension becomes practically unavoidable. It is precisely this level of decision that current institutional policy across the sector tends to leave to individual academic judgement without corresponding support.

THEORETICAL FOUNDATIONS: EXPLAINING ACADEMIC PREPAREDNESS

Understanding what academic preparedness for artificial intelligence-driven assessment requires cannot rest on a single theoretical lens, nor should it be accepted uncritically from any one. This section reviews four established perspectives: Technological Pedagogical Content Knowledge, the Artificial Intelligence Assessment Scale, diffusion of innovations theory, together with the Technology Acceptance Model, and the more recent literature on artificial intelligence literacy, while examining the limitations each brings when applied to a resource-constrained, historically unequal higher education sector.

Technological Pedagogical Content Knowledge

Technological Pedagogical Content Knowledge, commonly abbreviated as TPACK, was developed by Mishra and Koehler (2006) as an extension of Shulman's (1986) concept of pedagogical content knowledge. Shulman had argued that effective teaching depends on understanding how a particular concept can best be taught within a specific disciplinary context, rather than on subject knowledge or teaching methods considered in isolation. Mishra and Koehler extended this insight to a period when technology was becoming an unavoidable component of professional teaching knowledge, proposing that an academic must develop knowledge across three interacting domains: content knowledge, pedagogical knowledge, and technological knowledge.

The value of the framework lies in the intersection of these domains rather than in any one of them alone. Applied to artificial intelligence-driven assessment, TPACK implies that preparedness cannot be reduced to knowing how to operate ChatGPT or a similar tool. An academic must also understand how a given tool interacts with the conventions of their discipline, and whether its use supports or quietly undermines the pedagogical purpose of a particular task. Generative artificial intelligence used to provide formative feedback on expository writing calls on a markedly different configuration of knowledge than the same tool used to generate practice problems in a quantitative discipline.

This intersection is, however, precisely where the framework has attracted its most sustained criticism. Archambault and Barnett (2010), analysing survey responses from almost six hundred online teachers, found that the boundaries between TPACK's constituent domains were difficult to separate empirically, with only the technology factor emerging clearly, rather than the pedagogy, content, and technology distinctions the model assumes. This is not a minor technical objection. If academics and researchers cannot reliably distinguish where pedagogical knowledge ends and technological pedagogical knowledge begins, then TPACK functions better as an organising vocabulary for reflection than as a precise diagnostic tool for identifying what a given academic still needs to learn, a limitation this chapter treats as a reason for caution rather than a reason to discard the framework altogether.

A further, more context-specific limitation concerns resource-constrained environments. TPACK was developed and largely validated in settings where reliable access to a range of technologies could be assumed. Within historically disadvantaged South African institutions, where connectivity and access to licensed software remain uneven (Maimela & Mbonde, 2025), the technological knowledge component of the framework is not simply a matter of individual learning. However, it is bounded by what infrastructure actually makes available. An academic may possess sound pedagogical judgement about how a given generative artificial intelligence tool ought to be used and still be unable to exercise that judgement in practice, a gap that TPACK, framed as an individual competency model, does not itself account for. This is one reason the conceptual model developed later in this chapter treats institutional readiness as a distinct, encompassing condition rather than folding infrastructural access into technological knowledge as though it were simply another skill an individual academic could acquire.

The Artificial Intelligence Assessment Scale

A second, more directly practical resource is the Artificial Intelligence Assessment Scale, developed by Perkins et al. (2024) for the ethical integration of generative artificial intelligence into assessment design. The scale sets out a graduated series of levels, ranging from tasks in which no artificial intelligence use is permitted through to tasks in which full, open use of generative artificial intelligence is expected and assessed as part of the task itself, with the appropriate level determined by the specific learning outcomes a given assessment is meant to serve. Furze et al. (2024), reporting on a pilot implementation of the scale, found that framing artificial intelligence use as a matter of graduated, task-specific permission gave academics a considerably more workable vocabulary for redesigning assessment than the compliance-oriented policies that had characterised most institutions' initial response to ChatGPT.

The scale is not, however, a solution that implements itself. Its pilot evaluation was conducted in a single, well-resourced institutional setting, and applying it meaningfully assumes that an academic already has the assessment literacy to judge which level best suits a given learning outcome, as well as institutional permission to depart from a uniform, module-wide assessment policy. Where quality assurance systems still assume a single approved assessment plan for an entire module, as is common across much of South African higher education, an academic wishing to apply different levels of the scale to different tasks within the same module may find the scale conceptually clear but administratively difficult to enact. For South African higher education, the scale offers a practical route beyond the detection-and-prohibition orientation that Chaka et al. (2024) identify in current institutional policy, but only when paired with the institutional and quality-assurance flexibility discussed later in this chapter.

Diffusion of Innovations and the Technology Acceptance Model

A third lens is provided by Rogers's (2003) diffusion of innovations theory, which treats technology adoption as a social process unfolding through identifiable stages, knowledge, persuasion, decision, implementation and confirmation, and shaped by the perceived characteristics of the innovation itself, including its relative advantage, its compatibility with existing practice, its complexity, and the visibility of its results to colleagues. Many South African academics first encountered generative artificial intelligence not through institutional training but through students submitting work suspected of containing machine-generated content, an entry point that already frames the technology, for some, as a problem to be managed rather than a tool to be adopted. Diffusion of innovations theory is useful here because it makes clear that academic preparedness is not solely a matter of individual skill acquisition; it also depends on institutional conditions, infrastructure, leadership visibility and workload allowance, which make experimentation feasible in the first place. Maimela and Mbonde (2025) apply this same theory directly to the South African case, and their finding that historically black institutions face systemic barriers to artificial intelligence adoption regardless of individual staff willingness is a direct empirical illustration of the theory's central claim.

A closely related account is offered by the Technology Acceptance Model, developed by Davis (1989), which identifies perceived usefulness and perceived ease of use as the two principal determinants of whether an individual adopts a given technology. Cabero-Almenara et al. (2024), applying an extended technology acceptance framework to university teachers' beliefs about generative artificial intelligence, found that teachers holding constructivist pedagogical beliefs were considerably more inclined to adopt these tools than colleagues holding more transmission-oriented views of teaching. This finding matters for academic development because it suggests that preparedness initiatives framed purely as technical training are unlikely to succeed on their own; they need to engage with academics' underlying beliefs about what teaching and learning are for.

Artificial Intelligence Literacy and Related Literacies

A fourth, more recent body of scholarship distinguishes artificial intelligence literacy from the neighbouring concepts of digital literacy, assessment literacy and ethical competence, and this distinction has direct relevance for academic preparedness even though it is not always made explicit in the higher education assessment literature. Long and Magerko (2020) define artificial intelligence literacy as a set of competencies that enable individuals to understand how artificial intelligence systems function, to evaluate their outputs critically, and to interact and collaborate with them effectively, a definition subsequently organised by Ng et al. (2021) into four component dimensions: knowing and understanding artificial intelligence, using and applying it, evaluating and creating with it, and navigating its ethical implications.

This literature clarifies a distinction that the discussion of academic preparedness benefits from making explicit. Digital literacy, in its older, broader sense, concerns competence with digital tools and information in general. Assessment literacy, as discussed further below, concerns an academic's understanding of validity, reliability, fairness and constructive alignment. Artificial intelligence literacy sits conceptually between these, and closer to technological knowledge in TPACK terms, but with a specific emphasis that TPACK does not fully capture: the capacity to interrogate why a generative system produced a particular output, including the biases and gaps in its training data, rather than to operate the interface competently. An academic can be highly digitally literate, in the sense of using a wide range of software confidently, while possessing limited artificial intelligence literacy in this more specific sense, and the distinction matters because the two competencies require different forms of professional development. The conceptual model developed later in this chapter situates artificial intelligence literacy explicitly within the technological and pedagogical fluency dimension, because critical evaluation of machine-generated output is, in TPACK terms, precisely the kind of judgement that sits at the intersection of technological and content knowledge, rather than a separate, free-standing competency.

Reading the Frameworks Together, and Against Each Other

None of these four perspectives, taken alone, offers a complete account of academic preparedness, and reading them together also exposes some genuine tension rather than a tidy synthesis. TPACK and the emerging artificial intelligence literacy literature both foreground disciplinary and pedagogical judgement, but TPACK's empirical fuzziness (Archambault & Barnett, 2010) means it functions better as an organising heuristic than as a measurable competency; the Artificial Intelligence Assessment Scale offers a workable design tool but assumes an institutional flexibility many South African universities do not yet provide; diffusion of innovations theory and the Technology Acceptance Model explain variation in adoption but say comparatively little about what academics should actually do differently once they have adopted. A further, more uncomfortable tension sits beneath all four frameworks: each was developed with an implicit assumption that generative artificial intelligence enhances teaching and assessment once academics are sufficiently prepared to use it well, yet the South African evidence on academic integrity and disciplinary identity reviewed above suggests that some academics reasonably regard artificial intelligence enhancement and academic integrity as being in genuine, not merely apparent, tension for certain forms of assessment. A conceptual model that layers these four frameworks together without acknowledging that tension would understate a real disagreement within the field about what artificial intelligence-driven assessment is ultimately for. The derivation that follows attempts to hold this tension explicitly rather than resolve it prematurely.

This critical reading also has a bearing on how the four frameworks should be weighted rather than merely combined. TPACK and artificial intelligence literacy scholarship are most directly relevant to what an individual academic needs to know, but the empirical fuzziness that Archambault and Barnett (2010) identify means that neither should be treated as offering a checklist against which an academic's readiness can be definitively measured. The Artificial Intelligence Assessment Scale is most directly relevant to assessment redesign, but its institutional preconditions mean it serves more as an aspiration for what South African quality assurance systems could eventually support than as a description of what most academics can currently implement without institutional negotiation. Diffusion of innovations theory and the Technology Acceptance Model are most directly relevant to explaining why adoption varies. However, they were developed to describe adoption of innovations generally rather than of a technology that, as the South African integrity literature suggests, some academics have principled reasons to adopt only partially or conditionally. None of this diminishes the value of the four frameworks; it simply means that a model built from them needs to be explicit about which frameworks it draws on for which purpose, a task that the derivation below attempts directly.

DEVELOPMENT AND JUSTIFICATION OF THE CONCEPTUAL MODEL

Before introducing the conceptual model itself, it is worth setting out explicitly how it was derived, why it takes the particular shape it does, and how it relates to comparable frameworks that already exist internationally, since a model that appears without this justification risks reading as an assertion rather than a reasoned synthesis of the literature reviewed above.

A reasonable question to ask of any conceptual model of this kind is why it proposes three academic dimensions rather than four, five or more. The answer follows directly from the theoretical review above rather than from an arbitrary preference for parsimony. Each candidate dimension considered during development was tested against a single criterion: does the literature reviewed in this chapter treat it as a distinct body of professional knowledge requiring its own form of development, or as an instance, application or precondition of a dimension already identified. Technological and pedagogical fluency, assessment design capability and academic integrity each passed this test, in the sense that each is grounded in a distinct theoretical tradition, TPACK and artificial intelligence literacy scholarship, the Artificial Intelligence Assessment Scale, and the South African empirical and decolonial literature on authorship and epistemic justice, respectively, and each requires a recognisably different form of professional development to strengthen. Candidates who did not pass this test, considered in more detail below, were folded into an existing dimension rather than retained as additional categories.

The model's three academic dimensions, technological and pedagogical fluency, assessment design capability and academic integrity, map directly onto three bodies of theory reviewed in the preceding section: TPACK and artificial intelligence literacy scholarship jointly ground the first dimension; the Artificial Intelligence Assessment Scale grounds the second; and the South African empirical literature on authorship, disciplinary identity and epistemic justice (Maistry & Singh, 2025; Pramjeeth & Ramgovind, 2024; Le Grange, 2016; Mohamed et al., 2020) grounds the third. Institutional readiness is deliberately not presented as a fourth, coequal academic capability alongside these three. Diffusion of innovations theory treats institutional and infrastructural conditions as the context within which individual adoption decisions occur rather than as an additional decision an individual academic makes (Rogers, 2003), and Maimela and Mbonde's (2025) South African findings make the same point empirically: an individual academic's technological and pedagogical fluency, however well developed, cannot translate into practice where institutional infrastructure and policy enactment do not permit it. The model, therefore, represents institutional readiness as an encompassing, enabling condition, illustrated in Figure 1 as a surrounding context rather than a fourth internal box, precisely to avoid implying that institutional and individual factors sit at the same conceptual level or can substitute for one another.

This derivation also clarifies why other candidate dimensions considered during the model's development were not retained as separate categories. Digital infrastructure and technical support are treated as components of institutional readiness rather than as a standalone technological dimension, since the evidence reviewed above indicates that infrastructure functions as an enabling condition for individual capability rather than a capability in its own right. Artificial intelligence literacy and assessment literacy are treated as internal to the technological and pedagogical fluency and assessment design capability dimensions, respectively, rather than as free-standing fifth and sixth dimensions, on the grounds argued above that they are better understood as the specific content of existing dimensions than as conceptually distinct capabilities. Student-facing concerns, including students' artificial intelligence literacy and students' experiences of artificial intelligence-supported feedback, are treated in this chapter as downstream consequences of academic preparedness rather than as components of it, since the chapter's scope is explicitly academic development rather than student development. However, the two are clearly related. The point is returned to in the future research section below.

It is also important to be explicit about where this model sits relative to existing international frameworks, since South African higher education is not the first sector to have attempted this kind of synthesis. Chan (2023), drawing on a large-scale survey of staff and students at Hong Kong universities, proposed an AI Ecological Education Policy Framework organised around three dimensions: pedagogical, governance, and operational. That framework and the one proposed here share a basic structural intuition, that pedagogical capability alone cannot explain institutional readiness for artificial intelligence, and both frameworks separate an academic, teaching-facing dimension from an institutional, infrastructural one.

They differ in emphasis and origin. Chan's framework was derived from a large, primarily quantitative dataset within a single, comparatively well-resourced higher education system, and is oriented towards policy formulation at the institutional level; it does not distinguish, as the present model does, between assessment design capability and the underlying academic integrity concerns that a given assessment decision raises, treating both as aspects of a single governance dimension. The model proposed in this chapter separates these two because the South African evidence reviewed above suggests that assessment redesign and integrity reasoning draw on genuinely different bodies of knowledge, assessment literacy on one hand and a contextually specific understanding of authorship and disciplinary identity on the other, and conflating them risks treating academic integrity as a compliance matter to be resolved once assessment has been redesigned, rather than as an ongoing area of professional judgement in its own right. The present model is also explicitly derived for, and conceptually tested against, a lower-resource, historically unequal system, which is why institutional readiness receives the structurally more prominent, encompassing treatment described above rather than functioning as one dimension among several.

The resulting model, then, is not offered as an entirely novel invention with no relationship to prior scholarship, nor as a simple restatement of TPACK, the Artificial Intelligence Assessment Scale or Chan's (2023) framework considered separately. Its contribution lies in the particular combination and relative weighting of these elements for a specific and, until now, under theorised context: a higher education sector in which the academic capabilities required for artificial intelligence driven assessment are reasonably well described by existing international literature, but in which the institutional conditions that determine whether those capabilities can be exercised are distributed as unevenly as South African higher education infrastructure itself, a distribution existing frameworks developed elsewhere do not foreground to the same degree.

A CONCEPTUAL MODEL OF ACADEMIC PREPAREDNESS

Figure 1 presents the model that follows from this derivation. Institutional readiness surrounds and enables the three interacting academic dimensions, technological and pedagogical fluency, assessment design capability and academic integrity, each of which is elaborated below.

Figure 1. A conceptual model of academic preparedness for artificial intelligence-driven assessment, showing institutional readiness as an enabling condition surrounding three interacting academic dimensions.

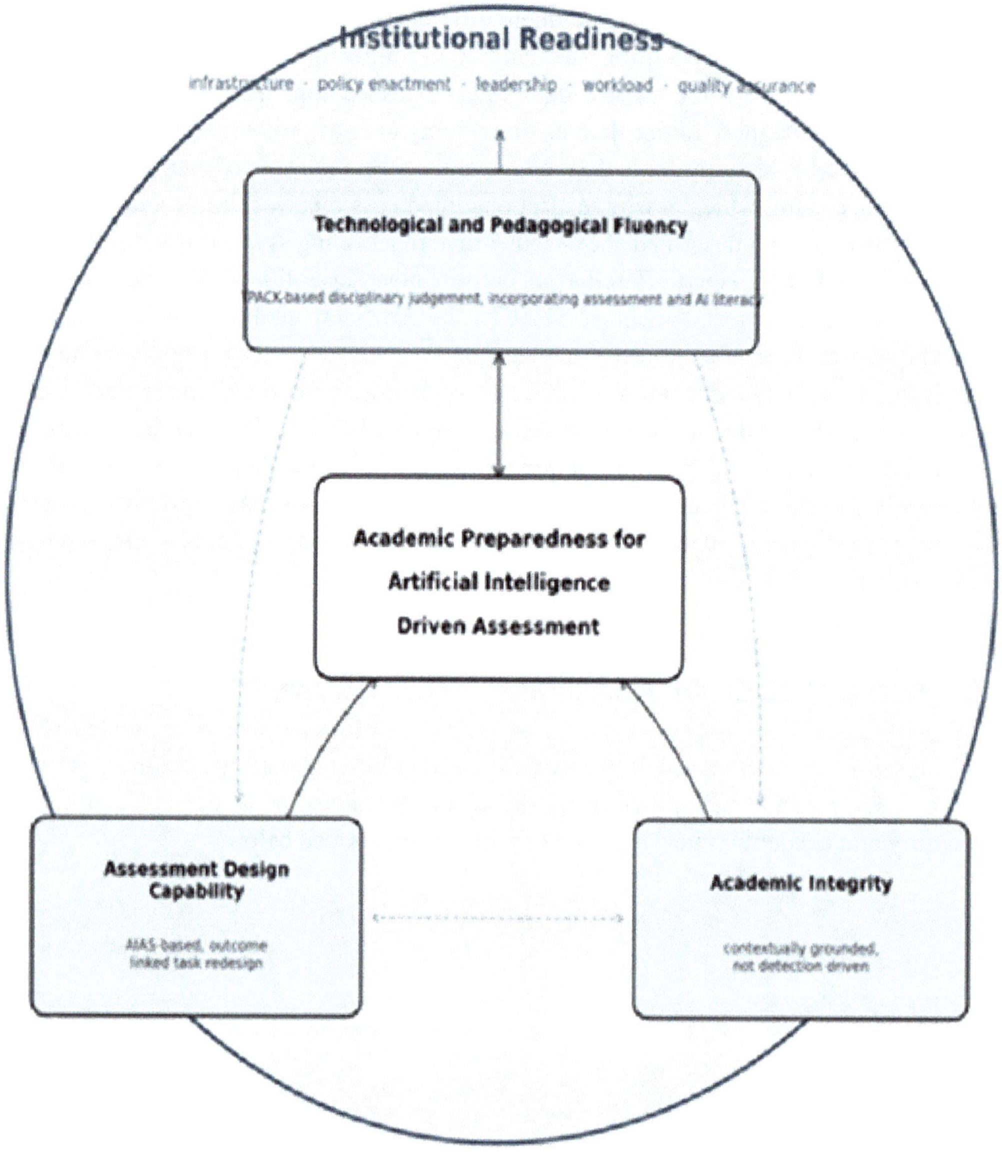

Technological and Pedagogical Fluency

This dimension concerns the capacity to judge which generative artificial intelligence tools, if any, are appropriate for a specific content area and pedagogical purpose, in the sense of this judgement as defined by TPACK, together with the more specific critical evaluation capacity described in artificial intelligence literacy scholarship. Understanding how ChatGPT works in general terms does not, by itself, tell an academic whether it is appropriate to allow its use in a particular assignment, still less how to redesign that assignment. Hence, the tool supports rather than substitutes for the intended learning.

Fluency of this kind is shaped by contextual factors that vary considerably across the South African sector. Reliable internet connectivity remains unevenly distributed, and academics differ in their prior experience of educational technology. Institutional investment compounds these differences: universities that provide licensed platforms and structured, discipline-specific training create the conditions under which academics can experiment with confidence, while academics without this investment develop fluency largely on their own initiative.

A useful working test of whether an academic has developed this fluency, rather than superficial familiarity with a particular interface, is whether they can explain to a colleague why a given tool is or is not appropriate for a specific task in terms that refer to the discipline and the intended learning outcome, rather than to the tool's general capabilities. An academic teaching financial reporting needs to know whether a generative artificial intelligence tool can be trusted to apply current accounting standards correctly; an academic teaching engineering design might instead use artificial intelligence deliberately to generate several plausible design solutions, precisely so that students can practise the comparative evaluation a professional engineer would need to perform. Neither judgment transfers cleanly to the other discipline, which is exactly the point TPACK was designed to make and which a discipline-neutral training session is structurally unable to address.

Assessment Design Capability

The second dimension, understood through the graduated logic of the Artificial Intelligence Assessment Scale, is the capacity to redesign assessment tasks around explicit, outcome-linked decisions about permitted use of artificial intelligence, rather than a reactive prohibition applied uniformly across a module. This requires assessment literacy, an understanding of validity, reliability, fairness, authenticity and constructive alignment (Biggs & Tang, 2022), which many academics were never explicitly taught, having learned assessment design largely through disciplinary apprenticeship.

Academics with strong assessment design capability respond to the weakened assurance value of unsupervised coursework not by abandoning it but by widening their repertoire: authentic assessment built around real-world problems, portfolio assessment tracing learning over time, oral examinations requiring students to explain and defend their reasoning, and structured collaborative tasks in which artificial intelligence use is an explicit and assessed part of the process. As noted above, this capability also has direct workload implications that the South African literature tends to underplay; redesigning a single high stakes assignment typically requires reconsidering the brief, the rubric and the feedback process together, and academic development that strengthens this capability without securing institutional recognition of the time involved is likely to produce well informed academics who nonetheless lack the capacity to act on what they have learned.

Applying the Artificial Intelligence Assessment Scale within a single module illustrates why the graduated logic matters more than it might first appear, while also illustrating the scale's practical limits. A first-year assignment intended to develop a student's own analytical writing might sit at the restrictive end of the scale, with artificial intelligence use excluded, so the underlying skill can actually be assessed. A later assignment in the same module, designed to develop a student's capacity to evaluate machine-generated output critically, might sit near the permissive end. Both decisions can be defended on pedagogical grounds specific to what each task demonstrates, in a way that a single, module-wide rule cannot. As noted in the theoretical review above, however, applying the scale this way assumes a quality-assurance environment flexible enough to approve task-by-task variation within a single module, a precondition that Furze et al.'s (2024) pilot setting provided but that is not yet standard practice across South African institutions.

A Contextually Grounded Understanding of Academic Integrity

The third dimension takes seriously the concerns South African academics themselves have raised regarding authorship and disciplinary identity (Maistry & Singh, 2025; Pramjeeth & Ramgovind, 2024), while resisting a purely punitive or detection-driven framing of academic integrity. This extends well beyond preventing plagiarism in its traditional sense; it requires clarity on transparency, fairness, privacy, and accountability, and on what counts as legitimate assistance when a student uses artificial intelligence to brainstorm or edit rather than to generate a submission wholesale.

A contextually grounded approach also has to reckon with concerns more specific to the South African and wider African setting. Generative artificial intelligence systems remain prone to fabricated references and forms of bias inherited from their training data. Mohamed et al. (2020) argue, from a decolonial theoretical position, that artificial intelligence systems developed predominantly within Western research institutions risk encoding and perpetuating existing global power asymmetries rather than merely reflecting a neutral technical limitation that better data could straightforwardly correct. Read alongside Le Grange's (2016) argument that South African curriculum decolonisation requires more than adding African content to an otherwise unchanged Western framework, this suggests that academic integrity in the South African context cannot be separated from a broader question about whose knowledge systems a given artificial intelligence tool actually represents. South African academics accordingly need a form of critical awareness that goes beyond the generic caution urged in most international guidance, and a willingness to model that scepticism for students rather than presenting artificial intelligence output as a neutral or authoritative source.

The Interdependence of the Model

The three academic dimensions do not operate independently, and institutional readiness does not sit apart from them as an unrelated backdrop; it actively determines whether each can be exercised in practice, as the dashed feedback loops in Figure 1 indicate. An academic may possess considerable technological and pedagogical fluency yet be unable to translate it into assessment redesign in the absence of institutional support to revise the assessment structure of a heavily subscribed module. A university may publish an ambitious generative artificial intelligence policy without the accompanying investment in academic development that would allow individual academics to enact that policy's aspirations. Treating the three academic dimensions as mutually reinforcing and institutional readiness as the enabling condition surrounding all three directs academic development practice away from one-off technical training sessions and towards sustained, discipline-embedded support that addresses pedagogical belief, assessment design, and institutional context together.

DISCUSSION: A SECTOR STILL BUILDING ITS RESPONSE

The South African evidence reviewed in this chapter suggests a sector that has moved relatively quickly to articulate policy positions on generative artificial intelligence but comparatively slowly to build the academic development infrastructure needed to enact those positions with pedagogical integrity. This pattern echoes a warning present in the broader international literature well before generative artificial intelligence existed in its current form. Zawacki-Richter et al. (2019) observed that research and practice in artificial intelligence in higher education had developed with insufficient attention to educators' preparedness. Popenici and Kerr (2017) cautioned more generally that the pace of technological change in higher education tends to outstrip institutions' capacity to reflect critically on its implications before adopting it. The South African case examined here suggests both observations remain apposite.

A further consideration specific to the South African context concerns feedback. Boud and Molloy (2013) distinguish between a model of feedback in which the academic functions as the sole driver of a corrective loop and a model of sustainable assessment in which students are supported to develop their own capacity for evaluative judgement over time. Generative artificial intelligence is frequently promoted for its capacity to deliver rapid, individualised feedback at scale, a capability of obvious relevance in large-enrolment South African modules where staff-to-student ratios can make timely individual feedback difficult to sustain through conventional means. If academic preparedness is understood only as using these tools to accelerate the first, academic-driven model of feedback, the opportunity to put generative artificial intelligence in service of the second, more sustainable model is likely to be missed. This framing has received comparatively little explicit attention in the South African literature reviewed here. It illustrates the broader diagnosis this chapter advances: a sector faster to legislate than to build capacity, and a feedback culture that risks defaulting to the more limited of two available uses of generative artificial intelligence, both of which reflect a tendency to treat generative artificial intelligence as a problem requiring rapid institutional response rather than an occasion for slower, more deliberate reconsideration of what assessment is for.

A related discussion point concerns the tension explicitly noted in the theoretical review above between generative artificial intelligence as an enhancement to teaching and as a challenge to academic integrity. The South African evidence does not resolve this tension, and this chapter does not claim it can be resolved in general terms, since the appropriate balance appears to depend on the specific assessment task, the discipline and the learning outcome in question, precisely the reasoning the Artificial Intelligence Assessment Scale is designed to support. What the evidence does suggest is that academic development, which presents generative artificial intelligence as straightforwardly beneficial, without acknowledging that some academics have defensible pedagogical reasons for caution, is likely to be received with justified scepticism by exactly the colleagues whose engagement is most needed for assessment redesign to spread across a department rather than remaining confined to a small number of early adopters.

IMPLICATIONS FOR ACADEMIC DEVELOPMENT PRACTICE

The model developed above carries several practical implications for academic development units. Interventions should be discipline-embedded rather than generic, since the pedagogical and content-specific judgement TPACK foregrounds cannot be adequately developed through sector-wide workshops detached from an academic's own subject matter. An accounting lecturer, an engineering lecturer and a literature lecturer face genuinely different judgements about what a given generative artificial intelligence tool is good for, and a single, discipline-neutral training session is unlikely to serve any of them well.

Training should also introduce academics to graduated, task specific frameworks such as the Artificial Intelligence Assessment Scale, while being honest with academics about the scale's own institutional preconditions, so that staff are equipped to make and justify their own assessment design decisions rather than defaulting to blanket prohibition, an approach the South African evidence suggests is already proving difficult to enforce (Chaka et al., 2024; Sevnarayan, 2024).

Development should further engage explicitly with the differing conceptions of the university's purpose that appear to underlie South African academics' divergent responses to generative artificial intelligence, rather than treating resistance as a simple deficit of technical skill correctable through training alone (Maistry & Singh, 2025). Academics who understand assessment primarily as inducting students into a disciplinary community are likely to need different support from academics who understand assessment primarily as preparation for a technologically mediated workplace.

Finally, consistent with the model's treatment of institutional readiness as an enabling rather than a coequal dimension, academic development cannot be treated as a matter of individual capacity building alone. Sustained investment in infrastructure, workload recognition for assessment redesign, and quality assurance processes flexible enough to accommodate task-by-task variation in permitted artificial intelligence use are necessary complements to any training intervention, particularly at historically under-resourced South African institutions, where the digital divide documented by Maimela and Mbonde (2025) is likely to be at its most pronounced.

These four implications point towards a single, more general recommendation: academic development centres should treat artificial intelligence-driven assessment as an ongoing programme of work with a recognised budget and a named responsible unit, rather than as a policy question that can be considered resolved once a guideline document has been approved. The evidence reviewed throughout this chapter suggests that institutions making the most tangible progress are those that have explicitly made this distinction, rather than those with the most detailed policy wording.

INSTITUTIONAL AND POLICY IMPLICATIONS

The implications of this analysis extend beyond individual institutions to the sector as a whole. National higher education bodies, including Universities South Africa, the Council on Higher Education and the Department of Higher Education and Training, are well placed to encourage a degree of coordination that individual institutions cannot achieve alone, while still respecting institutional autonomy over how artificial intelligence is integrated into specific curricula. Coordinated attention to consistent ethical principles, shared quality assurance standards, and deliberate resource sharing could meaningfully reduce duplication of effort, a consideration of particular importance for historically disadvantaged institutions with limited internal capacity to develop these resources independently.

At the institutional level, universities that have so far concentrated their efforts on publishing regulatory guidelines now have reason to move towards more comprehensive strategies that integrate teaching, assessment and academic development rather than treating each as a separate policy stream. Academic development centres are well-positioned to serve as the institutional hub for this work, provided they receive the additional capacity, rather than an unfunded expansion of an existing mandate, that genuinely discipline-embedded support requires. Quality assurance processes deserve particular attention here, since they are often the point at which an ambitious policy either becomes real practice or remains a document with little bearing on what happens in a given module. Institutions that update review processes alongside their generative artificial intelligence policy, so that task-by-task variation in permitted use is not treated as a departure from approved practice that requires lengthy re-approval, are better placed to let assessment redesign actually take hold.

FUTURE RESEARCH DIRECTIONS

Several directions for future research follow from the analysis developed in this chapter. Most existing South African studies examine perceptions, attitudes or institutional policy; comparatively few examine how academics actually redesign assessment in practice. Empirical studies that examine academic development interventions as they are actually implemented, rather than as they appear in policy documents or academic self-reports, would meaningfully extend the evidence base on which this chapter has drawn.

The three-dimensional model proposed here would also benefit from direct empirical testing against academics' actual assessment practices, potentially through structural equation modelling or mixed-methods research that examines how the dimensions interact with institutional readiness rather than treating institutional factors as a simple moderating variable. Comparative research extending Maimela and Mbonde's (2025) historically white and historically black institutional comparison to a wider set of South African universities would help establish how far the institutional readiness dimension generalises across the sector, and what forms of targeted investment might narrow the gap it identifies. Longitudinal research would add a dimension largely missing from current cross-sectional studies, tracing how academics' confidence and assessment practices change as institutional experience with artificial intelligence accumulates over several years.

The model itself would also benefit from deliberate testing against Chan's (2023) AI Ecological Education Policy Framework and comparable international models, using matched data collection instruments across institutions in different resource settings, so that the extent to which the two frameworks converge or diverge in practice, rather than only at the level of conceptual comparison offered in this chapter, can be established empirically.

Research is also needed on student learning outcomes rather than technology adoption alone, and, following the scope limitation acknowledged in the model's derivation above, on how student artificial intelligence literacy relates to and is shaped by academic preparedness, a relationship this chapter has treated as downstream but has not examined directly. Finally, research examining whether generative artificial intelligence tools can support the sustainable, learner-driven model of feedback that Boud and Molloy (2013) describe, rather than a purely academically driven acceleration of existing feedback practices, would help clarify one of the more significant unresolved pedagogical questions raised in this chapter. Questions of epistemic justice deserve equally sustained attention: whether artificial intelligence narrows or widens educational inequality in the South African context, and how African knowledge systems might be represented more fully within artificial intelligence supported learning, are not peripheral concerns but central to whether artificial intelligence driven assessment advances or undermines the decolonial project that continues to define South African higher education (Le Grange, 2016; Mohamed et al., 2020).

CONCLUSION

This chapter has argued that preparing South African academics for artificial intelligence-driven assessment requires considerably more than technical training in the use of generative artificial intelligence tools, and more than the institutional policy documents that have proliferated across the sector since 2023. Drawing critically on Technological Pedagogical Content Knowledge, the Artificial Intelligence Assessment Scale, diffusion of innovations theory and artificial intelligence literacy scholarship, and reading these against South African and African decolonial literature, the chapter has derived and justified a conceptual model in which academic preparedness rests on three interacting dimensions, technological and pedagogical fluency, assessment design capability and academic integrity, situated within institutional readiness as an enabling condition rather than a fourth, co-equal capability.

The model's contribution, made explicit in the derivation section above, is not that it introduces entirely new theoretical elements. TPACK, the Artificial Intelligence Assessment Scale and comparable international frameworks such as Chan's (2023) AI Ecological Education Policy Framework already exist and already inform practice elsewhere. Its contribution is a specific, justified synthesis for a sector in which the academic capabilities required for artificial intelligence driven assessment are reasonably well described by existing literature, but in which institutional readiness is distributed as unevenly as digital infrastructure itself, a distribution that existing frameworks developed in better resourced systems do not foreground, and one that Maimela and Mbonde's (2025) South African evidence shows to be empirically consequential rather than a theoretical nicety.

The South African evidence reviewed here indicates a sector that has responded quickly at the level of policy but unevenly at the level of practice, with academic development structures, workload recognition and infrastructural investment lagging behind the pace at which generative artificial intelligence has entered student and academic life alike. Closing this gap will require academic development that is discipline-embedded rather than generic, that engages honestly with academics' differing conceptions of what a university education is for, and that treats institutional readiness as a condition for individual capability building rather than an afterthought. Without this fuller conception of preparedness, artificial intelligence-driven assessment in South African higher education risks remaining, as the evidence reviewed in this chapter suggests it already may, a matter of policy on paper, while considerably behind practice in the classroom.

REFERENCES

Archambault, L. M., & Barnett, J. H. (2010). Revisiting technological pedagogical content knowledge: Exploring the TPACK framework. *Computers & Education, 55*(4), 1656–1662. DOI: 10.1016/j.compedu.2010.07.009

Biggs, J., & Tang, C. (2022). *Teaching for quality learning at university* (5th ed.). Open University Press.

Boud, D., & Molloy, E. (2013). Rethinking models of feedback for learning: The challenge of design. *Assessment & Evaluation in Higher Education, 38*(6), 698–712. DOI: 10.1080/02602938.2012.691462

Cabero-Almenara, J., Palacios-Rodríguez, A., Loaiza-Aguirre, M. I., & Andrade-Abarca, P. S. (2024). The impact of pedagogical beliefs on the adoption of generative AI in higher education: Predictive model from UTAUT2. *Frontiers in Artificial Intelligence, 7*, 1497705. Advance online publication. DOI: 10.3389/frai.2024.1497705 PMID: 39484153

Chaka, C., Shange, T., Nkhobo, T., & Hlatshwayo, V. (2024). An environmental review of the generative artificial intelligence policies and guidelines of South African higher education institutions: A content analysis. *International Journal of Learning. Teaching and Educational Research, 23*(12), 487–511. DOI: 10.26803/ijlter.23.12.25

Chan, C. K. Y. (2023). A comprehensive AI policy education framework for university teaching and learning. *International Journal of Educational Technology in Higher Education, 20*(1), 38. Advance online publication. DOI: 10.1186/s41239-023-00408-3

Cotton, D. R. E., Cotton, P. A., & Shipway, J. R. (2024). Chatting and cheating: Ensuring academic integrity in the era of ChatGPT. *Innovations in Education and Teaching International, 61*(2), 228–239. DOI: 10.1080/14703297.2023.2190148

Council on Higher Education. (2024). *VitalStats public higher education 2022*. Council on Higher Education.

Davis, F. D. (1989). Perceived usefulness, perceived ease of use, and user acceptance of information technology. *Management Information Systems Quarterly, 13*(3), 319–340. DOI: 10.2307/249008

Dwivedi, Y. K., Kshetri, N., Hughes, L., Slade, E. L., Jeyaraj, A., Kar, A. K., Baabdullah, A. M., Koohang, A., Raghavan, V., Ahuja, M., Albanna, H., Albashrawi, M., Aljalil, M., Al-Nuaimi, B., Al-Zubaidi, F., Balakrishnan, J., Barlette, Y., Basu, S., Bose, I., & Wright, R. (2023). So what if ChatGPT wrote it? Multidisciplinary perspectives on opportunities, challenges and implications of generative conversational artificial intelligence for research, practice and policy. *International Journal of Information Management, 71*, 102642. Advance online publication. DOI: 10.1016/j.ijinfomgt.2023.102642

Furze, L., Perkins, M., Roe, J., & MacVaugh, J. (2024). The AI Assessment Scale (AIAS) in action: A pilot implementation of GenAI-supported assessment. *Australasian Journal of Educational Technology, 40*(4), 38–55. DOI: 10.14742/ajet.9434

Ifenthaler, D., & Yau, J. Y. K. (2020). Utilising learning analytics to support study success in higher education: A systematic review. *Educational Technology Research and Development, 68*(4), 1961–1990. DOI: 10.1007/s11423-020-09788-z

Le Grange, L. (2016). Decolonising the university curriculum. *South African Journal of Higher Education, 30*(2), 1–12. DOI: 10.20853/30-2-709

Long, D., & Magerko, B. (2020). What is AI literacy? Competencies and design considerations. In *Proceedings of the 2020 CHI Conference on Human Factors in Computing Systems* (pp. 1–16). Association for Computing Machinery. https://doi.org/DOI: 10.1145/3313831.3376727

Maimela, C., & Mbonde, P. (2025). Artificial intelligence in South African universities: Curriculum transformation and decolonisation—aid or obstacle? *Frontiers in Sociology, 10*, 1543471. Advance online publication. DOI: 10.3389/fsoc.2025.1543471 PMID: 40697567

Maistry, S. M., & Singh, U. G. (2025). University research supervisors' responses to generative AI amid institutional policy lag. *Alternation African Scholarship Book Series, 22*, 155–176. DOI: 10.29086/978-0-9869938-3-1/2025/AASBS22/8

Mishra, P., & Koehler, M. J. (2006). Technological pedagogical content knowledge: A framework for teacher knowledge. *Teachers College Record, 108*(6), 1017–1054. DOI: 10.1111/j.1467-9620.2006.00684.x

Mohamed, S., Png, M. T., & Isaac, W. (2020). Decolonial AI: Decolonial theory as sociotechnical foresight in artificial intelligence. *Philosophy & Technology, 33*(4), 659–684. DOI: 10.1007/s13347-020-00405-8

Ng, D. T. K., Leung, J. K. L., Chu, K. W. S., & Qiao, M. S. (2021). Conceptualising AI literacy: An exploratory review. *Computers and Education: Artificial Intelligence, 2*, 100041. Advance online publication. DOI: 10.1016/j.caeai.2021.100041

Perkins, M., Furze, L., Roe, J., & MacVaugh, J. (2024). The Artificial Intelligence Assessment Scale (AIAS): A framework for ethical integration of generative AI in educational assessment. *Journal of University Teaching & Learning Practice, 21*(6), 49–66. DOI: 10.53761/q3azde36

Popenici, S. A. D., & Kerr, S. (2017). Exploring the impact of artificial intelligence on teaching and learning in higher education. *Research and Practice in Technology Enhanced Learning, 12*(1), 22. Advance online publication. DOI: 10.1186/s41039-017-0062-8 PMID: 30595727

Pramjeeth, S., & Ramgovind, P. (2024). Generative artificial intelligence (AI) tools in higher education: A moral compass for the future? *African Journal of Inter/Multidisciplinary Studies, 6*(1). https://doi.org/DOI: 10.51415/ajims.v6i1.1560

Rogers, E. M. (2003). *Diffusion of innovations* (5th ed.). Free Press.

Sevnarayan, K. (2024). Exploring the dynamics of ChatGPT: Students' and lecturers' perspectives at an open distance e-learning university. *Journal of Pedagogical Research, 8*(2), 212–226. DOI: 10.33902/JPR.202426525

Shulman, L. S. (1986). Those who understand: Knowledge growth in teaching. *Educational Researcher, 15*(2), 4–14. DOI: 10.3102/0013189X015002004

UNESCO. (2023). *Guidance for generative AI in education and research.* UNESCO. https://unesdoc.unesco.org/

van den Berg, G., & du Plessis, E. (2023). ChatGPT and generative AI: Possibilities for its contribution to lesson planning, critical thinking and openness in teacher education. *Education Sciences*, *13*(10), 998. Advance online publication. DOI: 10.3390/educsci13100998

van Wyk, M. M., Adarkwah, M. A., & Amponsah, S. (2023). Why all the hype about ChatGPT? Academics' views of a chat-based conversational learning strategy at an open distance e-learning institution. *Open Praxis*, *15*(3), 191–205. DOI: 10.55982/openpraxis.15.3.563

Zawacki-Richter, O., Marín, V. I., Bond, M., & Gouverneur, F. (2019). Systematic review of research on artificial intelligence applications in higher education: Where are the educators? *International Journal of Educational Technology in Higher Education*, *16*(1), 39. Advance online publication. DOI: 10.1186/s41239-019-0171-0

Chapter 16

Authentic Assessment for Learning in African Languages in the Era of Generative AI:

Pedagogical Possibilities, Ethical Tensions, and Epistemic Justice

Nthabiseng Blandina Khoalenyane
http://orcid.org/0000-0003-3964-5255
University of Zululand, South Africa

Tinashe Charles Matiyenga
http://orcid.org/0009-0004-1476-2441
University of Zululand, South Africa

ABSTRACT

Assessment plays a pivotal contentious role in language education, in African contexts, where colonial-era epistemologies and monolingual standards have shaped prevailing practices. Assessment frameworks for African languages often mirror those designed for dominant global languages, neglecting learners' sociolinguistic realities. Concurrently, the rise of generative artificial intelligence tools has catalysed discussions about academic integrity and assessment validity, in English-medium higher education. This chapter addresses a significant gap in the discourse on African languages and generative AI by examining how authentic assessment and assessment for learning can be redefined in these contexts. The chapter suggests that GenAI can serve as a transformative catalyst that challenges conventional definitions of knowledge, performance, and learning. By foregrounding ethical, linguistic, and epistemic concerns unique to Africa, this chapter aims to contribute insights into the pedagogical possibilities of decoloniality that emerge when integrating AI into African language education.

1. INTRODUCTION

The rapid expansion of digital technologies has reshaped educational practice worldwide, and assessment has become one of the most contested domains of change (Mavengere et al., 2021; Matiyenga

DOI: 10.4018/979-8-3373-8939-4.ch016

& Khoalenyane, 2025a; Muzindutsi et al., 2025). Designers often fail to exploit the affordances of new tools, and innovators sometimes transplant outdated, exam-centred models onto digital platforms. This mismatch highlights the need to rethink how technology can meaningfully enhance assessment, an imperative particularly urgent in African language education, where systems shaped by colonial epistemologies, monolingual norms and high-stakes regimes continue to prioritise standardised written forms over learners' lived linguistic practices. Even where multilingualism is officially endorsed (for example, South Africa), assessment frameworks are frequently adapted from those used for dominant global languages and remain misaligned with learners' sociolinguistic realities and communicative repertoires (Xeketwana & Robinson, 2026). Such misalignment undermines instruction and neglects translanguaging practices that can support deeper cognitive engagement and more meaningful language learning (Karamoko & Naounou, 2026).

Languages are not neutral tools: they shape cognition, perception, and cultural experience, thereby mediating what counts as legitimate knowledge (Downey & Gillett, 2023; Mai & de Rooij, 2023). Colonial languages often embody historical and economic value systems that privilege global mobility and market outcomes over local epistemologies and cultural continuity (Meighan, 2023; Matiyenga & Khoalenyane, 2025b). These hierarchies, often described as colonialingualism, sustain power asymmetries that marginalise indigenous and minority languages; assessment functions as a regulatory mechanism that legitimises particular practices and defines academic competence.

Generative artificial intelligence (GenAI) and large language models (LLMs), such as ChatGPT, Claude, and Gemini, introduce both challenges and opportunities for assessment (Ajani et al., 2024; Khoalenyane & Ajani, 2024). Debates have centred on academic integrity, authorship and validity, but much of this discourse focuses on English-medium higher education in the Global North. The implications of GenAI for authentic assessment and Assessment for Learning (AfL) in African languages remain under-theorised. Moreover, LLMs often reflect data and design choices that privilege high-resource languages and standardised varieties, reproducing linguistic hierarchies and cultural biases in their outputs.

This chapter addresses that gap by examining how authentic assessment and AfL for Conversational Sesotho can be reimagined in the age of GenAI. Rather than treating GenAI solely as a threat to assessment credibility, it explores the technology's potential as a catalyst for pedagogical renewal. Authentic assessment, tasks that mirror real-world communicative practices and sociocultural contexts, resonates with the communicative and relational character of many African languages. Research shows that tools developed for monolingual populations require careful adaptation in multilingual settings (Lanteigne et al., 2021; Reilly et al., 2023; Matiyenga &Khoalenyane, 2026), and South Africa's linguistic complexity underscores the need for assessment instruments that reflect local communicative practices (Simonsen & Southwood, 2021). Thoughtful GenAI integration can support formative feedback, dialogic learning, multilingual drafting and iterative revision, practices that deepen proficiency and critical engagement while preserving the educator's role in ensuring quality and ethical use (Ajani & Matiyenga, 2025; Darmawan & Sabata, 2025; Lee et al., 2026).

AI integration also raises ethical and epistemic concerns in African educational contexts (Nazira et al., 2025). Global data infrastructures commonly marginalise African languages; LLMs trained on high-resource languages may flatten dialectal variation, reproduce biases and overlook culturally embedded meanings. In low-resource contexts, AI outputs can lack nuance or privilege standardised varieties over community forms, thereby reinforcing existing linguistic hierarchies.

The chapter therefore advocates a principled, contextually grounded approach to AI integration that foregrounds epistemic justice, cultural integrity and linguistic diversity. It outlines how educators can design assessment practices that leverage GenAI affordances while preserving sociocultural richness, using conceptual analysis and practical examples to show how authentic assessment and AfL can be strengthened in digitally mediated contexts.

In sum, this chapter contributes to debates on decolonising language education and rethinking assessment in digitally evolving African contexts. It argues that the future of African language assessment lies not in resisting technology but in deliberately shaping it so that innovation supports, rather than erodes, linguistic equity, cultural identity and meaningful learning.

2. AUTHENTIC ASSESSMENT AND ASSESSMENT FOR LEARNING (AFL): CONCEPTUAL FOUNDATIONS

Assessment is not merely a mechanism for measuring learning; it shapes what is valued, legitimised, and reproduced within educational systems (Grønset & Kvam, 2025). It conditions curriculum-making by mediating the balance between developing students' skills and grounding them in disciplinary knowledge. From a sociological perspective, assessment embeds values and expectations within schooling. Broadfoot's analysis of national assessment policies illustrates how such policies affect pupils and teachers, underscoring the need for a sociological understanding of assessment's role in shaping educational experiences and outcomes (Broadfoot, 2021). Thus, assessment functions as a mechanism that legitimises particular forms of knowledge and learning practices.

Students can be active agents in this process: assessment practices may reinforce or contest existing power dynamics (Ezennia et al., 2024). Student partnership in assessment (SaPA) reconceives assessment as a democratic practice in which learners participate in designing and reviewing assessment policy and practice (Nieminen et al., 2025). This participatory orientation highlights the relational and political nature of assessment and shows that what is valued can be contested and redefined.

In African language education, conventional assessment has often prioritised standardised, decontextualised knowledge, privileging written accuracy and grammatical conformity over communicative competence, cultural nuance, and lived linguistic practice (Vogt & Antia, 2024). There is growing recognition, including in South Africa, of the need to move beyond such models (Melvill, 2024). This requires clearer construct definition (e.g., academic literacy) and validation grounded in applied linguistics rather than narrow technical debates about validity, so that tests are responsible and contextually relevant (Weideman, 2022). Reconsidering assessment through the lenses of authentic assessment and AfL offers a foundation for more contextually responsive and epistemically just pedagogies.

2.1 Authentic Assessment: Meaning, Purpose, and Relevance

Authentic assessment requires learners to apply knowledge and skills in tasks that mirror real-world contexts and meaningful social practices. It responds to limitations of traditional testing by emphasising contextualised, relevant tasks that enhance engagement and transfer, an issue made especially salient by disruptions such as COVID-19 and the arrival of generative AI (Papanastasiou et al., 2025). Well-designed, authentic tasks align with professional and societal practices and allow students to bring personal and systemic perspectives into their work (Ravi & Besharat, 2026).

Rather than testing isolated linguistic forms, authentic assessment situates language use within communicative, cultural, and relational settings: dialogues, storytelling, community interviews, oral presentations, problem-solving conversations, and culturally situated writing tasks (Liao et al., 2023). The Understanding by Design (UbD) framework of Wiggins and McTighe advocates assessment focused on meaningful performance and deep understanding rather than rote recall (Wiggins, 1990; Brown, 2004; McTighe et al., 2020; Marron, 2024). This encourages curriculum and assessment design that promotes transfer and coherence.

Critiques of traditional assessment highlight its failure to capture complex, real-world skills (Lestari, 2021; Kandlbinder, 2025). Authentic assessment aims to evaluate competencies such as autonomy, motivation, self-regulation, and metacognition—attributes associated with employability and meaningful learning and can be applied formatively and summatively (Villarroel et al., 2018; Ukashatu et al., 2021). Evidence indicates authentic methods can increase engagement and deepen understanding (Lestari, 2021), but implementation barriers remain, including unclear definitions and entrenched testing traditions; thus, curriculum redesign and staff development are necessary (Villarroel et al., 2018; Ukashatu, 2021).

In African language contexts, authentic assessment matters because of the following:

- *Contextual relevance*: Many African languages are rooted in oral traditions: storytelling, praise poetry, and dialogic interaction that transmit cultural values and norms; ignoring these forms narrows legitimate knowledge (Regassa & Mitiku, 2024).
- *Cultural integrity*: Authentic tasks enable learners to draw on indigenous knowledge, proverbs, idioms, and local narratives, recognising the performative, audience-oriented nature of many genres (Otiono, 2021).
- *Holistic competence*: Assessment can prioritise communicative effectiveness, pragmatic appropriateness, and cultural positioning over narrowly defined grammatical precision, aligning assessment with constructivist and communicative approaches.

Authentic assessment, therefore, resists colonial-linguistic norms that equate legitimacy with standardised written forms.

2.2 Assessment for Learning (AfL): A Formative Paradigm

Where authentic assessment focuses on task design, AfL emphasises the function of assessment within the learning process. AfL positions assessment as an ongoing enquiry that gathers evidence about learning goals to inform teaching and support student development. It encourages learners to reflect on their current status, identify next steps, and plan how to achieve goals, thereby fostering self-regulation and ownership (Padmanabha, 2021). Central to AfL are clarifying learning intentions and success criteria, eliciting evidence through interactive tasks, providing actionable feedback, encouraging self-regulation and metacognition, and activating peers as learning resources, principles articulated in the work of Black and Wiliam (2009).

In African language education, AfL can counter high-stakes, exam-driven systems that marginalise learners' linguistic identities by making assessment dialogic and relational, consistent with communal knowledge practices.

2.3 Intersections Between Authentic Assessment and AfL

Authentic assessment and Assessment for Learning (AfL) are distinct yet mutually reinforcing. Authentic tasks situate learners in meaningful, real-life contexts that require demonstration of relevant skills and competencies (Hu & Lee, 2023). AfL uses the evidence produced in those tasks to guide teaching and learning, providing feedback, prompting reflection, and enabling iterative improvement (Swaffield, 2011). Combined, these approaches transform assessment from a one-off judgment into a contextually grounded, dialogic, process-oriented practice that privileges learners' sociolinguistic realities.

In practice, this integration can take the form of iterative oral storytelling with feedback cycles, conversational role-plays followed by self- and peer-assessment, or community projects evaluated with negotiated rubrics, all of which foreground language as lived practice and support progressive learner autonomy.

2.4 Implications for African Language Education

Reconceptualising assessment through authentic and formative lenses is vital in postcolonial contexts where traditional systems often reproduce hierarchies associated with standardised varieties and colonial schooling (Sharma, 2026). These approaches enable recognition of dialectal diversity, integration of oral and multimodal forms, validation of community-based knowledge, and greater learner agency.

In technologically evolving environments, including those shaped by generative AI, grounding assessment in authenticity and formative purpose helps prevent reliance on superficial performance metrics (Jurāne-Brēmane, 2023) and aligns digital tools with the goals of meaningful communication, critical reflection, and culturally situated learning.

In sum, authentic assessment and AfL offer a theoretical and pedagogical basis for reimagining African language assessment beyond colonial legacies and exam-centric regimes, shifting the focus from linguistic conformity to communicative competence, cultural relevance, and learner agency.

3. GENERATIVE AI AND LANGUAGE ASSESSMENT: GLOBAL DEBATES, AFRICAN SILENCES

The rapid spread of generative artificial intelligence (GenAI) has unsettled assumptions about authorship, originality, and the integrity of assessment (Askari, 2025; Holmner et al., 2025). Systems such as ChatGPT, Claude and Gemini can generate essays, simulate dialogue, translate, mimic registers, and provide feedback with fluency that blurs the boundary between human and machine production. This capacity raises concerns about plagiarism, intellectual property and the validity of conventional written assessments, prompting intense debate in higher education about how to preserve accountability and academic rigour (Askari, 2025).

3.1 Global Debates: Integrity, Authorship, and Validity

Two broad responses have emerged. One frames GenAI as a threat: AI-facilitated text generation undermines the reliability of take-home assignments and unsupervised written tasks, leading some institutions to revert to proctored exams, oral assessments or AI-detection tools, each with its own limitations (Amrane-Cooper et al., 2024; Felipe et al., 2025; Chkarka & Fatmi, 2026). The other adopts an integrative stance, treating GenAI as a pedagogical resource that can prompt redesigns of assessment toward process, reflection, critique of AI outputs and multimodal engagement (Wang & Zhan, 2024). This view recommends faculty development, student partnerships, and policy guidance to address bias, overreliance, and digital inequality (Kurtz et al., 2024; Bower et al., 2024; Chan & Colloton, 2024).

Most of this debate assumes high-resource languages with extensive digital corpora; those assumptions do not map easily onto African-language contexts.

3.2 African Silences: Structural and Linguistic Marginalisation

African languages are frequently marginalised within global AI ecosystems. LLMs are predominantly trained on high-resource languages, which encode dominant ideologies and flatten dialectal and cultural variation. Many indigenous languages remain low-resourced in digital terms despite wide use, a condition compounded by limited digitisation, infrastructure and ethical concerns about data ownership. Algorithmic and epistemic biases thus disadvantage African languages and cultural identities (Yin, 2025; Ketere, 2025; Midigo, 2025). Initiatives such as the Masakhane Project in South Africa demonstrate participatory strategies for building corpora and improving representation, but progress is uneven and often dependent on external funding.

This marginalisation produces a double bind for African language educators: they confront the same integrity concerns as educators elsewhere while also contending with AI systems that poorly reflect local linguistic realities.

3.3 Validity in Low-Resource Language Contexts

Language assessment theory traditionally emphasises validity, reliability, fairness, and authenticity. GenAI complicates these core assessment principles:

- Validity: Does AI-assisted output measure language proficiency or prompt-engineering skill?
- Reliability: Are AI responses consistent across dialects and registers?
- Fairness: Do disparities in access and AI literacy produce inequitable advantages?
- Authenticity: Does AI undermine genuine communicative competence or simulate legitimate mediation practices?

In African-language contexts, concerns about validity are amplified by limited AI training data. African AI systems often reflect linguistic hierarchies embedded in global data infrastructures, thereby reinforcing colonial legacies and marginalising indigenous epistemologies and pedagogical values. This situation calls for a decolonial and Afrocentric approach to AI development and assessment, emphasising the inclusion of African languages and culturally relevant frameworks to ensure that AI tools are socially responsive and contextually grounded (Nazira et al., 2025).

An AI system generating Conversational Sesotho, for example, may default to standardised or hybridised forms, inadvertently privileging particular varieties while marginalising others. Assessment practices that rely uncritically on AI-generated feedback or exemplars risk reinforcing linguistic hierarchies already embedded in colonial educational systems.

3.4 Ethical and Epistemic Concerns

Beyond technical validity, GenAI raises deeper epistemic questions. Language is not simply a medium of expression; it encodes cultural memory, worldview, and social relations. When AI systems generate text in African languages, they do so through statistical modelling rather than lived cultural embeddedness. These models are built on large datasets and generate narrative text based on patterns learned from the data, without intrinsic cultural awareness or contextual lived experience (Ku & Hool, 2024). This can produce grammatically coherent yet culturally thin outputs. This limitation is inherent in the design of large language models (LLMs), which rely on probabilistic associations rather than cultural or experiential knowledge.

There is also the risk of linguistic homogenisation. If educators adopt AI-generated templates as benchmarks of correctness, dialectical variation and creative expression may be constrained. Such outcomes would contradict decolonising efforts aimed at recognising plural epistemologies and sociolinguistic diversity.

At the same time, dismissing AI outright may foreclose opportunities. In contexts where educational resources are scarce, GenAI tools could support formative feedback, vocabulary development, conversational simulation, and multilingual drafting. The question, therefore, is not whether AI should be present, but how it is integrated and regulated.

3.5 From Threat Narrative to Transformative Possibility

Reframing GenAI in African language assessment necessitates moving beyond a simplistic binary of outright prohibition or uncritical adoption (Chan & Hu, 2023; Chan & Colloton, 2024; Matsilele & Tshuma, 2025). This approach aligns with the broader discourse on GenAI's integration in professional and educational contexts, where nuanced frameworks are advocated to balance innovation with ethical and contextual considerations. Instead of prohibition or blanket acceptance, assessment practices should pursue principled integration grounded in authentic assessment and Assessment for Learning (AfL).

When assessment emphasises oral interaction, community-based tasks, iterative reflection, and culturally situated communication, the simplistic outsourcing of learning to AI becomes less viable. Educators can also incorporate AI in critical and pedagogically productive ways: for example, by asking learners to evaluate, edit and contextualise AI-generated texts, thereby promoting metalinguistic awareness and critical digital literacy. Such approaches reorient assessment from a focus on final products to a focus on learning processes, and from detecting AI use to discerning students' understanding and skills.

3.6 Addressing the Silence

The relative absence of African language perspectives in global AI–assessment debates reflects broader structural inequities in research production and technological development. African languages and their sociolinguistic dynamics are often underrepresented in AI discourse, which is often dominated by Western-centric frameworks and universalist principles. This marginalisation reflects a gap between academic knowledge and the lived realities of African linguistic and cultural contexts, as well as the limited inclusion of African epistemologies in global AI ethics and policy discussions (van Norren, 2023). Addressing this silence requires context-specific empirical research on AI performance in African languages; policy frameworks attuned to multilingual realities; investment in local-language corpora and digital infrastructure; and pedagogical innovation that centres on cultural and epistemic integrity.

This discussion makes it evident that Generative AI will continue to reshape educational landscapes. Therefore, the critical task for African language educators is not merely to respond defensively, but to intervene proactively, ensuring that assessment reforms advance linguistic justice rather than reproduce global hierarchies.

What is further evident is that global debates on GenAI and assessment are vibrant yet uneven. African languages occupy the periphery of these conversations. Bringing them to the centre is both a pedagogical necessity and an epistemic imperative.

4. KEY CONCERNS IN AFRICAN LANGUAGE CONTEXTS

While generative AI introduces new possibilities for assessment innovation, its integration into African language education surfaces context-specific concerns that extend beyond general debates about plagiarism or authorship (Nazira et al., 2025). These concerns are structural, linguistic, cultural, and epistemic. Addressing them requires situating technology within the historical and socio-political realities that shape African language education systems.

4.1 Linguistic Marginalisation and Digital Inequality

Most African languages are considered low-resource in computational linguistics. About 88% of them are severely underrepresented or entirely ignored by natural language processing (NLP) technologies, even though they make up nearly one-third of the world's languages (Issaka et al., 2025). This low-resource designation stems from a shortage of high-quality datasets, which impedes the development of effective language models and speech-recognition systems. As a result, the digital corpora needed to train robust models are limited, unevenly distributed, or missing altogether. Consequently, AI outputs may reflect hybridised or anglicised forms, misrepresent or ignore dialectal variation, and inconsistently generate technical vocabulary.

In assessment contexts, such distortions have implications for fairness and validity. Learners may be evaluated against AI-influenced norms that do not accurately reflect authentic community usage. Furthermore, disparities in access to devices, connectivity, and AI literacy may deepen existing educational inequalities, particularly in rural or under-resourced communities.

4.2 Standardisation Versus Linguistic Diversity

African languages often exhibit rich dialectal diversity and fluid boundaries between oral and written registers. Sesotho has several regional and social varieties shaped by geography and contact with neighbouring languages. A standardised form is used in formal education and writing, but everyday speech shows noticeable dialectal differences.

Example: Lexical variation

The word for "child" may vary slightly across dialects:

- *Standard Sesotho*: *ngoana* (child)

- Some speakers in border areas influenced by Setswana may pronounce or adapt it closer to *ngwana*.

Example: Variation in greeting forms
Formal written Sesotho typically uses:

- *Lumela* – "Hello"

In informal spoken contexts, speakers may extend or modify greetings:

- *Lumelang* – respectful or plural greeting
- *U phela joang?* – "How are you?"

In conversational settings, shortened or blended forms may occur:

- *O kae?* – literally "Where are you?", used pragmatically as "How are you?"

These variations show how spoken interaction prioritises social meaning and context over rigid standard forms.

Sesotho also demonstrates a flexible relationship between oral expression and written language, especially in storytelling, praise poetry, and everyday discourse.

Example: Oral storytelling
Repetition and expressive particles are common in oral narratives:

- *Eaba ngoana oa tsamaea, a tsamaea, a tsamaea…* ("Then the child walked, walked, walked…")

Such features maintain rhythm and audience engagement but are typically reduced in formal written texts.

Example: Discourse markers in speech
Spoken Sesotho frequently uses particles that organise conversation:

- *Joale* – "so / then"
- *Hantle* – "well / indeed"
- *Kea tseba* – "I know"

Example in conversation:

- *Joale, re se re tla qala mosebetsi hosane.* ("So, we will start the work tomorrow.")

These markers appear less frequently in formal academic writing but are essential to spoken interaction and the negotiation of meaning.

Sesotho speakers often operate in multilingual environments (including isiZulu, Xitsonga, and English), leading to code-switching and translanguaging. For instance:

- *Re ts'oanetse ho 'submit-a assignment' hosane.* ("We have to submit the assignment tomorrow.")

Here, the English verb "submit" is integrated into Sesotho grammar with the verbal suffix *-a*, demonstrating how oral communication adapts flexibly to modern academic contexts.

Dialectal diversity and oral–written fluidity express important implications for language education and assessment. Rigid adherence to standardised written forms can overlook the communicative practices learners bring from their communities. Recognising dialectal variation and oral discourse patterns supports more inclusive pedagogies.

However, assessment systems, often shaped by colonial schooling models, tend to privilege standardised varieties. The introduction of generative AI risks reinforcing this tendency: large language models frequently default to formal variants, and if their outputs are treated as authoritative, they may marginalise non-standard dialects, undermine oral and performative traditions, and narrow acceptable forms of expression. In contexts where language revitalisation and cultural preservation are urgent, such technological homogenisation poses a significant risk.

Sesotho thus exemplifies the dynamic nature of African languages, where regional dialects, oral traditions, and multilingual interactions shape everyday communication and call for policies that acknowledge and support linguistic diversity rather than privileging a single standard.

4.3 Cultural Nuance and Contextual Meaning

Language is embedded in cultural practices, social hierarchies, and historical memory. Many African languages encode relational norms, respect markers, idiomatic expressions, and proverbs that carry layered meanings.

Sesotho, like many Bantu languages, encodes respect and social relationships through specific linguistic forms. Politeness and hierarchy are reflected in pronoun use, greetings, and forms of address.

Example: Respectful greetings

A common greeting in Sesotho is:

- *"Lumela"* – Hello (singular)

When addressing elders or multiple people, speakers use:

- *"Lumelang"* – Hello (plural/respectful form)

The plural form is used to signal respect and social distance, even when addressing a single elder. This linguistic practice reflects the cultural principle of *hlompho* (respect), which structures many interpersonal interactions in Southern African societies.

Another example:

- *"Ntate"* – Father / respectful address for an older man
- *"Mme" /'me–* Mother / respectful address for an older woman

These forms go beyond literal kinship and are used to acknowledge social status and relational positioning within a community.

Sesotho also contains idiomatic expressions whose meanings cannot be interpreted literally but convey culturally embedded messages.

Example: Idiom

- *"Ho ja bophelo."* Literal translation: "to eat life." Meaning: to enjoy life or live fully.

Another example:

- *"O ja ka matsoho a mabeli."* Literal translation: "He/she eats with two hands."

Meaning: someone who takes excessive advantage of opportunities or benefits.

Such expressions illustrate how meaning in Sesotho is often context-dependent and metaphorical, drawing on shared cultural knowledge.

Proverbs (*maele*) play a central role in Sesotho discourse, particularly in teaching moral lessons and guiding social behaviour.

Example:

- *"Motho ke motho ka batho."* Translation: A person is a person through other people.

This proverb reflects the philosophy of collective identity and social interdependence, often associated with the broader African concept of Ubuntu.

Example:

- *"Nyane e tshwanetse ho mamela e kholo."* Translation: The young must listen to the elders.

The proverb reinforces respect for age and experience as important social values.

Example:

- *"Tsoho la motho ke moriana."* Translation: A person's help is medicine.

The saying emphasises the importance of solidarity and mutual support within communities.

In many communicative situations, these expressions function indirectly. Rather than stating criticism or advice directly, a speaker may use a proverb or idiom to convey meaning diplomatically. For instance, when advising someone to cooperate with others, a speaker might say:

- *"Motho ke motho ka batho."*

The listener understands the underlying message without explicit instruction. Such communicative practices highlight how African languages often rely on shared cultural interpretation.

These linguistic features have important implications for language assessment in educational contexts. Standardised tests that emphasise literal comprehension or rigid grammatical correctness may fail to capture learners' ability to interpret culturally embedded meanings such as proverbs and idioms.

For example, a student who correctly interprets the cultural meaning of *"Motho ke motho ka batho"* demonstrates deep linguistic competence, even if the response is expressed in a different phrasing than expected.

Assessments should measure learners' ability to interpret idioms and metaphors; grasp social/pragmatic meaning; and apply proverbs appropriately. For example, an assessment question might ask students to explain the meaning of a proverb and describe a situation in which it would be used.

Suggested task types include oral interpretation, storytelling, and discussions of proverb usage, which recognise linguistic competence as including cultural knowledge and communicative appropriateness, not only written accuracy.

AI systems trained on limited or decontextualised data can produce grammatically correct but culturally shallow outputs. In tasks requiring storytelling or culturally situated dialogue, such limitations become apparent. Overreliance on AI-generated scaffolds risks diluting culturally grounded expression; educators should avoid substituting computational fluency for cultural authenticity. Sesotho exemplifies how respect markers, idioms, and proverbs encode complex cultural meanings. Incorporating these features into assessment and pedagogy better captures learners' full communicative competence.

4.4 Epistemic Authority and Knowledge Hierarchies

Assessment determines what counts as valid knowledge (Li et al., 2026). Uncritical integration of AI risks reshaping notions of correctness and authority in ways that can marginalise indigenous linguistic practices. AI-generated responses may be perceived as more legitimate than learner-produced vernacular; teachers may unconsciously align marking criteria with AI outputs; and learners may internalise AI-generated language as the benchmark of proficiency. Such dynamics can reproduce epistemic hierarchies and erode the status of local registers and communicative norms unless assessment practices explicitly safeguard linguistic diversity and contextual legitimacy.

In postcolonial contexts, where African languages have historically been positioned as inferior to colonial languages, this dynamic can reproduce epistemic subordination in digital form.

4.5 Academic Integrity and Pedagogical Redesign

Concerns about academic integrity affect all disciplines, but heavy-handed responses such as blanket bans or surveillance risk undermining the relational, trust-based pedagogies common in many African contexts. Rather than centring detection, educators should redesign assessment to make inappropriate AI substitution less likely and to foreground authentic competence.

Practical redesign strategies:

- Prioritise oral and interactive assessments (synchronous interviews, storytelling, presentations) that evaluate pronunciation, pragmatics, and real-time negotiation of meaning.
- Require iterative drafts with reflective commentary (portfolios, process journals) to reveal development and authorship.
- Use community-engaged and performance-based tasks (interviews with elders, proverb collection, multimodal artefacts) that produce context-specific outputs resistant to generic AI.
- Demand process documentation (audio/video recordings, annotated transcripts, timelines) as evidence of method and learning.

These measures align with authentic assessment and Assessment-for-Learning principles: they shift the focus from final products to processes, cultural competence, and situated practice, reducing incentives for the misuse of AI while preserving relational pedagogy. Educators should also set clear criteria, teach responsible use of technology, and sustain dialogue on authorship and purpose.

4.6 Educator Preparedness and Policy Gaps

Many educators in African-language contexts lack institutional guidance on AI (Khoalenyane & Ajani, 2024; Mokoena & Seeletse, 2025). Existing policies are often absent or borrowed from English-medium models without adaptation to local contexts.

Effective integration of AI into African language education depends on targeted professional development that equips educators to navigate both technological possibilities and cultural responsibilities. Critical AI literacy is essential. Educators must understand how current AI systems are trained, the kinds of biases and data gaps that affect outputs, and the limits of model competence, particularly for low-resource languages (Ahmed et al., 2025). This knowledge enables educators to interpret AI-generated content judiciously, to identify when outputs are likely unreliable, and to explain these limitations to learners.

Second, ethical integration strategies are required. Professional development should address questions of authorship, consent, data sovereignty, and the potential for epistemic harm. Educators need frameworks for deciding when and how to use AI tools in ways that respect community norms and preserve indigenous knowledge systems, including guidelines for protecting sensitive cultural material and crediting human contributors appropriately (Nguyen, 2025).

Third, awareness of language-specific technological limitations must be built into training. African languages exhibit features of dialectal variation, oral-oriented registers, proverbs, and performative speech, which many AI models do not handle well (Mabokela et al., 2025). Teachers should be familiar with which tasks (e.g., automated grading of nuanced oral performance) remain problematic, and how to adapt pedagogical aims and assessment designs accordingly. This awareness supports realistic expectations and prevents overreliance on inappropriate automation.

Finally, educators need a grounding in the principles of assessment redesign (Ahangama, 2026). Training should offer practical strategies for creating assessments that prioritise process, oral competence, and community engagement (e.g., portfolios, oral exams, performance-based tasks), and for using rubrics that value cultural and communicative competence as much as formal accuracy. Such a redesign reduces opportunities for inappropriate AI substitution while aligning evaluation with authentic learning outcomes.

Together, these strands of professional development prepare educators to make informed, context-sensitive decisions about AI, balancing innovation with cultural integrity and technological affordance with pedagogical purpose. Without targeted support, educators may oscillate between uncritical adoption and outright rejection, neither of which addresses the nuanced challenges of teaching, assessment, and language preservation in AI-enabled environments.

4.7 Moving Forward: Contextual Vigilance

The integration of generative AI into African language assessment demands careful, context-sensitive navigation. Language assessment traditionally relies on human evaluators, but AI offers potential improvements in objectivity, scalability, and personalisation (Al-Abbas et al., 2023). The central question is not whether AI should be used, but under what conditions it supports rather than undermines linguistic equity, cultural integrity, and epistemic plurality.

Key concerns in African language contexts highlight a broader imperative: technological innovation must be guided by pedagogical purpose, sociolinguistic awareness, and ethical accountability (Ncube, 2024; Aiseng, 2025; Nazira et al., 2025). If assessment is to serve decolonising and developmental goals, AI integration must be critically mediated to ensure that African languages are not merely included in digital systems but meaningfully represented, respected, and sustained.

5. REIMAGINING ASSESSMENT PRACTICES

If generative AI disrupts conventional written assessment, it also creates an opportunity to rethink what meaningful language assessment looks like in African contexts. Rather than defending traditional essay-based formats, educators can redesign assessments to foreground communicative authenticity, cultural relevance, and epistemic participation. This section outlines three interrelated shifts: oral and multimodal tasks, process-based assessment, and reflective-dialogic approaches.

5.1 Oral and Multimodal Tasks

Many African languages are deeply rooted in oral traditions: storytelling, praise poetry, debate, ritual speech, song, and communal dialogue. Yet formal assessment systems have often privileged written forms that mirror colonial schooling models. Rebalancing assessment to include oral and multimodal performances realigns evaluation with lived linguistic practices (Taylor, 2025).

Oral tasks should foreground interactive, context-sensitive language use that is difficult to replicate with generic AI. Suitable formats include structured conversational exchanges, community interviews, storytelling anchored in local contexts, dialogic problem-solving scenarios, and role-play simulations that mirror real-world communication.

Multimodal extensions enrich assessment and evidence of competence: audio recordings, video narratives, performance-based presentations, and digital storytelling projects capture prosody, gesture, multimodal meaning-making, and situated cultural knowledge. Together, these approaches prioritise authentic communicative performance and provide robust, verifiable records of learner competence.

Such formats reduce the likelihood of uncritical AI substitution, as they require embodied performance, contextual awareness, and relational interaction. They also value pragmatic competence, tone, register, and cultural nuance dimensions often flattened in AI-generated text.

Importantly, oral and multimodal assessment affirms African languages as living, relational systems rather than purely textual objects (Makalela & White, 2021). It shifts the focus from grammatical correctness alone to communicative effectiveness and sociocultural appropriateness.

5.2 Process-Based Assessment

Generative AI poses significant challenges to product-oriented assessment because it can rapidly produce polished outputs, complicating the verification of authorship and the authenticity of student work (Ahmed et al., 2024; Chan & Colloton, 2024). This inevitably undermines the validity of traditional assessments that rely on final products, as educators struggle to distinguish between students' original work and AI-generated content. To address these challenges, some approaches emphasise the need to move beyond static scoring of final products. For instance, integrating AI-generated interactive verification through targeted follow-up questions can help assess genuine student understanding and detect superficial reasoning or unverified AI use. This Human-AI collaboration framework combines automated scoring with adaptive questioning to enhance construct validity, thereby addressing the limitations of relying solely on polished AI-generated outputs (Lee et al., 2025).

A shift toward process-based evaluation restores the emphasis on learning trajectories rather than final artefacts. Process-based assessment emphasises learners' development and decision-making over singular products, providing evidence of authorship and evolving competence. Effective components include draft submissions with tracked revisions, annotated reflections that explicate linguistic and pedagogical choices, structured peer feedback cycles, cumulative portfolio development, and systematic documentation of research or conversational preparation stages. These elements support formative assessment, metacognitive awareness, and authentic appraisal of communicative and analytical skills.

By assessing the evolution of thought, educators gain insight into learners' metalinguistic awareness, strategic competence, and conceptual growth. This aligns closely with Assessment for Learning principles, in which feedback serves as a developmental scaffold rather than a terminal judgment.

In African language contexts, process-based approaches also allow learners to experiment with dialectal forms, idiomatic expressions, and culturally embedded references without fear of immediate penalisation. The emphasis shifts from performance anxiety to iterative refinement. Moreover, when AI tools are used, learners can be required to critically evaluate and edit AI outputs and to document how they adapted or rejected suggestions. This transforms AI from a shortcut into an object of analysis and critique.

5.3 Reflective and Dialogic Assessment

Assessment practices often position learners as passive recipients of grades. A dialogic model reframes assessment as a shared inquiry into learning. Reflection becomes central.

Reflective tasks elicit metacognitive and linguistic awareness in learners and can be administered in the target language to reinforce proficiency. Useful formats include learning journals written in the target language, oral self-assessment interviews, and written or recorded commentary on linguistic strengths and challenges. Comparative reflections on dialectal choices versus standard forms encourage critical awareness of register and identity. Finally, structured critical analyses of AI-generated suggestions help students evaluate technological affordances and limitations, fostering responsible and informed tool use.

Dialogic assessment involves structured conversations between the educator and the learner about performance criteria, improvement strategies, and linguistic identity. Such dialogue recognises learners as epistemic agents rather than objects of evaluation.

In multilingual African contexts, dialogic assessment can also create space for discussing language politics, code-switching practices, and the negotiation of standardisation norms. These conversations are pedagogically valuable in themselves, fostering critical language awareness.

5.4 Integrating Innovation with Integrity

Reimagined assessment practices must remain anchored in fairness, transparency, and clearly articulated criteria. Rubrics should reflect communicative competence, cultural appropriateness, creativity, and reflective depth, not merely surface-level accuracy. When oral, process-based, and reflective elements are combined, assessment becomes harder to outsource to AI, foregrounds learner voice and agency, preserves cultural and linguistic authenticity, and strengthens learners' epistemic participation (Hidson, 2024).

This does not eliminate the need for written tasks, but it diversifies the modes through which competence is demonstrated. Such diversification is particularly important in African language education, where oral knowledge systems and communal communication traditions remain central.

5.5 Toward Culturally Grounded Assessment Futures

Reimagining assessment is not simply a defensive response to technological change. It is an opportunity to realign evaluation with decolonising goals and sociolinguistic realities. By prioritising oral engagement, multimodal creativity, developmental processes, and dialogic reflection, educators can design assessment systems that are resilient to AI disruption while remaining faithful to the cultural and epistemic richness of African languages.

In this sense, generative AI becomes less a threat to assessment integrity and more a catalyst for pedagogical renewal, prompting educators to clarify what truly counts as meaningful language learning and how it should be recognised.

6. IMPLICATIONS FOR POLICY, TEACHER EDUCATION, AND RESEARCH

The integration of generative AI into African language assessment cannot be addressed solely at the classroom level. Its implications extend to policy formulation, teacher preparation, and long-term research agendas. If assessment is to remain authentic, equitable, and culturally grounded, systemic responses are required (Ketonen et al., 2025; Ezeh & Kehinde, 2026).

6.1 Policy Implications: From Reaction to Strategic Governance

Policy responses to generative AI have often been reactive, focusing narrowly on academic misconduct or prohibition (Ncube et al., 2026). In African language contexts, such approaches are insufficient. Policies must move beyond surveillance and detection toward principled integration grounded in linguistic equity and epistemic justice.

Key policy considerations must be attuned to local linguistic, educational, and ethical contexts. National and institutional AI guidelines should explicitly address African languages rather than simply transplanting English-medium templates, thereby recognising linguistic diversity, dialectal variation, and culturally specific pedagogical needs. Assessment reform frameworks from ministries and examination bodies should promote diversified modalities, oral, multimodal, and performance-based tasks that preserve authenticity when AI is present. Data equity initiatives are required: sustained investment in local-language corpora, tooling, and digital infrastructure will help guard against the continued digital marginalisation of African languages. Finally, robust ethical standards should set clear expectations for transparency, attribution, data governance, and appropriate uses of AI while avoiding punitive measures that would stifle legitimate, exploratory learning and teacher innovation.

Policy reform must also recognise that assessment systems often reproduce colonial linguistic hierarchies. AI governance should therefore align with broader commitments to multilingualism and language revitalisation.

6.2 Teacher Education: Building Critical AI Literacy

Educators are central mediators between technology and pedagogy. However, many educators in African language contexts have limited exposure to AI tools or lack structured professional development on the implications of AI (Mokoena & Seeletse, 2025).

Teacher education programmes should therefore incorporate comprehensive preparation that equips educators to navigate AI's pedagogical and ethical implications. This includes critical AI literacy so teachers understand how large language models operate, their limitations, and potential biases; assessment redesign skills that enable implementation of authentic, process-based, and dialogic assessment approaches compatible with AI-mediated practices; structured ethical reflection on authorship, linguistic representation, and shifts in epistemic authority; and practical opportunities for controlled, reflective experimentation with AI-supported feedback tools to evaluate affordances and mitigate harms. Such curricular integration should be experiential, interdisciplinary, and tied to institutional supports (policy guidance, infrastructure, and ongoing professional learning) to ensure responsible, contextually grounded adoption.

Importantly, professional development should not frame AI solely as a threat. Instead, it should empower teachers to make informed, contextually grounded decisions that preserve linguistic integrity while leveraging technological affordances.

6.3 Research Imperatives: Addressing African Silences

Current scholarship on generative AI and assessment is heavily skewed toward English-dominant contexts. African language education remains underrepresented in empirical studies, policy analyses, and technological design research.

Future research should prioritise systematic evaluation of AI performance in African languages, combining quantitative metrics with human judgments to assess accuracy, sensitivity to dialectal variation and code-switching, and fidelity to culturally specific pragmatic conventions. Equally important are empirical studies of learner interaction that investigate how students and educators adopt and use AI tools, examining pedagogical affordances such as personalised feedback alongside risks of overreliance, deskilling, and unequal access using mixed methods that integrate learning analytics, controlled studies, and qualitative inquiry.

Research on assessment validity must interrogate how AI-mediated inputs, responses, and scoring affect reliability, construct validity, inter-rater agreement, and differential functioning across language and dialect groups, and must propose technical and policy safeguards to preserve transparency and fairness in high-stakes contexts. Finally, scholarship grounded in decolonial and epistemic-justice perspectives should theorise AI through African-centred frameworks that reveal epistemic asymmetries in datasets and models, foreground community participation and linguistic sovereignty in corpus curation and model governance, and produce actionable recommendations for equitable dataset stewardship and policy.

Across these priorities, interdisciplinary approaches, open and reproducible practices, rigorous ethical safeguards, and investment in local capacity-building are essential. Collaborative partnerships between linguists, educators, technologists, and policymakers will be critical in generating contextually relevant evidence.

6.4 Institutional Leadership and Infrastructure

Universities and teacher training institutions must address the infrastructural implications of integrating AI into African language teaching and assessment. This includes investing in the development of multilingual digital resources and supporting the creation and maintenance of open-access corpora for African languages to ensure representative, high-quality data. Institutions should foster interdisciplinary research clusters that bridge AI, linguistics, education, and ethics to drive contextually informed innovation.

Finally, they need to establish robust ethical review protocols for AI-assisted assessment that address transparency, data governance, fairness, and the protection of learners' rights. Without institutional commitment, classroom-level innovations may remain fragmented and unsustainable.

6.5 Toward Sustainable and Just Language Futures

The intersection of generative AI and African language assessment is not a temporary disruption but part of a longer transformation of educational ecosystems. Policymakers, educators, and researchers must therefore adopt long-term, justice-oriented perspectives.

If guided by thoughtful governance, rigorous teacher preparation, and sustained investment in research, AI integration can materially strengthen multilingual education by providing scalable, context-sensitive instructional supports and expanding access to high-quality linguistic resources. It can enhance formative feedback processes through timely, personalised guidance that complements teacher judgment while enabling more frequent practice and targeted remediation. Broader availability of digital tools and open corpora can democratize access to under-resourced languages, supporting both learners and community efforts to document and revitalise linguistic heritage. Crucially, when developed in partnership with local stakeholders, these technologies can foster culturally grounded innovation that respects linguistic identity, promotes epistemic justice, and aligns pedagogical practices with community values.

Conversely, uncritical adoption risks deepening digital inequalities and reinforcing linguistic hierarchies. The task ahead is therefore not merely technological adaptation, but ethical and epistemic stewardship, ensuring that African language education remains vibrant, equitable, and resilient within rapidly evolving digital landscapes.

7. CONCLUSION: TOWARD ETHICAL, AUTHENTIC, AND FUTURE-FACING ASSESSMENT

The emergence of generative AI has disrupted long-standing assumptions about language assessment, authorship, and academic integrity. In African language education, however, this disruption intersects with deeper historical and structural questions, colonial legacies, linguistic marginalisation, epistemic inequality, and persistent misalignment between assessment frameworks and sociolinguistic realities. The challenge, therefore, is not simply technological adaptation, but pedagogical and ethical reorientation.

This chapter has argued that assessment in African language contexts must be reimagined rather than defended. Traditional product-oriented, text-heavy models are increasingly vulnerable to AI substitution and have long failed to capture the richness of lived language practices. By contrast, authentic assessment and Assessment for Learning (AfL) provide robust conceptual foundations for renewal. When assessment prioritises oral engagement, multimodal performance, iterative development, and reflective dialogue, it becomes more resistant to superficial automation and more responsive to cultural and linguistic diversity.

At the same time, generative AI cannot be dismissed outright. Tools such as ChatGPT and other large language models are already embedded in learners' digital environments. The question is not whether students will encounter these technologies, but how educational systems will shape their use. Ethical integration requires transparency, critical AI literacy, and clear pedagogical intent. It also demands vigilance against digital linguistic homogenisation, bias, and the reproduction of epistemic hierarchies.

Future-facing assessment in African languages should be guided by three interlocking commitments. First, ethical accountability requires mechanisms that ensure fairness, protect cultural integrity, and mandate responsible AI use, transparent governance, robust data stewardship, and safeguards against bias, which should be integral to design and deployment. Second, authenticity demands that assessment tasks be rooted in real-world communicative practices and community contexts, privileging multimodal, oral, and performance-based formats that capture meaningful language use beyond decontextualised item responses. Third, epistemic justice entails recognising African languages as legitimate vehicles of knowledge production: assessment frameworks must validate local epistemologies, support linguistic sovereignty in corpus and test design, and resist tokenistic or instrumental treatments that relegate these languages to peripheral roles. Together, these commitments call for participatory development processes, interdisciplinary research, and policy alignment to ensure assessments are equitable, contextually resonant, and supportive of linguistic and educational flourishing.

Reimagined assessment practices should affirm linguistic plurality, validate dialectal diversity, and encourage learners to engage critically with technological tools. Rather than positioning AI as an external threat, educators can harness it as an object of inquiry, reflection, and metalinguistic awareness. When learners are invited to critique, adapt, and contextualise AI-generated outputs, they develop deeper agency and discernment.

Ultimately, the future of African language assessment will depend on deliberate, context-sensitive innovation. Ethical and authentic assessment is not anti-technology; it is purpose-driven. It seeks to ensure that emerging tools serve educational values rather than uncritically redefine them. In this sense, generative AI becomes less a disruptor to be feared and more a catalyst prompting overdue transformation, encouraging educators to clarify what counts as meaningful learning, whose language practices are legitimised, and how assessment can support equitable participation in an evolving digital world.

REFERENCES

Ahangama, N. (2026). Designing assessments in the generative AI era: A tailored assessment framework for ICT tertiary education. *International Journal of Educational Technology in Higher Education*, *23*(1), 9. DOI: 10.1186/s41239-026-00582-0

Ahmed, I., Liu, W., Roscoe, R. D., Reilley, E., & McNamara, D. S. (2025). Multifaceted assessment of responsible use and bias in language models for education. *Computers*, *14*(3), 100. DOI: 10.3390/computers14030100

Ahmed, Z., Shanto, S. S., Rime, M. H. K., Morol, M. K., Fahad, N., Hossen, M. J., & Abdullah-Al-Jubair, M. (2024). The generative AI landscape in education: Mapping the terrain of opportunities, challenges, and student perception. *IEEE Access : Practical Innovations, Open Solutions*, *12*, 147023–147050. DOI: 10.1109/ACCESS.2024.3461874

Aiseng, K. (2025). Political economy of languages in South African higher education. *South African Journal of African Languages*, *45*(3), 418–425. DOI: 10.1080/02572117.2025.2468705

Ajani, O. A., Gamede, B., & Matiyenga, T. C. (2024). Leveraging artificial intelligence to enhance teaching and learning in higher education: Promoting quality education and critical engagement. *Journal of Pedagogical Sociology and Psychology*, *7*(1), 54–69. DOI: 10.33902/JPSP.202528400

Ajani, O. A., & Matiyenga, T. C. (2025). Enhancing critical analysis and argumentation skills in university students through multimodal approaches: A comprehensive study. *International Journal of Educational Reform*, •••, 10567879251326556. DOI: 10.1177/10567879251326556

Al-Abbas, H. U. A. I., Halim, H. H., & Nurjati, N. N. (2023). Harnessing the use of artificial intelligence in language assessment: A systematic comprehensive review. *Tell-Us Journal*, *9*(3), 723–745. DOI: 10.22202/tus.2023.v9i3.7366

Amrane-Cooper, L., Hatzipanagos, S., Marr, L., & Tait, A. (2024). Online assessment and artificial intelligence: Beyond the false dilemma of heaven or hell. *Open Praxis*, *16*(4), 687–695. DOI: 10.55982/openpraxis.16.4.752

Askari, M. (2025). Reclaiming authorship in the age of generative AI: From panic to possibility. *AI Magazine*, *46*(3), e70022. DOI: 10.1002/aaai.70022

Black, P., & Wiliam, D. (2009). Developing the theory of formative assessment. *Educational Assessment, Evaluation and Accountability*, *21*(1), 5–31. https://link.springer.com/article/10.1007/s11092-008-9068-5. DOI: 10.1007/s11092-008-9068-5

Bower, M., Torrington, J., Lai, J. W., Petocz, P., & Alfano, M. (2024). How should we change teaching and assessment in response to increasingly powerful generative Artificial Intelligence? Outcomes of the ChatGPT teacher survey. *Education and Information Technologies*, *29*(12), 15403–15439. DOI: 10.1007/s10639-023-12405-0

Broadfoot, P. (2021). *The sociology of assessment: Comparative and policy perspectives: The selected works of Patricia Broadfoot*. Routledge. DOI: 10.4324/9780429262609

Brown, J. L. (2004). *Making the most of understanding by design*. ASCD.

Chan, C. K. Y., & Colloton, T. (2024). *Generative AI in higher education: The ChatGPT effect*. Routledge. DOI: 10.4324/9781003459026

Chan, C. K. Y., & Hu, W. (2023). Students' voices on generative AI: Perceptions, benefits, and challenges in higher education. *International Journal of Educational Technology in Higher Education*, *20*(1), 43. DOI: 10.1186/s41239-023-00411-8

Chkarka, F., & Fatmi, H. (2026). Comparative Examination of Master's Students' and Faculty Members' Maintenance of Academic Integrity in the Age of AI. *Journal of Academic Ethics*, *24*(1), 1–23. DOI: 10.1007/s10805-025-09684-2

Darmawan, D., & Sabata, Y. N. (2025). Formative Assessment in Efl Classroom (A Bibliometric Analysis of Adopting Artificial Intelligence in Classroom-Based Assessment Practices). *BABASAL English Education Journal*, *6*(2), 147–159.

Downey, G., & Gillett, A. J. (2023). Linguistic relativity in cross-cultural context: Converging evidence from neuroanthropology. *Topics in Cognitive Science*, *15*(4), 693–697. DOI: 10.1111/tops.12660 PMID: 37165535

Ezeh, C. C., & Kehinde, O. J. (2026). Promising practices for culturally relevant assessment: A systematic review. *Diaspora, Indigenous, and Minority Education*, *20*(1), 53–69. DOI: 10.1080/15595692.2024.2341930

Ezennia, J. C., Matiyenga, T. C., & Mokoena, S. (2024). Students: A Vital Agent and Voice Towards Curriculum Transformation. *Educational Administration: Theory and Practice*, *30*(11), 469–476.

Felipe, A. L., Khwakhali, U. S., & Nguyen, T. N. (2025, July). A Framework for Assessment Design in the Era of Generative AI: Case Study of Take-Home Assignment in Software-related Courses. In *2025 10th International STEM Education Conference (iSTEM-Ed)* (pp. 1-6). IEEE.

Grønset, T. L., Eide, L., & Kvam, E. K. (2025). The role of assessment in teachers' curriculum making: Insights from Norwegian history teachers. *Curriculum Journal*.

Hidson, E. (2024). Participants' perceptions of video-enhanced dialogic assessment as reflective practice in international teacher education. *European Journal of Teacher Education*, *47*(2), 204–225. DOI: 10.1080/02619768.2024.2338847

Holmner, M., Hirsh, S., Meyer, A., Mierzecka, A., & Rorissa, A. (2025). The future of academic writing in the age of generative AI. *Proceedings of the Association for Information Science and Technology*, *62*(1), 1241–1243. DOI: 10.1002/pra2.1374

Hu, J., & Lee, P. G. (2023). Designing authentic assessment tasks for EFL courses. In *SHS Web of Conferences* (Vol. 168, p. 01025). EDP Sciences. DOI: 10.1051/shsconf/202316801025

Issaka, S., Wang, K., Ajibola, Y., Samuel-Ipaye, O., Zhang, Z., Jimenez, N. A., . . . Gabriel, S. (2025). The African Languages Lab: A Collaborative Approach to Advancing Low-Resource African NLP. *arXiv preprint arXiv:2510.05644*.

Jurāne-Brēmane, A. (2023). Digital assessment in technology-enriched education: Thematic review. *Education Sciences*, *13*(5), 522. DOI: 10.3390/educsci13050522

Kandlbinder, P. (2025). Signature concepts of authentic assessment. *Higher Education Research & Development*, *44*(4), 946–960. DOI: 10.1080/07294360.2024.2442613

Karamoko, I., & Naounou, A. (2026). Interactions Between English and Bambara in the Learning Process: Towards a Didactics of Complexity. *Language Policy in Africa, 2*(1).

Ketere, C. (2025). Decolonizing Artificial Intelligence: Reducing Algorithmic Biases in African Educational and Linguistic Contexts. *Journal of Contemporary Issues in Open Distance and E-Learning*, *2*(1), 18–37. DOI: 10.71060/7qk9nd52

Ketonen, L., Körkkö, M., & Pöysä, S. (2025). Authentic assessment as a support for student teachers' reflection. *European Journal of Teacher Education*, *48*(3), 467–488. DOI: 10.1080/02619768.2023.2229004

Khoalenyane, N. B., & Ajani, O. A. (2024). A systematic review of artificial intelligence in higher education, South Africa. *Social Sciences and Education Research Review*, *11*(1), 17–26.

Ku, A. Y., & Hool, A. (2024). Capabilities and limitations of AI Large Language Models (LLMs) for materials criticality research: AY Ku and A. Hool. *Mineral Economics*, •••, 1–9.

Kurtz, G., Amzalag, M., Shaked, N., Zaguri, Y., Kohen-Vacs, D., Gal, E., Zailer, G., & Barak-Medina, E. (2024). Strategies for integrating generative AI into higher education: Navigating challenges and leveraging opportunities. *Education Sciences*, *14*(5), 503. DOI: 10.3390/educsci14050503

Lanteigne, B., Brown, J. D., & Coombe, C. (2021). *Challenges in language testing around the world.* Springer Singapore. DOI: 10.1007/978-981-33-4232-3

Lee, S., Choe, H., Zou, D., & Jeon, J. (2026). Generative AI (GenAI) in the language classroom: A systematic review. *Interactive Learning Environments*, *34*(1), 335–359. DOI: 10.1080/10494820.2025.2498537

Lee, T., Lee, S., & Kim, S. (2025). Beyond Static Scoring: Enhancing Assessment Validity via AI-Generated Interactive Verification. *arXiv preprint arXiv:2512.12592.*

Lestari, L. (2021). The Effect of Implementing Authentic Assessment on Student Learning Activities and Outcomes. *Tekno-Pedagogi: Jurnal Teknologi Pendidikan*, *11*(1), 14–19. DOI: 10.22437/teknopedagogi.v11i1.32705

Li, C., Zhao, C., Wang, Y., & Hua, Y. (2026). How should AI knowledge be governed? Epistemic authority, structural transparency, and the case for open cognitive graphs. *arXiv preprint arXiv:2602.16949.*

Liao, L., Ye, S. X., & Yang, J. (2023). A mini review of communicative language testing. *Frontiers in Psychology*, *14*, 1058411. DOI: 10.3389/fpsyg.2023.1058411 PMID: 37089727

Mabokela, R. K., Primus, M., & Celik, T. (2025). Advancing sentiment analysis for low-resourced African languages using pre-trained language models. *PLoS One*, *20*(6), e0325102. DOI: 10.1371/journal.pone.0325102 PMID: 40471940

Mai, T. A., & de Rooij, A. (2023). Linguistic Relativity in Creative Thought: How Divergent Thinking in Response to Motion Events is Influenced by Satellite- and Verb-Framed Languages. *The Journal of Creative Behavior*, *57*(4), 742–760. DOI: 10.1002/jocb.615

Makalela, L., & White, G. (Eds.). (2021). *Rethinking language use in digital Africa: Technology and communication in sub-Saharan Africa* (Vol. 92). Multilingual Matters. DOI: 10.21832/MAKALE2309

Marron, L. (Ed.). (2024). *Cases on Authentic Assessment in Higher Education*. IGI Global. DOI: 10.4018/979-8-3693-1001-4

Matiyenga, T. C., & Khoalenyane, N. B. (2025a). The potential of digital tools in supporting the teaching and learning of African languages. In *Empowering pre-service teachers to enhance inclusive education through technology* (pp. 183–214). IGI Global Scientific Publishing. DOI: 10.4018/979-8-3693-8759-7.ch007

Matiyenga, T. C., & Khoalenyane, N. B. (2025b). The Transformative Influence of Indigenous Languages on African Englishes. In *African Englishes* (pp. 238–249). Routledge. DOI: 10.4324/9781003582403-17

Matiyenga, T. C., & Khoalenyane, N. B. (2026). Innovative Narratives: The Role of Digital Storytelling in African Language Teaching. In *Transforming Teacher Education Through Narrative Dynamism* (pp. 69-108). IGI Global Scientific Publishing.

Matsilele, T., & Tshuma, L. A. (2025). Generative AI in Africa: Transforming News, Practices, and Ethics. In *Generative AI in African News Media* (pp. 1-15). Routledge.

Mavengere, N., Pondiwa, S., Matiyenga, T. C., Manzira, F., & Mutanga, A. (2021). The 'New Normal' in Higher Education: Innovative teaching and learning technologies and practices during a crisis. *Advances in Computing and Engineering*, *1*(2), 37–46. DOI: 10.21622/ace.2021.01.2.037

McTighe, J., Doubet, K. J., & Carbaugh, E. M. (2020). *Designing authentic performance tasks and projects: Tools for meaningful learning and assessment*. ASCD.

Meighan, P. J. (2023). Colonialingualism: Colonial legacies, imperial mindsets, and inequitable practices in English language education. *Diaspora, Indigenous, and Minority Education*, *17*(2), 146–155. DOI: 10.1080/15595692.2022.2082406

Melvill, O. (2024). Reading for Content: How the CAPS Assessment Model for Home Language Literature Discourages Critical Thinking. *Scrutiny2*, *28*(3), 4-17.

Midigo, J. (2025). AI-Powered Innovations for Documenting and Revitalizing African Languages. *Cultural Arts Research and Development*, *5*(2), 26–41. DOI: 10.55121/card.v5i2.517

Mokoena, O. P., & Seeletse, S. M. (2025). AI in rural classrooms: Challenges and perspectives from South African educators. *International Journal of Current Educational Studies*, *4*(2), 30–52. DOI: 10.46328/ijces.199

Muzindutsi, P. F., Muguto, H. T., & Kunjal, D. (2025). Digital transformation and innovation in higher education: Rethinking online assessment integrity. *African Perspectives of Research in Teaching and Learning*, *9*(6), 820–835.

Nazira, H., Najma, A., Tania, R. V. D. M., Ute, S., George, E., Mei, L., & Sibongile, Z. (2025). Decolonising AI: A Pan-African collaboration. *African Perspectives of Research in Teaching and Learning*, *9*(5), 504–518.

Ncube, G. (2024). What is the place of African languages in knowledge production? [South African Journal of African Languages]. *International Journal of the Sociology of Language*, *2024*(289-290), 157–162. DOI: 10.1515/ijsl-2024-0033

Ncube, P. D., Dzvapatsva, G. P., Matobobo, C., & Ranga, M. M. (2026). Redefining student assessment in AI-infused learning environments: A systematic review of challenges and strategies for academic integrity. *AI and Ethics*, *6*(1), 68. DOI: 10.1007/s43681-025-00871-w

Nguyen, K. V. (2025). The use of generative AI tools in higher education: Ethical and pedagogical principles. *Journal of Academic Ethics*, *23*(3), 1435–1455. DOI: 10.1007/s10805-025-09607-1

Nieminen, J. H., Dollinger, M., & Zou, T. X. (2025). Student partnership in assessment: What works, for whom, why, and under what circumstances? *Review of Education*, *13*(1), e70059. DOI: 10.1002/rev3.70059

Otiono, N. (2021). A heritage of African oral literary performance studies. In *Oral Literary Performance in Africa* (pp. 1–20). Routledge. DOI: 10.4324/9781003111887-1

Padmanabha, C. H. (2021). Assessment for Learning, Assessment of Learning, Assessment as Learning. A Conceptual Framework. *i-manager's. Journal of Educational Psychology*, *14*(4), 14–21.

Papanastasiou, E. C., Giallousi, M., & Pitri, E. (2025). Re-Introducing Authentic Assessment in Classroom Assessment Courses: Finding Its Place in the 21st Century. *Education Sciences*, *15*(11), 1564. DOI: 10.3390/educsci15111564

Ravi, M., & Besharat, M. (2026). A holistic consideration of authentic assessments: Student perception of assessment design, delivery, flexibility and creativity. *European Journal of Engineering Education*, *51*(1), 25–42. DOI: 10.1080/03043797.2025.2480116

Regassa, M., & Mitiku, T. (2024). Orality in African Literary Works: An Interaction of Oromo Oral Literature with Written Poetry. *Research in African Literatures*, *54*(3), 111–130. DOI: 10.2979/ral.00019

Reilly, C., Chimbutane, F., Clegg, J., Rubagumya, C., & Erling, E. J. (Eds.). (2023). *Multilingual learning: Assessment, ideologies and policies in Sub-Saharan Africa*. Taylor & Francis. DOI: 10.4324/9781003311553

Sharma, D. (2026). From Colonial Schooling to Decolonial Futures: Transforming Education in the Pacific. *International Journal of Social Sciences, Language and Linguistics, 6*(01), 01-10.

Simonsen, H. G., & Southwood, F. (2021). Child language assessment across different multilingual contexts: Insights and challenges from South and North. In *Multilingualism across the Lifespan* (pp. 11–30). Routledge. DOI: 10.4324/9781003125815-3

Swaffield, S. (2011). Getting to the heart of authentic assessment for learning. *Assessment in Education: Principles, Policy & Practice*, *18*(4), 433–449. DOI: 10.1080/0969594X.2011.582838

Taylor, L. (2025). Contributing to Multimodal Construct Definition and Operationalization: Insights from Research into Language Assessment Accommodations. *Language Assessment Quarterly*, *22*(4-5), 609–622. DOI: 10.1080/15434303.2025.2601851

Ukashatu, A., Suleiman, M. M., & Mahmoud, M. A. (2021). Emerging issues in educational measurement: Authentic assessment. *JISAE: Journal of Indonesian Student Assessment and Evaluation*, *7*(2), 73–80. DOI: 10.21009/jisae.v7i2.23056

van Norren, D. E. (2023). The ethics of artificial intelligence, UNESCO and the African Ubuntu perspective. *Journal of Information. Communication and Ethics in Society*, *21*(1), 112–128. DOI: 10.1108/JICES-04-2022-0037

Villarroel, V., Bloxham, S., Bruna, D., Bruna, C., & Herrera-Seda, C. (2018). Authentic assessment: Creating a blueprint for course design. *Assessment & Evaluation in Higher Education*, *43*(5), 840–854. DOI: 10.1080/02602938.2017.1412396

Vogt, K., & Antia, B. E. (Eds.). (2024). *Multilingual Assessment: Finding the Nexus?* Peter Lang. DOI: 10.3726/b21992

Wang, L., & Zhan, S. (2024). How can generative AI benefit educators in designing assessments in computer science? *Education Research and Perspectives*, *51*, 82–101. DOI: 10.70953/ERPv51.2412004

Weideman, A. (2022). Context, construct, and validation: A perspective from South Africa. *Language Assessment Quarterly*, *19*(2), 124–141. DOI: 10.1080/15434303.2020.1860991

Wiggins, G. (1990). The case for authentic assessment. *Practical Assessment, Research & Evaluation*. https://scholarworks.umass.edu/pare/vol2/iss1/2/

Xeketwana, S., & Robinson, M. (2026). The teaching and learning of isiXhosa for communicative purposes in teacher education for the Foundation Phase. *Southern African Linguistics and Applied Language Studies*, *44*(1), 240–255. DOI: 10.2989/16073614.2024.2357325

Yin, F. (2025). Encoding/decoding in artificial intelligence: Global AI and local languages. [Top of Form Bottom of Form Top of Form Bottom of Form]. *Media Culture & Society*, *47*(8), 1691–1701. DOI: 10.1177/01634437251360381

Chapter 17
Human-AI Collaboration in Pedagogy and Ethical Assessment in GenAI-Integrated Education:
Learning Analytics With Privacy by Design

Sabyasachi Pramanik
http://orcid.org/0000-0002-9431-8751
Haldia Institute of Technology, India

ABSTRACT

This chapter proposes that human-AI cooperation in learning analytics and evaluation is not a neutral technological advancement, but rather a normative design problem. In order to provide validity, reliability, equity, privacy, and academic integrity as hard design constraints, it integrates concepts from psychometrics, algorithmic fairness, data protection legislation, socio-technical systems theory, and critical pedagogy. In order to mitigate the risks posed by generative AI to authorship, inclusivity, and trust, the chapter presents a risk and harm taxonomy, a privacy by design control matrix, and discipline-aware evaluation redesign patterns. Procurement, model stewardship, and quality assurance are reframed as cyclical, data-informed procedures that divide supervision among institutional actors via a staged governance and evidence planner. The chapter presents a justice-focused framework where AI serves as a contestable and augmentative partner that expands educational intelligence while still being answerable to students, teachers, and democratic communities.

1. OVERVIEW

1.1 Problem Area and Goals

A complicated issue area where assessment, grading, and learning analytics are increasingly coordinated via opaque computer infrastructures has been created by the rapid spread of generative and predictive artificial intelligence in education. Learning management systems, assessment writing platforms,

DOI: 10.4018/979-8-3373-8939-4.ch017

plagiarism detection services, and early warning dashboards increasingly include generative models, which have an impact on important choices regarding admission, advancement, and remediation. Validity, fairness, privacy (An, Y. et al 2025), and academic integrity are left vulnerable to unchecked automation at many institutions because the pace of deployment has outpaced the development of ethical, legal, and pedagogical safeguards. Instead of serving as ancillary compliance requirements, this chapter makes the case that these values must serve as strict design restrictions for human AI cooperation in assessment. Automated scoring and generative analytics are seen as socio-technical interventions that need to be supported by learner-centered safeguards, institutional responsibility, and empirical reasoning rather than by claims of technological inevitability or efficiency.

1.2 Audiences, Contexts, and Scope

The chapter covers higher education, open and online learning, vocational and professional education, and mandatory schooling under various national systems and regulatory frameworks. The study focuses on learning analytics pipelines and assessment procedures that leverage massive language models and machine learning to produce tasks, score work, determine risk, and coordinate feedback at scale. To ensure that the conceptual framework is applicable to both dominant and minority global contexts, these phenomena are studied in classroom settings, completely online programs blended learning environments, and cross-border collaborations. Classroom teachers, assessment creators, leaders of academic programs, registrars, quality assurance specialists, institutional data stewards, learning technologists, chief information officers, platform vendors, regulators (Tran, M. et. al 2025), accrediting agencies, and student representatives are among the readers who are targeted. In order to enable diverse professional groups to place their obligations within a common conceptual grammar, the text purposefully incorporates vocabulary from educational assessment, computer science, information law, organizational science, and critical social theory.

1.3 Important Terms, Conceptual Limits, and Presumptions

The definitions used in this chapter are quite specific and serve as the foundation for the arguments that follow. While learning analytics refers to the gathering, combining, and algorithmic analysis of learner-related data to support diagnosis, prediction, and intervention, assessment refers to structured procedures for producing evidence about learner knowledge, skills, dispositions, and performance. While predictive models infer probabilities of outcomes like dropout, course failure, or declining engagement, generative artificial intelligence (Kong, X. et. al 2025) describes models that synthesize novel outputs like text, code, or images that are statistically consistent with training corpora. While reliability pertains to stability and consistency across occasions, raters, and models, validity is defined as the coherence of interpretative arguments connecting observed performances, model outputs, and inferred constructs. Academic integrity is defined as a collection of standards pertaining to authorship, attribution, originality, and proper cooperation. Fairness includes both group parity and individual non-discrimination. Through the lenses of contextual integrity, legal processing, and data subject control, privacy is distinguished from confidentiality.

1.4 The Chapter's Approach and Contribution

Rather of being a technical implementation guide or an empirical meta-analysis, this chapter provides a narrative overview and conceptual synthesis. In order to create an integrated architecture for human-AI (Qu, Y. et. al. 2025) collaboration in assessment, it combines and reconfigures concepts from educational measurement, learning analytics, responsible artificial intelligence frameworks, privacy by design doctrine, institutional governance models, and critical pedagogical (Miao, W. et al. 2025) thought. The chapter converts multidisciplinary ideas into operational design principles, decision heuristics, and governance templates that may be implemented in specific institutional settings rather than reporting primary datasets or experimental outcomes. A set of privacy-preserving (Peters, M. et. al 2025) analytics patterns, a catalog of assessment redesign techniques responsive to generative tools, a governance and literacy scaffold that links policy, procurement, implementation, and classroom practice, and a granular risk and harm taxonomy customized for AI-powered assessment are the main contributions. Therefore, the chapter offers a conceptual framework that may direct local experimentation as well as strategic planning for organizations looking to connect automation with epistemic responsibility and educational equity.

1.5 Reading List and Chapter Structure

From abstract theoretical lenses to practical practice and assessment, the subsequent parts are arranged in a methodical manner. A synthetic table that links these lenses to specific educational judgments is produced at the end of Section 2, which establishes fundamental ideas for educational assessment, algorithmic fairness, normative ethics, and sociotechnical design. A thorough taxonomy of data, model, process, and inclusion hazards in AI-mediated evaluation is created in Section 3, and each category is linked to a family of control mechanisms. Data ethics and privacy in learning analytics pipelines are examined in Section 4, which elaborates on privacy via design architectures and contestability mechanisms. With a focus on discipline-specific trends and workload consequences, Section 5 examines academic integrity and the redesign of assessment ecologies in the age of generative systems. The governance, procurement, implementation, and AI literacy (Zhang, F. 2025) frameworks presented in Section 6 allocate decision-making authority, supervisory duties, and evidential requirements among institutional players. Section 7 offers a comprehensive conclusion that breaks down important pledges and presents future research, policy, and practice priorities while encouraging adaptation to various sectoral and geopolitical circumstances.

2. FUNDAMENTAL IDEAS AND ETHICAL PERSPECTIVES ON AI IN EDUCATION

2.1 Assessment of Education Building Blocks for AI-Mediated Evaluation

Since model outputs are only relevant when they can be connected to clearly defined notions, educational measurement offers the inferential framework that is necessary to justify any AI-mediated evaluation. Automated scorers must be closely examined for systematic variation unrelated to target abilities, such as verbosity, lexical ornamentation, or device type, as classical test theory explains how observed scores break down into signal and error. The link between item difficulty, learner competency, and answer patterns is explicitly made clear by item response theory and associated latent trait models.

This is crucial when generative systems are used to create custom tasks or modify item sequences. Evidence-centered design becomes an essential design language for feature selection in model training, prompt engineering, and rubric development because it offers a systematic grammar for aligning claims, evidence, and task characteristics. Theory of generalizability and multifaceted Rasch modeling allows for the rational calibration of human-machine scoring constellations and extends these concepts to a variety of sources of variation, such as institutional settings, AI models, and human raters.

2.2 Algorithmic Fairness Perspectives in Academic Settings

A collection of quantitative and qualitative perspectives that examine how AI (Dervić, M. et. al 2025) systems allocate mistake, opportunity, and load across diverse learner groups are provided by algorithmic fairness. While individual fairness emphasizes that similarly situated students should receive comparable decisions given comparable evidence, group fairness criteria like demographic parity, equalized odds, predictive parity, and calibration describe various ways in which conditional probabilities and error rates can be aligned across protected or structurally marginalized groups. This logic is extended by counterfactual fairness, which asks if a choice would stay the same if all causally admissible evidence stayed the same but a protected characteristic changed. Models trained on imbalanced corpora may amplify systematic construct-irrelevant variation across subgroups, as shown by differential item functioning and differential prediction studies imported from. In Table 1, which places fairness constructs alongside validity, justice, and care-oriented frameworks for educational decision making, these fairness lenses are synthesized with other viewpoints and connect with measurement theory and normative ethics.

2.3 Normative Ethical Frameworks for Decision Architectures in the Classroom

The axiological language used to determine whether the use of AI in analytics and evaluation is appropriate or inadequate is provided by normative ethical theories, which also interact intricately with the measurement and fairness lenses previously covered and compiled in Table 1. Consent procedures, transparency standards, appeal procedures, and non-instrumental treatment of students become non-negotiable (Li, W. et. al 2025) limits even in the face of extreme efficiency demands since deontological viewpoints prioritize obligations and rights. The emphasis on aggregate benefit and harm reduction in consequentiality thinking necessitates a methodical examination of learning gains, psychological safety, stigma, workload, and distributive implications across demographic strata. Virtue ethics places a strong emphasis on helping educators and designers develop professional qualities like courage, fairness, honesty, and practical wisdom. These qualities influence human oversight and the willingness to oppose damaging automation. In proctoring (Jaldemark, J. et al 2025), early warning, and mental health triage situations, care ethics emphasizes relational responsibility, attention, and response. The focus is shifted from formal equality to substantive freedoms, such the real chance to learn, participate, and challenge, by justice-oriented theories, such as capability-based accounts. Table 1 creates a multidimensional evaluative matrix for AI-mediated evaluation by integrating this diverse ethical vocabulary with measurement and fairness lenses, demonstrating that they are not mutually incompatible.

Table 1. Integrative Perspectives for Ethical Educational Evaluation and Analytics Choices

Theory or Lens	Fundamental Assessment Question	Common Failure if Ignored	Important Selection Nodes in Teaching	Informatics and Statistical Facts
Validity Based on Arguments	What conclusion about competency is justified?	False assertions based on surface-level performance indicators	Feature engineering, job description, and rubric development	Create exemplary evaluations, rater-model comparisons, and maps.
Fairness of Equal Odds	What is the distribution of mistake rates among groups?	Methodical over- or under-fagging of subgroups	Automatically overriding rules and early alert levels	Confusion matrices via grouping and thresholds sensitive curves
A Capability-Based Approach to Justice	whose actual learning freedoms are increased	Effective but unfair distribution of opportunity	Resource allocation, accommodating procedures, and modality alternatives	Trends of modality adoption and disparities in outcomes under various interventions
Relationships and Care Ethics (Memon, T.D. et. al 2025)	How are stress and vulnerability shared in relationships?	Deterioration of feeling included, faith, and chilling consequences	Procedures for interaction, communication, and assessment	Subjective accounts, grievance trends, and climate assessments
Learning via Universal Design	To what extent is participation by design accessible?	Culturally and neurologically diverse individuals' exclusion	Multidisciplinary choices, job layouts, and adaptive compliance	Audits of availability and achievement disparities by characteristics
Decolonialism and Critical Pedagogy	Which subjectivities and knowledges are accepted as legitimate?	Strengthening of deficiency framings and cognitive superiority	Feedback discussion, canon choosing, and rules of language	Conversation diagrams, involvement gradients, and material analyses

A multiplex of lenses that examine inference quality, distributive impacts, relational dynamics, accessibility, and epistemic fairness all at once are necessary for the ethical examination of AI-mediated assessment, as Table 1 illustrates. A unique but intersecting normative horizon is encoded in each row, and these horizons are mapped into actionable decision nodes and empirically tractable indicators in the columns. Institutions can move past ad hoc technology (Akin, A.I. et. al 2025) adoption and toward principled decision architectures by implementing such a matrix as a design artifact. There, model selection, prompt engineering, dashboard configuration, and intervention design are continuously examined through the lenses of validity, fairness, capability, care, universal design, and critical pedagogical questions. As a result, the table serves as a heuristic tool that controls discussions between engineers, educators, attorneys, ethicists, and student representatives. It also makes abstract ideas applicable to the daily management of AI systems in education.

2.4 Design and Sociotechnical Views on Human-AI Assemblies

In order to avoid both technological determinism and merely individual blame narratives, socio-technical views regard AI (Alfredo, R. et al. 2025) systems, institutional frameworks, and human actions as coevolving assemblages rather than distinct entities. While participatory design involves students, instructors, and support staff as co-designers rather than passive recipients of infrastructure, value-sensitive design translates ethical commitments into design requirements by explicitly expressing stakeholder values at the interface, workflow, and data schema levels. Human factors research sheds light on how educators' interpretations of dashboards, override suggestions, and react to warnings are influenced by cognitive load, alert fatigue, anchoring biases, and perceived legitimacy. This, in turn, modifies the actual effect of any analytic pipeline. Critical data studies reveal how data assemblages and visualization (Qian, Y. et. al 2025) grammars are used to create and naturalize categories like danger, engagement, or preparedness.

In order to ensure that the resultant human AI configurations satisfy accessibility standards, epistemic diversity, and power-sensitive governance structures, the multi-lens synthesis in Table 1 may be integrated into socio-technical design processes.

2.5 Practical Guidelines for Regular Educational Decisions Creating

The conceptual tools of measurement theory, fairness analytics, normative ethics, and sociotechnical design are translated by operational principles into manageable heuristics that educators, designers, and administrators may use to inform their daily choices. Students and staff must be able to comprehend in simple yet accurate terms what data are gathered, how models work, what types of uncertainty persist, and what options are available when outputs appear inaccurate or harmful in order for there to be transparency. Contestability demands that no grade, risk score, or flag produced by AI be regarded as definitive without the opportunity for human review, iterative discussion, and correction—with special emphasis to power and expertise imbalances. According to (Asghar, M.Z. et. al. 2025), reversibility necessitates the ability to review critical choices and reverse detrimental deployments without causing catastrophic disruption. In order to maintain proportionality and minimize data, analytics must be as thorough and detailed as the pedagogical stakes, and needless monitoring must be avoided. Data and models are kept within well-defined instructional goals and aren't used for conflicting disciplinary, commercial, or political agendas thanks to purpose restriction and contextual integrity.

3. TAXONOMY OF RISK AND DAMAGE IN AI-POWERED EVALUATION

3.1 Algorithmic Assessment Ecologies' Data Risks

When the empirical substrate that models learn from does not accurately reflect the complexity and variability of actual learner populations, data hazards in AI-powered assessments occur. While under-representation of students studying offline, part-time, or in marginalized linguistic communities creates systematic blind spots, sampling frames that over-represent specific regions, institutions, or delivery modes introduce structural bias into predictive and scoring functions. When models interpret archival labels as ground truth, legacy inequities—such as monitoring procedures, restrictive entrance filters, or linguistically biased grading conventions—that are often encoded in historical data are re-inscribed. Even when protected qualities are ostensibly removed, proxy variables—like device kind, geo-location, or access patterns by time of day—can function as latent encodings of socioeconomic class or handicap. Inconsistent human grading creates label noise that taints training goals and undermines fairness and dependability. These data risks combine with model and process risks to produce cascading damages that need ongoing monitoring, recalibration, and governance, as Table 2 subsequently summarizes.

3.2 Model Risks in Algorithms for Learning and Assessment

The particular inductive biases, optimization techniques, and architectural decisions that characterize how AI systems extrapolate from data to judgments in educational situations give rise to model dangers. When tasks, curricula, or cohorts change, over-parameterized architectures may memorize peculiar patterns instead of capturing fundamental structures, resulting in brittle performance. Construct validity is compromised by shortcut learning, which happens when models cling to surface-level correlates like response length, linguistic complexity, or template conformance rather than deeper conceptual comprehension. Teachers who accept projected probabilities as epistemically reliable are misled by overconfident misclassifications produced by poorly calibrated models. Large neural networks' limited openness and opacity make it difficult for teachers to challenge decision-making processes, which makes contestation and remediation more difficult. Advanced pupils may alter outputs without true mastery thanks to adversarial flaws such prompt obfuscation, text disturbance, or style transfer. These model-specific hazards demonstrate how technological robustness and educational integrity are inextricably linked, as seen in Table 2 together with data and process vulnerabilities.

3.3 System and Process Hazards in AI Orchestrations for Education

When AI components are incorporated into organizational cultures, policy frameworks, and institutional processes in ways that subtly skew professional judgment and shift accountability, system and process hazards result. When possibilities for critical evaluation are limited due to time constraints and increased workload, automation bias encourages instructors to consider model results as authoritative defaults. Institutional pressure to spread automation into areas that need complex human reasoning is created by misaligned incentive systems that value efficiency measures like turnaround time or personnel cost reduction. When suppliers, IT departments, and academic departments share duties for procurement, configuration, monitoring, and redress and no actor owns the whole lifecycle, this is known as fragmented accountability. When damages occur, retroactive analysis is further hampered by inadequate documentation, missing model cards, opaque vendor changes, and insufficient incident reporting. Table 2 demonstrates how organizational design decisions significantly influence the ethical trajectory of AI-enabled evaluation and formalizes these systemic hazards by connecting them to specific scenarios, diagnostic signals, and mitigating repertoires.

Table 2. Risk Management for Administration of Artificial Intelligence-Based Assessments of Education

Classification of Risk	Example of Situation	Principal Implications for Education	Early Indications of Diagnosis	Key Risk Reductions and Persistent Hazards
Delay in Appearance and Information Bias	Metropolitan universities with the majority of language predominate the training corpus	Systematic undervaluation of the proficiency of marginalized students	Grade skew by group and inconsistent performance among fresh batches	recurring restructuring, sampling stratification, and persistent structural bias
Speedy Training and Model Incorrect specification	Excellent results are correlated with answer length by the auto-grader.	An increase in lengthy but poorly thought-out submissions	Strong association between length and score, prominence of construct-insignificant elements	Obligation regularization, feature auditing, and residual concealed shortcuts
Erosion of Process Automation and Oversight	Algorithmic grading and risk ratings are rubber-stamped by staff.	loss of expert judgment and the proliferation of opaque errors	Extremely low overrule rates and cursory examination processes	Validation intervals, required modifications, and possible complacency
Negative Behaviours and Integrity Modification	Learners avoid scanners by using obscuring prompts.	Improper benefit for technologically skilled users and weak deterrent	Anomaly clusters and abrupt changes in linguistic style distributions	Procedure tracking, oral approval, and the ongoing cat-and-mouse interactions

continued on following page

Table 2. Continued

Classification of Risk	Example of Situation	Principal Implications for Education	Early Indications of Diagnosis	Key Risk Reductions and Persistent Hazards
Lacks in Availability and Language Restriction	Unusual look or tics are flagged as questionable by testing.	Inequality against students with disabilities or neurologically diverse traits	Flags that are out of proportion to certain characteristics or circumstances	Alternate methods of opt-out routes, and the possibility of ongoing prejudice
Loss of Organizational Confidence and Mental Damage	Notifications that have significant stakes that are delivered without human interaction	Increased stress, disinterest, and alienation from institutions	Signs of bad mood, withdrawal surges, and student complaints	Jointly developed message, mediated by humans outreach, and persistent mistrust

Risk in AI-powered (Ren, X. et. al 2025) evaluation is intrinsically multi-layered, as Table 2 shows. These layers include statistical representation, algorithmic inductive bias, organizational workflow design, integrity dynamics, accessibility infrastructures, and psychosocial milieu. While admitting residual vulnerability that cannot be completely removed, each row compactly encapsulates a unique risk constellation and links it to observable signals and potential mitigations. Institutions may transition from general risk registers to analytically grounded taxonomies that guide procurement criteria, pilot design, monitoring dashboards, and escalation paths by incorporating such a matrix into quality assurance procedures. The chart highlights the need of systems thinking in educational AI governance by highlighting the fact that much harm are emergent qualities of interactions between data, models, and organizational practices rather than characteristics of any one component.

3.4 Particular Risks to Validity and Reliability in Educational Automation

Threats to validity and reliability in AI-mediated evaluation go beyond traditional worries about measurement error and include new diseases brought about by automation itself. When models perform differently across handwritten submissions, typed responses, speech-to-text transcriptions, or multimodal artifacts, format effects occur, resulting in construct-irrelevant variance that is associated with modality rather than competence. When models trained primarily on global lingua franca corpora penalize code-mixing, regional variants, or non-standard syntax, they intensify linguistic supremacy by confusing language variety with inadequacy. Systematic divergence (Sposato, M. et. al 2025) between pedagogical objectives and algorithmic scoring is caused by misalignment between human-crafted rubrics and model-accessible characteristics, especially when latent features are not available for examination. When software upgrades, infrastructure modifications, or vendor retraining cycles subtly modify scoring behavior in the middle of the semester, reliability is also jeopardized. By emphasizing representation drift, shortcut learning, and process degradation, the categories in Table 2 subtly reflect these validity and reliability issues, indicating that psychometric vigilance has to be expanded into the algorithmic arena.

3.5 Linguistic justice, accessibility, and inclusion in AI-mediated evaluation

Since automated systems have the potential to exacerbate or lessen preexisting disparities in recognition and participation, inclusion, accessibility, and linguistic justice are essential components of harm analysis in AI-powered evaluation. The use of non-traditional data streams, like screen readers, eye-tracking devices, or orthographic simplification tools, by learners who depend on assistive technologies, alternative input modalities, or prolonged processing times is common and may not have been anticipated by model designers. Accent and dialect sensitivity in speech-to-text pipelines might skew contributions from certain ethnolinguistic populations disproportionately, resulting in incorrect scoring or categorization. Language models based on monolingual norms may perceive pedagogically rich code-switching and translanguaging activities as plagiarism or incoherence. Therefore, universal design principles and accessibility-focused design frameworks are essential supplements to the risk taxonomy in Table 2, which clearly identifies linguistic exclusion and accessibility deficits as separate risk categories requiring targeted mitigation techniques and structurally aware governance.

3.6 Early Warning, Monitoring, and Compensation for Damages Caused by AI

By establishing feedback loops that enable institutions to identify, diagnose, and address AI-induced harms before they solidify into systemic injustice, early warning, monitoring, and redress methods operationalize the risk taxonomy. Particularly for data and model concerns described in Table 2, drift detection frameworks that compare current model outputs with historical baselines across demographic strata might uncover representation changes, calibration errors, or emergent adversarial behavior. According to (Hu, Y. et al 2025), disagreement audits that methodically compare algorithmic and human decisions across stratified samples show where expert judgment and machine predictions deviate in predictable ways, suggesting either human bias, model bias, or complex interactions. Redress systems must include procedures for grade adjustment, record modification, and psychological help when damage is proven, as well as accessible appeal paths for students and procedural safeguards during investigations. In order for risk management to transition from static documentation to dynamic, justice-oriented stewardship of AI in educational assessment, institutional learning necessitates that these episodes feed into model retraining, policy revision, staff development, and vendor renegotiation.

4. LEARNING ANALYTICS PIPELINES: DATA ETHICS AND PRIVACY

4.1 Education's Legal Foundation, Purpose Specification, and Proportionality

Since every downstream conclusion inherits the legitimacy or illegitimacy of upstream collection, data ethics in learning analytics pipelines starts with a careful articulation of legal foundation, purpose definition, and proportionality. These abstractions must be concretized through specific documentation that differentiates between instructional, advisory, research, and disciplinary uses of data. Educational institutions operate under hybrid legal regimes that generally recognize public interest, contractual necessity, or legitimate interests as bases for processing. Each dataset, feature space, and model must be grounded in well-defined instructional objectives rather than nebulously stated goals for innovation or optimization, according to purpose definition. According to (Okada, A. et. al 2025), proportionality therefore functions as an intensity restriction, requiring that the degree of intrusiveness, temporal persistence, and granularity of logs stay proportionate to the educational stakes involved. Analytical ambition tends to grow with time, which puts pressure on function creep—the use of data initially gathered for support or feedback for surveillance, ranking, or exclusionary gatekeeping—and necessitates ongoing assessment.

4.2 Configurations for Role-Based Access, Data Minimization, and Retention

The initial set of levers that may be adjusted using the control typology subsequently synthesized in Table 3 are data minimization, retention, and role-based access, which together define the attack surface and abuse potential of learning analytics ecosystems. In order to replace ambient hoarding of behavioral exhaust with epistemically motivated curation, minimization necessitates an explicit feature selection discipline in which each field in a log or dataset is justified by reference to a particular analytic question. Instead of being aspirational statements, retention schedules should be encoded as actionable regulations inside storage systems and must be in line with academic calendars, accreditation criteria, and research governance. With fine-grained permissions that adhere to least-privilege principles, role-based and attribute-based access control frameworks must distinguish between instructors, advisors, institutional research teams, IT personnel, and outside vendors. Since role creep, shared credentials, and undocumented backdoors may subtly undermine the protective purpose of even well-designed access taxonomies, it is imperative that these settings be auditable.

4.3 Analytics Patterns and Architectural Strategies That Preserve Privacy

By converting abstract concepts into computationally enforced procedures, privacy-preserving analytics patterns aim to balance the normative requirements of data security with the epistemic hunger of learning analytics. By guaranteeing that dashboards and exports never reveal granular profiles for numerically tiny subgroups, aggregation thresholds and small cell suppression approaches lower the danger of re-identification while allowing for macro-level. Although careful parameter tuning is required to prevent analytic deterioration, differential privacy techniques limit the information leakage associated with every particular record by injecting calibrated noise into query replies or model updates. By distributing model training and prediction to local nodes, federated learning and on-device inference architectures enable institutions to benefit from shared model advancements without sharing raw data. When genuine datasets are too sensitive for widespread usage, synthetic data synthesis may help with tool development and pedagogical experimentation. Table 3, which arrays privacy-by-design protections across many layers of the learning analytics pipeline, combines these and other principles.

Table 3. Comprehensive Security by Design Measures for Analytical Training

Realm of Authority	Theory of Design	Modality of Deployment	Artefacts of Operations	Identifying pipelines and contractual provisions
Regulation of collecting data	Extreme Data Reduction	Purpose labelling, conditional authorization, and feature curation	Consent examples, data databases, and collecting structure	Permission absorption patterns and field reduction ratios
Design for Storing and Accessibility	Lower-Privilege Segmentation	Rational division, role-specific access, and encryption at rest	Vault rules, key administration logs, and access control groups	Occasions of escalated privileges and access anomaly warnings
Protections for Scientific Processes	Formalized Protection of Privacy	Federated learning, unique confidentiality, and aggregated thresholds	Model update procedures, noise measurements, and query governors	Utility lost standards and estimations of recovering probability

continued on following page

Table 3. Continued

Realm of Authority	Theory of Design	Modality of Deployment	Artefacts of Operations	Identifying pipelines and contractual provisions
Limits for Communication of Data and Transparency	The Interoperability of Purpose	Secured zones, pseudonymization, and data sharing contracts	Identifying pipelines and contractual provisions	Linkage risk evaluations and audits of contract fulfilment
Permission Experiences and Interface for Users	Negotiating Human Data with Intelligence	Stacked notifications, granular opt-outs, and student portals	Authorization documents, selection centres, and explanation boards	Outcomes of understanding tests and opt-out patterns
Technology for Transparency and Audit	Computational stewardship that is verifiable	Ethical evaluations, computational benefit analyses, and audit logging	Records of administration, audit trails, and evaluation assessments	Remedial closure data and event response times

Table 3 illustrates how privacy-by-design is a distributed property of collection norms, storage architectures, processing safeguards, sharing arrangements, user interfaces, and accountability infrastructures rather than being boiled down to a single technical component like encryption or de-identification. Every control domain combines operational artifacts that can be examined, versioned, and managed with specific implementation modalities and guiding design principles. Verification metrics then serve as a foundation for ongoing assessment, allowing organizations to identify practice-related drift, such as growing field counts, an increase in privilege escalation incidents, or a decline in understanding of consent notifications. By institutionalizing such a matrix, educational institutions internalize privacy as a design parameter in all analytics projects instead of using it as an ex-post compliance checklist. They also establish a vocabulary that allows educators, students, legal counsel, and technologists to co-specify acceptable risk envelopes.

4.4 Empowerment of Data Subjects, Contestability, and Student Rights

Privacy is transformed from an institutional duty into a lived sense of agency and procedural fairness for data subjects via student rights and contestability processes. Students need clear, understandable information in clear, concise language about the data being gathered, the inferential logics being used, and the implications for their academic paths. Students may examine their digital footprints and have a say in how they are handled using interfaces that provide personalized data displays, explanation panels, and preference settings. In order to be considered contestable, students must be able to contest analytical results, such risk scores or behavioral indicators, using open processes that provide prompt human review, evidence-based discussion, and well-reasoned conclusions. By ensuring that the negotiation between institution and learner is mediated through artifacts that respect cognitive diversity, linguistic variation, and power asymmetries, the architectural patterns in Table 3—particularly those related to user interface and consent experience—provide the infrastructural foundation for such empowerment.

4.5 Lineage, Accountability, and Pipeline Integrity in Institutional Ecosystems

The ability of institutions to track the flow of data, models, and choices via intricate analytics ecosystems in order to assign responsibility for benefits and damages is known as pipeline integrity and accountability. In addition to being integrated with model registries that monitor training datasets, hyperparameters, evaluation metrics, and deployment contexts, data lineage tooling should record the provenance of each dataset, including its source systems, transformation processes, and merges. Before large-scale deployment, algorithmic impact evaluations and organized ethical reviews provide deliberative spaces where possible risks are mapped against control repertoires, such those listed in Table 3. In order to enable post-hoc reconstruction of decision episodes, audit logging must record human interventions, overrides, and threshold alterations in addition to technical events like access and query execution. When ethical violations occur, repair tasks are not dispersed into organizational uncertainty thanks to a clear allocation of blame among governing boards, academic leadership, IT departments, and outside contractors.

4.6 Do-No-Harm Thresholds, Intervention Ethics, and Harm Mitigation

According to (Shen, Y. et. al 2025), intervention ethics deals with the point at which analytics results are converted into tangible actions, like outreach emails, counseling referrals, academic sanctions, or modifications to teaching practices. It also identifies the ethical thresholds below which non-intervention is preferable. Since false negatives may leave vulnerable students without help and false positives can cause stigma, anxiety, and self-fulfilling prophesies, early warning systems that identify students as at risk must strike a balance between sensitivity and specificity. Considering cultural norms and intersecting identities, communication methods must be carefully crafted such that messages express support and concern rather than surveillance and suspicion. According to (An, X. 2026), safeguarding procedures should specify who sees sensitive indications, how multidisciplinary teams coordinate actions, and how permission is acquired for escalation to external services. Since the cycle of prediction, action, and feedback might produce new data that are inherently ethically laden, intervention data must be reintegrated into the governance architecture shown in Table 3. Intervention ethics thereby bridges the gap between organizational practice, technological design, and the actual student experience.

5. RETHINKING ACADEMIC INTEGRITY AND ASSESSMENT IN THE GENERATIVE AI ERA

5.1 Integrity Threat Topologies in Learning Environments Overloaded with GenAI

A developing threat topology that combines new types of model-mediated authorship and cooperation with classic misbehavior shapes academic integrity in generative AI-saturated learning contexts. Students rethink contract cheating when they plan entire pipelines that assign prompts, iterative refinements, and style transfer to large language models or code assistants, resulting in outputs that seem unique but are only loosely based on individual comprehension. Conventional plagiarism criteria are disrupted by paraphrastic obfuscation, concept mixing, and citation fabrication, which also make similarity indexes less useful. According to (Bou Zeid, M. et. al 2026), collaborative prompt engineering and shared system prompts produce concealed collectives of practice that may fall somewhere between legal peer learning and covert collusion. Solution harvesting without conceptual foundation is made possible in quantitative domains by auto-solving environments and symbolic manipulators. Because these danger vectors are not uniform across disciplines or modalities, integrity risk profiles are explicitly differentiated by course context and cohort size in the redesign patterns synthesized subsequently in Table 4.

5.2 Limits of Adversarial Co-Evolution and Detection-Only Strategies

Detection-only strategies that use watermarking, stylometry, or classifiers to identify AI-generated work face adversarial and epistemic constraints, making them increasingly less defendable as primary integrity tools. When model architectures, decoding techniques, or training corpora change, classifiers trained on historical model outputs become fragile. This can be easily avoided by using multi-model blending, paraphrasing cascades, or prompt rewriting. Language competence, bilingualism, and neurodivergent communication patterns might confuse stylometric methodologies that look for discontinuities in lexical, syntactic, or rhetorical fingerprints, which present significant fairness problems. According to (Chen, S. et al. et. al 2025), binary authenticity labels distort the procession nature of writing, coding, and creating, where legitimate tool aid and illicit substitute coexist on a continuum. While false negatives weaken deterrent for well-resourced perpetrators, false positives erode trust and disproportionately punish students who already hold vulnerable institutional positions. Therefore, Table 4 moves the focus from ex post detection to ex ante assessment redesign, which rewards evident epistemic involvement and lowers the benefit of covert outsourcing.

5.3 Task Ecologies and Design-For-Integrity Assessment Patterns

In order to reduce dependence on brittle detection pipelines, design-for-integrity patterns reorganize assessment ecologies so that authentic learning trajectories, artefact provenance, and method transparency become key evidentiary objects. Since it is challenging to consistently fabricate the artefactual trace of struggle and revision, process-oriented assignments that call for time-stamped drafting histories, version control logs, analytical memos, or lab notebooks make it easier to distinguish real cognitive labor from artificial surface polish. While still adhering to scalability constraints through sampling and structured rubrics, oral micro-vivas, studio crits, code walkthroughs, and data defense discussions provide opportunities for embodied demonstration of understanding (Lee, GG. et. al 2025). Situated reasoning is encouraged and generic model reuse is made more difficult by contextualized tasks that rely on local datasets, field observations, organizational issues, or community briefs. In order to help educators and curriculum teams choose patterns that are both practical and pedagogically sound, Table 4 compiles these design moves into a comparative matrix that links disciplinary contexts, integrity risk profiles, and redesign archetypes to workload and learning implications.

5.4 Clear Normative Clarity and Transparent Policy Architectures for AI Use

By outlining how, when, and why students may incorporate AI tools into their academic work, transparent policy architectures stabilize expectations for both students and staff, converting design patterns into lived normative clarity. While regulations that blindly support generative assistance may undermine the concept of authorship, those that just forbid any AI usage are seldom enforced and run the danger of pushing tool use into covert areas. According to (Gryshko, S. et al. 2025), coherent frameworks instead define allowed, conditional, and prohibited uses across task types, such as ideation, outlining, language polishing, coding scaffolds, or citation generation, and they connect these categories to disclosure requirements. Rather than being optional extras, explicit comments on attribution, reflection on tool contributions, and documenting of prompts and outputs become essential assessment components. In order for teachers to understand and execute rules consistently across sections and programs, normative clarity also necessitates staff development. These regulations, when combined with the redesign templates in Table 4, build ecosystems where responsible AI usage is scaffolded instead of being seen as a danger that has to be controlled.

5.5 Integrity Redesign's Workload, Sustainability, Equity, and Accessibility

Any integrity-focused redesign must prioritize equity, accessibility, workload, and sustainability; otherwise, well-meaning practices run the danger of making the exact inequalities they are meant to lessen worse. In addition to taking into consideration students with disabilities, caregiving responsibilities, precarious employment, or limited connectivity, process-intensive tasks requiring extensive drafting, oral engagements, or fieldwork must also offer alternative pathways that preserve evidentiary richness without imposing an undue burden. Redesign must make use of sample techniques, peer evaluation, calibrated rubrics, and selective oral verification in order to survive, since teachers in massified institutions often function under extreme temporal and emotional demands. It is necessary to assess if technological needs for logging, version control, or recording are compatible with institutional infrastructure and privacy frameworks, including the constraints previously described in Table 3. Therefore, rather than being imposed as episodic compliance responses to generative AI disruption, sustainable integrity ecosystems arise when design-for-integrity patterns, transparent policies, and supportive technologies are co-optimized for fairness, feasibility, and long-term institutional learning.

6. AI LITERACY, GOVERNANCE, IMPLEMENTATION, AND ASSESSMENT

6.1 Institutional Polycentricity, Accountability Structures, and Decision Rights

The management of human-AI cooperation in evaluation necessitates a clear distribution of decision-making authority and accountability within a naturally stratified and polycentric organization. Technology, pedagogy, and welfare are partially under the purview of academic senates, governing boards, senior leadership teams, ethics committees, quality assurance units, information technology services, teaching and learning centers, and student unions. AI-mediated evaluation procedures fall back on unofficial power structures and vendor influence in the absence of a clear constitutional map outlining who authorizes pilots, approves enterprise tools, establishes assessment policies, and resolves disagreements. In order to maintain academic freedom and student participation, governance tools like charters, mandates, and terms of reference must clearly state how pedagogical authority, data stewardship, and financial accountability interact. Uncoordinated departmental experimentation and technocratic centralization may both be avoided using matrixed responsibility structures. One practical method for bringing these diverse players together around common implementation horizons and evidence duties is the phased perspective of stewardship roles, which is summarized later in Table 5.

6.2 Classification of Risk, Level of Oversight, and Tiers of Approval

Institutions may adjust the level of monitoring and approval processes for various AI applications in analytics and evaluation by using risk categorization as an organizing grammar. Treating auto-grading of low-stakes quizzes, high-stakes exam scoring, early alert models, admissions triage, remote proctoring and generative feedback assistants as a homogeneous category results in either excessive regulation or risky permissiveness because they do not pose a commensurate risk to rights, welfare or institutional reputation. Different criteria for paperwork, pilot length, impact assessment, external review, and executive authorization may be specified by a tiered regime that separates applications with low, medium, and high consequentiality. Tier assignment criteria might include elements like learner stakes, the degree of autonomy, the opacity of the underlying models, and the scope of deployment. In order to make governance a fundamental aspect of project management rather than an afterthought, the implementation planner that is shown in Table 5 later in this section incorporates risk directly into phase-specific tasks.

6.3 Ecologies of Procurement, Contracting, and Vendor Governance

Because they decide which capabilities, limitations, and asymmetries are built into the AI systems that educators and students must utilize, procurement and contracting become places of epistemic and ethical negotiation. Vendors should be required to disclose training data provenance, model families, evaluation protocols, subgroup performance, robustness characteristics, security posture, and options for on-premises or hybrid deployment in requests for proposals and evaluation rubrics. Data ownership, data residency, acceptable secondary uses, incident reporting schedules, audit rights, support expectations, model update cadences, and exit plans that include data and configuration portability must all be spelled out in contractual provisions. Black box offers that prevent meaningful examination or independent benchmarking should be rejected by institutions. Members of procurement committees should not only be knowledgeable about money and IT, but also about measurement, pedagogy, privacy legislation, and systems design. In order to reduce the possibility that contracts lock in detrimental structures, the phased governance schema in Table 5 encourages institutions to see procurement as part of a longer lifecycle of piloting, scaling, optimization, and external assurance.

6.4 Lifecycle Stewardship, Model Governance, and Operational Safeguards

The way AI systems operate in educational environments is shaped over time by operational protections and model governance, which convert abstract concepts into daily practices. In order to diagnose changes in assessment results or alert patterns, staff must be able to track when and how changes to models, thresholds, or interfaces occurred. This is made possible by version control, release management, and configuration documentation. Before complete integration, shadow mode deployments—where AI outputs are produced but not yet significant—offer a controlled environment for evaluating usability, validity, and fairness. Proposed changes may be reviewed by change advisory boards with pedagogical and ethical competence, especially when they impact high-stakes usage. Adversarial audits and red team exercises check systems for resilience and potential for abuse. Over-automation is prevented via obligatory override procedures and minimum supervision ratios. Instead of functioning as a one-time compliance event, these protections are part of a systematic implementation program that is compiled in Table 5 and presents governance as a staged, evidence-based approach.

6.5 Developing Leadership, Staff, and Faculty Capabilities for Ethical AI Stewardship

Since even the most complex governance frameworks fall apart if practitioners lack the literacy necessary to inhabit them, creating capacity for academics, staff, and leadership is a crucial component of responsible AI integration. To maintain academic integrity, analyze dashboards, rethink assessments, evaluate algorithmic outputs, and openly discuss risks, rewards, and uncertainties with students, educators need assistance. Competencies in measurement theory, fairness analytics, privacy by design techniques, and change management are necessary for quality officers and learning technologists. In addition to resisting vendor narratives that portray AI adoption as inevitable, senior executives must be able to balance trade-offs between innovation, cost, risk, and institutional values. These abilities may be institutionalized via mentorship programs, communities of practice, micro-credentials, and structured professional learning programs. Such projects may be arranged according to the staged roadmap in Table 5 so that training corresponds with the real-world difficulties that employees face at every stage, from large-scale optimization to exploratory piloting.

6.6 AI Literacy as a Course Outcome for Employees and Students

For both staff and students, AI literacy must be seen as a curricular goal that encompasses a complex collection of conceptual, procedural, and dispositional skills in addition to a technological skill set. From a conceptual standpoint, students and teachers need to know how models are trained, what data they consume, what patterns they encode, and where they fall short, including bias, delusion, and overconfidence. In terms of procedure, they need to be able to utilize AI tools for data exploration, coding, brainstorming, and drafting in an ethical manner. They also need to be able to record and attribute this usage within evaluation protocols. According to (Priyadarshini, V. et. al 2025), and others, AI literacy comprise the following dispositions: epistemic humility, critical curiosity, respect for intellectual labor, and attention to power dynamics encoded in data infrastructures. By integrating AI literacy goals into all subject areas and skill levels, it is ensured that knowledge of generative tools does not lead to blind dependence. Curricular AI literacy may develop alongside institutional infrastructure when it is in line with Table 5's governance stages, resulting in a mutually reinforcing ecosystem of control and competence.

6.7 Assessment, Ongoing Enhancement, and Meta-Governance in Educational AI

The meta-governance layer that decides whether AI-enabled assessment stays in line with institutional values and learner welfare over time is made up of evaluation and continual improvement. Institutions can triangulate the lived effects of AI systems beyond specific performance benchmarks by utilizing mixed-method evidence strategies that incorporate learning analytics, equity indicators, workload metrics, appeal rates, incident reports, and qualitative feedback from staff and students. External assessments by independent research groups, accrediting bodies, or comparable institutions may supplement periodic internal audits by offering comparative viewpoints and challenging insular thinking. Since frameworks that were suitable for early pilots may become restrictive or inadequate if AI technologies enter fundamental evaluation regimes, governance arrangements themselves need to be reviewed on a regular basis. The results of the evaluation should lead to clear choices on the continuation, modification, or retirement of systems and stakeholders must be informed of these decisions in a clear and concise manner. AI-mediated evaluation becomes a location of continuous reflexive learning rather than a fixed infrastructure destiny when institutions approach the cycle of evidence collection, discussion, and redesign as a standard organizational activity.

7. CONCLUSION

7.1 Integration of Design Commitments and Arguments

Only when human AI cooperation in assessment and learning analytics is seen as a normative design issue rather than as a neutral technological advancement or a cost-saving measure can it be justified from an educational standpoint. The chapter has made the case that academic integrity, validity, dependability, fairness, and privacy must function as binding constraints that shape workflows, structures, and institutional cultures from the beginning rather than as lingering compliance checks after technologies have become ingrained. A multiaxial language for examining what is being inferred, for whom, with what evidential foundation, and with what distributive implications is provided by measurement theory, algorithmic fairness analytics, normative ethics, and sociotechnical design. These abstractions are converted into workable infrastructures via risk taxonomies, privacy by design matrices, design for integrity task ecologies, and phased governance planners.

7.2 Prompt Institutional Guidance for Ethical AI-Human Cooperation

A number of immediate directions that operationalize the frameworks described in the previous sections may be adopted by institutions looking to go beyond reactive postures. First, they may formally establish risk tiring for AI applications in evaluation, impose clear permission and evidence requirements on each tier, and prohibit the implementation of high-stakes systems without impact analysis and shadow testing. Second, procurement procedures may be reoriented to match vendor incentives with institutional goals by encoding criteria for data governance, exit plans, subgroup performance reporting, and transparency in contracts. Third, by using the pattern logics of process visibility, contextualization, and multimodal evidence, curriculum and assessment teams may start revising the most risky courses, therefore decreasing reliance on fragile detection. Fourth, by using the control domains that were previously gathered into tabular form, privacy by design rules may be included into any analytics endeavor. In order to keep governance rooted in living reality rather than in abstract texts, institutions might lastly establish participatory forums where staff and students jointly analyze dashboards, policies, and experiences.

7.3 Prospects for GenAI-Integrated Education Research, Policy, and Practice

A forward-looking agenda for research, policy, and practice that acknowledges the emerging, globally networked character of educational AI is also outlined in the conceptual architecture created in this chapter. The long-term effects of AI-mediated assessment on learner identity, motivation, pedagogical relationships, and labor circumstances need more study. Multilingual and resource-constrained environments, which seldom influence benchmark datasets, require special attention. It is possible to determine which combinations of supervision structures, transparency standards, and participatory methods genuinely lessen damage and enhance learning rather than just transferring risk by conducting comparative studies of governance models, regulatory tools, and institutional cultures. To avoid locking educational institutions into opaque, monopolistic ecosystems, policy frameworks must address cross-border data flows, platform concentration, interoperability standards, and public interest requirements. Practice-oriented study might investigate how communities employ open, inspectable technologies to oppose extractive data practices, how educators incorporate AI into disciplinary epistemologies, and how students acquire critical AI literacy. Instead of emphasizing passive acceptance, these views present education as a place for democratic experimentation.

7.4 Concluding Thoughts on Human-AI Futures in Education Focused on Justice

A conscious reinterpretation of what constitutes creativity, success, and responsibility is necessary for a justice-oriented vision of human AI futures in education. Institutions may value innovations that increase the acknowledgment of marginalized knowledge, broaden substantive freedoms of learning, and shift epistemic power toward students and instructors, instead of applauding automation that speeds up grading or increases surveillance capability. The frameworks, matrices, and patterns created throughout the chapter serve as scaffolding for situated discourse where local histories, legal systems, and community goals are actively negotiated rather than being templates that can be used in any situation. In the end, the issue is not if AI will be used in analytics and evaluation, but rather whether it will enhance or undermine human dignity, solidarity, and intellectual advancement. Educational institutions may foster a culture where technical sophistication is inextricably linked to ethical reflexivity and civic responsibility by considering every model, measure, and dashboard as a tentative hypothesis about learners and learning, susceptible to review and correction.

REFERENCES

Akin, A. I. (2025). Developing AI Literacy in the Classroom: AI–Human Collaboration and Ethical AI. In Ibáñez, D. B., Gallardo-Echenique, E., Siringoringo, H., & Diez, N. L. (Eds.), *Communication and Applied Technologies. ICOMTA 2024. Smart Innovation, Systems and Technologies* (Vol. 427). Springer., DOI: 10.1007/978-981-96-0426-5_28

Alfredo, R., Milesi, M., Echeverria, V., Gašević, D., Buckingham Shum, S., Zhao, L., Yan, L., Jin, Y., Fan, J. X., Pammer-Schindler, V., Swiecki, Z., & Martinez-Maldonado, R. (2025). Co-designing AI-powered learning analytics: Bringing students and teachers together. *International Journal of Educational Technology in Higher Education*, *22*(1), 78. DOI: 10.1186/s41239-025-00572-8

An, X., Bai, J., Li, Y., Zhou, Y., Chai, C. S., & Hong, J. C. (2026). Development of an Artificial Intelligence Technology Pedagogical Content Knowledge (AI-TPACK) Scale for Human and AI Concurrently as Teachers: X. An et al. *The Asia-Pacific Education Researcher, 35*(3), 483-493. DOI: 10.1007/s40299-025-01045-2

An, Y., & James, S. (2025). Generative AI integration in K-12 settings: Teachers' perceptions and levels of integration. *TechTrends*, *69*(6), 1304–1317. DOI: 10.1007/s11528-025-01114-9

Asghar, M. Z., Iqbal, J., Özbilen, F. M., Abedin, J., Järvenoja, H., & Widanapathirana, U. (2025). The nexus of artificial intelligence literacy collaborative knowledge practices and inclusive leadership development among higher education students in Bangladesh China Finland and Turkey. *Discover Computing*, *28*(1), 172. DOI: 10.1007/s10791-025-09695-y

Bou Zeid, M., & Abouchedid, K. (2026). AI for educational innovation: Opportunities and challenges amidst protracted crises. *Education and Information Technologies*, *31*(6), 1553–1580. DOI: 10.1007/s10639-025-13867-0

Chen, S.. (2025). Bridging the AI Adoption Gap: Designing an Interactive Pedagogical Agent for Higher Education Instructors. In Cristea, A. I., Walker, E., Lu, Y., Santos, O. C., & Isotani, S. (Eds.), Lecture Notes in Computer Science: Vol. 15881. *Artificial Intelligence in Education. AIED 2025*. Springer., DOI: 10.1007/978-3-031-98462-4_22

Dervić, M., Bećirović, S., & Polz, E. (2025). Revolutionizing Pedagogy: The Transformative Influence of Artificial Intelligence on Educators' Practices. In Adarkwah, M. A., Amponsah, S., Huang, R., & Thomas, M. (Eds.), *Artificial Intelligence and Human Agency in Education: Volume One. Future Education and Learning Spaces*. Springer., DOI: 10.1007/978-981-96-7937-9_9

Gryshko, S., Terziyan, V., & Golovianko, M. (2025). Resilience Training in Higher Education: AI-Assisted Collaborative Learning. In Auer, M. E., & Rüütmann, T. (Eds.), *Futureproofing Engineering Education for Global Responsibility. ICL 2024. Lecture Notes in Networks and Systems* (Vol. 1281). Springer., DOI: 10.1007/978-3-031-83520-9_12

Hu, Y., Xu, Y., & Wu, B. (2025). A dual-pathway model of teacher-AI collaboration based on the job demands-resources theory. *Education and Information Technologies*, *30*(11), 15125–15146. DOI: 10.1007/s10639-025-13421-y

Jaldemark, J., Lundin, J., Säljö, R., Edwards, J., Gegenfurtner, A., Holmes, W., Järvelä, S., de Laat, M., Lindberg, Y., Littlejohn, A., Seufert, S., Specht, M., Svensson, L., Rapanta, C., Hayes, S., & Zeivots, S. (2025). A multidisciplinary research agenda for artificial intelligence, education, learning, and instruction. *Postdigital Science and Education*, *7*(4), 1414–1450. DOI: 10.1007/s42438-025-00602-8

Kong, X., Fang, H., Chen, W., Xiao, J., & Zhang, M. (2025). Examining human–AI collaboration in hybrid intelligence learning environments: Insight from the Synergy Degree Model. *Humanities & Social Sciences Communications*, *12*(1), 821. DOI: 10.1057/s41599-025-05097-z

Lee, G. G., Mun, S., Shin, M. K., & Zhai, X. (2025). Collaborative learning with artificial intelligence speakers: Pre-service elementary science teachers' responses to the prototype. *Science & Education*, *34*(2), 847–875. DOI: 10.1007/s11191-024-00526-y

Li, W., Liu, H., Huang, K., & Hussain, A. (2025). Reinforcement learning for human-ai collaboration: Challenges, mechanisms, and methods. *Cognitive Computation*, *17*(5), 146. DOI: 10.1007/s12559-025-10500-7

Memon, T. D., & Kwan, P. (2025). A collaborative model for integrating teacher and GenAI into future education. *TechTrends*, *69*(6), 1192–1206. DOI: 10.1007/s11528-025-01105-w

Miao, W., Zang, H., Liu, Q., Zheng, T., Zhou, Y., Liu, C., Yang, N., Zhang, H., Zhang, Y., Zhang, Y., Li, S., Zhang, S., & Zhang, H. (2025). From chaos to symbiosis: Exploring adaptive co-evolution strategies for generative AI and research integrity systems. *BMC Medical Ethics*, *26*(1), 120. DOI: 10.1186/s12910-025-01288-0 PMID: 41013533

Okada, A., Sherborne, T., Panselinas, G., & Kolionis, G. (2025). Fostering transversal skills through open schooling supported by the CARE-KNOW-DO pedagogical model and the UNESCO AI competencies framework. *International Journal of Artificial Intelligence in Education*, *35*(4), 1953–1998. DOI: 10.1007/s40593-025-00458-w

Peters, M. A., & Kourkoulou, D. (2025). AI, Pedagogy, and the Conditions of Knowledge. *Postdigital Science and Education*, *7*(4), 1478–1493. DOI: 10.1007/s42438-025-00599-0

Priyadarshini, V., Thandapani, G., Meena, S., Sarada, V., Aaryan, A., & Ravindran, D. (2025). The Human–Machine Collaboration: Leveraging AI for Ethical Learning and Effectiveness. In Qasem, I. (Ed.), *Data-Driven Decision Making for Sustainable Business Growth. Studies in Systems, Decision and Control* (Vol. 607). Springer., DOI: 10.1007/978-3-031-96530-2_21

Qian, Y. (2025). Pedagogical applications of generative AI in higher education: A systematic review of the field. *TechTrends*, *69*(5), 1105–1120. DOI: 10.1007/s11528-025-01100-1

Qu, Y., & Wang, J. (2025). The impact of ai guilt on students' use of ChatGPT for academic tasks: Examining Disciplinary Differences: Y. Qu and J. Wang. *Journal of Academic Ethics*, *23*(4), 2087–2110. DOI: 10.1007/s10805-025-09643-x

Ren, X., & Wu, M. L. (2025). Examining teaching competencies and challenges while integrating artificial intelligence in higher education. *TechTrends*, *69*(3), 519–538. DOI: 10.1007/s11528-025-01055-3

Shen, Y., Kang, B., & Münch, F. (2025). Human-Centered AI in Design: Examining Educational Paradigms for Creativity and Responsibility. In Schrepp, M. (Ed.), Lecture Notes in Computer Science: Vol. 15799. *Design, User Experience, and Usability. HCII 2025*. Springer., DOI: 10.1007/978-3-031-93236-6_5

Sposato, M. (2025). Artificial intelligence in educational leadership: A comprehensive taxonomy and future directions. *International Journal of Educational Technology in Higher Education*, *22*(1), 20. DOI: 10.1186/s41239-025-00517-1

Tran, M., Balasooriya, C., Jonnagaddala, J., Leung, G. K. K., Mahboobani, N., Ramani, S., Rhee, J., Schuwirth, L., Najafzadeh-Tabrizi, N. S., Semmler, C., & Wong, Z. S. (2025). Situating governance and regulatory concerns for generative artificial intelligence and large language models in medical education. *NPJ Digital Medicine*, *8*(1), 315. DOI: 10.1038/s41746-025-01721-z PMID: 40425695

Zhang, F., Gou, J., Shen, K. N., Camarinha-Matos, L. M., & Wang, Z. (2025). Effects of AI teammates on learning behavior in human-AI collaboration environments: A perspective on self-regulated learning. *Education and Information Technologies*, *30*(18), 26801–26825. DOI: 10.1007/s10639-025-13717-z

Chapter 18
Redefining Postgraduate Student–Supervisor Relationships and the Role of Supervisors in the Age of Artificial Intelligence

Luthando Mpho Molefe
http://orcid.org/0000-0001-8980-0984
University of KwaZulu-Natal, South Africa

Nokubongwa Ntuli
University of KwaZulu-Natal, South Africa

ABSTRACT

The advent of Artificial Intelligence (AI) in postgraduate research and education is rapidly unsettling traditional student-supervisor relationships, thereby reshaping the role of supervisors. While AI-powered tools such as Grammarly, QuillBot, and Thesify assist postgraduate students in idea generation and mapping, searching, reviewing and analysing complex data, and improving academic tone, they also highlight significant challenges, including the erosion of critical thinking and independence, as well as issues of accuracy and ethical dilemmas in higher education. Grounded in Foucault's (1979) power-knowledge dynamics, this chapter provides an analytical framework for understanding how AI restructures mentor-mentee dynamics, establishing a different set of circumstances—a shift from a mentor-novice framework to a hybrid model. Moreover, this work contributes to ongoing debates regarding the implications for supervisory roles and mentorship models for supervisors and students in higher education in the age of AI.

BACKGROUND AND INTRODUCTION

The relationship between postgraduate students and their supervisors, including the role of supervisors in higher education, is currently being reshaped by the advent of Artificial Intelligence (AI) in educational research and beyond. While generative AI offers significant benefits and support for these students,

DOI: 10.4018/979-8-3373-8939-4.ch018

such as scoping topics, enhancing academic writing and language skills, and personalising learning and concept simplification, it also introduces challenges related to academic integrity and ethical concerns, over-reliance, and the potential erosion of critical thinking skills.

Consequently, the transition from a traditional mentorship model to a hybrid approach necessitates a reframing of postgraduate education, research, and supervision. Accordingly, Chinhamo et al. (2026), Nkosi (2026), and Omodan (2025) contend that the role of supervisors in upholding the core principles and values of mentoring has gained prominence in the modern digital age. These fundamental tenets include, among others, the development of critical thinking and problem-solving skills, the establishment of personal-professional identity, and the fostering of academic integrity.

In this chapter, we begin by unpacking the relationships between novice postgraduate students and their supervisors and their significance in higher education and beyond. Second, we deconstruct the role of AI in postgraduate research and education, including the evolving role of supervisors in the context of digital transformation. Third, we present discussions of the theoretical lens through which we examine and analyse the shifting student-supervisor relationships and the role of supervisors within the scope of the emergence of AI in higher education and beyond. Fourth, we consider the outcomes these developments have had and may have for academic integrity and ethical considerations. Lastly, we explore the implications of these critical discussions for the evolving supervisory roles and mentorship models in higher education.

Subsequently, we address the following research questions:

(a) How are student-supervisor relationships and the role of supervisors redefined in the age of artificial intelligence?
(b) What model(s) can be used to enhance student-supervisor relationships and the shifting role of supervisors in the age of artificial intelligence?

NOVICE POSTGRADUATE STUDENT-SUPERVISOR RELATIONSHIPS IN HIGHER EDUCATION

Postgraduate Student and Supervisor Relationships at Play

Postgraduate student-supervisor relations are often characterised as critical, complex, and pedagogical partnerships that significantly influence academic development, retention, and student success. These relationships are typically characterised by a blend of academic guidance, personal support, and a sustainable interactive process through which individuals acquire the specialised knowledge, skills, values, and attitudes necessary for self-realisation and meaningful participation as members of society. Furthermore, they frequently entail the development of a personal-professional identity and the transformation from novice to competent research practitioner, positively shaping policy and practice for meaningful engagement.

Similarly, Bao et al. (2025) and Han and Jin (2025) assert that these relational ties are defined by the complexity of the relationships between students and their supervisors. They are marked by collaboration, knowledge sharing, and co-creation, including decision-making and emotional exchange. Furthermore, Han and Jin (2025) posit that research over the years has revealed that positive emotions in student-supervisor relationships can cultivate confidence, nurture engagement, and foster a sense of trust, while the opposite can hinder student development, growth, and academic success—resulting in bonds characterised by poor communication, conflict, and emotional distance.

Likewise, Dube (2025), Han and Jin (2025), and Adedokun and Oyetunde-Joshua (2024) contend that elevating student voices in student-supervisor relationships is crucial as it provides critical guidance for enhancing the robustness of supervision and improving the quality of existing and ever-evolving methods. Moreover, these scholars postulate that by revisiting how institutions operate (structure) and think (culture), as shaped by students' lived experiences, the supervision process can be bolstered to reconceptualise postgraduate students as partners and co-constructors of knowledge in postgraduate research and education.

Doctoral Student-Supervisor Relationships

Developing a researcher identity is often a complex, non-linear, and transformative process, frequently characterised by a shift from a student mindset to that of an independent scholar or scholarly practitioner. This transition encompasses not only the acquisition of knowledge and skills but also a social, cultural, emotional, and intellectual transformation, ultimately shaping how doctoral students perceive their primary role as researchers. Consequently, this journey necessitates doctoral supervisors who possess a multifaceted blend of academic and pedagogical expertise, interpersonal and emotional intelligence, mentoring abilities, professional development skills, cultural sensitivity, ethical conduct, and functional managerial capabilities.

Similarly, Kutsyuruba (2021) and Mainhard et al. (2009) argue that the success of doctoral students is contingent upon the efficacy of their relationships with supervisors, collaborative relationships, and communities of practice. These scholars further assert that effective student development and growth must exemplify a balance between autonomy and guidance, fostering a psychologically safe and trusting environment.

Mavrogalou-Foti et al. (2024) and Halse and Malfroy (2010) maintain that a supervisor's role is multidimensional, encompassing the co-construction of a subject of inquiry, monitoring progress, providing timely feedback on writing, ensuring the development of pertinent knowledge and skills, and offering emotional support. In a similar vein, Corcelles-Seuba et al. (2023) and Sverdlik et al. (2018) contend that social support afforded to doctoral students by relevant stakeholders—such as supervisors, peers, and the research community—is crucial, as it facilitates identity development, fosters a sense of belonging, and promotes collaboration. Subsequently, such robust support networks enhance academic engagement, provide guidance, and cultivate a greater sense of security—thereby facilitating academic growth and career preparation.

Furthermore, Ringo (2025), Lee (2019), and Lee and Murray (2015) assert that effective supervisors not only equip their students with academic guidance and support but also accompany them in developing essential research-oriented skills, including critical thinking, intellectual independence, research and methodological competencies, pedagogical and leadership skills, personal effectiveness, project engagement, professionalism, and future-oriented skills. Thus, these competencies represent a significant milestone for navigating the often complex research journey and can, if utilised appropriately, lead to heightened academic engagement and improved academic outcomes for both the present and future positioning.

Le et al. (2025), Ringo (2025), and Chu et al. (2024) contend that, in addition to bridging theory and practice within a supervisory relationship, as facilitated by supervisors, robust student-supervisor relationships are contingent upon the efforts and goal-oriented approaches of both parties. Consequently, a positive student-supervisor relationship is fundamentally rooted in trust, open and consistent communication, mutual respect, collaborative partnerships, and shared responsibilities towards common goals.

In a similar vein, Li et al. (2025), Ringo (2025), Samuel (2025), and Friesen et al. (2022) assert that the interpersonal bonds formed between supervisors and students extend beyond mere academic guidance; they are designed to encompass emotional support and personal-professional growth, which are crucial for alleviating feelings of isolation, frustration, and stress. Such support can lead to enhanced student engagement and improved academic outcomes. Furthermore, they argue that trust and the clear communication of responsibilities are imperative in co-creating positive and collaborative relationships between students and their supervisors. This, in turn, influences intellectual growth and success, fostering scientific innovation and advancement, as well as promoting the overall well-being of all stakeholders involved.

Conversely, Ringo (2025) and Yende (2021) argue that the personalised support extended to doctoral students facing various challenges by their supervisors is intended to provide tailored guidance to address unique obstacles. These approaches include active listening, the establishment of clear and mutually agreed-upon expectations, the provision of constructive feedback, and active engagement, along with tailored communication, among other strategies. Thus, these practices serve to enhance students' motivation, goal attainment, and emotional well-being. Therefore, acknowledging the importance of the aforementioned skills and striving to cultivate them can lay the foundation for a positive, meaningful, and enduring academic and research journey for supervisors and their postgraduate students.

Beginner Student-Supervisor Relationships

> *Personal uncertainties and feelings of novice researcher vulnerability are compounded by a lack of research skills and experience to draw knowledge of processes and understanding.* Kirk and Lipscombe (2019).

Beginner postgraduate students in higher education face a complex set of challenges as they navigate the uncharted terrain of the research space. These challenges are often categorised into personal and emotional, academic and research, and institutional-related challenges. The transition from structured undergraduate learning to postgraduate studies typically necessitates independence, self-directed learning, time management, and critical engagement with the subject matter, among other competencies.

Hoffman and Julie (2012), as well as Hoffman (2009), delineate the transition of undergraduate students to postgraduate learning through three interrelated characteristics, as follows:

(a) *Personal-emotional transition,* which refers to the complex and challenging journey characterised by a deep shift in the mindset, cultural and social outlook. Moreover, this repositioning includes social isolation and emotional disorientation as beginner postgraduate students redefine social and academic engagement, shifting identities and managing expectations.

(b) *Social transition* is characterised by a shift from a broader sociocultural setting to a more differentiated, professionalised, and sometimes isolated academic and research environments. Key aspects of this social change includes developing a new personal-professional identity, increased emotional challenges and building new networks and support systems.

(c) *Academic transition* refers to shifting from a 'traditional' structured learning to an independent, critical thinking and analysis, and decision-making skills. Moreover, this transition possess and requires increased academic demands, discipline-specific and research area knowledge, adjustment periods (personal-professional development), time management and support systems.

Therefore, it is crucial to support these types of students as they shift from being consumers of knowledge to taking a significant and critical step towards becoming knowledge generators, which is vital for their academic success and career progression in the academy and beyond. On the other hand, White (2024) and McLeod et al. (2019) argue that it is important to note that a number of postgraduate students return at a later stage to further their studies, and they often find the academic environment even more challenging and unfamiliar as they transition to independent and critical thinkers in the research space.

Moreover, Liu and Pullinger (2021) and Wozniak et al. (2009) assert that, with the continuous exploration and incorporation of new technological tools, systems, and methods such as AI, blockchain, and digital tools/simulation in research to advance scientific knowledge and untangle complicated issues, undertaking postgraduate studies has become a complicated process for these types of students. Therefore, they require support and guidance more than ever from key stakeholders such as supervisors and their institutions in navigating the unfamiliar terrain of the research atmosphere.

White (2024), Tran et al. (2022), Becker (2019), Bunney (2017), McPherson et al. (2017), and Tobell and O'Donnell (2013) further posit that the progression experiences of postgraduate students in higher education have been and continue to be overlooked in the literature, with significant studies focusing on the transition from high school to higher education institutions. This gap has, they argue, created assumptions that these students are familiar with the systems and possess pre-existing research skills, are naturally confident, independent thinkers, and hold a clear sense of personal-professional identity within postgraduate education and research.

In reality, this type of transition—a shift from an academic mindset and between professional and academic environments, along with associated ways of doing—is often marked by complexity and characterised by emotional stress and uncertainties. Therefore, these assumptions highlight the need for comprehensive and targeted transition support designed to help postgraduate students succeed as they navigate the uncharted waters of the research space.

THE ROLE OF ARTIFICIAL INTELLIGENCE IN POSTGRADUATE RESEARCH AND EDUCATION

AI in postgraduate research and education serves as a transformative tool that optimises engagement and performance. It assists students in brainstorming research ideas, refining research questions in alignment with their area of study, exploring multiple approaches to the phenomenon under scrutiny, conducting literature reviews and synthesis, and performing data analysis and processing. To this end, it facilitates the rapid assimilation of complex research objects, aids in identifying research gaps, and subsequently pushes the scholarly conversation forward. It streamlines academic writing and provides researchers with the opportunity to focus on strategic assessment, which enhances their critical thinking and decision-making skills.

Dai et al. (2023), Kipling et al. (2023), and Crossouard (2008) maintain that online discussion forums in postgraduate research provide a flexible platform for students to exchange varied viewpoints, refine reasoning, and narrow existing gaps. Moreover, these scholars argue that such active engagement can facilitate feedback from supervisors, thereby maximising postgraduate students' engagement in critical and meaningful learning. This engagement is crucial for student development and growth, strengthening student-supervisor relationships and improving students' academic outcomes.

Correspondingly, Crosta et al. (2024) contend that active engagement with these online forums fosters self-determination and independent learning among postgraduate students. Moreover, this amplifies critical thinking and problem-solving skills, thereby building adaptability and resilience, as well as lifelong learning skills for navigating the research space and professional environments. Equally, Yoshida et al. (2026) assert that online discussion forums serve as a platform for creating online research communities, thereby reinforcing student learning. This can be achieved through students engaging in academic interaction, knowledge sharing, building a community of support, and providing collaborative learning opportunities.

Furthermore, Yoshida et al. (2026) argue that online discussion forums, through learning management systems, provide mentors with the opportunity to manage and facilitate learning while at the same time allowing students to engage actively with their peers. This engagement is crucial for planning, time management, expected roles, implementation, and reflection for authentic learning. Therefore, these forums promote high-level cognitive engagement, critical thinking and problem-solving skills, and the active co-construction of knowledge, which is essential for active learning. Consequently, they provide sustained learning experiences for students in research and beyond.

AI-powered writing assistant tools like Grammarly, QuillBot, and Thesify have significantly changed the landscape of postgraduate research. These tools offer, among other features, dynamic text improvement, paraphrasing, summarising literature and analysis, and enhancing citations in alignment with the writing process. Abbas and Teyebi (2025) and Van Wyk (2025) argue that as AI technologies continue to evolve, their capacity to improve the research landscape is becoming increasingly clear and noticeable.

Abbas and Teyebi (2025, p. 136) further posit that:

> These generative AI tools signify a fundamental evolution in writing support; they do not merely correct but also co-author. Their capacity to respond interactively to user prompts, refine academic language, and simulate a scholarly tone renders them particularly appealing to doctoral students who are navigating the complexities of thesis writing, research article preparation, or grant proposals.

Correspondingly, Omodan (2025, p. 7) argues that:

> Software like Grammarly uses sophisticated machine-learning algorithms to provide real-time critiques on grammar, style, and overall coherence. Automated feedback mechanisms can therefore accelerate the drafting and revision cycle, allowing supervisors to spend more time on conceptual discussions and less on line-level editing.

Therefore, the use of AI-empowered writing assistants such as Grammarly and many others has proven to enhance postgraduate students' skills, thereby fostering self-confidence, academic writing standards, and improved productivity. These tools have also demonstrated their ability to aid brainstorming, outlining, engagement, and refining tone. Moreover, they boost accuracy and uplift self-assurance in drafting clear, professional, and well-structured academic pieces.

However, despite the numerous benefits associated with AI writing assistants, the presence and continuous advancement of these tools in higher education pose threats to academic integrity. These include concerns about the true identity of authorship, originality, erosion of critical thinking and future-focused skills, and ethical issues regarding data privacy and algorithmic bias. Therefore, postgraduate students, as individuals and as independent critical thinkers, along with the mentorship of their supervisors and institutional research spaces, need to tread carefully when using these tools in engaging with their research projects in higher education and beyond. We shall expand on this argument in one of the sections in this chapter.

GROUNDING THE STUDY: FOUCAULT'S POWER-KNOWLEDGE DYNAMICS

Michel Foucault (1979) argued that power and knowledge are indivisible and mutually constitutive. As a result, power-knowledge practices shape human behaviour by defining what is considered 'normal' or 'correct' as upheld by society. Moreover, power is not only oppressive but also productive, generating new understandings and insights, while knowledge constructs the truths that serve existing structures, thereby shaping reality, knowledge, and behaviours.

In the context of higher education, student-supervisor relationships, and postgraduate supervision in the age of AI, Foucault's (1979) power-knowledge framework emerges as a transformative tool that challenges the established norms of knowledge production. Likewise, Pitsoe and Vlădu escu (2024) argue that this "paradigm challenges the very bedrock of traditional perspectives on knowledge production. It boldly asserts that power and knowledge are not mere bedfellows; they are inextricably woven into the fabric of academic inquiry…this revolutionary perspective reshapes the understanding of academic knowledge, stripping away the illusion of neutrality and revealing the intricate dance between knowledge and the pervasive influence of power relations" (p. 42).

Foucault's (1979) theory of power-knowledge in the present study provides a critical lens for understanding how AI rearranges the dynamics between students and supervisors. It posits that in the age of AI, power is not only held by a human supervisor but is increasingly distributed across human management and digital platforms, thereby creating a different research environment—a blended model of supervision. AI tools like Grammarly, QuillBot, and ChatGPT can offer immediate and comprehensive feedback on students' work, including increased efficiency in literature reviews, data analysis, and writing. Meanwhile, human-centred pedagogical mentorship offers proactive oversight over passive review, critical evaluation skills, ethical awareness, digital literacy, adaptability, and human connection.

This allows researchers to manage complex data sets in reduced time frames, which challenges the traditional model of the supervisor as the sole expert knowledge holder. Therefore, students and supervisors need to embrace a hybrid model of supervision where human capacity, oversight, and AI-assisted tools play a critical role in actively engaging with research projects and ethical considerations.

ACADEMIC INTEGRITY AND ETHICAL CONSIDERATIONS

Academic integrity and ethical considerations in postgraduate research have become significantly more complex in contemporary times due to the rapid integration of AI, which extends beyond traditional plagiarism concerns to encompass issues of authorship, over-reliance, data privacy, and algorithmic bias. Key ethical challenges include the potential for AI to generate fabricated, angle-driven content and the erosion of critical thinking and problem-solving skills. Similarly, Mogoale et al. (2025) argue that the incorporation of AI in higher education can yield benefits when adhering to established rules and quality benchmarks. However, the overuse of AI-powered technologies may diminish students' abilities to think critically, creatively, and independently, thereby posing a threat to human capacity for active and independent thought.

Likewise, Okoth (2025) and Sangwa et al. (2025) assert that the over-reliance on AI tools by postgraduate students undermines the authentic definitions of meaningful engagement and advancements in research. Moreover, these scholars argue that excessive dependence on AI may erode critical oversight, including but not limited to complex problem identification, critical thinking and validation, creativity and innovation, and ethical judgements. Therefore, students must proceed with caution when integrating AI into their research projects.

Gaudu et al. (2026) contend that AI-powered tools such as ChatGPT and QuillBot introduce new challenges to academic integrity through issues of plagiarism. They argue that auto-generated content allows AI to formulate arguments based on prompts without engaging in high-level thinking and reasoning. Furthermore, while paraphrasing tools are designed to enhance articulation and refine text, their misuse may result in a loss of voice and contextual inaccuracies. Gaudu et al. (2026) also warn that unattributed AI assistance, wherein students utilise data generated from AI to support their academic arguments without proper citation or acknowledgement of the original ideas, misrepresents authorship. Consequently, these practices compromise academic integrity rather than serving, if appropriately applied, as a supportive tool for research by postgraduate students.

Khatri and Karki (2023) assert that the widespread recognition of AI in higher education has complicated the distinction between original content and that which is AI-generated. Moreover, this development poses significant challenges for higher education institutions in maintaining ethical standards, thereby emphasising a commitment to fairness, responsibility, and trust in the independent creation of knowledge. Additionally, Khatri and Karki (2023) argue that "the use of AI in grading and evaluation processes may also raise concerns about fairness and transparency, as the algorithms used may not be fully understood or accessible to students, potentially impacting the objectivity of assessments" (p. 4). Therefore, the responsible conduct of research must adhere to research ethics, academic integrity, and scientific rigour.

IMPLICATIONS FOR SUPERVISORY ROLES AND MENTORSHIP MODELS

The rapid integration of AI technologies in higher education research continues to cause a paradigm shift in traditional student-supervisor relationships, as students no longer rely solely on human capacity to guide their research projects. While AI provides essential advantages for postgraduate students conducting research, its use requires caution, ethical behaviour, and security sensitivity in upholding intellectual integrity. AI tools such as Grammarly, QuillBot, and ChatGPT can assist students with topic refinement, content generation, academic writing and editing, literature reviews, data analysis, and research efficiency. However, over-reliance on these tools negatively affects students' critical thinking skills, originality, and raises questions about academic integrity.

To address potential misapplications by students, research supervisors need to be AI literate. Over time, they must develop the ability to understand, evaluate, and ethically use AI tools for the benefit of both their students and themselves. For this reason, Nkosi (2026), Mbodila (2025), and Omodan (2025) believe that supervisors cannot effectively guide students who are using AI in the construction of their research projects if they themselves cannot use AI. Moreover, these scholars suggest that supervisors should attend training programmes that can assist them in better understanding and managing the complexities of modern research and supervision while upholding intellectual integrity.

Therefore, this calls for higher education institutions to and in collaboration with the independent statutory bodies, advocates for higher education and training sector – both public and private – to plan and implement structured initiatives designed to help supervisors and students enhance cognitive reasoning, establish ethical guidelines for AI use in research, and foster a paradigm shift towards a co-active mentorship model. Correspondingly, Mbodila (2025) argues that this will help supervisors to guide students carefully on the ethical use of AI, including teaching them about the dangers of plagiarism, the limitations of AI, how to properly acknowledge content generated by AI, and how to verify information found using AI-generated tools.

To maintain a functional relationship between postgraduate students and supervisors in this age of AI, supervisors need to meet with postgraduate students regularly to provide guidance and monitor their progress. This will align expectations, create a productive academic environment, and ultimately enable prompt feedback (Lee & Murray, 2015). Omodan (2025) believes that AI can assist supervisors with providing feedback by quickly identifying grammar and spelling mistakes and analysing large volumes of data. Therefore, detailed and regular feedback can strengthen student-supervisor relationships. Moreover, research conducted by Selwyn (2019) outlines that supervisors provide emotional support to students, which is an element that AI cannot offer. Omodan (2025) shares similar sentiments, stating that supervisors play an irreplaceable role in research as they offer emotional support to students who are under pressure, dealing with personal hardships, and struggling to find their identity in their work. Therefore, this transition—a shift towards a hybrid model—requires criticality, transparency, and AI-informed frameworks if students and supervisors are to thrive in this modern research era.

REFERENCES

Abbas, C., & Teyebi, S. (2025). From Grammarly to GPT: Exploring the use of AI-assisted academic writing tools among doctoral researchers. *Journal of Languages and Translation*, *5*(3), 134–150.

Adedokun, T., & Oyetunde-Joshua, F. (2024). Strengthening student-supervisor relationships: An examination of postgraduate students' perspectives on supervisory support. *JMSP (Jurnal Manajemen Dan Supervisi Pendidikan), 8*(2), 108–123. https://journal-fip.um.ac.id/index.php/jmsp/article/view/1804

Bao, J., Feng, D. W., Hu, G., & Wang, J. (2025). 'You could make original contributions, just like them!': Supervisory interactions and a doctoral student's academic identity construction. *Studies in Higher Education*, *50*(2), 349–364. DOI: 10.1080/03075079.2024.2338267

Becker, S., Johnson, D., & Britton, P. (2019). Mapping the challenges in making the transition to taught postgraduate study in psychology. *Psychology Teaching Review*, *25*(1), 1–5. https://www.bps.org.uk/publications/psychology-teaching-review. DOI: 10.53841/bpsptr.2019.25.1.12

Bunney, D. (2017). Facilitating the transition to postgraduate studies: What can we learn from the First Year Experience? *Journal of Academic Language and Learning*, *11*(1), A23–A38. https://journal.aall.org.au/index.php/jall/article/view/421

Chinhamo, E., Dzvapatsva, G. P., & Matobobo, C. (2026). Redefining postgraduate supervision in the age of AI: Balancing technology and human mentorship. In I. Kariyana & W. Sinkala (Eds.), *Artificial IntelligenceandPostgraduateSupervisioninHigherEducation* (pp. 38–54). ERRCD Forum. DOI: 10.38140/obp4-2026-03

Chu, X., Litifu, A., Zhu, Z., Ma, S., Zhou, Y., Gao, Q., Lei, L., & Wei, J. (2024). Supervisor's neuroticism and problematic Internet use among graduate students: The mediating role of supervisor-student relationship quality and the moderating role of fear of the supervisor's negative evaluation. *BMC Public Health*, *24*(1), 2238. DOI: 10.1186/s12889-024-19725-x PMID: 39154018

Corcelles-Seuba, M., Suñe-Soler, N., Sala-Bubaré, A., & Castelló, M. (2023). Doctoral student perceptions of supervisory and research community support: Their relationships with doctoral conditions and experiences. *Journal of Further and Higher Education*, *47*(4), 481–491. DOI: 10.1080/0309877X.2022.2142102

Crossouard, B. (2008). Developing alternative models of doctoral supervision with online formative assessment. *Studies in Continuing Education*, *30*(1), 51–67. DOI: 10.1080/01580370701841549

Crosta, L., Edwards, A., & Reis-Jorge, J. (2024). The use of social media and artificial intelligence tools by online doctoral students: Skills needed and challenges. *GILE Journal of Skills Development*, *4*(2), 19–36. DOI: 10.52398/gjsd.2024.v4.i2.pp19-36

Dai, Y., Lai, S., Lim, C. P., & Liu, A. (2023). ChatGPT and its impact on research supervision: Insights from Australian postgraduate research students. *Australasian Journal of Educational Technology*, *39*(4), 74–88. DOI: 10.14742/ajet.8843

Dube, M. C. (2025). Sustaining a healthy supervisor-student relationship: Students speak. *Journal of Culture and Values in Education, 8*(2),26-43. [REMOVED HYPERLINK FIELD]DOI: 10.46303/jcve.2025.18

Foucault, M. (1979). *Discipline and punish: The birth of the prison.* Penguin.

Friesen, S., Becker, S., & Jacobsen, M. (2022). Online doctoral student-supervisory relationships: Exploring relational trust. In Jacobsen, M., & Smith, C. (Eds.), *Online learning and teaching from kindergarten to graduate school* (pp. 282–306). Canadian Association for Teacher Education. [REMOVED HYPERLINK FIELD], DOI: 10.11575/PRISM/40509

Halse, C., & Malfroy, J. (2010). Retheorizing doctoral supervision as professional work. *Studies in Higher Education, 35*(1), 79–92. DOI: 10.1080/03075070902906798

Han, J., & Jin, L. (2025). Reconceptualizing supervisory relationships in graduate education: The role of interpersonal emotion regulation in supervisor-student interactions. *International Journal of Educational Research, 132*, 102650. DOI: 10.1016/j.ijer.2025.102650

Hoffman, J. C. (2009). *The academic transitional experience of postgraduate students in the Faculty of Community and Health Sciences at the University of the Western Cape* (Doctoral dissertation, University of the Western Cape).

Hoffman, J. C., & Julie, H. (2012). The academic transitional experiences of master's students at the University of the Western Cape. *Curationis, 35*(1), 1-8. [REMOVED HYPERLINK FIELD]DOI: 10.4102/curationis.v35i1.33

Khatri, B. B., & Karki, P. D. (2023). Artificial intelligence (AI) in higher education: Growing academic integrity and ethical concerns. *Nepalese Journal of Development and Rural Studies, 20*(01), 1–7. DOI: 10.3126/njdrs.v20i01.64134

Kipling, R. P., Stiles, W. A. V., de Andrade-Lima, M., MacKintosh, N., Roberts, M. W., Williams, C. L., Wootton-Beard, P. C., & Watson-Jones, S. J. (2023). Interaction in online postgraduate learning: What makes a good forum? *Distance Education, 44*(1), 162–189. DOI: 10.1080/01587919.2022.2150391

Kirk, M., & Lipscombe, K. (2019). When a postgraduate student becomes a novice researcher and a supervisor becomes a mentor: A journey of research identity development. *Studying Teacher Education, 15*(2), 179–197. DOI: 10.1080/17425964.2019.1587606

Kutsyuruba, B. (2021). The role of trust in doctoral student-supervisor relationships in Canadian universities: The students' lived experiences and perspectives. *Journal of Higher Education Theory and Practice, 21*(2), 125.

Lee, A. (2019). *Successful research supervision: Advising students doing research* (2nd ed.). Routledge., DOI: 10.4324/9781351234986

Lee, A., Jere, A., Du Plessis, L., Van Gerven, P. W., Heeneman, S., & Ross, S. (2025). Continuity of supervision: Balancing continuous and episodic relationships for assessment and learning. *Medical Education, 59*(6), 596–605. DOI: 10.1111/medu.15595 PMID: 39697042

Lee, A., & Murray, R. (2015). Supervising writing: Helping postgraduate students develop as researchers. *Innovations in Education and Teaching International, 52*(5), 558–570. DOI: 10.1080/14703297.2013.866329

Li, Y., Xu, W., & Chen, J. (2025). PhD student-supervisor relationship and its impacts: A perspective of the interpersonal relationship model. *Frontiers in Education, 10*, 1570137. DOI: 10.3389/feduc.2025.1570137

Liu, J., & Pullinger, D. (2021). STep up to masters: Supporting the academic skills transition for taught postgraduate students. *Journal of Information Literacy*, *15*(3), 100–118. DOI: 10.11645/15.3.3095

Mainhard, T., Van der Rijst, R., Van Tartwijk, J., & Wubbels, T. (2009). A model for the supervisor–doctoral student relationship. *Higher Education*, *58*(3), 359–373. DOI: 10.1007/s10734-009-9199-8

Mavrogalou-Foti, A. P., Kambouri, M. A., & Çili, S. (2024). The supervisory relationship as a predictor of mental health outcomes in doctoral students in the United Kingdom. *Frontiers in Psychology*, *15*, 1437819. Advance online publication. DOI: 10.3389/fpsyg.2024.1437819 PMID: 39444829

Mbodila, M. (2025). Postgraduate supervision in the age of ChatGPT: Redefining the role of supervisors. *Foundations and Trends® in Information Systems*, 9(2), 60-68.

McPherson, C., Punch, S., & Graham, E. A. (2017). Transitions from undergraduate to taught postgraduate study: Emotion, integration and ambiguity. *Journal of Perspectives in Applied Academic Practice*, *5*(2), 42–50. DOI: 10.14297/jpaap.v5i2.265

Mogoale, P. D., Pretorius, A., Mogase, R. C., & Segooa, M. A. (2025). Ethical considerations in artificial intelligence-driven environments for higher education. *South African Journal of Information Management*, *27*(1), 2007. Advance online publication. DOI: 10.4102/sajim.v27i1.2007

Nkosi, T. B. (2026). Supervision skills of supervisors in AI-enhanced environments: Perspectives on postgraduate supervision. In I. Kariyana & W. Sinkala (Eds.), *Artificial IntelligenceandPostgraduate-SupervisioninHigher Education* (pp. 93-110). ERRCD Forum. DOI: 10.38140/obp4-2026-06

Okoth, M. O. (2025, February 4). Use of AI in research and postgraduate supervision: Balancing efficiency and academic integrity. *Scholar Media Africa*. https://scholarmedia.africa/education/higher-ed-bar/use-of-ai-in-research-andpostgraduate-supervision-balancing-efficiency-and-academic-integrity

Omodan, B. I. (2025). Redefining the role of supervisors in the era of artificial intelligence: Implications for hybrid postgraduate research governance. *Cogent Education*, *12*(1), 2536534. Advance online publication. DOI: 10.1080/2331186X.2025.2536534

Pitsoe, V. J., & Vlădu escu, . (2024). A critical analysis of Foucault's power and knowledge in higher education research. *Social Sciences and Education Research Review*, *11*(1), 41–51. DOI: 10.5281/zenodo.15258133

Ringo, D. S. (2025). When relationships make a difference! Supervisor support and PhD students' academic performance in the journey: The moderating effect of supervisor-student relationship quality. *Cogent Education*, *12*(1), 2479403. Advance online publication. DOI: 10.1080/2331186X.2025.2479403

Samuel, M. T. (2025). Fostering trust in the postgraduate student-supervisor relationship: A crucial foundation for academic success. *TWIST, 20*(1), 436-444. https://twistjournal.net/twist/article/view/787

Sangwa, S., Nsabiyumva, S., Ngobi, D., & Mutabazi, P. (2025). Ethical AI integration in African higher education: Enhancing research supervision, grant discovery, and proposal writing without compromising academic integrity. *Grant Discovery and Proposal Writing Without Compromising Academic Integrity (June 30, 2025)*. DOI: 10.55677/ijhrsss/08-2025-Vol02I6

Selwyn, N. (2019). *Should robots replace teachers?: AI and the future of education*. John Wiley & Sons.

Sverdlik, A., Hall, N. C., McAlpine, L., & Hubbard, K. (2018). The PhD experience: A review of the factors influencing doctoral students' completion, achievement, and well-being. *International Journal of Doctoral Studies*, *13*, 361–388. DOI: 10.28945/4113

Tran, M. N., Hogg, L., & Marshall, S. (2022). Understanding postgraduate students' perceptions of plagiarism: A case study of Vietnamese and local students in New Zealand. *International Journal for Educational Integrity*, *18*(1), 3. DOI: 10.1007/s40979-021-00098-2

van Wyk, M. M. (2025). Postgraduate students' voices on leveraging Grammarly as an AI-powered tool in academic writing. *Journal of Education*, *98*(98), 103–123. DOI: 10.17159/2520-9868/i98a06

White, A. (2024). The *Transition In* framework: Supporting the transition of students into postgraduate taught study. *Innovations in Education and Teaching International*, *61*(4), 703–715. DOI: 10.1080/14703297.2023.2216682

Wozniak, H., Mahony, M. J., Lever, T., & Pizzica, J. (2009). Stepping through the orientation looking glass: A staged approach for postgraduate students. *Australasian Journal of Educational Technology*, *25*(2), 221–334. DOI: 10.14742/ajet.1151

Yende, S.J. (2021). Factors of effective postgraduate student-supervisor relationships at selected universities in South Africa. *Journal of African Education*, *2*(2), 135–155. DOI: 10.31920/2633-2930/2021/v2n2a6

Yoshida, M., Duangchinda, V., & Ruangrit, N. (2026). AI-supported learning in online discussion forums: A scoping review. *Electronic Journal of e-Learning*, *24*(1), 19–35. DOI: 10.34190/ejel.24.1.4409

Chapter 19
The Future of Learning:
AI-Driven Educational Platforms for Inclusive and Adaptive Education

Govind Sharma
http://orcid.org/0000-0002-5884-4674
Vivekananda Global University, Jaipur, India

Payal Shekhawat
Vivekanand Global University, Jaipur, India

Kunal Singh Shekhawat
Vivekanand Global University, Jaipur, India

Swarnim Shrivastav
Vivekanand Global University, Jaipur, India

ABSTRACT

This study investigate AI based education platform in the world of modern education system. This education platform provides assessment of individual abilities with quizzes and self-assessment model. This will create the learning environment for each connected with this platform and real time learning uniquely with proper feedback system. The experts will guide the students on each level and encourage them for the higher education with proper academic progression. This type of platform beneficial for students for proper engagement and advance level of learning method, predictive analysis and progress report on each level. This platform is easy to handle for educators and focus on unlimited time interaction with students. This will be fostering critical thinking and stimulating creativity while encouraging self-paced learning. This allows for less administrative hassle, gains insights for the tutors to check the student progress, and offers online meetings.

1. INTRODUCTION

In recent time the education system is transforming with support of AI tools. It offers the platforms for educators to create advanced algorithm, automate data driven learning experiences. AI provide the

DOI: 10.4018/979-8-3373-8939-4.ch019

efficient methods for engaging lessons, notes preparation and task progressions. Traditional education system has lacking of one size fit model, there is not accommodate single space for learner. The students of all levels with different learning ability can access here to improve individual learner. students of all ability levels with any levels of fast or slow learners are rarely able to fit easily or very rigid systems that may not support their strengths. AI based platforms truly incorporate with students and teachers for prepared the questions according to their levels and knowledge. The student's performance, learning behavior, and even IQ levels can set up pathways of learning specifically their career related program. AI base models made for each student and pathways change dynamically based on the learner's actual ongoing progress on the subject matter. These systems enable for every student to receive the perceptive content for goal at the precise moment, in the desired manner. AI is not only a advantage for student as well as good for teacher too that educates students. The administrative load reduced and less focus on grading will support to overall engagement of students. Institute are focus on the engagement on the other activities and marking according to all aspects. The institutions performance modifying the best solution with the data interpretation and advantage for all. The Predictive analytics and natural language processing (NLP) will be easy approach for teachers and students to achieve the best solution of each problem. Predictive analytics and natural language processing (NLP) should instruction and learning by identifying potential challenges for real-time solutions. AI's will provide the wide range of capabilities in education allows for all learners to partake in activities. Some features are like Text-to-speech, speech-to-text, real-time translations, and customized interfaces ensure equality and benefiting the system for special needs or minority language students. These factors specially gamification-algorithm-driven techniques made learning much more enjoyable and engaging, thereby instilling a firm interest in students to better serve their learning purpose. The features have to address the issues of data privacy, equity, and digital divides for the benefits of these platforms to accrue equally to all students, irrespective of their leaning toward any socio-economic background. All that the concerns are deployed with ethics for summarize and AI-based learning platforms provide a glimpse of the future of learning like bespoke, fair, and powered to succeed. The technology development can empowerment in study system of new comers and provide best environment for research also. It has the potential of challenging problem solution and education outcomes. This AI base education system increase the capacity of adaptability, creativity and learning. The advanced connection of Artificial intelligence has modern teaching and learning in education system. AI enhances educational experiences by providing immediate feedback and customized learning paths, as demonstrated by Woolf (2010) through intelligent tutoring systems (ITS). Recent AI technology like Dream box learning and smart sparrow line up the content according to level of mind IQ of users. AI technologies applied in education include adaptive learning platforms like Dream Box Learning and Smart Sparrow, which adjust content in real time based on student performance (Du Boulay, 2016). The NLP tools such as Grammarly and chatbots that help in language acquisition and grading; predictive analytics track progress and identify students needing support (Baker & Inventado, 2014). AI-enhanced gamification techniques which increase motivation for learner and benefits to prepare well documentation (Landers, 2019). (Holmes et al., 2019) Encouraged personalisation and improved accessibility for students with features such as text-to-speech and real-time captions. Supported scalability in educational delivery by allowing institutions to reach larger student populations more efficiently. The advantages of these technologies in well documentation and involve the students in other activities. Another advantage is that challenges such as data privacy concerns, algorithmic biases and the digital divide must be addressed to ensure ethical and equitable use of AI in education. (Rane, P. Choudhary & Rane, 2024) studied the frameworks of education 4.0 and 5.0 with integration of Artificial intelligence in the education industries. The education industry is witnessing revolutionary developments with Artificial Intelligence (AI). The culture of work and technology environment are changing, and education is changing in response. Education 4.0 is a paradigm shift to improve the educational process. Education 4.0 is technology particularly artificial intelligence is used develop customized learning environments. The AI technologies, including natural language processing and machine learning algorithms, to develop learning environments for students. It examined the frameworks of Education 4.0 and 5.0, the incorporation of Artificial Intelligence (AI) in the education industry is bringing about revolutionary developments. A more dynamic and progressive system is approaching to education with the transition from Education 3.0 to 4.0. This system may be useful in comparison of standardized, one-size-fits-all approaches to education system elaboration. this era Education 5.0 builds on the ideas of Education 4.0 and further integrates AI into education. Education 5.0 focus on the optimization of the learning journey by customizing assessments, pace, and material to each student's aptitudes and learning preferences. According to (Aniekan, Chukwudi, & Imoh, 2024) Artificial intelligence (AI) can revolutionize educational planning and emphasizes how it can improve institutional decision-making abilities. Artificial intelligence (AI) may greatly simplify and improve teaching methods; the study uses a qualitative approach that emphasizes a thorough document evaluation and analysis. Based on the idea this method investigates a range of AI applications, including predictive analytics for evaluating student performance. This method makes resources as efficiently as possible, and developing individualized learning programs that are catered to the needs of each individual student. The results show that AI technologies can result in better earning outcomes in each sector of education. AI technologies can result in better earning outcomes, more effective resource management, and the capacity to foresee and handle new educational difficulties by enabling more informed and data-driven decision-making. According to (Banerjee, 2024) [2] recent advancements in AI integration as the emergence of a new normal and effective AI techniques on outcome-based learning. The effects of AI techniques on outcome-based learning, action deliverables, and the adoption of best practices in the higher education environment were assessed. In the process, the study evaluates AI's effectiveness in enhancing the learning management systems. AI techniques have capacity to enhance qualities in higher education institutions and offers suggestions for better integration procedures. Goal-driven outcome-based learning and resource optimization are made possible by the development and spread of AI approaches. Goal-driven outcome-based learning and resource optimization in an inclusive and sustainable are adaption of best practices and their effective reinforcement. (Butt, 2024) discussed transformation of the educational field by providing individualized instruction based on the needs of each student. The conventional method of education system and strategies have short comes to full fill the requirements of varies skill students. (Duraes, D., Bezerra, R., & Novais, P. 2024)investigates the transformative potential of Artificial Intelligence (AI) within secondary education, focusing on the utilization of student assessment data and socioeconomic contextual information. The primary objective of this paper is to investigate the transformative potential of Artificial Intelligence (AI) within secondary education, with a specific focus on the utilization of student assessment data and socioeconomic contextual information. (B E Saaida, 2023) explores the potential impact of artificial intelligence (AI) on higher education. The integration of AI has the potential to enable adaptive learning systems to personalise learning, to provide real-time feedback and support, and to foster greater student engagement. Furthermore, AI-powered administrative systems can streamline tedious processes like admissions, registration and financial aid processing, allowing valuable resources to be directed toward more strategic initiatives. (Semi, et al., 2025) proposed an AI-based child learning system that uses ML and NLP to provide personalised and adaptive educational experiences to children.

Research Gap

Most of the existing research is mainly on higher education and online learning platforms. Secondary education requires specialised adaptive frameworks and they are very different from tertiary education. There is limited research on addressing the inclusive learning needs of slow learners at the same time by AI. Most of the literature that exists at this time is about predicting performance, not about supporting actual instructional decisions. Research on the integration of AI with Education 4.0 and Education 5.0 frameworks in secondary education institutions is not exhaustive.

This study attempts to fill these gaps with a series of investigations into how AI-enabled educational systems can facilitate student achievement and empower teachers by creating effective learning environments in secondary schools. Although the current literature has shown the effectiveness of AI in personalised learning and educational analytics, there is a substantial void in the development and evaluation of a holistic AI-driven educational ecosystem integrating adaptive learning, predictive analytics, stakeholder collaboration, inclusive education, and Education 4.0/5.0 principles on one platform. In this paper, an AI-based educational platform is proposed and tested to overcome these limitations by providing personalised learning experience, real-time monitoring of academic activities, and better collaboration among students, teachers, parents, and administrators.

2. RESEARCH AND DISCUSSION

The main purpose of the research is analysis of AI-powered educational platform that can improve the teaching and learning process for students, educators and parents. Personalised learning experiences Tracking student progress Helping teachers Parental involvement Real-time academic monitoring This research uses a qualitative and practice-based research approach to evaluate the effectiveness of an Artificial Intelligence (AI) based educational platform to enhance personalised learning, academic progress monitoring, and stakeholder engagement. The platform utilises Machine Learning (ML), Natural Language Processing (NLP), adaptive learning algorithms and predictive analytics to provide personalised learning for students and support teachers, parents and administrators with real-time data-driven insights.The present study evaluates the effectiveness of the Artificial Intelligence (AI) driven educational platform, which aims to enhance personalised learning, academic monitoring and stakeholder engagement using a qualitative and practice-based research methodology. The platform integrates Machine Learning (ML), Natural Language Processing (NLP), adaptive learning algorithms and predictive analytics to deliver personalised learning experiences for the students while giving teachers, parents and administrators real-time data-driven insights. The proposed AI-powered educational ecosystem comprises five interconnected modules:

(i) Student Module

Learner profiles, academic performance, pace of learning and cognitive ability are used to provide personalised learning paths through the student portal. The AI engine is constantly analysing the students' interactions and recommending:

Personalised Educational Resources

Adaptive quizzes & assessment

Custom Video Training

Activities to develop skills

The system adjusts the difficulty level of the content according to the learner's performance and engagement patterns.

(ii) Teacher Module

The teacher dashboard is an intelligent instructional support system. It enables educators to:

Monitor student progress

Generate performance analytics

Create tasks and evaluations

Get predictive alerts on at-risk learners

AI-based analytics help teachers make informed pedagogical choices and detect learning difficulties early.

(iii) Administrative Module

The admin dashboard gives you the centralised management of:

User profiles

Course structures,

Learning analytics

Institutional performance reporting

This module provides the necessary governance of the platform and the strategic planning of education.

(iv) Parent Engagement Module

The parent portal improves the home-school partnership by:

Academic reports in real time

Attendance tracking

Dashboards for tracking progress

AI-based recommendations for improving student achievement

The module enhances transparency and helps parents to be active participants in the learning process.

(v) Smart Digital Library

The intelligent library utilizes recommendation algorithms to provide:

Subject-specific learning materials

Digital books and notes
Interactive simulations
Multimedia educational resources

This study conducted quiz and assignment in explaining mode for continuous progress of students. This educational platform consists of:

- Student Login page
- Faculty Login Page
- An administrative panel
- Parent login page
- digital library for students

1. Student Dashboard

- This section was tested by creating mock student profiles.
- Each student was assigned different IQ levels, subjects of interest, and learning paces.
- The system responded by recommending specific learning materials, quizzes, and video lessons suited to that profile.
- We observed how the system dynamically changed content based on the student's progress and performance.

Figure 1. Student portal

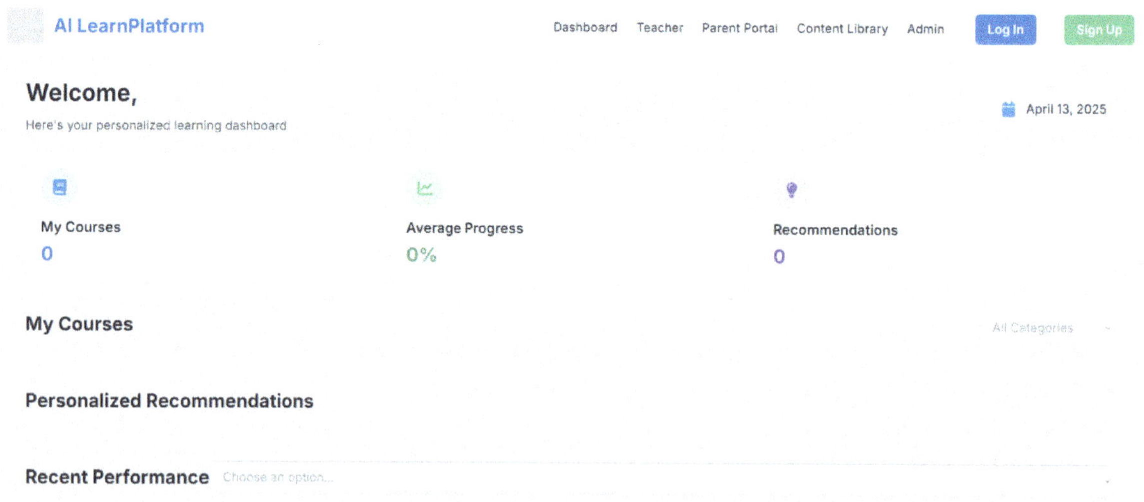

2. Teacher Dashboard

- We explored how teachers can view student progress reports and learning analytics.
- Teachers could upload content, assign tests, and receive real-time alerts about students who might be struggling.
- The platform's predictive tools allowed early identification of students who needed special attention.

Figure 2. Teacher portal

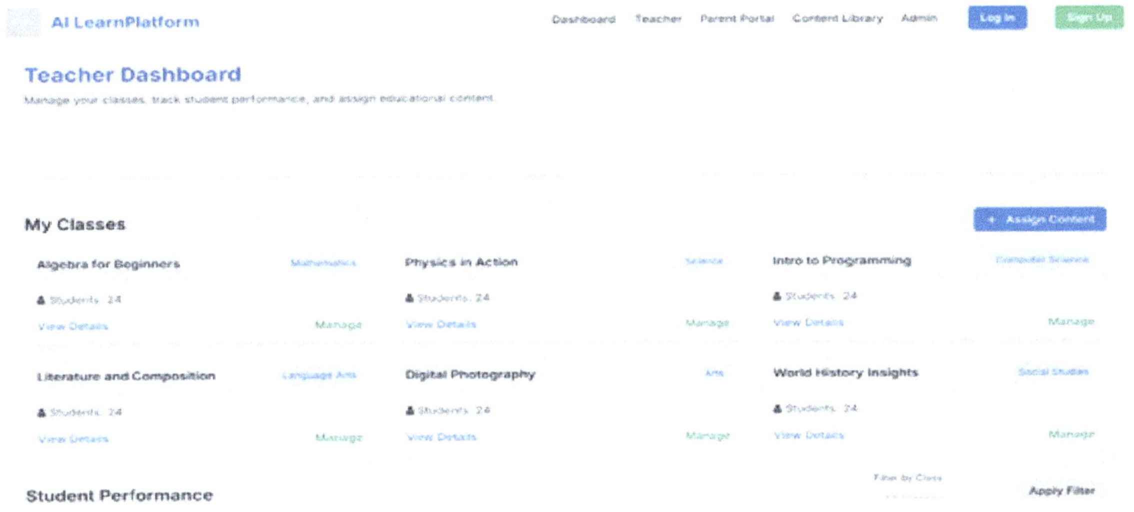

3. Admin Portal

- This section allows the management of all platform users—students, teachers, and parents.
- It provides full control over course content, permissions, platform analytics, and backend data.

Figure 3. Admin portal

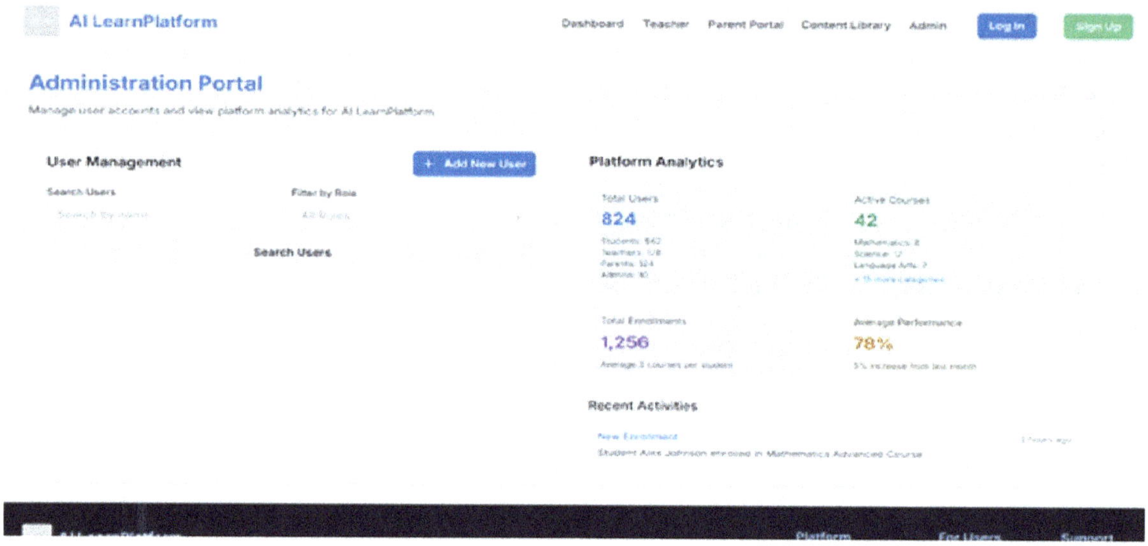

4. Parent Portal

- The parent interface provides academic reports, attendance tracking, and AI-based suggestions for improving student performance.
- It was tested by creating a mock parent account linked to a student to verify how well the communication and feedback systems work.

Figure 4. Parent portal

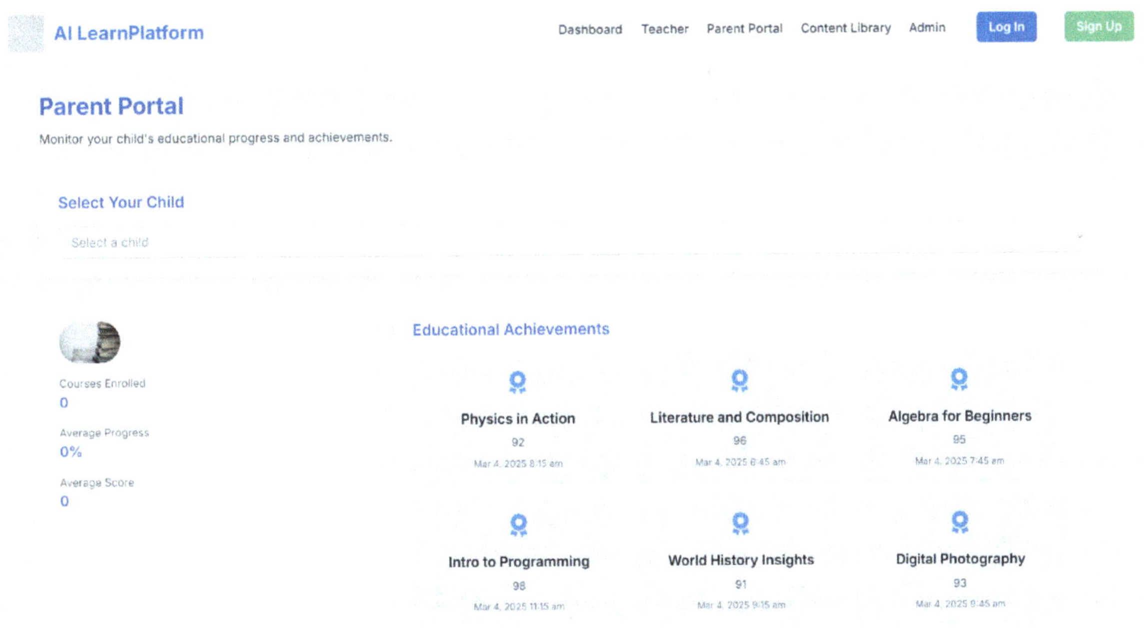

5. Smart Library

- This digital content section includes books, notes, videos, and interactive tools.
- The library content is filtered and suggested by AI based on student learning history and subject choices.

Figure 5. Smart Library

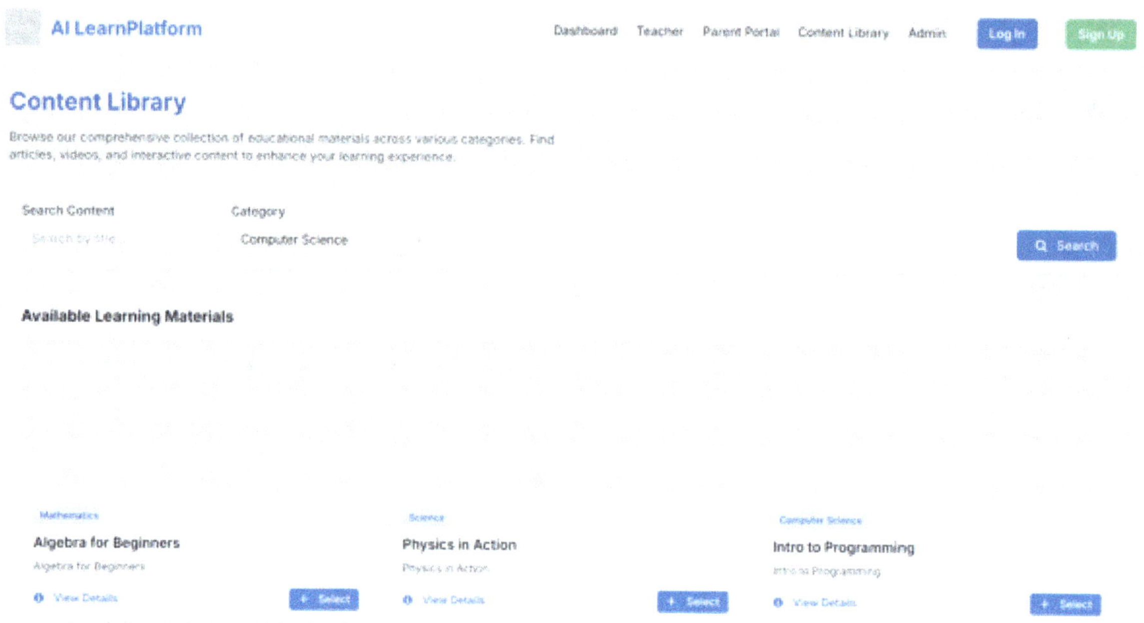

Technologies Employed

The platform integrates multiple AI technologies to support adaptive learning and intelligent decision-making.

Table 1. Tools and Technology Used

Technology	Function
Machine Learning	Performance prediction and learning analytics
Natural Language Processing	Chatbots, voice assistance, automated responses
Adaptive Learning Algorithms	Dynamic content personalization
Predictive Analytics	Early identification of struggling students
Gamification Engine	Student engagement and motivation
Recommendation System	Personalized content delivery

The platform is built using modern AI tools that include:

- **Machine Learning Algorithms** – to track and predict student performance.
- **NLP (Natural Language Processing)** – to support voice commands, text-to-speech, and auto-responses to student queries.

- **Adaptive Learning Algorithms** – which adjust lesson difficulty based on real-time student feedback.
- **Gamification Engines** – to make learning interactive and engaging through points, badges, and rewards.

Data Collection Methods

The following methods were used to analyse the effectiveness of the system:

·Simulation of user journeys of different types of students (slow learners, advanced learners, special needs students etc.). Interface testing by navigating through each module (Student, Teacher, Admin, Parent)

- Feedback from educators who have reviewed the dashboards. Notas manuales de cómo la plataforma manejaba el aprendizaje adaptativo en tiempo real

Research Questions Answered

This study aims to answer the following research questions:

1. To what extent can AI adapt content to suit the learning requirements of individual students?
2. Do teachers get the benefit of automated insights and predictive alerts?
3. How well do parents keep up with their child's academic progress?
4. Does the platform allow all learners from different backgrounds and different learning styles to access?

Limitations

While the system shows great potential, some limitations of the study include:

- Testing was limited to internal simulations and demonstrations.
- Real classroom deployment and user feedback from actual schools are planned in future phases.
- Some AI features such as real-time emotion recognition and speech interaction were not fully implemented yet.

New Frontiers in Higher Education Sustainability Practices

1. Introduction to Higher Education and Sustainability
2. The Evolution of Sustainability in Academic Institutions
3. Sustainable Campus Infrastructure and Green Buildings
4. Renewable Energy Initiatives in Universities
5. Waste Management and Recycling Programs in Higher Education
6. Water Conservation Practices in Universities

3. FUTURE SCOPE

The future scope of AI-powered AI platforms is vast and disruptive, and has the potential for absolutely transforming the evolution of technology. These AI platforms will not only be able to self-improve, where the algorithms optimize its own algorithms, tuning parameters, and improving performance, without human intervention, but also in a field completely related to meta-learning. The ability of one AI to learn from and improve other AIs will drastically reduce human tuning and vastly increase the number of people able to develop AIs. With this type of innovation, as AI-as-a-Service (AIaaS) will evolve and improve distinctions between just getting off-the-shelf domain-algorithms instead of having to create their own. Basically, we are talking about an improved off-the-shelf AI platform for use in almost every industry including, healthcare, finance, cybersecurity, and beyond. Another notable piece of technology evolving is autonomous decision-making systems. AI platforms will have the potential to use real-time analytics and make decisions in complicated situations such as smart factories, autonomous vehicles, or financial markets as new data are coming in. Further, collaborative AI ecosystems will become part of the future AI landscape. These ecosystems will consist of co-evolving and collaborative AI models operating collectively in the spirit of swarm intelligence in order to solve larger problems such as disaster responses, logistics, or simulations. Also, in the future AI systems, ethical and explainable AI will not only be part of the discussion, but built into the mannequin for tools to detect bias as part of AI development.

Research Contributions

The major contributions of this study are:

1. Development of a comprehensive AI-driven educational platform integrating students, teachers, parents, and administrators within a unified ecosystem.
2. Implementation of adaptive learning algorithms for personalized educational pathways.
3. Integration of predictive analytics for early identification of academically vulnerable students.
4. Promotion of inclusive education through AI-enabled accessibility tools.
5. Alignment of platform design with Education 4.0 and Education 5.0 frameworks.
6. Establishment of a scalable model suitable for secondary and higher educational institutions.

4. CONCLUSION

The paper argues that AI is able to improve the teaching and learning process and to offer highly personalised, adaptive and engaging educational experiences. The practical experience of simulation of platform student dashboards, smart libraries and dynamic learning is highlighting the content and improve the version of material. Student dashboards are evident that systems can dynamically adjust learning content based on individual needs, track performance, and support educators in real time. This system supports a data-driven educational ecosystem and enabling teachers to make decisions for reduce administrative burdens. It is beneficial for transforming the knowledge to real-time insights in children progress, encouraging collaborative involvement in the educational journey. The results are promising to acknowledges the need for real-world deployment feedback to further validate the effectiveness of the platform. The lack of emotion and speech interaction recognition is the limitation of AI base education system. We can conclude that AI in creating a future-ready education system. The study is inclusive, efficient and responsive role for learning and improve in the innovation teaching. AI-based platforms are well-positioned to shape the next generation of education and learning outcomes

REFERENCES

Aniekan, U. R., Chukwudi, U. M., & Imoh, S. G. (2024). Application of artificial intelligence in educational planning. *SSR Journal of Artificial Intelligence*, *1*(1), 27–35.

Baker, R. S., & Inventado, P. S. (2014). Educational data mining and learning analytics. In J. M. Spector, M. D. Merrill, J. Elen, & J. Bishop (Eds.), Handbook of research on educational communications and technology (pp. 673–689). Springer.

Banerjee, P., & Bhattacharya, D. (2024). Transforming the world of education through AI-enabled learning: A new normal. *The Business and Management Review*, *15*(1), 225–235. DOI: 10.24052/BMR/V15NU02/ART-21

Butt, A. (2024). AI in education: Personalizing learning with intelligent systems. *Journal of AI Spectrum*, *2*(1), 27–36.

Du Boulay, B. (2016). Artificial intelligence as an effective tool in education. *IEEE Intelligent Systems*, *31*(6), 76–81. DOI: 10.1109/MIS.2016.93

Duraes, D., Bezerra, R., & Novais, P. (2024). AI-driven educational transformation in secondary schools: Leveraging data insights for inclusive learning environments. In *Proceedings of the 2024 IEEE Global Engineering Education Conference (EDUCON)* (pp. 1–9). IEEE. DOI: 10.1109/EDUCON60312.2024.10578910

Holmes, W., Bialik, M., & Fadel, C. (2019). *The ethics of AI in education: Promises and risks*. Center for Curriculum Redesign.

Landers, R. N. (2019). Gamified learning in educational settings. *Journal of Educational Psychology*, *111*(8), 1167–1176.

Rane, N. L., Choudhary, S. P., & Rane, J. (2024). Education 4.0 and 5.0: Integrating artificial intelligence for personalized and adaptive learning. *Journal of Artificial Intelligence and Robotics*, *4*(2), 29–43.

Saaida, M. B. E. (2023). AI-driven transformations in higher education: Opportunities and challenges. *International Journal of Educational Research and Studies*, *5*(2), 29–36.

Semi, M. A., Uddin, M. B., Sultana, S., Tamanna, M., Uddin, A., & Ahmed, K. R. (2025). AI-driven education: Integrating machine learning and NLP to transform child learning systems. *International Journal of Advanced Computer Science and Applications*, *16*(1), 16–24. DOI: 10.14569/IJACSA.2025.0160603

Woolf, B. P. (2010). *Building intelligent interactive tutors: Student-centered strategies for revolutionizing e-learning*. Morgan Kaufmann.

Woolf, B. P., Burleson, W., Arroyo, I., Dragon, T., Cooper, D. G., & Picard, R. W. (2013). AI grand challenges for education. *AI Magazine*, *34*(4), 66–84. DOI: 10.1609/aimag.v34i4.2490

Compilation of References

Aardenburg, E., & Nel, A. (2019). Fatalism and dissidence in Dukuduku, KwaZulu-Natal, South Africa: Ongoing contestations over land, resources and identities. *Journal of Southern African Studies*, *45*(2), 393–411. DOI: 10.1080/03057070.2019.1619429

Abah, J. A., Terungwa, U. D., & Chinaka, T. W. (2025). Conceptualizing the Influence of Artificial Intelligence on Students' Academic Integrity. *Journal of Mathematics Instruction. Social Research & Opinion*, *4*(2), 257–290.

Abbas, C., & Teyebi, S. (2025). From Grammarly to GPT: Exploring the use of AI-assisted academic writing tools among doctoral researchers. *Journal of Languages and Translation*, *5*(3), 134–150.

Act, E. A. I. (2024). The EU artificial intelligence act. *European Union.*

Adedokun, T., & Oyetunde-Joshua, F. (2024). Strengthening student-supervisor relationships: An examination of postgraduate students' perspectives on supervisory support. *JMSP (Jurnal Manajemen Dan Supervisi Pendidikan)*, *8*(2), 108–123. https://journal-fip.um.ac.id/index.php/jmsp/article/view/1804

Adedoyin, O. B., & Soykan, E. (2020). Covid-19 pandemic and online learning: The challenges and opportunities. *Interactive Learning Environments*, •••, 1–13. DOI: 10.1080/10494820.2020.1813180

Agrawal, A., Banerjee, A. R. S., Jhariya, M. K., Garg, N., Hashmi, I., Brar, V., Gupta, D., & Mishra, D. K. (2025). AI-powered student assessment in higher education. In *Research Gate* (pp. 177–202). DOI: 10.4018/979-8-3373-2130-1.ch006

Agrawal, A., Bhadhouriya, S., Pandey, A. K., Bhadoriya, S., Shrivastava, D., Dubey, G., Dubey, M., Sengar, H., Shakywar, K., & Shrivastava, V. (2024). Transforming student assessment in higher education. In *Advances in Educational Technologies and Instructional Design Book Series* (pp. 363–386). DOI: 10.4018/979-8-3693-6170-2.ch013

Ahamed, F. I. (2025). The transformative role of artificial intelligence in modern education. *World Journal of Advanced Research and Reviews*, *26*(1), 3239–3247. DOI: 10.30574/wjarr.2025.26.1.1453

Ahangama, N. (2026). Designing assessments in the generative AI era: A tailored assessment framework for ICT tertiary education. *International Journal of Educational Technology in Higher Education*, *23*(1), 9. DOI: 10.1186/s41239-026-00582-0

Ahmed, I., Liu, W., Roscoe, R. D., Reilley, E., & McNamara, D. S. (2025). Multifaceted assessment of responsible use and bias in language models for education. *Computers*, *14*(3), 100. DOI: 10.3390/computers14030100

Ahmed, Z., Shanto, S. S., Rime, M. H. K., Morol, M. K., Fahad, N., Hossen, M. J., & Abdullah-Al-Jubair, M. (2024). The generative AI landscape in education: Mapping the terrain of opportunities, challenges, and student perception. *IEEE Access : Practical Innovations, Open Solutions*, *12*, 147023–147050. DOI: 10.1109/ACCESS.2024.3461874

Aiseng, K. (2025). Political economy of languages in South African higher education. *South African Journal of African Languages*, *45*(3), 418–425. DOI: 10.1080/02572117.2025.2468705

Ajani, O. A., Gamede, B., & Matiyenga, T. C. (2024). Leveraging artificial intelligence to enhance teaching and learning in higher education: Promoting quality education and critical engagement. *Journal of Pedagogical Sociology and Psychology*, *7*(1), 54–69. DOI: 10.33902/JPSP.202528400

Ajani, O. A., & Matiyenga, T. C. (2025). Enhancing critical analysis and argumentation skills in university students through multimodal approaches: A comprehensive study. *International Journal of Educational Reform*, •••, 10567879251326556. DOI: 10.1177/10567879251326556

Ajzen, I. (1991). The theory of planned behavior. *Organizational Behavior and Human Decision Processes*, *50*(2), 179–211. DOI: 10.1016/0749-5978(91)90020-T

Ajzen, I. (2011). The theory of planned behaviour: Reactions and reflections. *Psychology & Health*, *26*(9), 1113–1127. DOI: 10.1080/08870446.2011.613995 PMID: 21929476

Ajzen, I. (2014). The theory of planned behaviour is alive and well and not ready to retire: A commentary on Sniehotta, Presseau, and Araújo-Soares. *Health Psychology Review*, *9*(2), 131–137. DOI: 10.1080/17437199.2014.883474 PMID: 26209198

Akgun, S., & Greenhow, C. (2022). Artificial intelligence in education: Addressing ethical challenges in K-12 settings. *AI and Ethics*, *2*(3), 431–440. DOI: 10.1007/s43681-021-00096-7 PMID: 34790956

Akhtar, M. A. K., Kumar, M., & Nayyar, A. (2024). Transparency and accountability in explainable AI: Best practices. In *Towards ethical and socially responsible explainable AI* (Vol. 551, pp. 1–18). Springer., DOI: 10.1007/978-3-031-66489-2_1

Akin, A. I. (2025). Developing AI Literacy in the Classroom: AI–Human Collaboration and Ethical AI. In Ibáñez, D. B., Gallardo-Echenique, E., Siringoringo, H., & Diez, N. L. (Eds.), *Communication and Applied Technologies. ICOMTA 2024. Smart Innovation, Systems and Technologies* (Vol. 427). Springer., DOI: 10.1007/978-981-96-0426-5_28

Al-Abbas, H. U. A. I., Halim, H. H., & Nurjati, N. N. (2023). Harnessing the use of artificial intelligence in language assessment: A systematic comprehensive review. *Tell-Us Journal*, *9*(3), 723–745. DOI: 10.22202/tus.2023.v9i3.7366

Al-Amin, M., Saqui, F. Z., & Khan, M. R. (2024). Enhancing assessment systems in higher education. In *Advances in Educational Technologies and Instructional Design Book Series* (pp. 28–56). DOI: 10.4018/979-8-3693-2145-4.ch002

Alfaleh, M. (2026). Sustainable AI-Driven Assessment in Higher Education: A Systematic Review of Fairness, Transparency, Pedagogical Innovation, and Governance. *Sustainability (Basel)*, *18*(2), 785. DOI: 10.3390/su18020785

Alfredo, R., Milesi, M., Echeverria, V., Gašević, D., Buckingham Shum, S., Zhao, L., Yan, L., Jin, Y., Fan, J. X., Pammer-Schindler, V., Swiecki, Z., & Martinez-Maldonado, R. (2025). Co-designing AI-powered learning analytics: Bringing students and teachers together. *International Journal of Educational Technology in Higher Education, 22*(1), 78. DOI: 10.1186/s41239-025-00572-8

Alhalalmeh, A. H., & Al-Tarawneh, A. (2025). Artificial intelligence and the law: the complexities of technology and legalities. In A. Hannoon., & A Mahmood (Eds.). *Intelligence-Driven Circular Economy: Regeneration Towards Sustainability & Social Responsibility*, Volume 2 (pp. 641-649). Cham: Springer Nature Switzerland. DOI: 10.1007/978-3-031-74220-0_50

All India Council for Technical Education. (2020). *Approval process handbook.* AICTE.

Almutairi, M., Alamry, A., Rahman, G., & Mudhsh, B. A. (2025). The role of AI-powered learning analytics in enhancing EFL curriculum design and learning outcomes in higher education. *International Journal of Innovative Research and Scientific Studies, 8*(7), 477–487. DOI: 10.53894/ijirss.v8i7.10480

Al-Omari, O., Alyousef, A., Fati, S., Shannaq, F., & Omari, A. (2025). Governance and ethical frameworks for AI integration in higher education: Enhancing personalized learning and legal compliance. *Journal of Ecohumanism, 4*(2). Advance online publication. DOI: 10.62754/joe.v4i2.5781

Alone, V. N., & Mishra, K. C. (2025). Role of learning analytics and AI in measuring learning outcomes and student performance. In *Research Gate* (pp. 62–90). DOI: 10.71443/9789349552685-03

Alsaleh, A. (2024). The impact of technological advancement on culture and society. *Scientific Reports, 14*(1), 32140. DOI: 10.1038/s41598-024-83995-z PMID: 39738478

Altbach, P. G., Reisberg, L., & Rumbley, L. E. (2019). *Trends in global higher education: Tracking an academic revolution.* Brill., DOI: 10.1163/9789004406155

Amigud, A., & Lancaster, T. (2019). 246 reasons to cheat: An analysis of students' reasons for seeking to outsource academic work. *Computers & Education, 134*, 98–107. DOI: 10.1016/j.compedu.2019.01.017

Amrane-Cooper, L., Hatzipanagos, S., Marr, L., & Tait, A. (2024). Online assessment and artificial intelligence: Beyond the false dilemma of heaven or hell. *Open Praxis, 16*(4), 687–695. DOI: 10.55982/openpraxis.16.4.752

An, X., Bai, J., Li, Y., Zhou, Y., Chai, C. S., & Hong, J. C. (2026). Development of an Artificial Intelligence Technology Pedagogical Content Knowledge (AI-TPACK) Scale for Human and AI Concurrently as Teachers: X. An et al. *The Asia-Pacific Education Researcher, 35*(3), 483-493. DOI: 10.1007/s40299-025-01045-2

Ananny, M., & Crawford, K. (2018). Seeing without knowing: Limitations of the transparency ideal and its application to algorithmic accountability. *New Media & Society, 20*(3), 973–989. DOI: 10.1177/1461444816676645

Andrade, H., & Du, Y. (2005). Student perspectives on rubric-referenced assessment. *Practical Assessment, Research & Evaluation, 10*(1), 3. DOI: 10.7275/g367-ye94

Aniekan, U. R., Chukwudi, U. M., & Imoh, S. G. (2024). Application of artificial intelligence in educational planning. *SSR Journal of Artificial Intelligence, 1*(1), 27–35.

An, Y., & James, S. (2025). Generative AI integration in K-12 settings: Teachers' perceptions and levels of integration. *TechTrends*, *69*(6), 1304–1317. DOI: 10.1007/s11528-025-01114-9

Anyanwu, R., Le Grange, L., & Beets, P. (2015). Climate change science: The literacy of geography teachers in the Western Cape Province, South Africa. South African Journal of Education, 35(3), 1-9. Distance Education, 20(2). http://www.asianjde.com/ojs/index.php/AsianJDE/article/view/847

Apata, A. O., & Oyedele, M. O. (2025). Undergraduates' Application of ChatGPT in Academic Writing: Perceptions, Problems and Prospects. *International Journal of Social Sciences and Management Review*, *8*(3), 201–218. DOI: 10.37602/IJSSMR.2025.8312

Archambault, L. M., & Barnett, J. H. (2010). Revisiting technological pedagogical content knowledge: Exploring the TPACK framework. *Computers & Education*, *55*(4), 1656–1662. DOI: 10.1016/j.compedu.2010.07.009

Arday, J., & Mirza, H. S. (Eds.). (2018). *Dismantling race in higher education: Racism, whiteness and decolonising the academy*. Palgrave Macmillan., DOI: 10.1007/978-3-319-60261-5

Ardito, C. G. (2023). *Contra generative AI detection in higher education assessments*. arXiv. /arxiv.2312.05241DOI: 10.48550

Armitage, C. J., & Conner, M. (2001). Efficacy of the theory of planned behaviour: A meta-analytic review. *British Journal of Social Psychology*, *40*(4), 471–499. DOI: 10.1348/014466601164939 PMID: 11795063

Asghar, M. Z., Iqbal, J., Özbilen, F. M., Abedin, J., Järvenoja, H., & Widanapathirana, U. (2025). The nexus of artificial intelligence literacy collaborative knowledge practices and inclusive leadership development among higher education students in Bangladesh China Finland and Turkey. *Discover Computing*, *28*(1), 172. DOI: 10.1007/s10791-025-09695-y

Ashford-Rowe, K., Herrington, J., & Brown, C. (2014). Establishing the critical elements that determine authentic assessment. *Assessment & Evaluation in Higher Education*, *39*(2), 205–222. DOI: 10.1080/02602938.2013.819566

Askari, M. (2025). Reclaiming authorship in the age of generative AI: From panic to possibility. *AI Magazine*, *46*(3), e70022. DOI: 10.1002/aaai.70022

Awadallah Alkouk, W., & Khlaif, Z. N. (2024). AI-resistant assessments in higher education: Practical insights from faculty training workshops. []. Frontiers Media SA.]. *Frontiers in Education*, *9*, 1499495. DOI: 10.3389/feduc.2024.1499495

Ayanwale, M. (2023). Can Experience Determine the Adoption of Industrial Revolution 4.0 Skills in 21st Century Mathematics Education? *Research in Social Sciences and Technology*, *8*(1), 74–91. DOI: 10.46303/ressat.2023.6

Ayentimi, D., & Burgess, J. (2019). Is the fourth industrial revolution relevant to sub-Sahara Africa? *Technology Analysis and Strategic Management*, *31*(6), 641–652. DOI: 10.1080/09537325.2018.1542129

Ayoubi, M., Mehrabanfar, E., & Banaitis, A. (2018). Guidelines on designing conceptual framework for strategic management with application to the energy industry. *Administrative Sciences*, *8*(3), 27. Advance online publication. DOI: 10.3390/admsci8030027

Ayyoub, A. M., Khlaif, Z. N., Shamali, M., Abu Eideh, B., Assali, A., Hattab, M. K., Barham, K. A., & Bsharat, T. R. K. (2025). Advancing higher education with GenAI: Factors influencing educator AI literacy. *Frontiers in Education*, *10*, 1530721. Advance online publication. DOI: 10.3389/feduc.2025.1530721

Bai, J. Y. H., Zawacki-Richter, O., Bozkurt, A., Lee, K., Fanguy, M., Sari, B. C., & Marin, V. I. (2022). Automated essay scoring (AES) systems: Opportunities and challenges for open and distance education. In *Tenth Pan-Commonwealth Forum on Open Learning*. DOI: 10.56059/pcf10.8339

Baidoo-Anu, D., Asamoah, D., Amoako, I., & Mahama, I. (2024). Exploring student perspectives on generative artificial intelligence in higher education learning. *Discover Education*, *3*(1), 98. DOI: 10.1007/s44217-024-00173-z

Baker, R. S., & Inventado, P. S. (2014). Educational data mining and learning analytics. In J. M. Spector, M. D. Merrill, J. Elen, & J. Bishop (Eds.), Handbook of research on educational communications and technology (pp. 673–689). Springer.

Baker, R. S., & Hawn, A. (2022). Algorithmic bias in education. *International Journal of Artificial Intelligence in Education*, *32*(4), 1052–1092. DOI: 10.1007/s40593-021-00285-9

Ballier, N., Pachet, F., Safar, É., & Sagot, B. (2019). Automated language assessment. *Language Assessment Quarterly*, *16*(4-5), 335–354. DOI: 10.1080/15434303.2019.1674316

Banerjee, P., & Bhattacharya, D. (2024). Transforming the world of education through AI-enabled learning: A new normal. *The Business and Management Review*, *15*(1), 225–235. DOI: 10.24052/BMR/V15NU02/ART-21

Bao, J., Feng, D. W., Hu, G., & Wang, J. (2025). 'You could make original contributions, just like them!': Supervisory interactions and a doctoral student's academic identity construction. *Studies in Higher Education*, *50*(2), 349–364. DOI: 10.1080/03075079.2024.2338267

Barocas, S., & Selbst, A. D. (2016). Big data's disparate impact. *California Law Review*, *104*, 671–732. DOI: 10.15779/Z38BG31

Barrett, L. (2021). *Rejecting test surveillance in higher education*. SSRN Electronic Journal. DOI: 10.2139/ssrn.3871423

Başar, T., & Şahin, L. (2021). Technology integration in teaching English as a foreign language: A content analysis study. *Journal of Educational Technology & Online Learning*, *5*(1), 204–222. DOI: 10.31681/jetol.972577

Baskara, F. R., & Mukarto, M. (2023). Exploring the implications of ChatGPT for language learning in higher education. *Indonesian Journal of Applied Linguistics*, *13*(1), 105–117. DOI: 10.17509/ijal.v13i1.53393

Bates, T., Cobo, C., Mariño, O., & Wheeler, S. (2020). Can artificial intelligence transform higher education? *International Journal of Educational Technology in Higher Education*, *17*(1), 42. DOI: 10.1186/s41239-020-00218-x

Bayne, S. (2015). Teacherbot: Interventions in automated teaching. *Teaching in Higher Education*, *20*(4), 455–467. DOI: 10.1080/13562517.2015.1020783

Bayne, S. (2015). What's the matter with 'technology-enhanced learning'? *Learning, Media and Technology*, *40*(1), 5–20. DOI: 10.1080/17439884.2014.915851

Bayne, S., Evans, P., Ewins, R., Knox, J., Lamb, J., Macleod, H., & Sinclair, C. (2020). The manifold implications of manifold implications of manifold implications of manifold implications of algorithmic proctoring in higher education. *Teaching in Higher Education*, *25*(6), 675–691. DOI: 10.1080/13562517.2020.1760137

Bearman, M., & Ajjawi, R. (2023). Learning analytics and the limits of automated judgement in higher education. *Assessment & Evaluation in Higher Education*, *48*(4), 567–580. DOI: 10.1080/02602938.2022.2067421

Bearman, M., Dawson, P., Ajjawi, R., Tai, J., & Boud, D. (2022). Reconsidering assessment for learning in the age of artificial intelligence. *Assessment & Evaluation in Higher Education*, *47*(5), 676–691. DOI: 10.1080/02602938.2021.1930462

Bearman, M., Dawson, P., Ajjawi, R., Tai, J., & Boud, D. (Eds.). (2022). *Re-imagining university assessment in a digital world.* Springer., DOI: 10.1007/978-3-030-41956-1

Bearman, M., Nieminen, J. H., & Ajjawi, R. (2022). Designing assessment in a digital world: An organising framework. *Assessment & Evaluation in Higher Education*, *48*(3), 291–304. DOI: 10.1080/02602938.2022.2069674

Bearman, M., Ryan, J., & Ajjawi, R. (2022). Discourses of artificial intelligence in higher education: A critical literature review. *Higher Education*, *86*(2), 369–385. DOI: 10.1007/s10734-022-00937-2

Bearman, M., Tai, J., Dawson, P., Boud, D., & Ajjawi, R. (2024). Developing evaluative judgement for a time of generative artificial intelligence. *Assessment & Evaluation in Higher Education*, *49*(6), 893–905. DOI: 10.1080/02602938.2024.2335321

Bearman, M., Tai, J., Kent, F., Edouard, V., Nestel, D., & Molloy, E. (2022). What should we do about feedback? A participatory approach to feedback research. *Medical Education*, *56*(4), 384–392. DOI: 10.1111/medu.14702

Becker, S., Johnson, D., & Britton, P. (2019). Mapping the challenges in making the transition to taught postgraduate study in psychology. *Psychology Teaching Review*, *25*(1), 1–5. https://www.bps.org.uk/publications/psychology-teaching-review. DOI: 10.53841/bpsptr.2019.25.1.12

Belkina, M. (2025). Implementing generative AI in higher education teaching and learning: Case studies and integration strategies. *Computers & Education*, *185*, 104781. Advance online publication. DOI: 10.1016/j.compedu.2025.104781

Benjamin, R. (2019). *Race after technology: Abolitionist tools for the new Jim code*. Polity Press.

Benjamin, R. (2019). *Race after technology: Abolitionist tools for the new Jim Code*. Polity Press., DOI: 10.1093/sf/soz162

Berkel, N. van, Papachristos, E., Giachanou, A., Hosio, S., & Skov, M. B. (2020). A Systematic Assessment of National Artificial Intelligence Policies: Perspectives from the Nordics and Beyond. 1–12. DOI: 10.1145/3419249.3420106

Bernabei, M., Colabianchi, S., Falegnami, A., & Costantino, F. (2023). Students' use of large language models in engineering education: A case study on technology acceptance, perceptions, efficacy, and detection chances. Computers & Education. *Artificial Intelligence*, *5*, 100172. DOI: 10.1016/j.caeai.2023.100172

Bhatia, A., Bhatia, P., & Sood, D. (2024). Leveraging AI to transform online higher education: Focusing on personalized learning, assessment, and student engagement. *International Journal of Management and Humanities (IJMH) Volume-11 Issue-1.*

Bhavana, S., Jayashree, K., & Rao, T. V. N. (2024). Navigating AI biases in education. In *Advances in Educational Marketing* (pp. 135–160). Administration, and Leadership Book Series., DOI: 10.4018/979-8-3693-5443-8.ch005

Biggs, J., & Tang, C. (2011). *Teaching for quality learning at university* (4th ed.). Open University Press.

Binns, R. (2018). Fairness in machine learning: Lessons from political philosophy. *Proceedings of the 2018 Conference on Fairness, Accountability and Transparency, 81*, 149–159. https://doi.org/DOI: 10.1145/3287560.3287598

Bittle, K. (2025). Generative AI and academic integrity in higher education: A systematic literature review. *Information (Basel)*, *16*(4), 296. DOI: 10.3390/info16040296

Black, P., & Wiliam, D. (1998). Assessment and classroom learning. *Assessment in Education: Principles, Policy & Practice*, *5*(1), 7–74. DOI: 10.1080/0969595980050102

Black, P., & Wiliam, D. (2009). Developing the theory of formative assessment. *Educational Assessment, Evaluation and Accountability*, *21*(1), 5–31.

Black, P., & Wiliam, D. (2018). Classroom assessment and pedagogy. *Assessment in Education: Principles, Policy & Practice*, *25*(6), 551–575. DOI: 10.1080/0969594X.2018.1441807

Bloxham, S., & Boyd, P. (2007). *Developing effective assessment in higher education: A practical guide*. Open University Press.

Bou Zeid, M., & Abouchedid, K. (2026). AI for educational innovation: Opportunities and challenges amidst protracted crises. *Education and Information Technologies*, *31*(6), 1553–1580. DOI: 10.1007/s10639-025-13867-0

Bouakaz, L., & Khalid, S. (2025). AI in education: A sociological exploration of technology in learning environments. *Frontiers in Education*, *10*, 1700876. Advance online publication. DOI: 10.3389/feduc.2025.1700876

Boud, D. (1995). Assessment and learning: Contradictory or complementary? In Knight, P. (Ed.), *Assessment for learning in higher education* (pp. 35–48). Kogan Page.

Boud, D. (2000). Sustainable assessment: Rethinking assessment for the learning society. *Studies in Continuing Education, 22*(2), 151–167. DOI: 10.1080/713695728

Boud, D. (2008). How can practice reshape assessment? In *Assessment, learning and judgement in higher education* (pp. 1–15). Springer Netherlands., DOI: 10.1007/978-1-4020-8905-3_3

Boud, D., Ajjawi, R., Dawson, P., & Tai, J. (2018). *Developing evaluative judgement in higher education*. Routledge.

Boud, D., Ajjawi, R., Dawson, P., & Tai, J. (Eds.). (2018). *Developing evaluative judgement in higher education: Assessment for knowing and producing quality work*. Routledge., DOI: 10.4324/9781315109251

Boud, D., & Falchikov, N. (2006). Aligning assessment with long-term learning. *Assessment & Evaluation in Higher Education, 31*(4), 399–413. DOI: 10.1080/02602930600679050

Boud, D., & Falchikov, N. (2007). *Rethinking assessment in higher education*. Routledge.

Boud, D., & Falchikov, N. (2007). *Rethinking assessment in higher education: Learning for the longer term*. Routledge. DOI: 10.4324/9780203964309

Boud, D., & Molloy, E. (2013). Rethinking models of feedback for learning: The challenge of design. *Assessment & Evaluation in Higher Education, 38*(6), 698–712. DOI: 10.1080/02602938.2012.691462

Boud, D., & Soler, R. (2016). Sustainable assessment revisited. *Assessment & Evaluation in Higher Education, 41*(3), 400–413. DOI: 10.1080/02602938.2015.1018133

Bovill, C. (2020). Co-creation in learning and teaching: The case for a whole-class approach in higher education. *Higher Education, 79*(6), 1023–1037. DOI: 10.1007/s10734-019-00453-w

Bovill, C., Cook-Sather, A., Felten, P., Millard, L., & Moore-Cherry, N. (2016). Addressing potential challenges in co-creating learning and teaching: Overcoming resistance, navigating institutional norms and ensuring inclusivity in student–staff partnerships. *Higher Education, 71*(2), 195–208. DOI: 10.1007/s10734-015-9896-4

Bower, M., Torrington, J., Lai, J. W., Petocz, P., & Alfano, M. (2024). How should we change teaching and assessment in response to increasingly powerful generative Artificial Intelligence? Outcomes of the ChatGPT teacher survey. *Education and Information Technologies, 29*(12), 15403–15439. DOI: 10.1007/s10639-023-12405-0

Bozkurt, A. (n.d.). *GenAI et al.: Cocreation, authorship, ownership, academic ethics and integrity in a time of generative AI*. Open Praxis., DOI: 10.55982/openpraxis.16.1.654

Bretag, T. (2013). Challenges in addressing plagiarism in education. *PLoS Medicine, 10*(12), e1001574. DOI: 10.1371/journal.pmed.1001574 PMID: 24391477

Bretag, T. (2023). Academic integrity in the age of artificial intelligence. *International Journal for Educational Integrity, 19*(1), 1–3. DOI: 10.1007/s40979-015-0004-4

Bretag, T., Harper, R., Burton, M., Ellis, C., Newton, P., Rozenberg, P., Saddiqui, S., & van Haeringen, K. (2019). Contract cheating: A survey of Australian university students. *Studies in Higher Education, 44*(11), 1837–1856. DOI: 10.1080/03075079.2018.1462788

Broadfoot, P. (1996). *Education, assessment and society: A sociological analysis*. Open University Press.

Broadfoot, P. (2021). *The sociology of assessment: Comparative and policy perspectives: The selected works of Patricia Broadfoot*. Routledge. DOI: 10.4324/9780429262609

Brown, G., Bull, J., & Pendlebury, M. (2013). *Assessing student learning in higher education* (2nd ed.). Routledge. DOI: 10.4324/9781315004914

Brown, J. L. (2004). *Making the most of understanding by design*. ASCD.

Buckingham Shum, S., Ferguson, R., & Martinez-Maldonado, R. (2019). Human-centred learning analytics. *Journal of Learning Analytics, 6*(2), 1–9. DOI: 10.18608/jla.2019.62.1

Buele, J., & Llerena-Aguirre, L. (2025). Transformations in academic work and faculty perceptions of artificial intelligence in higher education. In *Frontiers in Education* (Vol. 10, p. 1603763). Frontiers Media SA. https://doi.org/DOI: 10.3389/feduc.2025.1603763

Bunney, D. (2017). Facilitating the transition to postgraduate studies: What can we learn from the First Year Experience? *Journal of Academic Language and Learning, 11*(1), A23–A38. https://journal.aall.org.au/index.php/jall/article/view/421

Buolamwini, J., & Gebru, T. (2018). Gender shades: Intersectional accuracy disparities in commercial gender classification. In *Conference on fairness, accountability and transparency* (pp. 77-91). PMLR. Available on https://proceedings.mlr.press/v81/buolamwini18a.html

Buolamwini, J., & Gebru, T. (2018). Gender shades: Intersectional accuracy disparities in commercial gender classification. *Proceedings of Machine Learning Research, 81*, 1–15.

Burrell, J. (2016). How the machine 'thinks': Understanding opacity in machine learning algorithms. *Big Data & Society, 3*(1), 1–12. DOI: 10.1177/2053951715622512

Butt, A. (2024). AI in education: Personalizing learning with intelligent systems. *Journal of AI Spectrum, 2*(1), 27–36.

Cabero-Almenara, J., Palacios-Rodríguez, A., Loaiza-Aguirre, M. I., & Andrade-Abarca, P. S. (2024). The impact of pedagogical beliefs on the adoption of generative AI in higher education: Predictive model from UTAUT2. *Frontiers in Artificial Intelligence, 7*, 1497705. Advance online publication. DOI: 10.3389/frai.2024.1497705 PMID: 39484153

Calo, R. (2017). Artificial intelligence policy: A primer and roadmap. *U.C. Davis Law Review, 51*(2), 399–435.

Carless, D. (2015). *Excellence in university assessment: Learning from award-winning practice*. Routledge., DOI: 10.4324/9781315740621

Carless, D., & Boud, D. (2018). The development of student feedback literacy: Enabling uptake of feedback. *Assessment & Evaluation in Higher Education, 43*(8), 1315–1325. DOI: 10.1080/02602938.2018.1463354

Carless, D., & Chan, K. K. H. (2023). Student perspectives on assessment feedback: Elaborating the conceptual framework of feedback literacy. *Studies in Higher Education*, *48*(1), 133–144. DOI: 10.1080/03075079.2022.2119655

Carless, D., & Winstone, N. (2023). Teacher feedback literacy and its interplay with student feedback literacy. *Teaching in Higher Education*, *28*(1), 150–163. DOI: 10.1080/13562517.2020.1782372

Chaka, C., Shange, T., Nkhobo, T., & Hlatshwayo, V. (2024). An environmental review of the generative artificial intelligence policies and guidelines of South African higher education institutions: A content analysis. *International Journal of Learning. Teaching and Educational Research*, *23*(12), 487–511. DOI: 10.26803/ijlter.23.12.25

Chan, C. K. Y. (2023). A comprehensive AI policy education framework for university teaching and learning. *International Journal of Educational Technology in Higher Education*, *20*(1), 38. Advance online publication. DOI: 10.1186/s41239-023-00408-3

Chan, C. K. Y., & Colloton, T. (2024). *Generative AI in higher education: The ChatGPT effect*. Routledge. DOI: 10.4324/9781003459026

Chan, C. K. Y., & Hu, W. (2023). Students' voices on generative AI: Perceptions, benefits, and challenges in higher education. *International Journal of Educational Technology in Higher Education*, *20*(1), 43. DOI: 10.1186/s41239-023-00411-8

Chan, C. K. Y., & Lee, K. K. W. (2023). The AI generation gap: Are Gen Z students more interested in adopting generative AI such as ChatGPT in teaching and learning than their Gen X and millennial generation teachers? *Smart Learning Environments*, *10*(1), 60. DOI: 10.1186/s40561-023-00269-3

Chand, V. S., Kostić, S., & Reis, A. (2020). Taxing Artificial Intelligence and Robots: Critical Assessment of Potential Policy Solutions and Recommendation for Alternative Approaches. *World Tax J.*, *12*(4). Advance online publication. DOI: 10.59403/2sjxe4d

Charles, T., & Alshamsi, A. (2025). Navigating challenges in technology integration for inclusive classrooms: Insights for pre-service teachers. In Ajani, O. A. (Ed.), *Empowering pre-service teachers to enhance inclusive education through technology* (pp. 87–126). IGI Global Scientific Publishing., DOI: 10.4018/979-8-3693-8759-7.ch004

Charles, T., & Hill, C. (Eds.). (2026). *Integrity, assessment, and collaboration in the AI classroom*. IGI Global Scientific Publishing., DOI: 10.4018/979-8-2600-0328-2

Charles, T., & Papadaki, M. (2025). Ethical leadership in technology integration and digital education. In Soles, B., & Meyerott, T. (Eds.), *Diverse leadership perspectives in education: From K–12 to higher education* (pp. 437–454). IGI Global Scientific Publishing., DOI: 10.4018/979-8-3693-6115-3.ch016

Chen, R., Wu, Y., Chen, Z., & Zhou, P. (2025). Advancing educational equity in rural China: The impact of AI devices on teaching quality and learning outcomes for sustainable development. *Frontiers in Psychology*, *16*, 1588047. Advance online publication. DOI: 10.3389/fpsyg.2025.1588047 PMID: 41267767

Chen, S.. (2025). Bridging the AI Adoption Gap: Designing an Interactive Pedagogical Agent for Higher Education Instructors. In Cristea, A. I., Walker, E., Lu, Y., Santos, O. C., & Isotani, S. (Eds.), Lecture Notes in Computer Science: Vol. 15881. *Artificial Intelligence in Education. AIED 2025.* Springer., DOI: 10.1007/978-3-031-98462-4_22

Chinhamo, E., Dzvapatsva, G. P., & Matobobo, C. (2026). Redefining postgraduate supervision in the age of AI: Balancing technology and human mentorship. In I. Kariyana & W. Sinkala (Eds.), *Artificial IntelligenceandPostgraduateSupervisioninHigherEducation* (pp. 38–54). ERRCD Forum. DOI: 10.38140/obp4-2026-03

Chkarka, F., & Fatmi, H. (2026). Comparative Examination of Master's Students' and Faculty Members' Maintenance of Academic Integrity in the Age of AI. *Journal of Academic Ethics*, *24*(1), 1–23. DOI: 10.1007/s10805-025-09684-2

Chukwu, C. O., Chukwu, J. C., & Odey, F. A. (2026). AI-Powered Learning Tools on Measurement of Student Engagement Across Academic Disciplines: Implications of Age and Gender. *Educational Point*, *3*(1), e144. DOI: 10.71176/edup/17782

Chu, T. S., & Ashraf, M. (2025). Artificial intelligence in curriculum design: A data-driven approach to higher education innovation. *Knowledge (Beverly Hills, Calif.)*, *5*(3), 14. DOI: 10.3390/knowledge5030014

Chu, X., Litifu, A., Zhu, Z., Ma, S., Zhou, Y., Gao, Q., Lei, L., & Wei, J. (2024). Supervisor's neuroticism and problematic Internet use among graduate students: The mediating role of supervisor-student relationship quality and the moderating role of fear of the supervisor's negative evaluation. *BMC Public Health*, *24*(1), 2238. DOI: 10.1186/s12889-024-19725-x PMID: 39154018

Coates, H., & Galán-Muros, V. (2019). *Performance measurement in universities: Learning from experience*. OECD Publishing.

Coghlan, S., Miller, T., & Paterson, J. (2021). Good proctor or "Big Brother"? Ethics of online exam proctoring in higher education. *Ethics and Information Technology*, *23*(3), 567–580. DOI: 10.1007/s10676-021-09576-1

Coghlan, S., Miller, T., & Paterson, J. (2021). Good proctor or "big brother"? Ethics of online exam supervision technologies. *Philosophy & Technology*, *34*(4), 1581–1606. DOI: 10.1007/s13347-021-00476-1 PMID: 34485025

Combrinck, C., & Loubser, N. (2025). Student self-reflection as a tool for managing GenAI use in large class assessment. *Discover Education, 4*(1), 72.| DOI: 10.1007/s44217-025-00461-2

Consumer Protection Act, 2019, No. 35, Acts of Parliament, India.

Cope, B., Kalantzis, M., & Searsmith, D. (2021). Artificial intelligence for education: Knowledge and its assessment in AI-enabled learning ecologies. *Educational Philosophy and Theory*, *53*(12), 1229–1245. Advance online publication. DOI: 10.1080/00131857.2020.1728732

Corcelles-Seuba, M., Suñe-Soler, N., Sala-Bubaré, A., & Castelló, M. (2023). Doctoral student perceptions of supervisory and research community support: Their relationships with doctoral conditions and experiences. *Journal of Further and Higher Education*, *47*(4), 481–491. DOI: 10.1080/0309877X.2022.2142102

Cotton, D. R., Cotton, P. A., & Shipway, J. R. (2024). Chatting and cheating: Ensuring academic integrity in the era of ChatGPT. *Innovations in Education and Teaching International*, *61*(2), 228–239. DOI: 10.1080/14703297.2023.2190148

Council on Higher Education. (2024). *VitalStats public higher education 2022*. Council on Higher Education.

Crawford, J., Cowling, M., & Allen, K. A. (2023). Leadership is needed for ethical ChatGPT: Character, assessment, and learning using artificial intelligence (AI). *Journal of University Teaching & Learning Practice, 20*(3), 02. DOI: 10.53761/1.20.3.02

Crenshaw, K. (1991). Mapping the margins: Intersectionality, identity politics, and violence against women of color. *Stanford Law Review*, *43*(6), 1241–1299. DOI: 10.2307/1229039

Crompton, H., & Burke, D. (2023). Artificial intelligence in higher education: The state of the field. *International Journal of Educational Technology in Higher Education*, *20*(1), 22. DOI: 10.1186/s41239-023-00392-8

Crossouard, B. (2008). Developing alternative models of doctoral supervision with online formative assessment. *Studies in Continuing Education*, *30*(1), 51–67. DOI: 10.1080/01580370701841549

Crosta, L., Edwards, A., & Reis-Jorge, J. (2024). The use of social media and artificial intelligence tools by online doctoral students: Skills needed and challenges. *GILE Journal of Skills Development*, *4*(2), 19–36. DOI: 10.52398/gjsd.2024.v4.i2.pp19-36

Cruvinel, L., Ascama, O. H., & Silva, M. M. (2026). *AI ethics in higher education: A review of ethical challenges*. Springer., DOI: 10.1007/978-3-032-01429-0_17

Cudjoe, E. K., & Adebayo, J. O. (2025). Investigating the Existence of AI Policy in Higher Education Institutions in Sub-Saharan Africa. *Proceedings of the Association for Information Science and Technology*, *62*(1), 1414–1417. DOI: 10.1002/pra2.1421

Cukurova, M., Luckin, R., & Kent, C. (2019). Impact of an artificial intelligence research frame on the perceived credibility of educational research evidence. *International Journal of Artificial Intelligence in Education*, *29*(4), 205–235. DOI: 10.1007/s40593-019-00182-x

Czerniewicz, L., Agherdien, N., Badenhorst, J., Belluigi, D., Chambers, T., Chili, M., de Villiers, M., Felix, A., Gachago, D., Gokhale, C., Ivala, E., Kramm, N., Madiba, M., Mistri, G., Mgqwashu, E., Pallitt, N., Prinsloo, P., Solomon, K., Strydom, S., & Wissing, G. (2020). A wake-up call: Equity, inequality and Covid-19 emergency remote teaching and learning. *Postdigital Science and Education*, *2*(3), 946–967. DOI: 10.1007/s42438-020-00187-4 PMID: 40477091

Czerniewicz, L., & Brown, C. (2013). The habitus of digital "strangers" in higher education. *British Journal of Educational Technology*, *44*(1), 44–53. DOI: 10.1111/j.1467-8535.2012.01281.x

Dai, K. (2026). Generative AI in higher education: A bibliometric review of the current landscape of research. Computers & Education. *Artificial Intelligence*, *8*, 100311. Advance online publication. DOI: 10.1016/j.caeai.2026.100311

Dai, Y., Lai, S., Lim, C. P., & Liu, A. (2023). ChatGPT and its impact on research supervision: Insights from Australian postgraduate research students. *Australasian Journal of Educational Technology*, *39*(4), 74–88. DOI: 10.14742/ajet.8843

Darmawan, A. H., & Azizah, S. (2020, January). Resistance to change: Causes and strategies as an organizational challenge. In *5th ASEAN conference on psychology, counselling, and humanities (ACPCH 2019)* (pp. 49–53). Atlantis Press. https://doi.org/DOI: 10.2991/assehr.k.200120.010

Darmawan, D., & Sabata, Y. N. (2025). Formative Assessment in Efl Classroom (A Bibliometric Analysis of Adopting Artificial Intelligence in Classroom-Based Assessment Practices). *BABASAL English Education Journal*, *6*(2), 147–159.

Data Protection Board of India. (2023). *Digital Personal Data Protection Act, 2023*. Government of India.

Davis, F. D. (1989). Perceived usefulness, perceived ease of use, and user acceptance of information technology. *Management Information Systems Quarterly*, *13*(3), 319–340. DOI: 10.2307/249008

Dawson, P. (2021). *Defending assessment security in a digital world: Preventing e-cheating and supporting academic integrity in higher education*. Routledge., DOI: 10.4324/9781003002970

Dawson, P. (2023). *ChatGPT and other AI chatbots: A threat or opportunity for academic integrity?* Centre for Academic Integrity., DOI: 10.5204/intechethics.v10i1.356

Dawson, P., Bearman, M., Bennett, S., Hall, M., Molloy, E., & Boud, D. (2023). Assessment reform for the age of artificial intelligence. *Assessment & Evaluation in Higher Education*, *48*(3), 357–370. DOI: 10.1080/02602938.2022.2130174

Dawson, P., Bearman, M., Boud, D. J., Hall, M., Molloy, E. K., Bennett, S., & Joughin, G. (2019). Assessment might be failing. Can we fix it? *Teaching in Higher Education*, *24*(3), 339–357. DOI: 10.1080/13562517.2018.1449742

Dawson, P., Bearman, M., Boud, D., Hall, M., & Molloy, E. (2020). Reframing assessment for a digital world. *Assessment & Evaluation in Higher Education*, *45*(4), 519–533. DOI: 10.1080/02602938.2019.1646270

Dawson, P., & Sutherland-Smith, W. (2018). Can markers detect contract cheating? Results from a pilot study. *Assessment & Evaluation in Higher Education*, *43*(2), 286–293. DOI: 10.1080/02602938.2017.1336746

Dawson, P., Sutherland-Smith, W., & Harris, B. (2019). Contract cheating, artificial intelligence and assessment design. *Assessment & Evaluation in Higher Education*, *44*(6), 847–857. DOI: 10.1080/02602938.2018.1527892

de Fine Licht, K. (2024). Generative artificial intelligence in higher education: Why the "banning approach" to student use is sometimes morally justified. *Philosophy & Technology*, *37*(3), 113. DOI: 10.1007/s13347-024-00799-9

Deepshikha, D. (2026). A systematic review on the future of educational assessment: AI-driven grading and personalised feedback in higher education. In *Artificial Intelligence in Education* (Vol. 2, No. 2, pp. 75-115). Emerald Publishing Limited.

Deepshikha, D. (2025). A comprehensive review of AI-powered grading and tailored feedback in universities. *Discover Artificial Intelligence*, *5*(1), 251. DOI: 10.1007/s44163-025-00517-0

Deneen, C. (2025). Artificial intelligence and educational assessment: Opportunities and threats. *Learning Letters*, *4*, 38–38. DOI: 10.59453/ll.v4.38

Dervić, M., Bećirović, S., & Polz, E. (2025). Revolutionizing Pedagogy: The Transformative Influence of Artificial Intelligence on Educators' Practices. In Adarkwah, M. A., Amponsah, S., Huang, R., & Thomas, M. (Eds.), *Artificial Intelligence and Human Agency in Education: Volume One. Future Education and Learning Spaces*. Springer., DOI: 10.1007/978-981-96-7937-9_9

Design-Based Research Collective. (2003). Design-based research: An emerging paradigm for educational inquiry. *Educational Researcher*, *32*(1), 5–8. DOI: 10.3102/0013189X032001005

Dhawan, S., & Batra, G. (2020). Artificial intelligence in higher education: Promises, perils, and perspective. Expanding Knowledge Horizon. OJAS, 11, 11–22. https://www.researchgate.net/publication/348910302_Artificial_Intelligence_in_Higher_Education_Promises_Perils_and_Perspective

Diallo, K., Smith, J. W., Okolo, C. T., Nyamwaya, D., Kgomo, J., & Ngamita, R. (2025). Case studies of AI policy development in Africa. *Data & Policy*, *7*, e15. Advance online publication. DOI: 10.1017/dap.2024.71

Diene, A. (2024). AI and equity in higher education. In *Advances in Computational Intelligence and Robotics Book Series* (pp. 1–12). DOI: 10.4018/979-8-3693-1565-1.ch001

Dignum, V. (2021). The role and challenges of education for responsible AI. *London Review of Education*, *19*(1). Advance online publication. DOI: 10.14324/lre.19.1.01

Dockens, A. L., & Shelton, K. (2025). AI for formative and summative assessment. In *Advances in Computational Intelligence and Robotics Book Series* (pp. 353–386). DOI: 10.4018/979-8-3373-5102-5.ch013

Dogan, S., Nalbantoglu, U. Y., Celik, I., & Agacli Dogan, N. (2025). Artificial intelligence professional development: A systematic review of TPACK, designs, and effects for teacher learning. *Professional Development in Education*, *51*(3), 519–546. DOI: 10.1080/19415257.2025.2454457

Dollinger, M., Lodge, J. M., & Coates, H. (2019). Co-creation in higher education: Towards a conceptual model. *Journal of Industry-University Collaboration*, *3*(1), 3–18. DOI: 10.1108/JIUC-01-2019-0003

Downey, G., & Gillett, A. J. (2023). Linguistic relativity in cross-cultural context: Converging evidence from neuroanthropology. *Topics in Cognitive Science*, *15*(4), 693–697. DOI: 10.1111/tops.12660 PMID: 37165535

Drinan, P. M., & Gallant, T. B. (2008). Plagiarism and academic integrity systems. *Journal of Library Administration*, *47*(3–4), 125–140. DOI: 10.1080/01930820802186472

Du Boulay, B. (2016). Artificial intelligence as an effective tool in education. *IEEE Intelligent Systems*, *31*(6), 76–81. DOI: 10.1109/MIS.2016.93

Dube, M. C. (2025). Sustaining a healthy supervisor-student relationship: Students speak. *Journal of Culture and Values in Education, 8*(2),26-43. [REMOVED HYPERLINK FIELD]DOI: 10.46303/jcve.2025.18

Duraes, D., Bezerra, R., & Novais, P. (2024). AI-driven educational transformation in secondary schools: Leveraging data insights for inclusive learning environments. In *Proceedings of the 2024 IEEE Global Engineering Education Conference (EDUCON)* (pp. 1–9). IEEE. DOI: 10.1109/EDUCON60312.2024.10578910

Dwivedi, Y. K., Kshetri, N., Hughes, L., Slade, E. L., Jeyaraj, A., Kar, A. K., Baabdullah, A. M., Koohang, A., Raghavan, V., Ahuja, M., Albanna, H., Albashrawi, M., Aljalil, M., Al-Nuaimi, B., Al-Zubaidi, F., Balakrishnan, J., Barlette, Y., Basu, S., Bose, I., & Wright, R. (2023). So what if ChatGPT wrote it? Multidisciplinary perspectives on opportunities, challenges and implications of generative conversational artificial intelligence for research, practice and policy. *International Journal of Information Management*, *71*, 102642. Advance online publication. DOI: 10.1016/j.ijinfomgt.2023.102642

Eaton, S. E. (2020). Academic integrity in online learning: What to do when students cheat. *Canadian Journal of Higher Education*, *50*(2), 1–14. DOI: 10.47678/cjhe.v50i2.188901

Eaton, S. E. (2021). *Academic integrity in Canada: An enduring and essential challenge*. Springer., DOI: 10.1007/978-3-030-83255-1

Eaton, S. E. (2023). Artificial intelligence and academic integrity: Striking a balance. *International Journal for Educational Integrity*, *19*(1), 1–8. DOI: 10.1007/s40979-023-00144-1

Eaton, S. E. (2023). *Plagiarism in higher education: Tackling tough topics in academic integrity*. Springer.

Eaton, S. E., & Turner, K. L. (2020). Exploring academic integrity and mental health during COVID-19: Rapid review. *Journal of Contemporary Education Theory & Research*, *4*(1), 35–41.

Eaton, S. E., & Turner, K. L. (2022). Exploring academic integrity and artificial intelligence in higher education. *International Journal for Educational Integrity*, *18*(1), 11. Advance online publication. DOI: 10.1007/s40979-022-00110-0

Edwards, L., & Veale, M. (2017). Slave to the algorithm? Why a "right to an explanation" is probably not the remedy you are looking for. *Duke Law & Technology Review*, *16*(1), 18–84. DOI: 10.31228/osf.io/97upg

Elshall, A. S., & Badir, A. (2025). Balancing AI-assisted learning and traditional assessment: The FACT assessment in environmental data science education. *Frontiers in Education*, *10*, 1596462. Advance online publication. DOI: 10.3389/feduc.2025.1596462

Entschew, E. M. (2024). Discriminatory data yields discriminatory systems: When AI biases harm human beings. In *Edward Elgar Publishing eBooks* (pp. 37–65). DOI: 10.4337/9781803928241.00009

Eraut, M. (2000). Non-formal learning, implicit learning and tacit knowledge in professional work. *The British Journal of Educational Psychology*, *70*(1), 113–136. DOI: 10.1348/000709900158001 PMID: 10765570

Es-sarghini, A., & Boumahdi, A. (2026). Introducing sentinel assessment: An AI-powered approach for evaluating writing competence in French as a Foreign Language. *Language Education & Assessment*, *9*, 103686–103686. DOI: 10.29140/lea.v9.103686

Eubanks, V. (2018). *Automating inequality: How high-tech tools profile, police, and punish the poor*. St. Martin's Press.

European Commission. (2021). *Proposal for a regulation laying down harmonised rules on artificial intelligence*. Artificial Intelligence Act.

Ezeh, C. C., & Kehinde, O. J. (2026). Promising practices for culturally relevant assessment: A systematic review. *Diaspora, Indigenous, and Minority Education, 20*(1), 53–69. DOI: 10.1080/15595692.2024.2341930

Ezennia, J. C., Matiyenga, T. C., & Mokoena, S. (2024). Students: A Vital Agent and Voice Towards Curriculum Transformation. *Educational Administration: Theory and Practice, 30*(11), 469–476.

Fadlelmula, F. K., & Qadhi, S. M. (2024). A systematic review of research on artificial intelligence in higher education: Practice, gaps, and future directions in the GCC. *Journal of University Teaching & Learning Practice, 21*(6), 146–173. DOI: 10.53761/pswgbw82

Fakokunde, A. (2025). Ethics, privacy, and transparency in AI-assisted teaching: Evaluating NoteGrade. ai against global standards. *Preprints.org*. DOI: 10.20944/preprints202509.1148.v1

Fakunle, S. O., Okunola, J. L., & Ajani, B. K. (2023). Technological Advancement, Globalization, and Developing Countries. In *The Palgrave Handbook of Global Social Change*. Palgrave Macmillan., DOI: 10.1007/978-3-030-87624-1_160-1

Falchikov, N., & Boud, D. (2007). The role of assessment in preparing for lifelong learning: Problems and challenges. In *Research Gate* (pp. 97–110). DOI: 10.4324/9780203942185-14

Farazouli, A., Cerratto-Pargman, T., Bolander-Laksov, K., & McGrath, C. (2024). Hello GPT! Goodbye home examination? An exploratory study of AI chatbots' impact on university teachers' assessment practices. *Assessment & Evaluation in Higher Education, 49*(3), 363–375. DOI: 10.1080/02602938.2023.2241676

Farooqi, S. A. (2025). Ethical framework for AI in education. In *Advances in Computational Intelligence and Robotics Book Series* (pp. 153–188). DOI: 10.4018/979-8-3373-5550-4.ch007

Felder, R. M., & Brent, R. (2016). *Teaching and learning STEM: A practical guide*. Jossey-Bass.

Felipe, A. L., Khwakhali, U. S., & Nguyen, T. N. (2025, July). A Framework for Assessment Design in the Era of Generative AI: Case Study of Take-Home Assignment in Software-related Courses. In *2025 10th International STEM Education Conference (iSTEM-Ed)* (pp. 1-6). IEEE.

Felten, E., Raj, M., & Seamans, R. (2019). The variable impact of artificial intelligence on labor: The role of complementary skills and technologies. *Proceedings - Academy of Management, 2019*(1), 11925. DOI: 10.5465/AMBPP.2019.11925abstract

Fischer, I. (2024). Making sense of generative AI for assessments: Student engagement and learning implications. *Teaching in Higher Education, 29*(4), 456–472. DOI: 10.1080/13562517.2024.15226x

Fishman, T. (Ed.). (2016). *The fundamental values of academic integrity* (3rd ed.). International Center for Academic Integrity.

Fisk, G. D. (2024). AI or human? Finding and responding to artificial intelligence in student work. *Teaching of Psychology, 52*(3), 314–318. DOI: 10.1177/00986283241251855

Floridi, L., & Cowls, J. (2022). A unified framework of five principles for AI in society. *Machine learning and the city: Applications in architecture and urban design*, 535-545. https://doi.org/DOI: 10.1002/9781119815075

Floridi, L., Cowls, J., Beltrametti, M., Chatila, R., Chazerand, P., Dignum, V., Luetge, C., Madelin, R., Pagallo, U., Rossi, F., Schafer, B., Valcke, P., & Vayena, E. (2018). AI4People An ethical framework for a good AI society: Opportunities, risks, principles, and recommendations. *Minds and Machines*, *28*(4), 689–707. DOI: 10.1007/s11023-018-9482-5 PMID: 30930541

Fortuna, A., Prasetya, F., Samala, A. D., Rawas, S., Criollo-C, S., Kaya, D., Raihan, M., Andriani, W., Safitri, D., & Nabawi, R. A. (2025). Artificial intelligence in personalized learning: A global systematic review of current advancements and shaping future opportunities. *Social Sciences & Humanities Open*, *12*, 102114. DOI: 10.1016/j.ssaho.2025.102114

Foucault, M. (1977). *Discipline and punish: The birth of the prison*. Pantheon Books.

Foung, D., Lin, L., & Chen, J. (2024). Reinventing assessments with ChatGPT and other online tools: Opportunities for GenAI-empowered assessment practices. *Computers and Education: Artificial Intelligence*, *6*, 100250. Advance online publication. DOI: 10.1016/j.caeai.2024.100250

Friesen, S., Becker, S., & Jacobsen, M. (2022). Online doctoral student-supervisory relationships: Exploring relational trust. In Jacobsen, M., & Smith, C. (Eds.), *Online learning and teaching from kindergarten to graduate school* (pp. 282–306). Canadian Association for Teacher Education. [REMOVED HYPERLINK FIELD], DOI: 10.11575/PRISM/40509

Fuchs, K. (2023). Exploring the opportunities and challenges of NLP models in higher education: Is ChatGPT a blessing or a curse? *Frontiers in Education*, *8*, 1166682. DOI: 10.3389/feduc.2023.1166682

Funda, V., & Piderit, R. (2024, March). A review of the application of artificial intelligence in South African Higher Education. In *2024 Conference on Information Communications Technology and Society (ICTAS)* (pp. 44-50). IEEE. DOI: 10.1109/ICTAS59620.2024.10507113

Furze, L., Perkins, M., Roe, J., & MacVaugh, J. (2024). The AI Assessment Scale (AIAS) in action: A pilot implementation of GenAI-supported assessment. *Australasian Journal of Educational Technology*, *40*(4), 38–55. DOI: 10.14742/ajet.9434

Gamage, K. A., Dehideniya, S. C., Xu, Z., & Tang, X. (2023). ChatGPT and higher education assessments: More opportunities than concerns? *Journal of Applied Learning & Teaching*, *6*(2), 358–369.

García-López, I. M., & Trujillo-Liñán, L. (2025). Ethical and regulatory challenges of generative AI in education: A systematic review. *Frontiers in Education*, *10*(2), 115–130. DOI: 10.3389/feduc.2025.1565938

García, O., & Wei, L. (2014). *Translanguaging: Language, bilingualism and education*. Palgrave Macmillan., DOI: 10.1057/9781137385765

Gautam, D. A. S. (2024). Impact of National Assessment and Accreditation Council (NAAC) on Higher Education Institutions (HEIs) in India. *International Journal of All Research Education and Scientific Methods*, *12*(8). Advance online publication. DOI: 10.2139/ssrn.4932646

Gay, G. (2018). *Culturally responsive teaching: Theory, research, and practice* (3rd ed.). Teachers College Press.

Gefen, D., Karahanna, E., & Straub, D. W. (2003). Trust and TAM in online shopping: An integrated model. *Management Information Systems Quarterly*, *27*(1), 51–90. DOI: 10.2307/30036519

Gilliard, C., & Culik, A. (2016). Digital redlining, access, and privacy. *Journal of Information Ethics*, *25*(2), 24–36.

Gilliot, J.-M., & Hénaff, P. (2021). Surveillance technologies and academic integrity: A critical analysis of online proctoring systems. *European Journal of Open. Distance and E-Learning*, *24*(1), 1–14.

Gnambs, T., Stein, J. P., Appel, M., Griese, F., & Zinn, S. (2025). An economical measure of attitudes towards artificial intelligence in work, healthcare, and education (ATTARI-WHE). *Computers in Human Behavior: Artificial Humans*, *3*, 100106. DOI: 10.1016/j.chbah.2024.100106

Gnanaprakasam, J., & Lourdusamy, R. (2024). The role of AI in automating grading: Enhancing feedback and efficiency. In *Artificial intelligence*. DOI: 10.5772/intechopen.1005025

González-Calatayud, V., Prendes-Espinosa, P., & Roig-Vila, R. (2021). Artificial intelligence for student assessment: A systematic review. *Applied Sciences (Basel, Switzerland)*, *11*(12), 5467. DOI: 10.3390/app11125467

Government of India. (2020). National [Ministry of Education.]. *Educational Policy*, •••, 2020.

Gravett, K., & Ajjawi, R. (2022). Belonging as situated practice. *Studies in Higher Education*, *47*(7), 1386–1396. DOI: 10.1080/03075079.2021.1894118

Green, B. (2021). Data science as political action: Grounding data science in a politics of justice. MIT Press. DOI: 10.23919/JSC.2021.0029

Grønset, T. L., Eide, L., & Kvam, E. K. (2025). The role of assessment in teachers' curriculum making: Insights from Norwegian history teachers. *Curriculum Journal.*

Gryshko, S., Terziyan, V., & Golovianko, M. (2025). Resilience Training in Higher Education: AI-Assisted Collaborative Learning. In Auer, M. E., & Rüütmann, T. (Eds.), *Futureproofing Engineering Education for Global Responsibility. ICL 2024. Lecture Notes in Networks and Systems* (Vol. 1281). Springer., DOI: 10.1007/978-3-031-83520-9_12

Gu, J., Chen, J., & Yan, Z. (2026). Fostering feedback literacy by scaffolding self-regulated feedback: A comparative study of GenAI and human peers. *Frontiers in Education*, *10*, 1736446. Advance online publication. DOI: 10.3389/feduc.2025.1736446

Halse, C., & Malfroy, J. (2010). Retheorizing doctoral supervision as professional work. *Studies in Higher Education*, *35*(1), 79–92. DOI: 10.1080/03075070902906798

Han, B., Nawaz, S., Buchanan, G., & McKay, D. (2023). Ethical and pedagogical impacts of AI in education. In *Lecture Notes in Computer Science* (pp. 667–673). DOI: 10.1007/978-3-031-36272-9_54

Han, J., & Jin, L. (2025). Reconceptualizing supervisory relationships in graduate education: The role of interpersonal emotion regulation in supervisor-student interactions. *International Journal of Educational Research, 132*, 102650. DOI: 10.1016/j.ijer.2025.102650

Hassan, Z. Y. (2025). AI-Driven Horizons: Shaping the Future of Global Quality Assurance in Higher Education. *AI and Ethics, Academic Integrity and the Future of Quality Assurance in Higher Education*, 105.

Henderson, M. (2025). Comparing generative AI and teacher feedback: Complementary roles in higher education assessment. *Journal of Learning Analytics, 12*(1), 144–158. DOI: 10.18608/jla.2025.12212

Heng, T. T. (2018). Different is not deficient: Contradicting stereotypes of Chinese international students in US higher education. *Studies in Higher Education, 43*(1), 22–36. DOI: 10.1080/03075079.2016.1152466

Hidson, E. (2024). Participants' perceptions of video-enhanced dialogic assessment as reflective practice in international teacher education. *European Journal of Teacher Education, 47*(2), 204–225. DOI: 10.1080/02619768.2024.2338847

Hinojo-Lucena, F. J., Aznar-Díaz, I., Cáceres-Reche, M. P., & Romero-Rodríguez, J. M. (2019). Artificial intelligence in higher education: A bibliometric study on its impact in the scientific literature. *Education Sciences, 9*(1), 51. DOI: 10.3390/educsci9010051

Hoffman, J. C. (2009). *The academic transitional experience of postgraduate students in the Faculty of Community and Health Sciences at the University of the Western Cape* (Doctoral dissertation, University of the Western Cape).

Hoffman, J. C., & Julie, H. (2012). The academic transitional experiences of master's students at the University of the Western Cape. *Curationis, 35*(1), 1-8. [REMOVED HYPERLINK FIELD]DOI: 10.4102/curationis.v35i1.33

Holmes, W., Bialik, M., & Fadel, C. (2019). *Artificial intelligence in education promises and implications for teaching and learning*. Center for Curriculum Redesign. https://discovery.ucl.ac.uk/id/eprint/10139722

Holmes, W., Bialik, M., & Fadel, C. (2019). *Artificial intelligence in education promises and implications for teaching and learning*. Center for Curriculum Redesign. https://discovery.ucl.ac.uk/id/eprint/10139722/

Holmes, W., Bialik, M., & Fadel, C. (2019). *Artificial intelligence in education: Promises and implications for teaching and learning*. Center for Curriculum Redesign.

Holmes, W., Bialik, M., & Fadel, C. (2019). *The ethics of AI in education: Promises and risks*. Center for Curriculum Redesign.

Holmes, W., Persson, J., Chounta, I. A., Wasson, B., & Dimitrova, V. (2022). *Artificial intelligence and education: A critical view through the lens of human rights, democracy and the rule of law*. Council of Europe Publishing., DOI: 10.1007/978-3-031-32883-1_1

Holmes, W., & Porayska-Pomsta, K. (2022). *The ethics of artificial intelligence in education: Practices, challenges, and debates*. Routledge., DOI: 10.4324/9780429329067

Holmner, M., Hirsh, S., Meyer, A., Mierzecka, A., & Rorissa, A. (2025). The future of academic writing in the age of generative AI. *Proceedings of the Association for Information Science and Technology*, *62*(1), 1241–1243. DOI: 10.1002/pra2.1374

Hook, J., Junor, A., Sell, C., & Sapsed, C. (2024). Navigating integrity and innovation. In *ASCILITE Publications* (pp. 165–172). DOI: 10.14742/apubs.2024.1234

Hopfenbeck, T. N., Zhang, Z., Sun, S. Z., Robertson, P., & McGrane, J. A. (2023). Challenges and opportunities for classroom-based formative assessment and AI: A perspective article. *Frontiers in Education*, *8*, 1270700. Advance online publication. DOI: 10.3389/feduc.2023.1270700

Hu, J., & Lee, P. G. (2023). Designing authentic assessment tasks for EFL courses. In *SHS Web of Conferences* (Vol. 168, p. 01025). EDP Sciences. DOI: 10.1051/shsconf/202316801025

Hutson, J. (2024). Rethinking plagiarism in the era of generative AI. *Journal of International Communication*, *3*(2). Advance online publication. DOI: 10.54963/jic.v3i2.220

Hutson, J., Jeevanjee, T., Graaf, V. V., Lively, J., Weber, J., Weir, G., Arnone, K., Carnes, G., Vosevich, K., Plate, D., Leary, M., & Edele, S. (2022). Artificial intelligence and the disruption of higher education: Strategies for integrations across disciplines. *Creative Education*, *13*(12), 3953–3980. DOI: 10.4236/ce.2022.1312253

Hu, Y., Xu, Y., & Wu, B. (2025). A dual-pathway model of teacher-AI collaboration based on the job demands-resources theory. *Education and Information Technologies*, *30*(11), 15125–15146. DOI: 10.1007/s10639-025-13421-y

IFEDAYO, A. E. (2025). A CRITICAL ANALYSIS OF AI-POWERED MOBILE LEARNING SYSTEMS FOR ENHANCED EDUCATIONAL OUTCOMES IN NIGERIAN UNIVERSITIES. *International Journal of Library Science and Educational Research*. DOI: 10.70382/caijlser.v9i8.042

Ifenthaler, D., & Schumacher, C. (2016). Student perceptions of privacy principles for learning analytics. *Educational Technology Research and Development*, *64*(5), 923–938. DOI: 10.1007/s11423-016-9477-y

Ifenthaler, D., & Yau, J. Y. K. (2020). Utilising learning analytics to support study success in higher education: A systematic review. *Educational Technology Research and Development*, *68*(4), 1961–1990. DOI: 10.1007/s11423-020-09788-z

Ilieva, G., Yankova, T., Ruseva, M., & Kabaivanov, S. (2025). A framework for generative AI-driven assessment in higher education. *Information (Basel)*, *16*(6), 472. DOI: 10.3390/info16060472

Ilieva, G., Yankova, T., Ruseva, M., & Kabaivanov, S. (2025). A framework for generative AI-driven assessment in higher education. *Preprints.org*. DOI: 10.20944/preprints202505.0800.v1

Information Technology Act, 2000, No. 21, Acts of Parliament, India.

Instruments, O. L. (2019). *Recommendation of the council on artificial intelligence*. Organization for Economic Cooperation and Development.

Isaifan, R. J., Tawalbeh, A., & Hasna, M. O. (2025, October). From principles to practice: a novel matrix for evaluating AI-powered learning platforms based on the UNESCO Ethical Impact Assessment tool. In *Frontiers in Education* (Vol. 10, p. 1640780). Frontiers Media SA. https://doi:DOI: 10.3389/feduc.2025.1640780

Issaka, S., Wang, K., Ajibola, Y., Samuel-Ipaye, O., Zhang, Z., Jimenez, N. A., . . . Gabriel, S. (2025). The African Languages Lab: A Collaborative Approach to Advancing Low-Resource African NLP. *arXiv preprint arXiv:2510.05644*.

Jaakkola, E. (2020). Designing conceptual articles: Four approaches. *AMS Review*, *10*(1-2), 18–26. DOI: 10.1007/s13162-020-00161-0

Jabareen, Y. (2009). Building a conceptual framework: Philosophy, definitions, and procedure. *International Journal of Qualitative Methods*, *8*(4), 49–62. DOI: 10.1177/160940690900800406

Jackson, S., & Panteli, N. (2022). Trust or mistrust in algorithmic grading? An embedded agency perspective. *International Journal of Information Management*, *69*, 102555. DOI: 10.1016/j.ijinfomgt.2022.102555

Jafar, S. H., Oyedele, O. M., Nawaah, D., & Bolanle, A. S. (2025). Exploring Leadership Challenges for Adoption of Digital Innovation and Sustainability, Singh, R., Corvello, V., Coniglio, I.M. and Khan, S. (Ed.) *Innovation Ecosystems and Sustainable Technologies* (*Emerald Studies in Sustainable Innovation Management*), Emerald Publishing Limited, Leeds, pp. 253-269. DOI: 10.1108/978-1-83662-368-720251012

Jaldemark, J., Lundin, J., Säljö, R., Edwards, J., Gegenfurtner, A., Holmes, W., Järvelä, S., de Laat, M., Lindberg, Y., Littlejohn, A., Seufert, S., Specht, M., Svensson, L., Rapanta, C., Hayes, S., & Zeivots, S. (2025). A multidisciplinary research agenda for artificial intelligence, education, learning, and instruction. *Postdigital Science and Education*, *7*(4), 1414–1450. DOI: 10.1007/s42438-025-00602-8

Jin, Y., Yan, L., Echeverria, V., Gašević, D., & Martinez-Maldonado, R. (2025). Generative AI in higher education: A global perspective of institutional adoption policies and guidelines. *Computers and Education: Artificial Intelligence*, *8*, 100348. Advance online publication. DOI: 10.1016/j.caeai.2024.100348

Joshi, P., Santy, S., Budhiraja, A., Bali, K., & Choudhury, M. (2020). The state and fate of linguistic diversity and inclusion in the NLP world. *Proceedings of the 58th Annual Meeting of the Association for Computational Linguistics*, 6282-6293. DOI: 10.18653/v1/2020.acl-main.560

Joshi, R. D., Dhakal, C. K., & Pradhan, D. C. (2021). Addressing educational inequalities in the Global South through open and distance learning. *Asian Association of Open Universities Journal*, *16*(2), 201–215. DOI: 10.1108/AAOUJ-02-2021-0029

Jurāne-Brēmane, A. (2023). Digital assessment in technology-enriched education: Thematic review. *Education Sciences*, *13*(5), 522. DOI: 10.3390/educsci13050522

Kahn, L., Everington, L., Kelm, K., Reid, I., & Watkins, F. (2022). Proctoring anxiety and digital surveillance in higher education. *Computers and Education Open*, *3*, 100068. DOI: 10.1016/j.caeo.2022.100068

Kaminski, M. E. (2019). The right to explanation, explained. *Berkeley Technology Law Journal*, *34*(1), 189–218. DOI: 10.15779/Z38TD9N83K

Kandlbinder, P. (2025). Signature concepts of authentic assessment. *Higher Education Research & Development*, *44*(4), 946–960. DOI: 10.1080/07294360.2024.2442613

Karamoko, I., & Naounou, A. (2026). Interactions Between English and Bambara in the Learning Process: Towards a Didactics of Complexity. *Language Policy in Africa, 2*(1).

Kasneci, E., Seßler, K., Küchemann, S., Bannert, M., Dementieva, D., Fischer, F., Gasser, U., Groh, G., Günnemann, S., Hüllermeier, E., Krusche, S., Kutyniok, G., Michaeli, T., Nerdel, C., Pfeffer, J., Poquet, O., Sailer, M., Schmidt, A., Seidel, T., & Kasneci, G. (2023). ChatGPT for good? On opportunities and challenges of large language models for education. *Learning and Individual Differences*, *103*, 102274. DOI: 10.1016/j.lindif.2023.102274

Kayyali, M. (2025). AI in higher education. In *IGI Global* (pp. 57–82). DOI: 10.4018/979-8-3373-2685-6.ch003

Keet, C. M., Alberts, R., Gerber, A., & Chimamiwa, G. (2017). Enhancing web portals with ontology-based data access: The case study of South Africa's accessibility portal for people with disabilities. *OTM Confederated International Conferences*. Springer. DOI: 10.1007/978-3-319-69459-7_36

Kerr, I., & Earle, J. (2022). Prediction, preemption, and policy: Artificial intelligence and the challenges of accountability. *Law, Innovation and Technology*, *14*(1), 1–26. DOI: 10.1080/17579961.2022.2036955

Ketere, C. (2025). Decolonizing Artificial Intelligence: Reducing Algorithmic Biases in African Educational and Linguistic Contexts. *Journal of Contemporary Issues in Open Distance and E-Learning*, *2*(1), 18–37. DOI: 10.71060/7qk9nd52

Ketonen, L., Körkkö, M., & Pöysä, S. (2025). Authentic assessment as a support for student teachers' reflection. *European Journal of Teacher Education*, *48*(3), 467–488. DOI: 10.1080/02619768.2023.2229004

Khasawneh, M. A. S., & Khasawneh, Y. J. A. (2023). *Achieving assessment equity and fairness: Identifying and eliminating bias in assessment tools and practices.*

Khatri, B. B., & Karki, P. D. (2023). Artificial intelligence (AI) in higher education: Growing academic integrity and ethical concerns. *Nepalese Journal of Development and Rural Studies*, *20*(01), 1–7. DOI: 10.3126/njdrs.v20i01.64134

Khlaif, Z. N., Alkouk, W. A., Salama, N., & Abu Eideh, B. (2025). Redesigning assessments for AI-enhanced learning: A framework for educators in the generative AI era. *Education Sciences*, *15*(2), 174. DOI: 10.3390/educsci15020174

Khoalenyane, N. B., & Ajani, O. A. (2024). A systematic review of artificial intelligence in higher education, South Africa. *Social Sciences and Education Research Review*, *11*(1), 17–26.

Kickbusch, S., Ashford-Rowe, K., Kemp, A., Boreland, J., & Huijser, H. (2025). Beyond detection: Redesigning authentic assessment in an AI-mediated world. *Education Sciences*, *15*(11), 1537. DOI: 10.3390/educsci15111537

Kipling, R. P., Stiles, W. A. V., de Andrade-Lima, M., MacKintosh, N., Roberts, M. W., Williams, C. L., Wootton-Beard, P. C., & Watson-Jones, S. J. (2023). Interaction in online postgraduate learning: What makes a good forum? *Distance Education*, *44*(1), 162–189. DOI: 10.1080/01587919.2022.2150391

Kirange, D. Y., & Chaudhari, Y. N. (2025). A review of data-driven decision-making approaches in curriculum design. *International Journal of Innovative Research in Engineering, 26–29*. Advance online publication. DOI: 10.59256/ijire.20250604004

Kirk, M., & Lipscombe, K. (2019). When a postgraduate student becomes a novice researcher and a supervisor becomes a mentor: A journey of research identity development. *Studying Teacher Education, 15*(2), 179–197. DOI: 10.1080/17425964.2019.1587606

Kitchin, R. (2017). Thinking critically about and researching algorithms. *Information Communication and Society, 20*(1), 14–29. DOI: 10.1080/1369118X.2016.1154087

Kizilcec, R. F., Huber, E., Papanastasiou, E. C., Cram, A., Makridis, C. A., Smolansky, A., Zeivots, S., & Raduescu, C. (2024). Perceived impact of generative AI on assessments: Comparing educator and student perspectives in Australia, Cyprus, and the United States. Computers & Education. *Artificial Intelligence, 7*, 100269. DOI: 10.1016/j.caeai.2024.100269

Kizilcec, R. F., & Lee, H. (2022). Algorithmic fairness in education. *Educational Psychologist, 57*(1), 1–15. DOI: 10.1080/00461520.2021.1971742

Kizilcec, R. F., & Lee, H. (2022). Algorithmic fairness in education. In *The ethics of artificial intelligence in education* (pp. 174–202). Routledge., DOI: 10.4324/9780429329067-10

Klinger, D. A., DeLuca, C., & Miller, T. (2015). The evolving culture of assessment. *Assessment in Education: Principles, Policy & Practice, 22*(4), 395–411.

Knight, P. T. (2001). *A briefing on key concepts: Formative and summative, criterion and norm-referenced assessment. Assessment Series*. Learning and Teaching Support Network.

Knight, S. (2022). Building, understanding and using trust in learning analytics: Introducing the BUILD-LAT project. *Journal of Learning Analytics, 9*(3), 1–6. DOI: 10.18608/jla.2016.33.1

Köbis, N., & Mossink, L. D. (2021). Artificial intelligence versus human decision-making: Accountability and responsibility in AI systems. *AI & Society, 36*(3), 747–755. DOI: 10.1007/s00146-020-01039-x

Kolade, O., Owoseni, A., & Egbetokun, A. (2024). Is AI changing learning and assessment as we know it? Evidence from a ChatGPT experiment and a conceptual framework. *Heliyon, 10*(4), e25953. Advance online publication. DOI: 10.1016/j.heliyon.2024.e25953 PMID: 38379960

Kong, X., Fang, H., Chen, W., Xiao, J., & Zhang, M. (2025). Examining human–AI collaboration in hybrid intelligence learning environments: Insight from the Synergy Degree Model. *Humanities & Social Sciences Communications, 12*(1), 821. DOI: 10.1057/s41599-025-05097-z

Kotsiantis, S., Zaharakis, I., & Pintelas, P. (2004). Machine learning: A review of classification and combining techniques. *Artificial Intelligence Review, 26*(3), 159–190. DOI: 10.1007/s10462-007-9052-3

Ku, A. Y., & Hool, A. (2024). Capabilities and limitations of AI Large Language Models (LLMs) for materials criticality research: AY Ku and A. Hool. *Mineral Economics*, •••, 1–9.

Kuleto, V., Ilić, M., Dumangiu, M., Ranković, M., Martins, O. M., Păun, D., & Mihoreanu, L. (2021). Exploring opportunities and challenges of artificial intelligence and machine learning in higher education institutions. *Sustainability (Basel), 13*(18), 10424. DOI: 10.3390/su131810424

Kumar, A. B., & Sanjaya, K. (2025). AI and social justice. In *Advances in Social Networking and Online Communities Book Series* (pp. 163–190). DOI: 10.4018/979-8-3693-9904-0.ch008

Kumar, R. (2024). Beyond reproach: Navigating usage, detection, and future pathways of AI in education. *Brock Education Journal, 33*(3). Advance online publication. DOI: 10.26522/brocked.v33i3.1173

Kundu, A., & Bej, T. (2025). Empowering Students' Autonomy in EFL Learning: AI Innovations in Schools of the Global South. *The Electronic Journal on Information Systems in Developing Countries, 91*(6), e70041. Advance online publication. DOI: 10.1002/isd2.70041

Kurtz, G., Amzalag, M., Shaked, N., Zaguri, Y., Kohen-Vacs, D., Gal, E., Zailer, G., & Barak-Medina, E. (2024). Strategies for integrating generative AI into higher education: Navigating challenges and leveraging opportunities. *Education Sciences, 14*(5), 503. DOI: 10.3390/educsci14050503

Kutsyuruba, B. (2021). The role of trust in doctoral student-supervisor relationships in Canadian universities: The students' lived experiences and perspectives. *Journal of Higher Education Theory and Practice, 21*(2), 125.

LaFrance, J. (2025). The power and perils of AI-driven assessment in higher education. In *Advances in Computational Intelligence and Robotics Book Series* (pp. 267–296). DOI: 10.4018/979-8-3693-7873-1.ch010

Lahusen, C., Maggetti, M., & Slavkovik, M. (2024). Trust, trustworthiness and AI governance. *Scientific Reports, 14*(1), 20752. DOI: 10.1038/s41598-024-71761-0 PMID: 39237635

Lancaster, T., & Clarke, R. (2016). Contract cheating: The outsourcing of assessed student work. *Handbook of academic integrity*, 639-654. https://doi.org/DOI: 10.1007/978-981-287-098-8_17

Lancaster, T. (2023). AI tools that can write code: Challenges for academic integrity in computing education. *ACM Inroads, 14*(2), 30–35. DOI: 10.1145/3597095

Lancaster, T., & Cotarlan, C. (2021). Contract cheating by STEM students through a file sharing website: A COVID-19 pandemic perspective. *International Journal for Educational Integrity, 17*(1), 1–16. DOI: 10.1007/s40979-021-00070-0

Landers, R. N. (2019). Gamified learning in educational settings. *Journal of Educational Psychology, 111*(8), 1167–1176.

Lanteigne, B., Brown, J. D., & Coombe, C. (2021). *Challenges in language testing around the world.* Springer Singapore. DOI: 10.1007/978-981-33-4232-3

Le Grange, L. (2016). Decolonising the university curriculum. *South African Journal of Higher Education, 30*(2), 1–12. DOI: 10.20853/30-2-709

Lee, T., Lee, S., & Kim, S. (2025). Beyond Static Scoring: Enhancing Assessment Validity via AI-Generated Interactive Verification. *arXiv preprint arXiv:2512.12592.*

Lee, A. (2019). *Successful research supervision: Advising students doing research* (2nd ed.). Routledge., DOI: 10.4324/9781351234986

Lee, A., Jere, A., Du Plessis, L., Van Gerven, P. W., Heeneman, S., & Ross, S. (2025). Continuity of supervision: Balancing continuous and episodic relationships for assessment and learning. *Medical Education, 59*(6), 596–605. DOI: 10.1111/medu.15595 PMID: 39697042

Lee, A., & Murray, R. (2015). Supervising writing: Helping postgraduate students develop as researchers. *Innovations in Education and Teaching International, 52*(5), 558–570. DOI: 10.1080/14703297.2013.866329

Lee, D., Arnold, M., Srivastava, A., Plastow, K., Strelan, P., Ploeckl, F., Lekkas, D., & Palmer, E. (2024). The impact of generative AI on higher education learning and teaching: A study of educators' perspectives. Computers & Education. *Artificial Intelligence, 6*, 100221. DOI: 10.1016/j.caeai.2024.100221

Lee, G. G., Mun, S., Shin, M. K., & Zhai, X. (2025). Collaborative learning with artificial intelligence speakers: Pre-service elementary science teachers' responses to the prototype. *Science & Education, 34*(2), 847–875. DOI: 10.1007/s11191-024-00526-y

Lee, S., Choe, H., Zou, D., & Jeon, J. (2026). Generative AI (GenAI) in the language classroom: A systematic review. *Interactive Learning Environments, 34*(1), 335–359. DOI: 10.1080/10494820.2025.2498537

Lee, V. R., Pope, D., Miles, S., & Zárate, R. C. (2024). Cheating in the age of generative AI: A high school survey study of cheating behaviors before and after the release of ChatGPT. *Computers and Education: Artificial Intelligence, 7*, 100253. DOI: 10.1016/j.caeai.2024.100253

Lestari, L. (2021). The Effect of Implementing Authentic Assessment on Student Learning Activities and Outcomes. *Tekno-Pedagogi: Jurnal Teknologi Pendidikan, 11*(1), 14–19. DOI: 10.22437/teknopedagogi.v11i1.32705

Li, C., Zhao, C., Wang, Y., & Hua, Y. (2026). How should AI knowledge be governed? Epistemic authority, structural transparency, and the case for open cognitive graphs. *arXiv preprint arXiv:2602.16949.*

Liang, W., Yuksekgonul, M., Mao, Y., Wu, E., & Zou, J. (2023). GPT detectors are biased against non-native English writers. *Patterns (New York, N.Y.), 4*(7), 100779. DOI: 10.1016/j.patter.2023.100779 PMID: 37521038

Liao, L., Ye, S. X., & Yang, J. (2023). A mini review of communicative language testing. *Frontiers in Psychology, 14*, 1058411. DOI: 10.3389/fpsyg.2023.1058411 PMID: 37089727

Lillis, T., & Curry, M. J. (2010). *Academic writing in a global context: The politics and practices of publishing in English.* Routledge., DOI: 10.4324/9780203852217

Lim, T., Gottipati, S., & Cheong, M. L. F. (2023). Ethical considerations for artificial intelligence in educational assessments. In *Advances in Educational Technologies and Instructional Design Book Series* (pp. 32–79). DOI: 10.4018/979-8-3693-0205-7.ch003

Li, M., & Gao, W. (2025). Exploring How Human Capital Development Promotes Economic Transformation. *Journal of Organizational and End User Computing, 37*(1), 1–22. DOI: 10.4018/JOEUC.388939

Liu, J., & Pullinger, D. (2021). STep up to masters: Supporting the academic skills transition for taught postgraduate students. *Journal of Information Literacy*, *15*(3), 100–118. DOI: 10.11645/15.3.3095

Li, W., Liu, H., Huang, K., & Hussain, A. (2025). Reinforcement learning for human-ai collaboration: Challenges, mechanisms, and methods. *Cognitive Computation*, *17*(5), 146. DOI: 10.1007/s12559-025-10500-7

Li, Y., Xu, W., & Chen, J. (2025). PhD student-supervisor relationship and its impacts: A perspective of the interpersonal relationship model. *Frontiers in Education*, *10*, 1570137. DOI: 10.3389/feduc.2025.1570137

Lodge, J. M., Howard, S., Bearman, M. L., Dawson, P., Agostinho, S., Buckingham Shum, S., Deneen, C., Ellis, C., Fawns, T., Gniel, H., Harper, R., Henderson, M., Liu, D. Y. T., Markauskaite, L., McLean, J., Perrotta, C., Schuwirth, L., & Slade, C. (2023). Assessment reform for the age of artificial intelligence. Tertiary Education Quality and Standards Agency. https://www.teqsa.gov.au/sites/default/files/2023-09/assessment-reform-age-artificial-intelligence-discussion-paper.pdf

Lodge, J. M., Kennedy, G., Lockyer, L., Arguel, A., & Pachman, M. (2018). Understanding difficulties and resulting confusion in learning: An integrative review. *Frontiers in Education*, *3*, 49. DOI: 10.3389/feduc.2018.00049

Long, D., & Magerko, B. (2020). What is AI literacy? Competencies and design considerations. *Proceedings of the 2020 CHI Conference on Human Factors in Computing Systems*, 1-16. DOI: 10.1145/3313831.3376727

Longworth, J. (2021). Benjamin Ruha (2019) *Race after technology: Abolitionist tools for the new Jim Code*. Medford: Polity Press. 172 pages. eISBN: 9781509526437. *Science & Technology Studies*, *34*(2), 92–94. DOI: 10.23987/sts.102639

Lubinga, S., Maramura, T. C., & Masiya, T. (2023). The fourth industrial revolution adoption: Challenges in South African higher education institutions. *Journal of Culture & Values in Education*, *6*(2), 1–17. DOI: 10.46303/jcve.2023.5

Luckin, R. (2018). *Machine Learning and Human Intelligence. The future of education for the 21st century*. UCL institute of education press.

Luckin, R. (2017). Towards artificial intelligence-based assessment systems. *Nature Human Behaviour*, *1*(3). Advance online publication. DOI: 10.1038/s41562-016-0028

Luckin, R., Holmes, W., Griffiths, M., & Forcier, L. B. (2016). *Intelligence unleashed: An argument for AI in education*. Pearson.

Luft, J. A., Jeong, S., Idsardi, R., & Gardner, G. (2022). Literature reviews, theoretical frameworks, and conceptual frameworks: An introduction for new biology education researchers. *CBE Life Sciences Education*, *21*(3), rm33. Advance online publication. DOI: 10.1187/cbe.21-05-0134 PMID: 35759629

Luo, J. (2024). A critical review of GenAI policies in higher education assessment: A call to reconsider the "originality" of students' work. *Assessment & Evaluation in Higher Education*, *49*(5), 651–664. DOI: 10.1080/02602938.2024.2309963

Luo, J., Zheng, C., Yin, J., & Teo, H. H. (2025). Design and assessment of AI-based learning tools in higher education: A systematic review. *International Journal of Educational Technology in Higher Education, 22*(1), 42. DOI: 10.1186/s41239-025-00540-2

Lye, C. Y., & Lim, L. (2024). Generative artificial intelligence in tertiary education: Assessment redesign principles and considerations. Education Sciences, 14(6)*. *Education Sciences, 569*(6), 569. Advance online publication. DOI: 10.3390/educsci14060569

Lyon, D. (2018). *The culture of surveillance: Watching as a way of life*. Polity Press.

Mabokela, R. K., Primus, M., & Celik, T. (2025). Advancing sentiment analysis for low-resourced African languages using pre-trained language models. *PLoS One, 20*(6), e0325102. DOI: 10.1371/journal.pone.0325102 PMID: 40471940

Macfarlane, B., Zhang, J., & Pun, A. (2014). Academic integrity: A review of the literature. *Studies in Higher Education, 39*(2), 339–358. DOI: 10.1080/03075079.2012.709495

Madge, C., Breines, M. R., Dalu, M. T. B., Gunter, A., Mittelmeier, J., Prinsloo, P., & Raghuram, P. (2019). WhatsApp use among African international distance education (IDE) students: Transferring, translating and transforming educational experiences. *Learning, Media and Technology, 44*(3), 267–282. DOI: 10.1080/17439884.2019.1628048

Maimela, C., & Mbonde, P. (2025). Artificial intelligence in South African universities: Curriculum transformation and decolonisation—aid or obstacle? *Frontiers in Sociology, 10*, 1543471. DOI: 10.3389/fsoc.2025.1543471 PMID: 40697567

Maina, M. F. (2025). *Enhancing personalized formative feedback in higher education: A GenAI-powered tool design and implementation.* In *Proceedings of the EDEN Annual Conference 2025: Shaping the Future of Education in the Age of AI.*

Mainhard, T., Van der Rijst, R., Van Tartwijk, J., & Wubbels, T. (2009). A model for the supervisor–doctoral student relationship. *Higher Education, 58*(3), 359–373. DOI: 10.1007/s10734-009-9199-8

Main, P. (2025). AI and student assessment. *International Journal of Science and Research Archive, 16*(2), 305–313. DOI: 10.30574/ijsra.2025.16.2.2225

Maistry, S. M., & Singh, U. G. (2025). University research supervisors' responses to generative AI amid institutional policy lag. *Alternation African Scholarship Book Series, 22*, 155–176. DOI: 10.29086/978-0-9869938-3-1/2025/AASBS22/8

Mai, T. A., & de Rooij, A. (2023). Linguistic Relativity in Creative Thought: How Divergent Thinking in Response to Motion Events is Influenced by Satellite- and Verb-Framed Languages. *The Journal of Creative Behavior, 57*(4), 742–760. DOI: 10.1002/jocb.615

Májovský, M., Černý, M., Netuka, D., & Mikolov, T. (2024). Perfect detection of computer-generated text faces fundamental challenges. *Cell Reports. Physical Science, 5*(1), 101769. Advance online publication. DOI: 10.1016/j.xcrp.2023.101769

Makalela, L., & White, G. (Eds.). (2021). *Rethinking language use in digital Africa: Technology and communication in sub-Saharan Africa* (Vol. 92). Multilingual Matters. DOI: 10.21832/MAKALE2309

Makeleni, S., Mutongoza, B. H., & Linake, M. A. (2023). Language education and artificial intelligence: An exploration of challenges confronting academics in global south universities. *Journal of Culture and Values in Education*, *6*(2), 158–171. DOI: 10.46303/jcve.2023.14

Malagoudar, A. F., & Karadi, A. A. (2025). Transforming Student Learning Through Artificial Intelligence: Evidence from Personalization, Accessibility, and Pedagogical Innovation. *International Journal for Multidisciplinary Research*, *7*(6), 1–17. https://www.ijfmr.com/papers/2025/6/65191.pdf. DOI: 10.36948/ijfmr.2025.v07i06.65191

Maluleke, A. F. (2025). AI adoption in African higher education: A systematic review of benefits and ethical implications. *Interdisciplinary Journal of Education Research*, *7*(2), a05–a05. DOI: 10.38140/ijer-2025.vol7.2.05

Mangubat, F. M., & Mangubat, F. (2025). Consequences, Trends, and Future Directions in Using AI in Science Education: Is it a Boon or a Bane? *Research Square*. DOI: 10.21203/rs.3.rs-7708506/v1

Mariyono, D., & Mistar, J. (2025). Digital Education Strategies in Anaesthesiology: A Systematic Review and SWOT Analysis. DOI: 10.21203/rs.3.rs-7476309/v1

Marron, L. (Ed.). (2024). *Cases on Authentic Assessment in Higher Education*. IGI Global. DOI: 10.4018/979-8-3693-1001-4

Marzouk, Z., Rakovic, M., Liaqat, A., Vytasek, J., Samadi, D., Stewart-Alonso, J., & Nespenak, M. (2021). What might equity-oriented proctoring systems look like? Critiquing online exam proctoring in the age of COVID. *Canadian Journal of Learning and Technology*, *47*(4), 1–32. DOI: 10.21432/cjlt27854

Mateen, H. (2018). Weapons of math destruction: How big data increases inequality and threatens democracy. *Berkeley Journal of Employment and Labor Law*, *39*(1), 285–292. https://www.jstor.org/stable/26732553

Matiyenga, T. C., & Khoalenyane, N. B. (2026). Innovative Narratives: The Role of Digital Storytelling in African Language Teaching. In *Transforming Teacher Education Through Narrative Dynamism* (pp. 69-108). IGI Global Scientific Publishing.

Matiyenga, T. C., & Khoalenyane, N. B. (2025b). The Transformative Influence of Indigenous Languages on African Englishes. In *African Englishes* (pp. 238–249). Routledge. DOI: 10.4324/9781003582403-17

Matsilele, T., & Tshuma, L. A. (2025). Generative AI in Africa: Transforming News, Practices, and Ethics. In *Generative AI in African News Media* (pp. 1-15). Routledge.

Matthews, K. E., Dwyer, A., Hine, L., & Turner, J. (2019). Conceptions of students as partners. *Higher Education*, *76*(6), 957–971. DOI: 10.1007/s10734-018-0257-y

Mavengere, N., Pondiwa, S., Matiyenga, T. C., Manzira, F., & Mutanga, A. (2021). The 'New Normal' in Higher Education: Innovative teaching and learning technologies and practices during a crisis. *Advances in Computing and Engineering*, *1*(2), 37–46. DOI: 10.21622/ace.2021.01.2.037

Mavrogalou-Foti, A. P., Kambouri, M. A., & Çili, S. (2024). The supervisory relationship as a predictor of mental health outcomes in doctoral students in the United Kingdom. *Frontiers in Psychology*, *15*, 1437819. Advance online publication. DOI: 10.3389/fpsyg.2024.1437819 PMID: 39444829

Mbodila, M. (2025). Postgraduate supervision in the age of ChatGPT: Redefining the role of supervisors. *Foundations and Trends® in Information Systems*, 9(2), 60-68.

McCabe, D. L., Butterfield, K. D., & Treviño, L. K. (2012). *Cheating in college: Why students do it and what educators can do about it*. Johns Hopkins University Press.

McCabe, D. L., & Pavela, G. (2004). Ten principles of academic integrity. Change. *The Magazine of Higher Learning*, *36*(3), 10–15. DOI: 10.1080/00091380409605574

McConvey, K., Guha, S., & Kuzminykh, A. (2023). A human-centered review of algorithms in decision-making in higher education. In *Proceedings of the ACM Conference* (pp. 1–15). DOI: 10.1145/3544548.3580658

McGeechan, G. J., & Haste, A. (2026). Authentic assessments as a strategy to address generative AI use in assessment: A case study. *Assessment in Education: Principles, Policy & Practice*. Advance online publication. DOI: 10.14293/FFL26.000027.v1

McPherson, C., Punch, S., & Graham, E. A. (2017). Transitions from undergraduate to taught postgraduate study: Emotion, integration and ambiguity. *Journal of Perspectives in Applied Academic Practice*, *5*(2), 42–50. DOI: 10.14297/jpaap.v5i2.265

McTighe, J., Doubet, K. J., & Carbaugh, E. M. (2020). *Designing authentic performance tasks and projects: Tools for meaningful learning and assessment*. ASCD.

Meighan, P. J. (2023). Colonialingualism: Colonial legacies, imperial mindsets, and inequitable practices in English language education. *Diaspora, Indigenous, and Minority Education*, *17*(2), 146–155. DOI: 10.1080/15595692.2022.2082406

Melvill, O. (2024). Reading for Content: How the CAPS Assessment Model for Home Language Literature Discourages Critical Thinking. *Scrutiny2, 28*(3), 4-17.

Memarian, B., & Doleck, T. (2024). A review of assessment for learning with artificial intelligence. *Computers in Human Behavior: Artificial Humans*, *2*(1), 100040. DOI: 10.1016/j.chbah.2023.100040

Memon, T. D., & Kwan, P. (2025). A collaborative model for integrating teacher and GenAI into future education. *TechTrends*, *69*(6), 1192–1206. DOI: 10.1007/s11528-025-01105-w

Mhlanga, D. (2021). Artificial intelligence in the industry 4.0, and its impact on poverty, innovation, infrastructure development, and the sustainable development goals: Lessons from emerging economies? *Sustainability (Basel)*, *13*(11), 5788. DOI: 10.3390/su13115788

Mhlanga, D. (2023). Open AI in Education, the Responsible and Ethical Use of ChatGPT Towards Lifelong Learning. In *FinTech and Artificial Intelligence for Sustainable Development*. Sustainable Development Goals Series. Palgrave Macmillan., DOI: 10.1007/978-3-031-37776-1_17

Mhlanga, D., Denhere, V., & Moloi, T. (2022). COVID-19 and the Key Digital Transformation Lessons for Higher Education Institutions in South Africa. *Education Sciences*, *12*(7), 464. DOI: 10.3390/educsci12070464

Miao, F., & Cukurova, M. (2024). *AI competency framework for teachers*. UNESCO. UNESCO official publication

Miao, F., & Holmes, W. (2021). Artificial intelligence and education. Guidance for policy-makers. https://unesdoc.unesco.org/ark:/48223/pf0000376709

Miao, F., Shiohira, K., & Lao, N. (2024). *AI competency framework for students*. UNESCO. UNESCO official publication

Miao, F., & Holmes, W. (2021). *AI and education: Guidance for policy-makers*. UNESCO Publishing., DOI: 10.54675/PCSP7350

Miao, F., & Holmes, W. (2023). *Guidance for generative AI in education and research*. UNESCO., DOI: 10.54675/EWZM9535

Miao, W., Zang, H., Liu, Q., Zheng, T., Zhou, Y., Liu, C., Yang, N., Zhang, H., Zhang, Y., Zhang, Y., Li, S., Zhang, S., & Zhang, H. (2025). From chaos to symbiosis: Exploring adaptive co-evolution strategies for generative AI and research integrity systems. *BMC Medical Ethics*, *26*(1), 120. DOI: 10.1186/s12910-025-01288-0 PMID: 41013533

Midigo, J. (2025). AI-Powered Innovations for Documenting and Revitalizing African Languages. *Cultural Arts Research and Development*, *5*(2), 26–41. DOI: 10.55121/card.v5i2.517

Mikalef, P., Conboy, K., Lundström, J. E., & Popovič, A. (2022). Thinking responsibly about responsible AI and the 'dark side' of AI. *European Journal of Information Systems*, *31*(3), 257–268. DOI: 10.1080/0960085X.2022.2026621

Mill, J. S. (2016). Utilitarianism. In *Seven masterpieces of philosophy* (pp. 329–375). Routledge.

Mintz, Y., & Brodie, R. (2019). Introduction to artificial intelligence in medicine. *Minimally Invasive Therapy & Allied Technologies*, *28*(2), 73–81. DOI: 10.1080/13645706.2019.1575882 PMID: 30810430

Mishara, P. (2024). The ethical implications of AI in education: Privacy, bias, and accountability. *Journal of Informatics Education and Research*, *4*(2). Advance online publication. DOI: 10.52783/jier.v4i2.1827

Mishra, P., & Koehler, M. J. (2006). Technological pedagogical content knowledge: A framework for teacher knowledge. *Teachers College Record*, *108*(6), 1017–1054. DOI: 10.1111/j.1467-9620.2006.00684.x

Mishra, S. (2025). Artificial intelligence as a mediator between educator and learner: The new paradigm shift. *International Journal of Research and Innovation in Applied Science*, *10*(7), 91–95. DOI: 10.51584/ijrias.2025.100700008

Mittelstadt, B., Allo, P., Taddeo, M., Wachter, S., & Floridi, L. (2016). The ethics of algorithms: Mapping the debate. *Big Data & Society*, *3*(2), 1–21. DOI: 10.1177/2053951716679679

Mittelstadt, B., Russell, C., & Wachter, S. (2019). Explaining explanations in AI. *Proceedings of the ACM Conference on Fairness, Accountability, and Transparency*, 279–288. https://doi.org/DOI: 10.1145/3287560.3287574

Mogoale, P. D., Pretorius, A., Mogase, R. C., & Segooa, M. A. (2025). Ethical considerations in artificial intelligence-driven environments for higher education. *South African Journal of Information Management, 27*(1), 2007. Advance online publication. DOI: 10.4102/sajim.v27i1.2007

Mohamed, S., Png, M. T., & Isaac, W. (2020). Decolonial AI: Decolonial theory as sociotechnical foresight in artificial intelligence. *Philosophy & Technology, 33*(4), 659–684. DOI: 10.1007/s13347-020-00405-8

Mokoena, O. P., & Seeletse, S. M. (2025). AI in rural classrooms: Challenges and perspectives from South African educators. *International Journal of Current Educational Studies, 4*(2), 30–52. DOI: 10.46328/ijces.199

Molloy, E., Boud, D., & Henderson, M. (2020). Developing a learning-centred framework for feedback literacy. *Assessment & Evaluation in Higher Education, 45*(4), 527–540. DOI: 10.1080/02602938.2019.1667955

Moon, M. J. (2023). Searching for inclusive artificial intelligence for social good: Participatory governance and policy recommendations for making AI more inclusive and benign for society. *Public Administration Review, 83*(6), 1496–1505. DOI: 10.1111/puar.13648

Moorhouse, B. L., Yeo, M. A., & Wan, Y. (2023). Generative AI tools and assessment: Guidelines of the world's top-ranking universities. *Computers and Education Open, 5*, 100151. DOI: 10.1016/j.caeo.2023.100151

Mosha, N. F. V., Chigwada, J., Ketchiwou, G. F., & Ngulube, P. (2026). A systematic review of artificial intelligence in higher education institutions (HEIs): Functionalities, challenges, and best practices. *Education Sciences, 16*(2), 185. DOI: 10.3390/educsci16020185

Moulavinafchi, A., Alhaideri, S. A. A., & Alfawwaz, S. N. M. (2026). The impact of an AI-powered Flipped classroom on grammar competence and language anxiety in EFL learners. *International Journal of Instruction, 19*(1), 105–130. DOI: 10.29333/iji.2026.1916a

Murgatroyd, S. (2024). Artificial intelligence and future of higher education. [REPED]. *Revista Paraguaya de Educación a Distancia, 5*(1), 4–11. DOI: 10.56152/reped2024-vol5num1-art1

Muringa, T. P. (2025). Exploring ethical dilemmas and institutional challenges in AI adoption: A study of South African universities. *Frontiers in Education, 10*, 1628019. DOI: 10.3389/feduc.2025.1628019

Murugesan, S., & Cherukuri, A. K. (2023). The rise of generative artificial intelligence and its impact on education: The promises and perils. *Computer, 56*(5), 116–121. DOI: 10.1109/MC.2023.3253292

Mutongoza, B. H., & Olawale, B. E. (2022). Safeguarding academic integrity in the face of emergency remote teaching and learning in developing countries. *Perspectives in Education, 40*(1), 234–249. DOI: 10.18820/2519593X/pie.v40.i1.14

Muzindutsi, P. F., Muguto, H. T., & Kunjal, D. (2025). Digital transformation and innovation in higher education: Rethinking online assessment integrity. *African Perspectives of Research in Teaching and Learning, 9*(6), 820–835.

Nakajima, G. T. (2025). *Impact of AI Tools On Students' Learning and Academic Integrity: A Case Study at Africa University.*

Nakidien, T., Singh, M., & Sayed, Y. (2021). Teachers and teacher education: Limitations and possibilities of attaining SDG 4 in South Africa. *Education Sciences, 11*(2), 66. DOI: 10.3390/educsci11020066

Naraliev, A. (2025). The Impact Of Ai-Powered Tools On Language Learning And Assessment In Higher Education. In *International Conference on Global Trends and Innovations in Multidisciplinary Research* (Vol. 1, No. 4, pp. 146-149).

Nazira, H., Najma, A., Tania, R. V. D. M., Ute, S., George, E., Mei, L., & Sibongile, Z. (2025). Decolonising AI: A Pan-African collaboration. *African Perspectives of Research in Teaching and Learning, 9*(5), 504–518.

Ncube, G. (2024). What is the place of African languages in knowledge production? [South African Journal of African Languages]. *International Journal of the Sociology of Language, 2024*(289-290), 157–162. DOI: 10.1515/ijsl-2024-0033

Ncube, P. D., Dzvapatsva, G. P., Matobobo, C., & Ranga, M. M. (2026). Redefining student assessment in AI-infused learning environments: A systematic review of challenges and strategies for academic integrity. *AI and Ethics, 6*(1), 68. DOI: 10.1007/s43681-025-00871-w

Nedungadi, P., Tang, K.-Y., & Raman, R. (2024). The transformative power of generative artificial intelligence for achieving the sustainable development goal of quality education. Sustainability, 16(22)*. *Sustainability (Basel), 9779*(22), 9779. Advance online publication. DOI: 10.3390/su16229779

Newton, P. M. (2016). Academic integrity: A quantitative study of confidence and understanding in students. *Studies in Higher Education, 41*(5), 1–17. DOI: 10.1080/03075079.2014.966111

Newton, P. M. (2018). How common is commercial contract cheating in higher education and is it increasing? A systematic review. *Frontiers in Education, 3*, 67. DOI: 10.3389/feduc.2018.00067

Newton, P. M., & Boud, D. (2023). The post-pandemic university and the post-pandemic student: The role of evidence in shaping policy and practice. *Higher Education Research & Development, 42*(1), 3–17. DOI: 10.1080/07294360.2022.2130160

Ng, D. T. K., Leung, J. K. L., Chu, K. W. S., & Qiao, M. S. (2021). Conceptualising AI literacy: An exploratory review. *Computers and Education: Artificial Intelligence, 2*, 100041. Advance online publication. DOI: 10.1016/j.caeai.2021.100041

Nguyen, A., Ngo, H. N., Hong, Y., Dang, B., & Nguyen, B. P. T. (2022). Ethical principles for artificial intelligence in education. *Education and Information Technologies, 28*(4), 4221–4241. DOI: 10.1007/s10639-022-11316-w PMID: 36254344

Nguyen, J. G., Keuseman, K. J., & Humston, J. J. (2020). Minimize online cheating for online assessments during COVID-19 pandemic. *Journal of Chemical Education, 97*(9), 3429–3435. DOI: 10.1021/acs.jchemed.0c00790

Nguyen, K. V. (2025). The use of generative AI tools in higher education: Ethical and pedagogical principles. *Journal of Academic Ethics, 23*(3), 1435–1455. Advance online publication. DOI: 10.1007/s10805-025-09607-1

Nguyen, T. H., Tran, D. N., Vo, D. L., Mai, V. H., & Dao, X. Q. (2022). AI-powered university: Design and deployment of robot assistant for smart universities. *Journal of Advances in Information Technology*, *13*(1). Advance online publication. DOI: 10.12720/jait.13.1.78-84

Nieminen, J. H., Dollinger, M., & Zou, T. X. (2025). Student partnership in assessment: What works, for whom, why, and under what circumstances? *Review of Education*, *13*(1), e70059. DOI: 10.1002/rev3.70059

Nikolic, S., Daniel, S., Haque, R., Belkina, M., Hassan, G. M., Grundy, S., Lyden, S., Neal, P., & Sandison, C. (2023). ChatGPT versus engineering education assessment: A multidisciplinary and multi-institutional benchmarking and analysis of this generative artificial intelligence tool to investigate assessment integrity. *European Journal of Engineering Education*, *48*(4), 559–614. DOI: 10.1080/03043797.2023.2213169

Nkobane, J. G. (2025). Benefits and Challenges of Utilizing Automation and Artificial Intelligence in Auditing Firms in South Africa. In International Conference of Accounting & Business, 667 – 682. Springer DOI: 10.1007/978-3-031-84885-8_36

Nkosi, T. B. (2026). Supervision skills of supervisors in AI-enhanced environments: Perspectives on postgraduate supervision. In I. Kariyana & W. Sinkala (Eds.), *Artificial IntelligenceandPostgraduate-SupervisioninHigher Education* (pp. 93-110). ERRCD Forum. DOI: 10.38140/obp4-2026-06

Noble, S. U. (2018). *Algorithms of oppression: How search engines reinforce racism*. NYU Press., DOI: 10.18574/nyu/9781479833641.001.0001

Nwafor, O. F., & Ezeugo, C. R. (2025). Roles of AI-Powered Assessments in Enhancing the Professional Development of Academic Staff in Public Universities in Rivers State. *International Journal of Educational Management, Rivers State University.*, *1*(2), 170-180.

Nyathi, P. A. (2024). Exploring tensions between conservationists and African subsistence farmers in the Dukuduku forest area, KwaZulu-Natal, in the 1980s and 1990s. *IAHRW International Journal of Social Sciences Review*, *12*(1), 33–41.

O'Neil, C. (2016). *Weapons of math destruction: How big data increases inequality and threatens democracy*. Crown.

Ocaña-Fernández, Y., Valenzuela-Fernández, L. A., & Garro-Aburto, L. L. (2019). Inteligencia artificial y sus implicaciones en la educación superior. *Propósitos y Represent.*, *7*(2). Advance online publication. DOI: 10.20511/pyr2019.v7n2.274

OECD. (2026). *OECD Digital Education Outlook 2026: Exploring effective uses of generative AI in education*. OECD Publishing., DOI: 10.1787/062a7394-

Ogwueleka, F. N. (2025). Plagiarism detection in the age of artificial intelligence: current technologies and future directions. *AI & Ethics, Academic Integrity & the Future of Quality Assurance in Higher Education*, 10.

Okada, A., Sherborne, T., Panselinas, G., & Kolionis, G. (2025). Fostering transversal skills through open schooling supported by the CARE-KNOW-DO pedagogical model and the UNESCO AI competencies framework. *International Journal of Artificial Intelligence in Education, 35*(4), 1953–1998. DOI: 10.1007/s40593-025-00458-w

Okoth, M. O. (2025, February 4). Use of AI in research and postgraduate supervision: Balancing efficiency and academic integrity. *Scholar Media Africa.* https://scholarmedia.africa/education/higher-ed-bar/use-of-ai-in-research-andpostgraduate-supervision-balancing-efficiency-and-academic-integrity

Olawumi, K. B., & Mavuso, M. P. (2024). In-service teacher training programmes that promote education for sustainable development: A review of emerging literature. *Interdisciplinary Journal of Education Research, 6*, 1-20.2024: Vol 6, pp 1-20. DOI: 10.38140/ijer-2024.vol6.35

Olmos, M., & Corrin, L. (2011). Academic analytics in a medical curriculum. In *ASCILITE Publications* (pp. 930–941). DOI: 10.14742/apubs.2011.1731

Omari, E. B., Salifu Yendork, J., & Ankrah, E. (2022). University students' perspectives on the benefits and challenges of emergency remote teaching during the Covid-19 pandemic in Ghana. *Education and Information Technologies*, •••, 1–21. DOI: 10.1007/s10639-022-11401-0 PMID: 36406783

Omodan, B. I. (2025). Redefining the role of supervisors in the era of artificial intelligence: Implications for hybrid postgraduate research governance. *Cogent Education*, *12*(1), 2536534. Advance online publication. DOI: 10.1080/2331186X.2025.2536534

Oravec, J. A. (2022). AI, biometric analysis, and emerging cheating detection systems: The engineering of academic integrity? *Education Policy Analysis Archives*, *30*. Advance online publication. DOI: 10.14507/epaa.30.5765

Organisation for Economic Co-operation and Development. (2019). *OECD principles on artificial intelligence.*

Organisation for Economic Co-operation and Development. (2021). *AI in education: Challenges and opportunities*. OECD Publishing.

Otiono, N. (2021). A heritage of African oral literary performance studies. In *Oral Literary Performance in Africa* (pp. 1–20). Routledge. DOI: 10.4324/9781003111887-1

Otterbacher, J. (2023). Why technical solutions for detecting AI-generated content in research and education are insufficient. *Patterns (New York, N.Y.)*, *4*(7), 100796. Advance online publication. DOI: 10.1016/j.patter.2023.100796 PMID: 37521044

Overono, A. L., & Ditta, A. S. (2025). The rise of artificial intelligence: A clarion call for higher education to redefine learning and reimagine assessment. *College Teaching*, *73*(2), 123–126. DOI: 10.1080/87567555.2023.2233653

Owan, V. J., Abang, K. B., Idika, D. O., Etta, E. O., & Bassey, B. A. (2023). Exploring the potential of artificial intelligence tools in educational measurement and assessment. *Eurasia Journal of Mathematics, Science and Technology Education*, *19*(8), em2307. DOI: 10.29333/ejmste/13428

Owen, R., Stilgoe, J., Macnaghten, P., Gorman, M., Fisher, E., & Guston, D. (2013). A framework for responsible innovation. *Responsible innovation: managing the responsible emergence of science and innovation in society*, 27-50. https://doi.org/DOI: 10.1002/9781118551424

Oyenuga, M. O., Andah, R. A., & Apata, S. B. (2026). AI and Assessment: Generating and Grading Foreign Language Assignments Automatically. In Dehghan, F. (Ed.), *Harnessing AI-Generated Content in Language Education* (pp. 123–152). IGI Global Scientific Publishing., DOI: 10.4018/979-8-3373-2721-1.ch006

Oyenuga, M. O., Apata, S. B., & Sulaiman, M. M. (2024). Pre-Service Teachers' Perceptions and Utilisation of Chatgpt in Higher Institutions using UTAUT Theory: Evidence from an Emerging Economy. *British Journal of Contemporary Education*, *4*(2), 28–42. DOI: 10.52589/BJCE-DBIT7S4T

Oyenuga, M. O., & Omale, S. A. (2024). Is Africa Jinxed? Exploring the Challenges of Technology Access and Adoption in Africa. *African Journal of Economic and Sustainable Development*, *7*(4), 142–161. DOI: 10.52589/AJESD-ULN1LRNF

Padmanabha, C. H. (2021). Assessment for Learning, Assessment of Learning, Assessment as Learning. A Conceptual Framework. *i-manager's. Journal of Educational Psychology*, *14*(4), 14–21.

Page, E., Meyers, G., & Billings, E. (2024). Theory to practice: An assessment framework for generative AI. Intersection: A Journal at the Intersection of Assessment and Learning, 5(4), 114–126. DOI: 10.61669/001c.124250

Panda, M., Dehuri, S., Patra, M. R., Behera, P. K., Tsihrintzis, G. A., Cho, S. B., & Coello, C. A. C. (Eds.). (2022). Innovations in intelligent computing and communication: First international conference, ICIICC 2022, Bhubaneswar, Odisha, India, December 16–17, 2022, Proceedings. Springer Nature.

Pangrazio, L., & Sefton-Green, J. (2021). Digital rights, digital citizenship and digital literacy: What's the difference? *Journal of New Approaches in Educational Research*, *10*(1), 15–27. DOI: 10.7821/naer.2021.1.616

Pangrazio, L., & Selwyn, N. (2019). 'Personal data literacies': A critical literacies approach to enhancing understandings of personal digital data. *New Media & Society*, *21*(2), 419–437. DOI: 10.1177/1461444818799523

Papanastasiou, E. C., Giallousi, M., & Pitri, E. (2025). Re-Introducing Authentic Assessment in Classroom Assessment Courses: Finding Its Place in the 21st Century. *Education Sciences*, *15*(11), 1564. DOI: 10.3390/educsci15111564

Pardo, A., Jovanovic, J., Dawson, S., Gašević, D., & Mirriahi, N. (2019). Using learning analytics to scale the provision of personalised feedback. *British Journal of Educational Technology*, *50*(1), 128–138. DOI: 10.1111/bjet.12592

Pardo, A., & Siemens, G. (2014). Ethical and privacy principles for learning analytics. *British Journal of Educational Technology*, *45*(3), 438–450. DOI: 10.1111/bjet.12152

Pasquale, F. (2015). *The black box society: The secret algorithms that control money and information.* Harvard University Press. DOI: 10.4159/harvard.9780674736061

Patel, S., & Ragolane, M. (2024). The implementation of artificial intelligence in South African higher education institutions: Opportunities and challenges. *Technium Education & Humanities*, *9*, 51–65. DOI: 10.47577/teh.v9i.11452

Peddi, S., & Manoharan, G. (2025). Ethical guidelines for the thoughtful implementation of AI in higher education. *EthAIca*, *5*, 409. DOI: 10.56294/ai2026409

Peddi, S., & Manoharan, G. (2026). Ethical Guidelines for the thoughtful Implementation of AI in Higher Education. *EthAIca: Journal of Ethics. AI and Critical Analysis*, (5), 409.

Perelman, L. (2014). When "the state of the art" is counting words. *Assessing Writing*, *21*, 104–111. DOI: 10.1016/j.asw.2014.05.001

Perera, P., & Lankathilake, M. (2023). AI in higher education: A literature review of ChatGPT and guidelines for responsible implementation.

Perkins, M. (2023). Academic integrity considerations of AI Large Language Models in the post-pandemic era: ChatGPT and beyond. *Journal of University Teaching & Learning Practice, 20*(2), 07. DOI: 10.53761/1.20.02.07

Perkins, M., Furze, L., Roe, J., & MacVaugh, J. (2024). The artificial intelligence assessment scale (AIAS): A framework for ethical integration of generative AI in educational assessment. *Journal of University Teaching & Learning Practice*, *21*(6). Advance online publication. DOI: 10.53761/q3azde36

Perkins, M., Roe, J., Postma, D., McGaughran, J., & Hickerson, D. (2023). Detection of GPT-4 generated text in higher education: Combining academic judgement and software to identify generative AI tool misuse. *Journal of Academic Ethics*, **•••**, 1–17. DOI: 10.1007/s10805-023-09505-5

Perla, L., & Vinci, V. (2023). Enhancing authentic assessment in higher education: Leveraging digital transformation and artificial intelligence. *AIxEDU, 1*.

Perrotta, C., & Selwyn, N. (2020). Deep learning goes to school: Toward a relational understanding of AI in education. *Learning, Media and Technology*, *45*(3), 251–269. DOI: 10.1080/17439884.2020.1686017

Peters, M. A., & Kourkoulou, D. (2025). AI, Pedagogy, and the Conditions of Knowledge. *Postdigital Science and Education*, *7*(4), 1478–1493. DOI: 10.1007/s42438-025-00599-0

Peterson, S. (2025). Generative AI and academic integrity: Developing frameworks for formative assessment and policy. *Frontiers in Education, 10*, 1610836. DOI: 10.3389/feduc.2025.1610836

Pisica, A. I., Edu, T., Zaharia, R. M., & Zaharia, R. (2023). Implementing artificial intelligence in higher education: Pros and cons from the perspectives of academics. *Societies (Basel, Switzerland)*, *13*(5), 118. DOI: 10.3390/soc13050118

Pitsoe, V. J., & Vlădu escu, . (2024). A critical analysis of Foucault's power and knowledge in higher education research. *Social Sciences and Education Research Review*, *11*(1), 41–51. DOI: 10.5281/zenodo.15258133

Polanyi, M. (1966). *The tacit dimension*. University of Chicago Press.

Popenici, S. A., & Kerr, S. (2017). Exploring the impact of artificial intelligence on teaching and learning in higher education. *Research and Practice in Technology Enhanced Learning*, *12*(1), 1–13. DOI: 10.1186/s41039-017-0062-8 PMID: 30595727

Pramjeeth, S., & Ramgovind, P. (2024). Generative artificial intelligence (AI) tools in higher education: A moral compass for the future? *African Journal of Inter/Multidisciplinary Studies, 6*(1). https://doi.org/ DOI: 10.51415/ajims.v6i1.1560

Praveenkumar, S., Anute, N., Vaissnave, V., Ragupathi, T., Fardale, S., Selvakumar, P., & Manjunath, T. C. (2025). Risks of AI bias and inequities in learning. In *Advances in Computational Intelligence and Robotics Book Series* (pp. 257–284). DOI: 10.4018/979-8-3373-2302-2.ch009

Price, M., & Kirkwood, A. (2014). Using technology for assessment for learning in higher education: Student expectations and experiences. *Technology, Pedagogy and Education*, *23*(3), 327–342. DOI: 10.1080/1475939X.2014.894623

Primi, R., Beaty, R. E., Benedek, M., Dumas, D., Organisciak, P., Patterson, J. D., Calico, T., & Piacentini, M. (2026). AI-Powered Scoring for Creative Thinking: Methods and Challenges in PISA Assessment. *The Journal of Creative Behavior*, *60*(1), e70082. DOI: 10.1002/jocb.70082

Prinsloo, P., & Slade, S. (2016). Student vulnerability, agency, and learning analytics: An exploration. *Journal of Learning Analytics*, *3*(1), 159–182. DOI: 10.18608/jla.2016.31.10

Prinsloo, P., & Slade, S. (2017). Big data, higher education and learning analytics: Beyond justice and ethics. In *Big data and learning analytics in higher education* (pp. 109–124). Springer., DOI: 10.1007/978-3-319-06520-5_8

Prinsloo, P., & Slade, S. (2017). Big data, higher education and learning analytics: Beyond justice, toward an ethics of care. *British Journal of Educational Technology*, *48*(1), 10–19. DOI: 10.1111/bjet.12441

Priyadarshini, V., Thandapani, G., Meena, S., Sarada, V., Aaryan, A., & Ravindran, D. (2025). The Human–Machine Collaboration: Leveraging AI for Ethical Learning and Effectiveness. In Qasem, I. (Ed.), *Data-Driven Decision Making for Sustainable Business Growth. Studies in Systems, Decision and Control* (Vol. 607). Springer., DOI: 10.1007/978-3-031-96530-2_21

Pusporini, W., & Nurdiyanto, H. (2024). Utilization of artificial intelligence in outcome-based curriculum evaluation and development. *Journal of Research in Social Science and Humanities*, *4*(2), 132–134. DOI: 10.47679/jrssh.v4i1.109

Qian, Y. (2025). Pedagogical applications of generative AI in higher education: A systematic review of the field. *TechTrends*, *69*(5), 1105–1120. DOI: 10.1007/s11528-025-01100-1

Quiambao, J. E. A. (2022). Thinking ethically: The utilitarianism approach in moral decision making. *International Journal of Multidisciplinary Research and Growth Evaluation*, *3*(3), 602–604. DOI: 10.54660/anfo.2022.3.3.30

Qu, Y., & Wang, J. (2025). The impact of ai guilt on students' use of ChatGPT for academic tasks: Examining Disciplinary Differences: Y. Qu and J. Wang. *Journal of Academic Ethics*, *23*(4), 2087–2110. DOI: 10.1007/s10805-025-09643-x

Radjabov, S., & Ravshanov, F. (2024). Implementation of AI-based algorithm and its complications and security constraints in higher education systems. In *IEEE Xplore Conference Proceedings* (pp. 1597–1602). DOI: 10.1109/icacite60783.2024.10616878

Ragolane, M., & Patel, S. (2024). Transforming Educ-AI-tion in South Africa: Can AI-Driven grading transform the future of higher education. *Journal of Education and Teaching Methods*, *3*(1), 26–51. DOI: 10.58425/jetm.v3i1.267

Rahiman, H. U., & Kodikal, R. (2024). Revolutionizing education: Artificial intelligence empowered learning in higher education. *Cogent Education*, *11*(1), 2293431. DOI: 10.1080/2331186X.2023.2293431

Rane, N. L., Choudhary, S. P., & Rane, J. (2024). Education 4.0 and 5.0: Integrating artificial intelligence for personalized and adaptive learning. *Journal of Artificial Intelligence and Robotics*, *4*(2), 29–43.

Ravi, M., & Besharat, M. (2026). A holistic consideration of authentic assessments: Student perception of assessment design, delivery, flexibility and creativity. *European Journal of Engineering Education*, *51*(1), 25–42. DOI: 10.1080/03043797.2025.2480116

Regan, P. M., & Jesse, J. (2019). Ethical challenges of edtech, big data and personalized learning: Twenty-first century student sorting and tracking. *Ethics and Information Technology*, *21*(3), 167–179. DOI: 10.1007/s10676-018-9492-2

Regassa, M., & Mitiku, T. (2024). Orality in African Literary Works: An Interaction of Oromo Oral Literature with Written Poetry. *Research in African Literatures*, *54*(3), 111–130. DOI: 10.2979/ral.00019

Reilly, C., Chimbutane, F., Clegg, J., Rubagumya, C., & Erling, E. J. (Eds.). (2023). *Multilingual learning: Assessment, ideologies and policies in Sub-Saharan Africa*. Taylor & Francis. DOI: 10.4324/9781003311553

Ren, X., & Wu, M. L. (2025). Examining teaching competencies and challenges while integrating artificial intelligence in higher education. *TechTrends*, *69*(3), 519–538. DOI: 10.1007/s11528-025-01055-3

Rimban, E. (2025). Ethics in the time of artificial intelligence: Rethinking integrity in the classroom. *Preprints.org*. DOI: 10.20944/preprints202505.0913.v1

Ringo, D. S. (2025). When relationships make a difference! Supervisor support and PhD students' academic performance in the journey: The moderating effect of supervisor-student relationship quality. *Cogent Education*, *12*(1), 2479403. Advance online publication. DOI: 10.1080/2331186X.2025.2479403

Rogers, E. M. (2003). *Diffusion of innovations* (5th ed.). Free Press.

Roll, I., & Wylie, R. (2016). Evolution and revolution in artificial intelligence in education. *International Journal of Artificial Intelligence in Education*, *26*(2), 582–599. DOI: 10.1007/s40593-016-0110-3

Ross, J., & Macleod, H. (2018). Surveillance, (dis)trust and teaching with plagiarism detection technology. In *Proceedings of the International Conference on Networked Learning, 11*, 235–242. DOI: 10.54337/nlc.v11.8760

Saaida, M. B. (2023). AI-Driven transformations in higher education: Opportunities and challenges. *International journal of educational research and studies, 5*(1), 29-36.

Saaida, M. B. E. (2023). AI-driven transformations in higher education: Opportunities and challenges. *International Journal of Educational Research and Studies*, *5*(2), 29–36.

Sadler, D. R. (1989). Formative assessment and the design of instructional systems. *Instructional Science*, *18*(2), 119–144. DOI: 10.1007/BF00117714

Sajja, R., Sermet, Y., Fodale, B., & Demir, I. (2026). Evaluating AI-powered learning assistants in engineering higher education with implications for student engagement, ethics, and policy. *Scientific Reports*, *16*(1), 7565. DOI: 10.1038/s41598-026-39237-5

Sakri, L. I., Kori, D. N., Joshi, S. S., Nayak, A. S., & Marigoudar, S. (2025). AI-Enabled Transformation of Online Learning through Personalization. *Journal of Engineering Education Transformations*, *39*(s1, is1), 26–33. DOI: 10.16920/jeet/2025/v39is1/25131

Saleem, T., Saleem, A., & Aslam, D. M. (2025). Integrating AI in Pakistani ESL classrooms: Teachers' practices, perspectives, and impact on student performance. *PLoS One*, *20*(9), e0333352. DOI: 10.1371/journal.pone.0333352 PMID: 41026767

Sampath, P. G. (2021). Governing Artificial Intelligence in an Age of Inequality. *Global Policy*, *12*(S6), 21–31. DOI: 10.1111/1758-5899.12940

Samuel, M. T. (2025). Fostering trust in the postgraduate student-supervisor relationship: A crucial foundation for academic success. *TWIST, 20*(1), 436-444. https://twistjournal.net/twist/article/view/787

Sandel, M. J. (2020). *The tyranny of merit: What's become of the common good?* Farrar, Straus and Giroux.

Sangwa, S., Nsabiyumva, S., Ngobi, D., & Mutabazi, P. (2025). Ethical AI integration in African higher education: Enhancing research supervision, grant discovery, and proposal writing without compromising academic integrity. *Grant Discovery and Proposal Writing Without Compromising Academic Integrity (June 30, 2025)*. DOI: 10.55677/ijhrsss/08-2025-Vol02I6

Saputra, I., Kurniawan, A., Yanita, M., Putri, E. Y., & Mahniza, M. (2024). The evolution of educational assessment: How artificial intelligence is shaping the trends and future of learning evaluation. *Indonesian Journal of Computer Science*, *13*(6). Advance online publication. DOI: 10.33022/ijcs.v13i6.4465

Sari, H. E., Tumanggor, B., & Efron, D. (2024). Improving educational outcomes through adaptive learning systems using AI. *International Transactions on Artificial Intelligence*, *3*(1), 21–31. DOI: 10.33050/italic.v3i1.647

Scarfe, P., Watcham, K., Clarke, A., & Roesch, E. (2024). A real-world test of artificial intelligence infiltration of a university examinations system: A "Turing Test" case study. *PLoS One*, *19*(6), e0305354. DOI: 10.1371/journal.pone.0305354 PMID: 38923941

Schlagwein, D., & Willcocks, L. (2023). 'ChatGPT et al.': The ethics of using (generative) artificial intelligence in research and science. *Journal of Information Technology*, *38*(3), 232–238. https://doi.org/ . DOI: 10.1177/02683962231200411

Schleicher, A. (2020). The impact of COVID-19 on education: Insights from education at a glance 2020. *OECD Journal: Economic Studies*, *2020*(1), 1–31.

Schoeman, F., & Seymour, L. F. (2022). Understanding the Low Adoption of AI in South African Medium Sized Organisations. In 43rd Conference of the South African Institute of Computer Scientists and Information Technologists, SAICSIT, 257–269.

Sellnow, D. D. (2025). Reflection-AI: Exploring the challenges and opportunities of artificial intelligence in higher education. *Frontiers in Communication, 10*, 1615040. DOI: 10.3389/fcomm.2025.1615040

Selwyn, N. (2019). *Should robots replace teachers? AI and the future of education*. Polity Press. https://research.monash.edu/en/publications/should-robots-replace-teachers-ai-and-the-future-of-education/

Selwyn, N. (2019). *Should robots replace teachers? AI and the future of education*. Polity Press.

Selwyn, N. (2019). *Should robots replace teachers? Artificial intelligence and the future of education*. Polity Press.

Selwyn, N. (2019). Should robots replace teachers? *British Journal of Educational Technology, 50*(3), 1033–1046.

Selwyn, N. (2019). *Should robots replace teachers?: AI and the future of education*. John Wiley & Sons.

Selwyn, N. (2019). What's the problem with learning analytics? *Journal of Learning Analytics, 6*(3), 11–19. DOI: 10.18608/jla.2019.63.3

Selwyn, N. (2022). *Education and technology: Key issues and debates* (2nd ed.). Bloomsbury Academic. DOI: 10.5040/9781350145573

Selwyn, N. (2024). On the limits of artificial intelligence (AI) in education. *Nordisk Tidsskrift for Pedagogikk og Kritikk, 10*(1). Advance online publication. DOI: 10.23865/ntpk.v10.6062

Selwyn, N., & Gašević, D. (2020). The datafication of higher education: Discussing the promises and problems. *British Journal of Educational Technology, 51*(2), 527–540. DOI: 10.1111/bjet.12946

Selwyn, N., Hillman, T., Bergviken Rensfeldt, A., & Perrotta, C. (2020). Digital technologies and the automation of education. In *The Routledge international handbook of sociology of education* (pp. 405–414). Routledge., DOI: 10.4324/9781315678825-37

Selwyn, N., O'Neill, C., Smith, G., Andrejevic, M., & Gu, X. (2021). A necessary evil? The rise of online exam proctoring in Australian universities. *Media International Australia, Incorporating Culture & Policy, 179*(1), 149–164. DOI: 10.1177/1329878X211005862

Selwyn, N., & Szili, A. (2025). The role of 'AI advocate'teachers in mediating technological change across Australian schools. *Teachers and Teaching*, •••, 1–16. DOI: 10.1080/13540602.2025.2596832

Semi, M. A., Uddin, M. B., Sultana, S., Tamanna, M., Uddin, A., & Ahmed, K. R. (2025). AI-driven education: Integrating machine learning and NLP to transform child learning systems. *International Journal of Advanced Computer Science and Applications, 16*(1), 16–24. DOI: 10.14569/IJACSA.2025.0160603

Sevnarayan, K. (2024). Exploring the dynamics of ChatGPT: Students' and lecturers' perspectives at an open distance e-learning university. *Journal of Pedagogical Research, 8*(2), 212–226. DOI: 10.33902/JPR.202426525

Shabalala, N. P., & Gumbo, M. (2023). Africanising distributed leadership in environmental education curriculum management. *Southern African Journal of Environmental Education, 39*. Advance online publication. DOI: 10.4314/sajee.v39.11

Sharma, D. (2026). From Colonial Schooling to Decolonial Futures: Transforming Education in the Pacific. *International Journal of Social Sciences, Language and Linguistics, 6*(01), 01-10.

Shay, S. (2008). Beyond social constructivist perspectives on assessment: The centring of academic judgement. *Teaching in Higher Education, 13*(5), 595–605. DOI: 10.1080/13562510802334970

Sheikh, F. (2024). AI-powered assessment and feedback: Enhancing student engagement and performance. *AI Edify Journal, 1*(4), 30–37.

Shen, Y., Kang, B., & Münch, F. (2025). Human-Centered AI in Design: Examining Educational Paradigms for Creativity and Responsibility. In Schrepp, M. (Ed.), Lecture Notes in Computer Science: Vol. 15799. *Design, User Experience, and Usability. HCII 2025*. Springer., DOI: 10.1007/978-3-031-93236-6_5

Shermis, M. D. (2014). State-of-the-art automated essay scoring: Competition, results, and future directions from a United States demonstration. *Assessing Writing, 20*, 53–76. DOI: 10.1016/j.asw.2013.04.001

Shermis, M. D., & Burstein, J. (2013). *Handbook of automated essay evaluation*. Routledge., https://psycnet.apa.org/record/2013-15323-000 DOI: 10.4324/9780203122761

Shishavan, H. B. (2024). AI in higher education. In *ASCILITE Publications* (pp. 118–126). DOI: 10.14742/apubs.2024.1205

Shulman, L. S. (1986). Those who understand: Knowledge growth in teaching. *Educational Researcher, 15*(2), 4–14. DOI: 10.3102/0013189X015002004

Shultz, L., & Guaglianone, L. (2015). Creating spaces for a global dimension in education: Policies and practices in Alberta. *Canadian and International Education. Education Canadienne et Internationale, 44*(1), 1–14. DOI: 10.5206/cie-eci.v44i1.9252

Siemens, G., & Baker, R. S. (2012). Learning analytics and educational data mining: Towards communication and collaboration. In *Proceedings of the 2nd International Conference on Learning Analytics and Knowledge* (pp. 252–254). ACM. DOI: 10.1145/2330601.2330661

Simonsen, H. G., & Southwood, F. (2021). Child language assessment across different multilingual contexts: Insights and challenges from South and North. In *Multilingualism across the Lifespan* (pp. 11–30). Routledge. DOI: 10.4324/9781003125815-3

Singh, R. J. (2023). Transforming higher education: The power of artificial intelligence. *International Journal of Multidisciplinary Research in Arts. Science and Technology, 1*(3), 13–18.

Siyi, C., Yu, Q., & Al-Samawi, A. (2023). Effects of digital education on human resource development. *Human Systems Management, 42*(6), 691–706. DOI: 10.3233/HSM-230111

Slade, S., & Prinsloo, P. (2013). Learning analytics: Ethical issues and dilemmas. *The American Behavioral Scientist, 57*(10), 1510–1529. DOI: 10.1177/0002764213479366

Slimi, Z., & Villarejo-Carballido, B. (2024). Unveiling the potential: Experts' perspectives on artificial intelligence integration in higher education. *European Journal of Educational Research, 13*(4), 1477–1492. DOI: 10.12973/eu-jer.13.4.1477

Snyder, H. (2019). Literature review as a research methodology: An overview and guidelines. *Journal of Business Research, 104*, 333–339. DOI: 10.1016/j.jbusres.2019.07.039

Song, N. (2024). Higher education crisis: Academic misconduct with generative AI. *Journal of Contingencies and Crisis Management, 32*(1). Advance online publication. DOI: 10.1111/1468-5973.12532

Sposato, M. (2025). Artificial intelligence in educational leadership: A comprehensive taxonomy and future directions. *International Journal of Educational Technology in Higher Education, 22*(1), 20. DOI: 10.1186/s41239-025-00517-1

Stilgoe, J., Owen, R., & Macnaghten, P. (2020). Developing a framework for responsible innovation. In Krimsky, S. F., & Powell, K. C. (Eds.), *The ethics of nanotechnology, geoengineering, and clean energy* (pp. 347–359). Routledge., DOI: 10.4324/9781003075028-22

Stoesz, B. M., & Eaton, S. E. (2023). Academic integrity policies of publicly funded universities in western Canada. *Educational Policy, 08959048231164209*. Advance online publication. DOI: 10.1177/08959048231164209

Stowell, J. R., & Bennett, D. (2010). Effects of online testing on student exam performance and test anxiety. *Journal of Educational Computing Research, 42*(2), 161–171. DOI: 10.2190/EC.42.2.b

Suchithra, V. G., & Arya, C. S. (2025). The study on ethics and biases in AI-powered education. *European Journal of Contemporary Education and E-Learning, 3*(2), 37–43. DOI: 10.59324/ejceel.2025.3(2).04

Sullivan, M., Kelly, A., & McLaughlan, P. (2023). ChatGPT in higher education: Considerations for academic integrity and student learning. *Journal of Applied Learning & Teaching, 6*(1), 1–10. DOI: 10.37074/jalt.2023.6.1.17

Sulthana, K. F., Rajeshwari, B. S., Ashok, M., & Joel, M. R. (2025). Ensuring fairness in AI-driven university assessments. In *Advances in Computational Intelligence and Robotics Book Series* (pp. 77–108). DOI: 10.4018/979-8-3373-6018-8.ch004

Sundnes, F. (2013). Scrubs and squatters: The coming of the Dukuduku forest, an indigenous forest in KwaZulu-Natal, South Africa. *Environmental History, 18*(2), 277–308. DOI: 10.1093/envhis/emt003

Surahman, E., & Wang, T. H. (2022). Academic dishonesty and trustworthy assessment in online learning: A systematic literature review. *Journal of Computer Assisted Learning, 38*(6), 1535–1553. DOI: 10.1111/jcal.12708

Surden, H. (2019). Artificial intelligence and law: An overview. *Georgia State University Law Review, 35*(4), 1305–1335.

Sutherland-Smith, W. (2008). *Plagiarism, the Internet, and student learning: Improving academic integrity*. Routledge. DOI: 10.4324/9780203928370

Sverdlik, A., Hall, N. C., McAlpine, L., & Hubbard, K. (2018). The PhD experience: A review of the factors influencing doctoral students' completion, achievement, and well-being. *International Journal of Doctoral Studies, 13*, 361–388. DOI: 10.28945/4113

Swaffield, S. (2011). Getting to the heart of authentic assessment for learning. *Assessment in Education: Principles, Policy & Practice, 18*(4), 433–449. DOI: 10.1080/0969594X.2011.582838

Swauger, S. (2020). *Our bodies encoded: Algorithmic test proctoring in higher education*. Hybrid Pedagogy., DOI: 10.21428/3f68b4f3.1fb6fa0e

Swauger, S. (2020). Software that monitors students during exams perpetuates inequity. *Teaching in Higher Education, 25*(1), 104–107. DOI: 10.1080/13562517.2019.1677821

Sweeney, L. (2013). Discrimination in online ad delivery. *Communications of the ACM, 56*(5), 44–54. DOI: 10.1145/2447976.2447990

Swiecki, Z., Khosravi, H., Chen, G., Martinez-Maldonado, R., Lodge, J. M., Milligan, S., Selwyn, N., & Gašević, D. (2022). Assessment in the age of artificial intelligence. *Computers and Education: Artificial Intelligence, 3*, 100075. DOI: 10.1016/j.caeai.2022.100075

Tai, J., Ajjawi, R., Boud, D., Dawson, P., & Panadero, E. (2018). Developing evaluative judgement: Enabling students to make decisions about the quality of work. *Higher Education, 76*(3), 467–481. DOI: 10.1007/s10734-017-0220-3

Tan, M. J. T., & Maravilla, N. M. A. T. (2024). Shaping integrity: Why generative artificial intelligence does not have to undermine education. *Frontiers in Artificial Intelligence, 7*, 1471224. Advance online publication. DOI: 10.3389/frai.2024.1471224 PMID: 39512399

Tannock, S. (2017). No grades in higher education now! Revisiting the place of graded assessment in the reimagination of the public university. *Studies in Higher Education, 42*(8), 1345–1357. DOI: 10.1080/03075079.2015.1092131

Taylor, L. (2025). Contributing to Multimodal Construct Definition and Operationalization: Insights from Research into Language Assessment Accommodations. *Language Assessment Quarterly, 22*(4-5), 609–622. DOI: 10.1080/15434303.2025.2601851

Tehzeeb, N., & Raza, A. (2022). Understanding social and ethical implications of artificial intelligence. *Pakistan Journal of Social Research, 4*(4), 708–716. DOI: 10.52567/pjsr.v4i04.884

Tensen, D. (2025). Using AI to generate formative feedback in doctoral education. *Assessment & Evaluation in Higher Education*. Advance online publication. DOI: 10.1080/02602938.2025.2536558

Thai, H., Nguyen, M., Nguyen, H. T. T., Vo, D. T. H., Thanh, B. N., Nguyen, K., Ha, S., & Le, T. V. A. (2024). Educational technology and responsible automated essay scoring in the generative AI era. In *Practice, Progress, and Proficiency in Sustainability* (pp. 325–356). DOI: 10.4018/979-8-3693-2827-9.ch011

Tierney, W. G., & Sabharwal, N. S. (2017). Academic corruption: Culture and trust in Indian higher education. *International Journal of Educational Development, 55*, 30–40. DOI: 10.1016/j.ijedudev.2017.05.003

Tlili, A., Shehata, B., Adarkwah, M. A., Bozkurt, A., Hickey, D. T., Huang, R., & Agyemang, B. (2023). What if the devil is my guardian angel: ChatGPT as a case study of using chatbots in education. *Smart Learning Environments*, *10*(1), 15. Advance online publication. DOI: 10.1186/s40561-023-00237-x

Torrisí-Steele, G. (2025). AI and curriculum. In *Advances in Computational Intelligence and Robotics Book Series* (pp. 147–170). DOI: 10.4018/979-8-3373-2397-8.ch006

Tran, M. N., Hogg, L., & Marshall, S. (2022). Understanding postgraduate students' perceptions of plagiarism: A case study of Vietnamese and local students in New Zealand. *International Journal for Educational Integrity*, *18*(1), 3. DOI: 10.1007/s40979-021-00098-2

Tran, M., Balasooriya, C., Jonnagaddala, J., Leung, G. K. K., Mahboobani, N., Ramani, S., Rhee, J., Schuwirth, L., Najafzadeh-Tabrizi, N. S., Semmler, C., & Wong, Z. S. (2025). Situating governance and regulatory concerns for generative artificial intelligence and large language models in medical education. *NPJ Digital Medicine*, *8*(1), 315. DOI: 10.1038/s41746-025-01721-z PMID: 40425695

Trowler, P. (2014). Depicting and researching disciplines: Strong and moderate essentialist approaches. *Studies in Higher Education*, *39*(10), 1720–1731. DOI: 10.1080/03075079.2013.801431

Tsai, Y. S., Rates, D., Moreno-Marcos, P. M., Muñoz-Merino, P. J., Jivet, I., Scheffel, M., Drachsler, H., Delgado Kloos, C., & Gašević, D. (2020). Learning analytics in European higher education: Trends and barriers. *Computers & Education*, *155*, 103933. DOI: 10.1016/j.compedu.2020.103933

Tsai, Y. S., Whitelock-Wainwright, A., & Gašević, D. (2021). The privacy paradox and its implications for learning analytics. *LAK21: 11th International Learning Analytics and Knowledge Conference*, 71-81. DOI: 10.1145/3448139.3448155

Twabu, K., & Nakene-Mginqi, M. (2024, December). Developing a design thinking artificial intelligence driven auto-marking/grading system for assessments to reduce the workload of lecturers at a higher learning institution in South Africa. In *Frontiers in Education* (Vol. 9, p. 1512569). Frontiers Media SA. https://doi.DOI: 10.3389/feduc.2024.1512569

Twum-Danso Imoh, A., & Gupta, N. (Eds.). (2021). *Children's lives in an era of children's rights: The progress of the convention on the rights of the child in Africa*. Routledge., DOI: 10.4324/9781003111719

Ukashatu, A., Suleiman, M. M., & Mahmoud, M. A. (2021). Emerging issues in educational measurement: Authentic assessment. *JISAE: Journal of Indonesian Student Assessment and Evaluation*, *7*(2), 73–80. DOI: 10.21009/jisae.v7i2.23056

UNESCO. (2021). *Recommendation on the ethics of artificial intelligence.*

UNESCO. (2021). *Recommendation on the ethics of artificial intelligence*. https://bsu.buap.mx/b2m

UNESCO. (2023). *Guidance for generative AI in education and research*. UNESCO Publishing. https://www.unesco.org

UNESCO. (2023). *Guidance for generative AI in education and research.* UNESCO. https://unesdoc.unesco.org/

UNESCO. (2024). *AI competency framework for teachers*. United Nations Educational, Scientific and Cultural Organization., DOI: 10.54675/ZJTE2084

United Nations Educational, Scientific and Cultural Organization. (2021). *AI and education: Guidance for policymakers*. UNESCO.

University Grants Commission. (2020). *Guidelines on academic integrity and prevention of plagiarism*. UGC.

University of Hong Kong. (2023). *Interim guidance to staff and students on the use of generative AI*. https://tl.hku.hk/generative-ai/

Urzúa, C. A. C. (2025). Effects of AI-assisted feedback via generative models on student writing and self-monitoring. Education Sciences, 15(10)*, 1396. DOI: 10.3390/educsci15101396

Usher, M. (2025). Generative AI vs. instructor vs. peer assessments: A comparison of grading and feedback. *Assessment & Evaluation in Higher Education*, *50*(6), 912–927. Advance online publication. DOI: 10.1080/02602938.2025.2487495

van den Berg, G., & du Plessis, E. (2023). ChatGPT and generative AI: Possibilities for its contribution to lesson planning, critical thinking and openness in teacher education. *Education Sciences*, *13*(10), 998. Advance online publication. DOI: 10.3390/educsci13100998

van der Waldt, G. (2020). Constructing conceptual frameworks in social science research. *The Journal for Transdisciplinary Research in Southern Africa*, *16*(1), a758. Advance online publication. DOI: 10.4102/td.v16i1.758

van Norren, D. E. (2023). The ethics of artificial intelligence, UNESCO and the African Ubuntu perspective. *Journal of Information. Communication and Ethics in Society*, *21*(1), 112–128. DOI: 10.1108/JICES-04-2022-0037

van Wyk, M. M. (2025). Postgraduate students' voices on leveraging Grammarly as an AI-powered tool in academic writing. *Journal of Education*, *98*(98), 103–123. DOI: 10.17159/2520-9868/i98a06

van Wyk, M. M., Adarkwah, M. A., & Amponsah, S. (2023). Why all the hype about ChatGPT? Academics' views of a chat-based conversational learning strategy at an open distance e-learning institution. *Open Praxis*, *15*(3), 191–205. DOI: 10.55982/openpraxis.15.3.563

Vangibhuratha, S. K. (2025). The impact of generative AI on educational assessment. *International Journal of Innovative Research in Engineering & Multidisciplinary Physical Sciences*, *13*(4). Advance online publication. DOI: 10.37082/ijirmps.v13.i4.232678

Vashchenko, M., Taraniuk, L., Danko, Y., & Taraniuk, K. (2018). Assessment of the technological readiness of the countries of the world for the radical innovations. *Marketing & Management of Innovations*, *4*, 86–97. DOI: 10.21272/mmi.2018.4-08

Veale, M., & Edwards, L. (2018). Clarity, surprises, and further questions in the GDPR's "right to explanation". *Computer Law & Security Review*, *34*(2), 398–404. DOI: 10.1016/j.clsr.2017.12.002

Venkatesh, V., Morris, M. G., Davis, G. B., & Davis, F. D. (2003). User acceptance of information technology: Toward a unified view. *Management Information Systems Quarterly*, *27*(3), 425–478. DOI: 10.2307/30036540

Verwoerd, J. C. (2025). Balancing innovation and ethics: A framework for responsible AI integration in educational assessment. *Preprints.org*. DOI: 10.20944/preprints202508.1696.v1

Villarroel, V., Bloxham, S., Bruna, D., Bruna, C., & Herrera-Seda, C. (2018). Authentic assessment: Creating a blueprint for course design. *Assessment & Evaluation in Higher Education*, *43*(5), 840–854. DOI: 10.1080/02602938.2017.1412396

Villarroel, V., Boud, D., Bloxham, S., Bruna, D., & Bruna, C. (2020). Using principles of authentic assessment to redesign written examinations and tests. *Innovations in Education and Teaching International*, *57*(1), 38–49. DOI: 10.1080/14703297.2018.1564882

Vlachopoulos, D., & Makri, A. (2024). A systematic literature review on authentic assessment in higher education: Best practices for the development of 21st century skills, and policy considerations. *Studies in Educational Evaluation*, *83*, 101425. Advance online publication. DOI: 10.1016/j.stueduc.2024.101425

Vogel, C., Schwaibold, U., & Misser, S. (2015). 'Teaching and Learning for Climate Change'–The Role of Teacher Materials and Curriculum Design in South Africa. *Southern African Journal of Environmental Education*, *31*, 78–97.

Vogt, K., & Antia, B. E. (Eds.). (2024). *Multilingual Assessment: Finding the Nexus?* Peter Lang. DOI: 10.3726/b21992

Von Schomberg, R. (2013). A vision of responsible research and innovation. In Owen, R., Bessant, J., & Heintz, M. (Eds.), *Responsible innovation: Managing the responsible emergence of science and innovation in society* (pp. 51–74). Wiley., DOI: 10.1002/9781118551424.ch3

Wachter, S., Mittelstadt, B., & Floridi, L. (2017). Why a right to explanation of automated decision-making does not exist in the General Data Protection Regulation. *International Data Privacy Law*, *7*(2), 76–99. DOI: 10.1093/idpl/ipx005

Wang, L., & Zhan, S. (2024). How can generative AI benefit educators in designing assessments in computer science? *Education Research and Perspectives*, *51*, 82–101. DOI: 10.70953/ERPv51.2412004

Wang, S., Wang, F., Zhu, Z., Wang, J., Tran, T., & Du, Z. (2024). Artificial intelligence in education: A systematic literature review. *Expert Systems with Applications*, *252*, 124167. DOI: 10.1016/j.eswa.2024.124167

Wang, X., Sanders, H. M., Liu, Y., Seang, K., Tran, B. X., Atanasov, A. G., Qiu, Y., Tang, S., Car, J., Wang, Y. X., Wong, T. Y., Tham, Y. C., & Chung, K. C. (2023). ChatGPT: Promise and challenges for deployment in low- and middle-income countries. *The Lancet Regional Health. Western Pacific*, *41*, 100905. DOI: 10.1016/j.lanwpc.2023.100905 PMID: 37731897

Watson, G., & Sottile, J. (2010). Cheating in the digital age: Do students cheat more in online courses? *Online Journal of Distance Learning Administration*, *13*(1), 1–10.

Weber-Wulff, D., Anohina-Naumeca, A., Bjelobaba, S., Foltýnek, T., Guerrero-Dib, J., Popoola, O., Šigut, P., & Waddington, L. (2023). Testing of detection tools for AI-generated text. *International Journal for Educational Integrity*, *19*(1), 26. Advance online publication. DOI: 10.1007/s40979-023-00146-z

Weideman, A. (2022). Context, construct, and validation: A perspective from South Africa. *Language Assessment Quarterly*, *19*(2), 124–141. DOI: 10.1080/15434303.2020.1860991

Weng, X. (2024). A scoping review on current research status and trends in generative AI impact on higher education assessment. Australasian Journal of Educational Technology, 40(5)*, 9540. DOI: 10.14742/ajet.9540

White, A. (2024). The *Transition In* framework: Supporting the transition of students into post-graduate taught study. *Innovations in Education and Teaching International*, *61*(4), 703–715. DOI: 10.1080/14703297.2023.2216682

Whitelock, D., Gilbert, L., & Gale, V. (2015). *Technology enhanced assessment and feedback*. British Educational Research Association. DOI: 10.13140/RG.2.1.4548.8966

Whitley, B. E., & Keith-Spiegel, P. (2002). *Academic dishonesty: An educator's guide*. Lawrence Erlbaum Associates.

Whittemore, R., & Knafl, K. (2005). The integrative review: Updated methodology. *Journal of Advanced Nursing*, *52*(5), 546–553. DOI: 10.1111/j.1365-2648.2005.03621.x PMID: 16268861

Wickramasinghe, M., Gunawardena, L., & Padukkage, A. (2026). Ethical principles for artificial intelligence in education: A meta-review approach. *AI and Ethics*, *6*(1), 63–75. DOI: 10.1007/s43681-025-00878-3

Wiggins, G. (1990). The case for authentic assessment. *Practical Assessment, Research & Evaluation*. https://scholarworks.umass.edu/pare/vol2/iss1/2/

Williamson, B. (2017). Big data in education: The digital future of learning, policy and practice. *Sage (Atlanta, Ga.)*. Advance online publication. DOI: 10.4135/9781529714920

Williamson, B., Bayne, S., & Shay, S. (2020). The datafication of teaching in Higher Education: Critical issues and perspectives. *Teaching in Higher Education*, *25*(4), 351–365. DOI: 10.1080/13562517.2020.1748811

Williamson, B., & Eynon, R. (2020). Historical threads, missing links, and future directions in AI in education. *Learning, Media and Technology*, *45*(3), 223–235. DOI: 10.1080/17439884.2020.1798995

Williamson, B., Eynon, R., & Potter, J. (2020). Pandemic politics, pedagogies and practices: Digital technologies and distance education during the coronavirus emergency. *Learning, Media and Technology*, *45*(2), 107–114. DOI: 10.1080/17439884.2020.1761641

Williamson, B., & Hogan, A. (2020). Commercialisation and privatisation in/of education in the context of AI. *Globalisation, Societies and Education*, *18*(4), 1–17. DOI: 10.1080/14767724.2020.1718754

Williamson, B., & Hogan, A. (2020). Commercialisation and privatisation in/of education in the context of Covid-19. *Journal of Education Policy*, *35*(4), 487–507. DOI: 10.1080/02680939.2020.1752031

Winstone, N. E., & Carless, D. (2020). *Designing effective feedback processes in higher education: A learning-focused approach*. Routledge., DOI: 10.4324/9781351115940

Woolf, B. P. (2010). *Building intelligent interactive tutors: Student-centered strategies for revolutionizing e-learning*. Morgan Kaufmann.

Woolf, B. P., Burleson, W., Arroyo, I., Dragon, T., Cooper, D. G., & Picard, R. W. (2013). AI grand challenges for education. *AI Magazine*, *34*(4), 66–84. DOI: 10.1609/aimag.v34i4.2490

Wozniak, H., Mahony, M. J., Lever, T., & Pizzica, J. (2009). Stepping through the orientation looking glass: A staged approach for postgraduate students. *Australasian Journal of Educational Technology*, *25*(2), 221–334. DOI: 10.14742/ajet.1151

Wu, Z. (2026). Evaluating the impact of AI tools on academic performance and student satisfaction. *Journal of Computer Assisted Learning*, *42*(2), e70225. DOI: 10.1002/jcal.70225

Xeketwana, S., & Robinson, M. (2026). The teaching and learning of isiXhosa for communicative purposes in teacher education for the Foundation Phase. *Southern African Linguistics and Applied Language Studies*, *44*(1), 240–255. DOI: 10.2989/16073614.2024.2357325

Xia, Q., & Weng, X. (2024). A scoping review on how generative artificial intelligence impacts higher education assessment research. *International Journal of Educational Technology in Higher Education*, *21*, 68. Advance online publication. DOI: 10.1186/s41239-024-00468-z

Xu, H. (2026). AI-powered technologies in physical education: Impact on physical and psycho-emotional well-being of students. *The Journal of General Psychology*, *153*(1), 130–151. DOI: 10.1080/00221309.2025.2541585

Yalçin-Incik, E., & Incik, T. (2022). Generation Z students' views on technology in education: What they want what they get. *Malaysian Online Journal of Educational Technology*, *10*(2), 109–124. DOI: 10.52380/mojet.2022.10.2.275

Yang, H., & Kyun, S. (2022). The current research trend of artificial intelligence in language learning: A systematic empirical literature review from an activity theory perspective. *Australasian Journal of Educational Technology*, *38*(5), 180–210. DOI: 10.14742/ajet.7492

Yang, L. P., & Xin, T. (2022). Changing educational assessments in the post-COVID-19 era: From assessment of learning (AoL) to assessment as learning (AaL). *Educational Measurement: Issues and Practice*, *41*(1), 54–60. DOI: 10.1111/emip.12492

Yani, A., & Rosita, R. (2025). Integrating AI in outcome-based education. In *Advances in Computational Intelligence and Robotics Book Series* (pp. 133–162). DOI: 10.4018/979-8-3373-1062-6.ch005

Yan, L., Sha, L., Zhao, L., Li, Y., Martinez-Maldonado, R., Chen, G., Li, X., Jin, Y., & Gašević, D. (2024). Practical and ethical challenges of large language models in education: A systematic scoping review. *British Journal of Educational Technology*, *55*(1), 90–112. DOI: 10.1111/bjet.13370

Yazici, T. (2026). Artificial Intelligence Ethics in Communication: Challenges and Future Perspectives. Navigating Modern Digital Communication Ethics and Law, 33-74.

Yende, S. J. (2021). Factors of effective postgraduate student-supervisor relationships at selected universities in South Africa. *Journal of African Education*, *2*(2), 135–155. DOI: 10.31920/2633-2930/2021/v2n2a6

Yin, F. (2025). Encoding/decoding in artificial intelligence: Global AI and local languages. [Top of Form Bottom of Form Top of Form Bottom of Form]. *Media Culture & Society*, *47*(8), 1691–1701. DOI: 10.1177/01634437251360381

Yoshida, M., Duangchinda, V., & Ruangrit, N. (2026). AI-supported learning in online discussion forums: A scoping review. *Electronic Journal of e-Learning*, *24*(1), 19–35. DOI: 10.34190/ejel.24.1.4409

Zawacki-Richter, O., Marín, V. I., Bond, M., & Gouverneur, F. (2019). Systematic review of research on artificial intelligence applications in higher education: Where are the educators? *International Journal of Educational Technology in Higher Education*, *16*(1), 1–27. DOI: 10.1186/s41239-019-0171-0

Zhang, C., & Lu, Y. (2021). Study on artificial intelligence: The state of the art and future prospects. *Journal of Industrial Information Integration*, *23*, 100224. DOI: 10.1016/j.jii.2021.100224

Zhang, F., Gou, J., Shen, K. N., Camarinha-Matos, L. M., & Wang, Z. (2025). Effects of AI teammates on learning behavior in human-AI collaboration environments: A perspective on self-regulated learning. *Education and Information Technologies*, *30*(18), 26801–26825. DOI: 10.1007/s10639-025-13717-z

Zhang, J., & Wu, H. (2025). Reimagining South–South Higher Education Interactions Under "Triple Disruptions.". *Ecnu Review of Education*, *8*(3), 638–657. DOI: 10.1177/20965311251335986

Zhang, X. (2025). Fairness and effectiveness in AI-driven educational assessments: Challenges and mitigation strategies. *Journal of Innovation and Development*, *11*(1), 7–10. DOI: 10.54097/adcxze34

Zhang, Z., & Perez-Paredes, P. (2021). Chinese postgraduate EFL learners' self-directed use of mobile English learning resources. *Computer Assisted Language Learning*, *34*(8), 1128–1153. DOI: 10.1080/09588221.2019.1662455

Zhao, C. (2024). AI-assisted assessment in higher education: A systematic review. *Journal of Educational Technology and Innovation*, *6*(4). Advance online publication. DOI: 10.61414/jeti.v6i4.209

Zhao, J., Chapman, E., & Sabet, P. G. P. (2025). Generative AI and educational assessments: Synthesis of empirical evidence. *Educational Assessment*, *51*, 124–155.

Zhao, Y., Ni, Y., Zhou, R., & Wu, S. (2021). Accessibility and inclusion challenges in AI-based educational systems. *Computers & Education*, *168*, 104195. DOI: 10.1016/j.compedu.2021.104195

About the Contributors

Oluwatoyin Ajani holds a Doctor of Philosophy degree in Curriculum Studies, awarded by the University of Zululand, South Africa, and is currently a Senior Lecturer in Curriculum Studies and Education Studies at the University of KwaZulu-Natal, South Africa. His academic work is situated at the intersection of curriculum theory, teacher education, assessment practices, and higher education transformation, with a sustained focus on quality, inclusion, and contextual responsiveness within African education systems. Dr Ajani has an established record of scholarly contributions in peer-reviewed journals, edited books, and conference proceedings, with research interests that include digital pedagogy, artificial intelligence in education, inclusive curriculum design, and academic integrity in higher education. He has supervised postgraduate research at master's and doctoral levels, contributed to curriculum development and quality assurance initiatives, and serves as an editor and reviewer for international journals and academic publishers. His work consistently engages global debates while foregrounding South African higher education as a critical site for comparative and socially just educational inquiry.

***

Siham Abukhalaf is a PhD researcher at Deakin University, specialising in AI-integrated authentic assessments.

SalamAl-E'mari earned her Ph.D. in Cybersecurity from Universiti Sains Malaysia (USM) in 2022. She is the Chair of the Information Security Department and an Assistant Professor at the University of Petra (UoP). With expertise in Blockchain, Deep Learning, and Network Security, she has contributed significantly to cybersecurity research. She previously earned her Bachelor's and Master's in Computer Science from Yarmouk University, Jordan, shaping her strong foundation in security and technology.

Deepak Chahal is working as Professor in Department of Information Technology at Jagan Institute of Management Studies, Sector-5,Rohini, New Delhi, India. He has over 18 years of teaching and 3 years of research experience in IT. He has done MCA & PhD in Computer Science. He served as Editor of Springer CCIS Volumes conducted under acronym of ICICCT, the volumes are indexed in Scopus & DBLP. His area of interest includes Machine Learning, Big Data & Networking. He has published & reviewed various research & technical papers in reputed national & international journals. Most of the published papers are indexed in Scopus.

Tendai Charles is an Assistant Professor of Education at the British University in Dubai. He holds an MSc in Data Analytics & Social Statistics from the University of Manchester and a PhD in Education from the University of York. He is an accredited researcher with the Office for National Statistics and is a Fellow of the Royal Statistical Society. He is a post-positivist researcher who specialises in evidence-based education and uses computational statistics for secondary data analyses.

Rajesh Dhaka is Assistant Professor in the Department of Education Jagannath University, NCR, Bahadurgarh. She has 7 years of Teaching Experience at college level. She has awarded her doctoral degree from Jaipur National University, Jaipur & M.A, M.Ed. from M.D. University, Rohtak. She is the member of the panel of Evaluator, Paper- setter & External Examiner. Dr. Rajesh has attended various FDPs, Workshops, National and International Seminars, Conferences, Refresher Courses & Orientation Programme. She has published a number of Research Papers in the reputed Journals. She has also published book & chapters in various book.

Ntandokamenzi Dlamini is an academic in the Department of Curriculum and Instructional Studies at the College of Education, University of South Africa. Her work is on gender and technology and pedagogy improvement. She is dedicated to improving pedagogy and nurturing the next generation of teachers.

Fadi Fataftah is an information technology professional, researcher, and educator with expertise in cybersecurity, cloud computing, healthcare IT, virtual care, artificial intelligence, and emerging digital technologies. He holds a PhD in Information Technology from North-West University, South Africa, where his research focused on risk assessment for big data in cloud computing environments. He currently works in healthcare technology and virtual care within a Canadian hospital setting, focusing on clinical workflow analysis, virtual care implementation, testing, training, change-impact review, and secure digital health service delivery. He is also a sessional faculty member at University Canada West, teaching in Computer Science, information systems, and emerging technologies. His publications include peer-reviewed journal articles, IEEE conference papers, and book chapters related to cybersecurity, cloud security, artificial intelligence, business intelligence, digital transformation, cyber insurance, edge intelligence, digital twins, and healthcare technology.

Viji Gripsy J is an Associate Professor in the Department of Computer Science with Cognitive Systems at PSGR Krishnammal College for Women, Coimbatore. She has extensive experience in teaching, academic administration, curriculum development, research, and industry-oriented education. Her areas of interest include Artificial Intelligence, Machine Learning, Cognitive Computing, IoT, Cybersecurity, and emerging technologies. She has contributed to several research publications, book chapters, conferences, academic projects, and industry-academia initiatives, with a strong focus on innovative teaching, student skill development, and technology-driven education.

Neha Guliani, B.Tech, M.Tech, Pursuing Ph.D., is a distinguished academician with over 20 years of rich teaching experience in reputed Engineering Colleges and Management Institutes affiliated with government universities. She has strong subject expertise in Business Research and Business Ethics, Organizational Behaviour, Business Communication, and Soft Skills. She has an impressive research profile, having published 18 research papers in reputed national and international journals and conferences. Her teaching philosophy integrates strong theoretical foundations with practical, real-world applications, enabling students to develop robust academic understanding as well as professional competencies.

M. Hemalatha is an Associate Professor in the PG & Research Department of Computer Science at Sri Ramakrishna College of Arts & Science, Nava India, Peelamedu, Coimbatore, Tamil Nadu, India. She is actively engaged in teaching, research, and academic activities in the field of Computer Science. Her research interests encompass emerging areas of computing and interdisciplinary applications of information technology. She is committed to promoting research-oriented education, innovation, and the development of technical skills among students. She is also an active researcher with an ORCID profile (0000-0001-5345-2375), reflecting her contributions to the academic and research community.

Raman Joshi is a dedicated academician and researcher with over 19 years of teaching experience in the field of Computer Science and Engineering. He is currently serving as an Assistant Professor in the Department of Computer Science at Jagannath University, Jaipur. He holds a B.Tech in Computer Science, a Post Graduate Diploma from C-DAC, Bangalore, and an M.Tech in Computer Science. He is presently pursuing his Ph.D. in Computer Science, further strengthening his research and academic expertise. Mr. Yadav has published numerous research papers in reputed national and international journals and has presented his work at various conferences and seminars. He has actively participated in workshops and faculty development programs to stay updated with emerging technologies and academic advancements. His core areas of interest include Nature-Inspired Algorithms and Programming Languages. Alongside teaching, he is actively involved in research activities, curriculum development, and mentoring students, contributing significantly to academic excellence and innovation.

M. Sasi Kala is the Head of the Department of Data Science at PSGR Krishnammal College for Women, Coimbatore. She is actively involved in teaching, research, academic administration, and curriculum development in the field of Data Science and emerging technologies. With a strong commitment to academic excellence, she contributes to fostering innovation, research, and industry-oriented learning among students. As the department head, she plays a key role in guiding faculty members, mentoring students, promoting research activities, and strengthening the department's academic and professional initiatives.

Nthabiseng Khoalenyane is a lecturer and researcher in the Faculty of Education (Department of Languages and Social Sciences Education) at the University of Zululand. Her research interests span myriad areas, including language education, technology in education, tourism development, community involvement, and inclusive tourism. She has published several articles and book chapters in language education, technology in education, and tourism development. Her strong organisational and administrative skills, along with her ability to collaborate effectively as a team player, are evident in her experience co-authoring and coordinating projects.

Nontobeko Khumalo is an Associate Professor in the Department of Curriculum and Instructional Studies at the University of South Africa (UNSA), where she teaches undergraduate (B. Ed) students and supervises postgraduate students. She has co-authored several peer-reviewed articles and book chapters. She has also presented at several local, regional, and international Conferences and has been a co-researcher on national and international community engagement projects. Her research interests are teacher education, academic literacy, scholarship of teaching and learning, assessment, and curriculum studies.

Rohit Markan has a working experience of 25+ years in the field of Academics and Research. Guided a numerous research Scholars of M. Phil and Ph. D. Published number of Research Papers in Various journals and national and international Conferences.

Tinashe Matiyenga is a Post-Doctoral Research Fellow (PDRF) in the Department of Languages and Social Sciences, Faculty of Education, at the University of Zululand. He is an alumnus of NIHSS-CODESRIA and a Doctor of Literature and Philosophy (D. Lit et Phil) in English Language and Comparative Literature. His foundational research explores the intersection of linguistic and literary analysis, grounded in appraisal linguistics and the extended pragma-dialectical perspective. Tinashe's research interests are diverse, and he has published peer-reviewed works on discourse analysis, language education, technology in education, social media dynamics, language and the media, translanguaging, and language contact, all examined from a decolonial perspective.

Luthando Molefe is currently a Ph.D. candidate in the Discipline of Teacher Education and Professional Development at the University of KwaZulu-Natal's School of Education in South Africa. He recently served as a Visiting Student Researcher at the University of Northern Iowa's College of Education in the United States of America. His research interests include self-reflexive methodologies (autoethnography, narrative inquiry and self-study), arts-based research, professional learning, teacher professional development, natural sciences teachers and teaching, rurality and rural education and community-engaged scholarship. He has presented his research at a number of national and international conferences and he has successfully supervised numerous postgraduate students.

Welile Ntombifuthi Msimango is a veteran lecturer in the Department of Educational Foundations, Curriculum and Instructional Studies cluster, at the University of Zululand's Faculty of Education. She specializes in curriculum and instructional studies, with active involvement in teaching, postgraduate research supervision and community engagement. Msimango also contributes to institutional development through her service on various academic committees. Her research focuses on curriculum development, inclusive education, teacher education programmes and the integration of contemporary technologies in teaching and learning. As a recognized scholar, she is committed to advancing educational practice through scholarly publications and innovative approaches that respond to the evolving needs of South African and global education.

Naveen Nandal is an Associate Professor at DIHE, Rohini, Delhi. Dr. Naveen Nandal is a distinguished academic and research professional with over 12 years of experience in teaching, research, and analytics. Currently an Associate Professor at JIMS, Delhi, she has published over 80 research papers, authored six books, and holds several patents. She has contributed extensively to Scopus-indexed, ABDC, WOS, and peer-reviewed journals. She has served as Analytics Area Chair and Research & Publication Head, actively involved in curriculum design, faculty development, and research guidance. Dr. Nandal is a reviewer for Sage and Emerald publications, a founding member of the Research India Foundation, and has extensive experience delivering impactful training and mentoring in marketing, human resource management, and data analytics domains.

Nokuthula Nkosi is a Lecturer at the University of South Africa, where she teaches Sociology of Education at the undergraduate level and supervises Honours and Master's students. She holds a Master of

Education in Curriculum and Evaluation, a Bachelor of Arts in Historical Studies, and a Bachelor of Education, all from the University of Johannesburg. She is currently pursuing her PhD in Education at the University of Johannesburg. Her research interests include epistemic justice, rhizomatic education, knowledge democracy, and Social Sciences Education.

Nokubongwa Ntuli is a Life Sciences and Natural Sciences teacher at Georgetown High School in Pietermaritzburg, KwaZulu-Natal, South Africa. She is currently pursuing a Master's degree in the discipline of Science Education at the University of KwaZulu-Natal's School of Education. Her research interests include environmental education, natural sciences teaching and pedagogy, and sustainability within the science curriculum. Through her dual role as an educator and researcher, she investigates pedagogical approaches that advance environmental awareness and support meaningful scientific learning among diverse student populations in the South African context.

Patrick Nyathi is a History of Education Lecturer in the Department of Education Foundations at the University of South Africa (UNISA) and is currently a registered PhD student in History at the University of the Witwatersrand, Johannesburg, South Africa. His research interests include Environmental History, the history of education in South Africa, rural education in under-resourced environments, land dispossession, traditional leadership and forced removals.

Siyacela Nzuza is a lecturer in the Department of Curriculum and Instructional Studies at the University of Zululand, Faculty of Education. He specializes in Curriculum Studies, with a strong focus on teaching, postgraduate supervision and scholarly output. His research interests include curriculum development, teacher education programmes, inclusive education and the integration of emerging technologies in teaching and learning. He teaches a range of modules within the curriculum studies discipline and actively contributes to academic publications. Passionate about curriculum theory and practice, Nzuza is committed to advancing educational transformation through innovative pedagogy and evidence-based inquiry that addresses contemporary challenges in South African and global education.

Michael Oyenuga holds a PhD in Marketing and Communication and has over 25 years of experience in scholarly and practitioner roles, spanning education policy, digital transformation, and inclusive learning. His research interests cut across marketing, branding, consumer behaviour, education and sustainability. He is an Associate Professor and the pioneer Assistant Dean at the School of Business, Woxsen University, Hyderabad, India.

Sabyasachi Pramanik is a professional IEEE member. He obtained a PhD in Computer Science and Engineering from Sri Satya Sai University of Technology and Medical Sciences, Bhopal, India. Presently, he is an Associate Professor, Department of Computer Science and Engineering, Haldia Institute of Technology, India. He has many publications in various reputed international conferences, journals, and book chapters (Indexed by SCIE, Scopus, ESCI, etc). He is doing research in the fields of Artificial Intelligence, Data Privacy, Cybersecurity, Network Security, and Machine Learning. He also serves on the editorial boards of several international journals. He is a reviewer of journal articles from IEEE, Springer, Elsevier, Inderscience, IET and IGI Global. He has reviewed many conference papers, has been a keynote speaker, session chair, and technical program committee member at many international conferences. He has authored a book on Wireless Sensor Network. He has edited 8 books from IGI Global, CRC Press, Springer and Wiley Publications.

Azash S MD is an Assistant Professor (Senior Scale) at the School of Law, Presidency University, Bengaluru. With a prolific academic portfolio, he has authored 23 journal articles and contributed to two books. His scholarly work reflects a strong commitment to legal studies, contributing to the intellectual depth and academic reputation of the institution. Azash's research contributions underscore his emerging influence in the legal academic community.

Yousef Sanjalawe is an Assistant Professor specializing in Cybersecurity and Cloud Computing at the University of Jordan (JU), Jordan. He earned his PhD in Cloud Computing from Universiti Sains Malaysia (USM) in 2020, where his research focused on enhancing cloud service broker selection using optimization algorithms. Dr. Sanjalawe has extensive experience in academia, research, and professional training. He has supervised Ph.D. students in Cybersecurity, Cloud Computing, IoT, Fog Computing, Optimization, and Artificial Intelligence (AI). From 2023 to 2024, he served as the Chair of the Cybersecurity Department at the American University of Madaba (AUM), Jordan, and from 2022 to 2024, he was an Assistant Professor in Cybersecurity at AUM.

Ratan Sarkar is an Assistant Professor in the Department of Education, Tezpur University (A Central University), Assam, India. Previously, he served nearly seven years as Assistant Professor in the Department of Teachers' Training (B.Ed.), Prabhat Kumar College, Contai (Vidyasagar University), and as Guest Faculty at National Institute for Empowerment of Persons with Intellectual Disabilities, Regional Centre, Kolkata. He holds a Ph.D. in Education from Pondicherry University, an M.Ed. and M.Phil. in Special Education from Ramakrishna Mission Vivekananda Educational and Research Institute, Belur Math, and an M.A. in Education and Technology from Tata Institute of Social Sciences, Mumbai. He began his academic journey with a B.Ed. in Special Education (Jadavpur University) and a B.A. in English (Hons) from Siliguri College (University of North Bengal), Darjeeling. Dr. Sarkar has published extensively in leading journals (SAGE, Springer, Routledge, Wiley), authored books, chapters, and reviews, and led projects under the Ministry of Education, Govt. of India. His works on inclusive education, EdTech, disability studies, policy advocacy to advance equitable learning ecosystems.

Nidhi Shukla is a senior academician and Professor of Management with over two decades of teaching and research experience. She holds a PhD from the University of Lucknow and specializes in Marketing, Leadership, Entrepreneurship, and Strategic Management. Dr. Shukla has taught across reputed universities and has actively contributed to academic administration, women empowerment initiatives, and student development activities. She has published extensively in national and international journals, guided doctoral research, and is known for integrating management education with real-world and societal perspectives.

Suraj Yadav is a dedicated academician and researcher with over 19 years of teaching experience in the field of Computer Science and Engineering. He is currently serving as an Assistant Professor in the Department of Computer Science at Jagannath University, Jaipur. He holds a B.Tech in Computer Science, a Post Graduate Diploma from C-DAC, Bangalore, and an M.Tech in Computer Science. He is presently pursuing his Ph.D. in Computer Science, further strengthening his research and academic expertise. Mr.

Yadav has published numerous research papers in reputed national and international journals and has presented his work at various conferences and seminars. He has actively participated in workshops and faculty development programs to stay updated with emerging technologies and academic advancements. His core areas of interest include Nature-Inspired Algorithms and Programming Languages. Alongside teaching, he is actively involved in research activities, curriculum development, and mentoring students, contributing significantly to academic excellence and innovation.

Index

A

C

D

E

www.ingramcontent.com/pod-product-compliance
Lightning Source LLC
LaVergne TN
LVHW062029101126
852251LV00005B/64